The American Presidency

The American Presidency
Origins and Development, 1776-1993

SECOND EDITION

Sidney M. Milkis
Brandeis University

Michael Nelson
Rhodes College

A Division of Congressional Quarterly Inc.
Washington, D.C.

Copyright © 1994 Congressional Quarterly Inc.

Printed in the United States of America

Photo credits: 28, 62, 76, 100b, 112, 132, 137, 157, 162, 197, 248, 252, 268, 300, Library of Congress; 100a, 180, National Portrait Gallery; 210, 227, Theodore Roosevelt Collection, Harvard College Library; 292, National Archives; 321, George Tames—*New York Times;* 327, Cecil Stoughton—National Park Service; 349, Gerald R. Ford Library; 354, Frank Johnston—*Washington Post;* 363, Pete Souza—The White House; 381, David Valdez—The White House; 397, 403, R. Michael Jenkins—Congressional Quarterly; 423, Abbie Rowe—National Park Service, courtesy of Harry S. Truman Library; 426, Jimmy Carter Library.

Cover design by Tina Chovanec

Library of Congress Cataloging-in-Publication Data

Milkis, Sidney M.
    The American presidency : origins and development, 1776-1993 /
Sidney M. Milkis, Michael Nelson, — 2nd ed.
        p.   cm.
    Includes bibliographical references and index.
    ISBN 0-87187-949-2 — ISBN 0-87187-766-X (paper)
    1. Presidents—United States—History. 2. Executive power—United
States—History. 3. United States—Constitutional history.
4. United States—Politics and government. I. Nelson, Michael,
1949- . II. Title.
JK511.M56 1993
353.03'13—dc20   93-43358
                                                                           CIP

Dedicated, with love and gratitude, to

Carol Milkis
Lauren Milkis
David Milkis
Jonathan Milkis

Linda E. Nelson
Michael C. L. Nelson, Jr.
Samuel M. L. Nelson

CONTENTS

PREFACE

Encouraged by the strong response to the first edition of *The American Presidency: Origins and Development,* we have undertaken a second edition with some important objectives in mind. First, we wanted to take account of recent events—the Bush administration, the 1992 presidential election, and the early Clinton administration—and important new scholarship. Second, we wanted to extend the book's constitutional theme by including accounts of the passage of the Twelfth, Twentieth, Twenty-second, and Twenty-fifth amendments. Finally, we wanted to take the opportunity to refine the writing and analysis throughout the book. The chapter on Lincoln has been the most extensively revised, but we have carefully reviewed and rewritten every chapter.

In its first edition, *The American Presidency* was the first comprehensive one-volume history of the presidency to be written by political scientists in more than fifty years. Not since Wilfred E. Binkley first published *The Powers of the President: Problems of American Democracy* in 1937 has a similar effort been undertaken.

In this edition, we continue to tell the history of how the institution of the presidency was created and how it has developed during its more than two centuries of existence. We tell of what has remained constant in the office, mostly because of its constitutional design. We also tell of those nineteenth- and twentieth-century innovations that have endured.

We are less concerned about describing either the recurring, or cyclical, patterns in the history of the presidency or what is individual, or idiosyncratic, about particular presidents. Abraham Lincoln and Millard Fillmore receive their chapter and paragraphs, respectively, but more because of how they affected the presidency than because of the sorts of people they were. Similarly, although cycles of politics and policy are important aspects of presidential power, we believe that the institutional history of the presidency is a sufficiently important and neglected topic to merit a book all its own.

Some will ask: How pertinent is the presidency's first century and a half to its most recent half-century? The answers of many political scientists, at least until recently, have ranged from "hardly" to "not at all." Students of the modern presidency typically mark 1933, the year of Franklin D. Roosevelt's first inauguration, as the year 1 A.D. of presidential history.

Our argument—and our evidence—is different. Many of the most important institutional characteristics of the presidency date from the Constitutional Convention and the earliest days of the Republic, which we chronicle in Chapters 1-3. During the nineteenth century, highly significant patterns and practices of presidential conduct took shape: these we discuss in Chapters 4-7. As for the era of the modern presidency—that is, the era in which the president has replaced Congress and the political parties as the leading instrument of popular rule—we trace its origins to Theodore Roosevelt and Woodrow Wilson as much as to Franklin Roosevelt and his successors (Chapters 8-14). Put simply, TR and Wilson began the practices that strengthened the president as the nation's popular and legislative leader; then FDR consolidated, or institutionalized, the president's new leadership roles in ways that subsequent presidents have continued.

This book is an interpretive political history of the presidency as well as a factual one. We have worked hard to get our facts straight and to make our interpretations sound. Research scholars, we think, will be stimulated by much of what we report about the deep roots of modern American political institutions. Students will gain a solid undergirding for their study of the presidency, the Constitution, political development, and contemporary U.S. politics and government. We also hope that this book will find its home not only in reading rooms and classrooms but also in living rooms. After all, in a system of republican government such as ours, political history means our politics, our history.

We take pleasure and pride in the friendship and colleagueship that underlie our continuing collaboration on *The American Presidency*. The book is truly a joint intellectual endeavor. In our rough division of labor, Michael Nelson did "origins" and Sidney M. Milkis did "development." Specifically, Milkis drafted Chapters 3-12 and 14, and Nelson drafted Chapters 1, 2, and 15, the latter on the origins and development of the vice presidency. (We codrafted Chapter 13.) Nelson also wrote the original outline for the book and rewrote the entire manuscript into its final form.

We have many thanks to offer, not least to our wives and children, to whom this book is dedicated. Milkis thanks his students Matthew Van Atta and Jonathan Aronie for their invaluable support in carrying out research that went into Chapters 3-13. David Tarr, director of Congressional Quarterly's Book Department, and Joanne Daniels, formerly the director of CQ Press, encouraged us to write the book. As for Margaret Seawell Benjaminson, CQ's developmental editor and the project editor for this book, words fail us in our effort to thank her properly, a cliché that she no doubt would edit out if we let her have her way.

Others labored long and well on the second edition, and we thank them too: Brenda Carter and Shana Wagger, acquisitions editors; Laura Carter, production editor; Brad Clarke and Richard Davies, students whom Milkis thanks for research assistance on Chapters 6 and 14; and especially Sabra Bissette Ledent, who copyedited the book with good humor and great skill.

Sidney M. Milkis and Michael Nelson

CHAPTER 1

Setting the Stage

The American presidency was an invention of the Constitutional Convention of 1787, unlike any other national executive position in history. Its inventors—the fifty-five convention delegates—drew on their experience, philosophy, study of history, understanding of political reality, and individual and collective wits in designing the office.

The constitutional presidency that the convention created may be regarded as, in a sense, the office's "genetic code." Because of the Constitution, the presidency is a one-person office, and the president, who is elected for a fixed term by a uniquely national constituency, shares virtually all the powers of the national government with an equally distinct and independent Congress. The constitutional presidency contains, as does an individual's configuration of DNA molecules, some ingredients whose meaning has been clear and unchanging from the moment of conception, such as the sex of a baby and the thirty-five-year minimum age requirement for the president. The Constitution also contains sentences and phrases that are the legal equivalent of genetically rooted baldness: their meaning, although determined at the very beginning, could be discovered only later. "He shall take Care that the Laws be faithfully executed" first appeared as a passing constitutional reference—the fifth of six clauses in the single sentence that constitutes Article II, section 3. But in subsequent years it afforded the presidency a strong legal claim to such varied powers as acting against secession and directing the activities of the extensive federal bureaucracy. Finally, there are those attributes whose meaning can be found only in the vagaries of individual choice and environmental circumstance. Just as the relation of physical strength to well-being varies from person to person and situation to situation during a person's life, so, for example, has the president's constitutional power to "recommend to [Congress's] consideration such Measures as he shall judge necessary and expedient" been of varying importance to different presidents at different times.[1]

Antecedents

As with any invention, the presidency had antecedents, all of which influenced the form it took in the Constitution. The delegates to the convention had long experience with British executives—namely, the king in London and his appointed governors in the American colonies. After independence was declared in 1776, delegates had the benefit of a decade's worth of experience with governments of their own design, both the various state constitutions and the Articles of Confederation, which defined and created a national government. These experiences, more than anything else, set the stage for the calling of the convention that wrote the Constitution and thus created the presidency in the summer of 1787.

British and Colonial Executives

During their long years as colonists of Great Britain, Americans became well-acquainted with the British form of government, which may be described as a constitutional monarchy. Great Britain was headed by a king (or, less frequently, a queen) who usually assumed the throne through inheritance and reigned for life. The monarch's power was limited by Parliament, the British legislature. The king could order the nation into war, for example, but his order would prevail only if Parliament were willing to appropriate the funds to finance the effort. (Conversely, Parliament could pass laws, but the king could veto them.) Parliament was a bicameral legislature—it consisted of the House of Commons, which was an elected body, and the House of Lords, which was made up of hereditary peers with lifetime tenure.

The British form of government was more than just the most familiar one to the American colonists—many of them also regarded it as the best that human beings ever had devised. Basic liberties seemed better safeguarded by Britain's constitutional monarchy than by any other government in history; British wealth and power exceeded that of any other nation. Indeed, Great Britain seemed to have solved what traditionally had been regarded as an insoluble problem of classical political philosophy—the inherent limitations of each of the three basic forms of government that were identified by Aristotle: monarchy (rule by one person), aristocracy (rule by an elite group), and democracy (rule by the people). Because, as the problem usually was formulated, those who were entrusted to reign on behalf of the whole society ended up using power for their own selfish ends, monarchy inevitably degenerated into despotism, aristocracy into oligarchy, and democracy into anarchy, then tyranny. The British remedy, developed over several centuries, was to meliorate these tendencies both by blending elements of all three forms of government into one—monarchy in the king, aristocracy in the House of Lords, and democracy in the House of Commons—and by allowing each element to check and balance the powers of the others.

The governments of most of Britain's American colonies were similar in structure to the British national government: a governor, appointed by the king; an upper house of the legislature, which in most colonies was appointed by the governor; and a lower house of the legislature, elected by the people. Governors were armed with substantial powers, including the right to cast an absolute, or final, veto over colonial legislation, the right to create courts and appoint judges, and even the right to prorogue, or dissolve, the legislature. But politically astute governors exercised these powers cautiously because only the legislature was empowered to appropriate the funds to finance a colony's government and pay its governor's salary.

For all their virtues, the British and colonial governments were prone to abuse by executives who were hungry for power. King George III, who reigned during the American Revolution, used government contracts, jobs, and other forms of patronage as virtual bribes to ensure the support of members of Parliament. Some colonial governors employed similar practices to influence their legislatures.[2] In 1776 the colonists' anger over these abuses of power was expressed fervently in the Declaration of Independence, which is best known for its ringing preamble ("all men are created equal," "Life, Liberty and the pursuit of Happiness") but which consisted mainly of a long and detailed indictment of executive "injuries and usurpations, all having in direct object the establishment of an absolute Tyranny over these States."

The lesson many Americans learned from their experience with the British and colonial governments was that liberty is threatened by executive power and safeguarded by legislative power. As James Wilson, the Scottish-born Pennsylvanian who signed the declaration, fought in the revolutionary war, and later served as a delegate to the Constitutional Convention, observed:

> Before [the Revolution], the executive and judicial powers of the government were placed neither in the people, nor in those who professed to receive them under the authority of the people. They were derived from a different and a foreign source: they were regulated by foreign maxims; they were directed to a foreign purpose.

Need we be surprised, then, that they were objects of aversion and distrust? ... On the other hand, our assemblies were chosen by ourselves: they were guardians of our rights, the objects of our confidence, and the anchor of our political hopes. Every power which could be placed in them, was thought to be safely placed: every extension of that power was considered as an extension of our own security.[3]

State Constitutions

During the course of the revolutionary war, seventeen constitutions were written by the thirteen newly independent former colonies. (Some states began with one constitution, then quickly replaced it with another.) Revulsion against their experience with the British executive—the king in London and the royal governors in the state capitals—led almost all of the authors of state constitutions to provide for weak governors and strong legislatures. As James Wilson wryly observed, under independence, "the executive and the judicial as well as the legislative authority was now the child of the people; but to the two former, the people behaved like stepmothers. The legislature was still discriminated by excessive partiality; and into its lap, every good and precious gift was profusely thrown." [4]

Typically, state governors in the decade after independence was declared were elected by the legislature for a brief term (one year, in most cases) and were ineligible for reelection. They were forced to share their powers with a council of some sort, which made them, in the assessment of the historian Gordon Wood, "little more than chairmen of their executive boards." [5] (At the Constitutional Convention, Gov. Edmund Randolph of Virginia would oppose the proposal to make the presidency a unitary office by saying that, as governor, he was merely "a member of the executive.") Such powers as the governors had were meager. Most state constitutions made vague grants of authority to their chief executives and, by specifically denying them the right to veto legislation and to make appointments, rendered them incapable of defending even those modest powers from legislative encroachment. In his *Notes on the State of Virginia*, Thomas Jefferson described the result in his home state:

All the powers of government, legislative, executive and judiciary, result to the legislative body. ... The [state constitutional] convention, which passed the ordinance of government, laid its foundation on this basis, that the legislative, executive and judiciary departments should be separate and distinct, so that no person should exercise the powers of more than one of them at the same time. But no barrier was provided between these several powers. The judiciary and executive members were left dependent on the legislative for their subsistence in office and some of them for their continuance in it.[6]

The constitution of the state of New York offered a striking exception to the general practice of weak governors and strong legislatures. New York's governor was elected by the people, not the legislature, for a term of three years, not one, and, rather than being confined to one term, could be reelected as often as the people chose. (George Clinton, the first governor to be elected under the New York constitution, was elected six times, for a total of eighteen years.) The executive power of New York was unitary, exercised by the governor alone and not shared with a council. The governor was empowered to veto legislation, subject to a vote to override by the legislature, and to make appointments, subject to legislative confirmation. Finally, the powers of New York's governor were defined by the state constitution in detail, much as the powers of the president would be in the U.S. Constitution:

> Article XVIII. . . . The governor . . . shall by virtue of his office, be general and commander in chief of all the militia, and admiral of the navy of this state; . . . he shall have power to convene the assembly and senate on extraordinary occasions; to prorogue them from time to time, provided such prorogations shall not exceed sixty days in the space of any one year; and, at his discretion, to grant reprieves and pardons to persons convicted of crimes, other than treason and murder, in which he may suspend the execution of the sentence, until it shall be reported to the legislature at their subsequent meeting; and they shall either pardon or direct the execution of the criminal, or grant a further reprieve.
>
> Article XIX. . . . It shall be the duty of the governor to inform the legislature of the condition of the state so far as may concern his department; to recommend such matters to their consideration as shall appear to him to concern its good government, welfare and prosperity; to correspond with the Continental Congress and other States; to transact all necessary business with the officers of government, civil and military; to take care that the laws are executed to the best of his ability; and to expedite all such measures as may be resolved upon by legislature.

The Articles of Confederation

The decision by the Continental Congress to declare independence from Great Britain in the summer of 1776 was accompanied by another decision. Congress voted that, as stated in the motion by the Virginian Richard Henry Lee, "a plan of confederation [shall] be prepared and transmitted to the respective Colonies for their consideration and approbation." Such a step was militarily necessary. Although the Declaration of Independence made each of the states, in effect, an independent nation, they could not fight a common war against the British without some sort of common government.

But the states, jealous of their independence and reluctant to substitute a new central government (even one that was homegrown) for the British government they had just rejected, surrendered power grudgingly. They stipulated to their delegates in Congress that the confederation was to be no stronger than was absolutely necessary to conduct the Revolution. Reacting against their experience with British rule, the states also made clear that the confederation's executive component must be minimal. Nothing remotely resembling a national king would be tolerated.

On June 11, 1776, a Committee of Thirteen (one from each state) was formed in the Continental Congress to draft a plan of confederation. The committee, acting expeditiously, submitted its recommendation on July 12. More than a year later, on November 15, 1777, Congress adopted a revised version of the plan, calling it the Articles of Confederation and Perpetual Union. Ratification by the states came slowly, with the last state not voting its approval until March 1, 1781. But the articles were so much like the ad hoc arrangement that the states already were using under the Continental Congress that the delay in ratification, by itself, was of little consequence.

The Articles of Confederation more than embodied the states' dread of central government and executive power. Indeed, they hardly created a government at all—more like an alliance or, as the articles themselves put it, a "league of friendship." Each state, regardless of wealth or population, was represented equally in Congress. The president, chosen by Congress, was no more than a presiding officer. Eventually, Congress created departments headed by appointed officials—the burden of making all financial, diplomatic, and military decisions and of executing all legislative enactments was more than Congress as a body could handle—but the departments' activities underwent close legislative monitoring. In truth, few laws of consequence were passed by Congress because passage required the support of nine of the thirteen states. Amendments to the Articles of Confederation had to be approved unanimously.

In addition to a weak institutional structure, the articles undermined the power of the national government in other ways. Technically, Congress was empowered to declare war, make treaties and enter alliances, raise an army and navy, regulate coinage and borrow money, supervise Indian affairs, establish a post office, and adjudicate disputes between states. Funds and troops were to be supplied by each state according to its wealth and population. But Congress had no power to tax the states or to enforce its own laws. When, as often happened, one or two states balked at meeting an obligation, other states followed suit. "Each state sent what was convenient or appropriate," the historians Christopher Collier and James Lincoln Collier have observed, "which usually depended on how close to home the fighting was going on." [7]

After the revolutionary war was won and the common threat from the British was removed, states felt even less incentive to honor the requests of the national government.

National Problems

For all their weakness, the Articles of Confederation did not prevent the United States from winning independence from Great Britain. The revolutionary war effectively ended on October 17, 1781, when Gen. George Washington's American army and a French fleet, anchored off Yorktown, Virginia, forced the surrender of the British forces led by Charles Lord Cornwallis.

The problems of a weak, purely legislative national government became more apparent in the half-decade that followed victory. No longer united by a common foe, the states turned their backs almost completely on Congress and on one another.

Overlapping claims to western lands brought some states into conflict—Connecticut settlers and Pennsylvania troops even clashed violently in a disputed area. The western territories were the nation's most valuable resource, but until the states' rival claims were settled, it was difficult to develop and profit from them. On the East Coast, some states with port cities—New York, Massachusetts, South Carolina, and Pennsylvania—placed taxes on goods imported from overseas by merchants in neighboring states.

The nation also was burdened by a crippling debt. Money was owed to soldiers who had fought and to merchants who had provided supplies during the revolutionary war. Threatened with bankruptcy or foreclosure, many of these soldiers and merchants were angry and sometimes violent. By 1789, foreign creditors held more than $10 million in notes and were owed $1.8 million in unpaid interest. Unless paid, they were unwilling to engage in further trade with the United States. Yet Congress was unable to persuade the states to contribute to the Treasury. The total income of the national government in 1786, for example, was less than one-third of the interest due that year on the national debt.

The United States faced numerous problems outside its borders as well. The nation's northern, southern, and western boundaries were under siege, with only an ill-equipped, poorly financed, seven hundred-member army to defend them. British soldiers continued to occupy several Great Lakes forts that their government had promised to vacate under the Treaty of Paris, the 1783 pact that was supposed to have settled the revolutionary war. Similarly, Spain closed the Mississippi River to U.S. ships and made claim to land east of the river that, according to the treaty, rightfully belonged to the United States. Both

Spain and Britain encouraged American Indian raids on frontier settlements. (Spain, in particular, roused American Indians in Florida to harass settlers in Georgia.) Abroad, U.S. ships were preyed on by pirates in the Mediterranean Sea and were denied entry by Great Britain to its colonies in Canada and the West Indies, two lucrative markets for trade.[8]

In the midst of foreign and domestic difficulties, another problem developed that mixed elements of both. A currency crisis occurred in the United States, largely because Americans had gone on a buying spree after the revolutionary war was over, frantically importing such luxuries as clocks, glassware, and furniture from Great Britain. As money—that is, gold and silver—flowed out of the country to pay for these goods, it became scarce at home. Many debtors, especially farmers who had left the land to fight for independence and still had not been paid by the financially destitute national government, put pressure on the legislatures of their states simply to print vast sums of paper money that they could use to pay off their debts. Creditors, horrified at the prospect of being reimbursed in depreciated currency, fought back politically, with limited success. Most state legislatures, being both powerful and highly democratic, were more responsive to the greater number of debtors than to the smaller number of creditors.

Conclusion

Fear of executive power remained strong among Americans during the decade after independence was declared. But the problems that beset the United States under the strong legislative governments of the states and the weak legislative government of the Articles of Confederation taught certain lessons, particularly to conservatives and people of property. As the political scientist Charles Thach has written, "Experience ... during the period following the cessation of hostilities served ... to confirm the tendencies toward increasing confidence in the executive and increasing distrust of the legislature." Experience also taught certain lessons about the proper design of an effective executive:

> It taught that executive energy and responsibility are inversely proportional to executive size; that, consequently, the one-man executive is best. It taught the value of integration; the necessity of executive appointments, civil and military; the futility of legislative military control. It demonstrated the necessity of the veto as a protective measure ... [for] preventing unwise legislation. ... It demonstrated the value of a fixed executive salary which the legislature could not reduce. It discredited choice [of the executive] by the legislature, though without teaching clearly the lesson of popular choice. ... And, above all, it assured the acceptance of, if it did not create, a new concept of national government—the fundamental principles of which were the

ruling constitution, the limited legislature, and the three equal and coordinate departments.[9]

The Constitutional Convention

Of all the problems that plagued the new nation after independence, none seemed more amenable to solution than those involving commerce among the states. Few benefited, and many suffered, from the protectionist walls that individual states had built around their economies. The Virginia state assembly, at the urging of James Madison, one of its youngest members, called for a national trade conference to be held at Annapolis, Maryland, in September 1786 and urged all the other states to send delegations.

In some ways, the Annapolis Convention was a failure. Only three states (Virginia, New Jersey, and Delaware) sent full delegations; and seven states, suspicious of Virginia's intentions, boycotted the meeting altogether. The convention made no proposals to remedy the nation's trade difficulties. But the delegates who did come to Annapolis, notably Madison and General Washington's young revolutionary war aide, Alexander Hamilton of New York, rescued the enterprise by issuing a bold call to Congress to convene an even more wide-ranging meeting. They urged that the states be enjoined to choose delegates to "meet at Philadelphia on the second Monday in May next [1787], to take into consideration the situation of the United States, to devise such further provisions as shall appear to them necessary to render the constitution of the Federal Government adequate to the exigencies of the Union."

Congress initially was cool to the summons of the Annapolis Convention, but within weeks an event occurred that lent urgency to the nationalist cause. Mobs of farmers in western Massachusetts, saddled with debts and unable to persuade the state legislature to ease credit, closed down courts and stopped sheriffs' auctions in order to prevent foreclosure orders from being issued and executed against their land. Although similar outbreaks had occurred in other states, they had been suppressed easily; this one, dubbed Shays's Rebellion after one of its leaders, the revolutionary war hero Daniel Shays, threatened for a time to rage out of control. Around the country, people of property and, more generally, believers in law and order were shocked and horrified both at the class warfare that seemed to be breaking out and at the inability of the national government to maintain the peace. On February 21, 1787, Congress decided to act on the request of the Annapolis Convention:

> RESOLVED, That in the opinion of Congress it is expedient that on the second Monday in May next a Convention of delegates who shall have been appointed by the several states be held in Philadelphia for the sole and express purpose of revising the Articles of Confederation

and reporting to Congress and the state legislatures such alterations and provisions therein as shall when agreed to in Congress and confirmed by the states render the federal constitution adequate to the exigencies of government & the preservation of the Union.

The states were, of course, no more compelled to follow this summons of Congress than to follow any other—Rhode Island never did send delegates to the Constitutional Convention. But when a sufficient number of states—whether frightened by the prospect of further Shays's-style rebellions, concerned about the nation's growing domestic and international weakness, or inspired by the example of the nationally revered Washington, who decided to attend as a delegate from his native Virginia—selected delegations, other states fell into line for fear of having their interests ignored.

The Delegates

The Constitutional Convention has been variously described over the years: an "assembly of demigods" (Jefferson), a "miracle at Philadelphia" (author Catherine Drinker Bowen), and a "nationalist reform caucus" (political scientist John Roche), to cite but three descriptions.[10] The convention may have been all of these things and more, but, more mundanely, it also was a gathering of fifty-five individuals.

Who were the delegates? Self-selection had much to do with determining both who was chosen by the various states to represent them at the convention and who actually went. Political leaders who were committed to the idea that the system had to be dramatically improved leaped at the opportunity to attend the convention. Most of those who were basically satisfied with the status quo and who disapproved of the convention—including such prominent Americans as Patrick Henry and Richard Henry Lee of Virginia, Samuel Adams of Massachusetts, and George Clinton of New York—stayed away. (Henry said he "smelt a Rat.")[11] Had they attended and fought stubbornly for their position, observed the political scientist Clinton Rossiter, the convention "would have been much more perfectly representative of the active citizenry of 1787. It would also, one is bound to point out, have been crippled as a nation-building instrument."[12]

The fifty-five delegates generally were united, then, in their belief that a stronger national government was vital to the success of the new American nation. In part, this was because many of them had shared similar experiences. Forty-two were current or former members of Congress; twenty-one had risked life and livelihood by fighting in the revolutionary war; eight had signed the Declaration of Independence.

Collectively, the convention was young. Many of the delegates were "the young men of the Revolution," in the phrase of the historians

Stanley Elkins and Eric McKitrick—men who had come of age during the revolutionary decade of the 1770s, when the idea of building a nation was more inspiring than were traditional state loyalties.[13] Madison, at thirty-six, was older than eleven other delegates, including several who were to play significant roles in the proceedings, such as Gouverneur Morris of Pennsylvania (thirty-five), Virginia's governor Randolph (thirty-three), and Charles Pinckney of South Carolina, who was twenty-nine but said he was twenty-four so that he could claim the honor of being the youngest delegate. (That title went to Jonathan Dayton of New Jersey, who was twenty-six.) The average age of the delegates—even counting eighty-one-year-old Benjamin Franklin of Pennsylvania—was forty-three.

Other shared characteristics contributed to the delegates' common outlook on many fundamental issues. Almost all were prosperous— around half were lawyers, and another quarter owned plantations or large farms. (Only two delegates were small farmers, who made up 85 percent of the nation's white population.) Almost all the delegates lived in the long-settled coastal regions of their states; the backcountry frontier was hardly represented at the convention. The wealth of most of the delegates derived from personal property (government securities and investments in manufacturing, shipping, and land speculation). The prosperity of other delegates lay in real property, notably agricultural land and, in the South, slaves.[14]

Rules and Procedures

Congress had called upon the convention to assemble on Monday, May 14, 1787, but not until Friday, May 25, were the seven state delegations that were needed for a quorum present in Philadelphia. Although most of the other delegations arrived within a few days, some came much later.

The first order of business on May 25 was to elect a president, a word that, in the usage of the day, suggested a "presiding officer" more than a "leader" or "chief executive." Not surprisingly, George Washington was the delegates' unanimous choice. Washington spoke on only one minor issue during the convention—he rose on the last day to support a proposal to require that members of the House of Representatives represent at least thirty thousand people rather than forty thousand. (Not surprisingly, the delegates agreed unanimously.) But clearly Washington played more than a ceremonial role at the convention. According to the Colliers, "during that long, hot summer, this gregarious man was constantly having dinner, tea, supper with people, and one must assume of course that he was actively promoting his position," namely, a strong national government and a strong executive within that government.[15]

After Washington's election, a secretary was chosen—Maj. William Jackson of Pennsylvania. Jackson kept the convention's official journal, which was little more than a record of motions and votes. Fortunately, Madison decided to keep extensive notes of the delegates' debates and deliberations. Madison had been frustrated in his studies of other governments by the near-impossibility of determining what their founders had intended. Although he was acting on his own initiative, the other delegates knew what he was doing. In fairness to them, he decided to keep his notes secret until the last delegate died. This turned out to be himself. (Madison died in 1836, at the age of eighty-five.) Along with the rest of Madison's papers, his notes on the Constitutional Convention were purchased by Congress in 1837 and published in 1840.

The only other business of the convention's first day was to accept the credentials of the various state delegations. In doing so, the delegates implicitly agreed that the then-customary procedure of having each state cast an equal vote in any national body would be followed. Wilson of Pennsylvania was displeased by this arrangement (he felt that the larger states should have a greater voice), but he was persuaded by Madison and others that to alienate the small states at such an early stage would abort the entire proceedings.

On Monday, May 28, the delegates adopted additional rules and procedures. None was more important to the success of the convention than the rule of secrecy. The rule was simple: no delegate was to say anything to anyone, including members of his family, about the convention's discussions and deliberations.

Thomas Jefferson, then the U.S. ambassador to France, wrote John Adams, the ambassador to Great Britain, that he was appalled by "so abominable a precedent [as secrecy]. . . . Nothing can justify this but the innocence of their intentions and ignorance of the value of public discussions." But in a letter to Jefferson, Madison explained the delegates' decision. "It was thought expedient in order to secure unbiased discussion within doors, and to prevent misconceptions & misconstructions without, to establish some rules of caution which will for no short time restrain even a confidential communication of our proceedings." [16] In other words, secrecy permitted delegates to think through issues aloud and even to change their minds without appearing weak or vacillating. It also kept opponents of the convention from sensationalizing particular proposals or decisions in an effort to discredit the whole undertaking. Years later, Madison told the historian Jared Sparks that "no Constitution would ever have been adopted by the Convention if the debates had been made public." [17]

Another important rule that the convention adopted was to permit its decisions to be reconsidered at even a single delegate's request. Because issues could always be raised and decided again, those who were on the losing side of a crucial vote were encouraged to stay and try to persuade the other delegates to change their minds, rather than to walk out and return home in protest and frustration.

An Overview of the Convention

The Constitutional Convention was not a scripted or even an especially orderly proceeding. The delegates' decision to allow issues to be reconsidered, reinforced by their twin desires to build consensus among themselves and to create a government whose parts would mesh with one another, meant that the convention "could not, and did not, proceed in a straight line, neatly disposing of one issue after the next until all were dealt with. It moved instead in swirls and loops, again and again backtracking to pick up issues previously debated." [18]

Still, the Constitutional Convention was not a completely chaotic undertaking. Various plans (submitted by delegates) and committees (appointed by the convention) helped to order its deliberations. These plans and committees structured the work of the convention into seven main stages:

- The introduction of the Virginia Plan (May 29)
- The convention's decision to recast itself as a Committee of the Whole, originally for the purpose of considering the Virginia Plan in detail but later to evaluate Alexander Hamilton's plan and the New Jersey Plan as well (May 30-June 19)
- Clause-by-clause debate by the convention of the decisions of the Committee of the Whole (June 20-July 26)
- The work of the five-member Committee of Detail, which was appointed by the convention to produce a draft of the new Constitution that reflected the delegates' manifold decisions on particular issues (July 24-August 6)
- Systematic convention debate on the report of the Committee of Detail (August 7-31)
- The recommendations of the eleven-member Committee on Postponed Matters (or Committee of Eleven), which was created to propose acceptable solutions to the problems that continued to divide the delegates (August 31-September 8)
- Final adjustments, including the work of the Committee of Style, which was charged to write a polished and final draft of the Constitution, and last-minute tinkering by the convention, culminating in the signing of the proposed plan of government (September 9-17)

Virginia Plan (May 29). The Virginia Plan, introduced on May 29 by Governor Randolph but written mainly by Madison, offered a radical departure from the Articles of Confederation. The plan proposed to create a three-branch national government and to elevate it to clear supremacy over the states, partly by granting the new government the power to veto state laws that were in conflict with the Constitution or with national laws, and partly by grounding its authority squarely in the people.[19]

According to the Virginia Plan the heart of the national government would be a bicameral legislature, with the lower house apportioned by population and its members elected by the people, and the upper house elected by the lower house. The legislature's powers would include broad authority not just to pass laws but also to appoint judges and most other government officials and to conduct foreign policy.

A national judiciary, organized into "one or more supreme tribunals" and various "inferior tribunals" and appointed (with life tenure) by the legislature, would form a second branch. Its broad-ranging powers included "impeachments of any National officers."

The government also would have an executive branch, although it was vaguely defined in the Virginia Plan. The "national executive" (the plan left unresolved the question of whether this would be a person or a group) was "to be chosen by the National Legislature for a term of —— years." Its powers were obscure: "besides a general authority to execute the National laws, it ought to enjoy the Executive rights vested in Congress by the [Articles of] Confederation."

Finally, a "Council of revision," consisting of "the executive and a convenient number of the National Judiciary," was empowered to veto laws that were passed by the national legislature, subject to override if a vetoed law was repassed by an unspecified majority.[20]

The delegates' response to the Virginia Plan was remarkably placid, especially considering the radical departure in the direction of a strong national government that the plan proposed. "So sharp a break was Virginia asking the other states to make with the American past that one wonders why at least one stunned delegate ... did not rise up and cry havoc at the top of his lungs," Rossiter has written. "Instead, the delegates ended this [May 29] session by resolving to go into a 'committee of the whole house' " on the next day to "consider the state of the American union." [21]

Committee of the Whole (May 30-June 19). In becoming a Committee of the Whole, the convention was, in a sense, simply giving itself a different name—the same group of delegates made up the committee as made up the convention. But as a Committee of the Whole they could operate more informally. (To symbolize this change, Washington temporarily stepped down as president, and Nathaniel Gorham of Massachusetts was chosen to preside.) In addition, any decision made by the delegates while meeting as the committee would be in the form of a recommendation to the convention that would have to be voted on again.

From May 30 to June 13, the Committee of the Whole spent most of its time going over the Virginia Plan, clause by clause. Much of the plan was accepted. But some of it was altered, and some ambiguous provisions were clarified.[22] For example, the executive was defined as a unitary, or one-person, office. The executive would be elected for a single, seven-year term by the legislature and was subject to impeachment and removal on grounds of "malpractice or neglect of duty." The executive alone, not a council of revision, was empowered to veto laws that were passed by the legislature, subject to override by a two-thirds vote of both houses.

In deference to the states, the Committee of the Whole decided that members of the upper house of the national legislature (who had to be at least thirty years old) would be chosen by the various state legislatures. They would serve seven-year terms and be eligible for reelection. Members of the lower house, also eligible for reelection, would serve three-year terms. All members of the national legislature would be barred from holding any other government office, mainly to prevent conflicts of interest from arising. As for the courts, there would be only one "supreme tribunal," and judges who served on it or on such "inferior tribunals" as the national legislature might create would be appointed by the upper house of the legislature for lifetime terms.

New Jersey Plan. One plank of the Virginia Plan was especially controversial—the provision that both houses of the national legislature would be apportioned according to population. Delegates from the large states (specifically, those from Virginia, Massachusetts, Pennsylvania, and the three states whose populations were growing most rapidly—Georgia, North Carolina, and South Carolina) favored the idea. They split sharply with the delegates from the small states, who feared that their constituents would be hopelessly outnumbered in the legislature and who favored instead the existing arrangement, namely, equal representation in Congress for each state. A compromise plan, which was proposed by Roger Sherman of Connecticut on June 11, would have apportioned the lower house of the legislature according to population and the upper house on the basis of one state, one vote, but few delegates were ready yet for the compromise. Instead, small-state delegates responded to the Virginia Plan with a sweeping counterproposal of their own. It was introduced on June 15 by William Paterson of New Jersey.

The New Jersey Plan came in the form of amendments to the Articles of Confederation rather than as a new constitution. It proposed to add two new branches to the one-branch national government—a plural, or committee-style, executive, to be elected by Congress for a single term and "removeable by Cong[ress] on application by a majority of the Executives of the several States," and a supreme court, its judges to be appointed by the executive for lifetime terms. The plan also would declare national laws and treaties to be "the supreme law of the respective States" and would authorize the executive to use force if necessary to implement them. In addition, Congress would be empowered to regulate interstate and international commerce and to impose taxes. But the main purpose of the New Jersey Plan was an unstated one: to preserve the structure of Congress under the articles—a single house in which each state, regardless of size, would cast one vote.[23]

Hamilton's Plan. On June 18, Alexander Hamilton delivered a four-to-six-hour speech to the delegates in which he urged them to consider his plan for an avowedly British-style government.[24] "[H]e had no scruple in declaring," according to the notes kept by Madison, "supported as he was by the opinions of so many of the wise & good, that the British Government was the best in the world: and that he doubted much whether any thing short of it would do in America." [25]

Specifically, Hamilton proposed that, as in Great Britain, the national government be supreme. State governors would be appointed by the national legislature and granted the right to veto any laws passed by their own assemblies. Members of the upper house of the national legislature, like members of the British House of Lords, would serve for life. As to the executive, "the English model is the only good one on this subject," Hamilton asserted.[26] Although he did not suggest that the United States create a hereditary monarchy, Hamilton did propose that the executive be chosen by electors and granted lifetime tenure and vast powers, including "a negative on all laws about to be passed, ... the direction of war when authorized or begun, the sole appointment of the heads of the departments, the power of pardoning all offences except Treason," and, along with the Senate, the treaty-making power.

Although Hamilton's speech was dismissed by most of the delegates as being far beyond the bounds of what the people or the states would accept, several of his specific proposals were adopted later in the convention, notably those concerning the president's powers to grant pardons and to negotiate treaties. As for the New Jersey Plan, it was defeated on June 19 by a vote of seven states to three. Later that day, the Virginia Plan, as modified by the Committee of the Whole, was approved and referred to the convention for further consideration. The conflict between the delegates from the large and from the small states over apportionment in the national legislature, however, was far from resolved.

Convention Debate (June 20-July 26).   On June 20, with Washington again in the chair as president of the convention, the delegates began their clause-by-clause evaluation of the plan of government they had laid out as the Committee of the Whole.

Among the changes they voted in the plan were these:

- Members of the lower house of the legislature would be elected for a term of two years, not three; they also would be required to be at least twenty-five years old.
- The term for members of the upper house would be six years rather than seven. Their terms would be staggered so that one-third were elected every two years.
- The national legislature would not have the power to veto state laws, much to Madison's dismay. But, borrowing a plank from the New Jersey Plan, national laws and treaties would be "the supreme law of the respective States."
- A property requirement for members of the executive, legislative, and judicial branches would be established. (This idea later was abandoned.)
- Sufficient displeasure was expressed with the provision for legislative election of the president to a single, seven-year term as to guarantee that it would not remain in the final document, but no generally satisfactory alternative was agreed upon.

More than any other issue, legislative apportionment consumed the convention's time, attention, and endurance during these five weeks of debate. Delegates from the small states pressed relentlessly for equal representation of the states in Congress; delegates from the large states were equally adamant in their insistence on representation according to population.

A special committee, with members from all the states, was appointed on July 2 to propose a compromise. On July 5, after a break to celebrate Independence Day, the committee recommended a plan of equal representation for each state in the upper house, apportionment according to population in the lower house (with each slave counted as three-fifths of a person), and, as a sop to delegates from the large states who feared that the upper house would push for spending programs that would impoverish their states, exclusive power in the lower house to originate all legislation dealing with money.

For more than a week the delegates engaged in complex and sometimes bitter debate. New questions were raised, for example, about whether states yet to be admitted to the Union should receive as much representation as the original thirteen, how often a national census should be taken to measure population changes, and whether apportionment in the lower house should reflect wealth as well as people. On July 16, the convention voted narrowly to approve the main points of the special committee's proposal, sometimes called the Connecticut Compromise after its original advocate, Roger Sherman. On July 23, the delegates decided that each state should have two members in the upper house, with each member free to vote independently.

Committee of Detail (July 24-August 6). On July 24, the convention voted to appoint a Committee of Detail to review all of its actions and to draft a plan of government that incorporated them. The five-member committee included representatives of the three main regions of the country—Nathaniel Gorham of Massachusetts and Oliver Ellsworth of Connecticut (a protégé of Sherman) from New England, James Wilson of Pennsylvania from the middle states, and Edmund Randolph of Virginia and John Rutledge of South Carolina from the South. The committee worked while the rest of the convention adjourned until August 6.

One index of the committee's influence is that it took convention-passed resolutions amounting to twelve hundred words and transformed them into a draft constitution of thirty-seven hundred words.[27] The committee also drew from a wide range of other sources in compiling its report: the New Jersey Plan, the Articles of Confederation, the rules of Congress, some state constitutions (notably those of New York and Massachusetts), and a plan of government proposed by Charles Pinckney of South Carolina.[28]

Most of the memorable phrases in the Constitution were written by the Committee of Detail, including *state of the Union* and *We the People.* Institutions were named: the executive became the *president;* the national tribunal, the *Supreme Court;* and the legislature, *Congress,* with its upper house called the *Senate,* and the lower house, the *House of Representatives.*

For the most part, the committee, in keeping with its name, simply fleshed out the details of earlier convention decisions. It set procedures for the president's veto, defined the jurisdiction of the courts, and adjusted certain relations between the states. In some instances, however, the committee substituted its own judgments for the convention's. The power to impeach, for example, was vested in the House, with only the power to convict remaining in the Supreme Court. The property requirement for officeholders was omitted.

Perhaps the most important decision of the Committee of Detail was to transform general grants of power into specific ones. What had been Congress's broadly stated authority "to legislate in all cases for the general interests of the Union" became instead a list of eighteen enumerated powers, including the power to "lay and collect taxes," regulate interstate commerce, establish post offices, make war, elect a national treasurer, and set up inferior courts—all culminating in a sweeping grant "to make all laws that shall be necessary and proper for carrying into execution" these and "all other powers vested" in the government. The states were forbidden certain powers, notably to make treaties with other nations, to print money, and to tax imports.

The committee granted the president the power to recommend legislation to Congress, make executive appointments, receive ambassadors from other nations, issue pardons, "take care" that the laws be executed, and command the armed forces. An oath to "faithfully execute the office" of president also was included, as was a provision that the president of the Senate would exercise the powers and duties of the presidency if the president died, resigned, or became disabled. The judiciary—the Supreme Court and other, "inferior courts" to be created by law—was given jurisdiction in controversies between states or the citizens of different states and cases arising under the laws of the national government.

Finally, responding to a threat to walk out by Gen. Charles Cotesworth Pinckney of South Carolina (a cousin of Charles Pinckney), the committee forbade Congress to tax or ban the importation of slaves and the exportation of goods. In another concession to southern delegates, who feared that Congress might legislate navigation acts to require that American exports be transported on American ships (a boon to northern shipbuilders but a burden to southern agricultural exporters), the committee required that such acts would have to pass Congress by a two-thirds vote.

Convention Debate (August 7-31). As they had with the Virginia Plan and the report of the Committee of the Whole, the delegates reviewed the draft constitution that was proposed by the Committee of Detail clause by clause. Much of the draft was approved. Some parts, however, were modified, and others became matters of serious controversy.

Modifications. The delegates tinkered with several provisions of the committee draft.

* They enacted citizenship requirements for legislators (seven years for members of the House, nine years for senators), along with a requirement that legislators be inhabitants of the states they represented in Congress.
* They raised from two-thirds to three-fourths the majority of votes needed in both houses of Congress to override a president's veto. (Near the end of the convention, the delegates restored the two-thirds figure.)
* They judged that Congress's power to "make war" was too sweeping to protect the national security when Congress was out of session. The wording was revised to read "declare war."

• They prohibited Congress from passing both ex post facto laws—that is, retroactive criminal laws—and bills of attainder (laws that declare a person guilty of a crime without a trial).

• They barred the government from granting "any title of nobility" to any person and forbade government officials to receive "any present, emolument, office, or title of any kind whatever from any king, prince, or foreign state."

• They empowered Congress to call forth the militia of any state "to execute the laws of the Union, suppress insurrections, and repel invasions."

• They dropped the two-thirds requirement for Congress to pass navigation acts.

• They created a procedure to amend the Constitution: "on the application of the legislatures of two-thirds of the states in the Union for an amendment of this Constitution, the legislature of the United States shall call a convention for that purpose."

• They prohibited any religious test as a requirement for holding office.

• They expanded the president's oath to include these words: "and will to the best of my judgment and power preserve, protect, and defend the Constitution of the United States." (Still later, "to the best of my judgment and power" became "to the best of my ability.")

• The Committee of Detail had proposed that the new constitution take effect when ratified by a number of state conventions (not state legislatures) but had left the number unspecified. The delegates now voted to set it at nine.

Controversies. The draft constitution's slavery provisions came under fierce assault by northern delegates, both the three-fifths rule for counting slaves as part of the population and the prohibition against laws to ban the importation of slaves. Much of the North's concern derived from fear of slave rebellions, which might attract foreign invaders and, in any event, would require northern arms and money in order to be subdued. Southern delegates not only defended the provisions to protect slavery but also insisted that their states would not ratify any constitution that placed slavery in jeopardy.

As it had with the controversy between the large and small states, the convention appointed a special committee on August 22 to find a compromise solution. Two days later, the committee proposed that Congress be authorized, if it so decided, to end the importation of slaves after 1800; in the meantime, Congress could tax imported slaves at a rate no higher than ten dollars each. (A euphemism—not "slaves" but "such Persons"—was used in the Constitution.) General Pinckney persuaded the convention to change 1800 to 1808. The committee recommendation, as amended, was passed.

Controversies over two other matters caused the convention to bog down: the powers of the Senate (which delegates from the large states wanted to minimize and delegates from the small states wanted to maximize) and a cluster of issues regarding presidential selection. On August 31, nearing the end of its labors, the convention appointed a Committee on Postponed Matters, with a member from each state delegation, to resolve these vexing issues.

Committee on Postponed Matters (August 31-September 8). Beginning on September 4, the Committee on Postponed Matters, chaired by David Brearley of New Jersey, made several recommendations concerning the presidency.[29] It proposed a term of four years rather than seven, with no restriction on the president's eligibility for reelection. The president was to be chosen by an electoral college, not by Congress. To constitute the electoral college, each state would be assigned the right to select, by whatever means it chose, electors equal in number to its representatives and senators in Congress. The candidate who received the greatest number of electoral votes, assuming the support of a majority of electors, would become president; the candidate who finished second would become vice president. (This was the first mention of the vice presidency at the convention.) If no candidate received a majority, the Senate would select a president and vice president from among the five candidates who had received the greatest number of electoral votes.

As a corollary to its proposal for an electoral college, the committee recommended that certain responsibilities be assigned to the vice president—namely, to serve as president of the Senate, with the right to cast tie-breaking votes, and to act as president if the office became vacant before the expiration of the president's term. Finally, the committee recommended that qualifications for president be stated in the Constitution: the president would have to be at least thirty-five years old, a natural-born citizen of the United States (or a citizen at the time of the Constitution's enactment), and at least fourteen years a resident of the United States.

For several days, the delegates gave critical scrutiny to the committee's complex and surprising proposal for presidential selection. On September 7, they passed it after making only one substantial change: the House of Representatives, rather than the Senate, would choose the president in the event of an electoral college deadlock, with each state delegation casting one vote. The Senate still would choose the vice president if the electoral college failed to produce a winner.

Having approved the electoral college, the convention quickly took other actions to reduce the powers of the Senate in response to the demands of the delegates from the large states. The president was granted authority to make treaties and to appoint ambassadors, public ministers, consuls, Supreme Court justices, federal judges, and all other officers whose appointments were not otherwise provided for. The delegates decided to require Senate confirmation for all of these appointments; they also stipulated a two-thirds vote by the Senate to ratify treaties.

On September 8, the convention approved two final proposals of the Committee on Postponed Matters. The president was to be impeached by the House on grounds of "treason or bribery or other high crimes and misdemeanors against the United States" and, upon conviction by the Senate, removed from office. (The delegates added the vice president and other civil officers to the roster of those who were subject to impeachment but raised the requirement for Senate conviction from a simple to a two-thirds majority.) In addition, the House was empowered to originate "all bills for raising revenue."

Having thus completed (or so they believed) their work on the Constitution, the delegates ended their business on September 8 by voting to create a five-member Committee of Style to write a polished, final draft for them to sign. Among the committee's members were Madison, Hamilton, and Gouverneur Morris, who seems to have done most of its work.

Final Adjustments (September 9-17). Even as the Committee of Style labored, the convention continued to modify its earlier decisions. On September 10, Madison urged that special conventions not be a part of the process of amending the Constitution. Instead, he argued, amendments should be initiated either by a two-thirds vote of Congress or by two-thirds of the state legislatures. Subsequent approval by three-fourths of the states would be required for ratification. The Committee of Style incorporated Madison's idea into its draft.

On September 12, Hugh Williamson of North Carolina successfully moved that the requirement for overriding a president's veto be reduced from a three-fourths vote of each house of Congress to a two-thirds vote.

Meanwhile, more fundamental reservations about the Constitution were being expressed by some delegates. Randolph worried that the delegates had gone far beyond their original charter from Congress to propose revisions in the Articles of Confederation. He urged that the approval of not just state ratifying conventions but also of Congress and the state legislatures be sought for the proposed constitution, even if this process necessitated a second constitutional convention. His fellow Virginian, George Mason, objected to the absence from the Constitution of a bill of rights.

The Committee of Style reported to the convention on September 12.[30] Its draft not only reduced the number of articles from twenty-three to seven but also included some significant innovations. The most memorable of these was the preamble:

> We the People of the United States, in Order to form a more perfect Union, establish Justice, insure domestic Tranquility, provide for the common defence, promote the general Welfare, and secure the Blessings of Liberty to ourselves and our Posterity, do ordain and establish this Constitution for the United States of America.[31]

The Committee of Style also added a provision that barred states from passing laws to impair the obligations of contracts. Finally, a pair of vesting clauses for Congress and the president were written that, intentionally or not, suggested that the president might have executive powers beyond those enumerated in the Constitution. (See pp. 33-34.)

The committee's draft met with widespread approval from the delegates, but their tinkering continued. Congress was stripped of its power to choose the national treasurer. A provision was added that the Constitution could not be altered to deprive a state of equal representation in the Senate without the state's consent. And, at the initiative of Gouverneur Morris and Massachusetts delegate Elbridge Gerry, a compromise procedure for amending the Constitution was created that incorporated both the Committee of Detail's recommendation and Madison's plan. As finally agreed upon, a constitutional amendment could be proposed either by a two-thirds vote of both houses of Congress or by a convention that Congress was to call if two-thirds of the state legislatures requested one. In either case, three-fourths of the states would have to ratify an amendment for it to become part of the Constitution.

Randolph and Mason remained unhappy. Now joined by Gerry, they again expressed doubts about the magnitude of the changes that the convention was recommending. But their motion for a subsequent constitutional convention to consider the objections and suggestions that might be made at the state ratifying conventions was defeated by a vote of eleven states to none.

The convention's labors completed, the delegates assembled on September 17 to sign an engrossed, or final, copy of the Constitution. Forty-one of the original fifty-five delegates still were present at the convention; all but Randolph, Mason, and Gerry signed the document. Even then the delegates could not resist some fine tuning, unanimously approving a Washington-supported motion to alter slightly the apportionment formula for the House of Representatives.

Speaking first before, then after the signing ceremony, Benjamin Franklin offered the convention's most memorable benedictions. To the delegates, he presented a long speech (read by Wilson because of Franklin's frailty), which said in essence:

> Mr. President, I confess that there are several parts of this constitution which I do not approve, but I am not sure that I shall never approve them. For having lived long, I have experienced many instances of being obliged by better information, or fuller consideration, to change opinions even on important subjects, which I once thought right, but found to be otherwise. . . . I doubt too whether any other convention we can obtain may be able to make a better constitution. . . . It therefore astonishes me, Sir, to find this system approaching so near to perfection as it does; and I think it will astonish our enemies. . . . Thus I consent, Sir, to this constitution because I expect no better, and because I am not sure it is not the best.[32]

Later that day, according to an oft-repeated story, someone asked Franklin as he left the hall, "Well, Doctor, what have we got? A republic or a monarchy? " "A republic, if you can keep it," Franklin replied.

Notes

1. The idea is elaborated on in Erwin C. Hargrove and Michael Nelson, *Presidents, Politics, and Policy* (Baltimore, Md.: Johns Hopkins University Press, 1984), chap. 2.
2. Jack P. Greene, *Peripheries and Center: Constitutional Development in the Extended Polities of the British Empire and the United States, 1607-1788* (Athens, Ga.: University of Georgia Press, 1986), chap. 2.
3. Quoted in Charles C. Thach, Jr., *The Creation of the Presidency, 1775-1789* (Baltimore, Md.: Johns Hopkins University Press, 1969), 27.
4. Ibid.
5. Gordon S. Wood, *The Creation of the American Republic, 1776-1787* (Chapel Hill: University of North Carolina Press, 1969), 138.
6. Thomas Jefferson, *Notes on the State of Virginia*, ed. William Peden (Chapel Hill: University of North Carolina Press, 1955).
7. Christopher Collier and James Lincoln Collier, *Decision in Philadelphia: The Constitutional Convention of 1787* (New York: Ballantine, 1986), 5.
8. To a large degree, British hostility to the United States was caused, or at least rationalized, by the U.S. failure to comply with two provisions of the Treaty of Paris. One provision compelled the United States to reimburse British loyalists for property that had been seized from them during the war; the other required that prewar debts to British merchants be paid. Individual states actively resisted both of these requirements, and the national government was powerless to enforce them.
9. Thach, *Creation of the Presidency*, 49, 52-53.
10. Lester Cappon, ed., *The Adams-Jefferson Letters* (Chapel Hill: University of North Carolina Press, 1959), 1:196; Catherine Drinker Bowen, *Miracle at Philadelphia* (Boston: Little, Brown, 1966); and John P. Roche, "The Founding Fathers: A Reform Caucus in Action," *American Political Science*

Review 55 (December 1961): 799-816.

11. Quoted in Collier and Collier, *Decision in Philadelphia*, 74.
12. Clinton Rossiter, *1787: The Grand Convention* (London: MacGibbon and Kee, 1968), 141.
13. Stanley Elkins and Eric McKitrick, "The Founding Fathers: Young Men of the Revolution," *Political Science Quarterly* 76 (June 1961): 181-216.
14. The historian Charles A. Beard believed that the enactment of the Constitution, more than anything else, was a triumph of the "personalty"—that is, financial and commercial—interests over the "realty," or landed interests (*An Economic Interpretation of the Constitution* [New York: Macmillan, 1913]). A powerful critique of this once-influential theory was offered by Forrest McDonald in *We the People: Economic Origins of the Constitution* (Chicago: University of Chicago Press, 1958).
15. Collier and Collier, *Decision in Philadelphia*, 108.
16. Cappon, *Adams-Jefferson Letters* 1:196; Max Farrand, ed., *The Records of the Federal Convention* (New Haven, Conn.: Yale University Press, 1913), 3:35. All of Madison's notes on the convention are included in Farrand. A one-volume edition is: James Madison, *Notes of Debates in the Federal Convention of 1787* (Athens: Ohio University Press, 1966).
17. Roche has argued that the preservation of secrecy by the delegates is great testimony to their sense of shared enterprise: even when they disagreed strongly over particular issues, they were sufficiently committed to the effort to keep their objections within the convention's walls ("The Founding Fathers").
18. Collier and Collier, *Decision in Philadelphia*, 120.
19. The Virginia Plan may be found in Farrand, *Records* 1:20-22.
20. The Virginia Plan was one of two that were offered to the convention on May 29. Madison recorded in his notes for that day that Charles Pinckney of South Carolina also introduced a plan. But because Madison (who had long loathed Pinckney from their days together in Congress) neither described the Pinckney Plan nor included its text, scholars have had to try to reconstruct it as best they could from other documents (in particular, some notes found in the papers of James Wilson).

    The Pinckney Plan probably resembled the Virginia Plan in many ways. It, too, provided for a strong, three-branch national government. It seems to have been more specific regarding the executive, however. The executive was to consist of a single person (called "president") who would serve a seven-year term and be empowered, among other things, to recommend laws to the legislature, oversee the executive branch, and act as commander in chief of the military.

    Pinckney borrowed most of the elements of his plan from the Articles of Confederation, the Massachusetts constitution, and, especially, the New York constitution. Still, depending on how one does the counting, somewhere between twenty-one and forty-three specific contributions to the Constitution seem to have been made by Pinckney. (S. Sidney Ulmer, "James Madison and the Pinckney Plan," *South Carolina Law Quarterly* 9 [Spring 1957]: 415-444; S. Sidney Ulmer, "Charles Pinckney: Father of the Constitution?" *South Carolina Law Quarterly* 10 [Winter 1958]: 225-247; Collier and Collier, *Decision in Philadelphia*, 97.)
21. Rossiter, *1787*, 171.
22. The resolution of the Committee of the Whole may be found in Farrand, *Records* 1:235-237.

23. The New Jersey Plan may be found in ibid. 1:242-245.
24. Hamilton's Plan may be found in ibid. 1:291-293.
25. Ibid. 1:288.
26. Ibid. 1:289.
27. The Committee of Detail report may be found in ibid. 2:177-189.
28. See note 20.
29. The recommendations of the Committee on Postponed Matters may be found in Farrand, *Records* 2:497-499, 508-509.
30. The Committee of Style draft may be found in ibid. 2:590-603.
31. The preamble it replaced was blander and more state-centered: "We the people of the states of New Hampshire, Massachusetts," etc.
32. Farrand, *Records* 2:641-643.

CHAPTER 2

Creating the Presidency

During the course of the Constitutional Convention, the presidency developed along two major lines. First, the rather loosely designed executive of the Virginia Plan took on greater clarity and specificity. Second, the weak executive, subordinate to the legislature, that most of the delegates initially seem to have favored was made stronger. These two developments manifested themselves at the convention in a variety of specific issues of executive design, including number, selection, term, removal, institutional separation, and enumerated powers.

An Overview of the Creation
of the Presidency

The design of the executive was one of the most vexing problems of the Constitutional Convention. Other issues were more controversial, but they typically lent themselves to compromise solutions, as when small states split the difference with large states and provided for a bicameral legislature and the North and the South worked out the three-fifths rule for counting slaves. When it came to the nature and powers of the executive, however, the delegates labored in a realm of such intellectual and political uncertainty that the politics of compromise were largely irrelevant.

One problem the delegates encountered was that their experience offered several models of what they did not want in an executive but few models that they found attractive. The British monarch and the royal colonial governors had been, in their eyes, tramplers of liberty. The state constitutions that were written after independence provided for

George Washington, hero of the
Revolution and presiding officer
of the Constitutional Convention,
was to many people the personifi-
cation of the new Republic and of
the presidency.

nonoppressive governors but also rendered them weak to the point of
impotence. The national government of the Articles of Confederation,
such as it was, had no chief executive at all.

A second problem that stymied the delegates derived from their
general ambivalence about executive authority. They wanted an executive branch that was strong enough to check a runaway legislature, but
not so strong as to become despotic. This ambivalence was shared by the
American people, whose hatred of monarchy existed side by side with
their longing to make George Washington king. As the political scientist
Seymour Martin Lipset has shown, Washington was a classic example of
what the German sociologist Max Weber called a charismatic leader,
one "treated as endowed with supernatural, superhuman, or at least
specifically exceptional powers or qualities." [1] The historian Marcus
Cunliffe recorded:

> Babies were being christened after him as early as 1775, and while he
> was still President, his countrymen paid to see him in waxwork effigy.
> To his admirers he was "godlike Washington," and his detractors
> complained to one another that he was looked upon as a "demigod"
> whom it was treasonous to criticize. "Oh Washington!" declared Ezra
> Stiles of Yale (in a sermon of 1783). "How I do love thy name! How
> have I often adored and blessed thy God, for creating and forming
> thee into the great ornament of humankind!" [2]

But the public's longing for Washington—shared by many delegates,
although with more restraint—was just that: a longing for Washington,
not for a monarchy. "The first man put at the helm will be a good one,"

Benjamin Franklin of Pennsylvania told the convention. "No body knows what sort may come afterwards." [3]

Despite the delegates' difficulties, the presidency took shape as the convention wore on. For all their intellectual uncertainty, the delegates moved steadily in the direction of a clearly designed executive. For all their ambivalence, they made the executive stronger as well.

Greater Clarity

The political scientist Charles Thach noted in his book *The Creation of the Presidency* that Virginia delegate James Madison "has with much justice been called the father of the Constitution." But even as admiring a scholar as Thach conceded that "the claims for his paternity do not extend to the fundamentals of Article II." [4]

Madison himself claimed no paternity of the presidency. As he wrote to George Washington on April 16, 1787, less than a month before the scheduled opening of the convention, "I have scarcely ventured as yet to form my own opinion either of the manner in which [the executive] ought to be constituted or of the authorities with which it ought to be cloathed." [5] Madison's Virginia Plan offered the convention a shadowy and vaguely defined executive. Even the basic structure of the plan's executive—was it to be a single person, a chaired board, or a committee?—was unclear. In addition, the length of the executive's term was not specified, and its powers were not enumerated.[6]

Madison's fellow delegates seem to have shared his uncertainty. The only issues they resolved to their satisfaction during the convention's first two months were the unitary nature of the executive and its power to veto laws passed by the legislature, subject to override. The Committee of Detail, which began its work on July 24, helped matters some: it gave the executive the name of president, provided for succession, and enumerated its powers. But the main issues that divided the delegates—selection, term, and reeligibility—were not resolved until September, when the Committee on Postponed Matters proposed selection by an electoral college, a term of four years with no limit on reeligibility, and the creation of the vice presidency.

Greater Strength

For all the vagueness of its conception, the national executive of the Virginia Plan generally accorded with what most delegates at the start of the Constitutional Convention seem to have been looking for, namely, an agent of restraint in a basically legislative government. The executive in Madison's proposed government was weak (it was bound by a council and devoid of enumerated powers), but it certainly was stronger than in the government of the Articles of Confederation. The executive also was subordinate to the legislature, which was empowered to elect it. But it was not subservient, as demonstrated by its fixed term, the veto power, and the bar on legislative reductions of the executive's salary.

Dissatisfied with the convention's early consensus on a subordinate executive, a coterie of committed and talented delegates worked diligently and effectively to strengthen the office's constitutional power. They were led by two Pennsylvanians—James Wilson, who envisioned the executive as "the man of the people," and Gouverneur Morris, who regarded a properly constituted executive as "the great protector of the Mass of the people." [7] During the course of the convention, the pro-executive group won victory after victory.

Number of the Executive

The number of the executive was the first issue to rouse the delegates. The debate on number took two forms. First, should the executive be unitary or plural—that is, a single-person or a committee-style office? Second, should the executive be forced to consult with a council before exercising some or all of its powers?

Unitary or Plural?

The Virginia Plan said nothing about the number of the executive, perhaps because Madison had no clear opinion on the matter or perhaps because, like Roger Sherman of Connecticut, he initially felt that the legislature should be free to define, then redefine the executive as it saw fit.

On June 1, the convention, meeting as the Committee of the Whole, heard a motion from Wilson that the executive be a single person. According to Madison's notes, "a considerable pause ensu[ed]" as the usually talkative delegates lapsed into silence.[8] Historians differ as to why: Catherine Drinker Bowen attributes the pause to the delegates' awe at the prospect of creating a potentially kinglike office; Charles Mee suggests that they were uneasy about discussing the issue in the presence of George Washington, whom everyone presumed would be the leader of whatever executive branch was created.[9] After Franklin admonished his colleagues that they were obliged to speak freely, however, the debate was joined, and the issue became an early test for the pro-executive and anti-executive forces at the convention.

Edmund Randolph of Virginia and Sherman led the fight against Wilson's motion. Randolph, arguing that a single executive, by its nature, would be the "foetus of monarchy," proposed instead a three-person committee, with one member of the executive from each region of the country. Sherman, who regarded the ideal executive "as nothing more than an institution for carrying the will of the Legislature into effect," said he "wished the number might not be fixed, but that the legislature should be at liberty to appoint one or more as experience might dictate." [10]

Wilson defended his motion shrewdly. To be sure, he argued, a single executive would be a source of "energy" and "dispatch"—that is, of leadership and action—in the new government. But Wilson also urged that a single executive was indispensable to control executive power—how could responsibility for incompetence or for abuses of power be assigned to a committee? [11] These arguments were persuasive to most delegates. They feared monarchy but realized how much the national government had suffered under the Articles of Confederation from the diffusion of executive responsibility. As property owners, they also feared threats to the social order such as Shays's Rebellion and regarded a single executive as more likely to respond quickly and effectively to riot and discord than a committee would be.

On June 4, the convention voted overwhelmingly in favor of a unitary executive. One of Washington's few recorded votes was in favor of this motion.

A Council?

The Virginia Plan provided that a "council of revision" consisting of the executive and "a convenient number of the National Judiciary" would be empowered to veto laws passed by the legislature. All thirteen state constitutions provided for a council of some sort; Sherman, who voted in the end for the single executive, said that he had done so only because he assumed it would be forced to share power with a council. Wilson, however, opposed a council because he believed that it would dilute the virtues of the unitary executive—energy, dispatch, and responsibility.

The proposal for a council was tabled on June 4 after two Massachusetts delegates, Elbridge Gerry and Rufus King, injected a new argument into the debate. Gerry and King questioned the wisdom of having judges participate in making laws that they later would be asked to rule upon. Confusion also existed among the delegates about what effect a council would have on executive power. Some saw it as a check on the executive, but others, including Wilson and Madison, thought that a council would buttress the executive with the support of the judiciary, thus strengthening it in its relations with the legislature.

The council idea recurred in several guises throughout the convention. Morris and others tried at various times to persuade the convention to enact a purely advisory council, consisting mainly of the heads of the executive departments.[12] As late as September 7, George Mason of Virginia suggested that the House of Representatives or the Senate be charged to appoint an executive council with members from all regions of the country. ("The Grand Signor himself had his Divan," Mason noted from Ottoman history.)[13] But because no consensus ever formed about either the wisdom of having a council or the form that it should take, the idea simply was abandoned.

Selection and Succession

Wilson was as much opposed to the part of the Virginia Plan that provided for the executive "to be chosen by the National Legislature" as he was in favor of a unitary executive. Legislative selection would make the executive a creature of (and thus subservient to) the legislature, Wilson believed. On June 1, he proposed instead that the executive be elected by the people. Wilson said he realized that his idea "might appear chimerical," but he could think of no better way to keep the executive and legislative branches "as independent as possible of each other, as well as of the states." [14]

The delegates virtually ignored Wilson's proposal for popular election. In principle, the idea was too democratic for their taste. (They thought of democracy mainly as mob rule.) By requiring voters to pass judgment on candidates from distant states of whom they knew little or nothing, popular election seemed impractical as well. Mason stated both of these objections cogently: "It would be as unnatural to refer the choice of a proper character for chief Magistrate to the people, as it would, to refer a trial of colours to a blind man." [15]

Undiscouraged, Wilson returned to the convention on June 2 with a proposal for an electoral college to elect the executive. For purposes of election, each state would be divided into a few districts; the voters in these would choose electors, who in turn would gather to select an executive. A plan like Wilson's was briefly accepted on July 19 and ultimately was adopted in September, but at this stage of the convention it still seemed too novel.[16] The delegates voted instead to affirm the legislative selection provision of the Virginia Plan.

The decision for legislative selection, although it was reaffirmed in several votes taken in July and August, was not a happy one. The source of the unhappiness was that, in the delegates' minds, a legislatively selected executive could not be allowed to stand for reelection, lest the powers and patronage of the office be used for the purpose of, in effect, bribing legislators for their support. But the delegates also believed that eligibility for reelection was a valuable incentive to good performance in office and regretted that legislative selection of the executive ruled reeligibility out. The result was an ongoing search for a selection process that was desirable in its own right and that allowed for reelection. This was no easy task. Among the ideas the delegates considered and rejected, wrote the political scientist Clinton Rossiter, were some rather far-fetched ones:

> election by the state governors or by electors chosen by them, neither a scheme that could muster any support; nomination by the people of each state of "its best citizen," and election from this pool of thirteen by the national legislature or electors chosen by it, an unhelpful proposal of John Dickinson; election by the national legislature, with electors chosen by the state legislatures taking over whenever an executive sought reelection, a proposal of [Oliver] Ellsworth that found favor with four states; and, most astounding of all, election by a small group of national legislators chosen "by lot". . . .[17]

The search for an alternative to legislative selection became more urgent after August 24. Until that day, no consideration had been given to *how* the legislature was to choose the president. Now, by a vote of seven states to four, the convention approved a motion that Congress would select the president by a "joint ballot" of all the members of the House of Representatives and Senate. This decision, by giving the large states a clear majority in the presidential selection process (there would be many more representatives than senators), threatened to reignite the controversy between large and small states that already had split the convention once. To avert this catastrophe, Sherman, who originally had suggested the compromise between the large and the small states on legislative apportionment, moved on August 31 to refer the whole issue of presidential selection to the Committee on Postponed Matters.

On September 4, the committee proposed the electoral college as a method to elect the president, with no restriction on the president's right to seek reelection. The president would be selected by a majority vote of the electors, who would be chosen by the states using whatever methods they individually adopted. (The delegates expected that most states would entrust the selection of electors to the people.)[18] Each state would receive a number of electoral votes equal to its representation in Congress. If no presidential candidate received votes from a majority of electors, the Senate would elect the president from among the five highest electoral vote recipients. In addition, to prevent a "cabal" from forming in the electoral college, electors would never meet as a national body—instead, they would vote in their own state capitals, then send the results to the Senate for counting. Finally, to ensure that the electors would not simply support a variety of home-state favorites, each was required to vote for two candidates for president from two different states (an idea first proposed by Gouverneur Morris on July 25), with the runner-up in the presidential election filling the newly created office of vice president.

The proposal for an electoral college was generally well received by the delegates. As Fred Barbash has argued, it was the ideal political compromise, "baited" with something for virtually every group at the convention:

> For those in the convention anxious for the President to be allowed reelection, the committee made him eligible without limit.
> For those worried about excessive dependence of the President on the national legislature, the committee determined that electors chosen as each state saw fit would cast ballots for the presidency.
> For the large states and the South, the committee decided that the number of electors would be proportioned according to each state's combined representation in the House and Senate. . . .
> For the small states, the committee determined that when no candidate won a majority of electoral votes, the Senate would choose the president from among the leading contenders.[19]

Only one aspect of the proposed electoral college was controversial among the delegates, that of Senate selection of the president in the absence of an electoral college majority. Large-state delegates objected because the Senate underrepresented them in favor of the small states. What is more, not foreseeing the development of a two-party system, most delegates believed that after Washington (the obvious choice for the first president) left office, majorities seldom would form in the electoral college and the Senate would choose most presidents. Mason estimated that the electoral college would fail to reach a majority "nineteen times in twenty." [20]

Once again, Sherman proposed an acceptable compromise: let the House of Representatives elect the president when the electoral college failed to produce a majority, but assign each state delegation a single vote. The Senate still would choose the vice president. Quickly, on September 6, the convention agreed.

One issue that the creation of the vice presidency resolved, at least partially, was: What happens if the president dies, resigns, becomes disabled, or is impeached and convicted? The Committee of Detail was the first to deal with the matter. It recommended that the president of the Senate be designated "to discharge the powers and duties of [the Presidency] . . . until another President of the United States be chosen, or until the disability of the President be ended." When Madison and other delegates objected to this proposal because it might give the Senate an incentive to remove a president in favor of one of its members, the issue was referred to the Committee on Postponed Matters.

The committee proposed that the vice president, not a senator, be president of the Senate; it also designated the vice president as the official to step in when a vacancy occurred in the presidency. The convention agreed, but only after passing an additional motion that seemed to call for a special presidential election before the expiration of the departed president's term. Somehow this intention was lost when the Committee of Style wrote its final draft of the Constitution. No one caught the error. As a result, the convention left the Constitution vague on two important matters. First, was the vice president to become president in the event of the president's death, resignation, disability, or removal or merely to assume the powers and duties of the presidency? Second, was the vice president to serve out the unexpired balance of the president's term or only to fill in until a special election could be held to pick a new president?

Term of Office

Questions of length of term, eligibility for reelection, and selection were so interwoven in the minds of the delegates that they could not resolve any of them independently of the others. Indeed, one political scientist has compared their efforts to sort out these questions to a game of "three-dimensional chess." [21]

The Virginia Plan left the length of the executive's term of office blank—literally. ("Resolved, that a National Executive be ... chosen by the National Legislature for the term of —— years.") The plan also stipulated that the executive was "to be ineligible a second time." When these provisions came before the Committee of the Whole on June 1, a variety of alternatives were proposed, including a three-year term with no limit on reeligibility; a three-year term with two reelections allowed; and a seven-year term, with no reeligibility. Although the delegates approved the single seven-year term, the vote was narrow, five states to four.

Underlying the delegates' uncertainty was a basic choice between two provisions concerning the executive that they regarded as incompatible: eligibility for reelection or legislative selection. Mason well stated the reason that, in their view, one could not have both: if the legislature could reelect the executive, there would be a constant "temptation on the side of the Executive to intrigue with the Legislature for a re-appointment," using political patronage and illegitimate favors in effect to buy votes.[22]

On July 17, the convention voted for both legislative selection and reeligibility, but when James McClurg of Virginia pointed out the contradiction between these two decisions, ineligibility for reelection was reinstated. McClurg, supported by Morris and by Jacob Broom of Delaware, offered a different way out of the dilemma: election of the executive by the legislature for a life term. But this proposal seemed too reminiscent of a king to suit the other delegates.

On July 24 and 26, the convention voted again to have the legislature elect the executive for a single term. But the advantages the delegates saw in reeligibility were so powerful that the issue remained alive. Reeligibility not only would give the nation a way to keep a good executive in office, it also would give the executive what Morris called "the great motive to good behavior, the hope of being rewarded with a re-appointment." [23] As Alexander Hamilton of New York later argued in *Federalist* No. 72, even an executive whose behavior was governed by such personal motives as "avarice," "ambition," or "the love of fame" would do a good job in order to hold on to the office that could fulfill those desires.[24] "Shut the Civil road to Glory," warned Morris, "& he may be compelled to seek it by the sword." [25]

To complicate their task further, the delegates' decision between legislative selection and reeligibility implied a related decision between a shorter term for the executive and a longer term. If the executive were to be chosen by the legislature for a single term only, the delegates believed, the term should be long. If the executive were eligible for reelection, a shorter term was preferable.

In late August, the convention changed course for the last time. Effectively deciding against legislative selection of the president, the delegates created the Committee on Postponed Matters to propose an alternative. The committee's recommendation, adopted by the convention, was that the electoral college choose the president for a four-year term, with no limit on reeligibility.

Removal

During the course of the convention, the delegates decided to provide for situations in which the executive needed to be removed from office before the expiration of the term. Serious abuse of power by the president was one such situation—the remedy was impeachment. Disability was the other, but, even at the end of the convention, the delegates were less than clear about what ought to be done if the executive became disabled.

Impeachment

Although the Virginia Plan made no specific provision for impeaching the executive (it said only that the "supreme tribunal" would "hear and determine . . . impeachments of any National officers"), most of the delegates agreed from the outset that some mechanism should be included explicitly in the Constitution. Even proponents of a strong executive quickly came to realize that their goal could be achieved only if the other delegates felt confident that an out-of-control executive could be removed from office.

The convention's consensus on impeachment was revealed on June 2, when the Committee of the Whole quickly passed North Carolina delegate Hugh Williamson's motion that the executive be "removable on impeachment and conviction of malpractice or neglect of duty." [26] (Impeachment is comparable to indictment by a grand jury; it must be followed by a trial and conviction in order for the impeached official to be removed from office.) The consensus was confirmed and strengthened on July 19, when Morris suggested that if the executive were assigned a short term, there would be no need for impeachment—the passage of time would lead to the executive's removal soon enough. Morris was answered the next day by Gerry, Randolph, Franklin, and Mason, each of whom made clear that he regarded impeachment not only as a vital safeguard against and punishment for abuses of power, but also (at least in Franklin's view) as a way to remove tyrants without having to resort to assassination. Morris quickly retreated, declaring that he was persuaded by his colleagues' arguments.

The Committee of Detail tried to clarify Williamson's definition of the grounds for presidential impeachment, changing it from "malpractice or neglect of duty" to "treason, bribery, or corruption." It also created a mechanism for removal: "impeachment by the House of Representatives and conviction in the Supreme Court." The convention did not take up the impeachment provision of the committee's report until August 27, when Morris asked that it be tabled. He argued that if, as still seemed possible, the convention decided to create a council of revision for the president that included the chief justice of the Supreme Court, the Court should not be involved in the impeachment process. The delegates agreed to Morris's motion without objection. Later that week, on August 31, the Committee on Postponed Matters was formed and took charge of the impeachment issue.

The committee made its three-part recommendation on September 4: first, impeachment by the House; second, trial by the Senate, with the chief justice presiding; and third, impeachment on grounds of treason or bribery, but not the vague offense of "corruption." On September 8, Mason complained that simply to bar treason and bribery "will not reach many great and dangerous offenses," including certain "attempts to subvert the Constitution." He proposed that "maladministration" be added to the list of impeachable actions.[27] After Madison objected that in practice maladministration would mean nothing more than unpopularity in Congress, Mason replaced it with "other high crimes and misdemeanors." This phrase passed, despite Madison's continuing objection.

Two other modifications to the committee's impeachment proposal were made by the delegates on September 8. First, the majority required for Senate conviction was raised to two-thirds. Second, the vice president and "all civil officers of the United States" were made subject to impeachment in the same way as the president.

Disability

As thorough as the delegates were in considering the grounds for and process of presidential impeachment, they treated cavalierly the situation of a president who is disabled. The matter first was put before the convention on August 6, as part of a provision of the Committee of Detail's report that dealt mainly with succession. It read: "In the case of his ... disability to discharge the powers and duties of his office, the President of the Senate shall exercise those powers and duties, until another President of the United States be chosen, or until the disability of the President be removed."

On August 27, when this provision of the committee's report came before the convention, John Dickinson of Delaware complained that "it was too vague. What is the extent of the term 'disability' & who is to be the judge of it?" [28] The delegates decided to postpone their discussion of disability until another time, presumably intending to supply answers to these questions. In a historic case of oversight, that time never came. *Disability* was left an undefined term in the Constitution, nor was any process created either to determine if a president were disabled or to transfer the powers and duties of the presidency to a temporary successor. Instead, the Committee on Postponed Matters merely named the vice president, rather than the president of the Senate, as the successor to a disabled president and substituted *inability* for *disability*, without explaining what difference, if any, this substitution made.

Institutional Separation from Congress

Many of the delegates were very much influenced by the idea that in order to preserve liberty, government should be designed to incorporate the principle of separation of powers. Various political philosophers of the Enlightenment, including England's John Locke, had articulated this idea, but no version was more familiar to the delegates than that of the Frenchman, Baron de Montesquieu. Montesquieu, the author of *L'Esprit des Lois (The Spirit of the Laws,* 1748) was "the oracle who is always consulted and cited" on the subject of separation of powers, wrote Madison in *Federalist* No. 47. According to a passage from Montesquieu's book that the delegates knew well and that *Federalist* No. 47 quoted:

When the legislative and executive powers are united in the same person or body, there can be no liberty because apprehensions may arise lest *the same* monarch or senate should *enact* tyrannical laws to *execute* them in a tyrannical manner. ... Were the power of judging joined with the legislative, the life and liberty of the subject would be exposed to arbitrary control, for *the judge* would then be *the legislator*.[29]

The separation of powers principle did not require a strict division of labor, in which each branch of the government was assigned exclusive power to perform certain functions. Indeed, the Constitution assigns few powers to the federal government that are not shared by two or more branches. Separation of powers actually meant something more like "separation of institutions" to the delegates, a separation in which the membership of one branch does not overlap and cannot persecute the membership of another.[30]

From the beginning, the convention imposed two prohibitions to preserve institutional separation within the government. The first prohibition was against alterations in the incumbent executive's salary; the other was against simultaneous membership in the legislative and executive branches. Both prohibitions were stated in the Virginia Plan and remained substantially unaltered in the final Constitution.

Salary

Immediately after the clause stating that the executive shall be chosen by the legislature, the Virginia Plan provided that the executive shall "receive punctually at stated times, a fixed compensation for the services rendered, in which no increase or diminution shall be made so as to affect the Magistracy existing at the time of increase or diminution." In view of the Virginia Plan's brevity and generality, the detail in this provision is remarkable, as is the priority assigned to it. Clearly, Madison feared that a legislature either might infringe on the executive's independence by lowering or delaying the salary or might reward or entice the executive with an increase in salary.

During the course of the convention, the provision for executive salary was modified only slightly. (The delegates eventually added a provision that "he shall not receive within [his term of office] any other Emolument from the United States, or any of them.") On June 2, Franklin wrote (and Wilson read) a long, almost wistful speech to urge that the executive not be compensated at all because to attach a salary to the position "united in view of the same object" two "passions which have a powerful influence on the affairs of such men. These are ambition and avarice, the love of power, and the love of money. ... Place before the eyes of men a post of *honor* that shall be at the same time a place of *profit*, and they will move heaven and earth to obtain it." [31] The delegates gave Franklin's speech a courteous listening and no more. Their concern was to protect the executive from the legislature, not to create an office that only the rich could afford to occupy.

Membership

As with their ban on altering an incumbent president's salary, the delegates' commitment to separating membership in Congress and the executive branch did not waver. The Virginia Plan said that legislators were "ineligible to any office established by a particular State, or under the authority of the United States, except those peculiarly belonging to the functions of the first branch [the legislature], during the term of service, and for the space of —— after its expiration." The final document, although lifting the temporary bar on legislators holding executive office after they left Congress, included essentially the same provision: "no Person holding any Office under the United States, shall be a Member of either House during his Continuance in Office." The Constitution also prohibited members of Congress from serving as electors in presidential elections.

The delegates wanted to keep the membership of the legislative and executive branches separate to prevent the executive from bribing members of Congress for their support with jobs and salaries. On June 22, Pierce Butler of South Carolina, supported by Mason, "appealed to the example of G[reat] B[ritain] where men got into Parl[iamen]t. that they might get offices for themselves or their friends. This was the source of corruption that ruined their Govt." [32]

The office-holding issue was raised again on August 14, when John Mercer of Maryland took the opposite side of the question. He argued that since "[g]overnments can only be maintained by *force* or *influence*" and the president lacks force, then to "deprive him of influence by rendering the members of the Legislature ineligible to Executive offices" was to reduce the president to "a mere phantom of authority." [33] Unpersuaded, the delegates did not alter their earlier decision, either then or on September 3, when the further argument was made by Wilson and Charles Pinckney of South Carolina that honorable people would be reluctant to serve in government if the official presumption was that they were too corrupt to fulfill faithfully the responsibilities of more than one office.[34]

Nothing was said during the convention about judges holding executive offices. The New Jersey Plan would have prohibited them from doing so, but the subject never was discussed on the convention floor. Indeed, most of the proposals that individual delegates made for a council of revision included one or more federal judges as members. The political scientist Robert Scigliano has argued that allowing judges to hold executive office was not an oversight on the delegates' part. Instead, they regarded the executive and judicial powers as in some ways joined. (Both involved carrying out the law.) The delegates also believed that Congress would be the most powerful branch in the new government unless the executive and the judiciary could unite when necessary to restrain it.[35]

Enumerated Powers

The delegates were slow to enumerate the powers of either the presidency or the other branches of the government. Indeed, their initial inclination seems to have been to give each branch a general grant of powers rather than a specific list. The Virginia Plan, for example, empowered the legislature "to legislate in all cases to which the separate states are incompetent, or in which the harmony of the United States may be interrupted by the exercise of individual [state] Legislation." The executive, in addition to sharing the veto with a council, was to execute the national laws.

The advantage the delegates saw in a general grant of powers (which they approved both while meeting as the Committee of the Whole and soon afterward in convention) was that the alternative, a specific enumeration, risked limiting the government to a list of powers that the passage of time could render obsolete. But the convention was uneasy with its choice. "Incompetent" was a vague word, easily subject to abuse, but so was any other phrase they might invent for a general grant.

Reading the delegates' mood (if not their minds), the Committee of Detail included an enumeration of each branch's powers in the draft constitution that it presented to the convention. The committee anticipated the convention's reaction correctly. Although the delegates debated each proposed power separately, they never questioned the decision to enumerate.

The powers of the presidency are detailed in Article II of the Constitution (except for the veto power, which is in Article I, section 7). They are discussed here in the order of their appearance in the Constitution. Three other provisions that are examined in this section—the president's title, oath of office, and qualifications—also are spelled out in Article II.

Veto Power

The right to veto acts passed by the legislature was the only specific grant of power to the executive in the Virginia Plan. The states' recent experience with weak governors and powerful legislatures was proof enough to most delegates that the veto was indispensable to executive self-defense against legislative encroachments. Even so, they were initially reluctant to cede too much responsibility to the executive. The Virginia Plan provided that the executive could cast a veto only with the cooperation of a council of judges. Vetoes could be overridden (and the vetoed act become law) by vote of an unspecified majority of both houses of the legislature.

On June 4, Wilson and Hamilton urged the delegates, then meeting as the Committee of the Whole, to grant the executive an absolute veto—that is, a veto not subject to legislative override. Franklin, Sherman, Mason, and others rose in opposition to this suggestion, invoking their own and the public's memories of the British king and the royal governors, who had cast absolute vetoes against the acts of American legislatures in colonial times. "We are not indeed constituting a British Government, but a more dangerous monarchy, an elective one," warned Mason, who wanted to empower the executive merely to postpone the enactment of an offensive law in the hope that the legislature would decide to revise it.[36] Gerry found a middle ground that was acceptable to the delegates: an executive veto, subject to override by a two-thirds vote of each house of the legislature. The recommendation that the executive share the veto power with a council was tabled.

In its report of August 6, the Committee of Detail, although faithfully reflecting the decisions of the Committee of the Whole regarding the veto, also sought to clarify two unresolved issues. First, it assigned the right to cast vetoes to the president alone. Second, it stipulated that after a bill was passed and presented, the president would have seven days in which to respond. If the bill was neither signed nor vetoed by the president in that period, it would become law. An important exception was made, however, in order that Congress not try to get its way by adjourning before the president had a chance to cast a veto. If Congress adjourned within the seven-day period, the president had merely to ignore the bill for it to be vetoed. Such vetoes later came to be called "pocket vetoes."

On August 15 and 16, the convention voted to modify the Committee of Detail's report in ways that strengthened the president's veto power. The two-thirds requirement for congressional override of a veto was raised to three-fourths. In addition, the period in which a president could cast a veto was lengthened from seven days to ten days, not including Sundays. Finally, the convention decided that to prevent Congress from evading a veto by passing legislation and calling it something other than a "bill," the veto power would extend to "every order, resolution, or vote" of Congress.

Only one further modification was made in the veto. On September

12, in a gesture to delegates suspicious of presidential power that was designed to win their signatures on the Constitution, the convention voted to restore the two-thirds requirement for a legislative override.

"The Executive Power"

The Virginia Plan introduced the executive article by stating "that a national Executive be instituted." The Committee of the Whole modified this provision of the plan only by adding "to consist of a single person." The Committee of Detail, however, proposed "vesting" clauses for all three branches of government:

> The legislative power shall be vested in a Congress. . . .
> The Executive Power of the United States shall be vested in a single person. His stile shall be, "The President of the United States of America," and his title shall be, "His Excellency."
> The Judicial Power of the United States shall be vested in one Supreme Court, and in such inferior courts as shall, when necessary, from time to time, be constituted by the Legislature of the United States.

The vesting clause that the Committee of Detail proposed for the president was particularly important because it made clear that the powers of the presidency derived directly from the Constitution, not from discretionary grants by Congress. But the clause was less instructive on another important aspect of presidential power. As the political scientist Richard Pious has noted, " 'Executive Power' was a general term, sufficiently ambiguous so that no one could say precisely what it meant. It was possible that the words referred to more than the enumerated powers that followed, and might confer a set of unspecified executive powers." [37] First among these would be prerogative powers, which had been discussed at length in a book that was widely familiar among the delegates, John Locke's *Second Treatise on Government.* Locke had argued that in times of crisis, laws and constitutional provisions that were inadequate to the challenges at hand might temporarily have to "give way to the executive power, viz., that as much as may be, all the members of society are to be preserved." Prerogative, according to Locke, was "the people's permitting their rulers to do several things of their own free choice, where the law was silent, or sometimes, too, against the direct letter of the law, for the public good, and their acquiescing in it when so done." [38]

The theory that the powers of the presidency extend beyond those listed in the Constitution is supported by the language of the document itself, thanks to a "joker," as Thach has called it, that Morris, the chief draftsman for the Committee of Style, tossed into the final version. The committee's charge was merely to put the Constitution into polished language. "Positively with respect to the executive article," noted Thach, Morris "could do nothing." His pro-executive biases were so well known that any substantive changes would have been quickly detected. Morris left the vesting clause for the presidency unaltered ("the executive Power shall be vested in a President of the United States of America") but changed the vesting clause for Congress to read: "All legislative Powers *herein granted* shall be vested in a Congress of the United States" (emphasis added).

Thach suspects that Morris did his tinkering "with full realization of the possibilities"—namely, that presidents later could claim that the different phrasing of the branches' vesting clauses implies that there is an executive power beyond those "herein granted." (Otherwise, why would the Constitution not apply those restricting words to the president in the same way it does to Congress?) "At any rate," Thach concluded, "whether intentional or not, it admitted an interpretation of executive power which would give the president a field of activity wider than that outlined by the enumerated powers." [39]

Commander in Chief

Because nothing was said in the Virginia Plan about who would direct the armed forces, the delegates took it for granted during the early stages of the convention that Congress would be the controlling branch, as it had been under the Articles of Confederation. The issue did not come up for debate in the Committee of the Whole. The Committee of Detail, however, included a military role for the president in its enumeration of the suggested powers of each branch.

The committee proposed that the president "shall be commander in chief of the Army and Navy of the United States, and of the Militia of the several States." But it also suggested that Congress be empowered "to make war; to raise armies; to build and equip fleets; to call forth the aid of the militia, in order to execute the laws of the Union; enforce treaties; suppress insurrections, and repel invasions." The meaning of these various provisions confused the delegates when they took them up for consideration on August 17. Clearly, Congress's power to "make" war included directing the actual conduct of the fighting, but so did the president's power as "commander in chief of the Army and the Navy." Which branch, then, would actually order soldiers and sailors into action? Which would tell them where to go and what to do when they got there?

Debate on the convention floor concerning the powers of war was brief and went only part way toward resolving the ambiguities created by the Committee of Detail. Butler, doubting that Congress (or even the Senate alone) would be able to act quickly enough should a military need arise, urged the convention to vest the power to make war in the president alone, "who will have all the requisite qualities, and will not make war but when the Nation will support it." Madison and Gerry, agreeing that Congress might be unable to respond to foreign invasions promptly (perhaps because it was not in session) but not willing to entrust the president with such vast military powers, "moved to insert *'declare'* [war], striking out *'make'* war; leaving to the Executive the power to repel sudden attacks." Sherman agreed: "The Executive shd. be able to repel and not to commence war." [40] Madison and Gerry's motion passed.

As for control of the various state militia, on August 27 the convention approved without discussion a motion by Sherman that the president be commander in chief of the militia only "when called into the actual service of the U.S." Thus, the clause as finally written in the Constitution reads: "The President shall be Commander in Chief of the Army and Navy of the United States, and of the Militia of the several States, when called into the actual Service of the United States."

"Require the Opinion"

The Constitution includes a provision that empowers the president to "require the Opinion, in writing, of the principal Officer in each of the executive Departments, upon any Subject relating to the Duties of their respective Offices." This curious clause (Hamilton described it in *Federalist* No. 74 "as a mere redundancy in the plan, as the right for which it provides would result of itself from the office") [41] was proposed by the Committee on Postponed Matters and adopted by a unanimous vote of the state delegations on September 7. But the clause's origin lies in the Virginia Plan's proposal for an executive council, an idea that recurred frequently during the convention.

Although most delegates seem to have favored some sort of council, they never created one because they held such varied opinions about who should be on the council and whether its relationship to the president would be merely advisory or would involve the shared exercise of executive powers. One version of the council idea was included in a sweeping plan for the organization of the executive branch that Morris and Charles Pinckney introduced on August 20. The Morris-Pinckney plan provided that five departments would be created, to be headed by, respectively, a secretary of domestic affairs, of commerce and finance, of foreign affairs, of war, and of marine. All five of these "principal officers" would be appointed by the president and would serve at the president's pleasure. Together with the chief justice of the Supreme Court, they would constitute a Council of State whose purpose would be to assist the President in conducting the Public affairs. . . . The President may from time to time submit any matter to the discussion of the Council of State, and *he may require the written opinions of any one or more of the members:* But he shall in all cases exercise his own judgment, and either Conform to such opinions or not as he may think proper; and every officer abovementioned shall be responsible for his opinion on the affairs relating to his particular Department—(emphasis added).[42]

The Morris-Pinckney plan was not debated by the delegates, but the proposal to empower the president to require written opinions from individual department heads on matters relating to their responsibilities seems to have underlain the Committee on Postponed Matters' September 4 recommendation. Although on September 7 Mason, Franklin, Wilson, Dickinson, and Madison again urged that a council be created, their colleagues, frustrated by their inability to agree on a specific proposal and eager to conclude the convention's business, approved the committee's recommendation as written.

Power to Pardon

Hamilton was the first to suggest to the convention that it grant the president the power to pardon criminals. In his long and generally unpersuasive speech to the delegates on June 18, he urged that the executive "have the power of pardoning all offences except Treason; which he shall not pardon without the approbation of the Senate." [43] Perhaps persuaded by Hamilton's proposal, the Committee of Detail recommended that the president "shall have power to grant reprieves and pardons; but his pardon shall not be pleadable in bar of an impeachment" (that is, to prevent an impeachment).

Remarkably (because the pardon power is a power of kings and the only unchecked power the Constitution grants to the president), the delegates resisted efforts to modify the committee's recommendation in any substantial way. Sherman's August 25 motion to require the president to gain Senate consent for a pardon was defeated by a vote of eight states to one. Two days later, Luther Martin of Maryland moved to allow pardons only "after conviction"; he withdrew the motion when Wilson, using the crime of forgery as an example, objected that "pardon before conviction might be necessary in order to obtain the testimony of accomplices." On September 12, the Committee of Style clarified one aspect of the pardon power by limiting it to "offences against the United States"—that is, to violations of national rather than state law. A September 15 motion by Randolph to disallow pardons for treason ("The President may himself be guilty. The Traytors may be his own instruments.") was defeated by a vote of eight states to two after Wilson argued that if the president "be himself a party to the guilt he can be impeached and prosecuted." [44]

No thoroughgoing case for granting the pardon power to the president ever was offered at the convention, but Hamilton's defense of it in *Federalist* No. 74 may have reflected the delegates' thinking. Hamilton began by pleading the need for leeway in the criminal justice system to make "exceptions in favor of unfortunate guilt." As to pardons for treason, he wrote (perhaps with Shays's Rebellion in mind), "The principal argument for reposing the power of pardoning in this case in the Chief Magistrate is this: in seasons of insurrection or rebellion there are often critical moments when a well-timed offer of pardon to the insurgents or rebels may restore the tranquility of the commonwealth; and which, if suffered to pass unimproved, it may never be possible afterwards to recall." [45]

Power to "Make Treaties"

At the start of the convention most delegates seemed to assume that the power to make treaties with other countries would be vested in Congress. That had been the practice under the Articles of Confederation, and although the Virginia Plan said nothing explicitly about treaties, it did provide that "the National Legislature ought to be impowered to enjoy the Legislative Rights vested in Congress by the Confederation."

The first suggestion that the treaty power should be shared between the legislative and executive branches seems to have been made by Hamilton. Among the specific provisions of the plan of government he proposed on June 18 was that the executive should "have with the approbation and advice of the Senate the power of making all treaties." [46] The delegates did not discuss Hamilton's suggestion on the convention floor, and it appeared to be dead when the August 6 report of the Committee of Detail provided instead that "the Senate shall have power to make treaties." But the committee's proposal sparked heated debate.

Mason argued that an exclusive treaty-making power would enable the Senate to "sell the whole country by means of treaties." [47] Madison thought that the president, who represented all of the people, should have the power exclusively. Regional concerns also were expressed: Southern delegates worried that their states' right to free navigation of the Mississippi River might be surrendered in a future treaty; New Englanders expressed similar fears about the right to fish in the waters near Newfoundland. The delegates, having reached an impasse, referred the treaty issue to the Committee on Postponed Matters.

On September 4, the committee recommended that the president, "with the advice and Consent of the Senate," be granted the treaty-making power and that no treaty be approved "without the consent of two-thirds of the members [of the Senate] present." The provision for a two-thirds vote, which was designed to assuage the concerns of the southerners and New Englanders that they would be outnumbered on issues of regional importance, was highly controversial and provoked numerous motions to revise. One proposal would have deleted the two-thirds requirement in favor of a simple majority vote. Another would have strengthened the requirement by stipulating a two-thirds vote of the entire membership of the Senate, not just those who were present for the vote. Another would have included the House of Representatives in the ratification process. Yet another proposal—which initially passed and then was rejected—would have applied the simple majority rule to treaties whose purpose was to end a war. In the end, however, the committee's recommendation of a two-thirds vote of the senators present was accepted.

The proposal to involve the president with the Senate in treaty making was relatively uncontroversial, reflecting an alliance between pro-executive delegates and small-state delegates that had formed after the convention decided that states would be represented equally in the Senate. Only one motion was made to modify the president's role: Madison moved to allow two-thirds of the Senate, acting alone if it chose to do so, to conclude peace treaties. Madison worried that the president, who inevitably would derive unusual power and importance from a state of war, might be tempted to "impede a treaty of peace." His motion failed when Nathaniel Gorham of Massachusetts pointed out that Congress could end a war by simply refusing to appropriate funds to continue the fighting.[48]

Appointment and Commissioning Power

Article II, section 2, of the Constitution, as finally written, provides three methods for appointing federal judges and other unelected government officials: presidential appointment with Senate confirmation (the ordinary method); presidential appointment without Senate confirmation (when the Senate is in recess); and, when Congress so determines by statute, appointment of certain "inferior Officers" (officers subordinate to the heads of the departments or the courts of law) by the heads of the departments or the courts of law. Clearly the delegates moved a long way from both the Articles of Confederation, which vested the appointment power entirely in Congress, and the Virginia Plan, which proposed to continue that practice.

The appointment power was one of the first, last, and (in between) the most contentious issues at the convention. On June 1, meeting as the Committee of the Whole, the delegates did accept Madison's motion to modify the Virginia Plan slightly by adding to the then-limited powers of the executive the ambiguous phrase: "to appoint to offices in cases not otherwise provided for." [49] But this decision simply opened the door to stronger advocates of executive power, such as Wilson and Hamilton, who wished to make the appointment of judges, ambassadors, and other government officials a purely executive responsibility, with no involvement by the legislature at all.

Hot debate erupted periodically during the months of June and July about such issues as which branch of government would be most prone to favoritism in appointments and which would know the most about the qualifications of prospective appointees. Many delegates, mindful of how George III and his royal governors in the colonies had used government appointments as patronage plums to curry support among legislators, dreaded giving this power to even a home-grown executive.

On July 21, the delegates voted to confer on the Senate sole responsibility for the appointment of judges. The Committee of Detail added the appointment of ambassadors to the Senate's list of powers, then stipulated that Congress as a whole should elect the national treasurer (that is, the secretary of the Treasury). The committee also confirmed the convention's earlier decision that the president "shall appoint officers in all cases not otherwise provided for by this Constitution" and empowered the president to "commission all the officers of the United States." It remained unclear, however, where responsibility would lie for appointing the heads of the departments or other departmental officials and employees.

On August 24, during a period in which the delegates generally were turning more in the direction of increased presidential power, they passed a motion that, although not altogether clear, seemed to expand the president's right to make appointments, while leaving complete responsibility for choosing judges and ambassadors in the Senate's jurisdiction. The motion, offered by Dickinson, stated: the president "shall appoint to all offices established by this Constitution, except in cases herein otherwise provided for, and to all offices which may hereafter be created by law." [50] The delegates did not revisit, however, their August 17 rejection of Delaware delegate George Read's motion to allow the president to appoint the treasurer. They still wanted anything to do with money firmly in Congress's hands.

As with the treaty-making power, the Committee on Postponed Matters proposed in early September to increase further the president's role in the appointment process. Judges, ambassadors, ministers, and officers that the delegates had not already provided for—all would be appointed by the president with the advice and consent of the Senate. A simple majority vote of the senators present would suffice to confirm a presidential appointment. Wilson tried again to persuade the delegates to make appointments a unilateral power of the president (to involve the Senate, he argued, would foster "a dangerous tendency to aristocracy"), but his motion was unsuccessful.[51]

The convention accepted the committee's recommendation after making three additions on September 6, 14, and 15, respectively: the president was given the power to fill vacancies that occurred while the Senate was in recess, the power to appoint the Treasury secretary was transferred from Congress to the president, and control over certain forms of patronage was distributed between the two branches by giving Congress the power to "vest the appointment of such inferior officers as they think proper" in the president, the courts, or the heads of the departments.

Advisory Legislative Powers

In enumerating the proposed powers of the presidency, the Committee of Detail provided that: "He shall, from time to time, give information to the Legislature, of the state of the Union: he may recommend to their consideration such measures as he shall deem necessary, and expedient." The latter of these two provisions, both of which were uncontroversial, was modified slightly in response to an August 24 motion by Morris. He argued that the Constitution should make it "the *duty* of the President to recommend [measures to Congress], & thence prevent umbrage or cavil at his doing it." The convention approved Morris's specific suggestion that the words "he may" be replaced by "and." [52] Thus, the Constitution as finally written reads: "He shall from time to time give to the Congress Information of the State of the Union, and recommend to their Consideration such Measures as he shall judge necessary and expedient."

Powers to Convene and Adjourn Congress

The Committee of Detail recommended that the president be empowered to "convene them [the House and Senate] on extraordinary occasions"—that is, to call Congress into special session. Further, "In case of disagreement between the two Houses, with regard to the time of adjournment, he may adjourn them to such time as he thinks proper."

James McHenry of Maryland, wanting to grant the president the flexibility to call only the Senate back into session (presumably to consider a treaty or a presidential appointment), persuaded the delegates to amend the special session clause to that effect on September 8. The Constitution therefore reads: "he may, on extraordinary Occasions, convene both Houses, or either of them."

Power to "Receive Ambassadors"

The president's power to "receive Ambassadors" was proposed by the Committee of Detail. The committee joined this power to another—permission to "correspond with the supreme Executives of the several States" (the state governors)—which the convention rejected on August 25 as, according to Morris, "unnecessary and implying that the president could not correspond with others." [53] As for receiving ambassadors, the absence of debate or discussion by the delegates makes it unclear whether they meant this power to be substantive or merely ceremonial. In practice, the power to receive (or, in particular cases, refuse to receive) ambassadors has made the president the sole official recipient of communications from foreign governments and the sole maker of decisions about which governments the United States will recognize diplomatically.

"Take Care"

According to the Virginia Plan, the executive was to have "general authority to execute the National Laws." On June 1, Madison sought to revise this to read: "power to carry into effect the national laws . . . and to execute such other powers not Legislative nor Judiciary in their nature as may from time to time be delegated by the national Legislature." The stipulation about legislative and judicial powers reflected Madison's acceptance of a suggestion by Charles Cotesworth Pinckney, who felt it was important to prohibit explicitly "improper powers" from being delegated to the executive. The other South Carolina Pinckney (Charles) persuaded the delegates to strike the amendment as "unnecessary." [54] No further controversy over the "take care" clause ensued. The Committee of Detail's formulation—"he shall take care that the laws of the United States be duly and faithfully executed"—was adopted without discussion by the convention and survived virtually intact in the final Constitution: "he shall take Care that the Laws be faithfully executed."

Title

During the first two months of their deliberations, the delegates usually referred to the head of the executive branch as the "national executive," "supreme executive," or "governor." On August 6, the Committee of Detail, borrowing from Charles Pinckney, included the term "president" in its report to the convention. The title had been used for the presiding officer of Congress and of many other legislative bodies, including the convention itself. It was familiar and unthreatening to those who feared that the delegates might be creating a monarchical or tyrannical office. Once proposed by the committee, "president" was accepted without debate by the convention.

Oath of Office

"Before he enter on the Execution of his Office," the Constitution requires of the president, "he shall take the following Oath or Affirmation:—'I do solemnly swear (or affirm) that I will faithfully execute the Office of President of the United States, and will to the best of my Ability, preserve, protect and defend the Constitution of the United States.'" Although another provision of the Constitution states that all legislators, judges, and other officials of both the national government and the various state governments "shall be bound by Oath or Affirmation, to support this Constitution," the actual language of only the president's oath is included in the document. Some regard the wording of the presidential oath (it pledges the president to execute "the office" rather than the laws) as further support for the claim that there are implied powers of presidential prerogative in the Constitution.

Virtually no debate or discussion accompanied the writing of the president's oath by the Constitutional Convention. The first half of the oath was proposed by the Committee of Detail on August 6: "I —— solemnly swear (or affirm) that I will faithfully execute the office of President of the United States of America." On August 27, Mason and Madison moved that the phrase "and will to the best of my judgment and power preserve, protect and defend the Constitution of the U.S." be added to the oath. Wilson objected that a special presidential oath was unnecessary, but Mason and Madison's motion passed handily.[55] On September 15, the delegates substituted "abilities" for "judgment and power," but no discussion is recorded to explain this alteration.

Departing from the practice that prevailed in most of the states at the time, the convention barred the imposition of religious oaths on the president and other officials of the national government. Some state constitutions required an adherence to Christianity as a condition for serving as governor, others to Protestant Christianity. North Carolina, for example, insisted that its governor affirm the existence of God and the truth of Protestantism and hold no religious beliefs that were inimical to the "peace and safety" of the state. On August 30, Charles Pinckney moved that "no religious test shall ever be required as a qualification to any office or public trust under the authority of the U. States." Sherman said he thought the proposal was "unnecessary, the prevailing liberality being a sufficient security agst. such tests." Nonetheless, Pinckney's motion was approved.[56]

Qualifications

No statement of qualifications for president was included in the Constitution until September 7, when the convention, unanimously and without debate, approved the recommendation of the Committee on Postponed Matters that the president be thirty-five years or older, a natural-born citizen (or a citizen at the time of the Constitution's adoption), and a resident of the United States for at least fourteen years.

In all likelihood, the lateness of the convention's actions on presidential qualifications was the result of deliberation, not neglect. Throughout their proceedings, the delegates seem to have operated on the principle that qualifications for an office needed to be established only if qualifications for those choosing the person to fill the office were not.[57] Thus, as early as the Virginia Plan, qualifications, which were not stated for voters, were included for members of the national legislature. (Ultimately, it was decided that members of the House of Representatives must be at least twenty-five years old, seven years a U.S. citizen, and an inhabitant of the state; and that senators must be at least thirty years old, nine years a citizen, and an inhabitant of the state.) Conversely, qualifications for judges and other appointed offices never were included in the Constitution because they were to be selected by other government officials for whom qualifications were stated.[58]

Through most of the convention's deliberations, the majority of delegates remained wedded to the idea that Congress, a body of constitutionally "qualified" members, would elect the president. Thus, no need was seen to include qualifications for president in the Constitution. By mid-August, however, it was obvious that most of the delegates had changed their minds about legislative selection of the executive. Although they had not yet decided upon an alternative, whatever procedure they eventually devised to choose the president clearly would involve selection by an "unqualified" body because members of Congress were the only officials for whom constitutional qualifications were stated. This new election procedure, in turn, would necessitate the writing of qualifications for president. What is more, these qualifications would have to be high, since the delegates also seem to have agreed that the greater the powers of an office, the higher the qualifications for it should be.

On August 20, Gerry moved that the Committee of Detail be revived for the purpose of proposing a list of qualifications for president. Two days later, the committee did so: the president was to be thirty-five years old or older, a U.S. citizen, and an inhabitant of the United States for at least twenty-one years. On September 4, the Committee on Postponed Matters submitted a revised statement of qualifications: at least thirty-five, a natural-born citizen (or a citizen at the time of the Constitution's adoption), and no fewer than fourteen years a resident. The delegates approved the revised recommendation on September 7.

Each element of the presidential qualifications clause was grounded in its own rationale. The age requirement had two justifications. First, the delegates presumed, age would foster maturity. As Mason said in the debate on establishing a minimum age for members of the House of Representatives, "every man carried with him in his own experience a scale for measuring the deficiency of young politicians; since he would if interrogated be obliged to declare that his political opinions at the age of 21 were too crude & erroneous to merit an influence on public measures." [59] Second, the passage of years left in its wake a record for the voters to assess. According to John Jay, the author of *Federalist* No. 64,

> By excluding men under 35 from the first office [president], and those under 30 from the second [senator], it confines the electors to men of whom the people have had time to form a judgment, and with respect to whom they will not be liable to be deceived by those brilliant appearances of genius and patriotism which, like transient meteors, sometimes mislead as well as dazzle.[60]

The residency and citizenship requirements for president were grounded less in principles of good government than in the politics of the moment. The stipulation that the president must be at least fourteen years a resident of the United States was designed to eliminate from consideration both British sympathizers who had fled to England during the revolutionary war and popular foreign military leaders, notably Baron Frederick von Steuben of Prussia, who had emigrated to the United States to fight in the revolution. As to the length of the residency requirement, the Committee of Detail's recommendation of twenty-one years probably was reduced to fourteen because the longer requirement—but not the shorter—might have been interpreted as barring three of the convention's delegates from the presidency.[61]

The reason for requiring that the president be a natural-born citizen was similarly tied to contemporary politics. Rumors had spread while the convention was meeting that the delegates were plotting to invite a European monarch to rule the United States. Prince Henry of Prussia and Frederick, Duke of York, who was King George III's second son, were the most frequently mentioned names. The practice of importing foreign rulers was not unknown among the European monarchies of the day and would not have seemed preposterous to people who heard the rumor. The delegates, aware that the mere existence of an independent executive in the Constitution was going to provoke attacks from opponents who suspected that the presidency was a latent monarchy, seem to have believed that they could squelch at least the foreign king rumor by requiring that the president be a natural-born citizen of the United States.[62]

A property qualification for president was not included in the Constitution, even though most state constitutions required that their governors be property owners and the delegates had approved a similar requirement for president more than a month before they enacted the presidential qualifications clause. On July 26, the convention adopted a motion by Mason and the Pinckneys that a property qualification be stated for judges, legislators, and the executive. The Committee of Detail neglected the motion in its proposed draft of the Constitution, which provoked both a complaint and another motion from Charles Pinckney on August 10. John Rutledge of South Carolina, the chair of the committee, apologized and seconded Pinckney's motion. He said the committee had made no recommendations about property "because they could not agree on any among themselves, being embarrassed by the danger on one side of displeasing the people by making them high, and on the other of rendering them nugatory by making them low." [63]

In response, Franklin rose to attack the very idea of property qualifications. As Madison paraphrased Franklin's argument, "Some of the greatest rogues he was ever acquainted with, were the richest rogues." Pinckney's motion, Madison then noted, quickly "was rejected by so general a no, that the States were not called." [64] In truth, the practical difficulty of establishing an acceptable property requirement, more than any belief that such a requirement should not be included on principle, seems to explain why the Constitution was silent regarding property ownership by the president.

The Vice Presidency

The idea of an office like the vice presidency was not unknown among the delegates to the Constitutional Convention. During the period of British rule, several colonies had lieutenant governors (known as deputy governors or by another title) whose ongoing duties were minor but who stood by to serve as acting governor if the governor died, was replaced, or was ill or absent from the colony.

After independence, five states (New York, Connecticut, Rhode Island, Massachusetts, and South Carolina) included lieutenant governors in their constitutions. Each was elected in the same manner as the governor and was charged to act as governor when needed. New York's lieutenant governor also was the ex officio president of the state senate and was empowered to vote to break ties. Other states handled the matter of gubernatorial death, absence, or inability differently. In

Virginia and Georgia, for example, the head of the privy council, a cabinet-style body, was the designated gubernatorial successor; in Delaware and North Carolina it was the speaker of the upper house of the legislature; in New Hampshire, the senior member of the state senate.[65]

It is difficult to say whether the experience of the states had much influence on the decision of the Constitutional Convention to create the vice presidency. No reference was made to the state lieutenant governors in the convention debates. Nor was any proposal made to include a vice president in the Constitution until very late in the proceedings. Indeed, the invention of the vice presidency seems to have been an afterthought of the convention, a residue of its solution to the problem of presidential selection.

As noted earlier, the convention initially had decided that the legislature should choose the executive, but it eventually replaced legislative selection with the electoral college, in which each state was to pick presidential electors, who in turn would elect the president by majority vote. A possibly fatal defect of this procedure was that the electors simply would vote for a variety of local favorites, preventing the choice of a nationally elected president. But the committee remedied this potential problem by assigning each elector two votes for president, requiring that they cast at least one of their votes for a candidate who "shall not be an inhabitant of the same State with themselves," and attaching a consequence to both votes: the runner-up in the election for president would be awarded the newly created office of vice president.

Thus, as Hugh Williamson, a member of the Committee on Postponed Matters, testified, "such an office as vice-President was not wanted. He was introduced only for the sake of a valuable mode of election which required two to be chosen at the same time." [66] But, having invented the vice presidency, the committee proposed that the office also be used to solve two other problems that had vexed the convention.

The first was the role of president of the Senate. Some delegates had fretted that if a senator were chosen for this position, one of two problems inevitably would arise. If the senator were barred from voting on legislative matters except in the event of a tie (which was customary for presiding officers because it guaranteed that tie votes would be broken), the senator's state would be effectively denied half its representation on most issues. If the senator were allowed to vote on all matters, the state would be effectively overrepresented in the Senate, occupying two voting seats and the presiding officer's chair. The Committee on Postponed Matters recommended that, as a way around this dilemma, the vice president serve as president of the Senate, voting only to break ties. An exception was made for impeachment trials of the president, when the chief justice of the Supreme Court would preside over the Senate. (In an oversight, vice presidents were not barred from presiding at their own impeachment trials.)

The creation of the vice presidency also solved the problem of presidential succession. This, too, was a matter to which the convention turned rather late. The Virginia Plan and the New Jersey Plan had been silent about succession. On June 18, as part of his sweeping proposal for a national executive chosen by electors to serve for life, Hamilton had suggested that in the event of the executive's death, resignation, impeachment and removal, or absence from the country, the senator who served as president of the Senate should "exercise all the powers by this Constitution vested in the President, until another shall be appointed, or until he shall return within the United States, if his absence was with the Consent of the Senate and Assembly [House of Representatives]."

Sustained attention first was given to the succession question by the Committee of Detail. Deliberately or not, the committee followed Hamilton's lead in its August 6 report to the convention, providing that: "In the case of his [the president's] removal as aforesaid, death, resignation, or disability to discharge the powers and duties of his office, the President of the Senate shall exercise those powers and duties, until another President of the United States be chosen, or until the disability of the President be removed." Considerable dissatisfaction was voiced when the delegates discussed this provision of the committee report on August 27. Madison, who feared that the Senate would have an incentive to create presidential vacancies if its own president were the designated successor, suggested instead that "the persons composing the Council to the President" fill that role.[67] Morris offered the chief justice as successor. Finally, Williamson asked that the question be postponed. The convention agreed, placing the issue in the hands of the Committee on Postponed Matters.

The committee, which reported to the convention on September 4, proposed that: "in the case of his [the president's] removal as aforesaid, death, absence, resignation, or inability to discharge the powers or duties of his office the Vice President shall exercise those powers and duties until another President be chosen, or until the inability of the President be removed." Three days later, Randolph, in an effort to supplement the committee's proposal with one that would provide a method of presidential succession if there were no vice president, moved that: "The Legislature may declare by law what officer of the United States shall act as President in the case of the death, resignation, or disability of the President and Vice President; and such Officer shall act accordingly until the time of electing a President shall arrive." Madison moved to replace the last nine words of Randolph's motion with "until such disability be removed, or a President shall be elected." The motion passed, as amended.[68]

Madison's reason for amending Randolph's motion is clear: he wanted to allow Congress to call a special presidential election to replace a departed president, or, in his words, to permit "a supply of vacancy by an intermediate election of the President." Other evidence from the records of the convention suggests that most of the delegates intended that the president's successor would serve only as acting president until a special election could be called.[69] But sometime during the period September 8-12, when the Committee of Style was working to fulfill its charge to produce a smooth, final draft of the Constitution, that intention was, probably unwittingly, lost. The committee took the September 4 motion of the Committee on Postponed Matters and Randolph's September 7 motion and merged them into one passage, which, with minor modification, became paragraph 6 of Article II, section 1, of the Constitution:

> In Case of the Removal of the President from Office, or of his Death, Resignation, or Inability to discharge the Powers and Duties of the said Office, the Same shall devolve on the Vice President, and the Congress may by Law provide for the Case of Removal, Death, Resignation or Inability, both of the President and Vice President, declaring what Officer shall then act as President, and such Officer shall act accordingly, until the Disability be removed, or a President shall be elected.[70]

Clearly, the delegates' intentions regarding succession were obscured by the Committee of Style. Grammatically, it is impossible to tell—and in its rush to adjournment, the convention did not notice the ambiguity—whether "the Same" in this provision refers to "the said office" (the presidency) or, as the delegates intended, only to its "powers and duties." Nor can one ascertain if "until ... a President shall be elected" means until the end of the original four-year term or, again as intended, until a special election is held.[71]

The vice presidency was not a very controversial issue at the Constitutional Convention. On September 4, when the delegates were considering the Committee on Postponed Matters' proposal for the electoral college, Gorham worried that "a very obscure man with very few votes" might be elected because the proposal required only that the vice president be the runner-up in the presidential election, not the recipient of a majority of electoral votes. Sherman replied that any of the leading candidates for president would likely be qualified.

The role of the vice president as president of the Senate became the subject of minor controversy on September 7. Gerry, seconded by Randolph, complained about the mixing of legislative and executive elements: "We might as well put the President himself at the head of the Legislature. The close intimacy that must subsist between the President & vice-president makes it absolutely improper." Morris responded wryly that "the vice president then will be the first heir apparent that ever loved his father." Sherman added that "if the vice-President were not to be President of the Senate, he would be without employment." He also reminded the convention that for the Senate to elect a president from among its own members probably would deprive that senator of a vote. Mason ended the brief debate by branding "the office of vice-President an encroachment on the rights of the Senate; . . . it mixed too much the Legislative & Executive, which as well as the Judiciary departments, ought to be kept as separate as possible." [72]

Despite the objections, the convention voted overwhelmingly to approve the vice presidency. Interestingly, the delegates gave no serious attention to the vice president's responsibilities as successor to the president.

Ratifying the Constitution

Congress's original call for a convention in Philadelphia had charged the delegates only to propose amendments to the Articles of Confederation, not to design an entirely new system of government. By itself, the delegates' decision to ignore this charge ensured that controversy would ensue when, having met so long in secret, they published the Constitution in September. In addition, several provisions of the draft constitution, including the enhanced powers of the national government and the design of the legislative branch, were certain to be controversial. But nothing astonished the nation more than the convention's decision to recommend that a national executive be established— unitary, independently elected for a fixed term, and entrusted with its own grant of powers.

In the debates that the various state ratifying conventions held on the Constitution, Anti-Federalists (the label that was attached to those who opposed the Constitution) concentrated much of their fire on the presidency. Federalists rose to the office's defense and ultimately prevailed.

The Anti-Federalist Critique
of the Presidency

Anti-Federalists attacked the presidency as a disguised monarchy that, in collaboration with a supposedly aristocratic Senate, eventually would rule the United States much as the British king, assisted by the House of Lords, was said to rule England.

The most strenuous opposition to the presidency was registered by

Patrick Henry of Virginia. On June 7, 1788, speaking with unvarnished fervor, Henry voiced the Anti-Federalists' fears of a presidential monarchy to his state's ratifying convention:

> This Constitution is said to have beautiful features, but when I come to examine these features, Sir, they appear to me to be horridly frightful: Among other deformities, it has an awful squinting; it squints towards monarchy: And does this not raise indignation in the breast of every American?
>
> Your President may easily become a King; ... if your American chief, be a man of ambition, how easy it is for him to render himself absolute: The army is in his hands, and if he be a man of address, it will be attached to him; ... I would rather infinitely, and I am sure most of these Convention are of the same opinion, have a king, Lords, and Commons, than a Government so replete with such insupportable evils. If we make a King, we may prescribe the rules by which he shall rule his people, and interpose such checks as shall prevent him from infringing them: But the President, in the field, at the head of his army, can prescribe the terms on which he shall reign master, so far that it will puzzle any American ever to get his neck from under the galling yoke. ... And what have you to oppose this force? What will then become of you and your rights? Will not absolute despotism ensue? [73]

Other Anti-Federalists directed their fire at the close relationship they thought the Constitution fostered between the "monarchical" president and the "aristocratic" Senate, the two bodies that, without the involvement of the "democratic" House of Representatives, shared the powers of appointment and treaty making. A group of delegates at the Pennsylvania ratifying convention published a report on December 18, 1787, asserting that the Constitution's treaty-making provisions virtually invited foreign meddling. The Senate would consist of twenty-six members, they noted, two from each of the thirteen states. Fourteen senators would constitute a quorum for that body, of whom only ten were needed to provide a two-thirds vote to ratify a treaty proposed by the president. "What an inducement would this [small number] offer to the ministers of foreign powers to compass by bribery *such concessions as could not otherwise be obtained*," the Pennsylvania dissenters warned.[74]

Although monarchy was the Anti-Federalists' main fear, few features of the presidency were immune from their criticism. The Virginia and North Carolina ratifying conventions urged that a constitutional amendment be enacted to limit each president to no more than eight years in office in any sixteen-year period. New York governor George Clinton, writing as "Cato" in the *New York Journal* in November 1787, argued that the president's term was too long and cited Montesquieu's prescription for one-year terms. In addition, Clinton charged, the absence of a council meant that the president will "be unsupported by proper information and advice, and will generally be directed by minions and favorites." Instead of direct election by the people (which Clinton said he favored), the president "arrives to this office at the fourth or fifth hand." [75]

Interestingly, the presidency drew criticism from two future presidents: Thomas Jefferson, who observed archly in a letter to Madison that a president who could be reelected indefinitely and who commanded the armed forces "seems a bad edition of a Polish king," and James Monroe, who fretted about the possibility of a president being reelected into life tenure. The office also was attacked by two future vice presidents—Gerry, one of the three delegates to the Constitutional Convention who refused to sign the document, and Governor Clinton, who was jealous of the presidency's resemblance to his own powerful office. "This government is no more like a true picture of your own than an Angel of Darkness resembles an Angel of Light," Clinton warned his fellow New Yorkers. [76]

The Federalist Defense
of the Presidency

Proponents of the Constitution at the state ratifying conventions stressed both the virtues of the presidency and the restraints that the Constitution placed upon the office. In doing so, they relied heavily on the explanations and defenses of the Constitution that Hamilton, Madison, and Jay were putting forth in a series of eighty-five newspaper articles that Hamilton had commissioned. These articles, later gathered in a book called *The Federalist Papers,* appeared pseudonymously under the name "Publius" in several New York newspapers. Hamilton wrote around fifty of them, Madison around twenty-five, Jay five, and Hamilton and Madison jointly wrote the rest. The articles were reprinted and disseminated widely throughout the states. [77]

Hamilton wrote *Federalist* Nos. 69-77, which dealt with the presidency. [78] The first of these squarely addressed the Anti-Federalist charge that the presidency was a latent monarchy. Hamilton argued that, in contrast to the British king, who secured his office by inheritance and served for life, the president was elected for a limited term. The president could be impeached; the king could not. The king had an absolute veto on laws passed by Parliament; the president's veto could be overridden by Congress. The king could both declare war and raise an army and navy; the president could do neither. The king could prorogue Parliament for any reason at any time; the president could adjourn Congress only when the House of Representatives and the Senate could not agree on an adjournment date. The king could create

Alexander Hamilton, one of the authors of *The Federalist Papers*, was instrumental in defending the Constitution's provisions for a strong executive office.

offices and appoint people to fill them; the president could not create offices and could fill them only with the approval of the Senate.

Hamilton dissembled to some degree in drawing these contrasts. The powers he ascribed to the British monarch were more characteristic of the seventeenth century than of the eighteenth, during which time the influence of Parliament and the prime minister had grown. But *Federalist* No. 69 was effective in deflating the Anti-Federalists' caricature of the presidency. Indeed, Hamilton deftly argued that in many cases the power of the presidency was less than that wielded by Governor Clinton of New York.

Federalist No. 70, less defensive in tone than the first article, described the virtues of the presidency. Its theme was "energy," a quality that, according to Hamilton, is requisite to good government:

> It is essential to the protection of the community against foreign attacks; it is not less essential to the steady administration of the laws; to the protection of property against those irregular and high-handed combinations which sometimes interrupt the ordinary course of justice; to the security of liberty against the enterprises and assaults of ambition, of faction, and of anarchy.

Energy, in the government created by the Constitution, was provided by the presidency, Hamilton argued, mostly because of its unitary character. Unity provided the presidency with a whole host of virtues— "decision, activity, secrecy, and dispatch ... vigor and expedition." In contrast, a plural, or committee-style, executive would be riven by disagreements that would render it slow to act and prone to create factions. It also would be hard to hold a plural executive responsible for failure since each member of the executive could blame the others.

In *Federalist* Nos. 71-73, Hamilton defended the presidency as having additional qualities indispensable to energy. "Duration," the theme of No. 71, was one—the four-year term provided the president with enough time to act with firmness and resolve but was not so long as "to justify any alarm for the public liberty."

Hamilton claimed that the provision for reelection, which he discussed in No. 72, shrewdly acknowledged that "the desire of reward is one of the strongest incentives of human conduct." Without that incentive, a president would be tempted either to slack off on the job or, at the opposite extreme, to usurp power violently. Presidential reeligibility also allowed the nation to keep a president in office if it so desired.

"Adequate provision for its support" was a third energy-inducing quality of the presidency, according to Hamilton. Interestingly, he attached great importance to the prohibition that the Constitution placed on Congress not to raise or lower an incumbent president's salary. In the first part of No. 73, Hamilton argued that without such a bar, Congress could "reduce him by famine, or tempt him by largesse" and thus "render him as obsequious to their will as they might think proper to make him."

Later in No. 73, then in Nos. 74-77, Hamilton defended the enumerated powers of the presidency, which, along with unity, duration, and adequate support, were the indispensable ingredients of presidential energy. Far from being threatening, he argued, the office's constitutional powers were modest and essential to the operations of good government:

Veto. "The propensity of the legislative department to intrude upon the rights, and to absorb the powers, of the other departments has been already more than once suggested. ... [Without the veto, the president] might gradually be stripped of his authorities by successive resolutions or annihilated by a single vote. ... But the power in question has a further use. It not only serves as a shield to the executive, but it furnishes an additional security against the enaction of improper laws. ..."

Commander in Chief. "Even those [constitutions] which have in other respects coupled the Chief Magistrate with a council have for the most part concentrated the military authority in him alone. Of all the cares or concerns of government, the direction of war most peculiarly demands those qualities which distinguish the exercise of power by a single hand."

Treaties. "With regard to the intermixture of powers [between the president and the Senate,] ... the essence of the legislative authority is to enact laws, or, in other words, to prescribe rules for the regulation of the society; while the execution of the laws and the employment of the common strength, either for this purpose or for the common defense, seem to comprise all the functions of the executive magistrate. The power of making treaties is, plainly, neither the one nor the other. . . . It must indeed be clear to a demonstration that the joint possession of the power in question, by the President and Senate, would afford a greater prospect of security than the separate possession of it by either of them."

Appointment. "I proceed to lay it down as a rule that one man of discernment is better fitted to analyze and estimate the peculiar qualities adapted to particular offices than a body of men of equal or perhaps even of superior discernment. The sole and undivided responsibility of one man will naturally beget a livelier sense of duty and a more exact regard to reputation. He will, on this account, feel himself under stronger obligations, and more interested to investigate with care the qualities requisite to the stations to be filled, and to prefer with impartiality the persons who may have the fairest pretensions to them. . . . To what purpose then require the co-operation of the Senate? I answer, that the necessity of their concurrence would have a powerful, though, in general, a silent operation. It would be an excellent check upon a spirit of favoritism in the President, and would tend greatly to prevent the appointment of unfit characters. . . . The possibility of rejection would be a strong motive to care in proposing."

Other Powers. "The only remaining powers of the executive are comprehended in giving information to Congress on the state of the Union; in recommending to their consideration such measures as he shall judge expedient; in convening them, or either branch, upon extraordinary occasions; in adjourning them when they cannot themselves agree upon the time of adjournment; in receiving ambassadors and other public ministers; in faithfully executing the laws; and in commissioning all the officers of the United States. Except some cavils about the power of convening *either* house of the legislature, and that of receiving ambassadors, no objection has been made to this class of authorities; nor could they possibly admit of any."

The Vice Presidency in the Ratification Debates

"Post-convention discussion of the vice presidency was not extensive," noted the legal scholar John D. Feerick.[79] The only mention of the office in *The Federalist Papers* is in No. 68, written by Hamilton. Like the delegates' debate at the Constitutional Convention, this passage, too, is concerned mainly with the vice president's role as president of the Senate:

> The appointment of an extraordinary person, as Vice-President, has been objected to as superfluous, if not mischievous. It has been alleged, that it would have been preferable to have authorized the Senate to elect out of their own body an officer answering to that description. But two considerations seem to justify the ideas of the Convention in this respect. One is, that to secure at all times the possibility of a definitive resolution of the body, it is necessary that the President should have only a casting [tie-breaking] vote. And to take the Senator of any State from his seat as Senator, to place him in that of President of the Senate, would be to exchange, in regard to the State from which he came, a constant for a contingent vote. The other consideration is, that, as the Vice-President may occasionally become a substitute for the President, in the supreme Executive magistracy, all the reasons which recommend the mode of election prescribed for the one, apply with great if not with equal force to the manner of appointing the other.[80]

Hamilton may have been responding in part to the concerns raised by the Anti-Federalist Clinton. Clinton was later to serve as vice president in the administrations of presidents Jefferson and Madison, but in November 1787, writing as Cato, he argued that the vice presidency was both "unnecessary" and "dangerous." "This officer," warned Clinton, "for want of other employment is made president of the Senate, thereby blending the executive and legislative powers, besides always giving to some one state, from which he is to come, an unjust preeminence." [81]

Luther Martin of Maryland, who opposed ratification, expressed concern that a large state like neighboring Pennsylvania or Virginia typically would benefit from the vice president's Senate role:

> After it is decided who is chosen President, that person who has the next greatest number of votes of the electors, is declared to be legally elected to the Vice-Presidency; so that by this system it is very possible, and not improbable, that he may be appointed by the electors of a *single large state;* and a very undue influence in the Senate is given to that State of which the Vice-President is a citizen, since, in every question where the Senate is divided, that State will have two votes, the President having on that occasion a casting voice.

Mason, another convention delegate who opposed ratification in his own state, also complained about the vice president's right to vote in the Senate and the office's mix of legislative and executive responsibilities. His fellow Virginia Anti-Federalist, Richard Henry Lee, wondered about the absence of stated qualifications for the vice president.[82]

Defenders of the vice presidency made a virtue of the office's role as

Senate president. In their view, the vice president's election by the nation as a whole would be good for the Senate. "There is much more propriety to giving this office to a person chosen by the people at large," urged Madison, "than to one of the Senate, who is only the choice of the legislature of one state." William R. Davie of North Carolina felt that a nationally elected vice president would cast tie-breaking votes "as impartially as possible." Answering another argument of the Constitution's critics, Connecticut delegates Oliver Ellsworth and Roger Sherman wrote separately that the vice president did not wield a mix of legislative and executive powers, but rather that the vice presidency was a part of the legislative branch except in the event of a succession, at which time it entered the executive branch.[83]

In all, as Feerick concluded, the vice presidency "received scant attention in the state ratifying conventions. . . . The discussion of the vice-presidency that did occur centered mostly on the fact that the office blended legislative and executive functions." [84] As in the Constitutional Convention, almost nothing was said in the state debates about the vice president's duties as successor to the president.

Notes

1. Seymour Martin Lipset, *The First New Nation* (New York: Basic Books, 1963), chap. 1; Max Weber, *The Theory of Social and Economic Organizations* (New York: Oxford University Press, 1947), 358.
2. Marcus Cunliffe, *George Washington: Man and Monument* (New York: New American Library, 1958), 15.
3. Max Farrand, ed., *The Records of the Federal Convention* (New Haven, Conn.: Yale University Press, 1913), 1:103.
4. Charles C. Thach, Jr., *The Creation of the Presidency, 1775-1789* (Baltimore, Md.: Johns Hopkins University Press, 1969).
5. Robert A. Rutland and William M. E. Rachal, eds., *The Papers of James Madison* (Chicago: University of Chicago Press, 1975), 9:385.
6. Calvin C. Jillson argues that Madison's fellow Virginia delegates, not Madison himself, brought what little clarity there was to the executive provision of the Virginia Plan. See Jillson, *Constitution Making: Conflict and Consensus in the Federal Convention of 1787* (New York: Agathon Press, 1988), 42-47.
7. Farrand, *Records* 2:52, 523.
8. Ibid. 1:65.
9. Catherine Drinker Bowen, *Miracle at Philadelphia* (Boston: Little, Brown, 1966), 55; Charles L. Mee, Jr., *The Genius of the People* (New York: Harper and Row, 1987), 118.
10. Farrand, *Records* 1:66, 65.
11. Ibid. 1:65.
12. See, for example, ibid. 2:487-488.
13. Ibid. 2:541.

14. Ibid. 2:68, 69.
15. Ibid. 2:30.
16. Indispensable to the eventual adoption of the electoral college was Wilson's conversion of Madison, who declared on July 19 that "it is essential then that the appointment of the Executive should either be drawn from some source, or held by some tenure, that will give him a free agency with regard to the Legislature. This could not be if he was appointable from time to time by the Legislature" (Ibid. 2:56).
17. Clinton Rossiter, *1787: The Grand Convention* (London: MacGibbon and Kee, 1968), 199.
18. Richard P. McCormick, *The Presidential Game: The Origins of American Presidential Politics* (New York: Oxford University Press, 1982), 25.
19. Fred Barbash, *The Founding: A Dramatic Account of the Writing of the Constitution* (New York: Linden Press/Simon and Schuster, 1987), 182.
20. Farrand, *Records* 2:500.
21. John P. Roche, "The Founding Fathers: A Reform Caucus in Action," *American Political Science Review* 55 (December 1961): 810.
22. Farrand, *Records* 1:68.
23. Ibid. 2:33.
24. Alexander Hamilton, James Madison, and John Jay, *The Federalist Papers,* with an introduction by Clinton L. Rossiter (New York: New American Library, 1961), 437-448.
25. Farrand, *Records* 2:53.
26. Ibid. 1:88.
27. Ibid. 2:550.
28. Ibid. 2:427.
29. Hamilton, Madison, and Jay, *Federalist Papers,* 301, 303.
30. Richard E. Neustadt, *Presidential Power* (New York: Wiley, 1960), 35.
31. Farrand, *Records* 1:82.
32. Ibid. 1:376.
33. Ibid. 2:284.
34. The bar to overlapping membership strongly distinguishes the U.S. system of government from parliamentary systems, in which executive offices are customarily held by legislators. James Sundquist, *Constitutional Reform and Effective Government,* rev. ed. (Washington, D.C.: Brookings, 1992), 232-244.
35. Robert Scigliano, "The Presidency and the Judiciary," in *The Presidency and the Political System,* 3d ed., ed. Michael Nelson (Washington, D.C.: CQ Press, 1990), 471-499.
36. Farrand, *Records* 1:101.
37. Richard M. Pious, *The American Presidency* (New York: Basic Books, 1978), 29.
38. John Locke, *The Second Treatise on Government* (Indianapolis: Bobbs-Merrill, 1952), 91-96.
39. Thach, *Creation of the Presidency,* 138-139.
40. Farrand, *Records* 2:318.
41. Hamilton, Madison, and Jay, *Federalist Papers,* 447.
42. Farrand, *Records* 2:343-344.
43. Ibid. 1:292.
44. Ibid. 2:426, 626.
45. Hamilton, Madison, and Jay, *Federalist Papers,* 447, 449.
46. Farrand, *Records* 1:292.

47. Ibid. 2:309.
48. Ibid. 2:540.
49. Ibid. 1:67.
50. Ibid. 2:405.
51. Ibid. 2:522.
52. Ibid. 2:405.
53. Ibid. 2:419.
54. Ibid. 1:67.
55. Ibid. 2:427.
56. Ibid. 2:468. In 1853, Franklin Pierce affirmed—rather than swore—to faithfully execute the office of president. At the first inaugural ceremony, on April 30, 1789, George Washington began the practice of adding the words "so help me God" at the conclusion of the oath (Charles C. Euchner and John Anthony Maltese, *Selecting the President* [Washington, D.C.: Congressional Quarterly, 1992], 192-193).
57. Michael Nelson, "Constitutional Qualifications for the President," *Presidential Studies Quarterly* 17:2 (Spring 1987): 383-399.
58. During most of the convention, the appointment power belonged mainly to senators; toward the end, the president's role in appointments was enhanced substantially.
59. Farrand, *Records* 1:375.
60. Hamilton, Madison, and Jay, *Federalist Papers,* 391.
61. The three were Hamilton, Pierce Butler of South Carolina, and James McHenry of Maryland.
62. Another reason the convention decided to include a requirement of natural-born citizenship for the president may be found in a letter John Jay sent to George Washington on July 25. "Permit me to hint," Jay wrote, "whether it would not be wise and reasonable to provide a strong check on the admission of foreigners into the administration of our National Government, and to declare expressly that the command in chief of the American Army shall not be given to, nor devolve upon, any but a natural *born* citizen." On September 2, two days before the Committee on Postponed Matters proposed the natural-born-citizen requirement to the convention, Washington replied to Jay, "I thank you for the hints contained in your letter" (Farrand, *Records* 4:61, 76).
63. Ibid. 2:249.
64. Ibid.
65. John D. Feerick, *From Failing Hands: The Story of Presidential Succession* (New York: Fordham University Press, 1965), chap. 2.
66. Farrand, *Records* 2:537.
67. Ibid. 2:427.
68. Ibid. 2:535.
69. See Farrand, *Records* 2:137, 146, 163, 172.
70. On September 15, 1787, delegates discovered a clerical error in the committee's draft and changed "the period for chusing another president arrive" to "a President shall be elected."
71. For a thorough comparison of the convention's decisions on succession with the Committee of Style's rendering of them, see Feerick, *From Failing Hands,* 48-51. Feerick speculates that the committee may have omitted presidential "absence" from the list of situations that require a temporary successor because it was covered by the term *inability.*
72. Farrand, *Records* 2:537. In truth, it still is constitutionally unclear whether

the vice president is part of the legislative branch, the executive branch, both branches, or neither (Michael Nelson, *A Heartbeat Away* [Washington, D.C.: Brookings, 1988], chap. 4).

73. Quoted in Ralph Ketcham, ed., *The Anti-Federalist Papers and the Constitutional Convention Debates* (New York: New American Library, 1986), 213-214.
74. Ibid., 251.
75. Quoted in Cecelia M. Kenyon, ed., *The Antifederalists* (Indianapolis: Bobbs-Merrill, 1966), 302-309.
76. Quoted in Pious, *American Presidency,* 39.
77. The voices of other famous people were raised in defense of the Constitution. See, for example, Tenche Cox, "An American Citizen I," and Noah Webster, "A Citizen of America," in *The Debate on the Constitution,* Part One (New York: Library of America, 1993), 20-25 and 129-163, respectively.
78. All quotations from the *Federalist* may be found in Hamilton, Madison, and Jay, *Federalist Papers,* 414-464.
79. Feerick, *From Failing Hands,* 51.
80. Hamilton, Madison, and Jay, *Federalist Papers,* 414-415.
81. Quoted in Kenyon, *Antifederalists,* 305.
82. Feerick, *From Failing Hands,* 52, 53-54.
83. Quotes are drawn from ibid., 52-55.
84. Ibid., 53.

CHAPTER 3

The Presidency of
George Washington

The Constitution of 1787 provided a broad outline of the powers and duties of the president, leaving considerable leeway for individual presidents and future events to shape the executive office. By stating that "the executive Power shall be vested in a President of the United States of America" and that "he shall take Care that the Laws be faithfully executed," without in most cases stipulating what those executive responsibilities would be, the Constitution gave rise to two centuries of conflict about the proper extent of presidential authority. "The executive article fairly bristles with contentious matter," the political scientist Charles Thach has written, "and, until it is seen what decision was given to these contentions, it is impossible to say just what the national executive meant." [1]

It is impossible, for example, to determine from the words of the Constitution alone what were to be the appropriate relations of the chief executive to the chief officers of the executive departments, or those of Congress to the executive business. Similarly, the Constitution left unclear the extent of the powers that were implied by the executive's responsibilities in war and peace, as well as in diplomacy. [2]

In large measure presidents have been able to fill the interpretive void, as "presidentialists" at the convention such as James Wilson, Gouverneur Morris, and Alexander Hamilton, had hoped. "The president claims the silences of the Constitution," noted the political scientist Richard Pious. [3] The expansion of executive power did not come easily, however. The institutional design of the Constitution created congressional as well as presidential partisans, including such influential political leaders as Thomas Jefferson, James Madison,

70

Henry Clay, and Daniel Webster. This chapter and those that follow chronicle the major developments that have shaped both the idea of presidential power in U.S. history, including some furious debates about the proper definition of executive authority, and the institutional changes that have followed from those debates and other developments.

Many of the most important questions about the character and breadth of presidential authority were settled during the two terms served by George Washington. The nation's first chief executive was very aware that his actions could establish enduring precedents. "Few who are not philosophical spectators," Washington wrote early in his first term, "can realize the difficult and delicate part which a man in my situation has to act. . . . In our progress towards political happiness my station is new; and, if I may use the expression, I walk on untrodden ground. There is scarcely any part of my conduct which may not hereafter be drawn into precedent." [4]

Significant precedents for the proper conduct of the executive office were settled not only by the first president but also by the first Congress. In fact, its work from 1789 to 1791, as Thach has observed, "was simply the continuation of that done at the Constitutional Convention two years before." [5] Many of those who had framed the Constitution were on hand in New York, the government's temporary first capital, to put the new instrument into operation. In the two houses of the legislature there were eighteen former members of the convention, eight in the House of Representatives, including Madison, and ten in the Senate. "It is safe to say," the historian Charles Beard has written, "that four-fifths of the active, forceful leaders of the Convention helped to realize as a process of government the paper constitution they had drafted." [6]

In 1789 the delegates-turned-legislators brought to New York many of the same political beliefs, values, and prejudices that they had carried with them to Philadelphia in 1787. Thus, in a very real sense the first Congress may be regarded as a constituent assembly, charged with the task of giving form to the rather slender framework of the executive office that was fashioned during the Constitutional Convention. [7]

The Election of George Washington

The election of George Washington as the first president of the United States was never in doubt. Still, as one historian has written, "never was the election of a president so much a foregone conclusion and yet so tortuous in consummation." [8]

Although the electoral college met in the various states on February 4, 1789, its unanimous vote for Washington could not be official until the president of the Senate, temporarily elected for the purpose, opened the ballots in the presence of both the House and the Senate. One of the final acts of the outgoing government of the Articles of Confederation had been to summon the new Congress to convene in New York on March 4. But legislators were slow to arrive, and a quorum was still unachieved at the end of the month. Anyone other than Washington might have been in the capital in time for the opening of Congress, which finally occurred when the House obtained a bare quorum on April 1, the Senate on April 6. But the Father of His Country was concerned with the requirements of correct behavior, and since he would not be officially elected until a joint session of Congress tallied the votes of the electors, he waited for formal word in frustration at his Mount Vernon, Virginia, home and worried about the "stupor or listlessness" being displayed by the members of the newly formed legislative body on whom the success of the Constitution would largely depend.[9]

Ironically, the start of the government was further delayed by Washington himself, who, upon finally receiving notice of his election on April 14 from Secretary of the Congress Charles Thompson, took his time riding from Virginia to New York "lest unseemly haste suggest that he was improperly eager for the office." [10] Because he believed that the future of the government required its acceptance by the people, the president-elect was concerned with the way his progress through the states to the capital would be received.

Washington's caution went deeper than an awareness of the American people's fear of executive power. As the historian Gordon Wood has observed, Washington sought to live up to the "Cincinnatus myth of Roman legend," which celebrated the disinterested patriot who devoted his life to his country. Although studied, Washington's diffidence was not disingenuous; self-denial came naturally to him. After the peace treaty was signed that ended the revolutionary war and expressed British recognition of American independence, Washington surrendered his sword to Congress on December 23, 1783, and retired to his farm at Mt. Vernon. His retirement from power had a profound effect everywhere in the Western world. "It was extraordinary, it was unprecedented in modern times," Wood wrote, for "a victorious general [to surrender] his arms and [return] to his farm." [11] English military heroes such as Cromwell, William of Orange, and Marlborough all had sought political rewards commensurate with their military achievements; in contrast, Washington was sincere in his desire for all the soldiers, as he put it, "to return to our Private Stations in the bosom of a free, peaceful and happy country." [12] The American people recognized Washington's sincerity, and it filled them with respect, admiration, even awe. As Garry Wills has noted, Washington "gained power from his willingness to give it up." [13]

The popular adulation that greeted Washington in every hamlet as he traveled to New York made obvious his country's devotion to him. As he entered Philadelphia, for example, surrounded by military horsemen who had formed an escort fifteen miles from the city, some twenty thousand citizens "lined every fence, field, and avenue." At the city limits, infantry wheeled and artillery fired their cannon. These units then fell into line behind Washington, as did squads of citizens at every block until, as one newspaper account had it, "the column swelled beyond credibility itself." The parade finally reached the City Tavern, where Washington was honored with "a very grand and beautiful banquet." The evening was topped off by fireworks.[14] The nation's first president finally arrived in New York in time to be inaugurated on April 30.

The long and complicated business that was involved in both the election of Washington and his assumption of the responsibilities of the chief executive foretold of the major task of his administration: "To make the government which had been adopted, often by the thinnest of majorities, and in only eleven out of thirteen states, happily acceptable to the overwhelming majority of the entire population." [15] This was an ambitious task, one that required the construction of a unified and energetic national government on a political landscape that was traditionally inhospitable to strong central authority. That the "more perfect Union" framed by the Constitution included a strong presidency was particularly notable, even radical in the American context, for executive power had been the object of public distrust for a long time. In view of this tradition, the establishment of the presidency may have been impossible without the great popularity and propriety of General Washington. Indeed, Washington was, or so Madison wrote in 1789, the only aspect of the government that really caught the imagination of the people at the outset.[16]

Making the Presidency Safe for Democracy

Washington's awe-inspiring personality and popularity made him an indispensable source of unity and legitimacy for the newly formed government, but they also made him seem, to those who were suspicious of strong executive power, extremely dangerous. Thus, many of the conflicts that arose during Washington's administration and that of his successor, John Adams, involved efforts to make strong executive power compatible with republican government. These conflicts sometimes concerned the most routine of matters. For example, Washington's schedule became the subject of controversy at the outset of his administration, prompting him to distribute queries to his trusted advisers "on a line of conduct most eligible to be pursued by the President of the United States." The challenge, as Washington understood it, was to establish precedents for the conduct of the presidency that would allow the executive sufficient privacy to get his work done and distance to retain the respectability of the office, yet would avoid giving the impression that he disdained contact with the people. The course that Washington decided on satisfied neither those who wanted to insulate the president from excessive popular influence nor zealous republicans who wished to see an open executive office. Nevertheless, he revealed his great sensitivity to the importance of attaining public support and respect for the presidency through activities that, no matter how mundane, were of great symbolic importance:

> Washington established two occasions a week when any respectably dressed person could, without introduction, invitation, or any prearrangement, be ushered into his presence. One was the President's "levee," for men only, every Tuesday from three to four. The other was Martha's tea party, for men and women, held on Friday evenings. Washington would also stage dinners on Thursdays at four o'clock in the afternoon. To avoid any charges of favoritism or any contests for invitations, only officials and their families would be asked to the dinners, and these in an orderly system of rotation.[17]

An even more controversial issue of etiquette involved how the president should be addressed on formal occasions. A committee of the House of Representatives wanted him to be addressed simply, as in the Constitution, "the President of the United States." But in May 1789 the Senate, at the behest of Vice President John Adams, who was presiding over the upper chamber, rejected the House report. Adams, believing that "titles and politically inspired elegance were essential aspects of strong government," supported the title "His Highness the President of the United States and protector of their Liberties." This proposal proved controversial, and Madison led the opposition in the House to what he perceived to be the Senate's effort to apply nomenclature to the executive that would be "dangerous to republicanism."

Madison was supported in his opposition by President Washington, who felt that the whole business of titles was a bit silly and made known his annoyance at Adams's efforts "to bedizen him with a superb but spurious title." On May 27, in a letter to Jefferson, Madison reported with relief that calm had been restored in the legislature and the episode was ended; its only substantial result was the facetious presentation to the heavy-set Adams of the title "His Rotundity."[18] Thereafter, it was agreed that the chief executive should have no more elaborate a title than "the President of the United States."

Beneath all the bickering over etiquette and nomenclature lay serious matters of state. Some political leaders, such as Adams and Hamilton, believed that a strong executive was necessary to make the American experiment in self-government successful. Other important figures in the formation of American government, such as Jefferson and Madison, were concerned that too much reliance on the presidency would undermine the delicate system of checks and balances that had been worked out in Philadelphia in 1787. Madison had been an ally of Hamilton in the effort to strengthen the national government at the convention, and he played a critical part in fighting off legislative attempts to encroach on the executive domain during Washington's presidency. Yet concern about the domestic and international objectives that Hamilton pursued as Washington's secretary of the Treasury led Madison to oppose the expansion of executive power after 1790.

Thus, even minor controversies became important when they touched on the central principles of how a republican government ought to work. The fundamental issues that animated battles in such matters underlay virtually all of the conflicts that made the task of forming a new government such a delicate business. It was to Washington's great credit that he was able to mediate so effectively the disputes that surrounded the creation of the American presidency and, in doing so, to build a strong foundation for national unity.

Forming the Executive Branch

During Washington's first term, Congress passed bills to establish three major departments of government: State, Treasury, and War. The heads of these departments, in accordance with the Constitution, were nominated by the president and confirmed by the Senate. For secretary of state, Washington chose Jefferson, who as minister to France had shown himself to be an excellent diplomat. Hamilton, a recognized expert on finance and commerce, became head of the Treasury. Gen. Henry Knox, a diligent administrator who as chief of artillery had served Washington reliably during the revolutionary war, was selected to be the secretary of war.

Edmund Randolph of Virginia was Washington's choice as the first attorney general. At this time the office of attorney general occupied a unique position in the executive branch. It did not yet possess the status and dignity of a department, but the attorney general attended cabinet meetings and served as the legal adviser to the president and the department heads.[19]

In forming the executive branch, the Washington administration employed highly informal procedures. No rigid division of labor was established between the departments, nor did formal rules or strictly defined codes of behavior govern their internal operations. In general, executive administration was ad hoc and personal. Indeed, the notion of a "President's Cabinet" did not even take form during the early years of Washington's tenure. Washington did not use the word *cabinet* until

The first cabinet, selected by President Washington, included Secretary of War Henry Knox (on Washington's left), Secretary of the Treasury Alexander Hamilton, Secretary of State Thomas Jefferson, and Attorney General Edmund Randolph.

April 1793, and he did not call formal meetings of "the Heads of the Great Departments" until close to the end of his first term.[20]

Administrative informality did not mean, however, that there was no purpose to the appointments and procedures of Washington's presidency. Recognizing the need to invest his administration with talented and respected leaders whose presence would advance the acceptability of the new government, Washington sought the most admired people available to carry out its functions. Washington's three principal aides—Hamilton, Jefferson, and, in Congress, Madison—formed a remarkable constellation of advisers; indeed, they became the nation's most important political leaders in the generation after Washington. Nevertheless, strong disagreements arose among them, with Madison and Jefferson often allied against Hamilton. Washington not only recognized the varied talents of these three independent-minded leaders, but also was able to yoke them in a "single harness." His ability to do so and the general success that he achieved as an administrator helped "to plant in the minds of the American people the model of a government which commanded respect by reason of its integrity, energy, and competence."[21]

Washington's appointments to minor jobs also were intended to enhance the legitimacy of the fledgling national government. As the various enactments to create the departments became law during his first term, the president found himself with nearly a thousand offices to fill. Considering these appointments important, Washington devoted an enormous amount of time to them: "no collector of customs, captain of a cutter, keeper of a lighthouse, or surveyor of revenue was appointed except after specific consideration by the President." [22]

Although besieged by applicants, directly or through intermediaries, Washington "scrupulously declined to exploit the opportunity to create a patronage system." His appointments were made with little regard to party loyalty, personal relations, or family connections. The president's appointments were, in fact, only partisan in the sense that he chose persons "of known attachment" to the new government. Especially during the first year or two of his administration, Washington took care not to appoint former Tories or other persons whose loyalty to the new Constitution was doubtful. [23]

In general, as one historian has written, "Washington's rules of selection shone in statesmanlike splendor. The dominating standard was the rule of fitness." [24] In screening applicants for jobs, however, Washington did not employ the criteria of "merit" and "neutral competence" that have dominated civil service procedures during the twentieth century. He was concerned less with his appointees' expertise than with their strong commitment to the Constitution and reputation for good character. Apart from personal integrity, standing in one's local community was a principal ingredient of fitness, reflecting Washington's desire to cultivate a favorable opinion of the national government in the far-flung sections of the Union. Washington's personnel policies manifested his concern for the requirements of building a nation.

Presidential "Supremacy" and the Conduct of the Executive Branch

In addition to his hiring policies, Washington established a critical precedent to advance the view that authority over the executive branch belongs solely to the president. His philosophy of public administration prevailed against competing philosophies that foresaw either the Senate or individual cabinet officers sharing fully in the direction of the executive departments. [25]

The belief that the upper house of the legislature should be involved in the details of administration was especially strong in the American tradition, reaching far back into the colonial era. Indeed, a bill nearly passed Congress during Washington's first term that would have severely restricted the president's administrative authority. The bill, which involved the creation of the Department of State, raised the issue of where the power to dismiss an executive official should lie. Opponents of a strong presidency argued that the constitutional provision that presidents can appoint officials only with Senate approval implies that they can dismiss officials only with Senate approval. Washington and Madison, his chief congressional ally in this matter, responded that presidents would be rendered impotent if they were prevented from being the master of their own domain.

Madison successfully led the fight in the House against senatorial interference with presidential removals, but in the Senate the final vote was tied. Vice President Adams, as presiding officer, broke the tie in favor of the president's unilateral power to remove executive appointees from office. From then on, Congress followed Madison's lead by passing laws to establish the major departments of the government that were carefully designed to minimize the legislature's influence in the executive branch.[26]

Congress's eventual acquiescence to presidential supremacy over the executive departments was probably a tribute to Washington's demonstrated devotion to the principle of separation of powers. The president shared Madison's view that the chief executive should be supreme in matters pertaining to the conduct of the executive branch but restrained in matters that were rightfully the legislature's. Washington did make legislative recommendations to Congress, albeit sparingly, but he made no special effort to get his program enacted, "nor did he attempt during his first term to achieve by executive orders any matter that the strictest interpretation of the Constitution could regard as within the legislative domain." [27]

Hamilton had argued in *Federalist* No. 73 that an aggressive use of the veto was essential for the president to protect the office from legislative usurpation and to "furnish security against the enaction of improper laws." But Washington adhered to the view that the presidential veto power properly extended only to bills of doubtful constitutionality, not unwise policy.[28]

Washington's circumspect use of the veto did not mean that he was a weak president, intent on avoiding conflict with the legislature at all costs. Rather, the first president sought to win the trust of Congress and the people so that he and future presidents would be able to exercise power forcefully when it seemed most appropriate—that is, in managing the affairs of the executive branch and upholding the law. In view of the inherently uneasy relationship between executive power and popular rule, Washington feared that aggressive presidential efforts to dominate or undermine the legislative process might vindicate the fears of the

Anti-Federalists that an independent executive would tend toward monarchy. Washington's respect for Congress won him the trust of legislators, which eventually enabled him to carve out significant spheres of presidential influence. Just as Washington's self-denial at the end of the revolution was an important prelude to his ascent to the presidency, so did his restraint as the first president bestow legitimacy on the office he occupied.[29]

Washington's propriety in executive-legislative relations extended even to foreign policy. The president did not hesitate to assert his primacy in diplomatic affairs, but he worked hard to develop a line of communication with the Senate, which he believed was required by the Constitution's stipulation that the president seek that body's "Advice and Consent" on treaties. Washington initially interpreted this constitutional requirement to include consultation with the Senate before treaty negotiations with another country began. But Washington's first effort to involve the Senate fully in the making of a treaty occasioned an awkward and embarrassing incident that caused a very different precedent to be established.

Having drafted instructions for a commission that he had appointed, with Senate approval, to negotiate a treaty with the Creek Indians, Washington accompanied acting secretary of war Knox to the Senate chamber in August 1789, seeking "Advice and Consent." After Vice President Adams read the proposed treaty to the Senate, however, the president's appeal for consultation was greeted with an awkward silence that was broken only reluctantly by the senators, who proceeded to engage in a rather confused and feeble discussion of the treaty. Finally, Sen. William Maclay of Pennsylvania, sensing that there was "no chance of a fair investigation of subjects while the President of the United States sat there, with his Secretary of War, to support his opinions and overawe the timid and neutral part of the Senate," spoke in favor of a motion (offered by his fellow Pennsylvanian, Robert Morris) that the papers of the president be submitted to a Senate committee for study. As the senator sat down, Washington started up in what Maclay described as a "violent fret" and cried out: "This defeats every purpose of my coming here." [30] Although in the end Washington achieved his purpose—the Senate later ratified the treaty with only minor changes—he had to sit for a long time, listening to what struck him as a dull and irrelevant debate. When he left the Senate chamber, he was overheard to say that he would "be damned if he ever went there again."

The incident over the Creek Indians treaty revealed the great difficulty of establishing a forum for formal personal encounters between the chief executive and the legislature within the constitutional system of "separated institutions sharing powers." Washington "slam[med] the door" on similar encounters in the future—neither he nor any later president ever again consulted the Senate in person.[31] Most significant, Washington's failure to obtain the Senate's active cooperation in the preliminary work of making treaties firmly established the president's supremacy in matters of diplomacy. Presidents never did come to possess an unhampered treaty-making power, to be sure. Yet the Washington administration created a precedent that relegated the Senate to approving or rejecting treaties that the executive already had negotiated.

Presidential Nonpartisanship and the Beginning of Party Conflict

Washington's conduct as president embodied his understanding that the presidency was a nonpartisan office. Like most of the Framers of the Constitution, he disapproved of "factions" and did not regard himself as the leader of any political party. Washington believed that Article II of the Constitution encouraged the president to stand apart from the jarring partisan conflict that was inherent to a legislative body. As such, the president could provide a strong measure of unity and stability to the political system. This was a task that, by temperament and background, Washington was well-suited to perform. Although he insisted on being master of the executive branch, it was contrary to his principles to try to influence either congressional elections or the legislative process. The primary duty of the president, he believed, was to execute the laws.[32]

Washington's conception of the presidency did not survive even his own administration, however. Ultimately, disagreements within his brilliant constellation of advisers led to the demise of the nonpartisan presidency. Party conflict arose from the sharp differences between Hamilton and Jefferson, differences that began during Washington's first term and became irreconcilable during the second term. These differences became obvious in reaction to Hamilton's financial measures for the "adequate support of public credit," which he proposed, at the behest of the House of Representatives, in a series of reports to Congress in 1790 and 1791. In the reports, Hamilton called upon Congress to assume the war debts of the states, to create a national bank, and to enact a system of tariffs to protect infant industries in the United States.

All of these proposals, save for the protectionist tariff, were supported by Washington and passed by Congress. In turn, Hamilton's program allowed the United States, so lately on the verge of bankruptcy, to acquire sounder credit and a more stable financial system than all but a few European nations had. Yet Hamilton's measures, successful as they were, pushed Jefferson into barely disguised opposition to the Washington administration's domestic program, sowing seeds of formal party conflict that blossomed as soon as Washington's unifying influence departed from the government.

Jefferson did not oppose all of Hamilton's measures—for example, he approved the plan to pay the national government's domestic and foreign debts. He did have grave reservations about the national government assuming the states' debts, believing that such a policy would benefit securities speculators unduly. But Jefferson acquiesced even to this policy as part of a deal he worked out with Hamilton. The two agreed that the nation's capital would be transferred from New York to Philadelphia in 1790 for ten years, pending removal to the new federal city of Washington, which would be built on the Potomac River between Maryland and Jefferson's home state of Virginia. But Jefferson, and eventually Madison, opposed Hamilton's proposal for a national bank, which was contained in the Treasury secretary's December 1790 report to Congress. According to Jefferson and Madison, Hamilton's plan would establish national institutions and policies that transcended the powers of Congress.

Furthermore, Hamilton's initiatives presupposed a principal role for the president in formulating public policies and carrying them out. This view, Jefferson and Madison believed, made the more decentralized and republican institutions—Congress and the states—subordinate to the executive, thus undermining popular sovereignty and pushing the United States toward a British-style monarchy. In 1791 Madison warned:

> The incompetency of one Legislature to regulate all the various objects belonging to the local governments would evidently force a transfer of many of them to the executive department; whilst the increasing splendor and number of its prerogatives supplied by this source, might prove excitements to ambition too powerful for a sober execution of the executive plan, and consequently strengthen the pretext for an hereditary designation of the magistrate.[33]

Neutrality Proclamation of 1793

The rift between Hamilton and Jefferson was aggravated during Washington's second term by a foreign policy conflict over the war between Britain and France, which broke out in 1793. Fearing that the French Revolution of 1789 had gotten out of hand, degenerating into mob rule, Hamilton took the side of England, a nation for which he had deep sympathies. Jefferson and Madison endorsed what they believed to be the sacred republican cause of the French Revolution, viewing Hamilton's support of England as evidence of his supposed commitment to monarchy.

As with domestic policy, conflicts over foreign affairs were inextricably joined to contrasting perceptions of the appropriate extent of presidential power. The Anglo-French question provoked a bitter exchange of views about the executive's proper role in foreign affairs when President Washington issued the Neutrality Proclamation of 1793.

The proclamation declared that the duties and interests of the United States required "that they should with sincerity and good faith adopt and pursue a conduct friendly and impartial to the belligerent powers." It prohibited Americans from "committing, aiding, or abetting hostilities against any of the said powers, or by carrying to them any of those articles which are deemed contraband by the modern usage of nations." [34]

Even before Washington's policy was announced, Hamilton and Jefferson took predictable stands on the merits of the proclamation. In private councils, Jefferson advised the president against it on two grounds. First, he believed such a unilateral executive action to be unconstitutional—a declaration of neutrality was, in effect, a declaration that there would be no war, a decision that rightfully belonged to Congress. Second, he pointed out that, according to a 1778 treaty, the United States was obligated to provide for France any necessities of war that had to be brought across the Atlantic. In reply, Hamilton argued to the president that, in the absence of a declaration of war by Congress, the executive had full power to proclaim and enforce American neutrality. Moreover, he defended the policy on its merits, claiming that the tumultuous events in France had deprived that nation of any permanent government, thus abrogating the obligations of the 1778 treaty.

President Washington, as he had in domestic policy, basically sided with Hamilton on the neutrality issue, although he took pains to unify his administration in public support of the proclamation. To mollify Jefferson, the word *neutrality* was not used in the text. (Still, the sense was trre.) A more substantial concession to Jefferson was made when Washington, against Hamilton's recommendation, decided soon after to receive France's ambassador to the United States, Edmond Genêt, making the United States the first nation to receive an emissary from the new Republic of France. These concessions to the secretary of state notwithstanding, the proclamation was a victory for Hamilton, one that boldly asserted the executive branch's power of initiative in the conduct of foreign affairs.[35]

The private controversy over the neutrality proclamation became public after Washington announced his policy, prompting Hamilton to write a series of newspaper articles under the pseudonym "Pacificus." Madison, at the urging of Jefferson, replied to these articles in the "Helvidius" letters. The issues that the coauthors of *The Federalist Papers* broached in this exchange illuminated the fundamental nature of a conflict that was to occupy the nation's attention time and time again, not only in foreign affairs but also in other matters pertaining to the legitimate authority of the president.

In defending the neutrality proclamation, Hamilton put forth a sweeping justification for discretionary presidential power that sharply distinguished between the Constitution's grants of legislative and executive authority. Article I states: "All legislative Powers *herein granted* shall be vested in a Congress of the United States" (emphasis added). Article II seems to provide a much more general grant: "The executive Power shall be vested in a President of the United States of America." The absence in Article II of the words *herein granted,* Hamilton argued, clearly indicated that the executive power of the nation was lodged exclusively in the president, "subject only to the exceptions and qualifications which are expressed in the Constitution." [36]

In foreign affairs, the explicit constitutional restrictions on presidential power extended no further than the right of the Senate to ratify treaties and of Congress to declare war. These rights of the legislature, Hamilton insisted, did not hinder the executive in other matters of foreign policy, which "naturally" were the domain of the president.[37] Indeed, Hamilton set forth a theory of presidential power that not only delegated to the chief executive nearly absolute discretion in the conduct of foreign affairs but also proposed a broad conception of "emergency powers that later Presidents, particularly those in the twentieth century, would generously draw upon." [38]

Madison, replying as Helvidius, denied that foreign policy was "naturally" an executive power. The tasks of foreign policy—to declare war, to conclude peace, and to form alliances—were among "the highest acts of sovereignty; of which the legislative power must at least be an integral and preeminent part." In foreign as in domestic matters, Madison argued, republican government required that the president's power be confined to the execution of laws. To suggest, as Hamilton did, that foreign policy was within the proper definition of executive power was to imply that the executive branch had a legislative power. Such an argument was "in theory an absurdity—in practice a tyranny." [39]

Important as it was, the precedent established by the Washington administration that the president can unilaterally enunciate a policy of neutrality was less significant than the larger issue in the debate between his leading advisers, namely, whether the president was to be limited by the letter of the Constitution or to be considered a sovereign head of state, with the discretion to act independently of legal restraints unless the Constitution specifically enumerated exceptions and limitations. The debate between Pacificus and Helvidius turned on nothing less than "the classical debate between the broad and narrow construction, the loose and strict interpretations of the Constitution." [40]

The Whiskey Rebellion

The strains created by the controversy over the neutrality proclamation made inevitable an outbreak of open party conflict between the Federalists, who shared Hamilton's point of view, and the Democratic-Republicans, who shared Jefferson's. The full implications of this conflict became clear during the presidency of John Adams, who took office in 1797. But even Washington, during his second term, was confronted with serious problems born of partisan differences. These culminated in the first test of the president's power to "take Care that the Laws be faithfully executed."

In 1794 militant opposition to a national excise tax on the production of whiskey arose in several parts of the country, particularly in the four westernmost counties of Pennsylvania, where whiskey was so important to the local economy that it was used, like money, as a medium of exchange. Back-country Pennsylvanians had avoided paying the hated whiskey tax since it was first levied in 1791.[41] In the summer of 1794 resistance turned into mass defiance of the law, stimulated at least in part by a local Democratic-Republican organization, the Mingo Creek society. A federal marshal and an excise inspector were forced to flee the area in July, and for two weeks western Pennsylvania was agitated by impassioned meetings, radical oratory, threats to take Pittsburgh by force and oust all federal authority, and occasional acts of violence.

President Washington's response to the so-called Whiskey Rebellion was to issue a stern proclamation on August 7, 1794, demanding that the rebels "disperse and retire peaceably to their respective abodes" and warning "all persons whomsoever against aiding, abetting, or comforting the perpetuators of the ... treasonable acts."[42] Almost simultaneously, after satisfying the law by securing from Supreme Court justice James Wilson a certification that the situation was beyond the control of federal marshals or judicial proceedings, Washington requested the governors of Pennsylvania, New Jersey, Maryland, and Virginia to supply a militia army to put down the rebellion.

The governors complied with Washington's request. The army was assembled in Harrisburg, Pennsylvania, in September and promptly marched on western Pennsylvania, with Washington himself accompanying the troops. Pennsylvania governor Thomas Mifflin had argued against federal intervention, insisting that his state's authority was adequate to cope with the outbreak of lawlessness. But Washington was persuaded by Hamilton to suppress the insurrection with a massive display of force.

Hamilton was moved by more than either his conviction that Washington must assert unequivocally the supremacy of the national government when in conflict with local claims of independence or his concern with establishing the president's leadership in such situations. The secretary of the Treasury and leader of the Federalists also was motivated by partisan considerations, viewing the insurrection in rural Pennsylvania as an opportunity to discredit and crush his political enemies by identifying them with treason. Referring to local Democratic-Republican societies, Hamilton averred, in a letter to Washington on August 2, 1792, that "formal public meetings of influential individuals" had "fomented" the "general spirit of opposition" that produced the violence in the western counties. Democratic-Republican leaders such as Jefferson and Madison did not actively oppose the national government's intervention in the insurrection; indeed, members of the Democratic-Republican societies in Philadelphia and Baltimore volunteered in large numbers to join the federal force against the Whiskey Rebellion. Nevertheless, the Democratic-Republicans found themselves in a politically vulnerable position because of the activities of their brethren in the West. Most Americans seemed convinced that treason and rebellion had arisen from the opposition societies. The immediate result was that the Federalists won full control of Congress in the 1794 elections.[43]

For his part, Washington delayed using federal force until his protracted efforts to conciliate the Pennsylvania rebels were rejected, reflecting "his earnest wish to avoid a resort to coercion." [44] In the face of a Washington-led army, the rebellion, such as it was, disappeared. Only twenty rebels were found, and these were taken to the state capital in Philadelphia and charged with treason. Two were convicted, but Washington pardoned them, inasmuch as one was "insane" and the other a retardate.[45]

Although his show of force in Pennsylvania ended anticlimactically, Washington believed, as he reported to Congress on November 19, 1794, that the suppression of the insurrection "demonstrated [that the prosperity of the United States rested] on solid foundations, by furnishing an additional proof that [his fellow citizens understood] the true principles of government and liberty." [46] As the historian William M. Goldsmith has written, "the first President clearly understood that a government which cannot enforce its laws is no government at all, and he also realized that within the framework of our complex political system, with its deliberate distribution of power, it is the responsibility of the executive to see that the laws are obeyed." [47]

Nevertheless, the Whiskey Rebellion and the government's response exacerbated rather than ended the political conflicts that divided the United States in the 1790s. The suppression of the insurrection did not eliminate the Democratic-Republicans from politics, as Hamilton had hoped, but strengthened their determination to thwart

Federalist purposes. Jefferson and Madison now were confirmed in their suspicion that Hamilton intended to establish a powerful executive, including a standing army, that would subvert the Constitution. Moreover, as word of the actual events in western Pennsylvania spread throughout the country, the prestige of the Federalist party was badly damaged. Jefferson wrote to Madison on December 28, 1794, "that the information of our militia, returned from the Westward, is uniform, that tho the people there let them pass quietly, they were objects of their laughter, not of their fear; . . . that their detestation of the excise law is universal, and has now associated to it a detestation of government." Prophetically, Jefferson added that the time was coming when the Democratic-Republicans would "fetch up the leeway of our vessel." [48]

Still, conflict between the Federalists and the Democratic-Republicans never became as raw and disruptive as the Framers of the Constitution had feared that partisan strife would be. The enduring restraint of "factionalism" in the United States may be attributed in part to the forceful example of nonpartisanship that was offered by George Washington at a time when to maintain unity was critical to the survival of the new government. To some extent Washington sought to deal with the divisions between the Hamiltonians and the Jeffersonians by avoiding them, choosing to "preside" over the government rather than to lead and direct it.[49] As his response to the Whiskey Rebellion makes clear, Washington sometimes did take stands, usually on the Hamiltonian side of controversial issues. Yet Washington's extraordinary personal charisma and popularity, combined with his commitment to the development of a strong and independent legislature, restrained partisan strife for as long as he was president. Moreover, Washington's renunciation of party leadership left his successors a legacy of presidential impartiality that has never been completely eclipsed. Even after a formal party system emerged, the Washingtonian precedent demanded that the chief executive lead the nation, not just the party that governed the nation.

Notes

1. Charles Thach, *The Creation of the American Presidency: 1775-1789* (Baltimore, Md.: Johns Hopkins University Press, 1922), 140.
2. Richard M. Pious, *The American Presidency* (New York: Basic Books, 1979), 38.
3. Ibid., 333.
4. *The Writings of George Washington,* ed. John C. Fitzpatrick, 39 vols. (Washington, D.C.: Government Printing Office, 1931-1944), 30:496. For a comprehensive account of Washington's contribution to the constitutional presidency, see Glen A. Phelps, "George Washington: Precedent Setter," in

Inventing the American Presidency, ed. Thomas E. Cronin (Lawrence: University Press of Kansas, 1989).

5. Thach, *Creation of the American Presidency,* 141.
6. Charles A. Beard, *The Economic Origins of Jeffersonian Democracy* (New York: Macmillan, 1915), 105.
7. Thach, *Creation of the American Presidency,* 141, 142; Wilfred E. Binkley, *President and Congress* (New York: Knopf, 1947), 26-27.
8. James Thomas Flexner, *George Washington and the New Nation: 1783-1793* (Boston: Little, Brown, 1970), 171.
9. *Writings of George Washington* 30:280.
10. Forrest McDonald, *The Presidency of George Washington* (Lawrence: University Press of Kansas, 1974), 24.
11. Gordon S. Wood, "The Greatness of George Washington," *Virginia Quarterly Review* 68:2 (Spring 1992): 196-197.
12. Quoted in ibid., 197.
13. Garry Wills, *Cincinnatus: George Washington and the Enlightenment* (Garden City, N.Y.: Doubleday, 1984), 23.
14. This description of Washington's journey comes from the account provided in Flexner, *George Washington and the New Nation,* 174-181.
15. Ibid., 398. North Carolina and Rhode Island did not ratify the Constitution until November 21, 1789, and May 29, 1790, respectively.
16. Flexner, *George Washington and the New Nation,* 193.
17. Ibid., 196.
18. Ibid., 182-183; McDonald, *Presidency of George Washington,* 29-31; John Zvesper, *Political Philosophy and Rhetoric: A Study of the Origins of the American Party System* (New York: Cambridge University Press, 1977), 66; and James Madison to Thomas Jefferson, May 27, 1789, *The Writings of James Madison,* ed. Gaillard Hunt (New York: Putnam's, 1904), 5:370-372. See also Madison's letter to Jefferson of May 23, 1789, *Writings of James Madison* 5:369-370.
19. On the early history of the office of attorney general, see Leonard White, *The Federalists: A Study in Administrative History* (New York: Macmillan, 1948), 164-172.
20. McDonald, *Presidency of George Washington,* 39; Flexner, *George Washington and the New Nation,* 400.
21. Flexner, *George Washington and the New Nation,* 399; White, *Federalists,* 101.
22. White, *Federalists,* 106.
23. McDonald, *Presidency of George Washington,* 39.
24. White, *Federalists,* 258-259.
25. McDonald, *Presidency of George Washington,* 39.
26. Flexner, *George Washington and the New Nation,* 222; Thach, *Creation of the American Presidency,* 140-165.
27. Flexner, *George Washington and the New Nation,* 221.
28. Alexander Hamilton, James Madison, and John Jay, *The Federalist Papers,* with an introduction by Clinton L. Rossiter (New York: New American Library, 1961), 442-443.
29. Phelps, "George Washington: Precedent Setter," 266.
30. "Account by William Maclay of President George Washington's First Attempt to Obtain the Advice and Consent of the Senate to a Treaty," August 22, 1789, *The Growth of Presidential Power: A Documented History,* ed. William M. Goldsmith (New York and London: Chelsea, 1974),

1:392-396.
31. Flexner, *George Washington and the New Nation,* 215-218.
32. Ibid., 398-399.
33. "Consolidation," from the *National Gazette,* December 5, 1791, *Writings of James Madison* 6:67 (Madison's emphasis). As the political scientist John C. Koritansky has noted, the fears of Jefferson and Madison about Hamilton's thoughts and practices were not without foundation:

> The picture of the United States government that emerges from reflecting on Hamilton's thoughts is that of a constitutional monarchy. Jefferson [and Madison] knew whereof they spoke when they branded Hamilton a "monarchist" and "monocrat," even if Hamilton never himself referred to his own thought in those words after he had respectively repudiated the avowedly monarchical stance he had taken in the Philadelphia convention.

Koritansky, "Alexander Hamilton and the Presidency," in Cronin, *Inventing the American Presidency,* 296.
34. Printed in *Letters of Pacificus and Helvidius on the Proclamation of Neutrality of 1793* (Washington, D.C.: Gideon, 1845), 3.
35. McDonald, *Presidency of George Washington,* 126-127.
36. As revealed in Chapter 2, the difference in the vesting clauses probably was not intended by the Constitutional Convention.
37. *Letters of Pacificus and Helvidius,* 5-15.
38. Goldsmith, *Growth of Presidential Power* 1:398.
39. *Letters of Pacificus and Helvidius,* 53-64.
40. Goldsmith, *Growth of Presidential Power* 1:411.
41. The discussion of the Whiskey Rebellion relies heavily on McDonald, *Presidency of George Washington,* 145-147.
42. President George Washington, Proclamation of August 7, 1794 ("Final Warning of a Resort to Force"). Printed in Goldsmith, *Growth of Presidential Power* 1:246-248.
43. Alexander Hamilton to George Washington, August 2, 1794, *Papers of Alexander Hamilton,* ed. Harold C. Syrett (New York and London: Columbia University Press, 1986), 15-19. See also Thomas P. Slaughter, *The Whiskey Rebellion: Frontier Epilogue to the American Revolution* (New York: Oxford University Press, 1986), 163, 190-229; and Leland D. Baldwin, *Whiskey Rebels: The Story of a Frontier Uprising* (Pittsburgh: University of Pittsburgh Press, 1939), 259-272.
44. *Messages and Papers of the Presidents,* ed. James D. Richardson, 20 vols. (New York: Bureau of National Literature, 1897), 1:156.
45. McDonald, *Presidency of George Washington,* 145.
46. President George Washington, "Report to Congress on Success of Operation," November 19, 1794. Printed in Goldsmith, *Growth of Presidential Power* 1:253-255.
47. Ibid., 255.
48. *The Writings of Thomas Jefferson,* ed. Paul Leicester Ford (New York: Putnam's, 1895), 6:516-519; Binkley, *President and Congress,* 287-288.
49. McDonald, *Presidency of George Washington,* 114.

CHAPTER 4

The Rise of Party Politics and the Triumph of Jeffersonianism

The end of George Washington's administration marked the transformation of the presidency from a nonpartisan to a partisan institution. This change did not entail a complete metamorphosis; even the protagonists in the nation's first great party conflicts—John Adams, Alexander Hamilton, Thomas Jefferson, and James Madison—regarded partisanship with great disfavor. As the historian Richard Hofstadter has written, "the creators of the first American party system on both sides, Federalists and Republicans, were men who looked upon parties as sores on the body politic." [1]

Yet the bitter disputes that occurred in the wake of Washington's return to Mount Vernon made open party conflict a central part of the American presidency. Thereafter, presidents might try to rise above party, but partisanship had become an essential condition of effective presidential leadership.

Washington's Retirement and the Jay Treaty: The Constitutional Crisis of 1796

Near the end of 1795, the paramount political question for most public figures in the United States was whether Washington would accept a third term as president. The Constitution imposed no limit on presidential reeligibility, and Washington, although his political reputation was slightly tarnished by the partisan animosities that had divided his cabinet, could surely have remained in office had he chosen to do so.

Washington was anxious, however, to return to Mount Vernon. In September 1796, he announced his retirement, marking the event with the release of his Farewell Address, which was published without ceremony and never spoken to an audience. Although Washington did not intend that it do so, his voluntary retirement set a precedent for limiting presidents to two terms that endured for nearly 150 years. (The two-term limit eventually became law, with the ratification of the Twenty-second Amendment in 1951.) His decision eased somewhat the Jeffersonians' concerns about the dangerous aggrandizement of executive power. In fact, Washington's example converted Jefferson from his original belief that the president should serve only a single term.[2]

Washington's retirement also cleared the way for a more partisan form of presidential politics. As long as he was the president, Washington was able by dint of his prestige to restrain open party conflict. But Vice President Adams, although a distinguished and respected political leader, lacked Washington's stature as well as his reputation for impartiality. In the division between Federalists and Democratic-Republicans, Adams was clearly identified with the Federalists. His role in the controversy over the president's title (he had favored something exalted) and his well-known admiration for the British form of government marked him as a "monarchist" in the eyes of Jeffersonians. Thus, when Washington's decision to retire became known and Adams assumed the position of heir apparent, the presidential campaign of 1796 began in earnest.

The 1796 election, generally considered to be one of the most bitter and scurrilous in U.S. history, matched Adams and Thomas Pinckney, the Federalist nominee for vice president, against the Democratic-Republican ticket of Jefferson for president and Aaron Burr for vice president. The divisions between the parties were crystallized by the controversial Jay Treaty, which had been signed in London in November 1794.

The Jay Treaty won for the United States both a pledge from Britain to evacuate by 1796 its Northwest military posts, which had sustained British power on American soil since the Revolution, and a limited right for American vessels to trade with the British West Indies. As such, the treaty promised to secure America's territorial integrity and to ameliorate dangerous conflicts at sea. (Several skirmishes, a by-product of Britain's ongoing war with France, had brought the United States and Britain to the brink of war.) Yet, when some secret terms of the Jay Treaty were leaked to the Democratic-Republican press in late June 1795, a political firestorm ensued that made both John Jay (the chief justice of the United States who, as a presidential envoy, had negotiated the treaty) and the Washington administration the targets of vicious partisan attacks.

Democratic-Republican opposition to the Jay Treaty was animated by a strong dislike of the British, which was reinforced by Britain's use of its eight northwestern posts to arm Indians and rebellious slaves to attack settlers in the Northwest Territory. Democratic-Republicans, who were strongest in the South, also were enraged because the treaty provided no compensation to slave owners for the slaves who had been seized by the British at the end of the Revolution; nor did it create a mechanism to settle the pre-revolutionary war debts that Americans owed to British citizens, which placed southerners, especially, in jeopardy of having to repay private debts of long standing. In effect, the Jay Treaty became the issue through which the emerging polarization between Hamiltonians and Jeffersonians—based upon fundamental differences of ideology and economic interest—was nationalized and hardened into organized two-party conflict.[3]

Curiously, the real fight over the Jay Treaty was not in the Federalist-dominated Senate, which ratified it with little opposition on June 24, 1795, but in the House of Representatives. Because the treaty required that arbitration commissions be established to settle certain disagreements between the United States and Britain that were not resolved by the document itself, it could not be carried into effect without congressional appropriations. "Money bills," as the Constitution clearly specified, could originate only in the House. Whether the House, by virtue of its power over appropriations, properly shared the Senate's role in foreign affairs was a constitutional issue that had not yet been settled. Democratic-Republican House leaders, including such reluctant partisans as Madison and Pennsylvanian Albert Gallatin, sought to weld the widespread popular opposition to the treaty to Congress's own resentment of executive initiative. In doing so, they enjoyed the full support of Secretary of State Jefferson, who wrote on November 30, 1795, in a letter to Edward Rutledge, a friend in the South Carolina Legislature:

> I trust the popular branch of our legislature will disapprove of it [the Jay Treaty], and thus rid us of this infamous act, which is really nothing more than a treaty of alliance between England and the Anglomen of this country, against the legislature and people of the United States.[4]

The Democratic-Republicans succeeded in passing a House resolution on March 24, 1796, that requested the president to provide the House with all papers pertaining to the negotiation of the Jay Treaty. Gallatin, one of the Democratic-Republicans' most persuasive leaders, argued that the House had the right to make such a request

> because their cooperation and sanction was necessary to carry the Treaty into full effect, to render it a binding instrument, and to make it properly speaking, a law of the land; because they had full discretion either to give or to refuse that cooperation; because they

must be guided, in the exercise of that discretion, by the merits and expediency of the treaty itself, and therefore had a right to ask for every information which could assist them in deciding the question.[5]

Gallatin's aim was not merely to see the papers, or even to defeat the Jay Treaty and pave the way for the election of a Democratic-Republican president in 1796.[6] Gallatin, along with Madison and Jefferson, also wanted to assert the right of the House of Representatives to participate in the treaty-making process. They believed that if such a power belonged exclusively to the president and to the two-thirds majority of the Senate that was needed to ratify treaties, the president conceivably could act in concert with just twenty-two of the then-thirty-two senators to usurp all the powers of the House, for treaties had the same constitutional status as the laws of the land.

In view of the Jay Treaty's unpopularity, the Democratic-Republicans had a real chance to scuttle it, which would have imposed a significant limitation on the president's power to conduct foreign affairs. But Washington, on the verge of retirement, chose to make the House's request for papers the last great constitutional issue of his presidency. He replied to the resolution with "a thunderous refusal," as the historian Forrest McDonald has described it.[7] "To admit . . . a right in the House of Representatives to demand . . . papers respecting a negotiation with a foreign power," Washington asserted, "would be to establish a dangerous precedent." Except in matters pertaining to impeachment, "it does not occur that the inspection of papers asked for can be relative to any purpose under the cognizance of the House of Representatives."

Washington also lectured Congress on the Constitution. "Having been a member of the General Convention and knowing the principles on which the Constitution was formed," he observed pointedly, "the power of making treaties is exclusively vested in the President, by and with the advice and consent of the Senate, provided two-thirds of the senators present concur; and . . . every treaty so made and promulgated thenceforward became the law of the land." [8]

A constitutional impasse had been reached. The House claimed the right to see the papers but had no means to pry them from the president. There followed a debate, consuming the entire month of April 1796, about whether the House would appropriate the funds (roughly $90,000) that were needed to carry the treaty into effect. In the end, Washington's resolute stand eroded the initial Democratic-Republican majority in Congress. The enabling legislation for the treaty was approved at the end of April, by the close vote of 51 to 48.

Thus, the Democratic-Republicans' effort to transform hostility to the Jay Treaty into the central campaign issue of 1796 backfired. Their opposition to the treaty probably contributed to Adams's election as president in 1796 and to the Federalist gains in that year's congressional elections. The only solace the Democratic-Republicans could find in this latest defeat was that it rested on George Washington's influence, not the Federalist party's. Even the Federalists must have realized from the treaty controversy, wrote Jefferson, "that nothing can support them but the colossus of the President's merits with the people, and the moment he retires, that his successor, if a monocrat, will be overborne by the republican sense of his Constituents. . . ." [9]

With the final enactment of the Jay Treaty, a constitutional crisis, animated by bitter partisan strife, was averted. The incident did not settle permanently the question of the House's proper role in foreign affairs: after more than two centuries the right of the House of Representatives to participate not only in diplomacy but in all aspects of foreign policy is still a matter of serious debate. "But the precedent and correlative implications of the decision that Washington established in 1796," the historian William Goldsmith has observed, "would be difficult to erase." [10]

The 1796 Election

In spite of the strong disagreements that divided Federalists and Democratic-Republicans, the contestants in the partisan strife of the 1790s were reluctant warriors. Partisanship was still not considered respectable in American politics; indeed, candidates for president were not expected to seek the office actively. Neither Adams nor Jefferson made the slightest public effort to influence the outcome of the presidential election of 1796, even as they (Jefferson especially) worked behind the scenes to achieve the triumph of the parties they represented.

Nevertheless, party organizations dominated the election, conducting their campaigns through newspaper polemics, pamphlets, and political rallies. Indeed, the issues that the parties raised so divided the country as to threaten the hard-won national unity that the Constitutional Convention and the Washington administration had achieved. The Federalists branded Jefferson as an atheist who would destroy all organized religion. He also was accused of being an ardent friend of the French Revolution of 1789—a radical democrat who as president would allow republican government to deteriorate into the sort of mob rule that had brought the Reign of Terror to France. Democratic-Republicans, for their part, excoriated Adams as being immoderately pro-British, a monarchist who neither believed in democracy nor respected the Constitution.

The 1796 election ended with a narrow Federalist victory. Adams was elected president with seventy-one electoral votes. Jefferson's sixty-eight votes made him the vice president—the avowedly nonpartisan constitutional mechanism for selecting the president and the vice president had not yet been changed to accommodate the outbreak of partisan competition. The Constitution directed that every elector vote for two persons for president, with the second-place candidate becoming vice president. Because this mechanism did not easily allow a party ticket to be elected, the election of 1796 yielded an administration that was headed by the leaders of two hostile political organizations.

The Embattled Presidency of John Adams

John Adams became president in extraordinarily difficult circumstances. No other chief executive would have the unenviable task of succeeding a leader of Washington's stature. More significant, the foreign situation that Adams faced in 1797 was perilous. The Jay Treaty had greatly worsened U.S. relations with an aggressive French government that was, after Napoleon Bonaparte defeated Austria in October 1797, at the height of its power. French harassment of American commerce at sea made Britain's interference with U.S. shipping in 1793 seem mild. As Jefferson said, "The President [Washington] is fortunate to get off just as the bubble is bursting, leaving others to hold the bag." [11]

The virtual naval war with France was aggravated severely when Adams's diplomatic attempts to maintain Washington's policy of neutrality received an insulting and humiliating response from the French foreign ministry. The American mission to France, composed of Elbridge Gerry (a Democratic-Republican who was chosen by Adams to convince the opposition of the president's good intentions), John Marshall, and Charles Cotesworth Pinckney, became the target of high-handed manipulation by the French foreign minister, Talleyrand. Talleyrand sent three representatives of the French government (referred to in secret dispatches as "X, Y, and Z") to find out from the U.S. emissaries in Paris how much the United States was willing to pay in bribes to French officials and loans to the French government in order to secure a treaty.

When the so-called "XYZ affair" became public early in 1798, a furor erupted in the United States that seemed to make war with France inevitable. The controversy brought to a close the brief lull in sectional and political strife that had followed Adams's inauguration on March 4, 1797. The more extreme Federalists, or "Arch-Federalists," as they were called, urged that a large standing army be created, both to deter an invasion by France and to protect the nation from the Jeffersonians, whom they regarded as even more dangerous than the French. President

Adams, although far more moderate than the extremists in his party, also supported war preparations, especially the development of a larger navy.

To pay for the expanded military, higher taxes had to be imposed. The resentment that was caused by these taxes, especially the tax on whiskey, became a potent political issue for the Democratic-Republicans. Increasing animosity between Federalists and Democratic-Republicans even led to rumors of civil discord and southern secession. At the end of June 1797, an alarmed Jefferson wrote to Rutledge:

> The passions are too high at present, to be cooled in our day. You and I have formerly seen warm debates and high political passions. But gentlemen of different politics would then speak to each other, and separate the business of the Senate from that of society. It is not so now. Men who have been intimate all their lives, cross the street to avoid meeting, and turn their heads another way, lest they should be obliged to touch their hats.[12]

Adams's efforts to deal with the domestic and international crises of the late 1790s were hindered as much by members of his own party as by the opposition. Although the Democratic-Republicans, led by Vice President Jefferson, were expected to oppose Adams's actions, "the Federalists were often as recalcitrant or bitter toward the president." [13] His most influential critic within the party was Hamilton, who regarded Adams as being too moderate politically and therefore incapable of dealing with the nation's problems.

Adams was a Federalist, but he intended to follow Washington's example of remaining as much as possible above party. The president was willing to accept a war declared by France but hoped to avoid one. His primary objectives were to protect American commerce, through diplomacy and an expanded navy, and to force the French Republic to respect the American flag. Hamilton and his Arch-Federalist allies, however, wanted to exploit the foreign conflict in which the United States was entangled, not to contain it. Ultimately, these differences caused an irreconcilable split to occur within the Federalist party, prompting Jefferson to write in May 1797 that the "Hamiltons" were "only a little less hostile [to Adams] than to me." [14]

Hamilton severely tested the president's authority as chief executive in other ways.[15] He was determined to guide the policy of the government, even though he was not one of its members. Hamilton had retired from the Treasury at the end of January 1795, but during the latter days of Washington's second term and throughout Adams's tenure he remained the dynamic center of the Federalist party. Indeed, Hamilton's influence was enhanced in 1797 by Adams's decision to retain Washington's cabinet, a policy that the new president pursued both out of deference to the stature of his predecessor and because he believed that good government required the labor of able and experienced administrators.[16]

Three members of Washington's cabinet—Secretary of State Timothy Pickering, Secretary of War James McHenry, and Oliver Wolcott, who succeeded Hamilton as secretary of the Treasury—owed their positions in the government mostly to Hamilton. In all important questions they looked to him, not to President Adams, as the guide for their actions. Only Charles Lee, who as attorney general was the least powerful member of the cabinet, and Benjamin Stoddert, who joined the cabinet as the secretary of the newly established Navy Department in 1798, were loyal to Adams. Unity of executive policy was achieved only when the president happened to agree with Hamilton, a coincidence that was absent when war with France threatened.

Thus, there emerged throughout the Adams administration "an extraordinary situation in which the control of public policy became the prize of a struggle between a New York lawyer and a president who apparently was not fully aware of the activity of his rival." [17] The situation was aggravated by Adams's tendency to take long retreats from the capital (then in Philadelphia) in the erroneous belief that he could manage the affairs of government from his home in Quincy, Massachusetts.

The conflict between Adams and the Arch-Federalists culminated in 1799. Early that year, Adams prepared to send a second mission to France in an effort to avoid war. In February, without consulting the cabinet or even the secretary of state, he nominated William Vans Murray, the U.S. minister to the Netherlands, as minister plenipotentiary to the French Republic. Adams chose Murray because of his good relations with France; it was through Murray, in fact, that Adams had learned that France was willing to receive a new American mission and wanted to avoid war with the United States. The Federalist-controlled Senate, which was sympathetic to Hamilton's views, probably would have rejected the nomination, but Adams's quick and unilateral action caught its members by surprise. Instead, the Senate compromised by asking for a commission of three, to which the president consented.

Thwarting attempts by Secretary of State Pickering and others to postpone the sailing of the second mission, Adams first indicated that he was not opposed to a delay, then hurried the peace commission aboard an American frigate. The commission arrived in time to take advantage of France's uncertain political situation, the aftermath of a series of military defeats by the British. Although Adams's bold course aggravated his problems with the cabinet and the Federalist party, it achieved a commercial agreement with France that ended the threat of war, thus preserving the principle of neutrality toward Europe that he had inherited from George Washington.

More significant, Adams rescued the authority of the presidency. His political position was shaken by the peace mission controversy; in all likelihood it cost him any chance for reelection. But as Leonard White, a scholar of the early development of the American presidency, has written:

> the outcome was a resounding affirmation of the authority of the President as chief executive and of the subordination of the department heads to his leadership and direction. Adams confirmed the character of the presidency as the Constitutional Convention had outlined it and as Washington had already formed it—but only after events which stirred grave doubts concerning its future.[18]

Solidifying his leadership in the aftermath of the peace mission, Adams rid the cabinet of the two men who were the most disloyal to him. In May 1800, he asked for the resignation of McHenry, who gave it, and summarily removed Pickering when he refused to resign. Pickering thus became the first cabinet officer to be removed by a president.

The Alien and Sedition Acts

Although historians frequently have praised John Adams for upholding the authority of the presidency in the face of a badly divided cabinet and party, he has been widely condemned for his part in the passage and enforcement of the Alien and Sedition acts of 1798. The Alien Act gave the president authority to expel foreigners who were suspected of subversion; the Sedition Act made it a crime, punishable by fine or imprisonment, to bring "false, scandalous and malicious" accusations against the president, Congress, or the government.

The Alien Act generally was viewed as a defensible measure to support the national government's right of self-protection, even though it was taken to task severely by the Democratic-Republicans for vesting extraordinary powers in the president and thus for violating the principle of separation of powers. The sedition law, however, was widely denounced as unconstitutional. To be sure, it was not as oppressive as similar European statutes: it imposed on the prosecution the burden to prove an "intent to defame" and required a jury trial to convict. But the law was enforced in ways that confounded conspiracy against the government with legitimate political opposition. As such, it violated the First Amendment to the Constitution, which had been added in 1791 as part of the Bill of Rights, and which, among other things, forbade Congress to pass any law abridging the freedom of speech or press.

The passage and enforcement of the Alien and Sedition acts was an unhappy chapter in U.S. history. Although a much more drastic sedition law (the Espionage Act) was passed during World War I and was enforced by sentences far severer than those of Adams's day, the 1798 statute was enacted in peacetime. Moreover, the Sedition Act was marred by partisan intolerance. Unlike the Alien Act, which had considerable Democratic-Republican support, the Sedition Act was introduced, defended, and passed by Federalists in Congress and was signed into law by a Federalist president. Fourteen people were sentenced under the act; its enforcement was nothing less than a government-directed war against the opposition party press. Indeed, most sedition cases came to trial in 1800 and were tied directly to the presidential election. Thus, the sedition law degenerated into a Federalist instrument to stifle and even to destroy the Democratic-Republican party.

Adams had little sympathy for the more extreme purposes of the Alien and Sedition acts. He resisted Secretary of State Pickering's desire to use the alien laws to deport large numbers of noncitizens. He also opposed the Arch-Federalists' proposal to establish a large standing army. Adams's restraint was not unimportant. As Hofstadter has written, "If we can imagine a determined High Federalist President in the White House seizing upon the most intense moment of Anti-French feeling to precipitate a war, we can imagine a partisan conflict that would have cracked the Union." [19]

The "Revolution" of 1800

Although Adams's efforts to rise above party conflict may have avoided civil discord, they did not prevent his defeat by Jefferson in the election of 1800. Indeed, Adams's dislike of party politics inadvertently contributed to the creation of a formal two-party system. His avoidance of war with France and the triumph of the more moderate elements of the Federalist party helped to create sufficiently tolerant political conditions so that a peaceful transfer of power from one party to another could occur. But the coming of the Democratic-Republican party to power, an event that Jefferson referred to as "the Revolution of 1800," was preceded by an odd set of occurrences that precipitated a constitutional crisis and nearly abrogated the results of the presidential election.

As noted earlier, the original Constitution, which was written without political parties in mind, provided that the candidate with the largest majority of electoral votes would become president, and the runner-up would become vice president. In 1796, Federalists and Democratic-Republicans understood that Adams and Jefferson were the heads of their respective party tickets, and some agreement existed about the identity of each party's candidate for vice president. But the nominating structure that the parties had devised was not yet sufficiently developed to enforce party discipline in support of a ticket. Adams was elected president, but his opponent, Jefferson, became the vice president.

By 1800, however, formal party organizations were fully in place. A caucus of each party's members of Congress was held to choose its nominees for president and vice president; the caucus's decision then was coordinated with party organizations in the various states so that electors were selected as instructed agents, pledged to cast their two ballots for president for the party's presidential and vice-presidential candidates. Consequently, when in the close election of 1800 seventy-three Democratic-Republican electors were chosen (to sixty-five for the Federalists), each voted for both Jefferson and his running mate, Burr. (Apparently, one vote was supposed to be withheld from Burr, but this did not happen.) Jefferson and Burr ended up with the same number of electoral votes for president. According to the Constitution, it then fell to the lame duck Federalist majority in the House of Representatives to decide which Democratic-Republican—Jefferson or Burr—would become president.

Federalist leaders in Congress saw some advantage in making Burr president; he was a less principled and, therefore, perhaps a more pliable politician than the "fanatic," Jefferson. For his part, Burr refused to take the honorable steps required to correct the results of the electoral college, even though it was clearly understood throughout the party that Jefferson was the head of the ticket. The result was a deadlock. Under the Constitution a majority of the representatives in nine of the sixteen states was needed to elect the president, and neither party could produce the votes. The stalemate lasted through thirty-five ballots. Not until February 17, 1801, was Jefferson elected.

Interestingly, Jefferson's leading supporter in the House election was Hamilton, who not many months earlier had urged Gov. John Jay of New York to change the state's election laws in the Federalists' favor "to prevent an *atheist* in religion and a fanatic in politics from getting possession of the helm of State." Faced with a choice between Burr and Jefferson, however, Hamilton assured his colleagues that Jefferson was the safer man. Writing to Delaware representative James A. Bayard in January 1801, Hamilton portrayed Jefferson in remarkably astute terms, foretelling much about the Virginian's presidency: "I admit that his politics are tinctured with fanaticism; that he is too much in earnest with his democracy; that he has been a mischievous enemy to the principal measures of our past administration. . . ." But, Hamilton went on, Jefferson was neither an enemy of executive authority nor a slave to his principles. On the contrary, he was likely "to temporize" and to acquiesce in the prevailing, mainly Federalist, governing arrangements. (Jefferson also was incapable, unlike Burr, of being corrupted.)[20]

The House of Representatives decided the outcome of the election of 1800 after Thomas Jefferson (left) and Aaron Burr received the same number of electoral votes for president. The Twelfth Amendment, which required that separate ballots be cast for president and vice president, was subsequently passed to avoid future deadlocks.

Hamilton's intervention and that of a few other influential Federalists broke the deadlock in the House, along with Jefferson's tacit assurances that he would neither scuttle the navy nor summarily purge Federalist officeholders from the government.

Jefferson's triumph in the 1800 election marked the beginning of a critical realignment in American politics. The Democratic-Republicans became the nation's leading political party and remained so until 1828. During the last decade of his life, in a letter to the eminent lawyer and legal scholar Spencer Roane, Jefferson said that the "revolution of 1800," although effected peacefully in the course of a popular election, was "as real a revolution in the principles of our government as that of 1776 was in its form." [21]

In Jefferson's view, the principles of the revolutionary war had been perverted by the Federalists in their ardent commitment to expand the responsibilities of the national government. The Federalists' domestic and international initiatives required that the executive take on a dominant role in formulating and carrying out public policy that eventually would transform the president into a monarch. The task of the Democratic-Republican revolution was to restore republican government to the American polity by casting off the Federalist institutions and, according to Forrest McDonald, by "instill[ing] the people with the historical knowledge and true principles that would prevent them from losing their liberties again." [22]

The importance of the Democratic-Republican task was revealed clearly in Jefferson's first inaugural address, which pronounced a party program of reform that included a strictly limited role for the national government and, concomitantly, "support of the state governments in all their rights"; a "frugal" government, dedicated to economy in public expenditures; and the encouragement of agriculture over commerce. In laying out this program, Jefferson stressed that it commanded the allegiance of a majority of the people. Although he took care to pay homage to the rights of the minority against the "unreasonable will of the majority," Jefferson called for "a jealous care of the right of election by the people" and "absolute acquiescence in the decisions of the majority." [23]

Jefferson's War with the Judiciary

Jefferson's desire to preserve the integrity of majority rule animated his war with the federal judiciary. In a desperate attempt to maintain a foothold in the national government, the Federalists tried to "pack" the courts with judges of their own party before leaving office. The Judiciary Act of 1801, enacted just before Jefferson was inaugurated, created a number of new federal judgeships, which were hurriedly filled through "midnight" appointments by the outgoing Adams administration. To the Jeffersonians the judiciary constituted "the final barrier to be assaulted in the advance of popular government and political liberty." To the Federalists the courts represented "the last bastion of moderation and sanity arresting the progress of mob rule and anarchy." [24]

More was at stake in this dispute than partisan power, however. The Democratic-Republicans opposed the doctrine that the Constitution implicitly vests the courts with a broad authority to override the actions of elected officials on constitutional grounds. The Federalists, to the contrary, supported the judiciary's claim to be the ultimate arbiter of the Constitution. Although Jefferson and his followers did not challenge the courts' right of judicial review, they insisted that each branch of the government, and the state governments as well, shares equally the right to decide matters of constitutionality.

These issues of power and principle came to a head in the case of *Marbury v. Madison* (1803).[25] The case involved a request by one of the Federalists' midnight appointees, William Marbury, that the Supreme Court issue a writ of mandamus to force the Jefferson administration to deliver his commission as a justice of the peace in the new capital, Washington, D.C. Although Marbury's commission had been ratified by the Senate and signed by John Marshall, who was secretary of state at the time, it never was delivered. The Jefferson administration, scorning the midnight appointments as part of a Federalist plot to control the government, simply held on to it. The unenviable task of mediating this bitter and symbolically important dispute fell to John Marshall, himself an ardent Federalist and a last-minute appointee as chief justice of the Supreme Court.

The Jefferson administration expected the Court to lay itself open to political attack by issuing the writ that Marbury had requested. But in a brilliant piece of judicial statecraft, Marshall outmaneuvered the Democratic-Republicans, sidestepping the case's narrow partisan issues in order to establish the authority of the Supreme Court. Writing for a unanimous court, Marshall scolded the president for refusing to deliver an appointment to which Marbury was legally entitled, noting that even the president is not above the law. Yet Marshall denied Marbury his writ of mandamus by ruling that Section 13 of the Judiciary Act of 1789, under which Marbury had brought his suit, was unconstitutional: the section presumed to give the Supreme Court original jurisdiction in the matter, even though the Constitution provided that the Court's jurisdiction is purely appellate in all but a few kinds of cases. In effect, Marshall gave Jefferson a free hand to bar Federalist appointees from office, but only on the condition that the president accept the Court's power to judge the constitutionality of acts of Congress.[26]

Jefferson was unwilling to accept this condition, but so adroit was Marshall's ruling that the president had no way to disobey the chief justice and the judiciary, as he had hoped. When he failed in a subsequent effort to remove by impeachment Supreme Court Justice Samuel Chase, Jefferson's war with the judiciary came to an end. Indeed, developments during his first term seemed to make the war unnecessary: by 1804 much of the Democratic-Republican program that Jefferson had heralded in his first inaugural was completed. Nevertheless, although the judiciary weathered the storm of Jefferson's first term, the question that had given rise to the conflict between the president and the Court never was fully resolved. That question— whether ultimate authority on matters of constitutionality rests with elected officials in Congress and the White House or in a standard of "fixed" law as interpreted by the judiciary—has arisen again and again in U.S. history.

The Democratic-Republican Program and the Adjustment to Power

In important respects, the Democratic-Republican program was negative; a great deal of it aimed at repealing Federalist policies that the Jeffersonians believed had undermined the Constitution. In 1801,

Congress, which also had been captured by the Democratic-Republicans in the elections of 1800, repealed the provisions of the Alien and Sedition acts that had not already expired. In addition, Jefferson pardoned all ten persons (mostly Democratic-Republican newspaper publishers) who had been convicted under the Sedition Act, and Congress voted to repay with interest all the fines that had been levied as part of their sentences. During Jefferson's first term, Congress also abolished most of the internal taxes, including the unpopular excise and direct property taxes, that the Federalists had enacted in 1798 to help prepare for a possible war with France. As part of the same package, Congress reduced the size of the military establishment, severely cutting army and naval appropriations.[27]

Although Jefferson emphasized the need to restrain the national government, he was not narrowly doctrinaire about government's proper limits. His main concern was to make Washington more responsive to the will of the people. "His faith in the people," the historian Robert M. Johnstone has written, "gave to his views on power a flexibility that permitted the use of power in positive ways to emphasize the freedom *from* government." [28] In those areas in which actions by the national government were proper—that is, in matters pertaining to external affairs and the relations among the states—Jefferson believed that the government's powers should be exercised with energy and efficiency.

When circumstances required, Jefferson actually was willing to tolerate government actions that seemed to contradict his stated principles. Thus, in 1803 he consented to the purchase of the Louisiana Territory, which doubled the size of the United States, even though, as he granted in a letter to Sen. John Breckinridge, he did not think the Constitution provided "for our holding foreign territory, still less for incorporating foreign nations into our union." [29] In 1807, seeking to maintain the longstanding American commitment to neutrality between Britain and France, he imposed an embargo on all foreign commerce. Enforcement of the embargo involved coercion on a scale rivaling that of the notorious Alien and Sedition acts.

Jefferson's actions as president reflected a "duality that was to underlie the whole of the [Democratic-Republican] era and to account for many of its frustrations." [30] Tensions within the party's philosophy of government became evident in the Jeffersonians' conduct of the presidency. Opposing conceptions of executive power had once been at the center of the bitter conflict between the Federalists and the Democratic-Republicans. The Federalists had invested the president with broad responsibilities, fretted about legislative encroachments on executive power, and, especially in matters pertaining to foreign affairs, tried to minimize the checks on the president that the Constitution had granted to Congress. In contrast, the Democratic-Republicans had placed their faith in the people's representatives, believing that policy and financial decisions should originate in Congress. They also had sought to restrict executive discretion severely, not only in domestic matters but in foreign policy as well. As noted earlier, for example, during the battle over the Jay Treaty, Democratic-Republicans had asserted the right of the House of Representatives to deny the funds needed to implement a treaty, thus claiming for the lower house of Congress a virtual veto over foreign affairs.

In view of these discrepant views, one might have expected important changes to occur in the presidency when Jefferson and his party took control of the government. But the Democratic-Republicans did not undertake the sort of wholesale dismantling of executive power that would have made governing virtually impossible. Jefferson, with able support from his secretary of the Treasury, Albert Gallatin, exercised as much control of domestic policy as Hamilton had during the Washington administration. Hamilton's assurances to his Federalist colleagues in 1801 that Jefferson was "no enemy to the power of the executive" predicted accurately how Jefferson would act as president. Indeed, to enforce his embargo policy, Jefferson secured authority from a Democratic-Republican Congress that exceeded any grant of executive power ever made by the Federalists. Moreover, Jefferson used those powers with the kind of energy that he once had denounced as the mark of tyranny.[31] In important respects, then, the "revolution" of 1800 brought no sweeping alterations in the government's institutional arrangements.

Nevertheless, Jefferson's presidency marked an important change in the relationship between the president and the people.[32] His predecessors, Washington and Adams, had believed that the power of the presidency derived from its constitutional authority. Jefferson, although not rejecting this view, maintained that the strength of the office ultimately depended on the "affections of the people." He strongly implied in his first inaugural address that the program of the Democratic-Republican party should be enacted simply because a majority of the people had endorsed it in the 1800 election.[33]

Washington and Adams believed that some distance from the people was required if presidents were to perform their proper task, which was to moderate the clash of parties and interests that inevitably would occur in Congress. But Jefferson felt that the most effective and responsible way for the president to lead the government was through the very institutions that were rooted most firmly in a popular base, the House and the Senate. Rather than stand apart from developments in the legislature, he sought to direct them. Thus, in contrast to Hamilton's concept of a strong presidency, which emphasized the need for independent executive initiatives, Jefferson assumed the mantle of party leader in an effort to lead the separate branches of American government.

Informed by a clear conception of the presidency, Jefferson's administration wrought other important institutional changes in order to forge a closer relationship between the president and the people. One such change was to reduce the ceremonial trappings of the executive office. Jefferson stripped away much of the pomp and ceremony to which Washington and Adams had adhered, regarding excessive formality in the conduct of the presidency as incompatible with a popularly based government. Unlike Washington, Jefferson rode around the capital not in a coach attended by liveried outriders, but on his own horse, with only one servant in attendance. His clothing expressed republican simplicity, even to the point of offending some who regarded his appearance as unsuitable for a head of state. As one critic described Jefferson, "The President was in an undress—Blue coat, red vest ... white hose, ragged slippers, with his toes out, clean linnen, but hair disheveled." [34]

Jefferson's interest in removing the "monocratic" features from the executive office also spawned efforts to simplify the president's relations with Congress. His decision to submit his first annual message to Congress in writing rather than to deliver it orally was "a calculated political act, designed to ... reduce the 'relics' left by the Federalists and underline the return to sound republican simplicity." [35] Jefferson thus inaugurated the century-long practice of presidents sending their State of the Union messages to Congress to be read aloud by the clerk of the House.

Jefferson's adoption of a simpler presidential etiquette corresponded nicely with the transfer of the capital from Philadelphia to Washington, D.C., in 1800. The move left members of Congress, government officials, and foreign diplomats, who were accustomed to Philadelphia's well-developed culture and comforts, "stranded" on the banks of the Potomac. The historian Merrill D. Peterson described the rather primitive new city of Washington as "a village pretending to be a capital, a place with a few bad houses, extensive swamps, hanging on the skirts of a too thinly peopled, weak and barren country." [36] Yet Jefferson, who was never fully comfortable in cities, appreciated the change in setting. His informal style was compatible not just with his view of the executive office but also with the relatively rustic surroundings of Washington.

The rise of the new capital also symbolized the growth in people and territory in the United States. The population more than tripled between 1800 and 1830. The acquisition of the Louisiana Territory, which occurred during Jefferson's presidency, almost doubled the size of the United States. Territorial expansion continued to be supported by later Democratic-Republican presidents, committed as they were to the encouragement of agriculture over commerce. The nation had to expand whenever the opportunity arose "to make room for the generation of farmers yet unborn." [37] Furthermore, the political ascendance of the Democratic-Republicans represented the growth of the agrarian and frontier interests of the South and West to political parity with the older commercial and financial interests of the East, which had controlled national politics under the Federalists.

The close relationship between territorial expansion and the Democratic-Republican program explains Jefferson's willingness to embrace the Louisiana Purchase in disregard of his oft-expressed commitment to a strict construction of the Constitution. He pushed the Louisiana Treaty with France through the Senate, certain that constitutional niceties were less important than the opportunity to contribute so greatly to the good of the people. As such, the purchase of Louisiana, and the overwhelmingly favorable reaction it received around the country, sustained the Democratic-Republican effort to define the president as the agent of the people's best interests.[38]

The Limits of "Popular" Leadership

All this being said, popular presidential leadership had its limits during the Jeffersonian era. Neither Jefferson nor his three Democratic-Republican successors—James Madison (1809-1817), James Monroe (1817-1825), and John Quincy Adams (1825-1829)—tried to enhance their power by bartering patronage or other sorts of favors for legislation in Congress. Indeed, until 1829 presidents seldom used the "spoils" of federal appointments to enhance party unity or to obtain legislation.

In spite of the bitter competition between the Federalists and the Democratic-Republicans, Jefferson did not purge all of his partisan opponents from the executive branch. The turnover in federal jobholders was only one-third during his first two years in office and one-half during his entire first term. On the whole, the Democratic-Republicans continued to use Federalist methods of administration. "After a brief period of transition," Leonard White has written, "during which new men took over the most important posts, the same expectation of nonpartisan, lifetime service prevailed." [39]

Nor was it respectable during the Jeffersonian era for the president to appeal over the heads of Congress to the public.[40] Until the twentieth century, presidents usually exercised popular leadership indirectly, through their influence on the party mechanisms in Congress and the state governments.

Jefferson's refusal to take the controversial embargo issue to the people illustrates the limits on the acceptable techniques of presidential persuasion. Initially, he was able to get the embargo enacted by using his enormous popularity to exert influence indirectly upon Democratic-Republican leaders in Congress. Yet during the course of its fourteen-month existence, the embargo began to unravel. The severe restriction of foreign trade wreaked havoc on the commercial interests of New England and the planters of the South. It deprived the government of millions of dollars in revenue by barring nearly all imports. Perhaps most significant, the embargo made a travesty of the Democratic-Republicans' traditional opposition to a broad constitutional interpretation of the regulatory powers of the national government and, especially, of the executive. By its unprecedented concentration of power in the president, by its deployment of the navy for enforcement, and by its disregard of the Fourth Amendment's protection against unreasonable searches and seizures, the embargo policy "carried the administration to the precipice of unlimited and arbitrary power as measured by any American standard then known." [41]

Notwithstanding the controversy over the embargo, Jefferson never took the issue to the people. Although Democratic-Republican leaders received behind-the-scenes presidential directives, Jefferson presented "an imperturbable, almost sphinxlike silence to the nation." [42] To have done otherwise would have violated the custom that prohibited presidents from trying to influence public opinion directly. Congress ended the embargo in early 1809.

The Twelfth Amendment

Paragraphs 2 through 4 of Article II, section 1, of the Constitution, which created the electoral college method of choosing the president and the vice president, had been among the least controversial provisions of the Constitution, both during the late stages of the Constitutional Convention and in the ratification debates that followed. "The mode of appointment of the Chief Magistrate of the United States," wrote Alexander Hamilton in *Federalist* No. 68, "is almost the only part of the system of any consequence, which has escaped without severe censure, or which has received the slightest mark of approbation from its opponents." It is all the more ironic, then, that the electoral college was the first institution of the new system of government to undergo a major constitutional overhaul.

The source of the irony was the Constitutional Convention's faulty assumption that political parties would not arise and dominate presidential elections. Instead, the delegates had believed that states and ad hoc groups would nominate candidates for president. Individual electors would then vote for two of these candidates, one of them perhaps a local favorite but the other a leader of national stature. The most popular (and, presumably, the best-qualified) candidate would be elected as president and the second most popular as vice president. The delegates' expectations, however, were soon disappointed. The two political parties—the Federalists and the Democratic-Republicans—that formed during the Washington administration began within a very few years to nominate complete national tickets. In 1800 the inevitable happened, with the perverse tie vote in the presidential election between Jefferson and his Democratic-Republican running mate, Burr. To make matters worse, partisan mischief in the House almost overturned the voters' intentions. Some disgruntled Federalists, then, began plotting in advance of the 1804 election: if the Democratic-Republican ticket won, they decided, Federalist electors would cast one of their votes for the opposition party's vice-presidential nominee, thus electing him, not the presidential nominee, as president and the presidential nominee as vice president.[43]

Aware both of the unsuitability of the original Constitution's presidential election process to the new realities of party politics and of the Federalists' willingness to continue to exploit the process's weaknesses, the Democratic-Republican-controlled Congress voted to propose the Twelfth Amendment in December 1803. All but Massachusetts, Connecticut, and Delaware, the most ardent Federalist states, quickly ratified (no amendment except the Twenty-sixth, which in 1971 gave eighteen-year-olds the right to vote, has been ratified as rapidly) and the amendment became part of the Constitution in June 1804, in time for the presidential election.

The main effect of the Twelfth Amendment was to change a system in which electors cast two votes for president, with the candidate receiving the largest majority elected as president and the second place finisher elected as vice president, to a system in which the electors were charged to vote separately for president and vice president, with a majority of electoral votes required to win each office. The amendment also reduced the number of candidates from which the House would elect a president in the event no one received a majority of electoral votes for president. The reduction from the five highest electoral vote recipients to the three highest was an acknowledgment that a two-party system had developed, in which even three candidates were unlikely to receive electoral votes in most elections, and that the parties had taken over the presidential nominating function.

Authority to select a vice president in the event of an electoral college failure was lodged exclusively in the Senate, not partially as in the original Constitution. (The amendment empowered the Senate to choose from the two highest electoral vote recipients for vice president, with a majority of the entire membership of the Senate required for election.) The Constitution's age, residency, and citizenship requirements for the president were extended to the vice president. Finally, the amendment stated that if a vice president, but no president, had been chosen by the March 4 following the election, "the Vice President shall act as President as in the case of the death or other constitutional disability of the President."

Jefferson's Mixed Legacy

Like the Federalists, Jefferson understood the need for executive power; indeed, as president he resorted at times to an enlarged executive authority. But Jefferson altered the tone and manner of executive authority to make it consistent with the essence of popular rule, as he and the Democratic-Republicans understood it. In place of the wide-ranging discretion the Federalists had sought to bestow upon the executive (for which they found support in Article II of the Constitution), Jefferson intended to substitute a party program that, although implemented by the president, would be controlled by Congress and sanctioned by a popular election.[44]

Unlike Washington and Adams, therefore, Jefferson deemphasized the constitutional powers of the office, governing instead through his extraconstitutional role of party leader. The Jefferson administration encouraged the development of a disciplined party organization in Congress, with the president relying on his floor leaders in the House and Senate to advance his program. Another source of presidential influence was the party caucus, which was created by the Federalists but was used most extensively by the Democratic-Republicans. During Jefferson's tenure as president, conclaves of leaders from the executive and legislative branches formulated policy and encouraged party unity. Secretary of the Treasury Gallatin played an important part in these caucuses; Jefferson himself occasionally presided. Jefferson, in short, constructed a highly centralized partisan system within the government, but one that operated for the most part by conference, consultation, and free discussion rather than by harsher political methods.[45]

Yet the development of a party machinery made possible, as the legislative historian Ralph Harlow has written, "a radical change in the relationship between executive and legislature." Should the party's leaders in Congress somehow take charge of the machinery, they would be in a position to control the whole of executive administration.[46] That is precisely what happened when Jefferson left office. The institutions he had developed for executive leadership were turned to the advantage of Congress. The presidency after Jefferson shrank to the limited constitutional office that long had been prescribed by orthodox Democratic-Republican theory.

The Presidency of James Madison

The decline of presidential influence was especially evident during James Madison's administration. While he was president, major institutional developments transferred power from the executive to the legislative branch. One such development was the advent of the congressional nominating caucus as an independent source of power.

The Democratic-Republican caucus's nomination of Jefferson for president in 1800 and 1804 had been a foregone conclusion, but the caucus of 1808 had a real decision to make. Secretary of State Madison generally was regarded as Jefferson's heir apparent, but the leader of the small anti-Jefferson faction in the Democratic-Republican party, John Randolph, tried to secure the nomination of James Monroe. Although Madison was duly nominated and elected, the promises he had to make to win support from his party's members in Congress suggested that subsequent presidential nominations might well become occasions "to make explicit executive subordination to congressional president-makers." Indeed, some scholars believe that President Madison's renomination by the Democratic-Republican party in 1812 was delayed until he assured "War Hawks" in the congressional caucus that he supported their desire for war with Britain.[47]

The emergence of the Speaker of the House as an important leader in Congress and Henry Clay's extraordinary use of the office during the Madison presidency further reduced executive power in relation to Congress. Until Clay's election as Speaker in 1811, party leadership in the House usually was shared among several designated floor leaders; the Speaker was mainly a moderator. Clay changed this practice dramatically:

> Clay was chosen Speaker on an issue that President Madison was unable to grip, and with the intention of forcing national action despite the president's incapacity to act—war with Great Britain. Clay succeeded in this purpose, and until the last day of Madison's administration the initiative in public affairs remained with Clay and his associates in the House of Representatives.[48]

Under Clay's direction, the House strengthened its capacity to meet its broader legislative obligations by expanding the number and influence of its standing committees, which enabled each representative for the first time to specialize in an area of interest. Because the committees' activities were coordinated by the party leaders, the House became an effective legislative instrument. Indeed, from 1811 to 1825 Henry Clay was arguably the most powerful man in the government.

The decline of the presidency was demonstrated most dramatically during the War of 1812. War sentiment had been aroused by evidence that the British were supplying arms to hostile Indians on the American frontier, by British seizure of American ships and impressment (that is, conscription) of their crews, and, to some degree, by a desire to acquire territory in British Canada and Spanish Florida. The War Hawks, most of them Democratic-Republican members of Congress from the South and West whose constituents were suffering from Indian attacks and falling agricultural prices, fanned the flames of anti-British feeling. New England Federalists, traditionally pro-British and commercially tied to Great Britain through shipping and trading, opposed war but were outnumbered.

Madison's message of June 1, 1812, which urged Congress to declare war against Britain, was the first war message by a president. Later historical developments were to establish formidable wartime powers for the president, but Madison's command of the nation's military effort was singularly undistinguished. He was handicapped not only by his inability to influence Congress but also by personal qualities that were poorly suited to the tasks at hand. Madison's figure was slight, his manner was quiet (even somber), his speaking voice was weak, and the force of his personality, at best, was moderate. As Gaillard Hunt, a generally sympathetic Madison biographer, writes of the president's war leadership: "The hour had come but the man was wanting. Not a scholar in governments ancient and modern, not an unimpassioned writer of careful messages, but a robust leader to rally the people and unite them to fight was what the time needed, and what it did not find in Madison." [49]

From a military standpoint, the War of 1812 was the most unsuccessful in U.S. history. At the beginning of the war a relatively small British detachment that was stationed in Canada administered a series of disastrous defeats to the disorganized U.S. forces. The low point of the war occurred in August 1814: Madison had to evacuate the capital for three days to escape a British force of fewer than five thousand men, which moved unchallenged up the Chesapeake Bay and marched with little resistance into the heart of Washington, burning the Capitol, the White House, the Navy Yard, and most other public buildings.

The nation eventually was saved from disaster by Britain's decision not to prosecute the war on a massive scale. Morale was boosted belatedly by Gen. Andrew Jackson's victory at New Orleans on January 8, 1815, even though it had no effect on the outcome of the war since peace had been concluded two weeks earlier. In the wake of Jackson's triumph the American people greeted the end of the war with joy, which enabled Madison to retire as president with honor in 1817. New Orleans also rendered a fatal political wound to the pro-British Federalists, many of whom had opposed the war from the start. But the War of 1812 was at best a stalemate, one that revealed Madison's shortcomings as president.

Only a torrential rainstorm prevented the White House from being reduced to total ruin when, in 1814, British forces set fire to it and other public buildings during the War of 1812.

In important respects, Madison's failures transcended his personal limitations—they were attributable in part to the legacies he inherited from the Jefferson administration and from the Democratic-Republican tradition of which he had been one of the major architects. By opposing the creation of even a minimal standing army, Madison and Jefferson, preaching economy in government, had undone many of the military preparations that the Adams administration had undertaken. Their foreign policy depended on diplomacy to solve America's problems with France and Britain. When negotiations failed, the Democratic-Republicans were forced to rely on the 1807 embargo—an impractical policy of "peaceful coercion" that proved disastrous for the American economy without influencing either Britain or France to stop interfering with American ships. The collapse of his own embargo, enacted in 1812, left Madison no alternative but war when the British provocations continued, even though he knew that the country was neither prepared nor united for battle.

Years later, Madison recounted that he had hoped to overcome the nation's obvious unpreparedness by "throw[ing] forward the flag of the country, sure that the people would press onward and defend it." [50] Yet the rapid decline in the status of the presidency left Madison in a poor position to rally Congress or the people. Contrary to his expectations, the Democratic-Republican doctrine of hostility to centralized power was not abandoned by the party in wartime. Congress was willing to declare war but not to raise enough money to fight it. Moreover, the Madison administration's plan to use the state militia was scuttled by the state governments' lack of cooperation. The governors of Massachusetts and Connecticut, for example, refused to release their militia to fight the war. The president, long a strong advocate of states' rights, "offered no suggestion for stopping so grave a defiance of federal authority." [51]

Madison began to face up to the limitations of Democratic-Republican principles in his seventh annual message of December 1815, in which he recommended a number of policies to solidify the national resolve, including the chartering of the Second Bank of the United States. (The Democratic-Republicans had allowed the first bank to expire in 1811.) With no national bank in operation during the War of 1812, the federal government had lacked a convenient and stable source of currency, exacerbating a financial crisis that saw the national debt grow from $45 million in 1811 to $127 million by the end of 1815. Believing that a national bank was a necessary evil, one without which a sound currency was a chimera, Madison signed the bank bill into law in 1816. As the political scientist James Savage has written, the severe economic dislocations of the war persuaded Madison and the Democratic-Republicans to embrace "the ghostly presence of Hamilton's national bank, with all its potential for corrupting the republic." [52]

Madison never ceased to express profound concerns, however, about the potential abuses of executive power that he believed Hamilton had demonstrated during the 1790s. According to the historian Ralph Ketcham, "in every one of his critical relationships and decisions—in bringing the nation face to face with war, in dealing with Congress, in arranging his Cabinet and in enduring near-treasonable dissent—[Madison] acted in view of [Democratic-Republican] principles of executive leadership." [53] In the final analysis, these principles were not congenial to dynamic presidential leadership.

The Presidencies of James Monroe and John Quincy Adams

James Madison's Democratic-Republican successors, James Monroe and John Quincy Adams, were unable to restore to the presidency the strength that the office had lost after Jefferson's retirement. Monroe, although a forceful man, was prone to a formality and stiffness of manner that ill-qualified him for party leadership; like Washington and Adams, he was better suited to preside than to direct. Monroe also was hindered by a growing split within his party between "old" Democratic-Republicans, who inclined toward a strict construction of the Constitution, and "new" Democratic-Republicans, or National Republicans, who were more nationalistic in outlook. Monroe was identified with the former group; the latter, which was led by such prominent figures as Henry Clay, John C. Calhoun, and Monroe's successor, John Quincy Adams, dominated the party after the War of 1812.

Monroe, like Madison, was a protégé of Jefferson and thus was regarded as the legitimate heir of the "Virginia Dynasty" that had held the presidency since 1801. But the fragmentation of the Democratic-Republican party ensured that he also would be the last of the Jeffersonians. Monroe's nomination, in spite of the powerful support of Jefferson and Madison, was a difficult affair. Two other contenders, Secretary of the Treasury William Crawford of Georgia and Henry Clay, were closely identified with the nationalist wing of the party. Although Monroe was nominated and easily elected in 1816, the troubles he confronted in winning the endorsement of the congressional caucus foretold of the difficulties that he would face as president.

One of the major domestic issues during the Monroe administration was "internal improvements." The president informed Congress that, in his view, a constitutional amendment was required to empower the national government to construct roads and canals. Congress, led by Clay, passed a bill to repair the main east-west highway, known as the Cumberland Road, in defiance of Monroe. The president's veto of this bill signaled a breakdown in Democratic-Republican unity that was to plague Monroe throughout his two terms.[54]

Monroe's strong response to the Cumberland Road controversy was the exception rather than the rule. Following the practice of presidents since Washington, he vetoed only legislation that he deemed unconstitutional. Indeed, Monroe's deference to Congress went beyond custom; more than any of his predecessors, he believed in legislative supremacy. Hence, he abstained almost completely from involvement in the greatest issue of the day: the admission of Missouri as a state, which for the first time forced Congress to debate the status of slavery in the Louisiana Territory.

Now a private citizen, Jefferson observed the bitter debate about Missouri with great concern. Writing to Rep. John Holmes of Maine, he said, "This momentous question, like a fire-bell in the night, awakened and filled me with terror. I considered it at once the knell of the Union." [55] The Missouri Compromise of 1820 settled the slavery controversy for a time, but Monroe had virtually no hand in it, save for signing the final bill. Leonard White has written of Monroe's abstention from this struggle: "His course of action was perhaps politically wise, perhaps politically inevitable, but it abdicated leadership." [56] Indeed, the passive character of the Monroe administration prompted Supreme Court Justice Joseph Story to remark in 1818 that "the Executive has no longer a commanding influence. The House of Representatives has absorbed all the popular feeling and all the effective power of the country." [57]

Justice Story's lament was not as pertinent to foreign affairs as to domestic matters. The Constitution conferred powers on the president in foreign policy that, although sometimes challenged by Congress during the Jeffersonian era, remained essentially untarnished. Indeed, every Democratic-Republican president was a former secretary of state. Even Madison's notable failures during the War of 1812 did not prevent him from asserting the powers of the president as the wartime commander of the armed forces.[58]

Monroe reinforced the president's right to take the initiative in foreign affairs by issuing the Monroe Doctrine, which became one of the pillars of U.S. foreign policy in the nineteenth and twentieth centuries. The revolt of Spain's Latin American colonies between 1815 and 1823 had nearly liquidated the Spanish empire. The Monroe administration was alarmed by reports that other European powers, France in particular, had designs on several of the new Latin American nations. Simultaneously, Tsar Alexander I of Russia, noting the presence of a Russian trading station at Fort Ross in Bodega Bay, near San Francisco, issued a decree that claimed exclusive trading rights for Russia in the area north of the fifty-first parallel. In response, the president included in his State of the Union message to Congress on December 2, 1823, a sweeping statement that proclaimed the Americas independent from European interference:

> The occasion has been judged proper for asserting, as a principle in which the rights and interests of the United States are involved, that the American continents, by the free and independent condition which they have assumed and maintain, are henceforth not to be considered as subjects for future colonization by any European powers. [59]

Although the Monroe Doctrine was neither confirmed by Congress nor enforced by President Monroe, it was a significant document. Like the Declaration of Independence, the Monroe Doctrine codified the aspirations of the American people. As the historian W. P. Cresson has written, "It was a sincere expression of the belief in the superiority of American institutions and ideals, and the right of self-preservation, grounded in the conviction that the extension of European principles was dangerous to the peace and safety of the American system." [60]

The Monroe Doctrine also was an important statement, at a time of general executive weakness, that the president was paramount in the making of foreign policy. Monroe's defiant expression of hemispheric independence committed the United States to more burdensome diplomatic and military responsibilities, most of which inevitably would fall upon the chief executive. For a time, this commitment was without important effect, but its potential to become a guiding influence on foreign policy was realized by the end of the nineteenth century.[61]

The end of the Monroe presidency in 1825 marked the end of a political dynasty. Monroe was the last member of the famous Virginia "triumvirate"—Jefferson, Madison, Monroe—to serve as president. Each of these men played an important role in the formation and early history of the Republic; each was a founder of the Democratic-Republican opposition and a leader during its rise as a governing party. Monroe also was the last of the revolutionary presidents, the generation that had won the War of Independence. With the end of the Virginia dynasty, the Democratic-Republicans no longer were led by a national figure whose stature could hold the party together.

Ironically, political unity became all the more difficult to achieve because of the extraordinary electoral success of the Democratic-Republican party. To mobilize popular support for a governing party requires a credible opponent.[62] Yet during Monroe's first term as president, the Federalist party disappeared as a national organization; indeed, Monroe was unopposed for reelection in 1820.

No sooner was the Democratic-Republican party fully triumphant than it began to break apart. Even as Monroe was being inaugurated for the second time, the party, already badly fragmented by the issues that separated "old" and "new" Democratic-Republicans, was further divided by the ambitions of the many candidates who wanted to succeed him as president. In fact, the 1824 campaign may have begun as early as 1816. In 1818, John Quincy Adams, Monroe's secretary of state, observed that "political, personal and electioneering intrigues are intermingling themselves with increasing heat and violence." As a result, Adams lamented, the government was "assuming daily more and more a character of cabal, and preparation, not for the next presidential election, but for the one after. . . ."[63]

With the Federalists vanquished, the 1824 presidential election became a contest of individuals rather than of issues. Rival and sectional leaders, each supported by his own organization and following, ran for president in one of the most bitter and confusing campaigns in U.S. history. The results of the election stirred a storm of controversy, prompting a revolt against party nominating procedures that had been used for a quarter century. Moreover, John Quincy Adams, the eventual winner of the 1824 election, inherited an impossible governing situation. The Democratic-Republican era was brought to an end amid conflicts so acrimonious that they endured for a generation.

In 1824, for the second time in twenty years, an election was decided not by the voters but by the House of Representatives. Sen. Andrew Jackson of Tennessee, the hero of the Battle of New Orleans, received the most electoral votes, 99, but fell far short of the 131 needed for a majority and election. John Quincy Adams, who felt that as secretary of state he was the logical heir to the presidency, was second with 84 electoral votes. Monroe's secretary of the Treasury, William Crawford, had been the nominee of the Democratic-Republican caucus. But the party machinery had run down badly by 1824, and its support no longer was tantamount to election. Crawford came in third with 41 votes. The powerful Speaker of the House, Clay of Kentucky, was fourth with 37 votes.

According to the Twelfth Amendment, the failure of any candidate to secure a majority of electoral votes meant that the three highest vote-getters were to be considered by the House. This removed Clay as a candidate, but he still exercised considerable influence with his fellow representatives. He used that influence to help secure Adams's election, and the new president rewarded Clay by naming him secretary of state. Not surprisingly, Jackson's supporters were furious, charging that Adams and Clay had made a corrupt bargain to violate the will of the people. Although the charge of conspiracy probably was unfounded, the controversial election of 1824 ensured the demise of what had come to be called "King Caucus."

John Quincy Adams, the final president of the Jeffersonian era, was severely constrained by the general view that he was a "minority president." But Adams was a statesman of considerable talent and accomplishment. Not content to remain in the shadow of Congress, he undertook to renew the strength of his office. In fact, Adams was the first president in history to attempt to lead Congress openly toward an active program of legislative achievement.

In his first annual message to Congress, Adams recommended a broad array of internal improvements, a national university, an observatory, scientific exploration, and voyages of discovery. His three Democratic-Republican predecessors had held strong reservations about the constitutional power of Congress to mandate such enterprises and to appropriate the funds to pay for them. Madison and Monroe had followed Jefferson in believing that a constitutional amendment was needed before anything could be done. But Adams boldly rejected both this narrow construction of the Constitution and the deference his predecessors had shown to Congress in domestic affairs. He also eschewed the reservations of his cabinet members, who believed that his ambitious plans were impractical. After recounting the cabinet's resistance, Adams wrote in his diary, "Thus situated, the perilous experiment must be made. Let me make it with full deliberation, and be prepared for the consequences." [64]

John Quincy Adams was the first president "to demonstrate the real scope of creative possibilities of the constitutional provision to 'recommend to their [Congress's] consideration such measures as he shall judge necessary and expedient.' " [65] But Adams had no decisive mandate either from the country or from Congress. His stern and formal manner was ill-suited to the task of building a political coalition. A quarter-century of Jeffersonian presidents had not prepared the country for the sort of openly assertive executive leadership that Adams was attempting. Thus, most of his proposals were ignored or ridiculed.

Adams's influence, never very great, was effectively ended by the congressional elections of 1826. His political opponents, championing Jackson's opposition to the administration, won control of both the House and Senate, marking the first time that the executive and legislative branches of the government were controlled by different parties. The Democratic-Republican era ended with Congress, not the president, at the center of government power.[66]

Notes

1. Richard Hofstadter, *The Idea of a Party System* (Berkeley: University of California Press, 1969), 2.
2. Leonard White, *The Jeffersonians: A Study in Administrative History, 1801-1829* (New York: Macmillan, 1951), 30.
3. Forrest McDonald, *The Presidency of George Washington* (Lawrence: University Press of Kansas, 1974), 160.
4. Thomas Jefferson to Edward Rutledge, November 30, 1795, *The Writings of Thomas Jefferson*, ed. Paul Leicester Ford (New York: Putnam's, 1895), 7:39-40.
5. *Annals of the Congress of the United States* (Washington, D.C.: Gales and Seaton, 1849), 4th Cong., Part 1 (1795-1796), 465.
6. McDonald, *Presidency of George Washington*, 173.
7. Ibid., 173.
8. James D. Richardson, ed., *Messages and Papers of the Presidents*, 20 vols. (New York: Bureau of National Literature, 1897), 1:186-188.
9. Jefferson to James Monroe, July 10, 1796, in Ford, *Writings of Thomas Jefferson* 7:88-90.
10. William M. Goldsmith, ed., *The Growth of Presidential Power: A Documented History* (New York and London: Chelsea, 1974), 1:420-421. The power of the House in foreign affairs has become especially controversial since the Vietnam War, which undermined confidence in the presidency and prompted a rise in congressional assertiveness during the 1970s and 1980s. The Carter administration learned, to its dismay, that it could not ignore the House in the pursuit of its diplomatic initiatives. Although House approval was not necessary to ratify treaties, the lower chamber influenced treaty making during the Carter years through both the appropriations process and committee investigations, thus raising concerns about illegitimate House intrusion into the president's right to conduct foreign affairs. During the ratification process for the two Panama Canal treaties in 1977 and 1978, for example, three House committees held hearings that served as an important and controversial forum to generate support for and opposition to the treaties (see Robert J. Spitzer, "The President and Congress," in *Congressional Quarterly's Guide to the Presidency*, ed. Michael Nelson

[Washington, D.C.: Congressional Quarterly, 1989], 1100-1103). The debate over the House's intervention in the details of foreign affairs intensified during the Reagan years as partisan differences sharpened the constitutional struggles between the executive and legislative branches. The House's "micromanagement" of U.S. foreign policy toward Central America, especially, became the subject of considerable political conflict and public controversy. The Boland Amendment, a prohibition on the expenditure of federal funds to aid the contra rebels in Nicaragua, was a House rider to an appropriations bill, which the Reagan administration considered an abuse of Congress's budgetary power.

11. Jefferson to James Madison, January 8, 1797, in Ford, *Writings of Thomas Jefferson* 7:104-105.

12. Jefferson to Edward Rutledge, June 24, 1797, in ibid. 7:152-155.

13. Ralph Adams Brown, *The Presidency of John Adams* (Lawrence: University Press of Kansas, 1975), 25.

14. Jefferson to Elbridge Gerry, May 13, 1797, *The Portable Thomas Jefferson,* ed. Merrill D. Peterson (New York: Viking Press, 1975), 471-474.

15. Leonard White, *The Federalists: A Study in Administrative History* (New York: Macmillan, 1948), 237-252.

16. Brown, *Presidency of John Adams,* 26-27.

17. White, *Federalists,* 241.

18. Ibid., 237.

19. Hofstadter, *Idea of a Party System,* 110; for a balanced account of Adams's role in the passage and enforcement of the Alien and Sedition acts, see Brown, *Presidency of John Adams,* 122-127.

20. Alexander Hamilton to James A. Bayard, January 16, 1801, *The Papers of Alexander Hamilton,* ed. Harold C. Syrett (New York: Columbia University Press, 1977), 25:319-324; for a discussion of Hamilton's role in the 1800 election, see Hofstadter, *Idea of a Party System,* 136-140.

21. Jefferson to Spencer Roane, September 6, 1819, *The Writings of Thomas Jefferson,* ed. Albert Ellery Bergh (Washington, D.C.: Thomas Jefferson Memorial Association, 1903), 15:212-216.

22. Forrest McDonald, *The Presidency of Thomas Jefferson* (Lawrence: University Press of Kansas, 1976), 34.

23. Thomas Jefferson, "First Inaugural Address," March 4, 1801, in Peterson, *The Portable Thomas Jefferson,* 290-295.

24. Robert M. Johnstone, Jr., *Jefferson and the Presidency* (Ithaca, N.Y.: Cornell University Press, 1978), 162.

25. *Marbury v. Madison,* 1 Cranch 137.

26. McDonald, *Presidency of Thomas Jefferson,* 50-51.

27. Ibid., 41.

28. Johnstone, *Jefferson and the Presidency,* 46 (emphasis in original).

29. Jefferson to John Breckinridge, August 12, 1803, in Peterson, *The Portable Thomas Jefferson,* 494-497.

30. White, *Jeffersonians,* 3.

31. Ibid., 551.

32. The discussion of the change in the presidency during the Jeffersonian era is based on James Ceaser, *Presidential Selection: Theory and Development* (Princeton, N.J.: Princeton University Press, 1979), 88-122; and Johnstone, *Jefferson and the Presidency,* 52-75.

33. Ceaser, *Presidential Selection,* 102.

34. Quoted in Johnstone, *Jefferson and the Presidency,* 58.

35. Ibid., 58-59. See Jefferson to Nathaniel Macon, May 14, 1801, in Ford, *Writings of Thomas Jefferson* 8:51-52.
36. Merrill D. Peterson, *Thomas Jefferson and the New Nation: A Biography* (New York: Oxford University Press, 1970), 653.
37. McDonald, *Presidency of Thomas Jefferson*, 22.
38. Johnstone, *Jefferson and the Presidency*, 67-75.
39. White, *Jeffersonians*, 547.
40. Jeffrey Tulis, *The Rhetorical Presidency* (Princeton, N.J.: Princeton University Press, 1987).
41. Leonard W. Levy, *Jefferson and Civil Liberties: The Darker Side* (Cambridge, Mass.: Harvard University Press, 1963), 102.
42. Ibid., 96.
43. Richard P. McCormick, *The Presidential Game: The Origins of American Presidential Politics* (New York: Oxford University Press, 1982), 82-87.
44. On Jefferson's effort to recast executive power in a more popular form, see Gary J. Schmitt, "Thomas Jefferson and the Presidency," in *Inventing the American Presidency*, ed. Thomas E. Cronin (Lawrence: University Press of Kansas, 1989); and Ralph Ketcham, "The Jefferson Presidency and Constitutional Beginnings," in *The Constitution and the American Presidency*, ed. Martin Fausold and Alan Shank (Albany: State University of New York Press, 1991).
45. White, *Jeffersonians*, 48-59.
46. Ralph Volney Harlow, *The History of Legislative Methods in the Period before 1825* (New Haven: Yale University Press, 1917), 192; and White, *Jeffersonians*, 52.
47. White, *Jeffersonians*, 53-54. Madison's biographer, Gaillard Hunt, exonerates Madison of striking any bargain with party leaders in Congress to secure his renomination. But there is no doubt that the Democratic-Republican caucus sought assurances about Madison's willingness to send a war message to Congress before agreeing to his renomination (*The Life of James Madison* [New York: Russell and Russell, 1902], 316-319).
48. White, *Jeffersonians*, 55.
49. Hunt, *Life of James Madison*, 325.
50. Ibid., 318-319.
51. Ibid., 329-330.
52. James D. Savage, *Balanced Budgets and American Politics* (Ithaca and London: Cornell University Press, 1988), 98-99. See also Robert Allen Rutland, *The Presidency of James Madison* (Lawrence: University Press of Kansas, 1990), 68-70, 195-203.
53. Ralph Ketcham, "James Madison and the Presidency," in Cronin, *Inventing the American Presidency*, 360-361. Ketcham has argued that contemporary scholarly judgments of Madison as a weak president—such as his failure to be a dynamic leader, even during wartime—miss the philosophical and practical grounds of the president's conduct:

> It was not only uncongenial personally and in principle for Madison to move harshly against [the resistance to the War]; it was very nearly practically impossible as well. The federal system, which in Madison's own theory was the *only* republican way to govern a nation as large as the United States, gave state officials a multitude of ways to obstruct the national conduct of the war. Furthermore, republican theory forbade stifling the opposition or summarily denying civil liberties even during wartime; to do so was tantamount to losing the essential point (a free society) at the beginning and by default (ibid., 357-358 [Ketcham's emphasis]).

54. White, *Jeffersonians,* 38-41.
55. Jefferson to John Holmes, April 22, 1820, in Peterson, *The Portable Jefferson,* 567-569.
56. White, *Jeffersonians,* 39. The Missouri Compromise admitted Missouri to the Union without restricting slavery, allowed Maine to enter as a free state, and banned slavery from all western territories north of Missouri's southern border (latitude 36°30').
57. Quoted in ibid., 39.
58. Goldsmith, *Growth of Presidential Power* 1:378-386.
59. James Monroe, "State of the Union Address," December 2, 1823, in Richardson, *Messages and Papers of the Presidents* 2:778.
60. W. P. Cresson, *James Monroe* (Chapel Hill: University of North Carolina Press, 1946), 448.
61. Goldsmith, *Growth of Presidential Power* 1:455-456.
62. Ceaser, *Presidential Selection,* 102-103.
63. Charles Francis Adams, ed., *Memoirs of John Quincy Adams: His Diary from 1795 to 1848* (Philadelphia: J. B. Lippincott, 1874-1877; New York: AMS Press, 1970), 4:193.
64. Adams, *Memoirs of John Quincy Adams* 7:63.
65. Goldsmith, *Growth of Presidential Power* 1:325.
66. White, *Jeffersonians,* 42.

CHAPTER 5

The Age of Jackson

The presidency of John Quincy Adams took on the character of a long and acrimonious political campaign. Adams's own reelection effort began even before he was inaugurated in 1825 and continued for four years. As the president struggled in Washington with a recalcitrant Congress, a well-organized opposition formed around the country in support of Andrew Jackson, who was intent upon rectifying the so-called corrupt bargain between Adams and Henry Clay that had denied him the presidency in 1824.

By 1828, the confused political situation that underlay the previous presidential campaign, in which there were four candidates, had been replaced by a new party alignment. The Democratic-Republicans now were divided into two major factions. Adams and Clay, who stood for the national aspirations of the "new" Republicans (or National Republicans, as they sometimes were called), formed one group. Jackson and John C. Calhoun, who was vice president during Adams's administration, led the opposition, which dedicated itself to the "old" Democratic-Republican principles of states' rights and a narrow interpretation of the national government's constitutional powers. By 1832, these factions had developed further into, respectively, the Whig and Democratic parties, which dominated the American political landscape until the eve of the Civil War.

The Jacksonian Democrats had the better of this rivalry. From 1828 until 1856, Democratic control of the presidency was interrupted only two times, by the election of Whigs William Henry Harrison in 1840 and Zachary Taylor in 1848. Jackson's victory in the 1828 election was the culmination of a trend that had begun during the Jeffersonian era: the emerging agrarian and frontier interests of the South and West triumphed over the commercial and financial interests of the East. The purchases of Louisiana in 1803 and Florida in 1819 not only had added millions of acres to the territory of the United States but also had afforded greater influence to those who formerly had stood outside the regular channels of political power.

Jackson, in fact, was the first political "outsider" to become president of the United States. His predecessors in the presidency had undergone extensive apprenticeships in national politics and diplomacy. The hero of the battle of New Orleans had less formal education than any of them; moreover, he had little experience in Congress and none in public administration. Jackson was a "self-made man" who had risen from a small cabin in the piney woods of South Carolina to a plantation near Nashville, Tennessee, to the White House in Washington. A powerful symbol of his times, Jackson's principles and presence held sway in the country for nearly three decades. Appropriately, this period in America history has been called the "Age of Jackson." [1]

Jacksonian Democracy

The most important political theme of the Age of Jackson was the widespread desire for equality of opportunity, the belief that no one should have special privileges at the expense of anyone else. Jackson followed Jefferson in believing that to eliminate privilege, political leaders must strictly limit the role of the national government. Rapid territorial expansion had been accompanied by dynamic growth in society and the economy, which seemed to foster unbounded opportunity in all parts of the country. Within that expansive environment, Jacksonians believed that the best approach to government was to confine power as much as possible to the less obtrusive state governments. As Jackson's Democratic successor in the presidency, Martin Van Buren, stated in his first annual message to Congress in 1837:

> All communities are apt to look to government for too much. . . . But this ought not to be. . . . [T]he less government interferes with private pursuits the better for the general prosperity. . . . [I]ts real duty . . . is . . . to leave every citizen and every interest to reap under its benign protection the rewards of virtue, industry, and prudence. [2]

The Jacksonians' political philosophy encouraged a much bolder assault on national institutions and programs than the generally more flexible Jeffersonians had undertaken. Jackson withdrew the federal government from the realm of internal improvements. Military power, especially the army, was kept to a minimum. Jackson's fiscal policy was to hold down expenditures. The Bank of the United States, which Jeffersonians had learned to live with, was dismantled and its deposits were reinvested in selected state banks.[3]

Yet the Age of Jackson had its contradictory and compensating aspects when it came to the authority of the national government. The Jacksonians regarded the president as the "tribune" of the people, an idea that invested the executive, in a period of democratic aspiration, with tremendous influence. During the Jeffersonian era, presidents had begun to develop a closer relationship with the people. But this development took place in the context of political principles and institutional arrangements that generally supported the supremacy of the legislature. Jackson tried to establish a direct connection between the president and the people, thus challenging Congress's status as the national government's principal representative institution. As the historian Major L. Wilson has observed, "This gave him [Jackson] independent power and made the presidency rather than the Congress, the true organ of the nation's will." [4] The strengthened presidency "gave voice in a new age to the rising spirit of democratic nationalism," which sustained and strengthened the Union in the face of serious sectional conflicts over the tariff and slavery.[5]

Thus, although Jackson supported states' rights, he also personified and defended the sovereignty of the nation during his presidency, never more so than in the nullification crisis that arose near the end of his first term. In an effort to compel the federal government to accede to its demands for a lower tariff, South Carolina's legislature summoned a state convention on November 24, 1832, to declare the new 1832 tariff law "null and void." South Carolina cited Calhoun's nullification doctrine, which held that a state could declare any federal law that it deemed unconstitutional to be inapplicable within its borders. The ordinance of nullification that the South Carolina convention passed forbade federal officials to collect custom duties in the state after February 1, 1833, and threatened that the state would secede from the United States if the federal government responded by attempting to blockade Charleston or otherwise use force.

In the face of this threat to the Union, Jackson issued a ringing proclamation that vigorously rejected South Carolina's claim of a right to disobey a federal statute. For a state to presume to annul a law of the United States, the president argued, was "incompatible with the existence of the Union, contradicted expressly by the letter of the Constitution, unauthorized by its spirit, inconsistent with every principle on which it was founded, and destructive of the great object for which it was formed." [6] In 1861, Abraham Lincoln based his own response to southern secession on the same argument.

Jackson placed the responsibility to defend the Union squarely upon the president's shoulders. It was the people, acting through the state ratifying conventions, who had formed the Union, and the president—not Congress or the states—embodied the will of the people. Jackson's concept of the presidency "transcended the older categories of nationalism versus states' rights" and offered a new understanding of national sovereignty.[7]

The idea that the president is the direct representative of the people was grounded in ongoing political developments that were associated with Jacksonian democracy. The French author Alexis de Tocqueville, writing in the 1830s, regarded these developments as part of the expanding doctrine of popular sovereignty in the United States, which was the cornerstone of Jacksonian democracy: "The people reign over the American political world as God rules over the universe. It is the cause and the end of all things; everything rises out of it and is absorbed back into it." [8]

The Jacksonians' concept of "the people" was limited, to be sure; it did not apply to African Americans, women, or American Indians. But a dramatic surge of democratic reform in the 1830s had a profound effect on the presidency. Jackson's election as president in 1828 coincided with changes in state election laws that replaced legislatures with voters in the selection of presidential electors. In the first three presidential elections most electors had been chosen by the state legislatures. Electors were selected by popular vote in all but six states by 1824, and, in 1832, in all states but South Carolina, which retained legislative selection until the Civil War. Jackson was arguably the first president to be elected by the people, thus strengthening his conviction and that of his supporters that his mandate came directly from the source of all sovereignty.[9]

The president's claim to be the direct representative of the people also was advanced by the expansion of the electorate. The Jacksonians worked successfully to persuade the states to eliminate property qualifications for voting, thus establishing virtually universal white manhood suffrage by 1832. This development brought into the electorate farmers, mechanics, and laborers—"the humble members of society," as Jackson called them—who regarded the presidency under "Old Hickory's" superintendence as a rallying point. Their support rescued the executive office from the congressional dominance that had characterized presidential administrations from James Madison to John Quincy Adams. Indeed, with the collapse of the congressional nominating caucus in 1824, Jackson became the first president since George Washington to be chosen in an election that did not involve the national legislature. Taking office in 1829, Jackson found himself in a position, therefore, to revitalize the presidency with a new independence and energy.

The Rise of the Party Convention

The advent of the Jackson presidency was accompanied by important developments in the party system. The demise of "King Caucus" left a vacuum in the presidential nominating process that was filled by the national party convention. A convention was used by the Democrats in 1832 and was adopted by the Whigs after the presidential campaign of 1836. National convention delegates were selected by conventions in the states, which consisted in turn of local organizations of party members. Taken together, the new and elaborate Whig and Democratic organizations reached far beyond the halls of Congress and eventually penetrated every corner of the Union. Sustained by his party's far-reaching political network, Jackson became the first president to appeal to the people over the heads of their legislative representatives.[10]

Party reform did not by itself ensure a strong presidency. The party apparatus on which presidents depended for support was little more than a loose confederation of state and local organizations. Yet, because the president and the nominating convention rather than Congress were at the heart of the party's character and mission, strong leaders such as Jackson had an added source of influence. Moreover, partisanship in the Jacksonian era took root in the minds and habits of the American people to a previously unknown extent. Presidents became the beneficiaries of a stable foundation of popular support that made the loss of political initiative to Congress somewhat less likely.[11]

Jackson's Struggle with Congress

The transformation of the presidency from a congressionally to a popularly based office did not take place without a tremendous political struggle. The Whig party, although it won only two of eight presidential elections between 1828 and 1856, offered vigorous opposition to the Democrats. Proclaiming the ideas of Henry Clay and John Quincy Adams, the Whigs took a national approach to national problems. They advocated a program, known as the "American plan," to recharter the Second Bank of the United States, enact a protective tariff, and foster internal improvements. This program contradicted the states' rights policies of the Democrats, resting instead on a broad, Hamiltonian construction of the Constitution.

Yet the Whigs, who formed as a party of opposition to Jackson, resisted the expansion of executive power and defended Congress's traditional status as the principal instrument of republican government. President Jackson and the Democratic party firmly controlled the House, but the Senate, led by such forceful Whigs as Clay and Daniel Webster, often challenged both Jackson's policies and his claims to executive primacy. Although the Whigs did not control a majority of Senate seats, they forged a coalition with Calhoun and other southern Democratic senators, who resented Jackson's defense of the Union in the nullification crisis of 1832.

The conflict between the president and the Whigs came to a head in July 1832, when Jackson vetoed a bill to recharter the national bank four years before the old charter expired. A generation earlier, as a central element of Alexander Hamilton's domestic program, the Bank of the United States had been a major point of controversy between the Federalists and the Democratic-Republicans. Nevertheless, although Jefferson had attacked the bank as an unconstitutional expansion of the national government's power, he and his Democratic-Republican successors became reconciled to it once they were in office, viewing the bank as a necessary evil to sustain a stable national currency. The Second Bank of the United States had received a twenty-year charter from Congress in 1816, but its president, Nicholas Biddle, decided to apply for a recharter in 1832 at the urging of Clay and Webster. Clay, the Whigs' likely nominee for president in 1832, expected Jackson, whose dislike of the bank was well known, to veto the measure and thereby weaken his prospects for reelection. A considerable number of Democrats—especially in Pennsylvania, the home of the bank—supported the recharter legislation.

Jackson's veto of the bank bill on July 10, 1832, was, according to the historian Robert Remini, "the most important veto ever issued by a president." [12] Certainly the veto established a precedent that significantly strengthened the presidency. Beginning with Washington, Federalist and Democratic-Republican presidents had agreed that a veto should be cast only when the president believed that a piece of legislation was unconstitutional. In forty years under the Constitution only nine acts of Congress had been vetoed, and of these only three had dealt with important issues. Yet Jackson successfully vetoed twelve bills in eight years, even putting the "pocket veto" to use for the first time. He believed, and so stated in the message to Congress that accompanied the bank veto, that a president should reject any bill that he felt would injure the nation.

One implication of Jackson's interpretation of the veto power was that Congress now had to consider the president's opinions on bills before enacting them or risk a veto. Even though the rechartering of the bank had involved an "agent of the Executive branch of government," Jackson complained in his veto message, "neither upon the propriety of the present action nor upon the provisions of this act was the executive consulted." In demanding the right to be involved in the development of legislation, Jackson "essentially altered the relationship between the executive and legislative branches of government." [13]

Two other aspects of Jackson's veto message were significant. First, the message rearticulated Jefferson's belief that the president and Congress each possess coordinate power with the courts to determine questions of constitutionality. Jackson argued that the national bank was unconstitutional as well as unwise, a claim that his Whig opponents regarded as outrageous in view of Chief Justice John Marshall's decision in *McCulloch v. Maryland* (1819) that Congress had the constitutional power to charter a bank.[14] Webster charged that Jackson had claimed, in effect, "a universal power of judging over the laws and over the decisions of the judiciary" that was "nothing else but pure despotism."[15]

Jackson insisted, however, that in matters of constitutional interpretation the executive was no more bound by judicial rulings than by acts of Congress. Congress, the president, and the Court, he asserted, "must each for itself be guided by its opinion of the Constitution." To rely solely on judicial precedent was to allow for "a dangerous source of authority, and should not be regarded as deciding questions of constitutional power except where the acquiescence of the people and the states can be considered as well settled."[16] Thus, Jackson's veto message dramatically reopened the question, which seemingly had been resolved in 1803 by *Marbury v. Madison,* of the appropriate authority of the federal courts. His claim that the president and Congress, the popularly elected branches, could make constitutional determinations was yet another example of his determination to forge a stronger connection between the people and their government.

The other notable aspect of Jackson's war with Congress over the bank was the manner in which he laid the controversy before the American people. The last paragraph of Jackson's veto message, anticipating his impending campaign for reelection, stated that if he were "sustained by his fellow citizens," he would be "grateful and happy."

Concerned about the political effects of the bank war, Congress failed to override the president's veto. Jackson's overwhelming defeat of Clay in the 1832 election, which was fought in large measure over the bank issue, convinced even his political opponents, the weekly *Niles Register* reluctantly reported after the election, that when the president "cast himself upon the support of the people against the acts of both houses of Congress," he had been sustained. Never before had a chief executive gone to the people over the heads of their elected legislators. Jackson's victory confirmed his conviction that the president, not Congress, was the public's direct representative in Washington.[17]

The Aftermath of the Bank Veto

The Jacksonian revolution was extended in the aftermath of the bank veto. Vindicated by his reelection in 1832, Jackson decided to kill off the bank once and for all by withdrawing its public deposits and placing them in selected state banks. Because Congress refused Jackson's request for power to remove the bank's funds, the authority to do so remained with the secretary of the Treasury, who had been granted this right in the law that chartered the Second Bank in 1816.

When Secretary of the Treasury Louis McLane refused to transfer the deposits from the national to the state banks, Jackson nominated him to be the secretary of state and replaced him at the Treasury with William J. Duane. But Duane also resisted the president's requests to kill the bank and was dismissed within four months of taking office. His replacement, Roger B. Taney, formerly the attorney general, finally gave Jackson the cooperation he was looking for, which provoked the Senate to pass a censure resolution that accused the president of assuming "authority and power not conferred by the Constitution and laws." [18]

On April 15, 1834, Jackson countered the Senate's challenge with a written "Protest." In this message, which the Senate testily refused to have entered in its journal, the president declared that the resolution of censure was "wholly unauthorized by the Constitution, and in derogation of its entire spirit." He had been accused and, in effect, found guilty of an impeachable offense, Jackson objected. Although the Senate's censure did not remove the president from office, it subjected him to a "solemn declaration" that threatened to undermine his authority and to usurp the powers of the executive office. Thus, Jackson concluded:

> I do hereby *solemnly protest* against the aforementioned proceedings of the Senate as unauthorized by the Constitution, contrary to its spirit and to several of its expressed provisions, subversive of that distribution of the powers of government which it has ordained and established, destructive of the safeguards by which those powers were intended on the one hand to be controlled and the other to be protected, and calculated by their character and tendency, to concentrate in the hands of a body not directly amenable to the people a degree of influence and power dangerous to their liberties and fatal to the Constitution of their choice.[19]

Taken together, Duane's dismissal, Taney's removal of public deposits from the national bank, and the Senate's censure of Jackson raised a fundamental constitutional question: Can the president, using the constitutionally implied dismissal power, dictate how a discretionary power that Congress has vested exclusively in the head of a department shall be exercised? Whig leaders, notably Clay and Webster, defended Congress's right to vest truly independent authority in the Treasury secretary. Jackson claimed in response that the president was responsible "for the entire action of the executive department."

The Senate censure controversy—one battle in the longstanding war between the president and Congress for control of executive administration—was won decisively by Jackson. Because his protest message became the leading issue in the next round of Senate elections, Jackson's Democratic allies took control of the upper house in 1837. Then, as the historian H. A. Wise has written, "At once the work [of expunging from the record the Senate resolution of censure] began which hurled senators from their seats in order to fill them with the pliant and supple tools of executive power to draw black lines on that journal around that resolution which dared to censure President Jackson!" [20]

On January 16, 1837, weeks before leaving office, Jackson had the satisfaction of seeing the Resolution of Censure formally expunged from the Senate journal. The Senate's decision to recant not only signified a personal political triumph for Jackson, it also confirmed his broad interpretation of the president's power to control the executive branch.[21]

The Decline of the Cabinet

Within the executive branch, Jackson reduced the status of the cabinet. The dismissal of Duane, in fact, merely capped the administration's unprecedented record of cabinet instability. During Jackson's two terms as president, he had four secretaries of state, five secretaries of the Treasury, two secretaries of war, three attorneys general, three secretaries of the navy, and three postmasters general.

The cabinet's status also was diminished by Jackson's reliance during his first term upon the so-called Kitchen Cabinet, a group of unofficial advisers with whom the president conferred confidentially. They included Andrew J. Donelson, Jackson's ward and private secretary; Maj. William B. Lewis, a longtime friend who lived in the White House; Martin Van Buren, Jackson's principal party strategist, sometime cabinet member, and second-term vice president; Amos Kendall, formerly a newspaper editor; and Francis P. Blair, the editor of the *Globe*, a newspaper whose pages he used from 1830 to 1845 to support Democratic policies and to denounce the Whigs. The Kitchen Cabinet was depicted by Jackson's enemies within and outside the Democratic party as slipping into the president's study by way of the back stairs through the kitchen. In contrast, the traditional cabinet sometimes was called the "parlor cabinet."

According to critics of the administration, the Kitchen Cabinet consisted of men who were gifted in the arts of political manipulation but who advised the president badly on matters of policy and government. (This charge has been repeated whenever a president has gone outside formal channels for advice.) Yet Jackson's reliance on informal sources signified more the dominant sway he held over public affairs than any undue dependence on "shadowy" sources of influence. The only permanent member of the Kitchen Cabinet was Jackson himself— membership in the group shifted from moment to moment and from issue to issue. The decline of the formal cabinet during the Jackson administration marked the unprecedented prominence of the presidency between 1829 and 1837, not the rise of some other advisory body.[22]

The Limits of the Jacksonian Presidency

According to the Whigs, the main legacy of Jackson's presidency was a dangerous expansion of presidential prerogative. The bank controversy demonstrated, they argued, that the chief executive now possessed powers that dwarfed those of Congress and the judiciary, thus undermining the constitutional separation of powers. Indeed, it was during this controversy that the anti-Jackson party assumed the name of "Whig." Historically, the term derived from the party in England that opposed the power of the king and supported parliamentary superiority. Whigs in the United States meant by their name to imply that the Jackson wing of the Democratic-Republican party—the Democrats—had abandoned Jeffersonian principles in favor of an elected monarch, whom Whigs dubbed "King Andrew the First." [23]

The institutional legacy of Jackson's two terms as president, however, was much more ambiguous than his political opponents believed. Jackson did not simply expand the opportunities for unilateral executive action. His extension of executive powers depended upon the president's emergence as a popular leader, a role that was mediated in critical ways by the party organizations. Van Buren and other members of Jackson's Kitchen Cabinet built the first national party organization extensive enough to link presidential politics and governance with a collective body that could constrain excessive personal or programmatic ambition. In this sense, the leaders of the Democratic party considered Jackson's great personal popularity and power to be both a threat and an opportunity. As Van Buren wrote to Thomas Ritchie, the editor of the *Richmond Inquirer,* the general objective was to "substitute party principle for personal preference." [24] The success of this partisan project ensured that Jackson's "appeal to the people" in the bank controversy was not entirely direct; instead, the campaign was waged through the party.

The Party Press

The bank war and other political struggles during the Jackson presidency were carried on by the party press that emerged during the

BORN TO COMMAND.

OF VETO MEMORY.

HAD I BEEN CONSULTED.

KING ANDREW THE FIRST.

Jackson's extension of executive power led his opponents to caricature him in this 1832 cartoon as a monarch trampling the Constitution,
a ledger of Supreme Court decisions, and the watchwords *Virtue,
Liberty,* and *Independence.*

1830s. In this respect, Jackson's relationship with Democratic journalists such as Amos Kendall and Francis Blair added an important
dimension to his leadership: these men provided the president with a
new and acceptable tool for political influence by translating "White
House decisions into forceful language and announc[ing] them with
persuasive eloquence to the American people." [25] Blair's *Globe,* in fact,
became the official organ of both the Jackson and the succeeding Van
Buren administrations. As such, the newspaper enjoyed special access
to official political circles as well as financial support derived from
printing contracts and other perquisites that were controlled by the
government.

Every Democratic president from Jackson to James Buchanan
secured the solid support of at least one important newspaper. Yet the
"administration press" was also a Democratic press, dedicated to the
party's program and organization.[26] Hence, a more assertive presi-

dency was bound inextricably to a more aggressive and popular party press.

The "Spoils System"

Jackson also implanted a system of rotation into government personnel practices, using the president's power of removal to replace federal employees for purely partisan reasons. Until Jackson became president, the belief had prevailed that the government work force should be stable and politically neutral. Beginning in 1829, however, Jackson and his successors rejected this principle and deliberately removed or sanctioned the removal of thousands of subordinates for political reasons. The credo of the new patronage system was, as New York senator William L. Marcy put it, "to the victor belong the spoils of the enemy." [27]

In theory, the "spoils system" expanded the powers of the executive enormously. The president was now in a position, as Jackson's dismissal of Duane illustrated, to enforce conformity to administration policies within the executive branch. In practice, however, most patronage was controlled by the party organizations in a manner that actually circumscribed presidential leadership. When local party leaders demanded offices as a reward for rallying voters to the national ticket in congressional and presidential elections, even powerful chief executives were not inclined to refuse them. Moreover, to keep their jobs, many federal officeholders, particularly those who served in the widely scattered customhouses and post offices, were required to return part of their salaries to the local party organization that sponsored the office, to do party work at election time, and to "vote right." [28]

The postal system became the primary source of partisan favors. Beginning with Jackson, and continuing well into the twentieth century, it was common practice to appoint as postmaster general someone who would serve as the administration's principal patronage agent, representing the interests of the party to the president. Presidents who were insensitive to the demands of partisanship paid a severe political price. Buchanan, for example, was attacked by many Democratic leaders when he removed loyal Democratic officeholders who had been appointed by his predecessor, Franklin Pierce.[29]

The powers of the presidency that Jackson brought to life were constrained not only by the party system but also by the fundamental political doctrine that he espoused: to limit the activities of the national government. As Tocqueville wrote, "General Jackson's power is constantly increasing, but that of the president grows less. The federal government is strong in his hands; it will pass to his successor enfeebled." [30]

Martin Van Buren and the Panic of 1837

As Tocqueville prophesied, Jackson's successor, the able and politically shrewd Martin Van Buren, assumed office under the most difficult of circumstances. Indeed, Van Buren became the first president to have to face a domestic crisis. No sooner was he inaugurated in 1837 than the economy began a steep downward spiral, a decline that was at least in part the legacy of Jackson's assault on the national bank.

The Panic of 1837, as the crisis was called, was caused in large measure by speculation. A boom in western land, manufacturing, transportation, banking, and other enterprises, which began in 1825, caused financial credit in the national economy to become overextended. By removing federal deposits from the cautious Second Bank of the United States and placing them in politically selected state banks, the Jackson administration had contributed to the rapid expansion of credit. Then, conscious of the problems created by an overextended economy, Jackson issued a Treasury order, the so-called Specie Circular, in July 1836, requiring that hard currency be used to pay for all federal lands. This order aroused fears that Jackson and his successor would do all they could to contract the currency, thus causing privately-owned banks to call in loans, many of which could not be paid. Panic ensued. In early 1837, mercantile houses began to fail, and New Yorkers rioted to protest the high cost of flour. In short order, almost every bank in the country suspended specie payments. The state banking system that the Jacksonians had encouraged to replace the national bank collapsed, costing the Treasury some $9 million.

Van Buren was a more pragmatic politician than his predecessor, but he was sufficiently wedded to Jacksonian principles to resist government-sponsored solutions to the economic crisis. Van Buren rejected any proposal to revive the national bank. Similarly, he rejected the idea that the Treasury should provide a paper medium to facilitate domestic commerce. Like Jackson, Van Buren believed that the Treasury should attend to its own affairs and let businesses do the same.

Spurning the "constant desire" of the Whigs "to enlarge the power of government," Van Buren's response to the Panic of 1837 was modest. He proposed to establish an independent subtreasury, which would keep federal funds in federal vaults instead of depositing them in state banks. The subtreasury, however, was to have limited powers, leaving state banks free from federal regulation. Van Buren's proposal was not implemented until 1840: it was resisted for most of his tenure by a coalition of conservative Democrats and Whigs, most of whom wanted the national government to become more active in the economy.[31] The presidential election of 1840 took place in the midst of the depression, a crisis for which the Democratic party was held responsible.

The Jacksonian Presidency Sustained

The triumph of the Whig candidate, William Henry Harrison, in the election of 1840 posed a challenge not only to the Jacksonians' domestic program but also to their institutional achievements. The triumphant Whig party was united above all else by its opposition to the expansion of executive power that took place during the Jackson administration. Accordingly, Whig leaders such as Henry Clay and Daniel Webster saw the Panic of 1837 as an opportunity to reassert the powers of Congress.

Clay had been the obvious candidate to head the Whig ticket in 1840. He was both the architect of the anti-Jackson program and the real founder of the Whig coalition. But, believing General Harrison to be more electable than Clay, the Whigs nominated the aged (he was sixty-seven years old at the time of the election) hero of the War of 1812's Battle of Tippecanoe. Perhaps it consoled Clay and his allies to know that the general had proclaimed his support for the Whig assault on the executive in 1838, dedicating himself to a program that would limit the president to one term, free the Treasury from the president's control, and confine the exercise of the veto power to legislation that the president deemed unconstitutional.[32]

Although the 1840 campaign was not distinguished by serious discussion of the issues, Harrison did pledge publicly to step down after one term as president. In a speech delivered on September 10, 1840, at Dayton, Ohio, he stated:

> In the Constitution, that glorious charter of our liberties, there is a defect, and that defect is, the term of service of the President,—not limited. This omission is the source of all the evil under which the country is laboring. If the privilege of being President of the United States had been limited to one term, the incumbent would devote all his time to the public interest, and there would be no cause to misrule the country. . . . *I pledge myself before Heaven and earth, if elected President of the United States, to lay down at the end of the term faithfully that high trust at the feet of the people!*[33]

Harrison's inaugural address, which Webster and Clay helped to write, provided further reason to believe that the Whig victory in 1840 would undo Jackson's reconstruction of the presidency. Indeed, when Harrison deemed "preposterous" the idea that the president could "better understand the wants and wishes of the people than their representatives," Jacksonians suspected that designing Whig leaders had persuaded the politically inexperienced president in effect to accept the status of a figurehead, delegating the powers of the executive to Congress.[34]

Yet the Jacksonian executive survived the Whig challenge. The importance of the presidency was so firmly established in the popular mind by 1840 that the executive no longer could be restored to the weak position it had occupied during the latter stages of the Jeffersonian era. The Whigs, in fact, unwittingly contributed to the permanent transformation of the presidency by their conduct of the 1840 campaign. Jackson's political enemies had looked with disfavor on the popular campaign tactics that the Democratic party had employed during the three previous presidential elections. But having lost repeatedly to Jackson and Van Buren, the Whigs did everything in their power to "go to the people" in 1840. They bought newspapers in order to publish party propaganda, held great mass rallies, sent popular party leaders on speechmaking tours, and worked to mobilize as many voters as possible.

So intent were the Whigs on outdoing the Democrats' campaign in 1840 that they subordinated sober attention to the issues to slogans, songs, and symbols. Not only did "Tippecanoe and Tyler too" catch on (an alliterative slogan made possible by the nomination of Virginia's John Tyler for vice president), but a great deal of rabble-rousing occurred that for the first time made the log cabin an important symbol in presidential politics. A Democratic journalist had said scornfully of the rough-hewn General Harrison: "Give him a barrel of hard cider and . . . a pension of $2,000, and . . . he will sit the remainder of his days in his log cabin by the side of a . . . fire and study moral philosophy." Clever Whig propagandists pounced on this remark, turning it to their candidate's advantage. In no time, Harrison became "the log cabin and hard-cider candidate," an image that endeared him to many voters. Log cabin badges, log cabin songs, log cabin newspapers, and cider barrels were seen everywhere.

In the face of such campaigning, Martin Van Buren, whose origins actually were more humble than Harrison's but whose tastes, as displayed in the White House, were ostentatious, never stood a chance. Although the popular vote was close, its geographical distribution was such that Harrison received 234 electoral votes to the 60 that Van Buren received.[35]

The log cabin, hard cider campaign stimulated tremendous interest and enthusiasm around the country. Electoral turnout increased substantially: the 2.4 million voters who cast their ballots in 1840 constituted 80.2 percent of the eligible voters in the country, a percentage that since has been surpassed only twice, in 1860 and 1876.[36] Ironically, by accepting and expanding upon the Democrats' successful campaign techniques, the Whigs in effect ratified the Jacksonian concept of the president as popular leader. The Whig anti-executive doctrine notwithstanding, it no longer was possible for the presidency to be restored to its late Jeffersonian status, however inept a particular president might be.[37]

John Tyler, as the first vice president to succeed to the presidency, faced the constitutional question of whether he succeeded to the office or succeeded temporarily to the responsibilities of the office. His decisive actions preempted debate and established a firm precedent for succession to the presidency.

John Tyler and the Problem of Presidential Succession

The consolidation of the Jacksonian presidency became more pronounced after Harrison died only a month into his term. (He caught pneumonia while delivering, hatless, a ninety-minute inaugural address in the freezing rain.) Vice President John Tyler quickly took the oath as president, thus imposing a solution on the unresolved constitutional question of the vice president's right to assume the full status of the presidency when the office became prematurely vacant. Tyler also proved to be a less enthusiastic proponent of Whig theories than his predecessor, particularly with regard to the executive. Whig leaders soon were disappointed to discover that Tyler was no ally in their effort to dismantle the Jacksonian presidency.

Tyler's constitutional right to become president was far from certain. The succession clause of Article II was vague, stipulating only that in case of the president's death, resignation, removal, or inability to discharge the powers and duties of the office, "the Same" shall "devolve on the Vice President." This provision left in doubt whether Tyler remained vice president, merely acting as president until a special election could be held, or whether he succeeded fully to the office and title of the president of the United States for the remainder of Harrison's four-year term.

Tyler wasted no time asserting that he was the president in every sense of the word. Despite some rumblings from Congress, he had a judge swear him in soon after hearing that Harrison was dead and, within ten days, moved into the White House. Leaving absolutely no doubt that he intended to be his own man as president, Tyler went before "the people" in the form of an audience assembled in the capital on April 9, 1841, and gave an inaugural address after the manner of an elected president. Tyler's taking this opportunity to provide an "exposition of the principles" that would govern his administration was a signal to the country that he would not be content to stand in Harrison's shadow; it also was a warning to Whigs that Tyler did not intend to be a compliant servant to Clay, Webster, and the other party leaders. By acting boldly and decisively, Tyler established, in the absence of clear constitutional guidance, the firm precedent that an "accidental" president enjoys the same status as an elected president.[38]

The difficulties that Tyler faced in office went beyond the constitutional doubts that shrouded his succession to the presidency. His elevation also created a political impasse. Tyler represented a faction of the Whig party that dissented from many of the nationalist views preached by its leaders. In accordance with the common practice in American party politics, his nomination as vice president had been made in an effort to balance the Whig ticket—it was a gesture of compromise from the National Republican Whigs to the smaller southern states' rights wing of the party. Yet ticket balancing backfired when Tyler decisively seized the reins of office after Harrison's death and proceeded to exercise the powers of the Jacksonian presidency in a way that thwarted the Whig efforts to enact Clay's "American plan." [39]

Tyler's opposition to much of the Whig domestic program prompted him to cast more vetoes than any of his predecessors except Jackson. In 1841, he vetoed two successive bills that resembled the old bank legislation that Jackson had killed. The outburst of fury against Tyler after his second veto was extraordinary, expressing the Whigs' frustration at their inability to enact their program, even after winning a presidential election. Effigies of Tyler were burned by the thousands; his private secretary received hundreds of letters threatening assassination. In Washington every cabinet member except Secretary of State Webster resigned. Had Webster not resisted pressure from Senator Clay to join this so-called conspiracy, which included a Senate plan to prevent Tyler from reconstructing his cabinet, Tyler himself very likely would have been forced to resign.

The bank battles were only the beginning of the struggle between

Tyler and his party. His veto of a tariff measure in 1842 provoked the first effort in history to impeach a president. Tyler's assertive exercise of the veto power was irreconcilable with the Whig theory of executive subordination to Congress. Clay even proposed a constitutional amendment to permit Congress to override a veto by a simple majority vote.[40]

Tyler, claiming for the president a right to participate in the legislative process that was reminiscent of Jackson, defended his veto of the tariff bill on policy rather than on constitutional grounds. Responding both to Congress's accusation that he had misused the veto power and to the talk of impeachment, Tyler issued a strongly worded public message, stating that he represented "the executive authority of the people of the United States" and in "their name" protested "against every attempt to break down the undoubted constitutional power" of the presidency.[41] Like Jackson, too, Tyler argued that when a conflict developed between the president and Congress, it was for the people to decide who was right. When the Whigs were defeated in the congressional election of 1842, Tyler believed that he had been vindicated. Nothing came of the effort to impeach him, and Clay's proposal for a constitutional amendment to weaken the veto power was greeted with public indifference.

Thus, although Tyler lost his party's support and with it any chance to be nominated to run for president in 1844, he prevented a potentially damaging setback to the evolution of the executive office. As the presidential scholar Wilfred E. Binkley has written, Tyler "prepared the way for the completion of the movement toward executive leadership started by Andrew Jackson." [42]

The Presidency of James K. Polk

Few would have guessed as Tyler's term came to an end that his Democratic successor, James K. Polk, would lead a successful administration. Yet if Tyler saved the presidency from a debilitating setback, Polk moved the office forward, successfully asserting executive responsibilities that had been either resisted by or denied to his predecessors. Polk's achievements did not come easily. He headed a Democratic party that was beginning to break apart over the slavery issue and faced militant Whig minorities in both houses of Congress.

The First "Dark Horse" Candidate

Most Democratic leaders expected that former president Van Buren would be nominated to run again in 1844—until, that is, the issue of Texas annexation intervened. Just before the Whig and Democratic nominating conventions, Tyler's secretary of state, John C. Calhoun, concluded an annexation treaty with the Republic of Texas, which had fought and won its independence from Mexico. As a result, each party's leading presidential candidate, Van Buren and Clay, was forced to announce his views on the treaty. Texas was an issue that aroused serious disagreements between North and South about the desirability of expanding the cotton-growing and slave-holding territory of the United States.

Clay's opposition to annexation caused little controversy in the mostly northern Whig party. But when Van Buren took the same position, a firestorm erupted in the Democratic party. The Democrats and their hero, Andrew Jackson, had long supported territorial expansion—the cause was sacred to the emerging frontier interests of the South and the West. To defeat the Whigs the Democrats needed strong support in the South, where states' rights advocates looked westward to expand slavery. Yet Van Buren, best known as a pragmatic politician, chose to follow what he called "the path of duty" and resist the extension of slavery. His decision cost him any chance to return to the White House.

With Van Buren's candidacy seriously wounded, Gov. James K. Polk of Tennessee emerged at the deadlocked Democratic convention as a compromise choice between North and South—the first "dark horse" candidate in the history of American presidential elections. Polk did not even receive his first vote for the nomination until New Hampshire was polled on the eighth convention ballot. But New York's support on the ninth ballot started a stampede, as delegation after delegation rushed to transfer its votes to Polk and thus to demonstrate its loyalty to the winner.[43]

Reasserting Presidential Power

By a combination of shrewd political maneuvering and forceful statesmanship, Polk was able to overcome the centrifugal forces that dominated American politics during the mid-1840s. After winning the Democratic nomination, he stole one of the Whigs' main issues by disclaiming any intention to seek a second term. Yet during his four years in office, Polk vigorously and effectively asserted executive functions that reinforced, even expanded, the Jacksonian conception of presidential power. Most significant, he was the first president, including Jackson, to exercise close, day-to-day supervision over the executive departments.

Until Polk, routine and consistent executive influence had been especially absent from the president's relations with the Treasury Department. Presidents never had been granted legal responsibility to oversee the various departmental budget estimates that were submitted annually to Congress. Instead, in the Treasury Act of 1789 Congress had assigned to the secretary of the Treasury the duty to prepare and report estimates of government expenditures to the legislature. George Washington's Treasury secretary, Alexander Hamilton, did not even consult the president in this matter. Hamilton was distinctive, as was Albert Gallatin, who served in the Jefferson and Madison administrations, mainly in the initiative he took in budgetary policy making. Their successors as Treasury secretary only gathered together the departmental estimates and submitted them to Congress in one package. In 1839, for example, Van Buren's secretary of the Treasury, Levi Woodbury, refused to take any responsibility for making a composite budget or reviewing the estimates that were submitted to him by the other departments.[44]

One of Polk's major achievements in office was to coordinate the budget: for the first time in history, the president oversaw the formation of a fiscal policy. Not only did Polk review all budget requests, he insisted that the department heads revise their planned expenditures downward. Polk was forced to tighten fiscal control after the Mexican War began in 1846, especially since the government was operating under the reduced revenues of the Walker Tariff, which he considered one of the major accomplishments of his administration.[45] Furthermore, Polk, like his fellow Tennessean, Andrew Jackson, hated public debt and was philosophically committed to limiting government spending. Polk's success as, in twentieth century terms, the director of the budget was demonstrated by the tight fiscal rein he imposed on the war department at the end of the Mexican War. Polk directed his reluctant secretary of war, William Marcy, to force the department's bureau chiefs to accept a return to the prewar level of expenditures.[46]

The precedents that Polk tried to establish in fiscal policy were not followed by his nineteenth-century successors. (Abraham Lincoln was an exception.) But his assertion of the president's right and duty to control personally the departmental activities of the executive branch implanted the Jacksonian concept of the presidency more deeply in the American constitutional order. In the face of belligerent Whig opposition, Polk's last message to Congress proclaimed that "the people, by the Constitution, have commanded the President, as much as they have commanded the legislative branch of government, to execute their will." Indeed, Polk argued, the president occupied a special place as the people's representative, for "the President represents in the executive department the whole people of the United States, as each member of the legislative department represents portions of them."[47]

According to the historian George Bancroft, who served as his secretary of the navy, Polk succeeded "because he insisted on being its [the administration's] center and in overruling and guiding all his secretaries to act as to produce unity and harmony."[48] Perhaps Polk's most important contribution to the development of the presidency was his forceful performance as commander in chief during the Mexican War. War with Mexico had become inevitable after the annexation of Texas, which was admitted as the twenty-eighth state of the Union on December 29, 1845. Polk's determination to secure additional Mexican territory in New Mexico and California provoked further territorial disputes. Unable to negotiate a purchase, Polk determined to gain these territories by force. Mexico recklessly helped Polk in this endeavor by attacking U.S. troops on May 9, 1846, only four hours after he and his cabinet had resolved to ask Congress to declare war. Congress voted for war on May 13, 1846.

As the historian Leonard White has observed, "Polk gave the country its first demonstration of the *administrative* capacities of the presidency as a war agency." [49] To be sure, Polk did not push the office's power as commander in chief to its limits—this task was accomplished by Lincoln during the Civil War. Unlike Madison during the War of 1812, however, Polk did establish that a president without previous military experience could provide decisive wartime leadership. Polk insisted on being the final authority on all military matters. As White has written:

> He determined the general strategy of military and naval operations; he chose commanding officers; he gave personal attention to supply problems; he energized so far as he could the General Staff; he controlled the military and naval estimates; and he used the Cabinet as a major coordinating agency for the conduct of the campaign. He told the Secretaries of War and Navy to give their personal attention to all matters, even of detail, and to advise him promptly of every important step that was to be taken. The President was the center on which all else depended; Hamilton's doctrine of the unity of the executive power was seldom more truly exemplified. [50]

Polk's efforts as commander in chief were not without partisan motivation or serious blunders. A loyal Democrat, he was disconcerted that the war was making a hero of Gen. Zachary Taylor, a Whig and potentially a formidable presidential candidate in 1848. Thus, in a petty partisan action, Polk refused to sign an order for the troops to fire a salute in honor of Taylor's victory at Buena Vista, a settlement in the northeastern part of Mexico. The president's relations with Gen. Winfield Scott, the army's commander but also a Whig, were similarly governed by partisanship. Polk urged Congress, for example, to create the post of lieutenant general for the Democratic senator Thomas Hart Benton, so that a Democrat would supersede Scott as the commanding officer in the field. Benton's military experience was so limited that the Democratic Senate narrowly rejected the president's recommendation. [51]

Polk's problems with his generals could be traced in part to the close relationship between the Jacksonian presidency and the newly institutionalized party system. Partisan practices had become so imbedded in presidential politics during the 1830s and 1840s that they could not easily be put aside even in wartime. Because Scott and Taylor were regular army officers, Polk could do little about them. Volunteer regiments of state militia, however, which did much of the soldiering, fought principally under Democratic officers. The decision to call up the militia conformed to the Democratic party's longstanding opposition to a large standing army, which it regarded as contrary to the character of free institutions. But the dependence on volunteers was to plague Polk throughout the war. The president eventually was forced to recognize his error and, in December 1846, to ask for an increase in the regular army. Until Congress granted his request in February 1847, however, critical military operations near Mexico City were halted.[52]

Notwithstanding the limitations of partisan practices and doctrine, Polk's command in the Mexican War was, on the whole, very able. The general military strategy that he devised and directed won not just a decisive victory on the battlefield, but also the acquisition of New Mexico and California. Thus, Polk obtained the major objective of the war and became, except for Jefferson, the president who has brought the most territory into the national domain. By demonstrating that the president as commander in chief could plan and oversee the execution of war strategy, Polk effectively asserted the principle that the president is responsible for the military operations of the United States.[53]

The Slavery Controversy and the Twilight of the Jacksonian Presidency

Polk was the last president of the Jacksonian era whose time in office was not consumed by the slavery question. The annexation of Texas and the Mexican War greatly expanded the southwest territory of the United States. Most northerners objected strongly to the extension of slavery into the new territories. Meanwhile, southern whites were unwilling to distinguish this "free soil" position from outright abolitionism, interpreting every effort to bar slavery from the territories as a threat to slavery where it already existed in the South.

The slavery issue had almost divided the Democratic party in 1844 but was papered over by the compromise nomination of Polk. The spoils of the Mexican War made a similar rapprochement impossible in 1848. Van Buren, the organizational genius who had done so much to bring the original Democratic coalition together during the 1820s, now abandoned his party to run as the third-party, Free Soil candidate. Although Van Buren received only 10 percent of the popular vote, he drained support away from the Democratic candidate, Lewis Cass, thereby helping to elect the Whig nominee, Zachary Taylor.

Taylor, the hero of the Mexican War, probably would have won the presidential election in any case. But the Free Soil party drew enough votes to affect the outcome of many state elections, even gaining support from some prominent political leaders. Van Buren's campaign in 1848 also made it difficult for the Democrats and the Whigs to ignore the slavery issue any longer. In less than a decade, the party system that had dominated the Jacksonian era collapsed, and a new governing coalition emerged.

The Presidency of Zachary Taylor

Because of its strong base in the South, the Democratic party survived the slavery controversy and the Civil War, although in a greatly weakened condition. But Taylor's election in 1848 was the last major success of the Whig party, which expired soon after. The Whigs stood for national unity, an ideal that was rendered politically irrelevant by the slavery question. Moreover, the Whigs' opposition to an active presidency was proven unworkable by the last Whig to be elected president. Taylor's inaugural address was replete with Whiggish declarations about the need to limit executive power. But the brief Taylor administration (he died in July 1850, just sixteen months into his term) was hardly true to his promise of political self-denial. The slavery controversy and Jackson's legacy of presidential leadership had made a "hands-off" presidency impossible.[54]

More than anything else, President Taylor is remembered for his "consistent and unyielding" opposition to the Compromise of 1850, a congeries of legislative measures that preserved a temporary peace on the slavery issue. Taylor's opposition to the compromise, which imposed no restrictions on slavery in the formerly Mexican southwest territories and strengthened the national fugitive slave law, angered slave holders. (The compromise also admitted California to the Union as a free state and ended the slave trade in the District of Columbia.) Yet the president stood firm against southern threats of disunion. He told congressional leaders that he would take the field in person to restore the Union and would hang rebels "with as little mercy as he had hanged deserters and spies in Mexico."

The Presidency of Millard Fillmore

Taylor died before the crisis provoked by the Compromise of 1850 matured. His successor, Vice President Millard Fillmore of New York, restated traditional Whig assurances about executive restraint, yet proved no more willing than Taylor to leave critical domestic matters to Congress. Fillmore, however, was as determined to see the compromise enacted as his predecessor had been to defeat it. His support was politically important: one member of the House reported that between twenty and thirty representatives who before Taylor's death were adamantly opposed to the compromise did a dramatic about-face in response to Fillmore's support.[55]

Having seen the Compromise of 1850 through to enactment, the president determined to enforce the new and stringent Fugitive Slave Act vigorously. When Massachusetts refused to cooperate in the prosecution of citizens who violated the act, Fillmore declared that his administration would admit "no right of nullification North or South." In practice, however, the president was never able to find a reliable means of securing compliance with the law in those areas of the country where fugitive slaves were protected.[56]

The Presidency of Franklin Pierce

Although Fillmore's tenure demonstrated again that the Jacksonian era had transformed the presidency irrevocably, even the strengthened executive was no match for the crisis engendered by the slavery question. The final two presidents of the Jacksonian era, Franklin Pierce of New Hampshire and James Buchanan of Pennsylvania, were irresolute leaders who sought vainly to hold the northern and southern factions of their party together. Each tried to defuse, rather than come to terms with, slavery as a political issue. But it was too late for temporizing. National polarization over slavery was only aggravated by the efforts of Pierce and Buchanan to dispel the issue.

The Kansas-Nebraska Act of 1854 was the most telling of Pierce's failures to allay sectional conflict. This law, the brainchild of the influential Democratic senator from Illinois, Stephen Douglas, tried to remove slavery from the national political agenda by resting its status in each new territory on the principle of "popular sovereignty." According to this principle, as soon as the people of a territory obtained a territorial legislature, they would decide whether or not to allow slavery. Because the Kansas-Nebraska Act would apply popular sovereignty to the Great Plains territories of Kansas and Nebraska, the central ingredient of the 1820 Missouri Compromise, which prohibited slavery north of Missouri's southern boundary, latitude 36°30', would be repealed.

The debate on Douglas's popular sovereignty bill dragged on for three months. Pierce used all the powers of his office, including patronage, to ensure its passage. Party discipline among Democrats, supplemented by presidential influence, prevailed. On May 25, 1854, the Kansas-Nebraska Act passed the Senate by a comfortable margin and Pierce signed it into law. Within six months, however, it became apparent that the repeal of the Missouri Compromise had aggravated, not quelled, the slavery controversy and had divided the parties irrevocably. Ironically, Pierce's forceful leadership of the Democratic party hastened its demise as a governing institution.

The election of 1856 revealed the emergence of a new national political alignment. The Whigs' collapse after 1852 and the northern crusade against slavery in Kansas (that Nebraska would become a free territory was never in doubt) prompted a new party to form. Offering a platform that stood squarely against the expansion of slavery, the Republican party nominated John C. Fremont for president in 1856. Although the Republicans made a good showing, they received no support in the South and were not yet sufficiently organized in the North to overcome this handicap. Winning Indiana, New Jersey, California, Illinois, his home state of Pennsylvania, and all 112 southern electoral votes, the Democratic candidate, James Buchanan, was elected president.

The Presidency of James Buchanan

Buchanan, who was just as anxious as Pierce to defuse the slavery controversy, also was determined to avoid the political damage that Pierce had suffered by fighting for ameliorative legislation. In his inaugural address, Buchanan associated himself with an as-yet-unannounced Supreme Court decision, arguing that the proper resolution of the slavery question in the territories belonged to the federal judiciary. Referring to the pending suit by Dred Scott, a sixty-two-year-old slave who claimed that residence with his owner on free soil had made him a free man, Buchanan pledged that he would "in common with all good citizens ... cheerfully submit" to the decision of the Supreme Court.[57]

Such a pledge, Binkley has noted, "was a strange abdication of executive claims by a member of the party of Jackson, who ... had emphatically denied the right of the judiciary thus to determine public policies through the medium of court opinions." [58] In truth, Buchanan's avowed deference to the Supreme Court was disingenuous: he had privately urged Justice James Grier, a critical swing vote on the Court, to side with colleagues who wanted to deny both Congress and the territorial legislatures the right to prohibit slavery.[59]

Buchanan's attempt to end the agitation over slavery in surreptitious alliance with the Court failed miserably. The Court's decision in Dred Scott v. Sanford opened the entire West to slavery, regardless of what the people in the territories might want.[60] This aggressive foray into the realm of controversial policy not only damaged the prestige of the Court badly, it also opened the floodgates to an outpouring of sectional strife that fractured the Democratic party and catapulted an obscure Illinois Republican, Abraham Lincoln, to the presidency in the election of 1860.

Notes

1. Robert V. Remini, *Andrew Jackson and the Course of American Democracy, 1833-1845* (New York: Harper and Row, 1984), 7.
2. James D. Richardson, ed., *Messages and Papers of the Presidents*, 20 vols. (New York: Bureau of National Literature, 1897), 4:1561.
3. As the historian Marvin Myers has written, Jackson's political philosophy called for a return to the principles set forth in Jefferson's first inaugural address: ". . . a wise and frugal government, which shall restrain men from injuring one another, which shall leave them otherwise free to regulate their own pursuits of industry and improvement, and shall not take from the mouth of labor the bread it has earned. This is the sum of good government, and this is necessary to close the circle of our felicities." As such—and here the bank war was the critical case—the strengthening of the executive office during the Jacksonian period "mobilized the powers of government for what was essentially a dismantling operation." Myers, *The Jacksonian Persuasion* (Stanford, Calif.: Stanford University Press, 1957), 20-21.
4. Major L. Wilson, *The Presidency of Martin Van Buren* (Lawrence: University Press of Kansas, 1984), 13.
5. Ibid.
6. Richardson, *Messages and Papers of the Presidents* 3:1206.
7. Wilson, *Presidency of Martin Van Buren*, 13.
8. Alexis de Tocqueville, *Democracy in America*, ed. J. P. Mayer (Garden City, N.Y.: Doubleday, 1969), 60.
9. Wilfred E. Binkley, *President and Congress* (New York: Knopf, 1947), 67.
10. Edward S. Corwin, *The President: Office and Powers, 1787-1957*, 4th ed. (New York: New York University Press, 1957), 20-21.
11. Ibid.; also see Leonard D. White, *The Jacksonians: A Study in Administrative History, 1829-1861* (New York: Macmillan, 1954), 24-25.
12. Robert V. Remini, *Andrew Jackson and the Course of American Freedom, 1822-1832* (New York: Harper and Row, 1981), 369.
13. Richardson, *Messages and Papers of the Presidents* 3:1152; Remini, *Andrew Jackson and the Course of American Freedom*, 370.
14. *McCulloch v. Maryland*, 4 L. Ed. 579 (1819).
15. Quoted in Binkley, *President and Congress*, 72.
16. Richardson, *Messages and Papers of the Presidents* 3:1144-1145. On Jackson's view of the courts, see Robert V. Remini, "The Constitution and the Presidencies: The Jackson Era," in *The Constitution and the American Presidency*, ed. Martin Fausold and Alan Shank (Albany: State University of New York Press, 1991), 37-40.
17. Richardson, *Messages and Papers of the Presidents* 3:1154; *Niles Register*, November 17, 1832, quoted in White, *The Jacksonians*, 23; Remini, *Andrew Jackson and the Course of American Freedom*, 373.
18. Quoted in Binkley, *President and Congress*, 79.
19. Richardson, *Messages and Papers of the Presidents* 3:1311 (Jackson's emphasis).
20. H. A. Wise, *Seven Decades of Union* (Philadelphia: Lippincott, 1872), 137.
21. Binkley, *President and Congress*, 82-85; White, *Jacksonians*, 33-44.
22. White, *Jacksonians*, 92-95; Remini, *Andrew Jackson and the Course of American Freedom*, 315-330.
23. Binkley, *President and Congress*, 80.
24. Van Buren to Thomas Ritchie, January 13, 1827, Martin Van Buren Papers,

Library of Congress, Washington, D.C. For a discussion of Van Buren's concept of political leadership, see James W. Ceaser, *Presidential Selection: Theory and Development* (Princeton, N.J.: Princeton University Press, 1979), 157-166.

25. Remini, *Andrew Jackson and the Course of American Freedom*, 325.
26. On the development of the "administration press," see White, *Jacksonians*, chap. 15.
27. Quoted in ibid., 320. On the theory and practice of rotation during the Jacksonian era, see ibid., 33-44 and chaps. 16-17.
28. Ibid., 332-343.
29. Ibid., 313. The deleterious effects of the system of rotation on public administration often have been exaggerated. As Leonard White writes, "The consequences of rotation on the public service were unfortunate as a whole, but they were balanced in part by democratic gains, and because both Whigs and Democrats looked for character and competence among their partisans, and often found these qualities." Moreover, although the number of removals during the Jacksonian era was unprecedented, less than 10 percent of the federal work force was affected (Ibid., 308, 343).
30. Tocqueville, *Democracy in America*, 394.
31. On Van Buren's response to the Panic of 1837, see Wilson, *Presidency of Martin Van Buren*, chaps. 3-7; and Donald B. Cole, *Martin Van Buren and the American Political System* (Princeton, N.J.: Princeton University Press, 1984), chaps. 10-11.
32. Gen. William Henry Harrison to Rep. Harmer Denny, December 2, 1838, in *The Growth of Presidential Power: A Documented History*, ed. William M. Goldsmith (New York and London: Chelsea, 1974), 2:637-641.
33. Printed in Arthur Schlesinger, Jr., and Fred I. Israel, eds., *History of American Presidential Elections* (New York: Chelsea, 1971), 1:737-744 (emphasis in original).
34. Binkley, *President and Congress*, 89.
35. For a description of the 1840 campaign, see Stefan Lorant, *The Presidency: A Pictorial History of Presidential Elections from Washington to Truman* (New York: Macmillan, 1951), 143-162.
36. Goldsmith, *Growth of Presidential Power* 2:647.
37. Binkley, *President and Congress*, 108.
38. Robert J. Morgan, *A Whig Embattled: The Presidency under John Tyler* (Lincoln: University of Nebraska Press, 1954), 16-21.
39. Ibid., chap. 2; Binkley, *President and Congress*, 92-99.
40. Binkley, *President and Congress*, 98.
41. President John Tyler, Protest Message to the House of Representatives, August 30, 1842, in Goldsmith, *Growth of Presidential Power* 2:710.
42. Binkley, *President and Congress*, 99.
43. Van Buren probably would have been nominated in spite of his opposition to the annexation of Texas, save for the two-thirds rule that governed Democratic conventions. The need for Democratic nominees for president and vice president to win support from two-thirds, rather than a majority, of national convention delegates gave the South a de facto veto over party nominations until this rule was abolished in 1936. On the nomination of Polk as the first dark horse candidate, see Charles A. McCoy, *Polk and the Presidency* (Austin: University of Texas Press, 1960), chap. 2; on Van Buren's actions in 1844, see Cole, *Martin Van Buren and the American Political System*, chap. 13.

44. McCoy, *Polk and the Presidency*, 74-75; White, *Jacksonians*, 77-79.
45. Polk and the Democrats had long been committed to the passage of a low-tariff act. As Speaker of the House, Polk had supported presidents Jackson and Van Buren in their attempts to enact a low-tariff law. And he devoted several pages of his first State of the Union address to a proposal that advocated a general lowering of tariff rates and the placing of rates on an *ad valorem* basis. Polk's dedication to a revision of the tariff did not falter as war with Mexico approached. Instead, he pressured Congress to pass the Walker Act in 1846, considering this assault on protectionism his most important domestic accomplishment—a vital measure for codifying the Jacksonian idea of economic justice. "Just as [Jacksonians] interpreted territorial expansion as a way to diminish the threat of industrialization and urbanization," the historian Paul Bergeron has written, "so they also perceived protective tariffs as beneficial only to manufacturers and therefore detrimental to the working classes and to the vision of an agrarian America." Paul H. Bergeron, *The Presidency of James K. Polk* (Lawrence: University Press of Kansas, 1987), 185-186. Also see McCoy, *Polk and the Presidency*, 148-153.
46. White, *Jacksonians*, 81-82.
47. Richardson, *Messages and Papers of the Presidents* 6:2514-2515.
48. Quoted in Binkley, *President and Congress*, 100-101.
49. White, *Jacksonians*, 50 (White's emphasis).
50. Ibid., 51.
51. Ibid., 55-56; McCoy, *Polk and the Presidency*, 103.
52. McCoy, *Polk and the Presidency*, 119-120; White, *Jacksonians*, 66.
53. McCoy, *Polk and the Presidency*, 140.
54. Binkley, *President and Congress*, 103-105; White, *Jacksonians*, 48.
55. Binkley, *President and Congress*, 106.
56. White, *Jacksonians*, 522, 529.
57. Richardson, *Messages and Papers of the Presidents* 7:2962.
58. Binkley, *President and Congress*, 107.
59. Elbert B. Smith, *The Presidency of James Buchanan* (Lawrence: University Press of Kansas, 1975), 23-29.
60. *Dred Scott v. Sanford*, 19 Howard 1393 (1857).

CHAPTER 6

The Presidency of
Abraham Lincoln

Abraham Lincoln was the last nineteenth-century president to make an important contribution to the theory and practice of the executive. Lincoln's accomplishments were born of a national crisis that threatened to destroy the foundations of constitutional democracy in the United States. The leadership he displayed in navigating the uncharted waters of emancipation and total war won him the esteem of Americans as their finest president. The historical profession has shared in the celebration of Lincoln's statesmanship. A recent poll of 900 American historians rated Lincoln the "greatest" president in history.[1]

Whether Lincoln's talents and achievements strengthened or weakened constitutional democracy is a matter of some dispute. Indeed, Lincoln's record as president has led some scholars to adjudge him not only a forceful leader but also a dictator, albeit a benevolent one in most accounts.[2] As commander in chief, especially, Lincoln demonstrated the presidency's great potential to assume extraordinary powers during a national emergency. The Civil War began while Congress was in recess, and for nearly three months every act of Union resistance to the seceding states of the South was a presidential act, performed without legislative authorization. To be sure, Lincoln considered his early measures to be ad interim, emergency decisions, which would require subsequent ratification by Congress to become fully valid. Yet as the problems of emancipation and reconstruction later loomed, it became clear that Lincoln "believed the rights of war were vested in the President and that as president he had extraordinary legal resources that Congress lacked."[3] Lincoln also acted in ways that preempted normal judicial functions, suspending the writ of *habeas corpus* and declaring martial law in various places.

Conceding that Lincoln went far beyond the normal bounds of presidential power during the Civil War, the constitutional scholar James G. Randall nonetheless has argued that the president showed notable restraint and leniency in administering his wartime measures, befitting his high regard for individual liberty. By doing so, Lincoln used his extraordinary powers not to subvert democracy but to save it.[4] Lincoln certainly did not regard his presidency as a dictatorship. He defended his conduct by invoking a conception of the Constitution that, although respectful of procedural regularity and formal legality, was concerned above all with the president's responsibility to uphold the basic principles of the constitutional order. Thus, Lincoln's presidency not only marked a critical moment in political history but also raised anew, under conditions of unprecedented urgency, questions about the appropriate place of executive power in the American system of republican government.

It is ironic that Lincoln was the president who so forcefully extended the boundaries of the executive. Until the Kansas-Nebraska Act was passed and the Republican party founded in 1854, Lincoln had been a Whig whose political career was distinguished by his eloquent and forceful expression of his party's opposition to the Jacksonian Democrats' expansion of presidential power. Significantly, Lincoln's first important speech, delivered in January 1838 before the Springfield Young Men's Lyceum, took the form of an allegory against great political ambition. The Framers of the Constitution were men of ample ambition, he conceded, but their passion for personal achievement proved to be a force for good because it found outlet in a great and constructive enterprise—writing, ratifying, and implementing the Constitution. But what of succeeding generations?

Lincoln warned in his speech that the "perpetuity of our free institutions"—the survival of the Constitution—would be threatened by other leaders of great ambition who would not be content simply to uphold the work of the founding generation. Such men would disdain the well-worn path of constitutional government, Lincoln feared; they were members of the "family of the lion, or the tribe of the eagle" who would seek to use public office to remake politics and government in their own image. Then, in words that could be understood clearly as a condemnation of the Jacksonians' aggrandizement of executive power, Lincoln foretold of the danger of demagogy, a danger made greater by the rise of the slavery controversy. "It thirsts and burns for distinction," he said of excessive ambition, "and if possible, it will have it, whether at the expense of emancipating the slaves, or enslaving free people."[5] In the peroration of the Lyceum address, Lincoln urged that "a reverence for the constitution and laws" become the civil religion of the nation, a reverence that might serve as a bulwark against immoderate presidential ambition.[6]

In the mid-1840s, Lincoln's devotion to settled, standing law informed his opposition to James K. Polk's assertive leadership in initiating and prosecuting the war with Mexico. As a Whig member of Congress, Lincoln argued that the Constitution gave the "war making power to Congress," and that "the will of the people should produce its own result without executive influence."[7] Nor did Lincoln give any indication during his rise to political prominence as a leader of the Republican party in the late 1850s that he viewed bold presidential leadership as the appropriate means to resolve the slavery controversy.

Lincoln's pre-presidential commitment to executive restraint notwithstanding, he became as president the "towering genius," a member of the "tribe of the eagle," against whom his Lyceum appeal for a reverence of law was ostensibly directed. As Garry Wills has argued, Lincoln transcended the work of the Framers and, in the course of emancipating the slaves and fighting the Civil War, remade the American political system. To be sure, Lincoln never disavowed the Constitution. But his celebration of the Declaration of Independence, especially its guarantees of equality before the law and the consent of the governed, imparted a new meaning to the Framers' handiwork, a meaning that could no longer abide the principle of states' rights and the institution of slavery. According to Wills, "Lincoln not only put the Declaration in a new light as a matter of founding *law*, but put its central proposition, equality, in a newly favored position as a principle of the Constitution."[8]

In truth, Lincoln was, as the historian James McPherson has written, a "conservative revolutionary" who wanted to preserve the Union as the revolutionary heritage of the Framers. Preserving this heritage was the purpose of the Civil War. "My paramount object in this struggle," Lincoln wrote to Horace Greeley in the summer of 1862, "*is* to save the Union, and is *not* either to save or destroy slavery." Yet Lincoln believed that to save the Union not just for the moment but enduringly, slavery would have to become anathema to the national creed and be set on the road to extinction in law and policy.[9] Drawing on a verse in the Book of Proverbs—"A Word Fitly Spoken is like apples of gold in pictures of silver"—Lincoln praised the declaration's principle of "liberty to All" as the essence of political life in the United States. "The assertion of that principle, at that time," he wrote, "was the word 'fitly spoken,' which has proved an 'apple of gold' to us. The Union, and the Constitution, are the pictures of silver, subsequently framed around it. The picture was made, not to conceal, or destroy the apple; but to adorn and preserve it."[10]

It was the Civil War itself that generated the radical momentum that led to a redefinition of politics and government in the United States. But Lincoln's words and leadership directed the course of events during the fight for emancipation and union. In this sense he was a revolutionary statesman, albeit one who sought to preserve, rather than to abolish, the heritage of constitutional government in the United States.

Lincoln and the Slavery Controversy

The key to Lincoln's statesmanship was to be found in his position on slavery. Lincoln was no abolitionist; indeed, his relative moderation on the issue helped him to wrest the 1860 presidential nomination of his party away from the avowedly pro-emancipation William H. Seward, the former governor of New York and the most prominent national Republican leader.[11] Although Lincoln consistently proclaimed himself "naturally antislavery," he believed that the national government lacked the authority to abolish slavery where it already existed. As he wrote to a friend in Kentucky, Joshua A. Speed, in 1855, "I acknowledge *your* rights and my obligations, under the Constitution, in regard to your slaves. I confess I hate to see the poor creatures hunted down, and caught, and carried back to their stripes, and unrewarded toils; but I bite my lip and keep quiet." [12]

At the same time, Lincoln believed that the extension of slavery into the western territories should not be tolerated, for such a policy threatened to perpetuate and expand the vile institution as a "positive good." With the enactment of the Kansas-Nebraska Act in 1854, he could no longer "bite his lip." In opening new territory to slavery, Congress had violated the Framers' understanding that slavery was a "necessary evil" that must be contained and allowed to die a "natural death." This constitutional impropriety was compounded in 1857 by the *Dred Scott* decision, in which the Supreme Court declared unconstitutional any act to abolish slavery by Congress or the territorial legislatures.

Lincoln was especially distressed because the Kansas-Nebraska Act and *Dred Scott* overturned the Missouri Compromise of 1820, which had prohibited slavery in the northern part of the Louisiana territory. The spirit of the Missouri Compromise, Lincoln claimed, was true to the principles of the Declaration of Independence, as well as to the Constitution. The author of the declaration, Thomas Jefferson, had first given form to this spirit when he conceived the policy embodied in the Northwest Ordinance of 1787, which banned slavery in the five states—Ohio, Michigan, Indiana, Wisconsin, and Lincoln's own Illinois—that composed the old Northwest Territory. Lincoln wanted to restore the

Missouri Compromise not only for the sake of the Union but also for the "sacred right of self government" and the restoration of "the national faith." As he said in his Peoria address of 1854:

> Our republican robe is soiled, and trailed in the dust. Let us repurify it. Let us turn and wash it white, in the spirit, if not in the blood, of the Revolution. Let us turn slavery from its "moral rights" back upon its existing legal rights and its argument of "necessity." Let us return it to the position our fathers gave it, and there let it rest in peace.[13]

Thus, although his respect for the limits imposed by the Constitution deterred Lincoln from attacking the existence of slavery in the southern states, he, unlike Stephen Douglas, his opponent in the 1858 Illinois Senate election and the author of the Kansas-Nebraska Act, was unwilling to save the Union at the price of tolerating slavery's extension into the territories. To do so would create a crisis by depriving the Constitution of its moral foundation. Lincoln argued that the South should join the North in restoring the long-standing national compromise on slavery that was embedded in the Northwest Ordinance and the Missouri Compromise.

But the logic of Lincoln's own position on slavery would not be satisfied by political compromise. In portraying his opposition to slavery as an act of statesmanship to restore the country's basic values, Lincoln actually shifted the terms of debate. His call for a new and explicit connection between the declaration and the Constitution made a national struggle over the existence of slavery all but inevitable. As he said in his speech accepting the Illinois Republican party's nomination to the Senate in 1858:

> A House divided against itself cannot stand.
> I believe this government cannot endure, permanently, half *slave* and half *free*.
> I do not expect the Union to be *dissolved*—I do not expect the House to *fall*—but I do expect it will cease to be divided.
> It will become *all* one thing, or *all* the other.[14]

The 1860 Election

The 1860 election did not provide Lincoln with a mandate to resolve the moral crisis created by the slavery controversy: he was a "minority" president who received almost no votes in the South. With the old Whig and Democratic coalitions supplanted by a fiercely sectional politics, the election of 1860 became a fragmented contest among four candidates. The northern vote was split between the Republican Lincoln and Stephen Douglas, the official Democratic nominee; the southern electorate was divided between John C. Breckinridge of Kentucky, the standard-bearer of southern Democrats, and John Bell of Tennessee, who was nominated by the National Constitutional Union, a party that formed from the remnant of southern Whiggery. Although the balloting yielded a decisive electoral college victory for Lincoln, who carried every northern state but New Jersey, he won only 40 percent of the popular vote. If southern Democrats had voted for Douglas, he would have had a considerable majority. Lincoln's victory was greeted throughout the South with ominous threats of secession. In bidding farewell to the citizens of Springfield, Illinois, on the eve of his journey to the nation's capital, Lincoln said, "I now leave, not knowing when, or whether ever, I may return, with a task before me greater than that which rested upon Washington." [15]

Lincoln's likening of his task to that faced by the first president bespoke not only the troubles he anticipated but also his hope of igniting a renewed faith in freedom. "Washington fought for National Independence and triumphed," the Republican senator from Massachusetts, Charles Sumner, wrote in an 1865 eulogy on Lincoln. "Lincoln drew his reluctant sword to save those great ideas, essential to the character of the Republic, which unhappily the sword of Washington had failed to place beyond the reach of assault." [16]

Lincoln did not receive such fulsome praise from his Republican colleagues during his lifetime. Indeed, the troubles he faced upon his arrival in Washington were aggravated by the suspicion with which many of his party's leaders regarded him. Seward had led on the first two ballots at the 1860 Republican convention in Chicago. "His claim to the nomination," the historian Allan Nevins has written, "on grounds of governmental experience, long service to the free soil cause, and tested ability, seemed to outweigh those of anybody else." [17] But the delegates had turned to Lincoln on the third ballot, believing that his humble birth, homely wit, skill in debate, and geographical and political centrism would attract votes in the midwestern states, such as Illinois and Indiana, where the Democrats were strongest, as well as in the solidly Republican Northeast and West.

Seward and his allies disdained Lincoln, whose experience in national affairs was limited to one term in the House of Representatives and a strong but unsuccessful Senate campaign against Douglas in 1858. They regarded him as a "prairie lawyer," an "upstart" who had taken the nomination away from the Republican who was most fit to command. Lincoln placated Seward gracefully, even inviting him to become secretary of state. But the president-elect had a hard time persuading Seward and other easterners in his party that the man they had dismissed as a "backwoods president" could rise to meet the challenge of southern secession.[18]

Lincoln and Secession

In the face of such dire political circumstances, Lincoln's inaugural address on March 4, 1861, sought to reassure southerners that his would be a policy of forbearance, not coercion.[19] Despite the widespread southern fear that the election of a Republican president threatened their property, peace, and personal security, Lincoln observed, there had never been any "reasonable cause for such apprehension."[20] Indeed, restating his long-standing position, he renounced any "purpose, directly or indirectly, to interfere with the institution of slavery in the states where it exists."[21]

The "only substantial dispute" that faced the country, Lincoln asserted, was over the extension of slavery. "One section of the country believes slavery is *right* and ought to be extended," he said, "while the other believes it is *wrong* and ought not to be extended."[22] This moral dispute was not a matter that could be settled by "legal right," as the Supreme Court had claimed when it ruled in the *Dred Scott* case that Congress could not prohibit slavery in the territories. Rather, the new president argued, slavery was an issue to be settled in the court of public opinion, through the regular course of elections. Otherwise, "the people will have ceased to be their own rulers, having to that extent practically resigned their government into the hands of an eminent tribunal."[23]

Lincoln's words fell on many deaf ears. Ten weeks earlier, on December 20, 1860, South Carolina had become the first state to take itself out of the Union. Echoing its Ordinance of Nullification, which was issued during the 1832 tariff controversy, South Carolina claimed that secession was each state's constitutional right and declared itself restored to a "separate and independent place among nations." By the time of Lincoln's inauguration, six other Deep South states—Georgia, Alabama, Mississippi, Florida, Louisiana, and Texas—also had seceded. Lincoln, following Jackson's example, used his inaugural address to pronounce the secessionist movement as treasonous: "I hold that in contemplation of universal law and of the Constitution the Union of these states is perpetual . . . , that no state upon its own mere notion can lawfully get out of the Union."[24] The new president declared that he intended to defend and maintain the Union and to enforce federal laws in all the states, just as the Constitution enjoined him to do.

Lincoln's appeal for a peaceful resolution of the slavery controversy was quickly rejected by secessionist leaders.[25] Southern whites were unwilling to distinguish his call for a compromise from outright abolitionism. (They were more than half right: Lincoln's plea for compromise thinly veiled his own moral indignation against slavery.) On March 5, 1861, the day after his inauguration, rebel batteries in South Carolina surrounded Fort Sumter in Charleston harbor, making an outbreak of

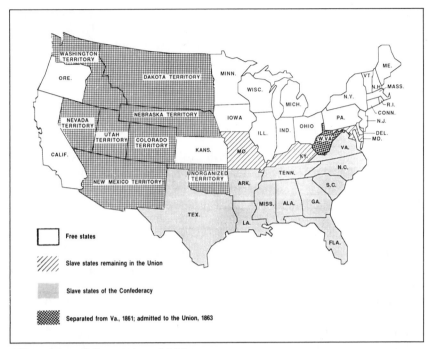

Alignment of the states, 1861.

hostilities inevitable. If the southern states' abandonment of the Union became violent and irrevocable, Lincoln believed that his oath to uphold the Constitution allowed him to take extraordinary measures, including the emancipation of the slaves, if that was what had to be done to restore the Union. As he wrote in an 1864 letter to the Kentuckian A. G. Hodges, domestic rebellion imposed on him the obligation to use "every dispensable means" to preserve "the nation, of which the Constitution was the organic law." It was senseless, Lincoln argued, to obey legal niceties while the very foundation of the law itself—the preservation of the Union—was threatened:

> Was it possible to lose the nation and yet preserve the Constitution? By general law, life and limb must be protected, yet often a limb must be amputated to save a life; but a life is never wisely given to save a limb. I felt that measures otherwise unconstitutional might become lawful by becoming indispensable to the preservation of the nation.[26]

Even more than Lincoln's words, the reaction of the southern states to his election dramatically confirmed the transformation of the presidency that had occurred during the Jacksonian era. Although a few southern leaders counseled against secession, arguing that Lincoln's powers would be limited, such advice meant nothing to people who had witnessed the expansion of executive power since 1829. To be sure, the president's authority was exaggerated in the popular mind. But the myth that the presidency was the all-important organ of the national government was symptomatic of the important precedents that, in effect, had made the office so powerful.

Lincoln's Wartime Measures

Lincoln did not hesitate to resort to "otherwise unconstitutional" measures after the rebels bombarded Fort Sumter on April 12, 1861. From that day until Congress convened on July 4, everything that was done to protect the Union and prosecute the war was done by or on the authority of the president.

The early stages of the Civil War marked the first dramatic example of a chief executive taking the law into his own hands; to that extent Lincoln waged a "presidential war." [27] Some of his actions, such as the mobilization of 75,000 state militia, were clearly within the proper bounds of the president's authority. Yet Lincoln went well beyond these bounds. Hoping to bring the insurrection to a speedy end, he imposed a naval blockade on the southern coast, enlarged the army and navy (adding 18,000 men to the navy and 22,000 to the army), and suspended the writ of *habeas corpus*. This suspension broadly empowered government officials who were acting under the president's authority: they could make arrests without warrant, for offenses undefined in the laws, without having to answer for their actions before the regular courts.

Many of Lincoln's measures raised grave doubts about the constitutionality of his prosecution of the war. The unauthorized enlargement of the military seemed to disregard blatantly Congress's clear constitutional power "to raise and support armies." Indeed, in referring to his proclamation of May 3, 1861, which called for enlistments in the regular army far beyond the existing legal limits, Lincoln frankly admitted that he had overstepped his authority. The president's critics also argued that because the power to suspend the writ of *habeas corpus* during a national emergency is mentioned in Article I of the Constitution, which defines the authority of the legislature, the right to exercise the power belongs to Congress. This was an especially controversial matter— Lincoln's suspension of *habeas corpus* struck at what the presidential scholar Edward Corwin has called "the greatest of all muniments of Anglo-American liberty." [28]

Not surprisingly, the severity of Lincoln's war measures prompted charges of "military dictatorship," even from some Republicans. The president's decision not to call a special session of Congress until Independence Day lent support to these charges.

In 1863, the constitutionality of Lincoln's conduct as president became an issue before the Supreme Court in the *Prize Cases*.[29] Ships had been captured by the Union navy for violating the president's proclamations of April 19 and 27, 1861, which imposed the blockade on the southern coast. In determining whether it was lawful for the navy to obtain these "prizes," the Court in effect decided the whole issue of the war's legality in its early stages. Shipping interests argued that a war begins only when Congress declares war, which it did not do until July 13, 1861. Accordingly, the argument continued, the actions Lincoln took to suppress the southern insurrection before convening the legislature, including the blockade order, were not valid.

Not unexpectedly, considering the urgent circumstances that prevailed in 1863, the Court brushed aside the shipping interests' constitutional claims. It upheld the legality of the war from the moment of Lincoln's blockade proclamation, sustaining completely the president's actions while Congress was in recess. Curiously, in rendering this decision, the Court drew attention to the legislation Congress passed on July 13 to ratify Lincoln's orders, yet refused to declare that the legislation was necessary. "If it were necessary to the technical existence of the war that it should have a legislative sanction," said the Court, "we find it in almost every act passed at the extraordinary session of . . . 1861." [30]

The Supreme Court's decision in the *Prize Cases* supported Lincoln's claim that his actions were justified not only by the threat the southern rebellion posed to public safety but also by his expectation that Congress eventually would approve what he had done. As Lincoln said in his "Special Session Message" to Congress on July 4, 1861:

> These measures, whether strictly legal or not, were ventured upon under what appeared to be a popular demand and a public necessity, trusting then as now, that Congress would readily ratify them. It is believed that nothing has been done beyond the constitutional competency of Congress.[31]

The extraordinary powers that were accorded to Lincoln can be understood only in terms of the extraordinary conditions he confronted. It was of considerable legal significance that, from the standpoint of the government in Washington, the Civil War began as an "insurrection," not a war. [32] Constitutionally, the president may not declare war but may proclaim the existence of a domestic rebellion, or insurrection. Lincoln believed, and Congress and the Supreme Court generally agreed, that organized and violent treasonous activity at home required quick and unilateral presidential action of a sort that might not be permissible in a formally declared war against a foreign nation. An internal rebellion, Lincoln proclaimed, may impose a special burden on the legal process because the execution of the laws is "obstructed . . . by combinations too powerful to be suppressed by the ordinary course of judicial proceedings."[33]

Lincoln's conception of the president's responsibility to suppress treasonous activity justified both the suspension of *habeas corpus* and the establishment of martial law in many areas of the country. Thus, not only did he claim sweeping powers to arrest and detain those who were suspected of rebellious activity, but citizens residing in some peaceful regions of the country were tried before military tribunals. As the Civil War progressed, Lincoln proclaimed even more comprehensive powers for the military authorities, without any apparent thought of seeking authorization from Congress.[34] For example, on September 24, 1862, an executive order declared that all rebels and insurgents and all persons who discouraged enlistment, resisted the draft, or were guilty of any disloyal practice were subject to martial law and to trial by either courts-martial or military commissions.[35]

The Supreme Court eventually challenged Lincoln's more far-reaching martial law measures, although not until the Civil War was over. In the case of *Ex Parte Milligan,* which was decided in 1866, the Supreme Court declared illegal the use of military tribunals to try citizens in districts that were remote from hostile armies.[36] Lamdin P. Milligan had been arrested on October 5, 1864, by order of Gen. Alvin P. Hovey, the Union commander at Indianapolis. Along with certain associates, Milligan was brought before a military commission and convicted of conspiracy to release rebel prisoners forcibly and march them into Kentucky and Missouri, where they could rejoin the Confederate army. The military commission sentenced Milligan to be hanged, but the case was brought to the Supreme Court on appeal.

In his opinion for the Court, Justice David Davis noted the significance of deciding the *Milligan* case after the war was over: "*Now* that the public safety is assured, this question, as well as others, can be discussed and decided without passion or the admixture of any element not required to form a legal judgement."[37] The Court proceeded to declare Milligan's trial and conviction by a military commission illegal, ruling that the constitutional guarantees of a fair trial could not be set aside merely because a state of insurrection existed. Rather, conditions had to be so grave as to close the civil courts and depose the civil administration. Martial law, the Court stated, "could never exist where the Courts are open" but had to be "confined to the locality of actual war."[38]

The *Milligan* case diluted somewhat the legal significance of the wartime precedents that were established by Lincoln's presidency. But the powers and prerogatives that Lincoln assumed during the Civil War demonstrated conclusively, as Corwin has written, "that in meeting the domestic problems that a great war inevitably throws up an indefinite power must be attributed to the president to take emergency measures." [39]

Although Lincoln took extreme measures, neither Congress nor the Court restrained him very effectively. Congress did challenge his suspension of *habeas corpus* in an 1863 statute, which directed that prisoners be released unless they were indicted in a civil court. Yet the law was ineffective. It did not put an end to extralegal imprisonments, nor did it succeed in shifting control of punishment from the military to the civilian tribunals. Similarly, while the war was still in progress the Supreme Court refused to interfere with the operation of a military commission in a case that was similar to *Milligan*.[40] In legal terms, the Civil War stands out as an exceptional period in American history, "a time when constitutional restraints did not fully operate and the rule of law largely broke down."[41]

Although Lincoln's grasping of the reins of power caused him to be denounced as a dictator, other aspects of his leadership demonstrated more obviously his faithfulness to the purposes for which the Union and the Constitution had been ordained.[42] The powers that Lincoln claimed were far-reaching, offering ample opportunity for abuse. But his exercise of these powers was remarkably restrained. In most cases a short military detention was followed by release or parole. As for martial law, military commissions almost always were used to try citizens in military areas for military crimes. Cases that, like *Milligan*, involved military trials for nonmilitary crimes in peaceful areas were few. Finally, Lincoln did nothing to obstruct the conduct of free and fair elections during the war.

Thus, the Constitution, although stretched severely, was not subverted during the Civil War. It is a "striking fact," as Randall has noted, "that no life was forfeited and no sentence of fine and imprisonment [was] carried out in any judicial prosecution for treason arising out of the 'rebellion.' "[43] Lincoln was driven by circumstances to exercise power more arbitrarily than any other president. Yet he was criticized for leniency as often as for severity.

The Emancipation Proclamation

Lincoln's concern with maintaining the integrity of the Constitution was revealed most clearly in his cautious handling of emancipation. The president had argued consistently that to abolish slavery where it existed was beyond the constitutional powers of Congress. Yet he also believed that the president's duties as commander in chief allowed him to grasp in war much that was forbidden in peace.[44] Even so, the celebrated Proclamation of Emancipation, which Lincoln issued on

Following the precedent established by James Polk in the Mexican War, Lincoln often gave highly detailed strategic and tactical orders to his field commanders.

January 1, 1863, was a more limited, cautious measure than his cabinet and the so-called Radical Republicans in Congress had hoped it would be. The proclamation did not proclaim a comprehensive and sweeping policy of emancipation; indeed, Lincoln earlier had declared unauthorized and void the declarations of two of his generals that slaves in captured territory were free. Instead Lincoln, who based his proclamation solely upon the "war power" and regarded it as "a fit and necessary war measure for suppressing rebellion," abolished slavery only in the unconquered parts of the Confederacy.[45]

As an act based on "military necessity," the Proclamation of Emancipation had an important practical effect. Emancipation struck at the very heart of the South's war effort by disrupting its labor force and by converting part of that labor force into a northern military asset. More than 100,000 former slaves became Union soldiers. "[S]ome of the commanders of our armies in the field who have given us our most important successes, believe the emancipation policy, and the use of colored troops, constitute the heaviest blow yet dealt to the rebellion," Lincoln wrote to the former mayor of Springfield, Illinois, James C. Conkling, in August 1863.[46] To be sure, there was grumbling and dissent by some northern soldiers, who said they had enlisted to fight for the Union, not for the "nigger." But most soldiers understood and accepted the policy. As a colonel from Indiana put it, whatever their opinion of slavery and blacks, his men "desire to destroy everything that gives the rebels strength." Therefore, "this army will sustain the emancipation proclamation and enforce it with the bayonet." [47]

Although emancipation became a critical part of Union war strategy, the proclamation neither condemned slavery outright nor guaranteed that it would be abolished after the war was over. Lincoln later vetoed the Wade-Davis Bill of 1864, which included the sort of sweeping emancipation and reconstruction measures that he still believed the federal government had no constitutional right to impose on the states. Yet the president seems to have realized that it was unthinkable to return blacks to slavery. When urged to do so by some northern Democrats, who argued that the coupling of emancipation with the Union was the only stumbling block to peace negotiations with the Confederacy, Lincoln countered that "as a matter of policy, to announce such a purpose, would ruin the Union cause itself." Why would black soldiers risk their lives for the Union, he asked, "with the full notice of our purpose to betray them?" The morality of such an act was even more troubling. If he were "to return to slavery the black warriors," Lincoln stated plaintively, "I should be damned in time and eternity for so doing." [48]

In fact, Lincoln had long believed that the Union and slavery were incompatible and that the nation was threaded together by a set of principles that required equality before the law. Those who signed the Declaration of Independence "did not mean to assert the obvious untruth, that all were actually enjoying that equality, nor yet, that they were about to confer it immediately upon them," Lincoln had said in his criticism of the *Dred Scott* decision. "They meant simply to declare the *right*, so that *enforcement* of it might follow as fast as circumstances should permit." [49] The Civil War created the circumstances—indeed, the necessity—to pursue a course of emancipation. Thus, Lincoln's presidential reconstruction policy, which he announced in December 1863, offered pardon and amnesty to white southerners who took an oath of allegiance both to the Union and to all wartime policies concerning slavery and emancipation. Reconstructed governments sponsored by Lincoln in Louisiana, Arkansas, and Tennessee abolished slavery in the Union-controlled areas of those states even before the war ended. [50]

Still, Lincoln was too respectful of procedural regularity and formal legality to abolish slavery by executive fiat. Instead, he worked to achieve abolition by constitutional amendment. In 1864, Lincoln took the lead in persuading the Republican convention to adopt a platform calling for an amendment to prohibit slavery anywhere in the United States. Because slavery was "hostile to the principles of republican government, justice, and national safety," declared the platform, Republicans vowed to accomplish its "utter and complete extirpation from the soil of the Republic." Full emancipation had thereby become an end as well as a means of Union victory.[51] But it was accomplished through regular constitutional procedures—in 1864 and 1865 Lincoln pressed the Thirteenth Amendment through a reluctant Congress. The ratification of the amendment in 1865 eliminated slavery "within the United States or any place subject to their protection."

Thus, Lincoln's disregard for legal restrictions on the war power went hand in hand with a deep and abiding commitment to the principles and institutions of the American Constitution. Lincoln did not become the tyrant he had warned against a quarter-century earlier in the Lyceum speech; instead, he invested his talent and ambition in strengthening the law by rooting it more firmly in a moral set of beliefs. As Lincoln said in his Gettysburg Address, the great task of the war was that the "nation—under God, shall have a new birth of freedom." [52]

The Election of 1864

As further evidence against the argument that Lincoln conducted the war in a dictatorial manner, full and free party competition continued in the election of 1864.[53] The stakes in this contest were great. Democrats charged that the war was hopeless: the Union army lost battles and the Confederacy persisted in rebellion because Republicans were elevating blacks over whites and the nation over the states and individuals. With enthusiastic support from the entire convention, the 1864 Democratic platform declared

> that after four years of failure to restore the Union by the experiment of War, during which under a pretense of a military necessity of war power higher than the Constitution, the Constitution itself has been disregarded in every part, and public liberty and private right alike trodden down, and the material prosperity of the country essentially impaired, justice, humanity, liberty, and the public welfare demand that immediate efforts be made for a cessation of hostilities, with a view of an ultimate convention of the States, or other peaceable means, to the end that, at the earliest practical moment, peace may be restored on the basis of the Federal Union of the states.[54]

Although the Democratic candidate, Gen. George B. McClellan, eventually disavowed the party's "peace before reunion" plank, he opposed the Emancipation Proclamation and wanted the Union to continue the fight only until the pre-secession status quo was restored. Thus, the Republicans held "the reasonable conviction," the historian Harold Hyman has written, "that a Democratic triumph would mean Confederate independence, the perpetuation of slavery, and the further fragmentation of the dis-United States." [55]

Lincoln and other Republican leaders believed that a Democratic victory was likely in 1864. Not only was there widespread public opposition to Lincoln's conduct of the war, but the custom of the previous three decades had been for the president to serve only one term. Since Jackson's victory in 1832, no president had been reelected— indeed, with the exception of Martin Van Buren in 1840, none even was nominated by his party for a second term. Six days before the Democratic convention, Lincoln was resigned to defeat, hoping only to defuse pressures for an immediate compromise with the Confederacy. "This morning, as for some days past," he admitted privately, "it seems exceedingly probable that the Administration will not be reelected. Then it will be my duty to so cooperate with the President-elect, as to save the Union between the election and inauguration; as he will have secured his election on such ground that he cannot possibly save it afterwards." [56]

In allowing the 1864 election to take place, the historian Herman Belz has argued, Lincoln "accepted a risk and permitted his power to be threatened in a way that no dictator, constitutional or not, would have tolerated." [57] During the campaign, rumors spread that, if defeated, Lincoln would refuse to accept the verdict of the people and instead would attempt to "ruin the government." Responding to these rumors at a public gathering in October, Lincoln stated that he was "struggling to maintain the government, not overthrow it." He then pledged that whoever was elected in November would be duly installed as president on March 4, 1865. Such a course was "due to the people," Lincoln said, "both on principle and under the Constitution." [58]

Even at the time, Lincoln's commitment to popular government could not be dismissed as empty rhetoric. The commitment had been expressed throughout the war in his support for the rights of free press and free conscience. Despite some notable and unfortunate exceptions, anti-Lincoln and anti-Union organs were, as a rule, left undisturbed. [59] "By all contemporary standards," Hyman has asserted, "the 1864 elections were free, and by contemporary standards fair as well." [60]

Seeing the alternatives clearly, the American people gave Lincoln 55 percent of the popular vote and an overwhelming electoral college majority of 212-21. Gen. William Tecumseh Sherman's timely capture of Atlanta and a spirited and effective Republican campaign, which accused the Democrats of seeking to return to the "hopeless imbecility and rapid progress of national dissolution," turned the tide in Lincoln's favor. Some Democrats charged fraud and corruption, but McClellan himself granted that Lincoln's claim to a second term was untainted. "For my country's sake I deplore the result," he reflected in a private statement, "but the people have decided with their eyes open." [61]

The election of 1864 was characterized by a remarkably spirited, even strident campaign in the midst of military hostilities, "adding not a little," as Lincoln granted after the election, "to the strain" caused by the civil insurrection. But as the president told a crowd of supporters who gathered at the White House to celebrate his victory on November 10, 1864, the election was necessary: "We cannot have free government without elections; and if rebellion could force us to forgo or postpone a national election, it might fairly claim to have already conquered and ruined us." The free and open presidential campaign, Lincoln concluded, "demonstrated that a people's government can sustain a national election in the midst of a great civil war. Until now, it has not been known to the world that this was a possibility." [62]

These were revealing words, for the principal task of Lincoln's presidency had been to demonstrate that a republican government could endure even a violent national struggle that threatened its survival. As Lincoln remarked on one occasion, "It has long been a grave question whether any government, not too strong for the liberties of its people, can be strong enough to maintain its existence in great emergencies." [63] His conduct of the Civil War seemed to answer this question in the affirmative. As Randall wrote, "In a legal study of the war the two most significant facts are perhaps these: the wide extent of the war powers; and, in contrast to that, the manner in which the men in authority were nevertheless controlled by the American people's sense of constitutional government." [64]

Lincoln's Legacy

The accomplishments of Abraham Lincoln's presidency could not have occurred without the Civil War. Had the South accepted Lincoln's initial call for a peaceful, gradual resolution of the slavery controversy, his extraordinary leadership probably never would have materialized. The Republican party he represented in the 1860 presidential election consisted mostly of former Whigs, who were dedicated to correcting the executive aggrandizement of the Jacksonians. Much of what Lincoln accomplished in consolidating presidential power during the Civil War, in fact, surprised his Republican colleagues in Congress, who, as described in the next chapter, acted forcefully to weaken the presidency after his assassination in 1865.

Lincoln, too, was respectful of Republican principles. Even in war, he did not abandon entirely the Whig view of executive power that he had expressed in the 1830s and 1840s. Consistent with this view, Lincoln denied that the president could veto bills merely because he disagreed with them; only legislation that he regarded as unconstitutional could be returned to Congress.[65] As the postwar Republican reformer Carl Schurz wrote of Lincoln:

With scrupulous care he endeavored, even under the most trying circumstances, to remain strictly within the constitutional limits of his authority; and whenever the boundary became indistinct, or when the dangers of the situation forced him to cross it, he was equally careful to mark his acts as exceptional measures, justifiable only by the imperative necessities of the civil war, so that they might not pass into history as precedents for similar acts in time of peace.[66]

The powers that Lincoln was willing to accumulate as commander in chief during the Civil War freed him to use the executive office energetically and to deal with the problem of slavery resolutely. At the same time, the end of hostilities led to a counterrevolution of sorts, which showed that Lincoln's stewardship, remarkable as it was, did not solve the problem of race in the United States. Nor did it expand executive power in a form that could survive the assault on it during the Reconstruction era. "By 1875," the political scientist Theodore Lowi has observed, "you would not know there had been a war or a Lincoln." [67]

Nevertheless, Lincoln and the Civil War made a lasting imprint on political life in the United States. Lincoln gave new meaning to the national community, investing it with a sense of purpose, even a religiosity, that marked a major change in the relationship between power and liberty. James McPherson has drawn on Isaiah Berlin's distinction between negative and positive liberty to explain the transformation wrought by the Lincoln presidency.[68] Negative liberty describes the intention of the original Constitution and the Bill of Rights—it requires, to use Jefferson's phrase, a "wall of separation" between government and society. Understood in this way, liberty is freedom from undue government interference.

Lincoln's indictment of slavery, and the changes in the Constitution that followed from it, brought forth a new, more positive view of liberty, in which the government had the affirmative obligation to ensure equality under the law. Lincoln's celebration of the declaration was embodied in the Civil War amendments to the Constitution, which abolished slavery (the Thirteenth Amendment), promised to blacks the right to vote (the Fifteenth Amendment), and, most important, guaranteed to all Americans the "privilege and immunities" of citizenship, "due process," and the "equal protection of the law" (the Fourteenth Amendment). These amendments changed the course of constitutional development in the United States. As McPherson has observed:

Eleven of the first twelve amendments to the Constitution limited the powers of the national government; six of the next seven dramatically expanded those powers at the expense of the states and individuals. In place of the "shall nots" of ten of the first eleven amendments, the six postwar amendments included the phrase "Congress *shall have the power* to enforce this article."[69]

The immediate consequences of this constitutional change were limited, to be sure. Lincoln's understanding of the equality that was guaranteed by the declaration was modest when compared to the collectivist aspirations of twentieth-century reform presidents such as Theodore Roosevelt, Franklin Roosevelt, and Lyndon Johnson. The reforms of the Civil War were tightly bounded by the nation's long-standing commitment to private property, limited government, and administrative decentralization. Lincoln's contribution was to establish the moral obligation of the national government to ensure equal opportunity. The Union's struggle, Lincoln told the special session of Congress in July 1861, was to maintain that "form and substance of government, whose leading object is, to elevate the condition of men—to lift artificial weights from all shoulders—to clear the paths of laudable pursuit for all—to afford all, an unfettered start, and a fair chance, in the race of life." [70]

Lincoln's words transcended emancipation and the Civil War. As president, he taught Americans that they were not merely a people dedicated to the unhindered pursuit of material satisfaction; they also were part of a moral community with mutual obligations. That lesson would never be entirely lost. Thus, Lincoln's presidency, which was almost entirely consumed by the necessities of war, revealed, as Charles Sumner proclaimed in his "Eulogy on Abraham Lincoln," that "ideas are always more than battles." [71]

Notes

1. Robert K. Murray and Tim H. Blessing, "The Presidential Performance Study: A Progress Report," *Journal of American History* 70:3 (December 1983): 535-555.
2. For a critical examination of the view that Lincoln's presidency was one of "constitutional dictatorship," see Herman Belz, *Lincoln and the Constitution: The Dictatorship Question Reconsidered* (Fort Wayne, Ind.: Louis A. Warren Lincoln Library and Museum, 1984).
3. James G. Randall, *Constitutional Problems under Lincoln,* rev. ed. (Urbana: University of Illinois Press, 1951), 514; see also Edward S. Corwin, *The President: Office and Powers, 1787-1957,* 4th ed. (New York: New York University Press, 1957), 23-24.
4. Randall, *Constitutional Problems under Lincoln,* 30-47; and "Lincoln in the Role of Dictator," *South Atlantic Quarterly,* 28 (July 1929): 236-252. See also Belz, *Lincoln and the Constitution,* 5-6.
5. J. B. McClure, ed., *Abraham Lincoln's Speeches* (Chicago: Rhodes and McClure, 1891), 21.
6. Ibid., 22.
7. Corwin, *The President: Office and Powers,* 451; Wilfred E. Binkley, *President and Congress* (New York: Knopf, 1947), 110.
8. Garry Wills, *Lincoln at Gettysburg: The Words That Remade America*

(New York: Simon and Schuster, 1992), 145 (Wills's emphasis).

9. James M. McPherson, *Abraham Lincoln and the Second American Revolution* (New York: Oxford University Press, 1991), 41; Lincoln to Greeley, August 22, 1862, *The Collected Works of Abraham Lincoln,* ed. Roy P. Basler (New Brunswick, N.J.: Rutgers University Press, 1953), 5:388.

10. Undated fragment, written in late 1860 or early 1861, *New Letters and Papers of Lincoln,* ed. Paul M. Angle (Boston: Houghton Mifflin, 1930), 241-242. Lincoln's reference was to Proverbs 25:11: "A word fitly spoken is like apples of gold in pictures of silver."

11. Allan Nevins, *The Emergence of Lincoln: Prologue to Civil War, 1859-1861* (New York: Scribner's, 1950), 233-239.

12. Lincoln to Speed, August 24, 1855, *The Political Thought of Abraham Lincoln,* ed. Richard N. Current (Indianapolis: Bobbs-Merrill, 1967), 80.

13. McClure, *Abraham Lincoln's Speeches,* 127.

14. Current, *Political Thought of Abraham Lincoln,* 95 (Lincoln's emphasis).

15. Basler, *Collected Works of Abraham Lincoln* 4:191.

16. Charles Sumner, *The Promises of the Declaration of Independence,* Eulogy on Abraham Lincoln (Boston: Ticknor and Fields, 1865), 9.

17. Nevins, *The Emergence of Lincoln,* 234.

18. Stephen B. Oates, *Malice Toward None: The Life of Abraham Lincoln* (New York: Harper and Row, 1977), 224.

19. Ibid., 218.

20. James D. Richardson, ed., *Messages and Papers of the Presidents,* 20 vols. (New York: Bureau of National Literature, 1897), 7:3206.

21. Ibid.

22. Ibid. 7:3211 (Lincoln's emphasis).

23. Ibid. 7:3210.

24. Ibid. 7:3208.

25. For an account of Lincoln's views on slavery and the Constitution, see Robert K. Faulkner, "Lincoln and the Constitution," in *Revival of Constitutionalism,* ed. James Muller (Lincoln: University of Nebraska Press, 1988).

26. John G. Nicolay and John Hay, eds., *Complete Works of Abraham Lincoln* (Harrogate, Tenn.: Lincoln Memorial University, 1894), 10:66.

27. Randall, *Constitutional Problems under Lincoln,* 51.

28. Corwin, *The President: Office and Powers,* 62.

29. *Prize Cases,* 2 Black 635 (1863). For a discussion of this case, see Randall, *Constitutional Problems under Lincoln,* 52-59.

30. *Prize Cases,* 67 U.S. 635 at 670.

31. Richardson, *Messages and Papers of the Presidents* 7:3225.

32. For a discussion of the importance of the legal distinction between an insurrection and a war against an independent nation, see Randall, *Constitutional Problems under Lincoln,* 59-73.

33. "Proclamation of April 15, 1861," in Richardson, *Messages and Papers of the Presidents* 7:3299.

34. Corwin, *The President: Office and Powers,* 145-147.

35. Richardson, *Messages and Papers of the Presidents* 7:3299.

36. *Ex Parte Milligan,* 4 Wall. 2 (1866). For a discussion of this case, see Randall, *Constitutional Problems under Lincoln,* 180-186.

37. *Ex Parte Milligan,* 4 Wall. 2 at 109 (emphasis in original).

38. Ibid., at 127.

39. Corwin, *The President: Office and Powers,* 234.

40. See the *Vallandigham* case (1 Wall. 243), decided in 1864, which found

acceptable the arrest and sentencing of a prominent antiwar agitator, who was detained for a speech that he gave in Mount Vernon, Ohio.

41. Randall, *Constitutional Problems under Lincoln*, 521.
42. Belz, *Lincoln and the Constitution*, 24.
43. Randall, *Constitutional Problems under Lincoln*, 91.
44. For a discussion of Lincoln's policy of emancipation, see Faulkner, "Lincoln and the Constitution."
45. Richardson, *Messages and Papers of the Presidents* 7:3359.
46. Lincoln to James C. Conkling, August 26, 1863, Basler, *Collected Works of Abraham Lincoln* 6:408-409.
47. Cited in McPherson, *Abraham Lincoln and the Second American Revolution*, 34-35.
48. Lincoln to Charles D. Robinson, August 17, 1864, and Lincoln interview with Alexander W. Randall and Joseph T. Mills, August 19, 1864, in Basler, *Collected Works of Abraham Lincoln* 7:499-500 and 7:506-507, respectively.
49. Current, *Political Thought of Abraham Lincoln*, 88-89 (Lincoln's emphasis).
50. McPherson, *Abraham Lincoln and the Second American Revolution*, 86.
51. Ibid.
52. Basler, *Collected Works of Abraham Lincoln* 7:23.
53. Belz, *Lincoln and the Constitution*, 15.
54. "Democratic Platform of 1864," in *History of American Presidential Elections*, ed. Arthur Schlesinger, Jr., and Fred I. Israel (New York: Chelsea, 1971), 2:1179-1180.
55. Harold M. Hyman, "Election of 1864," in ibid. 2:1167; see also Lord Charnwood, *Abraham Lincoln* (Garden City, N.Y.: Garden City Publishing Company, 1917), 414-415.
56. Quoted in Hyman, "Election of 1864," 1170.
57. Belz, *Lincoln and the Constitution*, 16.
58. Nicolay and Hay, *Complete Works of Abraham Lincoln* 10:244.
59. Randall, *Constitutional Problems under Lincoln*, chap. 9.
60. Hyman, "Election of 1864," 1175.
61. Quoted in ibid., 1175.
62. Nicolay and Hay, *Complete Works of Abraham Lincoln* 10:263-264.
63. Ibid. 10:263.
64. Randall, *Constitutional Problems under Lincoln*, 522.
65. Belz, *Lincoln and the Constitution*, 12. Lincoln took this position in refusing to veto a bill reducing fees paid to the marshal of the District of Columbia; see Basler, *Collected Works of Abraham Lincoln* 7:414-415.
66. Carl Schurz, "Abraham Lincoln," in *Abraham Lincoln*, ed. Carl Schurz (New York: Chautauqua Press, 1891), 72.
67. Lowi is cited in Michael Les Benedict, "The Constitution of the Lincoln Presidency and the Republican Era," in *The Constitution and the American Presidency*, ed. Martin Fausold and Alan Shank (Albany: State University of New York Press, 1991), 45.
68. McPherson, *Abraham Lincoln and the Second American Revolution*, 137; and Berlin, "Two Concepts of Liberty," in Isaiah Berlin, *Four Essays on Liberty* (New York: Oxford University Press, 1969).
69. McPherson, *Abraham Lincoln and the Second American Revolution*, 138 (McPherson's emphasis).
70. Current, *Political Thought of Abraham Lincoln*, 187-188.
71. Sumner, *Promises of the Declaration of Independence*, 40.

CHAPTER 7

The Reaction against Presidential Power: Andrew Johnson to William McKinley

Andrew Johnson, who was elected vice president with Abraham Lincoln in 1864, faced extraordinarily difficult circumstances when he succeeded to the presidency on April 15, 1865, the morning after Lincoln was shot by the Confederate zealot, John Wilkes Booth, at Ford's Theater in Washington. The Civil War had established the permanence of the Union and had emancipated the slaves, but with the end of hostilities in the spring of 1865 came the enormous problems of Reconstruction. How were the Confederate states to rejoin the Union? What would be the status of the emancipated slaves?

Lincoln and a majority of the Republicans in Congress agreed that the major objectives of Reconstruction were to destroy slavery and to deny political power to the leaders of the Confederacy. They disagreed, however, about how harsh Reconstruction policies had to be in order to plant liberty in soil tainted by slavery. Lincoln wanted to restore the Union as quickly as possible, without imposing extensive conditions for readmission on the rebellious states. The "Radicals" of his party, however, led by the Massachusetts senator Charles Sumner, believed that high-ranking Confederates should be punished severely for treason, southern states should not be granted full membership in the Union until they were thoroughly reconstructed and their loyalty was ensured, and blacks should be guaranteed the full rights of citizenship.

The conflict within the Republican party over Reconstruction remained unresolved as the war drew to an end. In 1863, Lincoln had promulgated a lenient program of reunification for the three Confederate states that already had been conquered by the Union army— Louisiana, Arkansas, and Tennessee. According to his plan, if even 10 percent of a state's voters took an oath of allegiance to the United States, the state could form a government and elect members of Congress. The Republican-dominated Congress, declaring that Reconstruction was a legislative, not an executive, function, rejected these terms as too lenient and refused to seat the newly elected legislators from the three southern states.

Congress's Reconstruction program was the Wade-Davis bill, which disenfranchised all high-ranking Confederates, stipulated that 50 percent of the voters in a rebel state must take a loyalty oath before elections could be held, and made the abolition of slavery a condition for readmission to the Union. Lincoln's pocket veto of this legislation in July 1864, accompanied by a message in which he argued that reunification should be an executive function, provoked the Republican leaders in Congress to issue the Wade-Davis Manifesto. The manifesto—a bold attack on Lincoln's Reconstruction program and a defense of the "paramount" authority of Congress—was reminiscent of the Whigs' assaults on Andrew Jackson.[1] Lincoln's landslide reelection in November took the wind out of the Radical Republicans' sails, but their strength was restored after he was assassinated. As the historian Wilfred E. Binkley has written:

> To those who had applauded the furious blast of the Wade-Davis Manifesto against Lincoln only to see its effect nullified by the triumphant re-election of the President it must have now seemed as if fate, through the assassin's bullet, had at last delivered the government into their hands. Their glee was but ill concealed.[2]

The Radicals initially had confidence in Johnson. Before Lincoln appointed him as military governor of Tennessee in early 1862 (a post he held until his nomination as Lincoln's running mate in 1864), then-senator Johnson had been one of them, serving on the Radical-dominated congressional Joint Committee on the Conduct of the War. This committee criticized Lincoln's wartime initiatives constantly, often charging that the president had usurped the rightful powers of Congress. Only a few hours after Lincoln died, the committee paid a visit to Johnson. Its chair, Sen. Benjamin Wade, the cosponsor of the Wade-Davis bill and manifesto, declared, "Johnson we have faith in you. By the gods, there will be no trouble now in running the government!"[3]

The Radicals' faith was short-lived. Johnson kept Lincoln's cabinet, spurning the Radicals' advice "to get rid of the last vestige of Lincolnism." Then, without consulting Congress, he ordered Lincoln's Reconstruction policies into effect in a series of executive proclamations during the late spring and summer of 1865. Congressional Republicans were furious but unable to respond. Congress was not scheduled to convene until December, and Johnson refused to call it into special session before then.

Johnson's bold, unilateral actions no doubt were influenced by the success that Lincoln repeatedly had had in executing major policy decisions while Congress was in recess, leaving the legislature with little choice but to ratify his *faits accomplis* when it returned to Washington.[4] But Johnson lacked both Lincoln's political skill and the latitude that the general sense of wartime urgency allowed. Congressional Republicans moved to establish their dominance over policy as soon as the regular session of Congress convened in December 1865.

Reconstruction and the Assault on Executive Authority

Johnson's struggle with Congress was aggravated by the sharp differences of principle that distinguished him from most Republicans. In contrast to Lincoln, who stood for strengthening the national government's authority to secure equality before the law, Johnson challenged Reconstruction legislation in the interest of preserving the rights of the states. To be sure, he was a strong defender of the Union; during the secession crisis of 1860-1861, Johnson was the only southern senator not to join the rebels. But in background and belief he was also a Jacksonian Democrat. Although he gave up that affiliation to join Lincoln's "Union" ticket in the 1864 presidential campaign, Johnson was never very comfortable in the Republican party.[5]

The new president's Jacksonian commitment to states' rights inclined him to oppose not just the Radicals but the moderate Republicans as well. Thus, in February 1866 Johnson vetoed a bill, sponsored by the moderate Republican senator Lyman Trumbull of Illinois, to continue the Freedman's Bureau. He argued in his message to Congress that in time of peace it would be unconstitutional to sustain the agency, which had been created during the war to promote the welfare of southern blacks. In vetoing Trumbull's bill, Johnson was challenging not just the Radicals but every Republican in Congress.

The ties between Johnson and the Republican party were broken irrevocably about a month later when he vetoed the Civil Rights Act, which, like the Freedman's Bureau, enjoyed unanimous support from congressional Republicans. This bill, parts of which were included in the Fourteenth Amendment, declared African-Americans to be citizens and bestowed on all persons born in the United States (except American Indians) an equal right to make and enforce contracts, to sue and be witnesses in the courts, to own land and other property, and to enjoy equal protection under the law.

Had Johnson supported the Civil Rights Act, he would have satisfied the North's desire to protect blacks in the South. Radical

Republicans considered any Reconstruction policy that did not impose some degree of black suffrage on the southern states as a condition for readmission tantamount to the perpetuation of "an Oligarchy of the skin." "At this moment," Sumner proclaimed in his eulogy on Lincoln of June 1865, "all turns on the colored suffrage in the rebel states." But although Lincoln had supported emancipation in principle, he had doubts about requiring immediate universal male suffrage.[6] His position was shared by moderate Republicans who did not insist on immediate black suffrage as long as policies were adopted that recognized, and initiated a movement toward, the fulfillment of the rights of African-Americans as full citizens.

Johnson's veto of the Civil Rights Act united both the party and public opinion against him. On April 6 the Senate voted 33-15 to repass the bill; three days later the House did the same, 122-41. Congress's passage of the Civil Rights Act over Johnson's veto was a landmark in constitutional development—the first time in history that the legislature had overridden a presidential veto on an important issue. The override was equally important as a political event: Congress, not the president, was now the master of Reconstruction.[7]

Johnson's staunch opposition to a national Reconstruction policy was motivated not only by ideology but also by his belief in the inherent inferiority of African-Americans. As a defender of the Union and a political enemy of the southern landed aristocracy, he supported the abolition of slavery. "This is your country as well as anybody else's," Johnson told a regiment of black soldiers that had gathered to pay him tribute in October 1865. "This country is founded upon the principle of equality."[8] Yet the president, who was born and spent the first seventeen years of his life in North Carolina, sometimes displayed a visceral attachment to white supremacy. "There is grave doubt," the historians LaWanda Cox and John Cox have written, that Johnson's "private views were ever completely emancipated from his heritage of Southern racial attitudes." Indeed, the president's private secretary recorded in 1868 that Johnson "has at times exhibited a morbid distress and feeling against negroes."[9]

Nevertheless, ideology and politics played a bigger role in molding Johnson's Reconstruction policy than did racial prejudice. In truth, Johnson's views on race relations were not inconsistent with those of the vast majority of whites of his time. Any attempt to impose civil rights on the South, he believed, not only would be unconstitutional but also would alienate southerners and, in all likelihood, most people in the North, where only five states in New England, with minuscule minority populations, gave blacks an unqualified right to vote. Johnson calculated that leaving the question of racial equality to the states would, at the end of the day, satisfy everyone but African-Americans, who scarcely counted politically, and the Radicals, whose principles and politics he abhorred.[10]

The midterm election of 1866 was widely regarded as a referendum on the question of which branch should control Reconstruction. The verdict of the voters was overwhelmingly in the Radical Republicans' favor. Disgusted when all the southern states that had been reconstructed by presidential proclamation rejected the Fourteenth Amendment, the voters routed Johnson's followers and gave the Radicals firm control over both houses of Congress. Particularly damaging to Johnson was that he had encouraged the southern states to reject the amendment.[11]

Spurred on by the mandate of the 1866 elections, Congress passed a series of measures in 1867 that not only deprived Johnson of his control over Reconstruction but also stripped his office of the authority to conduct the affairs of the executive department.

The Military Reconstruction Act replaced the southern state governments that Johnson had approved with military districts led by military commanders, who were granted almost complete independence from presidential direction.[12] Congress buttressed the commanders' autonomy by tacking onto the 1867 army appropriation bill riders that required the president and the secretary of war to transmit their orders through General of the Army Ulysses S. Grant and forbade the president to relieve, suspend, or transfer Grant without the Senate's consent. This direct challenge to the president's authority as commander in chief was instigated by Secretary of War Edwin Stanton, who, along with Grant, conspired with Republican congressional leaders to exclude Johnson from the administration of Congress's Reconstruction program.

Johnson vetoed the Military Reconstruction Act, charging that it would create an "absolute despotism" [13] in the South, and protested the riders that Congress attached to the army appropriation bill by claiming that they were "out of place in an appropriation act" and "deprived the President of his constitutional functions as Commander-in-Chief of the Army." [14] Congress overrode the veto and ignored the protest. Then, to prevent Johnson from reasserting control of Reconstruction, Congress arranged to stay in session permanently. This action both nullified the president's constitutional privilege to pocket veto legislation that was passed with fewer than ten days remaining in a session of Congress and usurped the president's authority to call (or not call) Congress into special session.[15]

Having stripped Johnson of his ability to influence legislation and the conduct of military government in the South, Congress next divested the president of his control over the personnel of the executive branch. In March 1867 Congress overrode Johnson's veto and passed the Tenure of Office Act, which prohibited the president from removing any Senate-confirmed official without first obtaining the Senate's approval. The act reversed the First Congress's decision in 1789 to uphold the president's authority to remove executive officials, which had prevailed without serious challenge for nearly eight decades. But the struggle against Johnson had reached the point where neither settled precedents nor explicit constitutional proscriptions would deter Radical Republicans any longer from attacking the rights of the executive.

By the spring of 1867 Johnson was nearly bereft of political power. He was helpless to block any legislation that Congress saw fit to pass. His only recourse was to appeal directly to public opinion. Thomas Jefferson and, especially, Jackson had sought to establish closer ties between the presidency and the public, but they had worked through the party organization to do so. Similarly, Lincoln had relied heavily on the Republican party to mobilize support for the war effort and his Reconstruction policies.[16] But Johnson, who had no party, decided to go over the heads of the party and congressional leaders, hoping that public rhetoric would restore his severely weakened presidency.

His was a vain hope. Johnson fancied himself a good orator, but, especially when goaded by hecklers, his forceful attacks on Congress were prone to excess. On the evening of February 22, 1866, Washington's birthday, he told a crowd that had marched to the White House to demonstrate its support for his veto of the Civil Rights Act that new rebels had appeared in the country, this time in the North. These men, the Radical leaders in Congress, "had assumed nearly all the powers of government" and had prevented the restoration of the Union. Johnson charged Thaddeus Stevens, the Pennsylvania representative who led the Radicals in the House, and Sumner, the president's major opponent in the Senate, with being just as traitorous as the leaders of the Confederacy.[17]

Johnson's rhetoric backfired. The vast majority of northerners were outraged and ashamed as they read, or read about, his speeches, most of which were closely patterned after the Washington's Birthday harangue. The public resented the attack on Stevens and Sumner, who, whatever else they might have been, were no traitors.[18] Moreover, the very purpose of Johnson's speeches—to rouse public opinion in support of his policies—was considered illegitimate, a form of demagogy that was beneath the dignity of the presidential office. The use of rhetoric by presidents to sway public opinion became acceptable, even expected, in the twentieth century. But during the nineteenth century presidential speechmaking of this sort was regarded as a violation of constitutional norms.[19]

Most of Johnson's speeches were delivered during a tour through the North, which he described as a "swing around the circle." The press quickly seized upon this expression as an object of derision and a subject for political cartoons. As the historian David Miller Dewitt has described the national reaction to Johnson's "swing":

> His want of dignity ..., his insensibility to the decorum due to his high office, his eagerness to exchange repartee with any opponent no matter how low, his slovenly modes of speech and his offenses against good taste, unfairly blazoned as they were before the country, disgusted many persons who were half-inclined to his policy; made many of the judicious among his supporters grow lukewarm; forced his warmest supporters to hang their heads for lack of apology; scattered abroad the ugliest scandals about his personal habits and irretrievably hurt his cause.[20]

The Impeachment of Andrew Johnson

Johnson's politically improper rhetoric not only strengthened his opponents but also served as the basis for one of the eleven articles of impeachment that were brought against him by the House of Representatives on March 2 and 3, 1868. Article X charged that the president had ignored the duties of his office by seeking to impugn Congress: Johnson allegedly had delivered "with a loud voice certain intemperate, inflammatory, and scandalous harangues ... amid cries, jeers, and laughter of the multitude then assembled. ..." [21] The charge of "bad and improper" rhetoric was not the main grounds for Johnson's impeachment; indeed, many members of Congress doubted that inflammatory speech, however despicable, was an impeachable offense. Yet, because custom placed severe limitations on direct popular leadership by nineteenth-century executives, the charge was not frivolous.

Johnson's dismissal of Secretary of War Stanton was the principal issue in the impeachment proceedings. In unilaterally firing Stanton, who in spite of his position in the cabinet was conspiring regularly with the president's enemies in Congress, Johnson disregarded the requirement for Senate authorization that was established by the Tenure of Office Act. His intention was to get the law into the courts to test its constitutionality. The House's 126-47 vote to impeach meant that the constitutional question would be decided, in effect, by the Senate, not the judiciary. For the first—and so far the only—time in history, a president had been impeached.

Johnson's impeachment trial, which lasted six weeks, threatened not only his presidency but also the independence of the executive office. The Senate proceedings resembled less a trial to determine if Johnson had committed "high Crimes and Misdemeanors" than a convention of the Radical Republican party to run Johnson out of office. Republican leaders did all they could to bring the pressure of public opinion to bear upon the Senate's deliberations. Moderate Republicans, who had broken with Johnson but who feared that to remove him from office would destroy the constitutional system of checks and balances, were threatened in the party press and by voters at home.[22]

Had Johnson been convicted under these circumstances, the power and prestige of the presidency may have suffered irreparable damage. But seven Republican senators stood up to the pressure of party discipline and public opinion, leaving the Radicals one vote shy of the two-thirds majority they needed to depose Johnson. The words of the recusant senator Trumbull expressed the belief of those who stood with Johnson that to convict the president would set a precedent for Congress to use the impeachment power cavalierly in the future:

> Once set the example of impeaching the President, for what, when the excitement of the hour shall have subsided will be regarded as insufficient causes, . . . and no future president will be safe who happens to differ with a majority of the House and two-thirds of the Senate on any measure deemed by them important, particularly if of a political character. Blinded by partisan zeal, with such an example before them, they will not scruple to remove out of the way any obstacle to the accomplishment of their purposes, and what then becomes of the checks and balances of the Constitution, so carefully devised and so vital to its perpetuity? They are all gone.[23]

As it turned out, the opposite precedent was established by Johnson's impeachment trial. The Senate's failure to convict Johnson in 1868 meant that a president could not be removed from office simply because of unpopularity or policy disagreements with Congress. Instead, the impeachment power was reserved to punish acts that could be clearly construed as illegal or willfully unconstitutional. Since the acquittal of Johnson no president has been impeached, although Richard Nixon surely would have been had he not resigned in 1974.

Ulysses S. Grant and the Abdication of Executive Power

The failure of the Senate to remove Andrew Johnson did not restore to strength either the president or the presidency. The remainder of Johnson's term was spent in a relatively quiet impasse with Congress. Nor did the election of Ulysses S. Grant in 1868 revive the power of the executive. If the American people, made uneasy by the president's subordination to Congress, thought they were electing a forceful leader in Grant, they were sorely mistaken. Although Grant's military career seemed to justify the belief that he had unusual executive ability, he was unable to transfer his talents from the battlefield to the White House. Lacking experience in civil administration, Grant had neither the detailed knowledge of the governmental process that a president requires to perform the tasks of chief executive nor the political experience a president needs to bend other leaders to his purposes.

Grant's shortcomings as a civilian leader were demonstrated almost immediately. The president had let it be known upon his election that he favored the repeal of the Tenure of Office Act and that he would not make any subcabinet appointments until Congress acted in accordance with his wishes. The House soon complied, but the Senate, still controlled by the Radical Republicans, approved a "compromise" amendment that essentially preserved its role in the removal of executive officials. Had Grant asserted himself in favor of repeal, he probably would have prevailed, considering the popularity and prestige he enjoyed at the time of his election. Instead, not realizing the implications of his decision, Grant capitulated to the Senate, which prompted Republicans in both houses to join ranks in support of the compromise. An advocate of repeal, former secretary of the navy Gideon Welles, expressed the disappointment of those who had hoped that Grant would restore the stature of the executive office: "The lawyers duped and cowed him. The poor devil has neither the sagacity and obstinacy for which he has credit, if he assents to this compromise, where the Executive surrenders everything and gets nothing." [24]

Grant's strategic error set the tone for his entire two terms as president: he never recovered the prestige and power that he lost in his first showdown with the Republican leaders.[25] Yet his acquiescence to the Senate on the question of whether to repeal the Tenure of Office Act no doubt was influenced by his concept of the presidency. Grant considered himself to be purely an administrative officer—"except on rare occasions he was, as President, disposed to accept without question the work of Congress as the authoritative expression of the will of the American people." [26]

Grant's understanding of executive leadership accorded well with that of the Republican leaders in the Senate, who embraced the old Whig principle of legislative supremacy. In Grant, unlike Lincoln or Johnson, congressional Republicans had a president whom they could manage. As a result, the Senate achieved its peak of power during the Grant administration. George F. Hoar, a Republican member of the House, described the Senate's attitude toward the president:

> The most eminent Senators—Sumner, Conkling, Sherman, Edmunds, Carpenter, Frelinghuysen, Simon Cameron, Anthony, Logan—would have received as a personal affront a private message from the White House expressing a desire that they should adopt any course in the discharge of their legislative duties that they did not approve. If they visited the White House, it was to give, not to receive advice. . . . Each

Despite a highly successful military career that suggested unusual executive ability, Gen. Ulysses S. Grant was unable to transfer that success from the battlefield to the White House.

of these stars kept his own orbit and shone in his sphere within which he tolerated no intrusion from the President or from anybody else.[27]

Grant's virtual abdication of presidential responsibility fostered not just weak leadership but patronage abuses and outright peculation. The most dramatic and probably the most damaging scandal involved the evasion of taxes on distilleries—the so-called Whiskey Ring. The Whiskey Ring included Gen. John A. McDonald, the collector of internal revenue in St. Louis who, with the collusion of Treasury officials and the president's private secretary, Gen. Orville E. Babcock, defrauded the government of millions of dollars. Perhaps the most disconcerting aspect of the scandal was Grant's effort to protect Babcock, who was acquitted on the strength of a deposition in his favor from the president.

The personally honest but hopelessly naive Grant repaid Secretary of the Treasury Benjamin H. Bristow's efforts to break the Whiskey Ring and to bring its perpetrators, including Babcock, to justice by making clear that Bristow no longer was welcome in the cabinet. (He resigned in 1876.) Babcock, however, received a presidential appointment as inspector of lighthouses.[28]

Grant's unfortunate conduct in the Whiskey Ring scandal notwithstanding, he was both aware of and concerned about the existing system of public administration. In early 1870 he called for civil service reform, declaring that "the present system [of party patronage] does not secure the best men and often not even fit men, for public place." [29] After receiving the necessary authority from Congress in March, Grant set up a board, soon known as the Civil Service Commission, and charged it to devise reformist rules and regulations. George William Curtis, the leader of the national civil service reform movement, was appointed to chair the commission, which also supervised the new competitive examination system for hiring in each department. Thus did one of the most corrupt presidential administrations in history make the first earnest attempt to reform the civil service.

Despite this promising beginning, most of what happened during Grant's second term thwarted the cause of civil service reform. The patronage system had long been dominated by individual members of Congress, who liked it that way. Sen. Roscoe Conkling of New York, the leader of the so-called Stalwart wing of the Republican party, led an assault on the new commission. He was supported not only by most leaders of his party but by patronage-seeking Democrats as well.

The rise of the Stalwarts reveals much about the political ambiance of the post-Civil War era. Like the Radicals, they initially were committed to the fundamental reconstruction of the South. But as the Civil War and its aftermath gradually faded in political significance, the defense of patronage and party organization became the Stalwarts' paramount concern. They were the product of a new political milieu, in which the needs of the party machinery, including spoils, took precedence over principle. As the historian Morton Keller has noted, the Stalwarts' emergence as the dominant faction of the Republican party signified the shift from a "politics of ideology to a politics of organization." [30]

Republicans who opposed the transformation of their party and who supported civil service reform turned in the early 1870s to a third party—the so-called Liberal Republicans. But Liberal Republicanism never flourished at the grass roots. After nominating the celebrated newspaper editor Horace Greeley to run (unsuccessfully) against Grant in 1872, Liberal Republicans became anathema to the president and thus were unable to work cooperatively with him to fend off the congressional attack on the Civil Service Commission. Stalwart Republicans and Democrats assailed the commission's rules as unconstitutional, aristocratic, and fatal to the ascendancy of any party.

Yielding, characteristically, to resistance from Congress, which refused to allocate funds for the Civil Service Commission in 1874, Grant abandoned the reform program. In strict accord with his belief that the legislature was the proper branch to determine policy, the president announced in his annual message on December 7, 1874, that if Congress did not pass a civil service reform law before adjourning, he would discontinue the system. Congress adjourned without taking action, and on March 9, 1875, Grant ordered that civil service examining boards throughout the country be abolished.[31]

The Fight to Restore Presidential Power

Grant retired from the presidency in 1877, leaving the office he had occupied for eight years at perhaps its lowest ebb. The Senate, its leaders believed, was "secure in its mastery over the executive." [32] Yet Grant's successor, Rutherford B. Hayes, was intent on emancipating the executive from congressional domination. During the Hayes administration, the powers of the presidency were defended persistently and effectively for the first time since the Civil War.

The Presidency of Rutherford B. Hayes

Although Hayes eventually brought more than a decade of executive decline to an abrupt end, his administration began in the least auspicious of circumstances. After eight years of Grant, a Republican defeat seemed certain in the election of 1876. In fact, Samuel J. Tilden, the Democratic candidate who as governor of New York had exposed the efforts of Boss Tweed and various political rings to corrupt the state's canal system, initially appeared to have won the election.[33] But the electoral votes of Oregon and of three southern states, which still were under military rule, were in doubt. Without them, Tilden had only 184 electoral votes; if Hayes carried all of the uncertain states he would have 185 votes and would win the election.

The four states—Oregon, Louisiana, Florida, and South Carolina— each sent two sets of electoral votes to Washington to be counted. Congress responded by setting up a fifteen-member electoral commission, eight Republicans and seven Democrats. At this point a deal—the so-called Compromise of 1877—apparently was worked out by Republican and southern Democratic leaders: in return for the Democrats' acquiescence to Hayes's election, the Republicans promised to remove the occupying forces from the South. Both sides kept their ends of the bargain. On March 2, 1877, the electoral commission, by a strict party vote, rejected the Democratic returns from the doubtful states and declared Hayes the winner by a margin of one electoral vote. Hayes, in turn, removed the federal troops from the South, thus putting an end to virtually all attempts to enforce the Fourteenth Amendment's guarantee of civil rights to every citizen, including the former slaves. Nor, thereafter, was any effort made to uphold the Fifteenth Amendment, which since 1870 had affirmed the right of U.S. citizens to vote, regardless of "race, color, or previous condition of servitude." [34]

Interestingly, Tilden maintained what Keller has called an "Olympian (or neurotic)" calm during the 1876 electoral dispute.[35] He kept busy during one critical month of the crisis by compiling a history of past electoral counts. When the issue finally was resolved against him, Tilden said he looked forward to private life "with the consciousness that I shall receive from posterity the credit of having been elected to the highest position in the gift of the people without any cares and responsibilities of the office." [36] Tilden's equanimity expressed not only an unusual willingness to forgo power but also his acceptance that the issue had been settled legitimately by negotiations between Democratic and Republican leaders. As Keller concluded, "The retreat from the purposive, ideological politics of the Civil War could not have been more complete." [37]

It is ironic that such an unsavory bargain brought to power a president who was uncompromisingly dedicated to breaking the Senate's grip on the executive office and to reforming the civil service. Hayes had been a reform-oriented governor of Ohio and had written a ringing endorsement of civil service reform in his letter accepting the Republican nomination. The president's appointing power, he declared, too often had passed improperly into the hands of members of Congress; the patronage system had degenerated into an intolerable hindrance to the proper discharge of the legislative business. In his inaugural address, Hayes proclaimed that civil service reform should be "thorough, radical, and complete." [38]

Congress, for its part, was uninterested in reform. By the end of Grant's second term the influence of senators and, to a lesser extent, representatives on executive appointments had become substantial. Hayes first offended Republican leaders in the Senate by making his cabinet nominations independently, without consulting them. This not only disrupted the Stalwarts' plans to dictate the composition of the cabinet, but, with the nomination of the former Confederate David M. Key as postmaster general, also aroused their patriotic wrath. The major insult that Hayes perpetrated upon the Senate, however, was his choice of the civil service reformer Carl Schurz to head the Department of the Interior, a position that members of Congress feared Schurz would use to wage war on patronage.

Even though Hayes's nominees were a distinguished and qualified group, the offended Senate "oligarchy" took their selection as a challenge. When the cabinet nominations were submitted to the Senate for confirmation, as required by the Constitution, the entire list was referred to committees for prolonged examination. Hoping that delay would force the president's hand, the Senate did not even exempt Sen.

John Sherman, whom Hayes had nominated as secretary of the Treasury, from this process, violating the custom that fellow senators, especially those as qualified as Sherman, be confirmed without investigation.

For the Senate to delay the confirmation of an entire cabinet was unprecedented, and a storm of indignation swept the country. The White House was flooded with telegrams and letters urging the president to stand firm. The Senate quickly capitulated to public opinion and, voting almost unanimously, confirmed every cabinet nominee. "For the first time since the Civil War," Binkley has written, "the Senate had been vanquished on a clear-cut issue between it and the President. The Senate had passed its zenith." [39]

Yet the great battle between Hayes and Congress was still to come. Having installed a cabinet of his own choice, the president set his sights on the patronage system. "Now for Civil Service Reform," Hayes wrote in his diary on April 22, 1877.[40] One of his first acts was to appoint independent commissions to investigate the federal customhouses in New York, San Francisco, New Orleans, and elsewhere. These federal outposts, which in effect were controlled by local party machines, had fallen into outrageous patterns of corruption in the course of collecting federal revenues. Although the investigations led to reforms in many areas of the country, the customhouse in New York, which collected more than two-thirds of all customs revenues and provided the federal government with about half of its income, continued to serve the party machines. The independent commission that investigated the New York customhouse found that employees were hired in response to political pressure; revealed a system of "assessments," in which employees were expected to contribute a percentage of their salaries to the party; and called attention to widespread incompetence and corruption among customhouse personnel.

After receiving the report on the New York customhouse, Hayes decided to replace its three highest officials—Collector Chester A. Arthur, Surveyor General George H. Sharpe, and naval officer Alonzo B. Cornell—all of whom were prominent members of the New York State Republican organization. Yet the president's intention was impeded both by custom and by law. One obstacle was the practice of "senatorial courtesy" that had taken root during the Civil War. Under this practice, which still exists, if senators of the president's party object to a nominee for federal office who lives or would serve in their state, they can rely on the support of their fellow senators to reject the nomination. The Stalwart New York senator Roscoe Conkling, for whom the New York customhouse was an important base of political power, invoked senatorial courtesy to deny confirmation to the nominees Hayes selected to replace the fired Republican spoilsmen.

The president's nominations were referred to the Senate Committee on Commerce. Conkling, who chaired the committee, invoked the Tenure of Office Act, which had been revised in 1869, and the session of Congress ended without the nominations being confirmed. Under the amended terms of the act, the Senate no longer was empowered to confirm a presidential removal, but until it approved the president's choice of a successor, the suspended official remained in office. Thus, when Hayes's nominations, which were greeted in the Senate with derisive laughter, were not approved, Arthur, Sharpe, and Cornell retained their federal posts. More important, Conkling and the New York Republican machine maintained their control of the federal customhouse.

The stubborn Hayes resolved to continue the fight. On December 12, 1877, he recorded in his diary, "In the language of the press, Senator Conkling has won a great victory over the administration. . . . But the end is not yet. I am right and I shall not give up the contest." [41] After Congress adjourned in 1878, Hayes again dismissed the three officials, replaced them temporarily with recess appointments, and in December sent to the Senate his nominations for the once-again vacant customhouse positions. Although Conkling was able to delay Senate action for two months, he finally defeated himself by delivering a bitter speech against the president, in which he alienated many senators by reading from the private correspondence of cabinet members.[42] The Senate voted to confirm Hayes's nominees on February 3, 1879.

In his letter of congratulation to Gen. E. A. Merritt, who was Arthur's replacement, the president established principles for the complete overhaul of the personnel system of the New York customhouse. Besides insisting that Merritt's office be conducted "on strictly business principles," Hayes required that the new collector confine patronage to the narrowest possible bounds. "Let no man be put out merely because he is a friend of the late collector," he wrote, "and no man be put in merely because he is our friend." [43]

Hayes's victory over Conkling came at great political cost. During the almost eighteen months that it took to remove Arthur, Cornell, and Sharpe, the president was virtually powerless as the administrative head of the government. Thus, even though Hayes's triumph restored to the executive some of the powers that it had lost since Lincoln's assassination, his administration was to be remembered mainly for "holding its ground, rather than for developing new frontiers." [44] Still, Hayes himself was satisfied with the blows he had struck against the senatorial group that for so long had directed the government. A year after winning his battle for control of the New York customhouse, Hayes wrote in his diary:

The end I have chiefly aimed at has been to break down congressional patronage. The contest has been a bitter one. It has exposed me to attack, opposition, misconstruction, and the actual hatred of powerful men. But I have had great success. No member of either house now attempts even to dictate appointments. My sole right to make appointments is now tacitly conceded.[45]

The Presidency of James A. Garfield

The struggle between the president and Congress to determine the conduct of the executive office was not ended by Hayes's defeat of Conkling. In fact, the battles for appointments that had dominated Hayes's term in office were renewed, with unexpected ferocity, during the first weeks of James A. Garfield's administration.

Party factionalism dominated American politics by the time of the election of 1880. Garfield was nominated by the Republican convention on the thirty-sixth ballot. He was chosen as a compromise between the Stalwarts, who were led by Conkling, and the moderate wing of the party (the so-called Half-Breeds), led by Sen. James G. Blaine of Maine.[46] The convention further bandaged party wounds by selecting Chester A. Arthur, Conkling's lieutenant and the deposed head of the New York customhouse, as its vice-presidential candidate. The Democrats too settled on a compromise candidate, the "pallid and unexceptional" Civil War general Winfield Scott Hancock of Pennsylvania, in a convention torn by factional disputes within the Indiana, New York, Ohio, and Pennsylvania delegations. Garfield won by a razor-thin margin—he received 9,457 more votes than Hancock out of the 9,219,467 cast. The closeness of the contest was not the result of a keen struggle over major issues; rather, it was the product of highly organized, closely balanced national parties bringing out their supporters.

Close elections were the norm throughout the post-Reconstruction era, signifying the public's ambivalence about both parties. In fact, no nineteenth-century president after Grant was reelected; no candidate even won a majority of the popular vote. The voters' unwillingness to support either parties or individuals decisively during this era reflected the dominance of a highly mobilized, intensely competitive form of factionalism, in which presidents were frequently ensnared in organizational battles over local interests and spoils.[47]

Garfield seemed well-suited to the new game of party politics. Unlike Hayes, he was by nature prone to conciliation and compromise; once in office, he hoped to work cooperatively with both factions of the Republican party. Yet against his will, Garfield was soon caught up in factional conflicts more severe than in the Hayes years. In the heat of these intramural squabbles, Garfield was forced to continue the assault against overly broad assertions of senatorial courtesy that his predecessor had begun.[48]

Garfield's attack on the Senate came in response to the Conklingites' attempt to dictate his choice for secretary of the Treasury. Stalwarts demanded that the president appoint Levi P. Morton, a New York banker. When Garfield resisted, arguing that the banker's Wall Street connections and extremely conservative economic views made him anathema to western Republicans, his conciliatory offer to name Morton as the secretary of the navy and to consider other recommendations for the Treasury was scorned. The Stalwarts' answer was unequivocal: Morton must be the secretary of the Treasury.

Garfield was not so conciliatory as to yield to such an aggressive challenge to executive authority. After generously recognizing the Conkling wing of the New York Republican party by placing many of its members in federal positions, he insisted on his own choices for the cabinet. Garfield now realized, as clearly as had Hayes, that the president's constitutional independence "could be preserved only by a bold challenge of the pretensions of the Senate and a duel to the finish with the most militant champion of senatorial courtesy." [49]

Garfield left no doubt of his intention to challenge the Senate when he nominated William H. Robertson as the collector of the port of New York. Robertson was Conkling's political enemy in New York and a friend of his major rival in national politics, Blaine. Robertson's appointment, then, was a more direct challenge to Conkling and to the practice of senatorial courtesy than Hayes ever had issued. Garfield wrote to his longtime friend, B. A. Hinsdale, the president of Hiram College:

> This [nomination] brings on the contest at once and will settle the question whether the President is registering clerk of the Senate or the Executive of the United States. . . . Summed up in a single sentence this is the question: shall the principal port of entry in which more than ninety percent of all our customs duties are collected be under the control of the administration or under the local control of the factional senator?[50]

Conkling marshalled the enormous weight of his political machine in an attempt to compel Garfield to withdraw Robertson's nomination. Vice President Arthur participated fully in these maneuvers, despite stiff criticism from the press. On the evening of April 14, 1881, Arthur eluded reporters and slipped into the White House for a private conversation with the president. He urged Garfield to withdraw Robertson's nomination on the grounds that it would badly fracture the Republican party in New York and consign its nominees to certain defeat. The president refused to budge. Afterward he wrote to Whitelaw Reid of the New York *Tribune*, "Of course I deprecate war, but if it is brought to my door the bringer will find me at home." [51]

When Conkling and his allies in the Senate attempted to outwit the president by preparing to confirm all of his nominees except Robertson, Garfield withdrew every other New York appointment. There would be no further nominations, Garfield insisted, until the issue of who controlled the executive office was settled. The president's bold maneuver left the Senate practically helpless and electrified his supporters. "At last," the Baltimore *American* trumpeted, "President Garfield has answered the question 'Who is president?' " [52] Garfield recorded in his diary, "The withdrawal of the New York appointments has brought me vigorous responses from many quarters and I think shows that the public do not desire the continuance of boss rule in the Senate." [53]

On May 16, 1881, seeing that Robertson's confirmation was inevitable, Conkling and his fellow New York senator, Thomas C. Platt, resigned, hoping that the state legislature would help them to save face by reelecting them. The legislature refused. After a long struggle, two other men were chosen to represent New York in the Senate.

Garfield's victory was complete. The Senate confirmed Robertson's nomination unanimously and Conkling never was restored to public office. The president's triumph, which ended the long struggle that had begun with Hayes's attempt to reform the New York customhouse, marked a "milestone in the revival of the power and prestige of the White House." Although the influence that senators wielded in suggesting persons for presidential appointments and rejecting objectionable nominees remained substantial, their claim to supersede executive discretion was ended.[54]

Chester A. Arthur and the Enactment
of Civil Service Reform

Garfield did not have time to pursue a comprehensive program of civil service reform. On July 2, 1881, in a Washington railroad station, a deranged lawyer named Charles J. Guiteau shot the president in the back. Guiteau, who apparently had expected to receive a presidential appointment, blurted out upon being arrested, "I am a Stalwart; now Arthur is president." When Garfield died, after lingering until September 19, Vice President Arthur indeed became the president.

Civil service reformers expected little from the New York Stalwart. Former president Hayes predicted that Arthur's former patron, Conkling, would be "the power behind the throne, superior to the throne." [55] But Garfield's assassination enflamed public opinion against the spoils system, and Arthur quickly realized that for him not to support civil service reform would jeopardize the dominant political position that the Republican party had enjoyed since the Civil War. The new president soon laid to rest the worst fears of those who had predicted that he would "turn the White House into a larger version of the New York Customhouse." [56] Intent on strengthening his political position in the country, Arthur, to the pleasant surprise of his critics, expressed support for limited civil service reform in his first annual message to Congress.

Arthur's commitment to reform was strengthened by the results of the 1882 congressional elections, in which the Democrats achieved dramatic gains. In his second annual message, the president called upon Congress to pass the Pendleton Act, which had been introduced in 1881 by the Democratic senator from Ohio, George Hunt Pendleton. The civil service reform bill contained measures, such as competitive examinations for government jobs and a ban on political assessments, that Arthur originally had opposed. But when Congress passed the act in early 1883, Arthur signed it. Thus did the president who once had been removed as the collector of the port of New York for flagrant partisan abuses launch the modern civil service in the United States.

The Pendleton Act was of limited application: its coverage extended only to employees in Washington and in major customhouses and post offices. The vast majority—all but 14,000 of 131,000 federal officeholders, including many postal workers—still were not covered. Indeed, control over the rich supply of remaining patronage jobs would be the primary source of conflict between Congress and Arthur's successor, Grover Cleveland.

Nevertheless, the enactment of civil service reform in 1883, the political scientist Leonard White has written, "was a fundamental turning point in the history of the federal administrative system." In addition to the support that it provided for merit hiring and its prohibition against on-the-job solicitations of campaign funds from federal employees, the Pendleton Act established a bipartisan, three-member Civil Service Commission, to be appointed by the president and confirmed by the Senate. The commission was vested with two important powers—to control hiring examinations and to investigate the enforcement of its rules. Finally, the president was authorized to extend the classified service by executive order. However limited its initial application, then, the Pendleton Act laid a solid foundation on which to build the civil service in succeeding decades.[57]

Grover Cleveland's First Term

Neither the Republicans' belated support for civil service reform nor their nomination for president of Speaker of the House James G. Blaine, the leader of the moderate, Half-breed faction of the party, could stave off defeat in the 1884 election. The Democrats' standard-bearer, Gov. Grover Cleveland of New York, won a narrow victory, thus becoming the first Democratic president in thirty-four years.

Moderates in every section of the country believed that Cleveland's election heralded the true end of the bitter conflicts that had been generated by the Civil War. Cleveland was anxious to prove them correct. As the head of the party that received its greatest support from the South, he appointed many southerners to high office, including two to his cabinet.

To be sure, the Republicans still were not willing to stop waving the "bloody shirt": they continued to paint the Democrats as unworthy of controlling the councils of power. Yet Cleveland's victory was proof that the post-Civil War political order would not be upset by the election of a Democratic president. The 1884 campaign and its aftermath confirmed that recent elections were more contests to control federal patronage than grand confrontations over national issues. The Democratic victory also indicated that the nation was turning its attention away from the legacy of the Civil War and toward tariffs, currency, and other economic controversies.[58]

Thus, the 1884 election brought no moratorium in the struggle between the president and Congress to control appointments to the federal government. By winning major victories against the Senate, Hayes and Garfield had restored some prestige to the presidency, which had been badly tarnished during the Johnson and Grant years. It fell to Cleveland, however, to fight the battle over appointments that finally brought about the repeal of the Tenure of Office Act.

The battle began when Cleveland attempted to reward with appointments loyal Democrats, who, after being out of office for so long, were hungry to partake of the spoils of patronage. The president certainly was no spoilsman; indeed, he had established a reputation for reform as mayor of Buffalo and governor of New York. He enforced the Pendleton Act and devoted an enormous amount of time to scrutinizing the qualifications of candidates for the federal positions that were not covered by the new civil service procedures. Cleveland's approach yielded a number of outstanding appointments and won him praise from civil service reformers.

Still, fashioning himself a Jacksonian Democrat, the president was no enemy to the patronage system. He certainly wanted to place deserving Democrats in posts that had been held by Republicans. Operating under the constraints of the amended Tenure of Office Act, however, the president was able merely to suspend, not to remove, federal employees from their jobs. In effect, Cleveland could replace officials only when the Senate was in session and approved his own nominees. This the Republican-controlled Senate was loath to do. As a result, of the 643 suspensions (and corresponding appointments) that Cleveland made during the early days of his presidency, the Senate, after being in session for three months, had considered only 17 and confirmed only 15.

The larger controversy between the president and the Senate was joined in a battle for the control of one particular office, that of the U.S. attorney in Alabama. When Cleveland suspended the incumbent, George M. Duskin, and nominated John D. Burnett to replace him, the Republican chair of the Senate Judiciary Committee, George F. Edmunds of Vermont, decided to subject the nomination to intense and protracted scrutiny. He asked Cleveland's attorney general to send to his committee all papers pertaining not just to Burnett's appointment but to Duskin's dismissal as well. Cleveland directed the attorney general to comply with the request for information about Burnett. But, determined to establish once and for all the president's right to remove federal officials without congressional interference, Cleveland refused to release any information about his decision to suspend Duskin.

Cleveland's refusal stung Senate Republicans, who responded with a resolution to condemn the administration for its unwillingness to cooperate. The president, in turn, sent a message to the Capitol that defended his actions and accused the legislature of infringing on his constitutional responsibilities as chief executive. Of the Senate's demand for information about his suspension of federal officials, Cleveland wrote:

> They assume the right of the Senate to sit in judgment upon the exercise of my exclusive discretion and executive function, for which I am solely responsible to the people from whom I have so lately received the sacred trust of office. My oath to support and defend the Constitution ... compel[s] me to refuse compliance with these demands.[59]

Cleveland's message to Congress dramatized his conflict with the Senate in a way that quickly caught the nation's attention. As in previous battles of this sort, public opinion supported the president. Recognizing that it was beaten, the Senate found a face-saving avenue of retreat. It was discovered that, during the controversy, Duskin's term had expired, which made his suspension by the president no longer necessary. Burnett's appointment as U.S. attorney was readily confirmed.

Cleveland's position on appointments was vindicated when, a few months later, with overwhelming support from both Democrats and Republicans, a bill to repeal the Tenure of Office Act was passed by Congress. "Thus," wrote Cleveland long after the event, "was an unhappy controversy happily followed by an expurgation of the last pretense of statutory sanction to an encroachment upon constitutional Executive prerogatives, and thus was a time-honored interpretation of the Constitution restored to us."[60]

Congressional Government and the Prelude to a More Active Presidency

During the twelve years that passed from the end of the Grant administration in 1877 until the end of Cleveland's first term in 1889, the post-Civil War decline of executive prestige was halted. The Senate's grip on the details of administration, especially the removal power, was loosened in the defeats administered by Hayes, Garfield, and Cleveland. And the struggle to rejuvenate the independence of the presidency was advanced by the enactment of civil service reform, which began the process of insulating federal appointments from the localistic concerns of party spoilsmen.

The achievements of Grant's successors notwithstanding, the presidency remained small in scale and limited in power during the latter decades of the nineteenth century. The president's control of the executive domain was restored, but the domain itself was still highly constricted. Late nineteenth-century presidents had little influence on government expenditures or on the policies that were pursued by the bureaus and departments of the executive branch.

In fiscal affairs, the end of the Civil War had marked a transition from emergency presidential control over the amounts and purposes of government spending to renewed efforts by Congress to reassert its authority. In response, Hayes and Cleveland had exercised the veto aggressively to ward off Congress's most egregious attempts to use spending bills to impose its will on the executive. For example, in 1879 Hayes successfully vetoed an army appropriation bill because it included riders attached by the Democrats to prohibit federal marshals from employing troops or armed civilians in the southern states to keep the peace at the polls in congressional elections. In so doing, Hayes established a powerful precedent against appropriation riders that encroach on the executive power.[61]

Yet the use of the veto to affect fiscal affairs was strictly a defensive measure. Indeed, until the Budget and Accounting Act was passed in 1921, presidential authority for taxing and spending was "almost, if not entirely, lacking." [62] Presidents, at least in peacetime, were never involved when department and agency spending estimates were made and seldom were consulted when those estimates were reviewed by the various congressional committees. The secretary of the Treasury was merely a compiler of budget requests, not a minister of finance. The absence of executive leadership in fiscal matters fostered irresponsible and disorderly budgets, made worse by Congress's practice of dispersing its decision-making authority on spending among a number of appropriations committees.

The president's ability to provide guidance in the policy-making process and to enlist congressional support for an administration program was also very limited during the latter part of the nineteenth century. Indeed, no president of this era advanced a theory of presidential power that supported legislative leadership.

Cleveland, for example, fiercely defended executive independence but did not believe that the president's legislative responsibilities went beyond recommending programs for Congress to consider. Even on an issue such as the tariff, which was central to the conflict between Democrats and Republicans in the 1880s, Cleveland made little effort to bend Congress to his will. After the Democrats fared poorly in the 1886 midterm elections, Cleveland delivered a forceful message that urged Congress, in conformance with Democratic principles, to reduce tariff rates sharply. But having done this much, the president did little more. As the historian John A. Garraty has written, "Like a great lethargic bear, Cleveland had bestirred himself . . . and shaken the political hive, but then he slumped back into querulous inactivity." [63] His tariff policy was rejected overwhelmingly by Congress, at considerable cost to his political reputation.

The Presidency of Benjamin A. Harrison

The narrow bounds that constrained presidential leadership during the latter decades of the nineteenth century led the political scientist Woodrow Wilson to declare in 1885, the second year of Cleveland's first term, that "unquestionably, the predominant and controlling force, the center and source of all motive and of all regulative power, is Congress." [64] Cleveland failed to challenge the principle of legislative supremacy, but his successor, Benjamin Harrison, enthusiastically endorsed it.

Harrison, a Republican senator from Indiana, won a very close election in 1888; in fact, Cleveland, by piling up large margins in the southern states, won a plurality of the national popular vote, even as he narrowly lost the large northern states and thus the electoral college. This unusual result (no discrepancy has occurred between the popular and the electoral vote outcomes since 1888) brought to the presidency a man who understood perfectly Congress's desire to control the conduct of government.

Harrison was one of the Senate leaders who had clashed with Cleveland over the president's removal power. He did not require much urging to accept the advice of the Republican senator John Sherman a few weeks after the election. "The President," Sherman wrote to Harrison, "should 'touch elbows with Congress.' He should have no policy distinct from his party and that is better represented in Congress than in the Executive." Suggesting that "Cleveland made a cardinal mistake in [seeking to dictate] a tariff policy to Congress," Sherman encouraged the new president to cultivate friendly relations with legislators and to follow rather than try to lead Republicans in the House and Senate.[65]

Thus, in spite of unquestioned industry and dignified supervision of executive affairs, Harrison's term in the White House marked a retreat in the recent struggle to revive the status of the presidency. Garraty wrote of his and his predecessor's conduct as president: "Cleveland had surrendered to the patronage system after a battle; Harrison embraced it from the start. Cleveland squabbled with Congress, and fumbled [in the tariff controversy] toward presidential leadership at least once; Harrison cheerfully submitted to being practically a figurehead." [66]

The absence of presidential leadership during Harrison's term and the triumph of the doctrine of congressional supremacy spawned efforts to reorganize the House and the Senate to perform their duties more efficiently. Before the 1880s, Congress had been primarily a deliberative body; by the end of the nineteenth century, it was a complex and well-disciplined institution that was organized to govern.

In the House, especially, lawmaking increasingly came under the control of the leadership—that is, the heads of the major committees and the Speaker. The Republican Speaker during Harrison's tenure, Thomas B. Reed, imposed rules on the House that greatly streamlined its chaotic proceedings. Confronted with the minority Democrats' use of the "disappearing quorum," in which members sat mute during attendance calls in order to deny the Speaker the quorum he needed to conduct business, Reed counted the recalcitrants whether they signified their presence or not. In 1891, the Supreme Court sanctioned the transformation of the House into a more disciplined legislative body by upholding the constitutionality of this and other "Reed rules," such as a ban on filibusters.[67]

Similar changes occurred in the Senate, so much so that the distinguished and critical English observer of American politics, James Bryce, wrote in 1890 that the upper house was "modern, severe, and practical." [68] Forceful leaders, such as Finance Committee chair Nelson Aldrich of Rhode Island and William B. Allison of Iowa, the chair of the Appropriations Committee, imposed controls on the Senate that resembled the ones "Czar" Reed had established in the House. As a result, Republicans were able to bring a previously unknown degree of partisan and procedural discipline to the Senate during Harrison's tenure.

The Harrison administration, then, was one in which Congress and the party organizations reigned supreme. A burst of important legislation during the first two years of Harrison's presidency, including the protectionist McKinley Tariff of 1890, marked the rise of party discipline and congressional efficiency.[69] As such, the Harrison years offered a striking example of Whiggish party government, now put into practice for the first time by the Republicans.[70]

Like the Whigs, the Republicans had long wanted to use the federal government to help achieve their economic objectives. The Republican program, which originally had been posed as a challenge to the slave economy of the South, was dedicated to industrial capitalism. Expressing support for private property with an ardor that was fully shared by the radicals of his party, Lincoln had said in 1863 that "property is the fruit of labor; . . . a positive good in the world. That some should be rich shows that others may become rich, and hence is just encouragement to industry and enterprise." [71] With the end of Reconstruction, the Republicans' dedication to industrial capitalism became their central party doctrine, embodied not only in protective tariffs but also in banking policies that provided capital for industrial development. The identification of the Republican party with business—although such a link had some political liabilities—was, on the whole, advantageous. The program of economic expansion through tariffs and publicly financed internal improvements was supported by a majority of voters.[72]

Yet developments were under way in the country that soon would render the Whig-Republican model of party government obsolete. Massive social and economic changes were increasing the scale and complexity of American life, producing jarring economic dislocations and intense political conflicts. In the face of change, pressures mounted for a new style of governance, one that would require a more expansive national government and the more systematic administration of public policy. The limited nineteenth-century polity, which could accommodate decentralized party organizations, political patronage, and a dominant Congress, began to give way to a new order that depended upon consistent and forceful presidential leadership. The rise of intensely ideological politics in the 1890s, culminating in the presidential contest between Democrat William Jennings Bryan and Republican William L. McKinley in 1896, and the growing role of the United States in world affairs, which began with the Spanish-American War of 1898, set the stage for a significant transformation of the presidency.

Grover Cleveland's Second Term

The effects of the new political order on the presidency first became apparent during the second term of Grover Cleveland, who defeated Harrison in the 1892 election. Cleveland owed his political comeback to the failure of the probusiness Republican party to assuage the nation's concerns about the economic dislocations caused by corporate industrialization. Although the Republican-controlled Fifty-first Congress both passed the Sherman Antitrust Act to ameliorate the concentration of economic power in massive corporations and responded to inflationist pressures by expanding the coinage of silver, it proved to be one of the most unpopular Congresses in history. In 1890, the Democrats swept the House elections by a huge margin—the prelude, as it turned out, to Cleveland's victory two years later. Yet when Cleveland and the Democrats were themselves caught by a severe economic depression in 1893, the Republicans regained control of Congress in the midterm elections of 1894.

The Democrats' political defeat notwithstanding, Cleveland responded to the Panic of 1893 by wielding the powers of the presidency more vigorously, albeit no more successfully, than any president since Lincoln. His call of a special session of Congress to secure the repeal of the Sherman Silver Purchase Act represented effective leadership in defense of the gold standard. Yet this dramatic departure from the hands-off approach to legislation that Cleveland had pursued during his first term cost him the support of his party. He not only alienated inflationist Democrats like Nebraska representative William Jennings Bryan but also insulted congressional leaders, who resented the president's aggressive intervention in domestic policy.

The Democratic party's repudiation of Cleveland was all but guaranteed by his intervention in the Pullman strike against the railroads in 1894. Without consulting John P. Altgeld, the Democratic governor of Illinois, Cleveland dispatched troops to Chicago, supposedly to protect federal property and "to remove obstructions to the United States mails." This action infuriated Altgeld, who proclaimed in a telegram to Cleveland that

> to absolutely ignore a local government in matters of this kind, when the local government is ready to furnish assistance needed, and is amply able to enforce the law, not only insults the people of this State by imputing to them an inability to govern themselves or an unwillingness to enforce the law, but is in violation of a basic principle of our institutions.[73]

Unimpressed, Cleveland replied "that in this hour of danger and public distress, discussion may well give way to active efforts on the part of all in authority to restore obedience to law and to protect life and property." [74]

Cleveland's intervention in the Pullman strike marked an important expansion of the president's domestic authority in peacetime. His use of federal troops was unprecedented, both in relying on constitutional, rather than explicit statutory, authority for his actions and in circumventing state officials from beginning to end. Nevertheless, the president's conduct was ringingly endorsed by the Supreme Court in the

Grover Cleveland, president from 1885 to 1889, lost the 1888 election but regained the White House in the election of 1892. He is the only president to serve two nonconsecutive terms.

Debs case, which upheld the arrest of Eugene V. Debs and other strike leaders for conspiring to obstruct the mails.[75] The Court ruled, in effect, that the president was authorized under his general executive powers, as stated in Article II of the Constitution, to take virtually any measure to protect the peace of the United States.[76]

Politically, Cleveland again paid a high price for his success. Although the conservative wing of the Democratic party praised the president, laborers and friends of labor turned against him and his party.[77] The rift between Democrats and workers was widened when the party's national convention nominated Bryan, a rural Nebraskan, for president in 1896 and fought the campaign mainly on the issue of "free silver," the proposal to expand the currency by basing it on silver as well as gold. Since the industrial cities were the fastest-growing part of the country, the heavy losses that the Democrats suffered among workers and other urban voters in 1896 precipitated a major political realignment in favor of the Republicans.[78]

The Presidency of William L. McKinley

The dramatic Republican triumph in the 1896 election brought an astute and skillful politician, Gov. William McKinley of Ohio, to the White House. McKinley's presidency often is regarded as an uneventful prelude to the vigorous and energetic administration of his successor, Theodore Roosevelt. But, continuing the forceful leadership shown by Cleveland during his second term, McKinley inaugurated important changes in the executive during his first four years. To be sure, McKinley's tenure was highly traditional in some respects. He, like Benjamin Harrison, was a Republican party professional who came to the presidency after a long political apprenticeship, spent mainly in Congress. Consequently, McKinley believed that good government could come only through a strong party organization. He also carried into office a deep and abiding respect for congressional primacy. Unlike Harrison, however, McKinley did not permit the executive to decline during his watch. Indeed, McKinley was the first post-Civil War president to take the political initiative without arousing the resentment of his party in Congress.[79]

Although active, McKinley's legislative leadership was of a kind that did not advance the cause of presidential power in enduring ways. His style of influence in Congress resembled that of Jefferson, who had quietly used the congressional caucus to enact the Democratic-Republican program nearly a century before. Jefferson's successors, of course, were unable to match his legislative influence, thus demonstrating the limits of party government as an instrument for sustained leadership.

The McKinley administration was dominated not by legislation, however, but by war and foreign policy. Here, as commander in chief and as chief diplomat, the president made his enduring mark on the office.

In 1898, a conflict arose with Spain over the desire of its colony, Cuba, for independence. McKinley favored a peaceful resolution, but he ultimately yielded to public sentiment, which, aroused by sensationalistic propaganda in the press, strongly favored war. Once having set his course for war, however, McKinley carried out a "day by day, and sometimes ... an hour by hour" supervision of the U.S. military effort that laid the foundation for more intense presidential involvement and greater executive control of foreign policy in the future.[80] The hostilities were so brief, the victory so complete, and, most important, the acquisition of Spanish territory in the Caribbean and Pacific so considerable that no postwar reaction set in against executive power, as it had after the Civil War.

The acquisition of the Philippines and the greater influence over Cuba that accompanied victory in the Spanish-American War broadened the international obligations of the United States in ways that subdued partisan differences. For the first time since George Washington, the president attained a status above party politics. Having territory in the Pacific also increased the interest of the United States in the Far East. American participation in China during the Boxer uprising of 1900 and the successful U.S. insistence upon an "open door" trade policy in Asia reinforced the public's view that the United States now occupied a new and prominent position in world affairs. Thus, the Spanish-American War was, in a very real sense, a landmark in the constitutional development of the executive.[81] As McKinley himself said to his secretary, "I can no longer be called the President of a party; I am now the President of the whole people." [82]

McKinley's tenure, then, marked an important transformation of the presidency. To be sure, his administration gave only a hint of what soon was to come. Committed to a limited role for the national government in domestic affairs, McKinley did not offer or endorse a positive program to deal with race relations, trusts, labor, the civil service, or other important issues of the day. Nor did he attempt to influence public opinion other than through the regular channels of party politics. Following in the tradition of the nineteenth-century executive, McKinley eschewed public rhetoric as a tool to influence policy; indeed, his speeches did not even allude to the Spanish-American War, the problem of racist "Jim Crow" laws in the South, or the U.S. policy toward the Philippines—all major issues that faced his administration.[83] Nevertheless, McKinley's influence with Congress and his role as world leader constituted an important preface to the more complete transformation of the executive that was about to take place in the twentieth century.

Notes

1. "The Wade-Davis Manifesto," August 5, 1864, in *History of American Presidential Elections*, ed. Arthur Schlesinger, Jr., and Fred I. Israel (New York: Chelsea, 1971), 2:1195-1196.
2. Wilfred E. Binkley, *President and Congress* (New York: Knopf, 1947), 128. For a discussion of the Reconstruction controversy that Johnson inherited, see Albert Castel, *The Presidency of Andrew Johnson* (Lawrence: University Press of Kansas, 1979), 17-20.
3. Quoted in Castel, *Presidency of Andrew Johnson*, 20.
4. Ibid., 31.
5. LaWanda Cox, *Lincoln and Black Freedom* (Columbia: University of South Carolina Press, 1981), 38.
6. Charles Sumner, *The Promises of the Declaration of Independence,* Eulogy on Abraham Lincoln (Boston: Ticknor and Fields, 1865), 56; Roy P. Basler,

ed., *The Collected Works of Lincoln*, 9 vols. (New Brunswick, N.J.: Rutgers University Press, 1953), 8:403-404; and Cox, *Lincoln and Black Freedom*, 38.

7. On the struggle between Johnson and Congress over civil rights legislation, see Castel, *Presidency of Andrew Johnson*, 68-76; and Binkley, *President and Congress*, 134-135.
8. Johnson cited in LaWanda Cox and John H. Cox, *Politics, Principle, and Prejudice, 1865-1866* (New York: Free Press, 1963), 153.
9. Ibid.
10. Castel, *Presidency of Andrew Johnson*, 29-30.
11. Binkley, *President and Congress*, 136-137.
12. Of this bill, Castel has written:

> This was—and still is—the single most dramatic piece of legislation to emerge from Congress. It placed millions of citizens under military rule in peace time, deprived hundreds of thousands of their political rights, and enfranchised a race which the vast majority of Americans at the time considered unqualified to participate in the government process.

Castel, *Presidency of Andrew Johnson*, 108.

13. James D. Richardson, ed., *Messages and Papers of the Presidents* (Washington, D.C.: Bureau of National Literature, 1911), 5:3700.
14. Ibid. 5:3870.
15. Binkley, *President and Congress*, 138.
16. Eric McKitrick, "Party Politics and the Union and Confederate War Efforts," in *The American Party Systems: Stages of Development*, 2d ed., ed. William Nisbet Chambers and Walter Dean Burnham (New York: Oxford University Press, 1975); and A. James Reichley, *The Life of the Parties: A History of American Political Parties* (New York: Free Press, 1992), 129-134.
17. Castel, *Presidency of Andrew Johnson*, 68-70.
18. Ibid., 70.
19. For a discussion of how the constitutional and political constraints on popular rhetoric during the nineteenth century contributed to Johnson's problems with Congress, see Jeffrey Tulis, *The Rhetorical Presidency* (Princeton, N.J.: Princeton University Press, 1987), 87-93.
20. David Miller Dewitt, *The Impeachment and Trial of Andrew Johnson* (Madison: State Historical Society of Wisconsin, 1967), 123-124.
21. "The House of Representatives Articles of Impeachment Against President Andrew Johnson," March 2-3, 1868, printed in *The Growth of Presidential Power: A Documented History*, ed. William M. Goldsmith (New York and London: Chelsea, 1974), 2:1068-1069.
22. Dewitt, *Impeachment and Trial of Andrew Johnson*, 517-518.
23. Quoted in ibid., 579.
24. Gideon Welles, *Diary of Gideon Welles* (Boston: Houghton Mifflin, 1911), 3:560.
25. Goldsmith, *Growth of Presidential Power* 2:1102.
26. Binkley, *President and Congress*, 147.
27. George F. Hoar, *Autobiography of Seventy Years* (New York: Scribner's, 1903), 2:46.
28. Leonard D. White, *The Republican Era: 1869-1901: A Study in Administrative History* (New York: Macmillan, 1958), 372-376.
29. President Ulysses S. Grant, "First Statement to Congress on Civil Service Reform," December 5, 1870, printed in Goldsmith, *Growth of Presidential*

Power, 2:986.
30. Morton Keller, *Affairs of State: Public Life in Late Nineteenth Century America* (Cambridge, Mass.: Harvard University Press, 1977), 266-268.
31. James D. Richardson, ed., *Messages and Papers of the Presidents* (New York: Bureau of National Literature, 1897), 9:4254-4255; White, *Republican Era,* 281-287.
32. Binkley, *President and Congress,* 161.
33. The scandals that afflicted the federal government during the Grant administration were, as the historian Samuel Eliot Morison has written, merely "the summit of a pyramid of corruption in the Northern states." In New York City, William Marcy ("Boss") Tweed built a Democratic machine, known as Tammany Hall, that stole $100 million from the city treasury. A similar ring, which operated at the state level under the auspices of the Republican party (but included some Democrats as well), perpetrated systematic fraud in canal construction, with estimated losses to the state of nearly $1 million (Samuel Eliot Morison, *The Oxford History of the American People* [New York: New American Library, 1972], 3:36).
34. The Republicans' willingness to end Reconstruction reflected their disillusionment with the program's disorder and corruption. When the Republican governor of Mississippi telegraphed for federal troops to protect black voters from white "rifle clubs" during the state election of 1875, the attorney general rejected his request, declaring that

> the whole public are tired out with these annual outbreaks in the South, and the great majority are now ready to condemn any interference on the part of the government. . . . [P]reserve the peace by the forces in your own state, and let the country see that the citizens of Mississippi, who are largely Republican [that is, the black majority], have the courage to *fight* for their rights and to destroy the bloody ruffians who murder the innocent and unoffending freedmen.

Edwards Pierrepoint, cited in Richard Nelson Current, *Those Terrible Carpetbaggers* (New York: Oxford University Press, 1988), 321-322 (emphasis in original). In the so-called Revolution of 1875, white Mississippians drove blacks from the polls and regained control of the state government. Thus, Reconstruction was already collapsing before the Compromise of 1877. Hayes's withdrawal of federal troops from the South only accelerated the demise of Radical Republican policies. James M. McPherson, *Abraham Lincoln and the Second American Revolution* (New York: Oxford University Press, 1991), 148.
35. Keller, *Affairs of State,* 258.
36. Quoted in ibid.
37. Ibid.
38. Rutherford B. Hayes, "Inaugural Address," March 5, 1877, in Richardson, *Messages and Papers of the Presidents,* 1911 ed., 6:4396; Hayes's Letter of Acceptance (July 8, 1876) cited in White, *Republican Era,* 287.
39. Binkley, *President and Congress,* 155.
40. Charles Richard Williams, ed., *Diary and Letters of Rutherford B. Hayes,* 5 vols. (Columbus: Ohio State Archeological and Historical Society, 1924), 3:430 (April 22, 1877).
41. Ibid. 3:454 (December 12, 1877).
42. Binkley, *President and Congress,* 157.
43. President Rutherford B. Hayes, "Letter to General E. A. Merritt Defining Criteria for Appointments to the New York Customhouse," February 4, 1879, in Goldsmith, *Growth of Presidential Power* 2:1112.

44. Ibid. 2:1113.
45. Williams, *Diary and Letters of Rutherford B. Hayes* 3:612-613 (July 14, 1880).
46. The Stalwarts labeled Blaine's followers as "Half-breeds," implying that they were deficient in Republican loyalty. In reality, the partisanship of the Blaine wing, although it paid lip service to civil service reform, was just as strong as that of the Stalwarts.
47. Keller, *Affairs of State*, 266-268.
48. John A. Garraty, *The New Commonwealth: 1877-1890* (New York: Harper and Row, 1968), 268-273.
49. Binkley, *President and Congress*, 158-159, 172; Theodore Clarke Smith, *James Abram Garfield: Life and Letters* (New Haven: Yale University Press, 1925), 2:1103-1104.
50. Quoted in Smith, *James Abram Garfield* 2:1109.
51. Quoted in Thomas C. Reeves, *Gentleman Boss: The Life of Chester Alan Arthur* (New York: Knopf, 1975), 227.
52. Quoted in ibid., 229.
53. Smith, *James Abram Garfield* 2:1127.
54. Garraty, *New Commonwealth*, 273; White, *Republican Era*, 34-35; and Binkley, *President and Congress*, 159-160.
55. Williams, *Diary and Letters of Rutherford B. Hayes* 4:23.
56. Garraty, *New Commonwealth*, 276.
57. White, *Republican Era*, 393; also see 301-302.
58. Garraty, *New Commonwealth*, 287; Keller, *Affairs of State*, 546.
59. President Grover Cleveland, "Message to the Senate on the President's Power of Removal and Suspension," March 1, 1886, in Goldsmith, *Growth of Presidential Power* 2:1121.
60. Grover Cleveland, *Presidential Problems* (New York: Century, 1904), 76.
61. White, *Republican Era*, 38.
62. Ibid., 66.
63. Garraty, *New Commonwealth*, 295.
64. Woodrow Wilson, *Congressional Government* (New York: Meridian Books, 1956; Boston: Houghton Mifflin, 1885), 31.
65. John Sherman, *Recollections of Forty Years in the House, Senate and Cabinet* (Chicago: Werner Company, 1895), 2:1032.
66. Garraty, *New Commonwealth*, 305.
67. Keller, *Affairs of State*, 302-303.
68. James Bryce, *The American Commonwealth* (London: Macmillan, 1891), 1:115.
69. Keller, *Affairs of State*, 306.
70. Binkley, *President and Congress*, 182.
71. Lincoln, cited in Reichley, *The Life of the Parties*, 128.
72. Ibid., 155.
73. Governor John P. Altgeld, "Telegram to President Grover Cleveland on the Use of Federal Troops in Illinois," July 5, 1894, in Goldsmith, *Growth of Presidential Power* 2:1155.
74. President Grover Cleveland, "Telegram to Governor John P. Altgeld on the Use of Federal Troops in Illinois," July 6, 1894, in ibid. 2:1157.
75. *In re Debs*, 158 U.S. 564.
76. Edward S. Corwin, *The President: Office and Powers*, 1787-1957, 4th ed. (New York: New York University Press, 1957), 134.
77. J. Rogers Hollingsworth, *The Whirligig of Politics: The Democracy of*

Cleveland and Bryan (Chicago: University of Chicago Press, 1963), 24-25.

78. Garraty, *New Commonwealth*, 306.
79. Binkley, *President and Congress*, 189.
80. Lewis L. Gould, *The Presidency of William McKinley* (Lawrence: University Press of Kansas, 1980), 93.
81. Binkley, *President and Congress*, 191.
82. Quoted in Charles S. Olcott, *William McKinley* (Boston: Houghton Mifflin, 1916), 2:296.
83. Tulis, *Rhetorical Presidency*, 87. "Jim Crow" was the term applied to state laws enacted during the late 1890s and early 1900s, mainly in the South, that systematically excluded African-Americans from public life and restricted them to segregated and generally inferior public facilities. The Jim Crow system was part of the unhappy legacy of the Compromise of 1877, although a decade and a half of relatively responsible "home rule" subsequently prevailed in the South before it succumbed to extreme racism. See C. Van Woodward, *The Strange Career of Jim Crow* (New York: Oxford University Press, 1957).

CHAPTER 8

Progressive Politics and Executive Power: The Presidencies of Theodore Roosevelt and William Howard Taft

During the last three decades of the nineteenth century, major changes in American society placed greater burdens upon the national government, and particularly upon the presidency.[1] The population of the United States doubled between 1870 and 1900; urbanization and immigration increased at extraordinary rates. These changes were accompanied by a shift in the economy from local, small-scale manufacturing and commerce to large-scale factory production and mammoth national corporations. The technological breakthroughs and the frenzied search for new markets and new sources of capital that were associated with rapid industrialization caused unprecedented economic growth—indeed, from 1863 to 1899 the index of manufacturing production rose by more than 700 percent. But dynamic growth also generated a wide range of problems that seriously challenged the capacity of the American political system to respond.

Industrial development was accomplished at the expense of other social and political values, which were sacrificed in the unchecked pursuit of economic progress. The concentration of wealth at the turn of the century yielded giant "trusts" that, according to reformers, constituted uncontrolled and irresponsible units of power within American society. These industrial combinations aroused fears that opportunity would be less equal in the United States because growing corporate might would threaten the freedom of individuals to earn a living. Moreover, many believed that the great business interests had captured and corrupted the men and methods of government for their own profit.

The first wave of protest against the financial exploitation and political corruption that industrial growth unleashed was the agrarian

Populist revolt, which culminated in William Jennings Bryan's failed campaign for the presidency in 1896. The Progressive Era took shape as populism collapsed; it was a period of urban and middle-class protest against many of the same forces of expanding industrialization and unrestrained finance capitalism that had vexed the Populists. Because it represented the fastest-growing segments of the population, progressivism had a major influence on the nation. As the historian Richard Hofstadter has noted, it "enlarged and redirected" agrarian discontent, bringing about industrial reforms and changes in government institutions that "affected in a striking way . . . the whole tone of American political life." [2]

One effect of the progressive transformation was a modified understanding of the responsibilities of the national government. Hitherto, American society had been strongly committed to individualism and limited government. The Populist and Progressive reactions to industrialization did not displace these traditions, to be sure. Many industrialists, bankers, and political leaders continued to adhere to the "laissez-faire" creed, eschewing government regulation of business, transportation, and finance. They did so, however, in the face of a rising progressive philosophy. Elihu Root, who served in Theodore Roosevelt's cabinet, clearly stated this philosophy in an address to the New York Bar Association in 1912:

> The real difficulty appears to be that the new conditions incident to the extraordinary industrial development of the last half-century are continuously and progressively demanding the readjustment of the relations between the great bodies of men and the establishment of new legal rights and obligations not contemplated when existing laws were passed or existing limitations upon the powers of the government were prescribed in our Constitution. . . . The relations between the employer and employed, between the owners of aggregated capital and the units of organized labor, between the small producer, the small trader, the consumer, and the great transporting and manufacturing and distributing agencies, all present new questions for the solution of which the old reliance upon the free action of individual wills appears quite inadequate. And in many directions the intervention of that organized control which we call government seems necessary to produce the same result of justice and right conduct which obtained through the attrition of individuals before the conditions arose.[3]

The Progressive movement helped to bring about important changes in the office of the president. Although the executive had developed significantly in the hands of strong leaders such as Washington, Jefferson, Jackson, and Lincoln, the roles and powers of the president remained tightly restricted until the twentieth century. Indeed, "congressional government" was the prevailing theme of late

nineteenth-century politics in America. The presidencies of Grover
Cleveland and William McKinley suggested that a more forceful style of
presidential leadership might be emerging, but they did not alter
fundamentally the condition of legislative dominance that had existed
since Lincoln's assassination in 1865.

Theodore Roosevelt changed the old pattern. Dedicated to a
progressive concept of government, he advocated and practiced an
active form of presidential leadership that broadly extended the reach
of executive influence. In his aggressive pursuit of a policy agenda and,
especially, in his active courting of public opinion, TR (who was the first
president to be known by his initials) recast the presidency. In both
foreign and domestic affairs, he established critical precedents that
charted a path for future presidents, such as Woodrow Wilson and TR's
cousin, Franklin D. Roosevelt, to follow and widen in bringing about a
more complete transformation of the American presidency. As the
historian William Goldsmith has written, "Theodore Roosevelt transformed the presidential office from its inert nineteenth century pattern
into a veritable cockpit of political leadership for social reform." [4]

Theodore Roosevelt and the Expansion of Executive Power

On September 6, 1901, President McKinley was shot by an anar-
chist while attending the Pan-American Exposition in Buffalo, New
York. When McKinley died on September 14, Vice President Theodore
Roosevelt became president. Disregarding the warning of friends that he
would seem but a "pale copy of McKinley," Roosevelt announced that
he intended to continue unchanged McKinley's policies and cabinet. "If
a man is fit to be President," TR wrote in his autobiography, "he will
speedily so impress himself in the office that the policies pursued will be
his anyhow, and he will not have to bother as to whether he is changing
them or not. . . ." [5]

The prospect of Roosevelt impressing himself upon the executive
office greatly troubled the politicians and other men of affairs who
dominated national politics at the turn of the century. The conservative
leaders of the Republican party, especially, feared that the young
president (at forty-two he was the youngest person ever to assume the
office) was not to be trusted. Throughout his political career, including
his tenure as governor of New York, Roosevelt had been known as a
progressive and impetuous leader, one who lived uneasily with the
patronage practices and probusiness policies of his party. Indeed, during
Roosevelt's two years as governor he was so troublesome to the party
regulars of his state that they took pains to remove him from their midst
by securing his nomination for vice president in 1900.

"Anything can happen now that that damn cowboy is in the White

House," complained Mark Hanna, the chair of the Republican National Committee, when his friend McKinley died. Conservatives in New York and Washington publicly hoped for the best but privately agreed with Hanna. They now wished that they had heeded the Republican chair, who, when presented with the suggestion that Roosevelt be chosen as McKinley's running mate, had blurted out, "Don't you realize that there's only one life between that madman and the White House?" [6]

Roosevelt's plain-speaking and unconventional style aside, he was not the "madman" that Hanna feared. TR was no enemy to business or party interests. Like most progressive reformers, he accepted the new industrial order, wanting only to curb its worst abuses through government regulation. Without moderate reform, Roosevelt believed, the connection between citizens and their leaders that was the essence of republican government would be dangerously attenuated. "Sweeping attacks upon all property, upon all men of means, without regard to whether they do well or ill, would sound the death knell of the Republic," he wrote, "and such attacks become inevitable if decent citizens permit rich men whose lives are corrupt and evil to domineer in swollen pride, unchecked and unhindered, over the destinies of the country." [7]

Theodore Roosevelt's Concept of Presidential Power

In both foreign and domestic matters, the presidential scholars Samuel and Dorothy Rosenman have written, "Roosevelt extended executive authority to the furthest limit permitted in peacetime by the Constitution—if not further." [8] After leaving office, Roosevelt himself described the extension of executive authority as the principal ingredient of his remarkably successful tenure as president. "The most important factor in getting the right spirit in my administration," he wrote in his *Autobiography*, "was my insistence upon the theory that the executive power was limited only by specific restrictions and prohibitions appearing in the Constitution or imposed by Congress in its constitutional powers." [9]

Believing that the delimitation of presidential power during the nineteenth century had rendered the American political system impotent and subject to capture by "special interests," Roosevelt proclaimed that the president was "a steward of the people bound actively and affirmatively to do all he could for the people, and not content himself with the negative merit of keeping his talents undamaged in a napkin." [10]

Roosevelt's confidence that the president possessed a special mandate from the people made him a conscious disciple of Andrew Jackson. Unlike Jackson, however, Roosevelt wanted to join popular leadership to a greater sense of national purpose—a "new nationalism" that foretold of an unprecedented expansion of the government's responsibility to secure the social and economic welfare of the nation. As he explained many years later:

> My belief was that it was not only his [the President's] right but his duty to do anything that the needs of the nation demanded unless action was forbidden by the Constitution or by the laws. Under this interpretation of executive power I did and caused to be done many things not previously done by the President and the heads of the departments. I did not usurp power, but I did greatly broaden the use of executive power. In other words, I acted for the public welfare, I acted for the common well-being of all our people, wherever and in whatever manner was necessary, unless prevented by direct constitutional or legislative provision.[11]

In important respects, Roosevelt's exposition of executive power drew upon the defense of a broad discretionary authority for the president that Alexander Hamilton had articulated in 1793 under the pen name "Pacificus." To justify George Washington's issuance of the Neutrality Proclamation, Hamilton had offered a theory of the presidency that, for the most part, was politically unacceptable until Roosevelt entered the White House. "The general doctrine of our Constitution," Hamilton argued, "is that the executive power of the nation is vested in the President; subject only to the exceptions and qualifications which are expressed in the instrument." [12] Washington, Jackson, and Lincoln had taken a broad view of the president's authority, especially in a time of national crisis. Roosevelt, however, was the first chief executive to embrace the Hamiltonian position as the proper recipe for the day-to-day administration of government.

Yet TR's acceptance of Hamiltonian principles certainly was not complete. Hamilton supported an energetic executive because he thought that it would curb, not abet, popular influence. Similarly, Gouverneur Morris, wrote Roosevelt in a biography of Hamilton's friend and political ally, embodied "both the virtues and the shortcomings of the Federalist school of thought." Morris, Roosevelt argued, "championed a strong national government, wherein he was right; but he also championed a system of class representation, leaning toward aristocracy, wherein he was wrong." [13]

In contrast to the Hamiltonian concept of executive nationalism, Roosevelt expressed and embodied the Progressives' aspiration to establish the president as an agent of social and economic reform. He looked with favor on the statesmanship of Lincoln, whose uncompromising defense of the Union served the "high purpose" of achieving equality of opportunity. "Men who understand and practice the deep underlying philosophy of the Lincoln school of American political thought," wrote TR, "are necessarily Hamiltonian in their belief in a strong and efficient National Government and Jeffersonian in their belief in the people as the ultimate authority, and in the welfare of the people as the end of government."[14] As the progressive reformer Herbert Croly put it, the aim of Roosevelt's new nationalism, and of the corresponding expansion of executive power, was "to give a democratic meaning and purpose to the Hamiltonian tradition and method."[15]

From Theory to Practice: The Beginning of the Rhetorical Presidency

Roosevelt's determination to use the presidency to serve the interests of the people, as he understood them, brought about a number of significant changes in the conduct of the executive office. Arguably, the most important of these changes was to advance the president's role as the leader of public opinion. In doing so, Roosevelt ushered in the "rhetorical presidency"—that is, the use of popular rhetoric as a principal technique of presidential leadership.[16] TR was an irrepressible, if not always eloquent, speaker, and is said to have been the first to describe the presidency as a "bully pulpit."[17]

The rise of the rhetorical presidency signified a dramatic transformation of the founding theory and the early history of the executive. The Framers of the Constitution had explicitly proscribed popular leadership. Thus, during the nineteenth century, direct presidential efforts to rouse public opinion in support of policy initiatives were considered illegitimate, a form of demagogy that was beneath the dignity of the office. Roosevelt's "stewardship" theory of the executive, however, demanded that a stronger popular connection be forged. Accordingly, on a number of occasions TR appealed directly to the people to bring pressure to bear on members of Congress who were reluctant to support his policies.

Much of Roosevelt's legislative program was designed, as TR put it, to "subordinate the big corporation to the public welfare."[18] But the Republican party in Congress was led by conservatives—notably Nelson Aldrich of Rhode Island and Eugene Hale of Maine in the Senate and Speaker Joseph Cannon of Illinois in the House—who distrusted anything that was progressive. Roosevelt sided with the "stand patters" (they also were called the "Old Guard") in their support of the gold standard and in their recognition of the need, after the Spanish-American War, for a strong American presence in world affairs. Domestic policy was different. As TR later wrote of his relationship with the Republican Old Guard, "Gradually I was forced to abandon the effort to persuade them to come my way, and then I achieved results only by

Theodore Roosevelt ushered in the "rhetorical presidency"—the use of popular rhetoric as a principal technique of presidential leadership.

appealing over the heads of the Senate and House leaders to the people, who were the masters of both of us." [19]

The Hepburn Act.   Perhaps the most important product of Roosevelt's popular appeals was the Hepburn Act of 1906. The act enhanced the power of the Interstate Commerce Commission (ICC) to regulate railroad shipping rates and to enforce compliance with its regulations.[20] Previous laws had failed to prevent the railroads from favoring the largest, most ruthless industrial corporations.[21] Faced with enormous fixed costs—such as the interest on huge bonded debts and the depreciation on large and expensive equipment—the railroads, to ensure having enough money to meet their overheads, acceded to the demands of corporations like the Standard Oil Company, the Armour Company, and the American Sugar Refining Company for lower freight rates than were charged to smaller shippers.

Although rate discrimination had been forbidden by the Elkins Act of 1903, the offenders usually were able to obscure any violations with deceptive bookkeeping methods, which the ICC had no authority to control. Major shippers also obtained special favors by arranging to receive inordinately large fees from the railroads for the use of private cars—such as oil or refrigerator cars—and of private sidings and terminals that the corporations owned.

Determined to remedy these conditions, Roosevelt proposed that Congress give the ICC the power to regulate railroad accounts, private railway equipment, and, most important, railroad rates. In his annual message, which he sent to Congress in December 1904, Roosevelt urged legislators to draft a law that would forbid railroads to provide large shippers with discriminatory rebates and would empower the ICC to impose ceilings on railroad rates in order "to keep the highways of commerce open to all on equal terms." [22]

The president's proposal was received favorably by the House of Representatives, which quickly passed railroad rate legislation in early 1905. But it ran into trouble in the Senate, where the conservative Committee on Interstate Commerce conducted long public hearings, mostly to receive opposing testimony from railroad executives. The committee managed to waste enough time to prevent the Senate from considering the bill before the summer recess.

The railroads' strategy was shrewd. "The House was the only one of the two bodies elected directly by the people," one contemporary observer wrote, "and was therefore regarded contemptuously by the railroads and conservatives generally as reflecting the mob; while the Senate, being elected by state legislatures, was regarded as a safe city of refuge." [23] (Senators were not elected by the people until the Seventeenth Amendment was enacted in 1913.)

But Roosevelt was shrewder still. As the Senate hearings proceeded, the president left Washington for a long vacation in the West. Speculation arose that he had given up on rate regulation. [24] In fact, Roosevelt's trip through the Midwest and Southwest in April and May of 1905 turned out to be a campaign for the Hepburn bill.

The president fired his first rhetorical blast in Chicago, where, speaking before the Iroquois-Republican Club on May 10, he called on the federal government to "take an increasing control over corporations." The first step, Roosevelt argued, "should be the adoption of a law conferring upon one executive body the power of increased supervision and regulation of the great corporations engaged primarily in interstate commerce of the railroads." The ICC should have "ironclad" powers to set rates, which could be suspended by the courts only if they proved to be confiscatory. [25] This speech and similar addresses in Dallas, San Antonio, and Denver received extensive and favorable coverage in the press.

Roosevelt's campaign resumed with a swing through the Southwest in the early fall of 1905 and culminated in his annual message to Congress in December. The annual message boldly reaffirmed the president's commitment to railroad regulation, insisting on the need "to prevent the imposition of unjust and unreasonable rates." [26] Although his argument was addressed formally to Congress, Roosevelt had a larger audience in mind, and the pressure of public opinion eventually overcame the Senate's resistance to the Hepburn Act. Secretary of War William Howard Taft told his brother that the president of the Rock Island line had admitted to him in a confidential talk that the senators he had counted on for "allegiance," although privately still opposed to the Hepburn bill, were yielding because the president had so "roused the people that it was impossible for the Senate to stand against the popular demand." [27]

When Congress reconvened in 1906, the House, once again, passed the railroad law quickly, in early February. This time, however, on May 18, Roosevelt's bill also was passed by the Senate. Indeed, only three senators voted against it.

The Hepburn Act was a landmark in the history of the federal regulation of private industry. As the historian John Morton Blum has written, "it challenged the most cherished prerogative of private management, the most hoary tenet of free enterprise—the ability freely to make prices." [28] Remarkably, considering the previous history of the presidency, the Hepburn Act passed even though it was opposed from beginning to end by the leadership of the president's own party.

TR and the Press. Roosevelt's remarkable victory in the battle for the Hepburn Act was helped considerably by the press. He was the first president to recognize the press's value as a medium to communicate with the people and the first to understand that journalistic support had to be pursued actively and continually. It was TR's good fortune that his presidency coincided with the development of mass-circulation newspapers and popular magazines. Before the 1890s, the "party organ" style of journalism, which had prevailed since the Jacksonian era, and primitive printing technology had tended to complement each other. At the beginning of the twentieth century, however, "cheap and rapid manufacture made possible and even necessary a *mass* market beyond the confines of one faction, party, or following." As the political scientist Elmer Cornwell has written, "the press inevitably became large-scale enterprise, and journalistic independence followed logically." [29]

One group of journalists, the so-called muckrakers—the label was original with Roosevelt—occupied an especially important place in early twentieth-century politics. They wrote mainly for new and low-priced magazines such as *McClure's*, a fifteen-cent monthly publication whose influence on public opinion was hardly less important than that of Roosevelt himself. The president's term for these writers evoked their relentless efforts to expose corruption in the relations between government and business. According to a writer in the August 1905 issue of the *Atlantic Monthly:*

They expose in countless pages the sordid and depressing rottenness of our politics; the hopeless apathy of our good citizens; the remorseless corruption of our great financiers and business men, who are bribing our legislatures, swindling the public with fraudulent stock schemes, adulterating our food, speculating with trust funds, combining in great monopolies to oppress and destroy small competitors and raise prices. . . . They show us our social sore spots, like the three cheerful friends of Job.[30]

Roosevelt's grasp of the political potential of the new media is revealed especially by his use of the mass-circulation magazines. The president endorsed the muckrakers with reservations. He believed that by fixing their gaze exclusively on the "vile and debasing," they neglected the achievements of the constructive elements of society.[31] Nevertheless, he took advantage of the literature of exposure, which brought to light so many of the evils to which he was responding. Partly by inspiring intimates in the press to write articles, and partly through the force of his personality and ideas, TR "kept the pages of the popular magazines glowing with support" for his crusades.[32] As the journalist Mark Sullivan noted, "Roosevelt, in marshalling public opinion for the railroad rate bill, had, as always, help from the magazine writers."[33]

Roosevelt's triumph in the matter of rate regulation signaled a change in the executive: the president's most important political relationship soon would be with the public rather than with his party or with Congress. But Roosevelt also believed that a balance must exist between presidential initiative and congressional deliberation in order to maintain the American system of government. Accordingly, even as he insisted that the modern president had to assume a more prominent place in public affairs than in the nineteenth century, TR worked assiduously to win support in Congress by cooperating with his party's leaders in the Senate and the House.

In fighting for the Hepburn Act, for example, Roosevelt directed his energies not just to the podium but also, more craftily, to the halls of Congress. He feigned interest in a bill to revise and reduce the tariff, then traded his abandonment of a threatened endorsement of that proposal for congressional support of his most important objective, railroad regulation. In late November 1904, the president sent Speaker of the House Cannon, "that arch priest of protection," a draft of a special message to Congress that urged tariff revision. Shortly thereafter Roosevelt delivered his annual message, in which nothing was said of the tariff. As TR wrote to a friend: "On the interstate commerce business, which I regard as a principle, I shall fight. On the tariff, which I regard as a matter of expediency, I shall endeavor to get the best results I can, but I shall not break with my party."[34]

At the other end of Pennsylvania Avenue, Cannon—already on

record against regulating the railroads—gave the Hepburn Act a clear track, and when other conservatives rose to fight the bill, Roosevelt revived the tariff issue until they retreated. The Old Guard in the House regarded the tariff as the linchpin of the Republican program of industrial development. Ultimately, therefore, they acquiesced to TR's desire for railroad regulation in order to preserve what they regarded as vital: the hallowed protection of American industry. By 1906, Roosevelt had abandoned all efforts to reduce tariffs, but it was mainly a bargaining instrument that he abandoned. "For eighteen months, however," Blum has written, "he employed adroitly the specter of tariff revision." [35]

Even in the Senate, which was less responsive than the House to Roosevelt's legislative maneuvers, the president worked cleverly to prevent a complete rupture within his party. When the Republican leader Aldrich assigned the responsibility to manage the Hepburn bill to a Democrat, Sen. Ben Tillman of South Carolina, Roosevelt responded by encouraging the progressives of both parties to maneuver the legislation out of committee and onto the Senate floor. Then, after it became clear that this new coalition lacked the votes to enact railroad reform, the president worked out an agreement with the Republican leaders by modifying his position on the judicial review of ICC findings. Although he opposed a broad grant of administrative authority to the judiciary, Roosevelt agreed to let the courts define what scope of review was proper. This concession overcame the last obstacle to Senate passage of the Hepburn Act.

Thus, in leading Congress Roosevelt exercised artfully the resources of office and person. He succeeded in part because of his remarkable political gifts and his willingness to compromise to attain his major objectives. But the president's commitment to constitutional government, which included an appreciation of Congress and his party, also was significant. Roosevelt began and ended his "swings around the circle" before Congress took up the Hepburn bill. He did not speak directly to the people on the eve of crucial votes, nor did he attack members of Congress during the debate. As Blum has written, "Roosevelt's impressive ability to work within the structure of government, like his facility in managing the party, depended less on his arresting manner than on his appreciation of the institutions that shaped American political life." [36]

Roosevelt and Policy Leadership

The rise of the rhetorical presidency that began during the Roosevelt administration went hand in hand with an expansion of the executive's responsibility to guide the formation of public policy. The ability of the president to lead an often factious and defiant Congress in policy matters had been very limited during the latter half of the nineteenth century. McKinley's successful party leadership and the executive responsibilities in foreign policy that arose in the aftermath of the Spanish-American War suggested a more active role for the president. But only with the advent of the Progressive Era and the enormously effective stewardship of Theodore Roosevelt was a fundamental challenge posed to the sway that Congress and the party organizations held over the affairs of state. Lord Bryce had forecast such a development in 1890, observing that "the tendency everywhere in America to concentrate power and responsibility in one man is unmistakable." [37]

By itself, Roosevelt's ability to get a considerable part of his program enacted in the absence of a national crisis and in spite of the tepid support, and sometimes the obstructive resistance, of the Republican party indicated that a new era of presidential leadership had arrived. Thereafter, government action would be much more likely to bear the president's personal stamp than in the past.

Roosevelt's all-out campaign for the Hepburn Act and the progressive principles that it embodied came to symbolize his whole domestic policy. While in office, Roosevelt called his program the "Square Deal," proclaiming that the proper function of government was to maintain a "just balance" between management and labor, between producer and consumer, and between extremists on both sides of the political divide.[38]

Toward the end of his presidency and, more decidedly, during his years as the leader of the Progressive movement after he left the White House, Roosevelt insisted that the government could not confine itself simply to mediating issues of wealth. Writing in 1913, he seemed to anticipate the welfare state that later was associated with the presidential initiatives of his cousin Franklin. "The nation and government," TR argued, "within the range of fair play and a just administration of the law, must inevitably sympathize with the men who have nothing but their wages, with the men who are struggling for a decent life, as opposed to men, however honorable, who are merely fighting for larger profits and autocratic control of big business." [39]

However defined, Roosevelt's enunciation of the Square Deal was important to the development of the modern presidency because it invoked principles of fairness as he, rather than his party or Congress, understood them. Several presidents would define their administrations in similar terms: Woodrow Wilson's New Freedom, Franklin D. Roosevelt's New Deal, Harry S. Truman's Fair Deal, Lyndon B. Johnson's Great Society, Ronald Reagan's Opportunity Society.[40] The effort, routine after Roosevelt, to advertise a catchy phrase to symbolize the president's programmatic philosophy was symptomatic of a new style of presidential leadership. In this new style, the executive, not Congress, assumed the major burden of formulating public policy.

Significantly, Roosevelt first used the term *Square Deal* during the 1904 presidential campaign, to describe his vigorous intervention (undeterred by the absence of either precedent or legislation to justify his involvement) in a nationwide coal strike. Rather than follow the example of Cleveland, who sent troops to break up the Pullman strike of 1894, Roosevelt called representatives of the coal industry and the miners to the White House, asking both sides to agree, in the interest of the health and welfare of the nation and as a matter of patriotism, to accept binding arbitration.

When the coal industry balked at Roosevelt's proposal, even lecturing the president about the folly of "negotiating with the fomenters of anarchy," TR prepared to take more drastic action. If he could not persuade labor and management to accept arbitration voluntarily, the president would appoint a settlement board without their consent and arrange for the governor of Pennsylvania to request federal assistance to keep the peace and order. Roosevelt also intended to have federal troops "seize the mines and run them as a receiver for the government." [41]

By previous constitutional interpretation dating back to the *In re Debs* decision in 1894, the president had the authority to send soldiers into a state to ensure that the national government could exercise duly authorized powers, such as to deliver the mail. Nowhere was the president's right to seize and operate private property even hinted at in the Constitution, much less specified. As it happened, such action did not prove necessary: an agreement finally was reached to end the strike, and a five-member commission, appointed by the president, arbitrated the points at issue between the miners and the coal industry. Yet Roosevelt's avowed willingness to act exemplified his style as the "steward of the people." Dedicated to expanding the national government to guarantee a "just balance" between rival claims in society, Roosevelt became the first president in history to recognize the rights of labor in an industrial dispute. [42] As the historian George Mowry has written: "By both his actions and threats Roosevelt had moved the government away from its traditional position of isolation from such economic struggles. The government by precedent if not by law, had become a third force and partner in major labor disputes." [43]

Roosevelt and Civil Service Reform

Roosevelt sought not only to expand presidential power but also to "professionalize" administration and thus to prepare the executive branch for its growing responsibilities. He believed that only continuous, disinterested administration, not the dicta of the bench or the give and take of partisan and sectional conflict in Congress, could properly direct the development of American industrial society.[44]

In Roosevelt's view, an orderly system of administrative control required a career civil service. To this end the president prevailed on Congress early in his tenure to increase the Civil Service Commission's budget so that it could be an effective supervisory body.[45] He also moved quickly to reinforce the commission's status as an agent of the executive, endowing it with new policing powers to ensure that employees were hired according to the civil service rules. William Dudley Foulke, a member of Roosevelt's civil service board, concluded in 1920 that Roosevelt "was the only President who from beginning to end of his career could be relied on to enforce the civil service act by taking by the scruff of the neck and kicking out of office anyone who violated it." [46]

Strengthening the Civil Service Commission went hand in hand with the extension of merit protection. Under Roosevelt's administration the coverage of the merit system for hiring, promotion, and tenure was pushed almost to the limits of the Pendleton Act. By the end of his incumbency approximately 60 percent of the civil service was included, even as the federal work force expanded from approximately 275,000 in 1901 to around 365,000 in 1909.

Most important, the Roosevelt administration marked the dividing line between the old commitment to party patronage in public affairs and the modern recognition that nonpolitical administration was a principal tool of governance. Americans never have carried the idea of a nonpolitical civil service to the same lengths as the British; indeed, the Jacksonian heritage still lingers. But by the end of Roosevelt's term in office, merit had begun to supplant spoils. Presidential leadership, previously dependent on patronage-seeking state and local party machines, now required careful attention to administrative management, sometimes to foster economy and efficiency and sometimes to bolster the power of the increasingly active federal government.

The new challenge for the president was to take charge of the large and disparate administrative apparatus. As the political scientist Stephen Skowronek has written, "A state building sequence that began with Roosevelt's determination to forge 'a more orderly system of control,' ended with the consolidation of a new governmental order defiant of all attempts at control." [47] After the 1930s, especially, presidential efforts to control the new structure of administration would become a continuing source of constitutional controversy, as well as of raw and disruptive conflict between the president and Congress.

The President as World Leader

Roosevelt's innovative and path-breaking activism in domestic affairs, important as it was, pales by comparison with his conduct of foreign policy. In domestic matters, TR led boldly, but only in the interest of moderate reform. In foreign affairs, he believed that new conditions dictated a more decisive break with the past. The course that he favored required a significant expansion of the executive's power to direct the country's international relations without interference from Congress. Although the president's authority to initiate foreign policy and to negotiate treaties had become settled practice during the nineteenth century, Roosevelt also asserted primacy in the execution of such policy, even when clear support from the legislature was lacking.

TR's executive theory had a policy purpose. The acquisition of territories from Spain gave the United States a new position in world affairs after 1898. Roosevelt was determined to build on this position and make the United States a world power. "It is a contemptible thing," he wrote in his autobiography, "for a great nation to render itself impotent in international action, whether because of cowardice or sloth, or sheer inability or unwillingness to look into the future." [48]

When Roosevelt looked into the future, he saw a more energetic and ambitious American foreign policy. "Whether we desire it or not," Roosevelt told Congress in his first annual message, "we must henceforth recognize that we have international duties no less than international rights." [49] Just as many progressives believed that laissez faire must give way to a greater sense of national purpose in domestic affairs, they also urged that the general nineteenth-century commitment to international isolation be abandoned in favor of the doctrine of manifest destiny, which proclaimed for the United States a natural right to expand as much as was necessary for freedom and republican government to prosper and survive. Progressives couched the doctrine in ethical terms, arguing that to extend American territory and influence was not imperialism but its opposite. Roosevelt himself was in hearty accord with the Progressive writer Herbert Croly's assertion that "peace will prevail in international relations, just as order prevails within a nation, because of the righteous use of superior force—because the power which makes for pacific organization is stronger than the power which makes for warlike organization." [50]

Practical considerations also prompted a more active foreign policy. The expansion of U.S. territory in the Caribbean and the Pacific required a dominant military presence in Central and South America, a new emphasis on the Pacific basin, and an isthmus canal so that naval power could move efficiently between the Atlantic and Pacific oceans.

The Panama Canal

Roosevelt considered the canal to be especially important. On December 3, 1901, in his first annual message to Congress, he said, "No single great material work which remains to be undertaken on this continent is of such consequence to the American people as the building of a canal across the isthmus connecting North and South America." [51] Panama, the site that eventually was chosen for this project, belonged to Colombia, which, to Roosevelt's surprise and embarrassment, was not willing to allow the United States to build the canal on the president's terms. A complicated round of diplomacy and intrigue ensued that revealed some of the most important characteristics of the Roosevelt era in American foreign policy.

On January 22, 1903, Secretary of State John Hay negotiated and signed a treaty with the Colombian minister in Washington, Thomas Herran. Under the Hay-Herran Treaty, the New Panama Canal Company, which was to construct the project, would receive $40 million from the United States, $10 million from Colombia, and an annual subsidy of $250,000 per year. Complete sovereignty in the three-mile canal zone, however, would belong to the United States in perpetuity. These conditions were rejected by the Colombian dictator, José Manuel Marroquin, and by the Colombian Senate. Several alternative agreements were proposed to the United States, all of which would have provided better financial terms for Colombia and recognized its sovereignty over the canal zone.

Instead of negotiating further, Roosevelt applied direct diplomatic pressure to Colombia. He threatened to turn to Nicaragua as an alternative site for the canal but to no avail. Undeterred, albeit enraged, by Colombia's refusal to cooperate, Roosevelt took by force what he had failed to achieve by diplomacy. He gave tacit support to the efforts of investors in the New Panama Canal Company to foment a secessionist revolution in Panama. Close associates of Roosevelt were even less restrained. The *New York Post* reported in mid-September that many prominent administration officials were "in favor of intimating to the Panamanian revolutionists that if they will maintain resistance long enough ... this government will see to it that they are not run over by the superior forces of Colombia." [52]

Roosevelt did indicate clearly that if a Panamanian revolution occurred and was unsuccessful, he would take possession of the isthmus anyway. Standing on the tenuous legal foundation of an 1846 treaty with Colombia, in which both countries had guaranteed the right of transit across the isthmus, TR was prepared to recommend to Congress that the United States occupy the canal zone; he actually drafted a paragraph to that effect in early October, to be included in his 1903 annual message to Congress.[53] When the more cautious Mark Hanna, who was now a leading figure in the Senate, was informed of this plan, he counseled patience. The president's answer typified his preference for decisive action:

> I think it is well worth considering whether we had not better warn those cat-rabbits that great though our patience has been, it can be exhausted. . . . I feel, that we are certainly justified in morals and . . . justified in law, under the treaty of 1846, in interfering summarily and saying that the canal is to be built and that they shall not stop it.[54]

A successful revolution in Panama made it unnecessary for Roosevelt to attack Colombia. But the president did aid and protect the revolution when it broke out on November 3, 1903. An American warship, the U.S.S. *Nashville*, docked in Colón on the eve of the uprising and, during the subsequent fighting, prevented Colombian troops from reinforcing their outnumbered brethren in Panama. On November 6, Panama became an independent nation, recognized within ninety minutes by the United States. Soon after, the Panamanian government signed a treaty to grant canal rights to the United States in return for the $10 million that Roosevelt originally had offered to Colombia.

Roosevelt's course of action in the canal zone controversy applied his stewardship theory of the presidency to foreign policy. He was not reluctant to act quickly and independently, even when congressional support and the legal foundation for his maneuvers seemed very uncertain. Roosevelt treated constitutional criticisms of his policy with disdain. "At different stages of the affair," he wrote, "believers in a do-nothing policy denounced me as having 'usurped authority'—which meant, that when nobody else could or would exercise efficient authority, I exercised it." [55]

Roosevelt built the canal, proclaiming some years later that having done so was "by far the most important action that I took in foreign affairs during the time I was President." [56] Still, Colombia felt cheated and outraged and continued to press its claims for justice. Later, over former president Roosevelt's protest, an apology was extended to Colombia by the Wilson and Harding administrations, along with an indemnity award of $25 million. Yet, as the historian William Goldsmith has written, "the wounds inflicted in this incident were never really eradicated. . . . An unfortunate pattern of overbearing American domination in Latin American affairs was established, and even when [interventionist policies] were at least partially abandoned in later years, the memory remains to plague future American Presidents." [57]

The Roosevelt Corollary.   The taking of the Canal Zone signified a new policy toward Latin America, one that entailed an expanded

American role in foreign affairs and enlarged presidential powers to support this role. The basic plan for a new Caribbean and Latin American policy had been worked out by McKinley and his secretary of state, John Hay. But under Roosevelt the new policy was greatly extended; it also was given a precision it previously had lacked.[58]

The desire to dominate the Caribbean was buttressed by the concern of Roosevelt and others in Washington that many of the independent republics of Central and South America had weak governments with chaotic finances, thus offering a standing invitation to Europe to intervene. Venezuela, for example, had borrowed heavily from Europe, then refused to pay the debt. In December 1902, Germany, Italy, and England undertook to blockade Venezuela in an effort to extract payment; Germany even threatened to take possession of certain Venezuelan cities or customhouses. Roosevelt persuaded all the parties to submit their cases to the Hague Court, an international tribunal, but not before he increased the strength of the American fleet in the Caribbean and described to the Germans how vulnerable they were to U.S. naval power on the western side of the Atlantic Ocean.[59]

Later, when a similar problem developed in Santo Domingo, Roosevelt decided to modify significantly the Monroe Doctrine. After a corrupt dictatorship left Santo Domingo bankrupt and unable to pay its debts, a revolution ensued. In the early winter of 1903, France, Germany, and Italy threatened to intervene; by the end of the year a German naval squadron was rumored to be sailing across the Atlantic to protect German interests in the Caribbean. Roosevelt, facing an election in 1904, responded cautiously at first. Before long, however, he began to formulate a policy that would proclaim the duty of the United States to intervene in the affairs of Latin American countries that it felt had acted wrongfully or been rendered impotent by the mismanagement of their political affairs. The president announced this policy in December 1904 in his annual message to Congress. The Roosevelt Corollary to the Monroe Doctrine, as it became known, was a bold statement of future U.S. conduct toward the debt-ridden, unstable governments of Latin America:

> It is not true that the United States feels any land hunger or entertains any projects as regards the other nations of the western hemisphere save such as are for their welfare. All that this country desires is to see the neighboring countries stable, orderly and prosperous.... If a nation shows that it knows how to act with reasonable efficiency and decency in social and political matters, if it keeps order and pays its obligations, it need fear no interference by the United States. Chronic wrongdoing, or an impotence which results in a general loosening of the ties of civilized society may in America, as elsewhere, ultimately require intervention by some civilized nation, and in the western hemisphere the adherence of the United States to

the Monroe Doctrine may force the United States, however reluctantly, in flagrant cases of such wrongdoing or impotence, to the exercise of an international police power.[60]

The Roosevelt Corollary altered the Monroe Doctrine, which had denied to Europeans the right to intervene in the Americas, by sanctioning U.S. intervention.[61] Less than a month after Roosevelt announced the new policy, worsening conditions in Santo Domingo led him to translate his words into action. In early 1905, confronted on the one side with a nation that faced bankruptcy and on the other with European powers demanding satisfaction for their accounts, Roosevelt forced an agreement on Santo Domingo to establish an American financial protectorate over the island. The arrangement required the United States to prevent any European interference with the Dominican customhouses but also to collect the custom revenues. Forty-five percent of the revenue was then turned over to the Dominican government, and 55 percent was deposited in a New York account for the benefit of the creditors.

Roosevelt sent the treaty to the Senate for ratification, declaring that to enact it promptly would forestall more drastic action in the future. But the Senate did not share the president's sense of urgency and failed to vote on the treaty. To a degree, the Democrats and some Republicans believed that commercial diplomacy was inherently mischievous, but resentment of the president's acting unilaterally to develop a new foreign policy also contributed to the Senate's unwillingness to support him. Roosevelt responded by implementing the Dominican protectorate as an executive agreement, which further antagonized his legislative critics. The executive agreement was two years old before the Senate finally acquiesced and approved the treaty with minor modification in 1907.

The eventual success of Roosevelt's Caribbean policy strengthened both his personal political position and, ultimately, the institutional status of the president in foreign affairs. In the past, it had not been uncommon for Congress, especially the Senate, to intervene in foreign policy. Indeed, the political scientist Woodrow Wilson wrote in 1885 that the executive's authority often was jeopardized by the Senate's "irresponsible exertion of ... semi-executive powers in regard to the foreign policy of the government." [62] The role that Theodore Roosevelt staked out for the president was not bounded by specific provisions of the Constitution, statutes passed by Congress, or even the Senate's power to ratify treaties. "The Constitution did not explicitly give me power to bring about the necessary agreement with Santo Domingo," Roosevelt wrote in 1913. "But, the Constitution did not forbid my doing what I did. I put the agreement into effect, and I continued its execution for two years before the Senate acted; and I would have continued it until the end of my term, if necessary, without any action by Congress." [63]

The Russo-Japanese War. The departure from the nineteenth-century doctrine of isolation that Roosevelt's Latin American policy signified was revealed even more clearly by TR's bold initiatives in Asia, especially his unprecedented intervention in the conflict between Russia and Japan over China in 1905.

After Russia moved troops into China in 1902—an action that, among other things, threatened the U.S. Open Door policy of free trade in China—Japan staged a devastating surprise attack in 1903 on the Russian fleet anchored at Port Arthur.[64] Because Roosevelt considered Russia the greater imperialistic threat in Asia, his sympathies lay with Japan. Indeed, the Japanese were fortified by the president's secret verbal assurances that the United States would support Japan if any of the European powers aided Russia. This extraordinary commitment also included an agreement by Japan to recognize U.S. jurisdiction in the Philippines in return for U.S. recognition of Japan's claim to Korea.[65] Thus, for the first time a president committed the United States to possible future military action, and to the recognition of one nation's claim upon another nation's territory and sovereignty, without consulting the Senate.

Roosevelt's audacious diplomacy ended in triumph. Although the president favored Japan as a counterweight to Russia's designs on China, he feared that too great a Japanese victory might endanger the peace of the entire Pacific area. When fighting in the Russo-Japanese War tilted dramatically in Japan's favor, Roosevelt arranged, without the knowledge of the cabinet, Congress, or even most of the State Department, for Russia and Japan to meet in a peace conference at Portsmouth, New Hampshire. There the president managed, through what Mowry has called "patient, tactful and brilliant diplomacy," to bring about the Peace of Portsmouth in September 1905. The agreement achieved a balance of power in Asia that satisfied the interests not only of the warring nations but also, because the Open Door policy was maintained, of the United States.[66] Roosevelt's policy was further advanced in 1907 when, again without consulting Congress or the cabinet, he sent the U.S. battle fleet on a cruise around the world, a daring and brilliant maneuver that roused public support for an expanded navy and demonstrated to the Japanese the intention and ability of the United States to protect its interests in Asia.[67]

Roosevelt's approach to international affairs, although singularly successful, did not complete the recently begun task of establishing the United States as a world power. His effort to expand both America's role in the world and the executive responsibility in foreign affairs took place without sustained and serious discussion by either the American people or their representatives in Congress. As Goldsmith has written, "Theodore Roosevelt set the stage for the American President to play a world historical role that in many instances successive Presidents were neither capable of nor inclined to follow, nor were the American people prepared to support it." [68]

The Troubled Presidency of William Howard Taft

Roosevelt was a remarkably popular and influential president. Indeed, had TR decided to stand for a another term in 1908, he almost certainly would have been renominated and most likely would have been reelected. "Few informed people in the country," Mowry has written, "seriously doubted the outcome of the election if Roosevelt decided to stand again." [69]

The decision to step down as president was not easy. But Roosevelt had promised in November 1904 that he would not run again. The three and a half years he already had served, after succeeding to the presidency in 1901, constituted his first term, Roosevelt had stated on election night, and because he considered the custom that limited presidents to two terms to be a wise one, he would not be "a candidate for or accept another nomination." [70]

Roosevelt's decision not to go back on his promise in 1908, although he clearly was tempted to do so, revealed his commitment to the traditions and institutions of constitutional government. TR believed strongly that the powers of the president needed to be expanded for the good, indeed for the survival, of the nation. But he also knew that representative government would be poorly served if too much power were concentrated in one person. His "act of abnegation," Mowry has claimed, "was among his greatest contributions to his country." [71]

Self-denial, however, did not prevent Roosevelt from selecting William Howard Taft, his secretary of war and closest adviser during the second term, as his successor. Nor did it stop him from "throwing his hat in the ring" in 1912 and challenging Taft's renomination, charging that his friend and fellow Republican had betrayed the progressive principles he was elected to uphold. Indeed, it is fair to say that Taft spent his entire four years as president uncomfortably in the shadow of Theodore Roosevelt.

Taft sincerely intended to carry on the policies of the Roosevelt administration, and he had some success in doing so. But Taft was ill-suited, by philosophy and personality, to match TR's stewardship of the executive office. As the historian Paolo Coletta has written, "while under the spell of the dynamic Roosevelt, Taft had appeared to be a progressive cut from the full Roosevelt cloth. With Roosevelt gone he would return to his basic conservative self and thereby earn the odium of the progressives as one who had deserted the cause." [72]

In the wake of Roosevelt's presidency, Taft seemed an anachronism. Although never saying so publicly, Taft disapproved of TR's theory that it is the president's duty "to do anything that the needs of the nation demand, unless such action is forbidden by the Constitution or the law." Taft's philosophy of executive power, like the understanding that had prevailed during most of the nineteenth century, eschewed a broad interpretation of the president's discretionary powers. As he wrote some years after leaving office:

> The true view of the executive function ... is that the President can exercise no power which cannot be reasonably or fairly traced to some specific grant of power or justly implied or included within such express grant as necessary and proper to its exercise. Such specific grant must be either in the Constitution or in an act of Congress passed in pursuance thereof. There is no undefined residuum of power which he can exercise because it seems to be in the public interest.... [73]

Because he construed the executive power narrowly, Taft denied that to be president required him to exercise either popular or policy leadership. He rejected the notion that he bore a special mandate from the people and refused to make any serious effort to court public opinion or the press. One Taft aide, who also had served with Roosevelt, noted the stark contrast between the two presidents in their relations with the press: "Mr. Roosevelt understood the necessity of guiding the press to suit one's ends; President Taft has no conception of the press as an adjunct to his office." [74]

Taft also rejected the TR-style "swings around the circle" as a device either to publicize his programs or to bring public pressure to bear upon Congress. Such speaking tours as Taft undertook came at the urging of his aides, and were made with considerable reluctance. "The Taft administration," Cornwell has noted, "represented a hiatus in the presidential leadership of opinion, if not actually a retrograde step." [75]

Taft and Congress

Taft dedicated himself to an ambitious legislative program that would institutionalize in law the reforms that Roosevelt's vigorous and independent executive action had begun. "Mr. Roosevelt's function has been to preach a crusade against certain evils. He has aroused the people to demand reform," Taft wrote on February 23, 1909, just before his inauguration. "It becomes my business to put such reform into legal execution by the suggestion of certain amendments of the statute in the governmental machinery." [76]

One important area in which the direction of reform remained unclear was natural resources. Roosevelt had asserted aggressively the idea that the president is the steward of the public welfare in matters of conservation. His administration set aside some 43 million acres of national forest, hoping to protect what was left of the country's woodlands from excessive commercial exploitation. By 1908, however, Congress had blocked further progress in the conservation program. Farmers, grazers, and water power interests in the West, where most of the forests were, won legislation to transfer from the president to Congress the authority to establish national forests in several western states. Tensions reached a breaking point when Roosevelt and the head of the forest service, Gifford Pinchot, prepared a "midnight forests" proclamation that protected 16 million acres just before the bill went into effect.

Roosevelt's proclamation not only drove a wedge between the executive and legislative branches, it also failed to resolve the dispute about the appropriate federal role in managing natural resources. In an effort to make conservation policy a matter of settled, standing law, Taft prepared a special message in 1909 that asked Congress to pass a bill to codify Roosevelt's executive order. As he wrote to the California conservationist William Kent, "We have a government of limited power under the Constitution, and we have got to work out our problems on the basis of law." [77]

But Taft's passive view of presidential power shaped his pursuit of the bill in Congress. He had serious misgivings about interfering in the legislative process, telling the Senate majority leader, Nelson Aldrich, "I have no disposition to exert any other influence than that which it is my function under the Constitution to exercise. . . ." [78]

Although Taft's position on conservation prevailed, his broader policy of forbearance in legislative matters cost him dearly, especially during the early days of his presidency. Indeed, his passivity gave the appearance that he was in accord with the conservative Republican leadership in Congress, which caused an irrevocable split to occur between the president and the Roosevelt administration alumni whom Taft had allowed to stay in office. Pinchot felt that Taft's unwillingness to act in the absence of explicit authority crippled progressive policies. "After T.R. came Taft," Pinchot later wrote. "It was as though a sharp sword had been succeeded by a roll of paper, legal size." [79]

Taft's modest definition of executive power governed his relations with Congress even on those policies that were closest to his heart. Of all the campaign promises he made in 1908, the president was probably the most serious about wanting to reduce tariff rates. He considered the Republican party's long-standing attachment to protectionism unfortunate. Roosevelt had done nothing about tariffs except to use them as a

William Howard Taft, who served as Theodore Roosevelt's secretary of war, was elected president in 1908. Although he intended to continue the policies of the Roosevelt administration, he was accused by progressives of betraying their principles.

bargaining chip in his fight for the Hepburn Act. Yet, although Taft cared deeply about reform, he stood by passively in 1910 as Congress watered down his proposal to alter the nation's protectionist policies. Senate Republicans added more than eight hundred amendments to the strong tariff reform bill that had been passed by the House. Taft simply signed the version that came out of the House-Senate conference committee, even though it closely resembled the Senate bill.[80]

Faced with a similar challenge, Roosevelt almost certainly would have abandoned his party's congressional leadership, worked to build a bipartisan progressive coalition, and, failing that, appealed to the people. Taft, however, remained loyal to the Republican organization, even claiming that the Payne-Aldrich tariff, as the final legislation was called, was "really a good bill." Progressive Republicans, most of whom bucked the president and their party's leaders to vote against the measure, disagreed.[81] As a result, Taft lost the political initiative, and, Coletta has noted, "the wounds inflicted in the acrid tariff debate never healed." [82]

Public deference to Congress did not necessarily foreclose an impressive legislative record. Jefferson and McKinley had worked quietly within party councils to exercise considerable influence in Congress. But Taft lacked the political skill to provide this kind of leadership. His pre-presidential experience was confined to judicial and administrative offices. Like Herbert Hoover in 1929, Taft came to the White House relatively unversed in public and legislative politics.[83]

Taft also suffered from changing political conditions. The Republican party was badly divided between an increasingly stubborn conservative, probusiness majority and a large and growing progressive minority that was bent on reform. By force of personality and popular support, Roosevelt had held the party together, even when his progressivism, which grew stronger during his presidency, made the cleavage between the Old Guard and the insurgent Republicans more distinct. In contrast, Taft's feeble efforts to mediate the differences between conservatives and reformers only aggravated his situation.

The outbreak of virtual civil war in the Republican party began with a progressive revolt in the House of Representatives. Unwilling to tolerate any longer the conservative policies and arbitrary leadership of Speaker Cannon, Republican insurgents, led by Rep. George Norris of Nebraska, united with Democrats in March 1910 to strip the speakership of most of its powers. Although Cannon was not removed from the chair, his influence was limited substantially. No longer would the Speaker control the members' committee assignments or the all-important Rules Committee, which set the House's legislative agenda. Even the Speaker's constitutional role as presiding officer was narrowed by new rules that limited his discretionary parliamentary prerogatives.[84]

The weakening of the party leadership, long a bulwark of congressional government, ultimately hastened the fundamental transfer of power from Congress to the White House that first had become noticeable during Roosevelt's presidency. The same progressive revolt that toppled the speakership in the House also undermined the foundations of party government in the Senate, depriving the leaders of their control of legislative deliberations. Power in both houses of Congress devolved to the committees, especially the committee chairs, who became specialized masters of legislation. Congress grew steadily less able to meet the growing responsibilities of the national government.

Unable to obtain reform from a fractious Congress, the American people demanded that the president provide strong leadership both in congressional and in party matters. Governor-elect Woodrow Wilson of New Jersey described the situation well when he said on November 5, 1910,

If I were to sum up all the criticisms that have been made of the gentleman who is now President of the United States, I could express them all in this: The American people are disappointed because he has not led them. . . . They clearly long for someone to put the pressure of the opinion of all the people of the United States upon Congress.[85]

Taft, his narrow construction of executive power notwithstanding, was sensitive to the new public demands. Very late in his term he suggested that the executive and legislative branches be brought closer together by giving cabinet members nonvoting seats in Congress. He also endorsed a presidential commission's call for the president to hold the various departments and agencies to a comprehensive budget program.[86] Taft submitted the first executive budget in 1913, just before he went out of office.[87]

Taft's proposals to strengthen the executive were ignored by Congress. But they revealed that even he had come to recognize that Roosevelt's dynamic leadership and the changing character of the country had placed more responsibility in the presidency than during the nineteenth century.

The Election of 1910

Ironically, Taft's most dramatic assertion of presidential leadership proved to be his political undoing. In the 1910 congressional primaries the president tried to purge progressives from the Republican party. Taft had criticized Roosevelt for meddling in the legislative process. Yet, oddly enough, Taft's intervention in his party's nominating process marked an unprecedented effort by a president to influence congressional support for his legislative program.

Taft had tried first to mediate between the badly divided factions of the Republican party. But the progressives' opposition to his legislative program, especially the Payne-Aldrich tariff, provoked him to join the conservatives' effort to influence the 1910 primary elections. Although Taft took no public position in these contests, he distributed party patronage on the basis of loyalty to the administration's program. Moreover, a rumor spread widely that the president was helping Speaker Cannon and Senate Republican leader Aldrich raise money to send out to the prairie states "a group of standpat evangelists to wrestle with all the districts possessed of the progressive devil." [88] Strong confirmation of this rumor came when the Republican congressional campaign committee flooded progressive constituencies with sharp attacks on their representatives and senators.

Taft's aggressive, albeit surreptitious, intervention in the primaries was manifestly unsuccessful. Not only were almost all of the progressive Republicans whom he opposed renominated, but their insurgent allies defeated conservative incumbents in several primaries. In the wake of these reversals came the great disaster of the November elections. In

1910, for the first time in sixteen years, the Democratic party took control of the House of Representatives. Republicans retained a majority in the Senate, but their control was nominal. Indeed, progressive Republicans now held the balance of power between the regular Republicans and the Democrats.[89]

Taft's purge campaign revealed not just the limits of his personal influence but also the imposing institutional obstacles to party discipline in national politics. To be sure, the decline of the party leadership's influence in Congress required more assertive presidential efforts to bring together the elected branches of the government. But Taft's approach to this problem, his purge campaign, was undertaken in concert with a Republican Old Guard that was steadily losing power in the country. Furthermore, although Congress had been weakened as an institution by the progressives' revolt against the party leadership, the American people were not ready to support an executive assault on their local members of Congress.

The failed purge campaign of 1910 and the deep irritation at Taft that it roused in Theodore Roosevelt set the stage for a disastrous party split in the 1912 presidential election. Thereupon it fell to the beneficiary of the Republican schism, Woodrow Wilson, to devise new and more acceptable ways to bring together the executive and legislative branches of the government.

Notes

1. For a very useful review of the effect of the Progressive movement on the presidency, see William M. Goldsmith, ed., *The Growth of Presidential Power: A Documented History* (New York and London: Chelsea, 1974), 2:1277-1349.
2. Richard Hofstadter, *The Age of Reform: From Bryan to F.D.R.* (New York: Knopf, 1956), 5.
3. Quoted in Samuel Eliot Morison, *The Oxford History of the American People* (New York: New American Library, 1972), 3:130-131.
4. Goldsmith, *Growth of Presidential Power* 3:1293.
5. Theodore Roosevelt, *The Works of Theodore Roosevelt* (New York: Scribner's, 1926), 20:340.
6. Hanna is quoted in Samuel and Dorothy Rosenman, *Presidential Style: Some Giants and a Pygmy in the White House* (New York: Harper and Row, 1976), 1.
7. Roosevelt, *Works* 20:450.
8. Rosenman and Rosenman, *Presidential Style*, 123.
9. Roosevelt, *Works* 20:347.
10. Ibid. 20:347.
11. Ibid.
12. Alexander Hamilton and James Madison, *Letters of Pacificus and Hel-*

vidius on the Proclamation of Neutrality (Washington, D.C.: Gideon, 1845), 10.

13. Roosevelt, *Works* 7:328.
14. Ibid. 20:414. Of course, Lincoln's defense of the Union and audacious use of executive power occurred during the stress of a domestic rebellion. His understanding of the national government's powers and of executive prerogative in less dire circumstances was far more circumscribed than Roosevelt's.
15. Herbert Croly, *The Promise of American Life* (New York: Macmillan, 1909; New York: Dutton, 1963), 169. Roosevelt did not actually use the term *New Nationalism* until it appeared in a speech he delivered after his presidency. But this speech, given on August 31, 1910, in Osawatomie, Kansas (*Works* 17:5-22), expressed ideas that had long been part of Roosevelt's thoughts and that had animated his actions as president.
16. Elmer E. Cornwell, Jr., *Presidential Leadership of Public Opinion* (Bloomington: Indiana University Press, 1965), 9. Also see Jeffrey Tulis, *The Rhetorical Presidency* (Princeton, N.J.: Princeton University Press, 1987), 97-116.
17. As the political scientist William Muir has noted, there is no direct evidence that Theodore Roosevelt ever spoke or wrote this term. In fact, just how the phrase "bully pulpit" became identified with TR is a mystery. See William Ker Muir, Jr., *The Bully Pulpit: The Presidential Leadership of Ronald Reagan* (San Francisco: Institute for Contemporary Studies, 1992), 44, n227.
18. Roosevelt, *Works* 20:416.
19. Ibid. 20:342.
20. For a discussion of Roosevelt's campaign on behalf of the Hepburn Act, see Tulis, *Rhetorical Presidency*, 97-116; and Cornwell, *Presidential Leadership of Public Opinion*, 24-26.
21. John Morton Blum, *The Republican Roosevelt* (Cambridge, Mass.: Harvard University Press, 1954), 74-75.
22. Roosevelt, *Works* 15:225.
23. Mark Sullivan, *Our Times: 1900-1925* (New York: Scribner's, 1939), 3:226.
24. George Mowry, *The Era of Theodore Roosevelt: 1900-1912* (New York: Harper, 1958), 201.
25. "Address delivered before the Iroquois Club, at a banquet in Chicago, May 10, 1905," in *The Roosevelt Policy*, ed. William Griffith (New York: Current Literature, 1919), 1:266-273; also see Mowry, *Era of Theodore Roosevelt* 201.
26. Roosevelt, *Works* 15:274-286.
27. Quoted in Mowry, *Era of Theodore Roosevelt*, 203.
28. Blum, *Republican Roosevelt*, 91; also Mowry, *Era of Theodore Roosevelt*, 205.
29. Cornwell, *Presidential Leadership of Public Opinion*, 10.
30. George W. Alger, "The Literature of Exposure," *Atlantic Monthly*, August 1905, vol. 96, 210.
31. Roosevelt derived the term *muckraker* from the description in John Bunyan's *Pilgrim's Progress* of the Man with the Muck-Rake. "Now it is very necessary that we should not flinch from seeing what is vile and debasing," TR said of the journalists who practiced the literature of exposure.

There is filth on the floor, and it must be scraped up with the muck-rake; and there are times and places where this service is the most needed of all the services that can be performed. But the man who never does anything else, who never speaks or thinks or writes save of his feats with the muck-rake, speedily becomes, not a help to society, not an incitement to good, but one of the most potent forces for evil.

Address at the laying of the cornerstone of the office building of the House of Representatives, Washington, D.C., April 14, 1906, found in Willis Fletcher Johnson, ed., *Theodore Roosevelt: Addresses and Papers* (New York: Sun Dial Classics, 1908), 311.

32. Sullivan, *Our Times* 3:83-84.
33. Ibid. 3:240.
34. Quoted in Blum, *Republican Roosevelt*, 81.
35. Ibid., 85.
36. Ibid., 87. The political scientist Jeffrey Tulis has noted, "Roosevelt abandoned nineteenth century practice, to be sure, but he did so in a way that retained nineteenth century objectives and accommodated that 'nineteenth century' institution, the Senate" (Tulis, *Rhetorical Presidency*, 106-107).
37. James Bryce, *The American Commonwealth* (London: Macmillan, 1891), 2:712.
38. Roosevelt, *Works* 20:482; Rosenman and Rosenman, *Presidential Style*, 47.
39. Roosevelt, *Works* 20:471.
40. Tulis, *Rhetorical Presidency*, 96.
41. A full account of Roosevelt's activities during the strike appears in a letter he wrote to Gov. Winthrop Murray Crane of Massachusetts, who was a concerned and apprehensive observer. See Roosevelt to Crane, October 22, 1902, in *Letters of Theodore Roosevelt*, ed. Elting Morrison (Cambridge, Mass.: Harvard University Press, 1951), 3:359-360.
42. Mowry, *Era of Theodore Roosevelt*, 138; Rosenman and Rosenman, *Presidential Style*, 73.
43. Mowry, *Era of Theodore Roosevelt*, 140.
44. Blum, *The Republican Roosevelt*, 105.
45. William H. Harbaugh, "The Constitution of the Theodore Roosevelt Presidency and the Progressive Era," in *The Constitution and the American Presidency*, ed. Martin Fausold and Alan Shank (Albany: State University of New York Press, 1991), 73-76.
46. William Dudley Foulke, *Roosevelt and the Spoilsmen* (New York: National Civil Service Reform League, 1925), 100. Also see Paul Van Riper, *History of the United States Civil Service* (Evanston, Ill.: Row, Peterson, 1958), 189.
47. Stephen Skowronek, *Building a New American State: The Expansion of National Administrative Capacities, 1877-1920* (New York: Cambridge University Press, 1982), 176.
48. Roosevelt, *Works* 20:491.
49. Ibid. 15:117.
50. Herbert Croly, *Promise of American Life*, 312.
51. Roosevelt, *Works* 15:114.
52. *New York Post*, September 8, 1903, 1.
53. Roosevelt, *Works* 20:510, 549-550.
54. Roosevelt to Marcus Alonzo Hanna, October 5, 1903, in Morrison, *Letters of Theodore Roosevelt* 3:625.
55. Roosevelt, *Works* 20:501.
56. Ibid.
57. Goldsmith, *Growth of Presidential Power* 2:1233.
58. Mowry, *Era of Theodore Roosevelt*, 155.
59. Goldsmith, *Growth of Presidential Power* 2:1233-1234.

60. Roosevelt, *Works* 15:256-257.
61. Mowry, *Era of Theodore Roosevelt*, 159.
62. Woodrow Wilson, *Congressional Government* (Boston: Houghton-Mifflin, 1885; New York: Meridian Books, 1956), 52.
63. Roosevelt, *Works* 20:490.
64. The Open Door policy was announced in September 1899 by Secretary of State John Hay. It asked the major powers that had imperialistic designs on Asia—notably, Great Britain, Germany, Russia, France, Italy, and Japan— to agree to support freedom of trade in the Orient. Great Britain was the only nation to accept Hay's proposals fully; the others agreed, but with reservations. Hay, however, chose to interpret their replies as acceptances and announced the Open Door policy to the world. When Russia's expansion in Manchuria after 1902 violated the Open Door policy, Roosevelt wanted to take action, but he did not think that the American people would support a military intervention in Asia. Thus, he welcomed Japan's attack on the Russian fleet in Port Arthur.
65. This agreement is described in a confidential memo to Roosevelt from Secretary of War William Howard Taft, July 29, 1905, in Goldsmith, *Growth of Presidential Power* 2:1246-1247. TR responded almost immediately, indicating that the agreement Taft had worked out with the Japanese prime minister, Count Taro Katsura, was "absolutely correct in every respect" and that he confirmed "every word you have said" (telegram from Roosevelt to Taft, July 31, 1905, in Morrison, *Letters of Theodore Roosevelt* 4:1293). See also Henry F. Pringle, *The Life and Times of William Howard Taft* (New York: Farrar and Rinehart, 1939), 1:297-299.
66. Mowry, *Era of Theodore Roosevelt*, 185.
67. Roosevelt describes his decision to send the U.S. fleet around the world in his autobiography. See *Works* 20:535-546.
68. Goldsmith, *Growth of Presidential Power* 2:1269.
69. Mowry, *Era of Theodore Roosevelt*, 226.
70. Ibid., 180; Roosevelt, *Works* 20:378.
71. Mowry, *Era of Theodore Roosevelt*, 227.
72. Paolo E. Coletta, *The Presidency of William Howard Taft* (Lawrence: University Press of Kansas, 1973), 48.
73. William Howard Taft, *Our Chief Magistrate and His Powers* (New York: Columbia University Press, 1916), 139-140.
74. Archie Butt, *Taft and Roosevelt: The Intimate Letters of Archie Butt* (Garden City, N.Y.: Doubleday, Doran, 1930), 1:30.
75. Cornwell, *Presidential Leadership of Public Opinion*, 27.
76. Taft to W. R. Nelson, February 23, 1909, cited in Coletta, *Presidency of William Howard Taft*, 45-46.
77. Cited in William Henry Harbaugh, *Power and Responsibility: The Life and Times of Theodore Roosevelt* (New York: Farrar Straus and Cudahy, 1961), 384.
78. Cited in Mowry, *Era of Theodore Roosevelt*, 245.
79. Quoted in Harbaugh, *Power and Responsibility*, 384.
80. Mowry, *Era of Theodore Roosevelt*, 246.
81. Ibid., 246.
82. Coletta, *Presidency of William Howard Taft*, 71.
83. Wilfred E. Binkley, *President and Congress* (New York: Knopf, 1947), 200. The only office that Taft ever ran for, except the presidency, was justice of the State Superior Court in Ohio.

84. For a discussion of the revolt in Congress against the regular party leadership, see Lawrence C. Dodd and Richard L. Schott, *Congress and the Administrative State* (New York: Wiley, 1979), 58-100.
85. Quoted in Ray Stannard Baker, *Woodrow Wilson: Life and Times* (Garden City, N.Y.: Doubleday, Doran, 1931), 3:181.
86. On Taft's budget proposals, see Goldsmith, *Growth of Presidential Power* 3:1471-1478; and Peri E. Arnold, *Making the Managerial Presidency: Comprehensive Reorganization Planning, 1905-1980* (Princeton, N.J.: Princeton University Press, 1986), 22-51.
87. Leonard White writes of James K. Polk's earlier coordination of budgetary appropriations: "The precedent established by Polk disappeared from view, and a new start had to be made many decades later on this aspect of presidential power" (Leonard White, *The Jacksonians: A Study in Administrative History, 1829-1861* [New York: Macmillan, 1956], 82).
88. George E. Mowry, *Theodore Roosevelt and the Progressive Movement* (Madison: University of Wisconsin Press, 1946), 98.
89. *New York Times*, November 10, 1910; Mowry, *Theodore Roosevelt and the Progressive Movement*, 106, 130.

CHAPTER 9

Woodrow Wilson and the Defense of Popular Leadership

After the Republicans lost control of the House of Representatives in the 1910 midterm election, it became apparent that William Howard Taft probably would not be reelected as president. The historian George Mowry has written of the 1910 election that it was "one of those significant divides in American history which signals a reversal in political trends before a complete transfer of power occurs." [1] Not only did the election weaken the Republicans, it also went far toward rehabilitating the Democrats. A number of Democratic progressives were elected to Congress, most of them unattached to William Jennings Bryan, the fiery rural Populist who had led the party to defeat in three of the last four presidential campaigns.

Among the new Democrats was Woodrow Wilson, formerly a professor and the president of Princeton University. In 1910, Wilson was elected as governor of New Jersey. Two years later, the Democratic national convention, after a long deadlock, nominated the erstwhile political scientist for president on the forty-sixth ballot. The nomination was secured when Bryan, in a symbolic passing of the scepter, threw his full support to Wilson, hoping thereby to thwart the anti-Wilson business interests of the East. Thus, after failing for two decades to offer a program that addressed the challenges of the Progressive Era, the Democrats suddenly found themselves led by an articulate and forward-looking scholar-politician. Wilson's victory in 1912 was only the third by a Democrat since the Civil War; moreover, enough Democrats were swept into Congress to give the party solid majorities in both the Senate and the House for the first time in more than fifty years.

The Democratic opportunity may not have been realized had the

Republicans not self-destructed in 1912. An intraparty progressive revolt against Taft and the Old Guard first gave rise to the insurgent candidacy of Wisconsin senator Robert La Follette, who challenged the president's bid for renomination. When La Follette failed to draw much support outside the Midwest, progressives turned to Theodore Roosevelt, who on February 21 announced, "My hat is in the ring." Persuaded that his candidacy was indispensable to the progressive cause and bored by four years of political inactivity, TR abandoned his pledge not to run again for president. That he had declined a "third cup of coffee" in 1908 did not mean that he never intended to drink coffee again, Roosevelt said.[2]

The Republican rank and file supported Roosevelt. In the thirteen states that selected convention delegates by primary, Roosevelt won 276 delegates, Taft 46, and La Follette 36. Of particular significance was Roosevelt's victory, by almost a 2-to-1 margin, in Taft's home state of Ohio.[3] But in 1912 most delegates still were selected at state conventions dominated by regular party leaders, who much preferred Taft's stolidity to the frenetic progressivism of Roosevelt.

When it became clear at the Republican national convention that Roosevelt would not be nominated, he and his followers walked out, reconvening in Chicago on August 5, 1912, as the Progressive party. In a speech that advanced the cause of a New Nationalism, Roosevelt called for "strong national regulation" of interstate corporations; social insurance in times of injury, sickness, unemployment, and old age; and constitutional reforms to establish a "pure democracy." The progressives' vision of democratic government was to be realized by enacting an easier method to amend the Constitution, universal use of the direct primary, voter initiatives, referenda on laws that the state courts declared unconstitutional, women's suffrage, and limits on the judicial power to issue labor injunctions.

Roosevelt's personal control of the Progressive party was extraordinary. The Progressive campaign thus foretold not only of the emergence of a more active and expansive national government but also of presidential campaigns conducted less by parties than by individual candidates. Roosevelt's appearance before the convention—the first in history by a presidential candidate—excited a fifty-two-minute standing ovation. His closing words—"We stand at Armageddon, and we battle for the Lord"—roused the delegates to an emotional state that could only be subdued by reverential singing of the "Battle Hymn of the Republic."[4]

The 1912 election was a triumph for progressivism, but it sent Wilson, not Roosevelt, to the White House. Although, like Lincoln, Wilson polled a minority of the popular votes, he won the election easily. The final tally awarded 6.3 million popular votes and 435 electoral votes to Wilson, 4.1 million popular votes and 88 electoral votes to Roosevelt, and 3.5 million popular votes and 8 electoral votes to Taft. Eugene V. Debs collected 900,000 votes, the highest total ever for a Socialist party candidate in a presidential election, but no electoral votes.

Above all, the 1912 election was a decisive rejection of the Republican Old Guard. Its candidate, the incumbent Taft, carried only Vermont and Utah; the combined popular vote of Wilson, Roosevelt, and Debs, each of them an advocate of progressive policies, was more than 75 percent.[5] The results enabled Wilson, although he was a minority president, to reap the benefits of a reform movement that was cresting just as he entered the White House. The new president seized the opportunity not just to advance progressive social and economic policies but also to extend further the restructuring of executive leadership that Roosevelt had begun.

Woodrow Wilson's Theory of Executive Leadership

Wilson had long wanted to reform radically the principles and institutions of American government in order to ameliorate what he regarded as a disconcerting lack of energy and consistency. In 1879, as a student of twenty-three, he published an article that called for major institutional reforms to establish closer ties between the executive and the legislature. At the time, Wilson believed that this connection could be forged best by enhancing the powers of Congress, which dominated politics during the latter part of the nineteenth century. Thus, he urged the United States to adopt the British cabinet system, which concentrated power in an executive board that was responsible to the legislature. Specifically, the young Wilson proposed that the Constitution be amended "to give the heads of the Executive departments—the members of the Cabinet—seats in Congress, with the privilege of the initiative in legislation and some part in the unbounded privileges now commanded by the Standing Committees."[6] The president, who, in Wilson's view, had been rendered virtually useless in the aftermath of the Civil War, would become a figurehead like the monarch in England.

Although Wilson never abandoned the idea that checks and balances should be replaced by an American version of the British Parliament, his views about presidential leadership changed dramatically. In the early 1900s, he argued that the best hope for leadership in the United States now lay in a strong presidency.[7] No doubt Wilson was influenced by the example of Roosevelt, whose vigorous and independent stewardship demonstrated the potential power of the executive. Wilson disagreed strongly with TR about certain institutional and policy matters, but he credited him for charting a new path of presidential leadership. "Whatever else we may think or say of Theodore Roosevelt," Wilson said in 1909, "we must admit he was an aggressive leader. He led Congress—he was not driven by Congress. We may not approve of his methods but we must concede that he made Congress follow him." [8]

Roosevelt's success persuaded Wilson that a new theory of government was needed to justify and make routine the forceful display of presidential leadership. Roosevelt had shown that it was not necessary to amend the Constitution to bring about a closer relationship between its elected branches; rather, the task was to use the existing powers of the executive more fully. "His office," Wilson said of the president, "is anything he has the sagacity and force to make it." [9] Roosevelt had done much to fulfill the promise of the presidency, but Wilson believed that TR was too inclined to act in defiance and to appeal over the head of Congress. A better strategy, Wilson argued, would be to break down the barriers between the president and Congress by making the president a strong party leader. In this way, constitutional government's various parts would work together in concert, but without violating the principles and institutions that protected the nation from an unhealthy aggrandizement of executive power. [10]

Because of the president's literally unique position to lead public opinion and the party, Wilson believed that he could encourage a high level of debate in election campaigns and in the councils of government, which all too often had been lacking. Unlike the members of Congress, who represent localities, the president is the only person whom an entire party nominates and the entire nation elects. Thus, Wilson wrote:

> The President represents not so much the party's governing efficiency as its controlling ideals and principles. He is not so much part of its organization as its vital link of connection with the thinking nation. He can dominate his party by being spokesman for the real sentiment and purpose of the country, by giving direction to opinion, by giving the country at once the information and the statements of policy which will enable it to form its judgments alike of parties and men. [11]

Wilson's theory of presidential power required a more comprehensive rethinking of the American constitutional order than did Roosevelt's stewardship model. As president, TR had accepted the constitutional system of checks and balances, seeking only to revive and modify Hamiltonian nationalism so that the government could address the problems of an industrial society. Even when Roosevelt roused the people to bring pressure to bear upon Congress, he did so in a way that was intended to preserve the independence of both branches. His deference to traditional constitutional practices was especially clear in domestic matters. TR's campaigns for legislation such as the Hepburn

Act were undertaken only as a last resort and always in a manner that showed respect for congressional deliberations.

Wilson agreed with Roosevelt that the president must direct more attention to national problems, but he believed that executive leadership would be ineffective or dangerous unless it was accompanied by a fundamental change in the government's working arrangements. Such a change would combine the usually separated branches of the government.[12] Most significant, the president's role as party leader would be strengthened. Instead of limiting executive power, as it had during much of the nineteenth century, the party system would be modified to enable the president to command Congress's support.

Wilson and Party Reform

As president, Wilson acted to perfect TR's methods of popular leadership and to apply them in a way that would establish him as the leader of Congress and the Democratic party. He was not completely successful in this endeavor, to be sure. But Wilson's two terms brought about major changes in the presidency. According to the Wilson biographer Arthur Link, "historians a century hence will probably rate the expansion and perfection of the powers of the presidency as his most lasting contribution." [13]

Wilson's desire to strengthen the president's position within party councils led him to examine closely the presidential nominating process, especially the convention system. The advent of national conventions, which had replaced the congressional caucus at the start of the Jacksonian era, to some extent had freed the president from an undue dependence on Congress. Wilson charged, however, that because the convention system was founded upon patronage-based state and local party organizations, it was ill-suited to modern conditions. Government in the twentieth century required a sense of purpose that could come only from national and programmatic political parties.[14]

Animated by his understanding of the presidency and the parties, Wilson became an advocate of the presidential primary. In his first annual message to Congress he urged "the prompt enactment of legislation which will provide for primary elections throughout the country at which the voters of the several parties may choose their nominees for the Presidency without the intervention of nominating conventions." [15] The direct primary, which had been advocated by progressive reformers since the turn of the century, already was used widely in elections around the country. Although Wilson's recommendation to establish a national primary made little headway in Congress, its democratic spirit continued to guide reformers, who fought throughout the twentieth century to weaken the grip of traditional party organizations on the presidency.

The Art of Popular Leadership

The national primary proposal was but one manifestation of Wilson's concern to increase the authority of the president and, by doing so, to provide the political system with a greater capacity for change. He also avowed the president's obligation as the voice of the people to bring public opinion to bear upon Congress. Roosevelt had demonstrated the value of this role, but, as Link has written, "Wilson used it to its fullest advantage and made it inevitable that any future president would be powerful only in so far as he established communication with the people and spoke effectively for them." [16]

In contrast to TR, who regarded popular rhetoric and "swings around the circle" as methods to be used infrequently and only in defense of specific pieces of legislation, Wilson believed that an ongoing effort to inspire the American people was the main ingredient of executive leadership. His effective use of oratory and other public messages set a new rhetorical standard: the president now was required to articulate a vision of the future and to guide the nation toward it. As Wilson announced in his first inaugural address:

> This the high enterprise of the new day: to lift everything that concerns our life as a nation to the light that shines from the hearthfire of every man's conscience and vision of the right. . . . We know our task to be no mere task of politics but a task which shall search us through and through, whether we be able to understand our time and the need of our people, whether we be indeed their spokesmen and interpreters, whether we have the pure heart to comprehend and the rectified will to choose our high course of action.[17]

At his best, Wilson was a spellbinder. "President Wilson probably has no equal in this country as an effective speaker," editorialized the *New York Times* in 1913.[18] Neither commanding in manner nor physically impressive, he was not a crowd pleaser in the usual sense. "In the campaign, as during the Presidency," Mowry has written, "there was between him and his countrymen something of the air of the classroom—something of the distance between a teacher and his pupils." [19] Nevertheless, although some in Wilson's audience may not have grasped the full meaning of his carefully crafted sentences, there was no mistaking their moral import or the conviction of the man who spoke them. Wilson not only understood the popular aspirations of his day but was able to translate them into words. In the course of doing so he consciously defended and, by example, established the legitimacy of public rhetoric as a principal tool of presidential leadership.

Wilson's desire to be in close touch with the people led him to make enduring innovations in the executive's relationship with the press and with Congress. Unlike Roosevelt, Wilson distrusted the press and was by temperament and philosophy unable to cultivate reporters personally. He was, however, the first president to have press conferences, which he held frequently during his first two years in office. In a sense, Wilson started regular press conferences *because* he distrusted the Fourth Estate. Less gregarious than Roosevelt, yet certain that regular contact with reporters was an essential part of his effort to take the people fully into his confidence, Wilson employed formal and restricted press conferences as an effective forum for relations with journalists.[20]

Nevertheless, Wilson did not rely on the press to communicate his views. The president's preferred devices for public leadership were speeches and formal messages. Wilson began his presidency by reviving the practice (which Jefferson had abandoned because it resembled too much the British monarch's speech from the throne) of appearing before Congress to deliver the State of the Union address and other important messages.

The White House's announcement on April 6, 1913, that Wilson himself would speak on tariff reform to the two houses of Congress on April 8 shocked some legislators. Especially concerned were certain of the president's fellow Democrats, who revered the Jeffersonian custom. Sen. John Sharp Williams of Mississippi, an original Wilson supporter, led the attack, concluding hopefully that the tariff message "would be the only instance of the breach of the perfectly simple, democratic and American custom of messages in writing which Thomas Jefferson instituted."[21] Williams's hope was disappointed: Wilson addressed Congress in person frequently. "As he no doubt foresaw," the political scientist Elmer Cornwell has written, "this forum would so concentrate public attention as to eliminate the likelihood that the newspapers would either slight or distort his message."[22]

Wilson's Relations with Congress

Appearances before Congress also served Wilson's desire to break down the walls that so long had divided the executive from the legislative branches. Part of his task was to educate and guide public opinion. But it also was important to establish customs and make symbolic gestures that would strengthen the president's ties to Congress. Wilson began his tariff address to the somewhat tense legislators by speaking directly to the symbolic purpose of his appearance:

> I am very glad indeed to have this opportunity to address the two
> houses directly and to verify for myself the impression that the

President of the United States is a person, not a mere department of
government hailing Congress from some isolated island of jealous
power, sending messages, not speaking naturally with his own voice—
that he is a human being trying to cooperate with other human beings
in a common service. After this pleasant experience I shall feel quite
normal in all our dealings with one another.[23]

Wilson's precedent-shattering speech was well received by Congress; it launched the first successful campaign for tariff reform since
before the Civil War. Other of his innovations also were significant, such
as the practice of visiting the Hill to meet personally with members of
Congress as legislative deliberations proceeded on an important bill.
Wilson followed his dramatic tariff address by appearing the next day in
the president's room of the Senate to confer with the Finance Committee, which was responsible for tariff legislation. No president since
Lincoln—and he in wartime—had ventured to make such a call.
Assessing Wilson's revolutionary approach to congressional relations,
his close associate Ray Stannard Baker wrote, "These vigorous innovations occasioned an enormous amount of publicity. The country at large
was vastly interested, amused, impressed." [24]

Nothing contributed more to Wilson's leadership of Congress than
the control he asserted over the House and Senate Democrats. The
Democrats were at least as divided between conservatives and progressives as the Republicans. Nevertheless, Wilson decided to work with his
party in Congress, rather than to govern with a coalition of progressive
Democrats and progressive Republicans, as he might have done. He
labored assiduously to formulate a comprehensive policy program and
to establish it as the party plan. He even persuaded the House
Democratic caucus to adopt a rule that bound its members to support
the administration's policies. Similar discipline was obtained in the
traditionally more individualistic Senate, where the party caucus declared important pieces of legislation such as the tariff bill to be party
measures and urged that it was the duty of all Democrats to support
them.[25]

Owing to his effective leadership, Wilson was able to drive through
Congress the major policies of his 1912 electoral platform, heralded by
him as the "New Freedom." The catchword expressed Wilson's own
understanding of progressivism, which he believed was rooted deeply in
the traditions of the Democratic party.

Roosevelt's New Nationalism had accepted the evolution of great
corporations both as inevitable and, with strict public regulation of their
activities by a powerful federal government, as desirable. In contrast,
Wilson wanted to free business from the plague of monopoly and special
privilege, thus making unnecessary a correspondingly dangerous centralization of power in the government. "As to monopolies, which Mr.

Roosevelt proposes to legalize and welcome," Wilson remarked during the 1912 campaign, "I know that they are so many cars of juggernaut, and I do not look forward with pleasure to the time when the juggernauts are licensed and driven by commissioners of the United States." [26] As the leader of the Democratic party, Wilson promised tariff reform, an overhaul of the banking and currency system, and a vigorous antitrust program that would "disentangle" the "colossal community of interest" and restore fair competition to the economy. [27]

To the astonishment of both Wilson's friends and his enemies, Congress approved most elements of the New Freedom agenda in 1913 and 1914. The Underwood Tariff Act became law in October 1913. The Federal Reserve Act, which reconstructed the national banking and currency system, followed in late December. Finally, two statutes were passed in 1914, the Clayton Anti-Trust Act and the Federal Trade Commission Act, to strengthen the government's authority to prevent unfair business competition.

Taken as a whole, Wilson's legislative achievements were remarkable. In contrast to TR, Wilson had turned his fractious party into a disciplined body. In the course of doing so, he enacted programs that progressives had been demanding for two decades. In his 1914 State of the Union address, the president reported proudly to Congress:

> Our program of legislation with regard to regulation of business is now virtually complete. It has been put forth, as we intended, as a whole and leaves no conjecture as to what is to follow. The road at last lies clear and firm before business. It is a road which it can travel without fear or embarrassment. [28]

The road for business was not as clearly or firmly charted as Wilson believed. The New Freedom program soon was compromised severely by the conservative judiciary, which still adhered to a restrictive view of the federal government's constitutional powers in the economy. In addition, Wilson's own administrative practices undermined the implementation of his progressive programs. Before becoming president, Wilson had declared his support for the merit system on numerous occasions; at the time of his election he was a vice president of the National Civil Service Reform League. As president-elect, Wilson promised to nominate "progressives—and only progressives" to federal jobs. But to the dismay of the president's supporters, old-style patronage practices dominated his appointments. [29] "The pity is," Secretary of the Navy Josephus Daniels wrote many years later, "that Wilson appointed some who wouldn't recognize a Progressive principle if he met it in the road." [30]

Wilson's approach to appointments was governed by the belief that to assault the patronage system would undermine party unity and ensure the defeat of his legislative program. The pressure to employ traditional partisan practices was great: the Democrats had been without federal patronage since Grover Cleveland left office in 1897. The problem was brought to the president's attention by Postmaster General Albert Burleson, whom Wilson included in the cabinet mostly because of his strong ties to Congress. When Wilson told Burleson at the beginning of his presidency that appointments would be made without the advice of the "professional politicians," the postmaster general urged otherwise:

> Mr. President, if you pursue this policy it means that your administration is going to be a failure. It means the defeat of measures of reform that you have next to your heart. These little offices don't amount to anything. They are inconsequential. It doesn't amount to a damn who is Postmaster at Paducah, Kentucky. But these little offices mean a great deal to senators and representatives in Congress. If it goes out that the President has turned down Representative So-and-so, and Senator So-and-so, it means that member has great trouble at home. If you pursue the right policy, you can make the Democratic party progressive....[31]

In the end Wilson was persuaded.

The decision to work through his party marked, Link has written, "one of the early decisive turning points in Wilson's presidential career."[32] It underlay the president's nearly absolute mastery of the Democratic party, especially its membership in Congress. "The corner stone of Wilson's entire conception of democratic administration in America was a closer relationship between the President and Congress," Ray Stannard Baker noted. "He must indeed lead, but they must follow. How was he to bring about the tremendous reforms that he had promised with his own party mutinous behind him? After all there is a political method."[33]

Wilson's political approach to appointments weakened the administration of the reform programs that he persuaded Congress to enact into law. Spoilsmen were less willing and less able to implement the president's New Freedom legislation than officials who were chosen for their talent and their commitment to progressive principles would have been. His decision to accept standard patronage practices was "the triumph of the professional politician over the idealist in the administration."[34]

Nevertheless, Wilson had transformed the presidency substantially. The office that only two decades earlier had seemed so unimpressive to Wilson the political scientist had been elevated to a position of unrivaled influence in the American political system. As the *New Republic* proclaimed in December 1914:

> Under Mr. Wilson the prestige of the presidency has been fully restored. He has not only expressly acknowledged and acted on this

obligation of leadership, as did Mr. Roosevelt, but he has sought to embody it in constitutional form. . . . In establishing regular forms of cooperation and a better understanding between the Presidency and Congress, Mr. Wilson is accomplishing an immediately beneficent constitutional reform.[35]

Wilson as World Leader

Roosevelt expanded the influence of the president and reduced the effectiveness of Congress in foreign affairs. Wilson did not shirk the office's new responsibilities. In a lecture delivered at Columbia University in 1907, he expressed the understanding of the executive's obligations in foreign affairs that was to govern his conduct as president:

> The president can never again be the mere domestic figure he has been throughout so large a part of our history. The nation has risen to the first rank in power and resources. . . . Our president must always, henceforth, be one of the great powers of the world, whether he act greatly or wisely or not. . . . We have but begun to see the presidential office in this light; but it is the light which will more and more beat upon it, and more and more determine its character and its effect upon the politics of the nation.[36]

Wilson's approach to foreign affairs, although just as ambitious as Roosevelt's, was somewhat more idealistic. TR's diplomatic initiatives were rooted in a mixture of progressive philosophy and *realpolitik* that sustained his administration's vigorous pursuit of U.S. strategic and economic interests. Wilson and his secretary of state, William Jennings Bryan, charted a more high-minded course, assuming somewhat naively, as Link has written, "that moral force controlled the relations of peace, that reason would prevail over ignorance and passion in the formation of public opinion, and that men and nations everywhere were automatically progressing toward an orderly and righteous international society."[37] Wilson was determined to pursue an energetic foreign policy but one that was based more upon altruism and less upon narrow considerations of the national interest than Roosevelt's had been.

Conflict with Mexico

Wilson's noble intentions did not prevent, and probably contributed to, his clumsy intervention in Mexico soon after becoming president. The incident was precipitated by his refusal to recognize the government of Victoriano Huerta, who in February 1913 had overthrown and arranged the murder of the Mexican reformer Francisco I. Madero. The Taft administration had delayed diplomatic recognition at the time, but only in the hope of obtaining concessions for American business interests in Mexico. Wilson, however, detested Dollar Diplomacy, as the approach that Taft adopted was called, and sought instead to impose political reforms on Mexico as the price of U.S. recognition. When Sir William Tyrell of the British Foreign Office, who was returning to England in November 1913, said to Wilson, "I shall be asked to explain your Mexican policy. Can you tell me what it is?" the president replied in his most decisive manner, "I am going to teach the South American Republics to elect good men!" As the historian Burton Hendrick has noted, "In its attitude, its phrasing, [this statement] held the key to much Wilson history." [38]

Wilson's determination to teach nations how to govern themselves led him to repudiate the historic presidential practice of recognizing all governments and to improvise for Mexico a radical new test for recognition. The test, as Wilson later put it, was one of "constitutional legitimacy," which implied the right of the president to determine whether the new government was adhering to its own constitution and, beyond even that, whether it was motivated by self-interest and ambition or by a sincere desire to eliminate despotism.[39] To Wilson the test seemed reasonable and honorable; to the Latin Americans it was meddling in their internal affairs.

Wilson achieved a diplomatic victory when he persuaded Britain and other European powers to withhold military and economic support from the Huerta regime. But, still not satisfied, he took measures, including the seizure of the port of Veracruz in April 1914, to support a counterrevolution instigated by the "constitutionalist" Venustiano Carranza. Then, when the triumphant Carranza would brook no advice and certainly no control from the American president, Wilson threw his support to Gen. Pancho Villa, an erstwhile Carranza ally whose defection prolonged Mexico's civil war for an additional three years. Wilson's clumsy interventions were resented deeply by the Mexican people, generating recurring threats of actual war.

The Mexican situation became especially dangerous after yet another shift in the U.S. diplomatic position. Villa, who proved no more amenable than Carranza or his predecessor to American control, began to extort ever-increasing financial contributions from U.S. companies in Mexico. In Washington, support for Villa gave way to diplomatic recognition of Carranza, whereupon Villa led raids into Texas that terrified American citizens. On March 15, 1916, Wilson sent a punitive expedition under the command of Brig. Gen. John J. Pershing in pursuit of Villa. Carranza, greatly alarmed at the size of the U.S. force in Mexico, even though it was hunting his enemy, demanded in an insulting note that Pershing withdraw. Eventually, after military skirmishes and the exchange of ultimatums, an agreement was worked out between Carranza and Wilson, and the president ordered Pershing's command to return to Texas on January 26, 1917. Carranza, whose stout resistance to the American government made him a hero to the Mexican people, was elected president on March 11, 1917. The United States recognized his government two days later.

Wilson's involvement in the Mexican revolution demonstrated his determination to play a constructive role in world affairs. But however well intentioned the intervention may have been, it did little to undo, and in fact further aggravated, the resentment that Roosevelt's more "realistic" policy in Central and South America had caused. According to Link, although Wilson helped to make possible the independence of the Mexican people, he "had interfered in the wrong way so often that he embittered Mexican-American relations for many years to come." [40]

Wilson's severest tests in foreign affairs came during and after World War I, which for the first time required a president to exercise executive power in conditions of global conflict. In many respects, Wilson's conduct during the war was exemplary; certainly, he contributed significantly to the evolution of the president's powers as a wartime leader. Yet the same stubbornness and idealism that Wilson displayed toward Mexico led ultimately to a tragic defeat in his pursuit of a program for postwar peace.

The Presidency and Total War

The United States formally entered World War I on April 6, 1917, when Wilson signed a proclamation that a state of war existed with Germany. Congress voted to declare war four days after hearing the president's moving and eloquent appeal, in which he reluctantly called on the United States to end its traditional position of neutrality in the face of European conflicts. "It is a fearful thing to lead this great peaceful people into war, into the most terrible and disastrous of all wars," said Wilson. "But, the right is more precious than peace, and we shall fight for . . . a universal dominion of right by such a concert of free peoples as shall bring peace and safety to all nations and make the world itself at last free." [41]

The fight to "make the world safe for democracy," as Wilson called it, placed new demands upon the war powers of the president. To wage a "total war" [42] successfully required the mass production of complex weapons; it also entailed the mobilization and, at a great distance from the United States, the deployment of troops on a grand scale. The president, therefore, was responsible for organizing and controlling the industrial economy and coordinating the transportation and communication industries so that they could meet the requirements of the military commitment. [43] All this was in addition to the president's traditional duties as commander in chief.

The need to impose wartime economic and social controls on

Woodrow Wilson was more successful promoting his foreign policy agenda during his European tour of December 1918 than he was during his September 1919 tour of the increasingly isolationist United States.

American society strained the settled procedures of constitutional government to an extent not seen since the Civil War. Perhaps conscious of the reaction against presidential authority that had set in after Lincoln's assassination, Wilson, whenever possible, sought explicit delegations of power from Congress. But he did not rely upon statutory power for everything he did as commander in chief. For example, when Congress failed to authorize him to arm merchant vessels, Wilson armed them anyway, realizing full well that he had the constitutional right to do so. But Wilson had believed from the start of his presidency that the full flowering of presidential authority required legislative support, even in wartime, when the expansive character of executive power was well established by constitutional doctrine and historical precedents.

Of the many delegations of power to the president that followed the U.S. declaration of war, the most striking was the Lever Food and Fuel Control Act of 1917. The Lever Act granted authority to Wilson "to regulate by license the importation, manufacture, storage, mining or distribution of necessaries"—in effect, to regulate the entire national economy. Because such a grant of power was without precedent, it was assailed by many legislators as the precursor to a dictatorship. To allay such concerns, the Senate added a provision to the act that created a bipartisan committee to oversee the conduct of the war.

Wilson attacked the Senate amendment vehemently. Hoping to kill it in the House-Senate conference committee, he fired off a letter to the bill's sponsor, Rep. A. F. Lever, to protest that the proposed oversight committee would "amount to nothing less than an assumption on the part of the legislative body of the executive work of the administration." Wilson invoked the "ominous precedent" of the Committee on the Conduct of the War, which Congress had constituted during the Lincoln administration. That committee, he argued, "was the cause of constant and distressing harassment and rendered [Lincoln's] task all but impossible." [44] By standing firm and by convincing legislative leaders like Lever to do the same, Wilson managed to have the amendment removed. The president signed the Lever Act on August 10, 1917, establishing once more his claim to congressional leadership.

The emergency powers that Wilson accrued during World War I were extraordinary. As the political scientist Edward S. Corwin has noted, the contrast between Wilson's and Lincoln's versions of wartime "dictatorship" was of "method," not of "tenderness for customary constitutional restraints." [45] Once having obtained his extraordinary authority from Congress, however, Wilson appointed competent managers—such as Bernard Baruch, who chaired the powerful War Industries Board; Herbert Hoover, who served as food administrator; and Secretary of the Treasury William Gibbs McAdoo, who managed the railroads—to handle the details of administration. Similarly, Wilson left the management of military affairs to his European commander, General Pershing; the president intervened only when large political and diplomatic considerations were involved. [46]

Wilson's style of delegating detailed tasks to trusted members of his administration, while he assumed responsibility for the overall direction of the war effort, suited his approach to government. It also was an understandable adaptation to the exigencies of modern warfare. By the twentieth century, the conduct of war had become too massive and complex an undertaking for the president to supervise closely, as Polk and Lincoln had done. It was by providing moral leadership to arouse and administrative appointments to sustain the nation's engagement in total war that Wilson contributed to the development of the president as the commander in chief. [47]

The need to prosecute the war successfully also brought to a halt the partisan patronage practices that had characterized Wilson's first term. To some extent, Wilson already had begun to turn his attention to administrative reform soon after his reelection in 1916. With the coming of war, partisan considerations were further subordinated to the task of strengthening the departments and agencies.[48] As the administrative historian Paul Van Riper has observed, the expansion of executive power during the war planted in Washington a subtle and suggestive idea that outlasted even the return of Old Guard Republicanism during the 1920s:

> [T]he Wilsonian period . . . left many satisfying memories of effective collective endeavor under the aegis of government. When the times would be more propitious, during the Depression and Second World War soon to follow, these memories, and the governmental mechanism and the administrative experiences upon which they were in part based, were to return in new forms and under new auspices.[49]

The Defeat of the League of Nations

Ironically, defeat marked Wilson's effort to lead in the area in which he believed his influence and talents could best be employed—the serving of peace. Wilson had been cautious in asserting his powers as commander in chief during the war because he did not want to jeopardize the opportunity to take charge at the peace table. As the historian Ernest R. May has argued, "From the first day of the war to the last, all that Wilson sought was a peace that could be secured by the League of Nations, a peace that would make the world safe for democracy." [50]

Wilson's plan for an international peace-keeping association was the most controversial of his Fourteen Points, the peace program that he formulated in early 1918. He hoped to persuade the Allies and the Senate to accept the program, which also included lenient terms for the defeated Axis powers. Although the president had to compromise on some points in the postwar peace negotiations, particularly those pertaining to the conditions that were to be imposed on Germany, the League of Nations was included in the Treaty of Versailles, which was signed by the major powers in June 1919.

Wilson had little doubt that he would be able to persuade the Senate to ratify the treaty. He had displayed throughout his presidency an almost unsurpassed ability to enlist public support for the causes he championed. Yet the same methods that had succeeded magnificently in passing the New Freedom program failed miserably in the fight for the League. The limits of Wilson's influence first became evident in the 1918 midterm election, before the treaty was signed. No sooner had the Fourteen Points been pronounced and peace negotiations begun than Congress, tiring of Wilson's independent course, began to challenge the president's conduct of foreign affairs. Roosevelt abetted the opposition by urging the Senate to repudiate the Fourteen Points. On October 24, 1918, TR sent a telegram to Republican leaders: "Let us dictate peace by hammering guns and not chat about peace to the accompaniment of the clicking typewriters." [51]

Flustered by the Republicans' efforts to discredit him on the eve of the November elections, Wilson tried to rally the nation in support of his war policy. The day after Roosevelt's telegram was released, the president made an unusual appeal to the voters. "If you have approved of my leadership and wish me to be your unembarrassed spokesman in affairs at home and abroad, I earnestly beg that you will express yourself unmistakably to that effect by returning a Democratic majority to both the Senate and the House of Representatives." [52]

Wilson's partisan campaign appeal was a serious political error. He was loudly criticized for suggesting that the Democrats had a monopoly on loyalty. During the war many Republicans had supported his leadership, while many Democrats had opposed him. Wilson, in fact, actually had begun his effort to secure a sympathetic Congress by interfering in the primaries of his own party; he actively sought to defeat the Democratic incumbents in five Southern states because they had opposed his policies. Wilson's intervention, like Taft's in 1910, was characterized more by quiet maneuvering within party councils than by active campaigning. He did write public letters against certain representatives and senators, however. In several important instances, Wilson was successful in defeating fellow Democrats who had voted against the declaration of war and the measures he had proposed for carrying it on.[53] But the intraparty purge campaign cast doubt on the president's claim during the general election that the return of a Democratic majority to both houses of Congress was essential for the successful prosecution of the war.

Moreover, the 1918 campaign, occurring as it did in the midst of an international crisis, seemed an inappropriate occasion for a president to appeal to party loyalty. But so intent was Wilson on leading through his party in Congress that he was seemingly incapable of nonpartisan statesmanship, even when the occasion so clearly called for him to support all who shared his views of foreign policy.

The Republicans made substantial gains in the election and, for the first time in eight years, took control of both houses of Congress. To be sure, elements other than Wilson's message contributed to the Republican victory. Workers resented high wartime taxes, consumers were irritated by controls, and farmers were unhappy with the price ceilings on their crops. But the president's tactic provided his critics with ammunition to conclude, as Roosevelt did soon after the election, that "our allies and our enemies and Mr. Wilson himself should all understand that Mr. Wilson has no authority whatever to speak for the American people at this time. His leadership has just been emphatically repudiated by them." [54]

After Woodrow Wilson fell gravely ill in September 1919 while
conducting a speaking tour of the country to gain support for the
League of Nations, his wife, Edith, shielded him from the daily
responsibilities of the presidency. She screened all papers, business,
and visitors while he recovered. The full extent of the power she
wielded at this time has never been conclusively determined.

The 1918 election, then, diminished the president's prestige abroad
and at home, adding immeasurably to the difficulties he was to
encounter at the postwar peace conference and, especially, with Congress. Although Wilson managed to salvage much of his program at
Versailles, he failed in Washington. The opposition to the treaty was led
by an implacable Wilson foe, the Massachusetts Republican Henry
Cabot Lodge, who, as a result of the election, chaired the Senate Foreign
Relations Committee. Unwilling to compromise with Lodge, Wilson left
the capital on September 3, 1919, on a month-long speaking tour of the
western states. He hoped to create, as he had in the past, a groundswell
in favor of his policies that would force the Senate to ratify the treaty.

Instead, Wilson's swing around the country reduced his influence
further. Conceivably, but not likely, the campaign would have succeeded had his health not broken toward the end of the grueling tour.
But the tide of public opinion had been moving against the president
since the 1918 election.[55]

Wilson's abortive campaign for the League was dramatic evidence that although the presidency had gained considerable influence since the turn of the century, the office still was constrained by a powerful, if no longer dominant, Congress and by the vagaries of popular opinion. Because of TR and Wilson, Americans no longer considered it inappropriate for the president to try to rouse public support with rhetoric. But there was certainly no guarantee that every campaign of persuasion would succeed. The 1920 presidential election, which the conservative, anti-League, Republican senator Warren Harding won by an overwhelming popular vote, and, soon after, the final Senate defeat of the Versailles treaty, were setbacks not only for progressivism but also for Wilson's theory of presidential power.

Notes

1. George Mowry, *The Era of Theodore Roosevelt: 1900-1912* (New York: Harper, 1958), 272.
2. Quoted in Edward S. Corwin, *The President: Office and Powers, 1787-1957*, 4th ed. (New York: New York University Press, 1957), 36.
3. George Mowry, "The Election of 1912," in *History of American Presidential Elections*, ed. Arthur Schlesinger, Jr., and Fred I. Israel (New York: Chelsea, 1971), 3:2146.
4. Theodore Roosevelt, *The Works of Theodore Roosevelt* (New York: Scribner's, 1926), 17:219; and Proceedings of the First National Convention of the Progressive Party, August 5, 6, and 7, 1912, Progressive Party Archives, *Theodore Roosevelt Collection*, Houghton Library, Harvard University. Also see Mowry, "The Election of 1912," 3:2151-2153, 2164.
5. William M. Goldsmith, ed., *The Growth of Presidential Power: A Documented History* (New York and London: Chelsea, 1974), 3:1343; also Mowry, "The Election of 1912," 3:2163-2165.
6. Woodrow Wilson, "Cabinet Government in the United States," *International Review* 7 (August 1879): 146-163, 150-151.
7. Wilson's mature views on presidential leadership and constitutional change are expressed in Woodrow Wilson, *Constitutional Government in the United States* (New York: Columbia University Press, 1908).
8. Quoted in David Lawrence, *The True Story of Woodrow Wilson* (New York: Doran, 1924), 39.
9. Wilson, *Constitutional Government in the United States*, 68-69.
10. Ibid., 71-72.
11. Ibid., 68.
12. Ibid., 68-69.
13. Arthur S. Link, *Wilson and the New Freedom* (Princeton, N.J.: Princeton University Press, 1956), 145.
14. James Ceaser, *Presidential Selection: Theory and Development* (Princeton, N.J.: Princeton University Press, 1979), 173.
15. Woodrow Wilson, "First Annual Message," December 2, 1913, in *The State of the Union Messages of the Presidents*, ed. Fred I. Israel (New York: Chelsea, 1966), 2548.

16. Link, *Wilson and the New Freedom*, 149.
17. Woodrow Wilson, *The Papers of Woodrow Wilson*, ed. Arthur S. Link (Princeton, N.J.: Princeton University Press, 1966-1985), 27:151. Wilson's contribution to popular leadership in the United States is assessed in Jeffrey Tulis, *The Rhetorical Presidency* (Princeton, N.J.: Princeton University Press, 1987), 117-144.
18. *New York Times*, April 9, 1913, 8.
19. Mowry, "The Election of 1912," 2155.
20. Elmer E. Cornwell, Jr., *Presidential Leadership of Public Opinion* (Bloomington: Indiana University Press, 1965), 32-44.
21. *New York Times*, April 8, 1913, 1.
22. Cornwell, *Presidential Leadership of Public Opinion*, 46.
23. Wilson, *Papers* 27:269-270.
24. Ray Stannard Baker, *Woodrow Wilson: Life and Letters* (London: Heinemann, 1932), 4:109.
25. Arthur S. Link, *Woodrow Wilson and the Progressive Era: 1910-1917* (New York: Harper and Row, 1954), 35.
26. Quoted in ibid., 21.
27. Woodrow Wilson, "Monopoly or Opportunity," in Goldsmith, *Growth of Presidential Power* 3:1334-1342, 1341.
28. Wilson, *Papers* 31:415.
29. Paul Van Riper, *History of the United States Civil Service* (Evanston, Ill.: Row, Peterson, 1958), 230; William Dudley Foulke, *Fighting the Spoilsmen* (New York: Arno Press, 1974; New York: Putnam's, 1919), 226-259.
30. Josephus Daniels to Franklin D. Roosevelt, December 15, 1932, Ray Stannard Baker Collection, Franklin D. Roosevelt File, Firestone Library, Princeton University.
31. Quoted in Baker, *Woodrow Wilson: Life and Letters* 4:45.
32. Link, *Wilson and the New Freedom*, 159.
33. Baker, *Woodrow Wilson: Life and Letters* 4:47.
34. Link, *Wilson and the New Freedom*, 160.
35. *New Republic*, December 5, 1914, 11-12.
36. Wilson, *Constitutional Government in the United States*, 78.
37. Link, *Wilson and the New Freedom*, 277.
38. Burton J. Hendrick, *The Life and Letters of Walter J. Page* (New York: Doubleday, Page, 1922), 1:204-205.
39. Link, *Wilson and the New Freedom*, 350; Sidney Warren, *The President as World Leader* (Philadelphia: Lippincott, 1964), 81.
40. Link, *Woodrow Wilson and the Progressive Era*, 144.
41. Wilson, *Papers* 41:526.
42. The concept of "total war" applied in part to the Civil War. The assault on slavery and the military tactics of Gen. William T. Sherman, who used military force against the civilian population of the rebel states, demonstrated the effectiveness of a plan of action that would destroy the enemy's economic system and demoralize the civilian population. See John Bennett Walters, "General William T. Sherman and Total War," *Journal of Southern History* 14 (1948): 447-480. In the twentieth century, however, the concept of total war took on a new, more expansive meaning. With the development of the modern state, war became an instrument of national policy that mobilized the society's entire population and resources for a prolonged conflict. Edward S. Corwin defines total war as "the politically ordered participation in the war effort of all personal and social forces, the

scientific, the mechanical, the commercial, the economic, the moral, the literary, the artistic, and the psychological" (Corwin, *Total War and the Constitution* [New York: Knopf, 1947], 24).

43. For a discussion of Wilson's leadership during World War I, see Goldsmith, *Growth of Presidential Power* 3:1699-1733.
44. Quoted in Baker, *Woodrow Wilson: Life and Letters* 7:185-186.
45. Corwin, *President: Office and Powers*, 237.
46. Goldsmith, *Growth of Presidential Power* 3:1705, 1711.
47. Ibid. 3:1706
48. Foulke, *Fighting the Spoilsmen*, 255-259.
49. Van Riper, *History of the United States Civil Service*, 282.
50. Ernest R. May, "Wilson (1917-1918)," in *The Ultimate Decision: The President as Commander in Chief*, ed. Ernest R. May (New York: Braziller, 1960), 131.
51. Warren, *President as World Leader*, 107.
52. Wilson, *Papers* 51:381.
53. *New York Times*, August 12, 1918, sec. 3, 1. Sidney M. Milkis, "Presidents and Party Purges: With Special Emphasis on the Lessons of 1938," in *Presidents and Their Parties: Leadership or Neglect?* ed. Robert Harmel (New York: Praeger, 1984), 154-157.
54. Quoted in Warren, *President as World Leader*, 108.
55. The failure of Wilson's campaign for the League was hardly a foregone conclusion, however. Indeed, before his health failed him Wilson was attracting large, enthusiastic crowds, and the opponents of the treaty were sufficiently concerned about his influence to send out Senators William E. Borah of Idaho and Hiram Johnson of California to give the other side of the argument. See Kendrick A. Clements, *The Presidency of Woodrow Wilson* (Lawrence: University Press of Kansas, 1992), 196.

CHAPTER 10

The Triumph of
Conservative Republicanism

The election of Warren Harding by a huge majority in 1920 signified the end of the Progressive Era. Ostensibly, the campaign that brought Harding to office was fought on the issue of the League of Nations. But in rejecting the League, so closely identified with the reform aspirations of Woodrow Wilson, voters were expressing their desire for quieter times after two decades of far-reaching and fundamental political change. The return to international isolation, which the repudiation of the League inaugurated, was accompanied by a return to laissez faire, a partial restoration of the wall that had separated government from society before the advent of progressivism.

Harding's election could be explained in no small part by his identification with the nation's longing for a moratorium on reform. In May 1920, he told the Home Market Club in Boston, "America's present need is not heroics, but healing; not nostrums but normalcy; not revolution but restoration . . . not surgery but serenity." [1]

The word *normalcy*, especially, attracted immediate and lasting attention; a "return to normalcy" became the theme of the Republican campaign.[2] Normalcy captured the temper of the times concerning not just public policy but the presidency as well. Harding capitalized on the popular reaction against what the Republicans called "executive autocracy." Meanwhile, a stricken President Wilson played into the opposition's hands. Before Congress adjourned in the summer of 1920, it passed an act to repeal around sixty wartime laws that conferred extraordinary powers on the executive. The repeal act was approved by the House of Representatives in a 343-3 vote and by the Senate unanimously. Nevertheless, after Congress adjourned Wilson pocket-vetoed the act, thereby retaining his war powers until Congress met again in December 1920. In doing so, the historian William Starr Myers noted, "President Wilson ... took one more step which decisively alienated the average American citizen." [3]

The Republicans resumed power in March 1921, militant in their determination to restore Congress and the party organization to their former stature. Leading the official committee that notified Harding of his nomination by the 1920 Republican convention, Senator Henry Cabot Lodge presented the candidate with something of an ultimatum. Alluding to the transfer of power from Congress to the White House that had occurred during the Wilson administration, Lodge reminded Harding that "the makers of the Constitution intended to coordinate the three great elements of government and strove to guard against either usurpation or trespass by one branch at the expense of the other." "In that spirit," the senator added, "*we all know well,* you will enter upon your great responsibility." [4]

Neither Harding nor his two Republican successors, Calvin Coolidge and Herbert C. Hoover, took exception to the sentiment that Lodge expressed. Their understanding of executive power owed more to William Howard Taft than to Theodore Roosevelt. In fact, the twelve-year tenure of these three presidents generally is regarded as the nadir of the presidency in the twentieth century. As before in U.S. history, strong executive leadership was followed by passivity and drift.

There was, however, no restoration of congressional government during the 1920s. Transformed social and economic conditions, as well as the precedents that Roosevelt and Wilson had established, did not allow for a return to the old order. As the political scientist Elmer Cornwell has observed, "the stature of the [executive] office in the eyes of the public, which had been growing since 1900, and was given powerful further impetus during the Wilson years, at least held its own if it did not actually continue to grow after 1920." [5] Even Harding's concept of normalcy did not entail turning back the clock entirely. As he wrote during the campaign, "The common people—the people of whom Lincoln said that God must have loved them, because he made so many of them—have seen themselves lifted to a new level in the social and economic scheme of the world; and our problems of the future will be to maintain them there." [6]

The Harding Era

In his acceptance speech for the Republican nomination for president, Harding tried to assuage the concerns of his Senate colleagues. The nominee pledged that, if elected, he would restore "party government as distinguished from personal government, individual, dictatorial, autocratic, or what not." [7] True to his promise as a candidate, President Harding made little effort to lead Congress. His expressed intention was to reign rather than rule: the president would announce his legislative program, which the Constitution directed him to do, but after that, lawmaking would be the work of Congress. On those rare occasions when Harding did take an interest in legislative matters, his actions almost always showed great deference to Congress. Harding's model was William McKinley, whose influence on Capitol Hill was achieved through quiet consultation and compromise with his party's leadership. [8]

But McKinley-style legislative leadership no longer was possible in the 1920s. The congressional revolt of 1910, which dethroned the Speaker, had weakened the ties of party in the House; gone were the days when the president and the Speaker could bring together the executive and legislative branches of the government through quiet consultation. The Senate, too, had been affected by the insurgent revolt against party leadership. Moreover, the enactment in 1913 of the Seventeenth Amendment, which provided that the people, not the state legislatures, would elect senators, further undermined party discipline in the upper chamber. The typical senator, one observer wrote in 1922, "came to think more in terms of himself and his reelection, nearly always an impelling motive, and less in terms of party." [9] Wilson's bold methods of party leadership had forged, at least for a time, new connections between the president and Congress. Harding's passivity guaranteed deadlock and confusion.

One consequence of the new president's forbearance was that his program to address the postwar economic problems, notably through higher tariffs and lower taxes, made little headway in the legislature; instead Congress became bogged down in disagreements over what to do. An old friend of the president, Malcolm Jennings, wrote him in the late summer of 1921 that effective "congressional action can only follow the establishment of dominant leadership upon your part." [10] Harding began to regret his pledge to defer to the legislative branch. As his policies foundered in Congress, he wrote to Jennings, "I find that I can not carry out my pre-election ideals of an Executive keeping himself aloof from Congress." [11]

Yet regret was unaccompanied by reform. Even when, to the astonishment of many, Harding went before Congress personally on July 12, 1921, to chide the House and, especially, the Senate for inaction, he did not follow through with the sort of forceful and painstaking efforts at public or personal persuasion that might have moved his fractious party to action. Harding did not bow down to Congress, but neither did he have the desire or the ability to lead it forward. [12]

Fresh from its defeat of the League, Congress was determined to direct foreign affairs during Harding's term. Most significant, the Senate took the initiative to curb the naval arms race that had preoccupied the major powers since the beginning of World War I. The rejection of the Versailles treaty had ensured that the nation's naval buildup would continue after the war; many public officials in the United States, including Harding, believed that the pursuit of naval supremacy was the only alternative to joining the League. Yet an arms race would be very expensive (especially because Great Britain and Japan were determined to match the U.S. deployments) and thus ran counter to the widespread desire for peace and economy.

Faced with this dilemma, the progressive Republican senator William Borah attached an amendment to the 1921 naval appropriation bill that called on the president to invite Great Britain and Japan to a naval disarmament conference. The rider passed Congress despite Harding's efforts to replace it with a weaker resolution. Harding was not opposed to having a conference, but he thought that it would be prudent to build up the American forces first. He also knew that one purpose of the Borah Amendment was to tie the president's hands.

Still, Harding was not one to engage Congress in a bitter and protracted struggle. Bowing to the legislative will, he called an international disarmament conference, which took place in Washington in late 1921 and early 1922. The Washington Naval Disarmament Conference worked out an agreement not only on naval armaments but on relations between the major Pacific powers as well. It was characteristic of Harding's presidency, however, that his outstanding foreign policy accomplishment was the result of a Senate initiative. As the presidential scholar Wilfred Binkley has written, "Nothing could be more indicative of how great had been the reaction against the Wilsonian type of executive." [13]

The Harding Scandals

Harding's presidency began slowly and ended disastrously. By 1923, it was clear that the country was paying a heavy price for his passive leadership and fawning deference to the regular party apparatus. The president's pledge to restore normalcy included a revival of enthusiasm for patronage appointments. The steady extension of the merit civil service that had begun with the passage of the Pendleton Act in 1883 and had continued ever since, especially during Roosevelt's presidency, went no further in the Harding administration. Wilson had been willing to manipulate the civil service when party patronage proved useful in getting his program through Congress. But Harding was the first (and only) twentieth-century president to embrace the spoils system as worthy in its own right. "By the middle of the summer of 1921 the spoils efforts of the Republicans began to assume the proportions of a sizable if not full-scale raid," the administrative historian Paul Van Riper has written.[14]

Nor was the Harding administration reluctant to manipulate the remaining unclassified service, which now constituted around one-fourth of the federal work force. Some of Harding's appointments were excellent, especially his selection of Herbert Hoover as secretary of commerce and of Charles Evans Hughes as secretary of state. Many others, however, were more reminiscent of the Grant era than of the twentieth century. Collectively, Harding's appointees produced the worst corruption of any administration since the advent of civil service reform.

The first disturbing situation to come to light involved Charles Forbes, the director of the Veterans' Bureau. In March 1923, Harding was told that Forbes had been selling items from the government's medical supply base in Perryville, Maryland, to private contractors at ridiculously low prices. He also was making undercover deals for hospital building contracts and site selections. Forbes resigned; his principal legal adviser, Charles F. Cramer, committed suicide.[15]

When the Veterans' Bureau scandal was followed soon after by another in the attorney general's office, Harding became convinced that his administration was deeply tainted with corruption. Fearing for his reputation and for the fortunes of his party, he is reported to have remarked to the journalist William Allen White, "My God, this is a hell of a job! I have no trouble with my enemies. I can take care of my enemies all right. But my damn friends, my God-damn friends, White, they're the ones that keep me walking the floor nights." [16]

Despondent and in poor health, the president decided to escape Washington on a cross-country speaking tour that would culminate in Alaska. In the course of his return trip, Harding fell ill of ptomaine poisoning, then pneumonia, and died of an embolism in San Francisco on August 2, 1923. Vice President Calvin Coolidge became president.

Mercifully, Harding's death preceded by a few months the uncovering of the Teapot Dome scandal, a complicated and subtle plot to defraud the government that was hatched and executed during his presidency. Teapot Dome, one of the most notorious political scandals in U.S. history, originated with the administration's effort to modify, and in some cases to reverse, the conservation policies of Roosevelt, Taft, and Wilson.[17] The prime mover in the affair was Harding's secretary of the interior, Albert B. Fall, who wanted to prevent the navy from continuing to withdraw petroleum-rich lands from private development, a policy that was designed to protect these lands and to provide a certain supply of oil for future naval emergencies. Fall, who was a strong advocate of private development, persuaded Secretary of the Navy Edwin Denby to turn over the management of the petroleum reserves to the Interior Department. In 1921 and 1922, Fall rapidly implemented a new program to lease the reserves to oil companies, which favored him in turn with loans and gifts.

Fall probably did not require payoffs to pursue most of his policies; the leasing program was in keeping with his own ideas about private development.[18] But the secretary's greed got the better of him, thus exposing his policies to attack from conservationists and their allies in the Senate. An exhaustive Senate investigation, which was chaired by Montana senator Thomas Walsh, disclosed that Fall had entered into a corrupt bargain with the oil companies of Edward L. Doheny and Harry F. Sinclair, granting them access to valuable petroleum deposits that President Wilson had reserved for the navy. The Elk Hill, California, oil reserve was leased to Doheny, and the Teapot Dome oil reserve in Wyoming to Sinclair. In return for the leases, Doheny and Sinclair built some pipelines and storage facilities for the navy on the West Coast and at Pearl Harbor. But Fall personally received at least $100,000 from Doheny and $300,000 from Sinclair.

Armed with these facts, and with other damaging revelations that were unearthed by the Senate committee's investigation, a special commission, appointed by President Coolidge, initiated criminal prosecutions in early June 1924. Sinclair, Doheny, and Fall, who had resigned as secretary of the interior before the scandal broke, were charged with conspiracy to defraud the government. The trials and legal maneuvering lasted almost six years, after which Fall was sentenced to a year in jail and a $100,000 fine, and Sinclair was sentenced to six months in jail. But Doheny was acquitted, a ridiculous verdict considering that Fall had been convicted of taking a bribe from him. The acquittal provoked the progressive Republican senator from Nebraska, George Norris, to remark, with reference to Doheny's expensive legal fees, that it is "very difficult, if not impossible to convict one hundred million dollars." [19]

Budget and Accounting Act of 1921

Harding's public reputation, which remained high while he was alive, suffered tremendously from the scandalous revelations that rocked the government after he died. But the Harding administration was not without its achievements. During his tenure, for example, the first national budget system was created, enhancing significantly the president's authority to oversee the expenditures of the executive departments and agencies. The Budget and Accounting Act of 1921 carried into effect the major recommendations of the 1913 Taft Commission.

The budget act required an annual, comprehensive executive budget, assigning to the president the responsibility to estimate both the government's financial needs and the revenues it expected to collect during the coming fiscal year. The act also established the Bureau of the Budget to support the president's use of the new budget authority. Although formally assigned to the Treasury Department, the Budget Bureau was intended to serve as a presidential staff agency. Finally, the budget act created the General Accounting Office as an auditing arm of Congress.

With the passage of the budget act, the president finally obtained legal authority to influence the allocation of expenditures in the executive branch. In exercising this authority the president still had to contend with both the powerful fiscal committees in Congress, especially the Ways and Means and the Appropriations committees, and the bureaucratic agency heads who for so long had dealt directly with Congress. But the president certainly was able to exert greater authority and direction in budgetary matters with the act than without it. Indeed, the scholar and civil servant Herbert Emmerich has judged the budget act to be "the greatest landmark of our administrative history except for the Constitution itself." [20]

Harding was not the first president to advocate a national budget system; both Taft and Wilson had supported measures to strengthen the executive's authority in fiscal affairs. Still, Harding did what Taft and Wilson were unable to do—he secured budget legislation from Congress. Moreover, Harding and the first director of the Budget Bureau, the capable Charles G. Dawes, made effective use of the powers that the new law had placed in the president's hands. Harding's 1920 call for a return to normalcy had included a pledge to reduce government spending. Dedicated as he was to fulfilling this pledge, Harding, acting somewhat out of character, managed to hold his cabinet to a stern fiscal program that by 1923 had achieved almost $2 billion in savings. [21]

Expansion of the President's Removal Power

Harding also made an indirect contribution to the president's control of administrative affairs by appointing William Howard Taft as chief justice of the Supreme Court in 1921. Taft's majority opinion in the case of *Myers* v. *United States*, which was decided in 1926, gave constitutional sanction to a sweeping interpretation of the president's removal power. [22] Although the repeal of the Tenure of Office Act in 1885 had eliminated one obstacle to presidential removal, nothing prevented Congress from deciding to enact a similar statute in the future. Indeed, in passing legislation to create federal offices and to establish the procedures for filling them, Congress had continued to limit the president's discretion through stipulations of tenure and other conditions.

The 1876 statute that was at issue in the *Myers* case required the president to obtain the advice and consent of the Senate before removing a first-class postmaster from office. On January 20, 1920, President Wilson had requested the resignation of Frank S. Myers, a first-class postmaster. When Myers refused to comply, Wilson removed him by order of the postmaster general.

The legality of Wilson's action was upheld—ironically, by a Supreme Court whose chief justice had endorsed, even while serving as president, a narrow theory of executive power. But Taft's opinion on behalf of a divided court displayed a boldness rarely seen during his tenure in the White House. Taft held that Wilson's order was valid and that the law that restricted the president's authority to remove postmasters was unconstitutional. Arguing that the removal power was inherently "executive," Taft insisted that the president must be able to control all executive officeholders, not just the highly placed ones. "The imperative reasons requiring an unrestricted power to remove the most important of his subordinates in their most important duties," the chief justice explained, "must ... control the interpretation of the Constitution as to all appointed by him." [23]

The *Myers* decision was the Court's first foray into the long struggle between the president and Congress for possession of the removal power. Issued by a conservative chief justice who had been appointed by a conservative president, *Myers* offered a startling constitutional endorsement of the expanding boundaries of executive authority. The Supreme Court eventually would restrict somewhat the application of Taft's ruling. But the *Myers* decision, following on the heels of the Budget and Accounting Act, was additional evidence that the presidency, regardless of who was president, was unlikely to return to its more modest nineteenth-century status.

Public Relations in the Harding Era

Neither Harding nor his successor, the taciturn Calvin Coolidge, regarded himself as a lawgiver or a tribune of the people in the sense that Roosevelt and Wilson had. But each found that he could not serve the laissez-faire economic policies that he embraced without taking a strong hand in the administration of the executive departments and agencies. Certainly, Harding's promise of economy in government could not have been fulfilled without the expanded fiscal powers that the president was granted by the Budget and Accounting Act. Moreover, the national government's involvement in domestic affairs could not have been reduced without public support. Thanks to TR and Wilson, public relations had become a critical ingredient of successful presidential leadership.[24]

Although Harding's presidency ended disastrously, he did manage to add to the arsenal of presidential techniques for leading public opinion. Having served as the editor and publisher of the *Marion Star* in Ohio before entering politics, Harding had a good sense of how the press worked. He developed an intimacy with journalists that greatly benefited both his 1920 presidential campaign and, until the scandals began to break in 1923, his image as president.

Good relations with the press were ensured by personal considerateness and conscious innovations. During the 1920 campaign, for example, a three-room cottage was built near the Harding home in Marion to accommodate the press. There Harding would meet with reporters daily to discuss political developments in frank, off-the-record fashion. Harding continued to cultivate the journalistic fraternity during the transition period, as he waited to be inaugurated. He was the first president to recognize that public opinion could be courted through leisurely as well as through formal and ceremonial activities, even to the extent of playing golf with particular correspondents.[25]

As president, Harding revived the practice of holding regular press conferences, which Wilson had begun but had allowed to taper off after 1915. In addition, it was under Harding that the "White House spokesman" device was invented to convey information from the administration to the public without attributing it to the president. Harding recognized that to hang this veil between himself and newspaper readers gave him room to maneuver that he otherwise would not have had. Finally, Harding was the first president to benefit from "photo opportunities." His administration issued identification cards to members of the newly formed White House News Photographers' Association that granted them access to all public and some private events at which the president appeared. Harding himself posed willingly for photographers several times a week.

Harding's conscious innovations in press relations helped to amplify the effects of his warm and engaging personality and to win support for his administration's policies. He also decided to retain Wilson's practice of delivering messages to Congress in person. Moreover, Harding immensely enjoyed speechmaking tours. The mounting burden of the rhetorical presidency led Harding to appoint the first presidential speech writer, the journalist Judson Welliver.[26]

Harding died before the American people realized his shortcomings. His intellectual weakness and dislike of hard work had always made the White House an uncomfortable place for him. Although he enjoyed the glamour and attention that recently had become part of the presidency, he found the responsibilities that accompanied the office's new stature to be unbearable. Poring over an immense stack of correspondence, Harding is reported to have lamented to an aide, "I am not fit for this office and should never have been here." [27]

Nevertheless, the death of Warren G. Harding, who had served barely two years in office and whom history would count as one of the least successful presidents, caused an extraordinary outpouring of national emotion. The crowds that came out to view the train carrying Harding's body to Washington were immense. As the historian Robert Murray has written, "Every town, every city, every hamlet turned out mourning people, standing silently or kneeling by the tracks and on the station platforms." [28]

The public reaction to Harding's death reflected the growing prominence of the presidency. Because of the minute journalistic surveillance of the president's activities that began during his administration, the stature of the office did not shrink but, to a surprising degree, continued to expand during the Harding era. "More than ever before," Cornwell has written, "thanks to the media and the use made of them on the President's behalf, the presidency was destined to blow up the man to heroic proportions and project this image constantly on the nation's screen." [29]

The "Silent" Politics of Calvin Coolidge

Calvin Coolidge was an unlikely heir to the increasingly public presidency. Plain in appearance, so sparing in speech that he was dubbed "Silent Cal," Coolidge's public persona was ordinary at a time when the executive office seemed to require persons of heroic demeanor. Yet, in spite of his limitations, or perhaps in part because of them, Coolidge was one of the most popular presidents in history.

Coolidge raised inactivity to an art. When it came to leading Congress or exerting his will on matters of public policy, Coolidge felt even less responsibility to act than had Harding. Less partisan than his immediate predecessor, Coolidge made little effort to join with Republican leaders in Congress to advance a legislative program. By philosophy and personality, Coolidge also was more doctrinaire than Harding in his opposition to the kind of bold measures that Wilson had undertaken to unite the separated branches of the government. "I have never felt it was my duty," Coolidge wrote in his autobiography,

> to attempt to coerce Senators or Representatives, or to take reprisals. The people sent them to Washington. I felt I discharged my duty when I had done the best that I could with them. In this way I avoided almost entirely a personal opposition, which I think was of more value to the country than the attempt to prevail through arousing personal fear.[30]

Restraint in legislative relations comported with Coolidge's general disdain for programmatic initiatives. "The key to an understanding of the presidential career of Calvin Coolidge is to be found in the fact that he had a distaste for legislation," Wilfred Binkley has written.[31] Like Harding, Coolidge believed that there already were too many federal programs and that the president's energies should be spent administering the government economically and efficiently. One of the few legislative measures that Coolidge promoted vigorously was the Mellon tax reduction plan of 1923, which took its name from the conservative Treasury secretary who served during the Harding and Coolidge administrations, Andrew Mellon.

Aside from bills that, like the tax cut, reduced the national government's involvement in the economy, Coolidge maintained a public silence about legislation that befitted a nineteenth-century president. Even in the matter of the protocol of the World Court, a treaty that Coolidge sent to the Senate for ratification, he gave neither encouragement nor direction to Republican senators. Instead, the president spoke barely a word as his supporters fought a valiant but, in the face of the isolationist mood that gripped the nation after World War I, a losing battle.

Coolidge's lack of success with Congress notwithstanding, he forged a strong bond with the American people. "No other president in our day and time," one commentator observed, "has had such close, such continuous and such successful relations with the electorate as Calvin Coolidge had."[32] To some degree, Coolidge had the virtues of his defects. His stern Yankee demeanor and business-like administrative style offered a welcome respite from the scandals that had rocked the government in 1923. He also benefited from the apparent prosperity of the postwar economy. The Harding-Coolidge economic program, with its emphasis on free markets at home and protection from abroad, put "business in the saddle."[33] For a time, business seemed competent for the task: throughout the spring of 1924, disclosures of the Harding administration scandals competed for attention on the front pages with news of increasing dividends, profits, and sales.[34] Good times seemed to call for a president who was content to "sit tight."

Coolidge's enormous popularity was grounded not just in his commitment to business but also in his ability to express that commitment in words that exalted the governing principles of the era. "The genius of this day was not altogether material," Coolidge said of the ascendant Republican party's faith in commerce. "It had its spiritual side, deep and significant. . . . Prosperity came to the people that they might have the resources for more of the refinements of life, more for the needs of education and religion, more to minister to the things of the soul. Power came to the nation that it might the better serve its own citizens and bear its share of the burden of civilization." Coolidge inspired the people by persuading them, as he put it in his 1925 inaugural address, that his program reflected "idealism in its most practical form." [35]

Coolidge's popularity was reinforced by his shrewd sense of public relations. Extraordinarily faithful in discharging what he felt to be his obligations to reporters, Coolidge held 520 press conferences during his five years in office, more each month than even the gregarious Franklin D. Roosevelt. Provisions for the comfort and convenience of correspondents reached new heights during his administration.[36] Not surprisingly, Coolidge's concern for the press corps won him a considerable measure of favorable coverage in the press.

On rare occasions, the president used his exceedingly cordial relations with reporters to exert legislative leadership. For example, in ten press conferences between December 1923 and June 1924, Coolidge urged Congress to enact the Mellon tax reduction plan. But much of Coolidge's public relations effort was designed to sell himself rather than his policies.

Characteristically, while Republican senators, without an encouraging word from the president, fought a losing battle for the administration's World Court treaty, Coolidge used a White House lunch with prominent editors and authors to disseminate benign personal impressions. "Instead of trying to guide Congress and impress his views on party leaders," a Washington correspondent wrote in 1926, "Mr. Coolidge devotes himself to playing the sort of politics he knows how to play, doing the sort of thing he can do—and in which he is far more interested than in the World Court proposal which was from the start more or less an annoyance to him." [37]

Coolidge had a keen understanding of the public's interest in the human side of the presidency. Convinced that news about his personal activities would pave the way for popular acceptance of his more serious pronouncements, the shy Coolidge threw open his private life to unprecedented public gaze. One contemporary reporter suggested that "he was probably the most photographed man who ever occupied the White House. It was a joke among photographers that Mr. Coolidge would don any attire or assume any pose that would produce an interesting picture. He was never too busy to be photographed; nor is it recorded that he ever resented any revelation as to his personal habits." [38]

Important as the newspapers were to Coolidge, his most significant contribution to the development of White House communications was his use of the radio. Lacking the "barnstorming ability" of his recent predecessors, Coolidge was blessed with a new medium, which he used effectively to enhance his image. "I am very fortunate I came in with the

Calvin Coolidge skillfully cultivated the press and generated favorable public opinion with photo sessions such as this March 1925 meeting with members of the Sioux Indian Republican Club.

radio," he told Sen. James Watson of Indiana. "I can't make an engaging, rousing, or oratorical speech to a crowd as you can, . . . but I have a good radio voice, and now I can get my messages across to them without acquainting them with my lack of oratorical ability." [39]

As with his courting of reporters, Coolidge used the radio less to rouse public opinion in support of his policies than to enhance his personal popularity. Had he not formed a strong bond with the voters in this way, Coolidge may not have been nominated for president by his party in 1924. The historian Gleason Archer has noted:

> It is probably true that radio played an exceedingly important part in the career of Calvin Coolidge. In six months [after he became president] the national election would be in its preliminary stages. In that brief time President Coolidge was so to impress himself upon the voters that no serious opposition to his re-election was to manifest itself. [40]

Coolidge's first significant public appearance as president was his State of the Union address, which he delivered to Congress on December 6, 1923. His speech was also the first presidential message to Congress to be broadcast, and Coolidge's clear, incisive, New England diction and the seeming wisdom of his message apparently made a profound impression on the national radio audience. [41] From then until the Republican convention in June 1924, Coolidge made certain to revisit the homes of the American people at least once each month through carefully prepared radio broadcasts.

Coolidge's overwhelming first-ballot nomination marked an important advance, as Coolidge himself recognized, in the emergence of the president as "the sole repository of party responsibility." [42] The conservative Republican senators who had controlled the party since 1912 had little regard for Coolidge; unlike Harding, the former governor of Massachusetts was not one of them. Yet they had little choice but to support the president's bid for a full term in 1924. As William Allen White wrote in 1925, "The reason why the senatorial group ceased hoping to defeat Coolidge for the Republican nomination was the obvious fact that Coolidge was getting stronger and stronger with the American people." [43] Noting that the radio in no small measure had made this possible, Cornwell has written: "Here was the first President in history whom more than a tiny fraction of the populace could actually listen to, and whose voice they could come to know at first hand. Small wonder that the man developed a tangible meaning for millions—more so perhaps than any of his predecessors." [44]

Herbert C. Hoover and the Great Depression

Coolidge demonstrated that the increasingly powerful and prominent executive office could be used as effectively by a president who wanted only to reign as by one who, like TR and Wilson, sought also to rule.[45] Coolidge was not simply a throwback to the Benjamin Harrison era. Instead, his tenure suggested how a president with a shrewd sense of politics and public relations could thrive in the new political conditions of the twentieth century, even one who was philosophically opposed to the expansion of government programs and executive power.

When Herbert Hoover, capitalizing on Coolidge's refurbishing of the presidency, defeated the Democrat Al Smith in the 1928 election, many expected that he would be an able—even a brilliant—leader. The "Great Engineer," as Hoover was called, brought to the White House a tremendous reputation for accomplishment and public service from his tenure as food administrator during the Wilson administration and as secretary of commerce under Harding and Coolidge. Dedicated to his Republican predecessors' probusiness program yet confident that knowledgeable and efficient administration in Washington could build a stronger foundation for national prosperity, Hoover seemed perfectly qualified to consolidate the gains of the postwar economic recovery.

Yet the same president who entered office amid such great expectations left four years later as the object of scorn and derision. This startling political reversal could be attributed in part to the Great

Depression, perhaps the worst economic crisis in the nation's history. The depression struck when the stock market crashed in October 1929, only seven months after Hoover was inaugurated. But the Hoover administration was in trouble even before the crash.

Much of Hoover's difficulty as president stemmed from the contrast between his desire to bring forth important changes in America's economy and society and his unwillingness or inability to undertake the tasks of leadership that could have made these changes possible. Like Harding and Coolidge, Hoover subscribed to a political philosophy that confined the national government to the few activities for which it had clear constitutional authority. But Hoover's fear of big government coexisted with his faith, born of the Progressive Era, in the government's ability to improve social and economic conditions.[46]

Early in his presidency, Hoover called a special session of Congress to recommend a significant program of reform. "No president in a hundred years, excepting Woodrow Wilson, had moved his administration so quickly and so extensively into domestic reform," the historian Martin Fausold has argued.[47] Hoover called for major changes in tariffs, taxes, conservation, and government organization.

Hoover also believed that his administration should mobilize industrial and civic organizations as a way to facilitate better economic coordination and enhanced economic opportunities. He was particularly concerned about several flaws in the nation's recent prosperity: the imbalance between high production and low consumption; the weak agricultural sector; the lack of efficient procedures in industry; feverish financial speculation, fueled by unsound currency and lending policies; and the inadequate organization of labor, which allowed a disproportionate share of corporate profits to go to owners and managers. The solutions to these problems, Hoover believed, lay not in expanding the national government but in using the presidency and the rest of the executive branch to encourage private institutions to develop more rational and just economic arrangements. As secretary of commerce, Hoover had worked successfully with trade associations and farm organizations. Now, as chief executive, he hoped to expand the bounds of these activities. "By his position," Hoover told the Gridiron Club on December 14, 1929, the president "must, within his capacities, give leadership to the development of moral, social, and economic forces outside of government which make for the betterment of our country."[48]

Hoover's philosophy and personality, however, rendered him incapable of providing the brand of leadership he advocated, especially after the hammer blows of the depression fell. Sharing Coolidge's respect for the autonomy of the legislature, Hoover did little to lead the special session of Congress that he had called in 1929. After leaving office, Hoover explained his reticence:

The encroachments upon our liberties may not be overt—by repeal of any of the Constitutional guarantees—but they may be insidious and no less potent through encroachment upon the checks and balances which make its security. More particularly does the weakening of the legislative arm lead to encroachment by the executive upon the legislative and judicial functions, and inevitably that encroachment is upon individual liberty.[49]

Despite the president's unassertiveness, a farm bill, at least, eventually was enacted. The Agricultural Market Act created the Federal Farm Board to administer loans so that agricultural cooperatives could help farmers to produce and market their crops. Before a bill that was acceptable to Hoover could pass, however, Republican leaders in the Senate had to quell a revolt by party insurgents. Against the president's wishes, western progressives had moved to subsidize farmers who were exporting commodities abroad at a price lower than the domestic rate. After weeks of deadlock, Congress approved the president's version of the agriculture measure, but with little help from Hoover. "There is some very bad leadership from the bottom of 16th Street," complained former secretary of agriculture William M. Jardine, referring to the White House.[50]

Congress was not so accommodating when the issue was tariffs. The president favored a limited revision of the tariff schedules that would aid only the stricken farmers. But a Senate resolution to confine tariff revision to the agricultural schedule was defeated by a single vote. Hoover, who in all likelihood could have swung the one vote he needed to prevail, refused even to try.[51] He then remained silent as Congress, particularly the Senate, proceeded to increase tariffs on nonfarm as well as on farm commodities, eventually passing a bill that raised tariffs to their highest levels in history. Hoover signed the protectionist Smoot-Hawley tariff, which he privately characterized as "vicious, extortionate, and obnoxious," in the face of ardent pleas from all parts of the country to veto it.[52] As the correspondent Walter Lippmann wrote, "The prospect of a controversy with his own party silenced him, and as far as one can judge by his public acts he abdicated all claims to leadership in the tariff battle." [53]

Hoover's refusal to lead the special session of Congress that he called in 1929 tempered the enthusiasm that had greeted his election. Coolidge's reticence had frustrated some, but his lack of involvement was in keeping with his indifference to programmatic achievement. Hoover's passivity, however, seemed inappropriate to his ambitions for the nation. As Fausold has remarked, "No activist president in this century has kept the distance from Congress as did Hoover...." [54] By the fall of 1929, even Republican leaders in Congress were criticizing Hoover's nonpolitical approach to the presidency. The press, although not yet willing to dismiss Hoover as a weak executive, was mystified. Assessing the president's aloofness from the special session of Congress, one commentator concluded that "a strange paralysis seemed to rest upon Mr. Hoover during the first year after Congress met." [55]

Hoover's "strange paralysis," which caused only concern and confusion during the early days of his presidency, provoked bitter jest and withering scorn after the onslaught of the depression. Dignified silence in the face of congressional interference with his program was one thing; for the president to remain above the fray when unemployment reached 25 percent of the work force seemed appalling and heartless. Yet Hoover resisted the growing public demands that he assume the mantle of legislative leader and work to produce a body of law that would authorize the executive departments and agencies to take more responsibility for economic coordination and social services.

The president's aloof stance became especially disabling after the Republicans lost control of Congress in the 1930 midterm election. When, subsequently, congressional Democrats refused to cooperate with him, Hoover chose to suffer in silence, bewailing their intransigence in the intimacy of his White House study but declining to go over their heads to the people. As he later wrote in his memoirs:

> I had felt deeply that no President should undermine the independence of the legislative and judicial branches by seeking to discredit them. The constitutional division of powers is the bastion of our liberties and was not designed as a battleground to display the prowess of presidents. They just have to work with the material that God—and the voters—have given them.[56]

The struggling president's constitutional principles, which kept him from exerting public leadership, were reinforced by personal qualities that ill-suited him for the tasks of legislative, party, and popular leadership. Like Grant, Hoover came to the presidency with no background in elected office. His experience had been as a builder of business-like economic and civic organizations, not as a politician working to forge legislative coalitions or a popular following. He was comfortable dealing with facts, which he could marshal to support a course of action.[57] But, as Lippmann wrote, Hoover was "diffident in the presence of the normal irrationality of democracy." [58]

Uncomfortable with politics and politicians, Hoover also proved unable to form close relationships with reporters or to build on Coolidge's pioneering efforts in radio broadcasting. In the history of presidential communications, Hoover's presidency was important mainly in a negative sense. He fought losing battles to keep both his private life and his negotiations on public policy screened from view. His administration "served to make painfully plain," Cornwell has observed, "the fact that no future President could hope to emerge from his White House ordeal unless he was prepared in talent and temperament to cope with and master the demands of an age of mass communications." [59]

Herbert Hoover was hardly the do-nothing president that Franklin Roosevelt and the Democrats labeled him in the 1932 election. He repeatedly encouraged efforts by various sectors of the economy to pursue more rational and just business practices. With the onset of the depression, he tried even harder to supply the leadership that the public more and more demanded.

But Hoover was only willing to go so far. He called for programs, such as the Reconstruction Finance Corporation, that would provide federal loans to banks, railroads, and certain agricultural organizations. But he would not offer bold political leadership to rouse popular support for these programs or to ensure their energetic operation. Similarly, Hoover marshalled the entire executive branch to encourage private and local groups to provide the needy with relief from the depression, but he rigidly refused to offer direct government aid. Seeking to come to terms with the great drought of 1930 and 1931, Hoover admonished the Red Cross to feed the people rather than have the federal government do it. When the Red Cross balked and Congress demanded that the government act, Hoover still demurred, stating simply that direct federal assistance was unconstitutional. It was a sorry spectacle: the president standing on a supposed constitutional prohibition, while Congress pleaded for basic human relief.[60]

In a sense, Hoover put traditional, nineteenth-century American political practices and principles to their greatest test. But his unalterable commitment to preserving these traditions even in the face of national calamity served only to discredit them. In this way, Hoover unwittingly laid the groundwork for a fundamental break with the politics and policies of the past.

The Twentieth Amendment

On February 6, 1933, less than a month before the end of Hoover's term, the Twentieth Amendment, also known as the "lame duck" amendment, became part of the Constitution. (It had cleared Congress in March 1932 and was ratified quickly by all the states.) The amendment was written mainly to shorten the time between the election of the president, vice president, and members of Congress and their entry into office. The hiatus for newly elected representatives and senators (unless the president called Congress into special session) had been thirteen months—from election day in November until the first Monday in December of the following year, the date established by Article I of the

Constitution as the initial meeting time for each Congress. The delay for presidents and vice presidents had been approximately four months, from election day until March 4, the inauguration date that was enshrined in a law passed by Congress in 1792.

Sen. George Norris, a Nebraska Republican and the main author of the Twentieth Amendment, sought to remedy three major flaws that he saw in the traditional arrangement, which he regarded as better-suited to the age when travel was difficult and time-consuming and the business of the federal government was relatively minor. The first flaw was the biennial lame duck session of Congress, which typically lasted from the December after the election until the following March and which included many outgoing members of the defeated party. Second, by not having Congress begin its term before the president, existing procedures empowered the lame duck Congress, not the newly elected one, to choose the president in the event of a deadlock in the electoral college. (This had happened in 1801 and 1825.) Third, Norris regarded four months as too long a time for the nation to have, in effect, two presidents—an outgoing incumbent and an incoming president-elect.

To remedy the lame duck and two-presidents problem, Section 1 of the Twentieth Amendment set noon on January 20 as the beginning of the president's and vice president's four-year terms and noon on January 3 as the start of the term for members of Congress. Norris used Section 3 of the amendment as a vehicle to address two other potential problems in the presidential and vice-presidential selection process. It provided that if a president-elect were to die before the start of the term, the vice president would be inaugurated as president. Section 3 also stated that if, by inauguration day, no presidential candidate had received either a majority of electoral votes or the support of a majority of state delegations in the House, the vice president-elect would become president until a president was chosen. (The same would be true if a president-elect were found to be unqualified by virtue of age, citizenship, or residency.) Other provisions of the amendment dealt with equally real but remote possibilities: for example, that a vice president-elect would not be chosen, or that either a winning presidential or vice-presidential candidate might die before receiving "elect" status when Congress counted the electoral votes in January.

As unlikely as some of the situations contemplated by the Twentieth Amendment are, two events that occurred near the time of its passage lent testimony to the amendment's wisdom. From November 1932 to March 1933, in the last of the four-month transitions, the nation endured a long and awkward interregnum between Hoover, the discredited and defeated incumbent president, and Franklin Roosevelt, his successor—all this in the midst of the Great Depression. On February

15, 1933—nine days after the amendment entered the Constitution—
President-elect Roosevelt was the object of an unsuccessful assassination attempt in Miami, Florida.

Notes

1. Quoted in Robert K. Murray, *The Harding Era: Warren G. Harding and His Administration* (Minneapolis: University of Minnesota Press, 1969), 70.
2. Confusion still exists about how the word *normalcy* originated. The best guess is that Harding meant *normality* but said *normalcy*.
3. William Starr Myers, *The Republican Party: A History* (New York: Century, 1928), 441.
4. Lodge cited in Andrew Sinclair, *The Available Man: The Life Behind the Masks of Warren Gamaliel Harding* (New York: Macmillan, 1965), 152 (Lodge's emphasis).
5. Elmer E. Cornwell, Jr., *Presidential Leadership of Public Opinion* (Bloomington: Indiana University Press, 1965), 60.
6. Warren Harding, "We Need a Newly Consecrated Americanism," *Independent*, October 1920, in *History of American Presidential Elections*, ed. Arthur Schlesinger, Jr., and Fred I. Israel (New York: Chelsea, 1971), 3:2437-2439. Also see *New York Times*, July 21, 1920, 7.
7. Quoted in Wilfred E. Binkley, *President and Congress* (New York: Knopf, 1947), 217.
8. Ibid.
9. George Rothwell Brown, *The Leadership of Congress* (New York: Arno Press, 1974; Indianapolis: Bobbs-Merrill, 1922), 258.
10. Quoted in Murray, *Harding Era*, 314.
11. Ibid., 128.
12. Ibid.
13. Binkley, *President and Congress*, 221. For a discussion of the events that led up to the Washington Naval Disarmament Conference, see Murray, *Harding Era*, 140-166; also Lindsay Rogers, "American Government and Politics: The Second, Third, and Fourth Sessions of the Sixty-Seventh Congress," *American Political Science Review* 18:1 (February 1924): 91-93.
14. Paul P. Van Riper, *History of the United States Civil Service* (Evanston, Ill.: Row, Peterson, 1958), 287.
15. Murray, *Harding Era*, 430.
16. William Allen White, *The Autobiography of William Allen White* (New York: Macmillan, 1946), 619.
17. On the events leading up to the Teapot Dome scandal, see J. Leonard Bates, *The Origins of Teapot Dome: Progressives, Parties, and Petroleum, 1909-1921* (Urbana: University of Illinois, 1963), esp. chaps. 13 and 14; and Burt Noggle, "The Origins of the Teapot Dome Investigation," *Mississippi Valley Historical Review* 64:2 (September 1957): 237-266.
18. Fall could not be dismissed as merely one of the "grafters" who attached themselves to the Harding administration. He was able to defend, on rational grounds, his belief that the public domain should be opened to private development. As he once told a critic, "Every generation from Adam and Eve down has lived better than the generation before. I don't know how

they'll do it—maybe they'll use the energy of the sun or the sea waves—but
. . . [they] will live better than we do. I stand for opening up every resource"
(quoted in Bates, *Origins of Teapot Dome*, 227-228).

19. George W. Norris, *Fighting Liberal: The Autobiography of George W. Norris* (New York: Macmillan, 1945), 233.
20. Herbert Emmerich, *Federal Organization and Administrative Management* (University, Ala.: University of Alabama Press, 1971), 40-41. For a discussion of the enactment and early history of the Budget and Accounting Act, see William M. Goldsmith, ed., *The Growth of Presidential Power: A Documented History* (New York and London: Chelsea, 1974), 3:1478-1495; and Peri E. Arnold, *Making the Managerial Presidency: Comprehensive Reorganization Planning, 1905-1980* (Princeton, N.J.: Princeton University Press, 1986), 53-55.
21. Murray, *Harding Era*, 178.
22. *Myers v. United States*, 272 U.S. 53 (1926).
23. Ibid., at 134.
24. Cornwell, *Presidential Leadership of Public Opinion*, 62. Much of the following discussion draws from Cornwell's interesting chapter on public relations in the Harding and Coolidge administrations.
25. Ibid., 63.
26. Ibid., 70.
27. Quoted in Murray, *Harding Era*, 418.
28. Ibid., 452.
29. Cornwell, *Presidential Leadership of Public Opinion*, 73.
30. Calvin Coolidge, *The Autobiography of Calvin Coolidge* (New York: Cosmopolitan Book Corporation, 1929), 232.
31. Binkley, *President and Congress*, 223.
32. William Allen White, *A Puritan in Babylon* (New York: Macmillan, 1938), v.
33. Edward S. Martin, "Shall Business Run the World?" *Harper's Magazine*, 150, February 1925, 381.
34. Murray, *Harding Era*, 505.
35. "The Destiny of America," delivered at Memorial Day services, Northampton, Mass., May 30, 1923, in Calvin Coolidge, *The Price of Freedom: Speeches and Addresses* (New York: Scribner's, 1924), 342; and Calvin Coolidge, "Inaugural Address," March 4, 1925, *Calvin Coolidge, 1872-1933*, ed. Philip R. Moran (Dobbs Ferry, N.Y.: Oceana, 1970), 65.
36. Cornwell, *Presidential Leadership of Public Opinion*, 74-75.
37. T.R.B., "Washington Notes," *New Republic*, 55, February 10, 1926, 326.
38. The reporter quoted is Jay C. Hayden of the *Detroit News*, who covered the White House for sixteen years. Hayden considered Coolidge to be as masterful as Theodore Roosevelt at the "human interest" game, although "the Coolidge process was more subtle" (*Literary Digest*, July 25, 1931, 8).
39. Quoted in Cornwell, *Presidential Leadership of Public Opinion*, 90.
40. Gleason L. Archer, *History of the Radio—To 1926* (New York: American Historical Society, 1938), 324.
41. Ibid., 323.
42. Coolidge, *Autobiography*, 231.
43. William Allen White, *Calvin Coolidge: The Man Who Is President* (New York: Macmillan, 1925), 137.
44. Cornwell, *Presidential Leadership of Public Opinion*, 92.
45. Ibid., 97.

46. Ellis Hawley, "The Constitution of the Hoover and F. Roosevelt Presidency during the Depression Era, 1900-1939," in *The Constitution and the American Presidency*, ed. Martin L. Fausold and Alan Shank (Albany: State University of New York Press, 1991), 89-91.
47. Martin L. Fausold, *The Presidency of Herbert C. Hoover* (Lawrence: University Press of Kansas, 1985), 56.
48. *Public Papers of the Presidents: Herbert Hoover*, March 4 to December 31, 1929 (Washington, D.C.: Government Printing Office, 1974), 472.
49. Herbert Hoover, *The Challenge to Liberty* (New York: Scribner's, 1934), 125-126.
50. Quoted in Fausold, *Presidency of Herbert C. Hoover*, 51.
51. Arthur W. MacMahan, "American Government and Politics: First Session of the Seventy-First Congress," *American Political Science Review* 24:1 (February 1930): 50-56; Binkley, *President and Congress*, 229-230.
52. Robert Allen and Drew Pearson, *Washington Merry-Go-Round* (New York: Horace Liveright, 1931), 66.
53. Walter Lippmann, "The Peculiar Weakness of Mr. Hoover," *Harpers Magazine*, 161, June 1930, 5.
54. Fausold, *Presidency of Herbert C. Hoover*, 49.
55. Quoted in Binkley, *President and Congress*, 229.
56. Herbert Hoover, *The Memoirs of Herbert Hoover: The Great Depression, 1929-1941* (New York: Macmillan, 1952), 3:104.
57. Binkley, *President and Congress*, 227-228.
58. Lippmann, "The Peculiar Weakness of Mr. Hoover," 5.
59. Cornwell, *Presidential Leadership of Public Opinion*, 113.
60. Fausold, *Presidency of Herbert C. Hoover*, 111.

CHAPTER 11

The Consolidation of the Modern Presidency: Franklin D. Roosevelt to Dwight D. Eisenhower

The 1932 election marked the beginning of a new political era. The Democratic candidate, Franklin Delano Roosevelt, became the first member of his party to be elected president with a majority of popular votes since Franklin Pierce in 1852. Roosevelt won forty-two states to six for the incumbent, Herbert C. Hoover; his majority among the voters was 22.8 million to 15.8 million. In the new Congress, Democrats outnumbered Republicans by 60 to 35 in the Senate and 310 to 117 in the House. FDR's victory indicated, in the opinion of the progressive Republican journalist William Allen White, "a firm desire on the part of the American people to use government as an agency for human welfare." [1]

Roosevelt did not disappoint this desire. He not only accepted the progressive reformers' commitment to regulate business in the public interest but also believed that it was the federal government's responsibility to guarantee the economic security of the people. His administration, then, brought the welfare state to the United States, years after it had become a fixture in other western nations.

The emergence of the welfare state was closely associated with a redefinition of the public's understanding of rights. FDR urged a fundamental rethinking of the American social contract, in which the national government would assume the responsibility to provide an adequate standard of living for all of its people. Roosevelt first spoke of the need to modernize elements of the old faith in his famous Commonwealth Club address, which he delivered during the 1932 campaign. In the address, FDR announced that the task of modern government was "to assist the development of an economic declaration of rights, an economic constitutional order." The traditional American emphasis on individual self-reliance should therefore give way to a new understanding of individualism, according to which the government acted as a regulating and unifying agency, guaranteeing to each person protection from the uncertainties of the marketplace.[2]

Roosevelt's commitment to build a modern state meant that the executive, as the leading national institution in American politics, would have to be strengthened. As FDR put it, "The day of enlightened administration has come."[3] This concept of presidential responsibility informed FDR's extraordinary leadership in expanding the federal government to meet the demands first of a domestic crisis, the Great Depression, and later an international one, the Second World War. His leadership had a profound effect on the presidency. The modern presidency, especially the executive office that took shape during the first half of the twentieth century, became an enduring fixture in the United States during Franklin Roosevelt's long tenure in the White House.

What is the modern presidency?[4] Many of the most important characteristics of the executive date from the Constitutional Convention and the earliest days of the Republic; during the nineteenth century, too, significant patterns and practices took shape. What marked the twentieth-century transformation of the executive was the emergence of the president, rather than Congress or the party organizations, as the leading instrument of popular rule, "the steward of the public welfare."

Acting on this modern concept of presidential power, Theodore Roosevelt and Woodrow Wilson inaugurated the practices that strengthened the president as popular and legislative leader. It fell to FDR, however, to consolidate, or institutionalize, the changes in the executive office that were initiated during the Progressive Era. Roosevelt's leadership was the principal ingredient in a full-scale realignment of the political parties, the first in history that placed presidential power at the heart of its approach to politics and government. After Roosevelt's long tenure, the new understanding of executive responsibilities would lead even conservative Republican presidents to wield the powers of their office according to the vision that was celebrated by their progressive forebears.

Franklin D. Roosevelt and the Modern Presidency

So great an impression did Franklin Roosevelt make on the American political system that in the most recent survey of historians, he ranked as the second greatest president in history, surpassed only by Abraham Lincoln.[5] Above all, FDR's high ranking owes to his efforts to lead the American people through the Great Depression. Roosevelt came to office in the fourth year of a world economic crisis whose persistence raised grave doubts about the viability of republican government—indeed, about the future of the Western world. The British historian Arnold Toynbee observed that 1931 was distinguished from previous years by one outstanding feature: "In 1931, men and women all over the world were seriously contemplating and frankly discussing the possibility that the Western system of society might break down and cease to exist." [6]

Americans had reason to share these doubts. As Roosevelt prepared to take the oath of office on March 4, 1933, the ranks of the unemployed numbered 15 million, about one-third of the work force. In thirty-two states, every bank had been closed by state government edict; bank operations in the remaining sixteen states were severely curtailed. On the morning of FDR's inauguration, the New York Stock Exchange closed its doors. In the face of increasing economic distress, Merle Thorpe, the editor of Nation's Business, wrote ominously: "Fear, bordering on panic, loss of faith in everything, our fellowman, our institutions, private and government. Worst of all, no faith in ourselves, or the future. Almost everyone ready to scuttle the ship, and not even 'women and children first.' " [7]

The national despair notwithstanding, Roosevelt's arrival in Washington was greeted with hope. Everyone who watched and waited, wrote the New York Times columnist Arthur Krock, was "ready to be enthusiastic over any display of leadership," eager to be convinced that the new president would exhibit the kind of bold and energetic initiative that the American people had demanded but not received from Hoover. [8]

Unlike Hoover, Roosevelt was admirably suited to lead by personality and background. His predecessor was aloof and uncomfortable with the demands of the presidency, but FDR believed that he belonged in the office. "The essence of Roosevelt's Presidency," the political scientist Clinton Rossiter has written, "was his airy eagerness to meet the age head on." [9] His confidence stemmed not only from a privileged, albeit challenging, upbringing in Hyde Park, New York, but also from an admirable political education: state senator, assistant secretary of the navy in the Wilson administration, vice-presidential candidate in 1920, and two-term governor of New York, then the largest state in the Union.

Roosevelt's faith in his own abilities was accompanied by a willingness to experiment, which he displayed throughout his presidency. The nation became aware of FDR's innovating spirit when, shattering precedent, he hired a small plane to take him to the Democratic national convention in Chicago to make his acceptance speech. In the past, major party nominees had stayed away from the convention, waiting to be notified officially of their nomination. [10] But FDR wanted to demonstrate dramatically that his physical disability (the year after the 1920 campaign he had been stricken with poliomyelitis) would not hinder him as a candidate or as president. "The convention rose enthusiastically to the voyageur of the skies" marvelled one reporter, "and accepted his method of travel and the fact that he endured its rigors so well as a proof of his venturesome spirit and fine physical equipment for the office of the President of the United States." [11]

Roosevelt also wanted to show his party and the nation that he would not hesitate to break even revered traditions that stood in the way of his vision of progress. "I have started out on the tasks that lie ahead by breaking the absurd traditions that the candidate should remain in professed ignorance of what has happened for weeks until he is formally notified of that event many weeks later," Roosevelt told the convention on July 2, 1932. "Let it also be symbolic that in so doing I broke traditions. Let it be from now on the task of our party to break foolish traditions." [12]

The Critical Early Days

Considerable excitement surrounded FDR's inauguration. In the cheers that greeted Roosevelt as the car carrying him and his predecessor approached the Capitol, "there seemed to be a tone of understanding," the *New York Times* reported, "that the motor bore not only two men, not only a Democrat elected to succeed a Republican whom he had defeated, but two antagonistic philosophies of government.... In the greeting there appeared to be a note of jubilation that the day had come when the new philosophy was to replace the rejected theories of the old." [13]

No such jubilation was evident in Roosevelt's demeanor that day. The president delivered a compelling, if solemn, inaugural address that spelled out in clear and uncompromising language both his indictment of the practices that he believed should be abandoned and his intention to act boldly to deal with the crisis at hand. Laying the blame for the depression squarely on the laissez-faire doctrines and halting leadership of his conservative Republican predecessors, Roosevelt summoned the nation to a higher purpose: "The money changers have fled from their high seats in the temple of our civilization. We may now restore that temple to ancient truths. The measure of that restoration lies in the extent to which we apply social values more noble than mere monetary profit." [14]

Just as boldly, the new president stated his determination to lead the nation to a more noble calling:

> It is to be hoped that the normal balance of Executive and legislative authority may be wholly adequate to meet the unprecedented task

before us. . . . But in the event that Congress shall fail to take [action]
. . . and in the event that the national emergency is still critical, I shall
not evade the clear course of duty that will then confront me. I shall
ask the Congress for one remaining instrument to meet the crisis—
broad executive power to wage a war against the emergency, as great
as the power that would be given to me if we were in fact invaded by a
foreign foe.[15]

Roosevelt lost no time translating his intentions into action. On
March 5, one day after taking the oath of office, he issued the "Bank
Holiday Proclamation," which suspended "the heavy and unwarranted
withdrawals of gold and currency from our banking institutions." The
bank edict, an unprecedented exercise of executive power in peacetime,
declared that from March 6 to March 9, banks in the United States
must suspend all transactions.[16]

During the final days of the Hoover administration, Secretary of
Commerce Ogden Mills had urged the president to call a bank holiday,
arguing that the authority to do so had been granted to the executive by
the Trading with the Enemy Act of 1917. But Hoover was reluctant to
act on his own initiative, especially when his attorney general questioned whether a wartime measure could be applied to a domestic
situation, no matter how grave. Hoover may have been willing to close
the banks if the president-elect had offered his public support, but
Roosevelt refused to assume responsibility for any action before becoming president.

Once sworn in, however, FDR did not hesitate to use the full powers
of his office to address the national emergency. He felt no reluctance to
attack the banking crisis with a World War I measure. On the same day
that he declared the bank holiday, Roosevelt issued another executive
order to call Congress into special session. Four days later, on March 9,
he introduced the Emergency Banking Bill, which marshalled the full
resources of the Federal Reserve Board to support the faltering banks,
thus restoring the people's confidence in the banking system. The bill
was the first to be passed during the extraordinary "One Hundred
Days" (from noon on March 9, to 1:00 a.m. on June 15, 1933), when
Congress passed a relentless succession of Roosevelt-sponsored laws.
Remarkably, the bank bill was enacted in fewer than eight hours; forty-
five minutes later, with photographers recording the scene, Roosevelt
signed it into law.

FDR promptly announced that he would go directly to the people
three days later, on Sunday evening, March 12, to explain in a radio
address what he had done about the banks and why he had done it. This
was the first of Roosevelt's so-called "fireside chats," which were a
revolutionary advance in the presidential use of the mass media.[17]
Calvin Coolidge and, less successfully, Hoover had spoken on the radio,

but only to broadcast fixed, formal pronouncements. The fireside chats were more relaxed. Their purpose was to shape public opinion in support of a specific piece of legislation or, as in the first talk, to enlist popular support for a particular course of action.

Of all the fireside chats that Roosevelt was to give (he delivered two or three during each year of his presidency), none was more successful than the first. Both Roosevelt's comfortable radio style and the phrasing of his message were ideally suited to his purpose of reassurance. "We had a bad banking situation," he said. "Some of our bankers had shown themselves either incompetent or dishonest in handling people's funds. They had used the money entrusted to them in speculation and unwise loans." But most bankers worked hard and well, Roosevelt argued; besides, the task at hand was not to lay blame for the crisis, but to ameliorate it:

> It was the government's job to straighten out the situation and do it as quickly as possible. And the job is being performed. . . . Confidence and courage are the essentials of success in carrying out our plan. You people must have faith; you must not be stampeded by rumors or guesses. Let us unite in banishing fear. We have provided the machinery to restore our financial system; it is up to you to support it and make it work.[18]

The bank bill and the fireside chat ended the banking crisis: there were no runs on the banks when they reopened on Monday morning, March 13. On the contrary, deposits far exceeded withdrawals as hoarded currency poured back into the vaults. A few days later, the New York Stock Exchange, closed since March 4, opened with the greatest single-day rise in memory. "Capitalism was saved in eight days," Roosevelt's aide Raymond Moley declared dramatically.[19]

Similar adulation was expressed not just by FDR's friends but also by his opponents. An "incredible change has come over the face of things here in the United States in a single week," editorialized the *Wall Street Journal*, because "the new administration in Washington has superbly risen to the occasion." To be sure, the *Journal* warned, only "a good beginning had been made" and "incalculable tasks" remained. But "there are times when a beginning is nearly everything."[20]

The first two weeks of Roosevelt's presidency marked an enduring change in the spirit of the country. In place of the despair and political paralysis of the Hoover years was an ebullient national mood and a refashioned executive, which forged a vital link between the government and the people. In the past, one thousand pieces of mail a day had arrived at the White House during peak periods. FDR's inauguration was greeted by 460,000 letters. One person had been able to handle Hoover's mail; a staff of fifty had to be hired to take care of Roosevelt's, which averaged 5,000 letters a day and, on birthdays, 150,000. As

William Hopkins, who worked in the White House correspondence section, remembered, "The mail started coming in by the truckloads. They couldn't even get the envelopes open." [21]

The New Deal

The early days of the Roosevelt administration brought the presidency into its own as the primary source of popular and legislative leadership. A close bond developed between Roosevelt and the American people during the struggle to end the depression. Moreover, the advent of the welfare state, which entailed a massive transfer of the responsibility to help those in need from the states and the private sector to the national government, created new responsibilities for the president. Roosevelt initiated this transfer, carefully preparing the nation for the revolutionary departures in public policy that took place during the 1930s.

The centerpiece of Roosevelt's program was the Social Security Act, which proposed to create a comprehensive federal system of old age and unemployment insurance. To sell social security was no easy task. Remarking on the unusual American commitment to individual self-reliance, Sen. Hugo Black of Alabama wrote to a member of the Roosevelt administration on June 19, 1934, "The public in our country has little conception of the possibilities of social insurance," and "there are few people in this country who realize such systems of social insurance have been adopted in most of the civilized countries in the world." [22]

Fourteen months after Black's letter, the Social Security Act sailed through Congress and was signed into law ceremoniously by the president. In the interim, FDR had nurtured public opinion carefully. He saw his task not as rousing popular pressure on Congress but as civic education, teaching the American people that social insurance was not alien to their values.

The development of a national industrial society, Roosevelt argued, made it no longer possible for individual financial security to be achieved within the familiar bonds of the small community and the family. Rather, the complexities of great communities and of organized industry required that the federal government help people to secure their welfare in time of need. To bring this lesson home, the president's fireside chat of June 28, 1934, included a folksy yet effective illustration: the remodeling of the White House office building (the West Wing), which he likened to the adoption of social insurance. After describing the wiring and plumbing and the modern means of keeping offices cool in the hot Washington summers that were being installed, Roosevelt noted: "It is this combination of the old and new that marks orderly peaceful progress, not only in building buildings, but in building government itself. Our new structure is a part of and a fulfillment of the old.... All that we do seeks to fulfill the historic traditions of the American people." [23]

Roosevelt's leadership involved, as one presidential scholar has written, "a careful process of grafting social security onto the stalk of traditional American values." [24] By the end of this process, Roosevelt had moved the nation beyond the traditional idea that rights embody only guarantees against government oppression to the new understanding, articulated in his Commonwealth Club address, that government also has the obligation to ensure economic security. It was just such an understanding that Roosevelt had in mind when, at the 1932 Democratic convention, he pledged himself to "a new deal for the American people." [25]

Significantly, the New Deal program, and its embodiment of a new individualism, was the principal message of Roosevelt's first reelection bid in 1936. The Democratic party's platform for that campaign, drafted by Roosevelt, was written as a pastiche of the Declaration of Independence. As the platform claimed with respect to the Social Security Act:

> We hold this truth to be self-evident—that the test of representative government is its ability to promote the safety and happiness of the people.... On the foundation of the Social Security Act we are determined to erect a structure of economic security for all our people, making sure that this benefit shall keep step with the ever increasing capacity of America to provide a high standard of living for all its citizens.[26]

The New Deal was a series of legislative acts, executive orders, and proclamations that sought not only to secure individual security but also to remedy the broader economic problems of the Great Depression. During Roosevelt's tenure as president, programs were established to aid the aged, the unemployed, the disabled, and the families with dependent children. Work projects were financed by the greatest single peacetime appropriation in history. For the first time the national government fostered unionization. When Roosevelt became president, almost no factory worker belonged to a labor union. By the time he left office, industrial unionism was firmly established, largely because of the National Labor Relations Act (the Wagner Act) of 1935, which empowered the government to enter factories to conduct elections so that workers could decide whether to join a union.

Finally, Roosevelt demanded that business recognize the superior authority of the federal government. Like his cousin Theodore, FDR fashioned himself as a conservative reformer who sought not to oppose private enterprise but to strengthen it by curbing business's most abusive practices and by ameliorating the most extreme conditions of economic inequality. But he was opposed in this effort by an unreconstructed segment of the American business community that denied to the federal government any right to regulate commercial activity. As the president complained in a letter to Harvard law professor Felix Frankfurter in February 1937, "It is the same old story of those who have property to fail to realize that I am the best friend the profit system ever had, even though I add my denunciation of unconscionable profits." [27]

Roosevelt's resentment of his critics in business was intense. "These economic royalists complain that we seek to overthrow the institutions of America," he told a roaring crowd at the 1936 Democratic convention. "What they really complain of is that we seek to take away their power." The time had come, Roosevelt insisted, "to overthrow this kind of power." The New Deal regulatory program greatly extended the responsibility of the federal government, especially the executive, to guarantee the average citizen "equal opportunity in the market place." [28] Describing a range of Roosevelt-sponsored regulatory laws, such as the Securities and Exchange Act and the Public Utility Holding Company Act, the historian William Leuchtenburg has written:

> Although the New Deal always operated within a capitalist framework, Roosevelt insisted that there was a national interest that it was the duty of the President to represent and, when the situation called for it, to impose. Consequently, the federal government in the 1930s came to supervise the stock market, establish a central banking system monitored from Washington, and regulate a range of business activities that had hitherto been regarded private.[29]

Not every major innovation in public policy during the 1930s originated in the White House. Some New Deal programs, such as the Tennessee Valley Authority, had long been on the public agenda but needed the impetus of a national crisis to be enacted.[30] Other parts of what Roosevelt called the new "economic constitutional order," such as the Wagner Act, redounded to the president's political benefit even though he had supported them only haltingly. That FDR was hailed for the initiatives of New York senator Robert F. Wagner and others signified the American people's growing tendency to think of the president as the government.

The 1936 election ensured that the important political changes that had occurred during Roosevelt's first term would endure. FDR's victory in 1932 had expressed the public's resentment of Hoover more than its approval of Roosevelt or of his party. But sweeping confirmation of Roosevelt's leadership and of the New Deal program came in 1936, when he won 60 percent of the popular vote—the largest plurality ever by a presidential candidate—and carried all but two small states. The 1936 election, which also strengthened the Democratic hold on both houses of

Congress, marked the Democrats' emergence as the nation's new majority party.

Institutionalization of the Modern Presidency

As Americans increasingly came to regard the presidency as the preeminent source of moral leadership, legislative guidance, and public policy, pressure mounted to increase the size and professionalism of the president's staff. A modest office from the time of its creation, the presidency developed after the 1930s into a full-blown institution.

Roosevelt hastened this development when he named three of the country's foremost scholars of public administration—Louis Brownlow, Charles E. Merriam, and Luther Gulick—to the newly formed President's Committee on Administrative Management. Concluding that "the President needs help," the Brownlow Committee, as it came to be called after its chair, proposed that the Executive Office of the President (EOP) be established, including not just the Bureau of the Budget but a new White House Office, to be staffed by loyal and energetic presidential aides whose public influence would be limited by their "passion for anonymity."

The committee also proposed to enhance the president's control of the expanding activities of the executive branch. By 1937, the Roosevelt administration confronted a bewildering array of sometimes autonomous agencies that offended its vision of a unified and energetic executive. Roosevelt, in fact, remarked shortly after the 1936 election that administrative management was the least successful aspect of his first term. He was glad that the Republicans had not hit on this weakness during the campaign.[31] The Brownlow Committee called for an overhaul of the executive branch, recommending that all of the more than 100 government agencies then in existence be integrated into twelve major departments, each of them under the virtually complete authority of the president. Thus would "the national will be expressed not merely in a brief, exultant moment of electoral decision, but in a persistent, determined, competent day-by-day administration of what the nation has decided to do."[32]

Roosevelt supported the Brownlow Committee's recommendations wholeheartedly. Congress, for its part, had little quarrel with the new EOP. But the proposal to overhaul the departments and agencies, which was embodied in the 1937 executive reorganization bill, provoked one of the most intense political controversies of FDR's presidency. His two-year battle for comprehensive administrative reform wrote a new chapter in the long-standing struggle between the executive and the legislature for the control of administration.

What gave the battle special intensity was that it occurred just as administration was becoming an important arena of public policy. As Gulick reported approvingly, the expansion of welfare and regulatory programs during the New Deal meant that the complex responsibilities of government increasingly were set forth in discretionary statutes, each of them little more than "a declaration of war, so that the essence of the program is in reality in the gradual unfolding of the plan in actual administration." [33] Thus, the struggle between the White House and Congress for control of the departments and agencies was no longer simply a squabble about patronage and prestige. The right to shape the direction and character of American public life also was at stake.

When Congress finally did enact the Executive Reorganization Act of 1939, it seriously limited the president's new administrative powers. For example, it restricted FDR's authority to overhaul the bureaucracy to two years and exempted twenty-one of the more important government agencies from reorganization. Nevertheless, the implementation of the 1939 statute by Executive Order 8248 effected many of the Brownlow recommendations. The order created the Executive Office of the President and moved several agencies under its umbrella. In addition to the White House Office, the EOP initially included the powerful National Resources Planning Board (a long-term planning agency) and the refurbished and strengthened Bureau of the Budget, which was transferred from the Treasury Department. Newly housed, the Budget Bureau began to acquire much greater powers, eventually attaining the responsibility to oversee the formation of the president's domestic program.

The creation of the EOP—because it enhanced the capacity of the president to manage the expanding activities of the executive branch—was an "epoch making event in the history of American institutions," wrote Gulick, and "perhaps the most important single step in the institutionalization of the presidency." [34] Roosevelt's successors have carried on their work through essentially the same executive office that he created. [35] Most significant, the 1939 reforms hastened the development of the "administrative presidency," which exercised extensive domestic power on behalf of the president through rule making and policy implementation. [36] To be sure, the absence of detail in Article II of the Constitution had always left the door open for independent presidential action. But the institutionalization of the presidency established a formal organizational apparatus with which presidents and their appointees could short-circuit the separation of powers, accelerating the transfer of authority from Congress to the executive.

Constitutional Crisis

The New Deal provoked a serious constitutional crisis toward the end of FDR's first term. Roosevelt argued that the modern presidency,

like the welfare state, was in keeping with sound constitutional principles. "The only thing that has been happening," he told the nation in a
fireside chat on May 7, 1933, "has been to designate the President as the
agency to carry out certain of the purposes of Congress. This was
constitutional and in keeping with past American traditions." [37]

Such was not the view, however, of the New Deal's opponents. "As
they saw it," the historian Ellis Hawley has written, "the balance and
separation of powers established by the Constitution were being de-
stroyed by a power-seeking presidency gathering into itself the power
that should be exercised by Congress and the states." [38]

Most important, the ranks of New Deal critics included not just
Roosevelt's enemies in Congress and business, but also, until 1937, a
majority of the Supreme Court. In 1935 and 1936, the Court struck
down more important national laws than in any comparable period in
history. Roosevelt, whose second-term inauguration was the first to be
held on January 20 under the Twentieth Amendment, responded on
February 5, 1937, with the most controversial action of his presidency,
the proposed "Court-packing" bill. The bill provided that for every
justice who failed to retire within six months of reaching the age of
seventy, the president could appoint a new justice. Six of the nine
justices already were seventy or older, which meant that Roosevelt
would be able to enlarge the Court to fifteen members by making new
appointments. Presumably, these new justices would overcome the
Court's resistance to the New Deal.

Although a number of strong presidents—notably Thomas Jefferson, Andrew Jackson, and Abraham Lincoln—had fought running
battles with the Court at one time or another, the intensity of the
response to FDR's Court plan was unprecedented. Day after day for the
next several months, stories about the Court-packing conflict rated
banner headlines in the nation's newspapers. The controversy aroused
debates in every corner of the country. In Beaumont, Texas, for
example, a movie audience cheered rival arguments about the Court bill
when they were shown on the screen.[39]

Roosevelt's plan sought to eliminate the final constitutional barrier
to a vast expansion of government activity and, thereby, to ratify the
president's power to direct the affairs of state. Significantly, the two
Supreme Court decisions that enraged FDR the most were *Humphrey's
Executor v. United States* and *Schechter Poultry Corp. v. United
States*, both of which imposed constraints on the president's personal
authority.[40] These decisions, which were handed down on May 27, 1935,
soon known to New Dealers as "Black Monday," threatened to derail
the institutional changes that Roosevelt believed were necessary to solve
the underlying problems of the depression.

The *Humphrey* case denied the president the right to remove appointees from the independent regulatory commissions, a legal power that Roosevelt and his advisers thought had been settled by tradition and affirmed by the *Myers* case of 1926.[41] The *Schechter* ruling was a direct challenge to the modern state. It declared that the discretionary authority that Congress had granted, at Roosevelt's request, to the National Recovery Administration, the leading economic agency of the early New Deal, was an unconstitutional delegation of legislative power to the executive.

Although the Court-packing bill failed in Congress, Roosevelt claimed that he had lost the battle but won the war, for the Court never again struck down another New Deal law. In fact, since 1937, the Supreme Court has not invalidated any significant federal statute to regulate the economy, nor has the Court judged any law to be an unconstitutional delegation of authority to the president.[42] Most of the judicial barriers to national and presidential power, then, have fallen.

But the bitter fight over Court-packing entailed a considerable political cost. The Court issue effectively brought Roosevelt's mastery of Congress and his party to an end. Moreover, it served as a lightning rod for the New Deal's opponents, sparking a resurgence of congressional independence and the formation of an enduring bipartisan "conservative coalition," consisting mainly of Republicans and southern Democrats, which would block nearly all presidential reform initiatives until the mid-1960s.

Roosevelt's first response to the new ideological fissure within Congress was to try to unseat entrenched conservative Democrats in the 1938 elections. He intervened in one gubernatorial and several congressional primary campaigns in a bold effort to replace recalcitrant Democrats with candidates who were "100 percent New Dealers." Although William Howard Taft and Woodrow Wilson had made limited efforts to rid their parties of uncooperative members, Roosevelt's campaign was conducted on an unprecedentedly large scale and, unlike the previous efforts, bypassed the regular party organization. The extent to which his action was regarded as a shocking departure from the norm was indicated by the label—"the purge"—that the press gave it. The term evoked Adolf Hitler's attempt to weed out dissenters from the German Nazi party and Joseph Stalin's elimination of suspected opponents from the Soviet Communist party.

The purge campaign failed, however; all but two of the incumbent Democrats whom Roosevelt opposed were renominated. Moreover, the campaign, which was widely condemned as an assault on the constitutional system of checks and balances, galvanized the political opposition to Roosevelt, apparently contributing to the heavy losses that the Democrats sustained in the 1938 general elections. Ironically, then, FDR's campaign only strengthened the conservative coalition. Peter

Gerry, a conservative Democratic senator from Rhode Island, wrote to North Carolina senator Josiah Bailey in September 1938:

> The victories of [conservative Democrats] have had even a greater effect than I had hoped for. They show that Roosevelt cannot control Senators for he does not have the weight with voters in his party that the New Dealers thought he possessed. They have also destroyed the picture of his being invulnerable. The Senate and the House will stiffen and the opposition to the New Deal has had a great stimulation to its morale.[43]

Since FDR's unhappy experience in 1938, presidents generally have shied away from open intervention in House and Senate primaries.[44]

Foreign Policy

The economic crisis that dominated Roosevelt's first two terms as president was displaced in the late 1930s by the approach and then the outbreak of the Second World War. Even before the United States declared war in December 1941, the growing U.S. involvement in the European and Asian conflicts intensified the concentration of power in the national government, its administrative apparatus, and the president. Significantly, it was the international crisis that led Roosevelt to stand for reelection in 1940. His victory made him the only president in history to break the two-term tradition; in 1944, during the latter stages of the war, he also won a fourth term. Only death in April 1945 cut short Roosevelt's protracted reign.[45]

In 1937, Roosevelt began to confront the mood of isolationism that had dominated the polity since the end of World War I.[46] Speaking in Chicago, he strongly attacked the aggression of Germany and Japan, whose armies had recently invaded the Rhine and China, respectively.

> The peace, the freedom and the security of ninety percent of the population of the world is being jeopardized by the remaining ten percent who are threatening a breakdown of all international order and law. Surely the ninety percent who want to live in peace under law and in accordance with moral standards that have received almost universal acceptance through the centuries, can and must find some way to make their will prevail.[47]

Although the immediate reaction to the president's speech was favorable, a severe backlash soon set in, demonstrating clearly that neither Congress nor the American people were yet prepared to intervene in Europe or the Far East. To some extent the clash between interventionists and isolationists became a clash between the president and Congress over who would control foreign policy, just as it had in the final days of the Wilson administration. But Roosevelt was more willing

Franklin Roosevelt made several trips overseas to confer with Allied leaders about military strategy and the postwar world. In 1945, Roosevelt conferred at Yalta with Winston Churchill, left, and Joseph Stalin.

than Wilson to act on his own, often with little warrant in statute or precedent. Ironically, his efforts were fortified by the very Court that had been such an obstacle to his domestic program.

In late 1936, in the case of *United States v. Curtiss-Wright Export Corp.*, the Supreme Court upheld a 1934 law that authorized the president to place an embargo on the sale of U.S.-made weapons to countries that were engaged in armed conflict. The law had been passed with the so-called Chaco war between Bolivia and Paraguay in mind, and Roosevelt quickly forbade the sale of arms to both countries. Weapons merchants challenged the measure as an unlawful delegation of legislative authority to the president; a federal district court agreed. But in a somewhat surprising opinion, written by the conservative justice George Sutherland, a near-unanimous Court laid down a sweeping doctrine of presidential authority in foreign affairs.

The Court held that the president's powers in domestic and foreign matters are fundamentally different. "The broad statement that the federal government can exercise no power except those specifically stated in the Constitution, and such implied powers as are necessary and proper to carry into effect the enumerated powers," Justice Sutherland wrote, "is categorically true only in respect to internal affairs." In foreign affairs, the actions of the federal government and, more specifically, of the president as the government's "sole organ" in international relations, depend neither on a specific grant of power from the Constitution nor on Congress. Because the executive's authority in foreign policy is "plenary and exclusive," the president enjoys a freedom from statutory restriction that "would not be admissible were domestic affairs alone involved." [48]

The *Curtiss-Wright* case established as constitutional doctrine the sweeping defense of the executive's prerogatives in foreign affairs that Alexander Hamilton had offered in 1793 to defend President Washington's Neutrality Proclamation. Along with the 1937 *Belmont* case, which justified the president's right to reach executive agreements with other countries (that is, quasi-treaties that are forged without the participation of the Senate), *Curtiss-Wright* made it virtually impossible to challenge Roosevelt's increasingly internationalist policies on constitutional grounds. [49]

Relying on his broad, Court-sanctioned understanding of the president's foreign policy authority, Roosevelt concluded the controversial Lend-Lease agreement with Great Britain in 1941. The agreement, which paved the way for the United States to send fifty naval destroyers to help England in its desperate battle with Nazi Germany, marked a departure from the official U.S. policy of neutrality. The constitutional scholar Edward Corwin charged that Roosevelt's conduct in this matter usurped authority that rightfully belonged to the legislature. "As a departure from neutral status," he wrote in a letter to the *New York Times*, "the President's action was a step toward war—and as such was an invasion of Congress's constitutional 'power to declare war.'" [50]

Corwin's argument ignored the steady growth of presidential power in foreign policy that had occurred since the turn of the century, but it raised serious questions that remain unanswered in American politics. "Even if Roosevelt's decision was the right one and the circumstances justified his extraordinary decision," the historian William Goldsmith has written, "it was undoubtedly the beginning of a period in which the continuous and incremental expansion of presidential power, and the concomitant erosion of congressional power and responsibility, let loose grave problems for the future." [51]

World War II greatly accelerated the flow of power to the executive, allowing Roosevelt to assert an inherent executive prerogative more boldly than he could have before Japan's December 7, 1941, attack on Pearl Harbor. Under conditions of total war, Roosevelt believed, the president was empowered not only to direct military operations abroad but to manage economic and social affairs at home. In a bold—critics said brazen—expression of his theory of power, Roosevelt demanded that an effective program of price and wage controls be created. "I ask the Congress," FDR said in his Labor Day message of September 7, 1942, "to take ... action by the first of October. Inaction on your part by that date will leave me with an inescapable responsibility to the people of this country to see to it that the war effort is no longer imperiled by threat of economic chaos." If Congress did not act, Roosevelt warned, "I shall accept the responsibility and I will act." [52]

Congress enacted the economic controls that the president demanded, and Roosevelt never had to follow through on his threat. The legislature's acquiescence, however reluctant, indicated, as Hawley has noted, that "as depression gave way to war, another expansion of presidential authority was underway, linked chiefly now to the creation of a national security and warfare state rather than a welfare one." [53]

The Modern Presidency Sustained: Harry S. Truman and Dwight D. Eisenhower

Franklin Roosevelt dominated American political life for more than a dozen years. His legacy included a more powerful and prominent executive office. But Roosevelt's long tenure also created serious concern about the dangers of concentrating too much power in the White House. Some political leaders stood poised after his death in 1945 to modify the constitutional and political changes that had greatly enhanced the powers of the presidency after 1933. But FDR had transformed politics in the United States permanently; he had taught most Americans to expect that the federal government would remain active in domestic and world affairs and that, within the government, the president would take the lead. Thus, the presidency's place in the American political system was an uneasy and unsettled one.

Harry Truman and the Roosevelt Inheritance

When the Senate adjourned at about five o'clock on April 12, 1945, Vice President Harry Truman made his way to the office of House Speaker Sam Rayburn to join his friends for their afternoon round of bourbon and water. No sooner had his drink been poured than the vice president received a telephone call from White House press secretary Steve Early, who told him to come to the executive mansion as soon as possible. Upon his arrival, Mrs. Roosevelt came up to Truman, put her arm around his shoulders, and said softly, "Harry, the president is dead." After a moment of shock, Truman recovered sufficiently to ask Mrs. Roosevelt: "Is there anything I can do for you? " She replied: "Is there anything we can do for you? For you're the one in trouble now." [54]

Eleanor Roosevelt was not the only one who felt that Truman was in trouble. With the country still at war, it seemed incomprehensible that anyone, let alone this "little man" from Missouri, as some of Truman's contemporaries disdainfully referred to him, could take Roosevelt's place as president of the United States. The journalist William White wrote of Truman, "For a time he walked, as completely as the smallest laborer who had been a 'Roosevelt man,' in the long shadow of the dead President." [55]

That Truman eventually was able to emerge from FDR's shadow had little to do with his ability to rouse the public. In this respect, the contrast between Truman and his predecessor was striking. "Truman possessed little or no charisma, struggled with an ego more fragile than most observers have understood, and had extreme distaste for the need to manipulate others," the historian Alonzo Hamby has written.[56] A poor speaker who was awkward in the presence of reporters, Truman suffered persistently low popularity: his public approval rating was less than 50 percent for the larger part of his tenure, including his entire final three years as president.[57]

In other respects, however, Truman was a solid successor to Roosevelt. He deeply believed in the changes that the New Deal had made in the United States. Although he was all too aware of his personal limitations, Truman also recognized that the legacy of both FDR's active personal style and the expanded government responsibilities that Roosevelt had brought about required active presidential leadership from his successors. Truman liked to say that "being a president is like riding a tiger. You have to keep on riding or be swallowed." [58]

The Fair Deal. When Truman assumed the presidency, some predicted that this supremely practical politician, who had been placed on the ticket as the nominee for vice president in 1944 mainly to appease southern and big-city Democrats, would readily adapt to the more conservative mood that the country had lapsed into during the twilight of the war. A close Roosevelt associate, Samuel Rosenman, informed the new president that his "conservative friends," particularly some of his former colleagues on Capitol Hill, believed that Truman was "going to be quite a shock to those who followed Roosevelt—that the New Deal [was] as good as dead—that [the country] was going back to 'normalcy' and that a good part of the so-called 'Roosevelt nonsense' now [was] over." [59]

Truman's twenty-one-point message to Congress on September 6, 1945, made clear that he would not be to Roosevelt what Harding had been to Wilson. The message, which introduced the "Fair Deal" agenda, marked the moment when Truman felt that he finally had assumed the office of president in his own right. "This legislative program," he wrote in his memoirs, "was a reminder to the Democratic party, to the country, and to the Congress that progress in government lies along the road to sound reform in our private enterprise system and that progressive democracy has to continue to keep pace with changing conditions." [60]

The Fair Deal was Truman's attempt to codify Roosevelt's vision of a complete economic constitutional order. In 1944, FDR had begun to lay out his goals for postwar America. "We have accepted," Roosevelt proclaimed in his 1944 State of the Union address, "a Second Bill of Rights under which a new basis of security and prosperity can be established for all—regardless of station, race, or creed." [61] To fulfill Roosevelt's vision, the federal government needed to guarantee everyone a useful and remunerative job, adequate medical care, a decent home, and a good education.

The program that Truman presented to Congress in 1945 was an appeal, as he put it, "to make the attainment of those rights the essence of post-war economic life." [62] He called for the extension of social security to more workers, an increased minimum wage, national health insurance, urban development, and full employment. But Congress approved few of Truman's twenty-one points, and the 1946 congressional election appeared to be a dramatic rejection of the Fair Deal. The Republicans campaigned on the theme that the country had "had enough" of Roosevelt-Truman-style liberalism. When, for the first time in sixteen years, the Democrats lost control of Congress, many concluded that the party could not survive the passing of FDR. [63]

But Truman marshaled all of the resources that his office had accrued during Roosevelt's tenure to prove otherwise. In the aftermath of the 1946 election, he fought every attempt by the Republican Eightieth Congress to dismantle the New Deal. Truman cast more than two hundred vetoes during his presidency, mostly on matters of tax and labor policy. The conservative coalition of southern Democrats and Republicans, the same alliance that had plagued FDR during his second term, often overrode these vetoes. But Truman's forceful defiance in the face of overwhelming legislative opposition, the political scientist Fred Greenstein has noted, "accustomed all but the most conservative national political actors to look at the president as the main framer of the agenda for political debate—even when much of the debate involved castigation of his proposals." [64]

Truman's most significant veto was of the Taft-Hartley bill, which was widely regarded as an attack on labor unions. [65] On June 20, 1947, Truman sent a stinging veto message to Congress to assert that the bill "would reverse the basic direction of our national labor policy." That evening he went on the radio to declare: "We do not need—and we do not want—legislation which will take fundamental rights away from our working people." [66] The Taft-Hartley veto, although it was overridden by Congress, caused organized labor to line up solidly behind Truman. It also earned him praise from middle-class liberals, most of whom passionately supported the unions. Truman "has given American liberalism the fighting chance that it seemed to have lost with the death of Roosevelt," *The Nation* editorialized.[67]

Shrewdly taking the political initiative, Truman turned the 1948 presidential election into a referendum on the Roosevelt era. When he surprised nearly everyone by winning a come-from-behind victory against his Republican opponent, Gov. Thomas E. Dewey of New York, Truman stepped at least partially out of FDR's shadow. Not only had the president saved the New Deal and rebuilt the Democratic coalition, but the assertiveness he displayed in his battles with Congress confirmed the preeminence of the modern executive in legislative affairs.

Truman never was able to end completely the legislative stalemate in domestic policy that had prevailed from the beginning of his presidency, but he could claim some successes: his social security, minimum wage, and public housing proposals were enacted during the Eighty-first Congress, which, as a result of the 1948 election, was again controlled by the Democrats. More important, his administration was remarkably successful in assembling a bipartisan foreign policy coalition in Congress. Postwar tensions between the United States and the Soviet Union, which had been allies against Nazi Germany, brought the world into an era of "cold war." Democrats and internationalist Republicans in Congress voted to authorize the Truman Doctrine to contain communist expansion, the Marshall Plan to rebuild Europe, and other postwar foreign policy initiatives that were designed to maintain the international commitments of the United States after the war.

Executive Power. Truman's battles with Congress encouraged him to stake out a substantial sphere for independent action. This course was consistent with his long-standing belief that the president should have considerable autonomous powers. On December 5, 1946, Truman established by executive order the President's Committee on Civil Rights (PCCR), which was authorized "to determine whether and in what respect current law enforcement measures and the authority and means possessed by Federal, State, and local governments may be strengthened and improved to safeguard the civil rights of the people." [68] The president was no zealot for minority rights, but, more than most elected officials of his day, he was determined to do something about racial segregation. When Congress failed to approve the legislation that he had recommended after receiving the PCCR's report, Truman did what he could on his own authority as chief executive. In

1948, for example, he issued an executive order to establish equal opportunity for all races in the armed services.

Truman's most daring and politically costly initiatives came in the realm of international relations. These included his decisions to use atomic weapons against Japan near the end of World War II and, in 1950, to commit troops to combat in Korea. The Korean intervention, which followed communist North Korea's invasion of South Korea in June 1950, was an important extension of the president's power as commander in chief. For the first time in history, U.S. troops were deployed in a full-scale war without a congressional declaration.

In part, Truman's intervention in Korea was a logical consequence of the postwar emergence of the United States as a superpower, actively and constantly engaged in international affairs. In 1945, the Senate overwhelmingly ratified the charter that established the United Nations (UN), and Congress passed the United Nations Participation Act, which made the United States subject to certain UN decisions. Truman invoked this act as the primary justification for his deployment of troops in Korea. Once the UN Security Council decided to help South Korea, the president argued, he had a duty to respond under Articles 39 and 42 of the UN Charter.

But Truman also defended his actions in Korea by claiming to have a sweeping presidential power to use the armed forces of the United States without consulting Congress. To be sure, Truman cited precedents from the administrations of earlier commanders in chief. But all of these precedents involved limited interventions to suppress piracy or to protect American citizens who were endangered by foreign disorders. Truman's real rationale was that the cold war against communism and the president's new responsibilities as the leader of the free world greatly diminished Congress's role in foreign policy. As he said in March 1951, "the congressional power to declare war has fallen into abeyance because wars are no longer declared in advance." [69]

Limits still existed on the powers of the modern presidency, however, even in foreign policy. Truman paid dearly in the coin of public and congressional criticism as the war in Korea dragged on inconclusively. Most important, his claim that the Korean conflict endowed the president with emergency economic powers was rebuffed by the Supreme Court during the steel dispute of 1952. For fear of alienating the unions, Truman refused to apply the Taft-Hartley Act, which empowered the president to impose a sixty-day cooling-off period on labor and management in industrial disputes to postpone a strike in the steel industry. Instead, he decided on April 8 to seize control of the steel mills, arguing that a "work stoppage would immediately jeopardize and imperil our national defense."

Less than two months later, the Court, in *Youngstown Sheet and*

Tube Co. v. Sawyer, disabused the president of his belief that he could do in a national emergency anything that the Constitution or Congress had not explicitly forbidden.[70] Justice Hugo Black argued in his opinion for the Court that Truman's seizure order was a de facto statute and that the Constitution did not provide the president with the lawmaking power:

> In the framework of our Constitution, the President's power to see that the laws are faithfully executed refutes the idea that he is to be a law maker. The Constitution limits his functions in the lawmaking process to the recommending of laws he thinks wise and the vetoing of laws he thinks bad. And the Constitution is neither silent nor equivocal about who shall make laws which the President is to execute. The first section of the first article says that "All legislative powers herein granted shall be vested in a Congress of the United States...." [71]

The Court's decision surprised many people. Truman could cite numerous precedents of the president intervening militarily in labor disputes. (Justice Black invoked no judicial or governmental precedents to the contrary in his opinion.) Theodore Roosevelt had threatened to seize and run the mines during the anthracite coal strike of 1902 if other methods of mediation failed.[72] Franklin Roosevelt seized the North American Aviation Plant at Inglewood, California, on June 9, 1941, six months before Pearl Harbor, arguing that his power to act derived from the "aggregate" of the Constitution and the laws.[73] Not since 1866 had the Supreme Court ruled against a president in the exercise of prerogative power, and in that case *(Ex parte Milligan)* the Court declared Lincoln's use of military tribunals during the Civil War to be invalid only after the war had ended.[74] Small wonder, then, that Truman believed he would be upheld, especially since the Court was stacked with Roosevelt and Truman appointees.

Nevertheless, only three justices—Chief Justice Fred Vinson and Justices Stanley Reed and Sherman Minton—agreed with Truman that his seizure of the steel mills was constitutionally permissible. The majority for the Court had decided, Vinson lamented, that

> the broad executive power granted by Article II to an officer on duty 365 days a year cannot ... be invoked to prevent a disaster. Instead the President must confine himself to sending a message to Congress recommending action. Under this messenger-boy concept of the Office, the President cannot even act to preserve legislative programs from destruction so that Congress will have something left to act upon.[75]

The Court's decision, however, did not circumscribe strictly the president's powers as commander in chief. Only Justices Black and William O. Douglas broadly questioned the president's emergency

Despite numerous precedents for military intervention in labor disputes, President Truman's seizure of steel mills during the Korean
War was widely denounced. The Supreme Court ruled the action
illegal.

powers. The opinions of the four other justices in the 6-3 majority
applied strictly to the case at hand, emphasizing that Congress had
explicitly rejected presidential seizure as a method to settle industrial
disputes when it passed the Taft-Hartley Act. Justice Robert S.
Jackson's concurring opinion offered a test for the Court to use when
weighing presidential powers against congressional action:

> When the president takes measures incompatible with the expressed
> or implied will of Congress, his power is at its lowest ebb, for then he
> can rely only upon his own constitutional powers minus any constitu-
> tional powers of Congress in the matter. Courts can sustain exclusive
> Presidential control in such a case only by disabling the Congress from
> acting upon the subject. Presidential claim to a power at once so
> conclusive and preclusive must be scrutinized with caution, for what is
> at stake is the equilibrium established by our constitutional system.[76]

The Supreme Court ordered Truman to return the mills to their
owners, even though a majority of the justices supported a broad

interpretation of the president's authority to mobilize the nation's resources to protect the United States against threats to its security. But, as Jackson argued, when the president's authority to command the instruments of force is "turned inward, not because of rebellion but because of a lawful economic struggle between industry and labor, it should have no such indulgence." [77] Such a struggle could not be interrupted by presidential prerogative but only by statutory procedures that were authorized by Congress.

The *Youngstown* case was "an important foundation," the historian Maeva Marcus has written, "for the reaffirmation of the proposition that the President is not above the law." [78] Truman's defeat in the steel crisis meant that he and his successors would have to exercise the expanded powers of the presidency more carefully, especially when their critics were numerous in Congress and among the public, as was true of Truman in 1952. Nevertheless, the Court did not strike a crippling blow to the president's powers as commander in chief. Indeed, the justices might have sustained Truman's seizure of the steel mills had Congress not provided the president with other ways to keep the mills running in the Taft-Hartley Act.

Truman and the Institution of the Modern Presidency. Truman's tenure reaffirmed the modern presidency. He demonstrated that a president without extraordinary political gifts or popularity could achieve important objectives, define the terms of national political debate, and control at least the main lines of domestic and foreign policy. In part, Truman succeeded because he was operating in the new political environment of big government: the welfare state at home and international leadership abroad inevitably concentrated major responsibilities in the White House.

But Truman also made an independent contribution to the development of the presidency by demonstrating that modern executive power could rest on something more solid than the personal resources of an extraordinary president such as FDR. Significantly, Truman both formalized and expanded the presidency as an institution.

Although Franklin Roosevelt had created the Executive Office of the President, his own staff was unstructured, reflecting his penchant for improvised, ad hoc arrangements. Truman, in contrast, was a systematic administrator. During his presidency, responsibilities within the White House Office were defined clearly. Truman also used the Bureau of the Budget (BOB) more extensively than did Roosevelt, relying heavily on the bureau in carrying out his executive and legislative duties. Truman assigned responsibility to the BOB to clear and coordinate all legislative requests that originated within the federal departments and to draft White House-sponsored legislation and executive orders.[79] As a result, Truman developed an advisory process in which policies came to him only for decision, not, as with FDR, for development.

Congress helped Truman (sometimes unintentionally) to institutionalize the presidency. Congressional statutes, for example, established the Council of Economic Advisers (CEA) in 1946 and the National Security Council (NSC) in 1947 to help the president to formulate fiscal and foreign policy, respectively. Congress also appropriated funds so that Truman could hire larger staffs to assist him. Although the NSC and CEA initially were conceived by many legislators to be a check on the president's autonomy in economic and security matters, Truman acted effectively to domesticate the councils—that is, to make them part of the president's team.

Truman's effort to strengthen the institutional presidency received surprising help from another source, former president Herbert Hoover. The Republican-controlled Eightieth Congress had appointed Hoover to head the Commission on the Organization of the Executive Branch of the Government. The task of the commission, as Republican leaders understood it, was to lay the groundwork for an assault on New Deal programs and to circumscribe the executive by foreclosing the possibility of another personalized, FDR-style administration. Yet Hoover, who had grappled with the problems of the presidency and the executive branch during the late 1920s and early 1930s, saw the need to fortify the modern office even though he wanted to repeal many of the modern government's programs.[80]

Thus, after much study the Hoover Commission recommended that the presidency be strengthened, not diminished. Its report, in fact, was very similar to the one that Brownlow and his colleagues had submitted in 1937 to support FDR's program of administrative reform. The president still needed help, the Hoover Commission argued, especially to supervise the far-flung activities of the enlarged executive branch. Its recommendations formed the basis of the 1949 executive reorganization act, which authorized Truman (who enthusiastically embraced the commission's report) to effect important changes in many of the departments and independent regulatory commissions.

Especially significant was Truman's Reorganization Plan No. 8, which he issued in 1950. Truman included provisions in the plan that eventually eroded the independent regulatory commissions' autonomy from presidential influence and thereby reduced the effect of the Court's ruling in *Humphrey's Executor v. United States* that the president may not remove a commissioner. The plan provided that the chairs of the regulatory commissions would be "appointed by the president and serve at his pleasure." The chairs in turn were granted considerable authority to appoint and supervise their commissions' staff and to oversee the daily business of their commissions. Consequently, presidents were better able to give direction to regulatory agencies than in the past.[81]

Hoover's endorsement of executive reorganization suggested that a political consensus gradually was emerging in support of the modern presidency. Republicans had "historically been against Presidents," one Truman aide noted, but Hoover's interest in the problems of administrative management offered bipartisan support for "the kind of Chief Executive office that will have enough authority and the right kind of organization to do the most difficult jobs."[82]

The Twenty-second Amendment

One of the political aftershocks of the New Deal and Fair Deal was the Twenty-second Amendment, which was proposed by the Republican-dominated Eightieth Congress in 1947 and ratified by the states in 1951. The amendment prohibits any person from being elected president more than two times. It also prevents vice presidents who succeed to the presidency from being elected more than once if they have served more than half of a departed president's four-year term. (If they have served less than half of a term, they may be elected two times on their own, for a maximum tenure of ten years). The amendment, although written in such a way as to exempt the incumbent Truman from its coverage, was a posthumous slap at Franklin Roosevelt, who had challenged the "two-term tradition" by being elected president four times.

The "Two-Term Tradition." The source of the two-term tradition was Thomas Jefferson, who was the first president to argue that no one should serve more than two terms. Responding on December 10, 1807, to a letter from the Vermont state legislature that requested him to run for a third term (six other states had sent similar letters), Jefferson replied, "If some termination of the services of the Chief Magistrate be not fixed by the Constitution, or supplied by practice, his office, nominally four years, will in fact become for life, and history shows how easily that degenerates into an inheritance." To strengthen his argument for a two-term limit, Jefferson invoked "the sound precedent set by an illustrious predecessor," George Washington.[83]

Jefferson's invocation of Washington for his argument was not altogether appropriate: Washington had stepped down voluntarily from the presidency after two terms, but as he explained in his Farewell Address, he did so not as a matter of principle but because he longed for "the shade of retirement."[84] Even so, Jefferson's defense of a two-term limit took root quickly in presidential politics. Indeed, the Whig party and many Democrats soon argued for a one-term limit. Of the first thirty presidents (Washington to Hoover), twenty served one term or less.

In the late nineteenth and early twentieth centuries, the issue of a third term arose only occasionally. Ulysses S. Grant (in 1876) and Woodrow Wilson (in 1920) would have liked to serve another four years but were too unpopular at the end of their second terms even to be renominated by their parties. In 1908, Theodore Roosevelt declined a certain renomination and, considering his great popularity, a probable reelection, calling the two-term limit a "wise custom." Four years later, however, he ran for president again, first as an unsuccessful contender for the Republican nomination, then as a third-party candidate.

The two-term tradition was broken by Franklin Roosevelt in 1940. In 1937, Roosevelt, although not flatly ruling out a third term, had declared that his "great ambition on January 20, 1941," was to "turn over this desk and chair in the White House" to a successor. But in 1939 World War II broke out in Europe, with little prospect that the United States would be able to remain above the fray. Waiting until the Democratic convention in July 1940, Roosevelt finally signaled his willingness to be renominated. The delegates jubilantly approved.

Public opinion polls had shown that the public was deeply divided about the propriety of Roosevelt's candidacy, and Republicans took up the cry "No Third Term!" on behalf of their nominee, business leader Wendell Willkie. Democrats rejoined that, in perilous times, the country would be foolish to "change horses in midstream." Roosevelt won the election, but by a much narrower popular vote margin than in 1936— five million votes, compared with eleven million. In 1944, with the United States and its allies nearing victory in World War II, Roosevelt won another term, by three million votes. Ill at the time of his fourth election, he died less than three months after the inauguration.

The Amendment Passes.   Congress had never been fully satisfied with the original Constitution's provision for unrestricted presidential reeligibility: from 1789 to 1947, 270 resolutions to limit the president's tenure had been introduced in the House and Senate.[85] But the Roosevelt years added a partisan dimension to this long-standing concern. In 1932, the Republicans, who had formed the nation's majority party since 1860, were driven from power by Roosevelt's New Deal Democratic coalition. Conservative Democrats, mostly southerners, lost control of their own party to liberals and northerners.

In the midterm elections of 1946, Republicans regained a majority of both houses of Congress. On February 6, 1947, less than five weeks after the opening of the Eightieth Congress, the House passed a strict two-term amendment to the Constitution by a vote of 285-121. Republicans supported the amendment unanimously (238-0); Democrats opposed it 47-121, with most of the Democratic yea votes coming from southerners. Five weeks later, on March 12, the Senate passed a slightly different version of the amendment (it allowed a president who had served one full term and less than half of another to seek an additional term) by a vote of 59-23. Republican senators, like their House colleagues, were unanimous in their support (46-0); Democrats opposed the amendment by a vote of 13-23. The differences between the two houses' versions were ironed out in favor of the Senate; final congressional passage took place on March 24, 1947.

Debate on the Twenty-second Amendment painted a thin gloss of philosophy over a highly partisan issue. Republicans contended that a two-term limit would protect Americans against the threat of an overly personalized presidency; besides, argued Rep. Leo Allen of Illinois, "the people should be given the opportunity to set limits on the time an individual can serve as Chief Executive." Democrats like Rep. Estes Kefauver of Tennessee rejoined that the people, "by a mere majority vote, have the opportunity of deciding every four years whether they want to terminate the services of the President if he stands for reelection." [86] Little, if any, consideration was given to the Constitutional Convention's carefully considered decision to place no restrictions on presidential reeligibility.

Once proposed by Congress, the Twenty-second Amendment received a mixed response from the states. Only one other amendment to the Constitution has taken longer to ratify than the three years, eleven months, required for the two-term limit.[87] Eighteen state legislatures—exactly half the needed number—approved the amendment in 1947, all of them in predominantly Republican states. Afterward, ratification proceeded slowly, with most victories coming in the South. Approval from the required three-fourths of the states was attained on February 27, 1951. Had the amendment not exempted Truman from its coverage, it might have foundered on the shoals of overt (instead of merely implicit) partisanship.

Dwight D. Eisenhower: The Reluctant Modern President

Like the Hoover Commission (and in contrast to the Twenty-second Amendment), the presidency of Dwight Eisenhower fostered the bipartisan acceptance of the modern presidency.[88] But like that of the commission, Eisenhower's contribution was reluctant. Although the Republican president had no intention of trying to dismantle the "Roosevelt Revolution," he came to the White House in 1953 with a very different perception of the executive office from Roosevelt's and with very different aspirations.

Eisenhower had served as supreme Allied commander in Europe (a position to which FDR appointed him) and was the most celebrated of the World War II generals. "Ike," as he was known to the nation, brought to the presidency a soldier's sense of duty. He was resolved not to lead the federal government into the new and the untried but to restore a sense of national calm after the controversy and frenetic activism of the Roosevelt and Truman years. In many ways Eisenhower was like Coolidge—he wanted to preside over a postwar healing process. "Eisenhower has been a sort of Roosevelt in reverse," the political scientist Richard Neustadt wrote in 1960. "Roosevelt was a politician seeking personal power; Eisenhower . . . came to crown a reputation not make one. He wanted to be arbiter, not master. His love was not for power but for duty—and for status." [89]

Eisenhower's concern for duty initially inclined him to accept the argument of some in his party that balance should be restored to the relationship between the president and Congress. He was no partisan Republican; in fact, some Democrats had tried to draft him to run for president in 1948, only to discover that he considered it so much his soldierly duty to remain above politics that he had never voted. But Eisenhower did accept the prevailing Republican doctrine that the proper relationship between Congress and the White House had been upset by his immediate Democratic predecessors. For example, as the first Republican president since 1933, Eisenhower decided not to submit a legislative program to Congress during his first year in office.

Some Americans regarded Eisenhower's constant professions of respect for Congress as refreshing evidence that the hallowed traditions of legislative government were being restored. Others, however, especially in the press, looked disdainfully upon what one observer called Eisenhower's "civic textbook concept of the three branches of the federal government." [90] Eisenhower found that reporters insisted on grading him at the end of his "First Hundred Days," and he did not fare well. In an article published in May 1953, the Washington *Reporter* correspondent Joseph Harsch observed: "The memory of Franklin Roosevelt's voracious seizure and joyous exercise of presidential power twenty years earlier contributes to a companion illusion of a man who slipped into the White House by the back door on January 20, 1953, and hasn't yet found his way to the President's desk." [91]

The Hidden Hand. Appearances to the contrary, Eisenhower was not simply sitting and watching history pass him by. He exercised power with much more relish and shrewdness than his contemporaries realized. His was a "hidden-hand" presidency, as Greenstein has called it, in which Ike exercised power behind the scenes, while presenting to the public the image of detachment from Washington's political machinations.[92] Eisenhower's approach to presidential leadership was an effort to escape an inherent difficulty of the modern presidency. On the one hand, the president was expected to be a chief of state who stood above politics, upheld the Constitution, and lent dignity to the national government. On the other hand, increasingly in the twentieth century the president was expected to get things done, to lead his party and Congress in the pursuit of a program. Ultimately, Eisenhower believed, the dignity and influence of the office were lost when the president not only led politically but also *appeared* to lead politically, as Truman had.

Ike's solution to the dilemma of modern executive leadership was not to abdicate responsibility for policy. Although Eisenhower was a domestic political conservative who had no desire to innovate except in modest, incremental ways, he believed that the New Deal had become a permanent component of modern American government. When his conservative brother Edgar criticized him privately for carrying on liberal policies, the president bluntly replied, "Should any political party attempt to abolish social security and eliminate labor laws and farm programs, you should not hear of that party again in our political history." [93] "Above all else," the historian Oscar Handlin wrote soon after Eisenhower left office, "Eisenhower made palatable to most Republicans the social welfare legislation of the preceding two decades. In the 1950s, the New Deal ceased to be an active political issue and became an accepted part of the American past. No other figure could have achieved that transformation." [94]

In foreign policy, too, Eisenhower carried on the policies of his Democratic predecessors. Unlike many Republicans, Eisenhower had long shared the internationalist perspectives of FDR and Truman. He was contemptuous of Republicans—notably the Ohio senator Robert Taft, his main rival for the party's presidential nomination in 1952— who urged that the United States withdraw from world affairs into a "fortress America." [95] Eisenhower decided to run for president, some said, not because he enjoyed politics but because he felt a duty to lead the internationalist wing of the Republican party and to preserve the postwar foreign policy that he, as the commander of the North Atlantic Treaty Organization (NATO), had helped to create.[96] "Observers sensed," Leuchtenburg has noted, "that even when Eisenhower did not acknowledge that he was FDR's legatee, he had the same internationalist aspirations." [97]

Eisenhower realized, then, that because of the New Deal legacy and the emergence of the United States as the leader of the free world it no longer was possible for the president simply to preside. Instead, the task, as he understood it, was to lead actively without seeming to lead, to remain quietly and persistently involved in political affairs while maintaining the public face of the congenial national hero.

The most instructive example of Eisenhower's hidden-hand approach to government was his handling of Sen. Joseph McCarthy. The nation was traumatized by the Wisconsin Republican's charges that Communists had infiltrated the federal government. Eisenhower refused publicly to attack McCarthy, who chaired the Senate Committee on Government Operations and its subcommittee on investigation, although he regarded McCarthy's "red-baiting" as demagogy of the worst sort. The president's critics claimed that by not upbraiding McCarthy, he abetted the senator in unjustly ruining many lives and careers. "Unopposed by the one public leader who could have discredited him," wrote Hamby, "McCarthy ran amok." [98]

But Eisenhower's public silence did not indicate timidity or tacit approval. Rather, he feared that to take on McCarthy publicly would undermine the dignity of the presidency and the unity of the Republican party, thereby jeopardizing his chances of pursuing an internationalist foreign policy. "I will not," Eisenhower told his brother Milton, "get into a pissing contest with that skunk." [99]

What the president did instead, working closely with his press secretary, James Hagerty, was to use the media and his congressional allies to ruin McCarthy's political effectiveness.[100] Through Hagerty, Eisenhower helped to manage the congressional hearings that culminated in McCarthy's censure by the Senate in December 1954. In addition, Eisenhower and Vice President Richard Nixon, although carefully avoiding any direct mention of McCarthy, condemned the kinds of actions in which the senator engaged.

Eisenhower's most notable reproof came when McCarthy's adherents purged libraries of politically controversial books and harassed educators. "Don't join the book burners," he told an audience at Dartmouth College. "Don't think you are going to conceal faults by concealing evidence that they ever existed.... How will we defeat communism unless we know what it is?" The right of the people to express ideas and to hear them, the president said, is "unquestioned, or it isn't American." [101] A few months later, Eisenhower proclaimed that teachers were loyal citizens who enjoyed "true freedom of thought, untrammelled by political fashion or expediency." [102] Although the president named no names in his speeches and press conferences, he said in response to a reporter's question that the ongoing Senate investigation threatened the very values that it claimed to be defending.[103]

As his handling of McCarthy illustrates, Eisenhower did not reject the modern presidency. Instead, he tried to manage its responsibilities in a way that suited his own strengths and political objectives. Despite criticism in the press, Eisenhower remained extraordinarily popular with the American people. Coolidge had shown thirty years earlier that presidential leadership of public opinion need not be exercised solely to achieve reform or innovation. Eisenhower's popularity indicated that, at least at times, the public still appreciated quiet leadership to preserve the status quo. "Among the qualities that the American government must exhibit is dignity," Eisenhower wrote in a 1960 letter to publisher Henry Luce. "In turn, the principal governmental spokesman must strive to display it." [104]

Eisenhower's Legacy. Eisenhower has been condemned frequently by presidential scholars for the work he left undone. "No president in history," wrote the political scientist Clinton Rossiter, "was ever more powerfully armed to persuade the minds of men and face up to the inevitable and then failed more poignantly to use his power." [105] The foundations of the welfare state and of America's international obligations were sustained during Eisenhower's tenure and, in some instances, such as social security, were extended. But to most liberals, Eisenhower, for all his popularity, failed as president by not rousing the country to redress its problems of civil rights, education, and social justice.

Critics have charged, in particular, that Eisenhower's approach to civil rights revealed a troubling deficiency in his understanding of presidential responsibility. In 1954, the Supreme Court decision in *Brown v. Board of Education of Topeka*, which struck down the doctrine of racially "separate but equal" public schools, raised the hopes of civil rights reformers that segregation finally had been routed.[106] But Eisenhower dampened these hopes by refusing to say whether he approved or disapproved of the decision. His equivocation probably slowed progress toward racial equality; certainly it helped to set the stage for the ugly racial incident that occurred in Little Rock, Arkansas, in 1957.

In September 1957, the governor of Arkansas, Orval Faubus, called up a state unit of the National Guard to thwart a federal court order to begin desegregating the all-white Central High School in Little Rock. Eisenhower made a determined effort to stay out of the Little Rock crisis, initially conducting only a single, inconclusive meeting with Faubus at the president's summer home in Newport, Rhode Island, on September 14. Upon returning to Arkansas, Faubus, who believed that Eisenhower was ill-informed and indifferent to the situation in his state, defied the president's private request to instruct the National Guard to enforce the court order; instead Faubus withdrew the guard from around the school. On September 23, nine black students were turned away from Central High School by a howling, hate-filled mob of segregationists from Arkansas and other states. Faubus continued to inflame the onrushing crisis with defiant rhetoric.

Eisenhower still was reluctant to interfere in Little Rock, believing that to use federal troops to enforce desegregation might cause the violence to spread. But when neither state nor local authorities dispersed the mob, the president could avoid responsibility no longer. Had he failed to act in the face of Arkansas's defiance of the court order, Eisenhower would have yielded to every segregationist governor the right to break the law. The unfortunate consequence of delay was that when Eisenhower did act, he was forced to deploy more military power domestically than any president in many decades. On September 24, a contingent of regular army paratroopers was dispatched to Little Rock. The next day Americans saw shocking photographs of troops wielding bayonets in an American city.

Many have found it difficult to understand Eisenhower's conduct in the Little Rock crisis. To his credit, however, he eventually did act firmly, thus establishing a precedent that would make it difficult for future presidents to deny the federal interest in the nation's schools and in race relations, which until then had been regarded as essentially local matters.[107]

Eisenhower also contributed to the institutionalization of the modern presidency. Drawing on his long experience with military staffs, the president enlarged and formally organized the White House Office. This is not to say that Eisenhower organized the White House along military lines, as many Washington observers erroneously concluded during his time in office. Instead, the enthusiasm that Ike had gained for careful organization as an army general predisposed him to entertain seriously the recommendation of the Brownlow and Hoover commissions to establish a clearer and more formal line of command between the White House and the rest of the executive branch.[108] He established a line of command and communications that ran from the president through a chief of staff (who reported directly to him) to the rest of the president's team and back again. Sherman Adams, who was the first chief of staff, worked zealously to free the president from the everyday demands of the White House and the rest of the executive branch.[109]

Eisenhower's modest programmatic ambitions notwithstanding, he also created the first White House office of legislative liaison. The liaison office was headed by Maj. Gen. Wilton B. Persons, a retired army officer who had handled Eisenhower's congressional relations when he served as the army's chief of staff and the NATO commander after World War II. The task of the liaison office was to promote the president's policies on Capitol Hill.

Although Eisenhower offered no program to Congress during his first year, pressure from several quarters soon forced him to become more actively involved in legislative matters. Eisenhower himself, having talked of "restoring the balance" between the branches, soon realized that even a conservative president who wanted mostly to curb policy innovation needed to have his views represented effectively to Congress. Thus, a presidential program accompanied the State of the Union message in January 1954, and Eisenhower and his legislative liaison office worked systematically to enact it. During his eight years as president, Ike became increasingly involved in legislative issues, such as the effort to create the federal interstate highway system. He even managed to work well with a Congress that, after 1954, was controlled by the Democrats.

Interestingly, Eisenhower's "special triumph" in congressional relations, as the historian Stephen Ambrose has noted, was to hold down defense spending.[110] The former military commander wanted to avoid an arms race with the Soviet Union, fearing that a military buildup would trigger uncontrollable inflation and eventually would bankrupt the United States, all without providing additional security. During his second term, Democrats in Congress, led by Sen. John F. Kennedy, criticized the president for putting a balanced budget ahead of the national defense. But Eisenhower, confident of his own military judgment, was unmoved. Inheriting a $50 billion annual defense budget from Truman, he reduced it to $40 billion.

After a doubtful start, then, Eisenhower upheld the modern presidency. His defense of the twentieth-century executive was never more apparent than in his active involvement in the campaign to defeat the Bricker Amendment, which would have curtailed the president's authority to conduct the nation's foreign policy. By the terms of the amendment, executive agreements with other nations would take effect only if they were approved by Congress and did not conflict with state laws. "The idea was, of course," noted the historian Elmo Richardson, "a belated response to Franklin Roosevelt's personal diplomacy." [111] The amendment's author, the Republican senator John Bricker of Ohio, and its adherents in Congress endorsed isolationist sentiments that, according to Eisenhower, threatened the future of both the United States and the Republican party.

In the Senate, mainly because of the president's personal influence, the Bricker Amendment fell one vote short of passage. The close vote indicated that many Americans still believed that the modern chief executive's exercise of initiative in foreign affairs was excessive. It was the reluctant modern president, "Dwight D. Eisenhower—nobody else," an embittered Senator Bricker claimed, who preserved the executive's right to make international agreements unilaterally.[112]

Notes

1. Quoted in Stefan Lorant, *The Presidency: A Pictorial History of Presidential Elections from Washington to Truman* (New York: Macmillan, 1951), 594.
2. Franklin D. Roosevelt, *Public Papers and Addresses*, ed. Samuel J. Rosenman, 13 vols. (New York: Random House, 1938-1950), 1:751-752.
3. Ibid 1: 752.
4. Many political scientists, most notably Fred I. Greenstein, consider Franklin Roosevelt to be the first "modern" president (see, for example, Fred I. Greenstein, "Introduction: Toward a Modern Presidency," in *Leadership in the Modern Presidency*, ed. Fred I. Greenstein [Cambridge, Mass.: Harvard University Press, 1988]). As Jeffrey K. Tulis argues, however, many of the characteristics of the executive that Greenstein identifies as distinctly modern, such as legislative leadership, found practical expression in the nineteenth century, if not earlier (see Jeffrey K. Tulis, *The Rhetorical Presidency* [Princeton, N.J.: Princeton University Press, 1987], esp. chap. 1).
5. Robert K. Murray and Tim H. Blessing, "The Presidential Performance Study: A Progress Report," *Journal of American History* 70:3 (December 1983): 542.
6. Arnold J. Toynbee, *Survey of International Affairs: 1931* (London: Oxford University Press, 1932), 1.
7. Quoted in Robert M. Collins, *The Business Response to Keynes* (New York: Columbia University Press, 1981), 28.
8. *New York Times*, March 4, 1933, 1.
9. Clinton Rossiter, *The American Presidency*, 2d ed. (New York: Harcourt, Brace and World, 1960), 145.
10. After bolting from the Republican party in 1912, Theodore Roosevelt had appeared before the gathering in Chicago that launched the Bull Moose campaign. But FDR was the first nominee to address a regular national convention.
11. *New York Times*, July 3, 1932, 1.
12. Roosevelt, *Public Papers and Addresses* 1:647-648.
13. *New York Times*, March 5, 1933, 3.
14. Roosevelt, *Public Papers and Addresses* 2:12.
15. Ibid. 2:15.
16. Ibid. 2:24-26.
17. The term *fireside chat* originated with Robert Trout of the Columbia Broadcasting System's Washington station, who introduced FDR on the occasion of his first radio address. At ten o'clock on the evening of March 12, 1933, Trout told sixty million people, seated before twenty million radios, that "the President wants to come into your home and sit at your fireside for a little fireside chat" (Kenneth S. Davis, *FDR: The New Deal Years, 1933-1937* [New York: Random House, 1986], 60).
18. Roosevelt, *Public Papers and Addresses* 2:65.
19. Raymond Moley, *After Seven Years* (New York: Harper and Brothers, 1939), 155.
20. *Wall Street Journal*, March 13, 1933; cited in Frank Freidel, *FDR: Launching the New Deal* (Boston: Little, Brown, 1973), 236.
21. Hopkins is quoted in Fred I. Greenstein, "Nine Presidents in Search of a Modern Presidency," in Greenstein, *Leadership in the Modern Presidency*,

299; also see James T. Patterson, "The Rise of Presidential Power before World War I," *Law and Contemporary Problems* 40:2 (Spring 1976): 53-57; and Louis Brownlow, *The President and the Presidency* (Chicago: Public Administration Service, 1949), 69-71.

22. Hugo Black to James Farley, June 19, 1934, box 34, folder "Roosevelt, Franklin D., 1934," James Farley Papers, Manuscripts Division, Library of Congress.

23. Roosevelt, *Public Papers and Addresses* 3:317-318.

24. Elmer E. Cornwell, Jr., *Presidential Leadership of Public Opinion* (Bloomington: Indiana University Press, 1965), 131.

25. Roosevelt, *Public Papers and Addresses* 1:659.

26. "Democratic Platform of 1936," in *National Party Platforms*, ed. Donald Bruce Johnson (Urbana: University of Illinois Press, 1978), 360. Evidence of FDR's dominant role in drafting the platform can be found in the President's Secretary file 143, folder: "Democratic Platform," Franklin D. Roosevelt Papers, Franklin D. Roosevelt Library, Hyde Park, New York.

27. Roosevelt to Frankfurter, February 9, 1937, Felix Frankfurter Papers, microfilm reel 60, Manuscripts Department, Library of Congress.

28. Roosevelt, *Public Papers and Addresses* 5:234.

29. Leuchtenburg, "Franklin D. Roosevelt: The First Modern President," in Greenstein, *Leadership in the Modern Presidency*, 27.

30. Greenstein, "Nine Presidents," 299. Congress created the Tennessee Valley Authority (TVA) in May 1933. The agency was authorized to sell electric power to states, counties, and municipalities; it also was empowered to construct dams on the Tennessee River. The TVA is widely regarded as one of the most successful New Deal programs, contributing greatly to flood control and to the dissemination of electric power throughout the southeast United States.

31. Louis Brownlow, *A Passion for Anonymity* (Chicago: University of Chicago Press, 1958), 392.

32. *Report of the President's Committee on Administrative Management* (Washington, D.C.: Government Printing Office, 1937), 53.

33. Luther Gulick, "Politics, Administration, and the New Deal," *Annals* 169 (September 1933): 64.

34. Quoted in Rossiter, *American Presidency*, 129.

35. A. J. Wann, *The President As Chief Administrator* (Washington, D.C.: Public Affairs Press, 1968), 187-188.

36. The term *administrative presidency* is drawn from Richard Nathan's book on the use of administrative strategies by modern presidents to pursue their policy objectives. See Richard Nathan, *The Administrative Presidency* (New York: Wiley, 1983).

37. Roosevelt, *Public Papers and Addresses* 2:161.

38. Ellis Hawley, "The Constitution of the Hoover and F. Roosevelt Presidency during the Depression Era, 1900-1939," in *The Constitution and the American Presidency*, ed. Martin L. Fausold and Alan Shank (Albany: State University of New York Press, 1991), 94.

39. William E. Leuchtenburg, "Franklin D. Roosevelt's Supreme Court 'Packing' Plan," in *Essays on the New Deal*, ed. Harold M. Hollingsworth and William F. Holmes (Austin: University of Texas Press, 1969), 76-77. The most recent study of the Court-packing fight is Michael Nelson, "The President and the Court: Reinterpreting the Court-Packing Episode of 1937," *Political Science Quarterly* 103 (Summer 1988): 267-293.

40. *Humphrey's Executor v. United States*, 295 U.S. 602 (1935); *Schechter Poultry Corp. v. United States*, 295 U.S. 495 (1935).
41. See Chapter 10.
42. Leuchtenburg, "Franklin D. Roosevelt's Supreme Court 'Packing' Plan," 115.
43. Peter Gerry to Josiah Bailey, n.d., Josiah William Bailey Papers, senatorial series, Political National Papers, box 476, folder "September to October, 1938," Manuscripts Division, William R. Perkins Library, Duke University, Durham, North Carolina.
44. For a detailed account of the 1938 purge campaign, see Sidney M. Milkis, "Presidents and Party Purges: With Special Emphasis on the Lessons of 1938," in *Presidents and Their Parties: Leadership or Neglect?* ed. Robert Harmel (New York: Praeger, 1984).
45. Because no other Democrat seemed capable of carrying forward the New Deal principles, many progressives began working for Roosevelt's renomination at the end of 1938. It was the foreign policy crisis, however, that finally persuaded Roosevelt to stand for reelection in 1940.
46. Hawley, "The Constitution of the Hoover and F. Roosevelt Presidency," 99-100.
47. Roosevelt, *Public Papers and Addresses* 6:410.
48. *United States v. Curtiss-Wright Export Corporation*, 299 U.S. 304 (1936).
49. *United States v. Belmont*, 301 U.S. 324 (1937). On Hamilton, see Chapter 3.
50. *New York Times*, October 13, 1940, section 4, 7.
51. William M. Goldsmith, *The Growth of Presidential Power: A Documented History*, 3 vols. (New York and London: Chelsea, 1974), 3:1774.
52. *Congressional Record*, 77th Cong., 2d sess., 1942, 7044.
53. Hawley, "The Constitution of the Hoover and F. Roosevelt Presidency," 101.
54. Harry Truman, *Memoirs*, 2 vols. (Garden City, N.Y.: Doubleday, 1955), 1:4-5; and William E. Leuchtenburg, *In the Shadow of FDR: From Harry Truman to Ronald Reagan*, rev. ed. (Ithaca and London: Cornell University Press, 1985), 1.
55. William S. White, "The Memoirs of Harry S. Truman," *New Republic*, November 7, 1955, 16.
56. Alonzo L. Hamby, "Harry S. Truman: Insecurity and Responsibility," in Greenstein, *Leadership in the Modern Presidency*, 42.
57. Ibid., 42-43.
58. Quoted in Larry Berman, *The New American Presidency* (Boston: Little, Brown, 1987), 212.
59. Truman, *Memoirs* 1:483.
60. Ibid., 1:485-486.
61. Roosevelt, *Public Papers and Addresses* 13:41.
62. *Public Papers of the Presidents of the United States: Harry S. Truman*, 14 vols. (Washington, D.C.: Government Printing Office, 1961-1966), vol. 1, September 6, 1945, 279.
63. Leuchtenburg, *In the Shadow of FDR*, 23.
64. Greenstein, "Nine Presidents," 306.
65. The Taft-Hartley Act outlawed the closed shop, made unions liable for damages caused by breaches of contract, enabled the president to declare a sixty-day cooling-off period before a strike, forbade unions to make political contributions or to exact excessive dues, and required elected union officials to take an oath that they were not Communists.

66. *Public Papers of the Presidents of the United States: Harry S. Truman,* vol. 3, June 20, 1947, 289, 299.
67. *The Nation,* vol. 164, June 28, 1947, 755.
68. President Harry S Truman, "Executive Order 9308 Establishing the President's Committee on Civil Rights," December 5, 1946, in *Growth of Presidential Power* 3:1568-1569.
69. *Public Papers of the President of the United States: Harry S. Truman,* vol. 11, March 1, 1951, 176.
70. *Youngstown Sheet and Tube Company v. Sawyer,* 343 U.S. 579 (1952).
71. Ibid., 343 U.S. 579 at 587.
72. See Chapter 8.
73. Pious, *The American Presidency,* 66; Edward S. Corwin, *The President: Office and Powers, 1787-1957,* 4th ed. (New York: New York University Press, 1957), 408-410.
74. Pious, *The American Presidency,* 67; see also Chapter 6 in this volume.
75. *Youngstown Sheet and Tube Co. v. Sawyer,* 343 U.S. 579 at 708.
76. Ibid., 343 U.S. 579 at 637; and Richard M. Pious, *The American Presidency* (New York: Basic Books, 1979), 64-69.
77. *Youngstown Sheet and Tube Co. v. Sawyer,* 343 U.S. 579 at 645.
78. Maeva Marcus, *Truman and the Steel Seizure Case: The Limits of Presidential Power* (New York: Columbia University Press, 1977), 248.
79. Greenstein, "Nine Presidents," 304.
80. Peri E. Arnold, *Making the Managerial Presidency: Comprehensive Reorganization Planning, 1905-1980* (Princeton, N.J.: Princeton University Press, 1986), 127.
81. Martha Derthick and Paul J. Quirk, *The Politics of Deregulation* (Washington, D.C.: Brookings, 1985), 61-74.
82. Truman's budget director James Webb, as quoted in Arnold, *Making the Managerial Presidency,* 142.
83. Quoted in Michael Nelson, *Historic Documents on Presidential Elections, 1787-1988* (Washington, D.C.: Congressional Quarterly, 1991), 102.
84. Indeed, Washington wrote in a 1788 letter that "I differ widely myself from Mr. Jefferson ... as to the expediency of rotation in that department [the presidency]." Edward S. Corwin, *The President: Office and Powers,* 4th ed. (New York: New York University Press, 1957), 333.
85. Paul G. Willis and George L. Willis, "The Politics of the Twenty-second Amendment," *Western Political Quarterly* 5 (September 1952): 469.
86. Ibid., 470.
87. The Twenty-seventh Amendment, which restricts Congress' ability to raise its members' salaries, was ratified in 1992, a record 203 years after Congress proposed it in 1789.
88. A second Hoover Commission was created by Congress in 1953. Republican leaders in the House and Senate hoped that this time the commission would not be sidetracked from its mission to reduce the size of the government. These hopes were realized. Although the first Hoover Commission had become interested primarily in improving the administrative management of the executive branch, the second concentrated on issues of policy and function. At the heart of the second Hoover Commission's recommendations was the idea that many of the Roosevelt-era programs and agencies had been counterproductive. But the commission's conservative ideological approach guaranteed that it would have little influence on the Eisenhower administration, which accepted most of the changes brought by the New

Deal. See Arnold, *Making the Managerial Presidency*, 166-227.
89. Richard Neustadt, *Presidential Power and the Modern Presidents: The Politics of Leadership from Roosevelt to Reagan*, 4th ed. (New York: Free Press, 1990), 139. The first edition of this volume was published in 1960 by Wiley.
90. Marquis Childs, *Eisenhower: Captive Hero* (New York: Harcourt, Brace, 1958), 179.
91. Joseph C. Harsch, "Eisenhower's First Hundred Days," *Reporter*, May 12, 1953, 9.
92. Fred I. Greenstein, *The Hidden-Hand Presidency: Eisenhower As Leader* (New York: Basic Books, 1982).
93. Quoted in Leuchtenburg, *In the Shadow of FDR*, 49.
94. Oscar Handlin, "The Eisenhower Administration: A Self-Portrait," *Atlantic Monthly*, vol. 212, no. 5, November 1963, 68.
95. Elmo Richardson, *The Presidency of Dwight D. Eisenhower* (Lawrence: University Press of Kansas, 1979), 14.
96. Erwin C. Hargrove, *The Power of the Modern Presidency* (Philadelphia: Temple University Press, 1974), 60.
97. Leuchtenburg, *In the Shadow of FDR*, 48.
98. Alonzo L. Hamby, *Liberalism and Its Challengers: FDR to Bush*, 2d ed. (New York: Oxford University Press, 1992), 126.
99. Quoted in Stephen E. Ambrose, "The Eisenhower Revival," in *Rethinking the Presidency*, ed. Thomas E. Cronin (Boston: Little, Brown, 1982), 107.
100. Greenstein, *Hidden-Hand Presidency*, chap. 5.
101. "Remarks at Dartmouth College Commencement Exercises," Hanover, N.H., June 14, 1953, *Public Papers of the Presidents of the United States: Dwight D. Eisenhower, 1953* (Washington, D.C.: Government Printing Office, 1960), 415.
102. "Address at the Sixth National Assembly of the United Church of Women," Atlantic City, New Jersey, October 6, 1953, ibid., 639.
103. Richardson, *Presidency of Dwight D. Eisenhower*, 55.
104. Quoted in Fred I. Greenstein, "Dwight D. Eisenhower: Leadership Theorist in the White House," in Greenstein, *Leadership in the Modern Presidency*, 104-105.
105. Rossiter, *American Presidency*, 163.
106. *Brown v. Board of Education of Topeka*, 347 U.S. 483 (1954).
107. Goldsmith, *Growth of Presidential Power* 3:1619.
108. Philip G. Henderson, *Managing the Presidency: The Eisenhower Legacy—From Kennedy to Reagan* (Boulder, Colo.: Westview, 1988), 17-24.
109. Greenstein, "Nine Presidents," 307-311.
110. Ambrose, "The Eisenhower Revival," 108.
111. Richardson, *Presidency of Dwight D. Eisenhower*, 51.
112. Quoted in Gary W. Reichard, *The Reaffirmation of Republicanism: Eisenhower and the Eighty-Third Congress* (Knoxville: University of Tennessee Press, 1975), 67.

CHAPTER 12

Personalizing the Presidency:
John F. Kennedy to Jimmy Carter

In his influential book *Presidential Power*, which was first published in 1960, Richard Neustadt, a former aide in the Truman White House, declared that "the same conditions that promote [the modern president's] leadership in form preclude a guarantee of leadership in fact." [1] Neustadt's study reaffirmed Woodrow Wilson's argument at the beginning of the twentieth century that the president is responsible for moving the United States to a higher level of political discourse and national action. But Neustadt cautioned that at mid-century this obligation fell upon the president with no assurance of "an influence commensurate with services performed." In fact, the modern president could count only on being a "clerk" whose help would be demanded but not always reciprocated by others. [2]

Neustadt's solution to the dilemma of the modern presidency was for each president to struggle to overcome the political obstacles that fetter the office. It was the president's personal task to resurrect the aggressive and skillful style of leadership that Franklin D. Roosevelt had displayed, so that the disparate parts of the political system—congressional leaders, cabinet officers, party officials, and others—would "feel obliged on their responsibility" to do what the president "wants done." [3] The relatively restrained approach to the office that Dwight D. Eisenhower had taken, his popularity notwithstanding, was judged by Neustadt to guarantee political stagnation.

John F. Kennedy read Neustadt's book—indeed, some pundits believed that it was the blueprint for the vigorous and innovative style of leadership that animated his presidency. But, as Fred Greenstein has noted, *Presidential Power* mostly clarified and defended the theory of good presidential leadership that already was current— namely, "that of an informal, Rooseveltian conduct of the presidency that contrasted with current perceptions of Eisenhower's operating manner." [4] Not surprisingly, then, the effort to expand the powers of the modern executive characterized not only the Kennedy administration but also the administrations of his two successors, Lyndon B. Johnson and Richard Nixon.

By the early 1970s, however, serious doubts had arisen about the compatibility of unrestrained executive power and the public interest. Developments during the Nixon era, especially, kindled the belief that a return to the traditional separation of powers was needed to restore responsible republican government.

John F. Kennedy and the Rise of "Personal" Leadership

Kennedy was elected president in 1960 to "get this country moving again," to lift the United States out of the complacency that seemed to have settled on it during the Eisenhower years. The combination of a sluggish economy, simmering civil rights problems, and the Soviet threat had created doubts about the country's future that led the voters back to the Democratic party. In addition, the still-popular Eisenhower, who disapproved of the Twenty-second Amendment and wanted a third term, was forbidden to run again—an ironic consequence of the Republican-inspired two-term limit.[5]

Running against Vice President Richard Nixon, Kennedy campaigned on a theme of change, tying that theme to the presidency itself. The nation could not afford a president in the 1960s, he declared, "who is praised primarily for what he did not do, the disasters he prevented, the bills he vetoed—a President wishing his subordinates would produce more missiles or build more schools." Instead, Kennedy insisted, the nation "needs a Chief Executive who is the vital center of action in our whole scheme of government." The president must be "willing and able to summon his national constituency to its finest hour—to alert the people to our dangers and our opportunities—to demand of them the sacrifices that will be necessary." [6]

On November 22, 1963, less than three years after he took the oath as president, Kennedy was assassinated by Lee Harvey Oswald in Dallas, Texas. His death traumatized the nation. All of the presidents who had died in office had been deeply mourned, but only Lincoln's death aroused as profound a sense of unfulfilled promise as Kennedy's. Forty-three years old at the time of his inauguration, Kennedy was the country's youngest elected president, and the striking down of such a vital, attractive leader in the prime of life left Americans with an extraordinary sense of personal loss. Yet despite his truncated term, or perhaps because of it, Kennedy enjoys a lasting place in American culture. As one historian has observed, Kennedy is "part not of history but of myth." [7]

Twenty years after his assassination, national surveys showed that Americans regarded Kennedy as the finest of the modern presidents. Remarkably, Kennedy edged out FDR in a 1987 Harris poll as the "best" president in domestic affairs, a result that, in truth, measured only the Kennedy mystique since JFK's legislative accomplishments were modest.[8] "Deprived of the place he sought in history," the columnist James Reston wrote a year after Kennedy's death, "he has been given in compensation a place in legend." [9]

Kennedy's popularity persists not only because of his tragic death but also because of certain qualities that he displayed as president. "Beyond question," the historian Carl Brauer has written, "Kennedy was inspirational in a way that few presidents have been." [10] Franklin Roosevelt's great achievement as a moral leader was to bring the United States through the dark days of the Great Depression and World War II; in a like manner, Kennedy sought to inspire the nation to meet the challenges of the postwar era. Roosevelt's New Deal, Kennedy said in his acceptance speech at the 1960 Democratic Convention, had "promised security and succor to those in need." But more prosperous times called for a New Frontier that was "not a set of promises" but "a set of challenges": "It sums up not what I intend to offer the American people, but what I intend to ask of them. It appeals to their pride, not their pocketbook—it holds out the promise of more sacrifice instead of security." [11]

Kennedy's inaugural address, the most important speech of his presidency, placed this challenge before the nation with eloquence and grace. Uplifting and optimistic in tone, it articulated a vision that greatly augmented the fragile basis of support he had received from the election (Kennedy's margin of victory was only 120,000 votes out of the nearly 69 million cast). Both liberals and conservatives found something to applaud in the new president's celebration of nationalism, spirit of sacrifice, and sense of mission. The best-remembered passages from the address emphasized these themes:

> In the long history of the world, only a few generations have been granted the role of defending freedom in its hours of maximum danger. I do not shrink from this responsibility—I welcome it. I do not believe that any of us would exchange places with any other people or any other generation. The energy, the faith, the devotion which we bring to this endeavor will light our country and those who serve it— and the glow from that fire can truly light the world.
> And so, my fellow Americans: ask not what your country can do for you—ask what you can do for your country.[12]

The First Television President

It was not just Kennedy's words that stirred the nation but also the vibrant and reassuring image he conveyed when delivering them. His administration marked a revolutionary advance in the use of television in politics. Although Eisenhower had been the first president to appear on television regularly, "it was under and because of Kennedy that television became an essential determinant—probably the essential determinant—of a president's ability to lead the nation." [13]

Kennedy's televised speeches were one element of his strategy of public communication. But after his inauguration, the president went before the cameras only nine times to deliver a prepared address. Convinced that citizens would tire quickly of formal speechmaking, JFK relied on the press conference as his principal forum for reaching the public. He was the first president to allow press conferences to be televised without restriction, recognizing that live, unedited broadcasts of his give and take with reporters would be a superb means of addressing the nation. Eisenhower's press conferences had been televised, but they were taped and the White House retained the power to revise them for broadcast. Ike's press secretary, James C. Hagerty, believed that live television was too dangerous—the president might misspeak. But Kennedy, who had benefited greatly from his televised debates with Nixon in 1960, regarded television as an ally.

Previous presidents, notably Theodore Roosevelt and Franklin Roosevelt, had used press conferences to cultivate the journalistic fraternity, which in turn had helped them to convey their purposes to the American people. But the live, televised press conference relegated reporters to the reluctant role of stage props. Under Kennedy's auspices the press conference became the functional equivalent of the fireside chat—that is, it afforded the president a relatively informal and personal way to reach the public, over the heads of both Congress and the proprietors of the media.

The public saw and heard more of Kennedy through press conferences than in any other way. Yet he held only sixty-four of them, fewer per month than either Roosevelt, Truman, or Eisenhower. "He realized the dangers as well as the possibilities of television," the historian James Giglio has written. "Overexposure became his major concern, particularly since an expanding news format provided more opportunities to cover the presidency." [14]

Kennedy's adept and well-timed media appearances made a positive impression on the American people; public opinion surveys gave him a 91 percent approval rating for his performance in press conferences. The keys to his success were careful preparation and an ability to project extremely well on television.[15] Kennedy's pleasing personality,

Partly because of Kennedy, the executive office became more powerful but also more politically isolated from Congress and party and
more burdened by public expectations.

quick wit, and impressive knowledge of government set a standard that
his successors have struggled to meet.[16]

The Personal Presidency

Woodrow Wilson believed that the "extraordinary isolation" of the
presidency, if used effectively, allowed the president both to inspire and
to benefit from public opinion. Wilson himself and FDR had done much
to advance the president's relationship with the people. But with
Kennedy and the advent of television, what the political scientist
Theodore Lowi has called the *personal presidency* came into its own.[17]

Kennedy's effective use of television was part of the personalization
of the presidency. His presidential campaign and his governing style
also established significant precedents that amplified the power of the
executive and set its activities apart from those of party politics, the
cabinet, the departments, and Congress.

All of Kennedy's campaigns for office, including his run for the presidency, were highly personal undertakings; indeed, they were managed by members of his family, especially his brother Robert. The success of Kennedy's organization, the "Kennedy Machine" as it was called, diminished the importance of the regular party organization. In winning the Democratic nomination for president in 1960, Kennedy outmaneuvered most of the established leaders of the party, whose initial attitude toward his candidacy was skeptical, if not hostile. To thwart them, he went outside the normal party channels, using political "amateurs" to round up votes in the state primaries and, after succeeding in that arena, to force the convention to accept him as its nominee. Kennedy's triumph changed presidential politics. Henceforth, campaigns for president would be directed by each candidate's personal advisers and strategists; coordination and liaison with the party would be of secondary importance.[18]

The Kennedy organization also made its mark on the government. Most members of JFK's campaign staff were appointed to similar positions in the White House Office, which contributed to the personalization of the president's staff. To reinforce this development, more responsibility for policy making was concentrated in the executive office than had been the practice in past administrations. The hitherto anonymous White House staff, now assigned to oversee the activities of the departments and agencies, began to develop into a veritable government unto itself. For example, Kennedy's assistant for national security, McGeorge Bundy, carried out many duties that traditionally had been reserved for the secretary of state; indeed, Bundy may have been more influential in foreign policy making than the secretary of state, Dean Rusk.[19] According to Robert Kennedy, JFK "felt at the end that the ten or twelve people in the White House who worked under his direction with Mac Bundy . . . really performed all the functions of the State Department."[20]

The Kennedy Legacy

Although John Kennedy was a very popular president during his brief stay in the White House and, in the public mind, has passed from life into enshrinement as the best of the modern presidents, many aspects of his presidency were unsuccessful. For example, his administration was responsible for the disastrous invasion of Cuba on April 17, 1961, by a brigade of some 1,400 anti-communist exiles from the regime of Fidel Castro. The rebels were crushed three days after landing in Zapata Swamp at Cuba's Bay of Pigs. Their failure to overthrow Castro was a humiliating defeat for Kennedy, who had been in office for less than one hundred days.

Kennedy also can be faulted for accelerating the deployment of nuclear missiles in order to fulfill a campaign promise to close the so-called "missile gap" with the Soviet Union. The nuclear buildup was carried out, even though an intelligence analysis conducted soon after Kennedy took office revealed that the missile gap was a myth; in fact, Soviet missile development was far behind that of the United States. Yet when the Soviets responded to Kennedy's buildup with a buildup of their own, the United States was forced into a spiraling arms race.[21]

Finally, the Kennedy administration initiated the ill-fated American involvement in Vietnam. Intense pressure to intervene had been brought to bear by the U.S. military when the French colonial government collapsed in July 1954. But Eisenhower had decided to stay out of Vietnam, certain that military victory was impossible. Kennedy also doubted the wisdom of direct involvement in Vietnam, but he sent more than 16,000 military advisers to assist the South Vietnamese army in counterinsurgency warfare, then encouraged a military coup against the government of Ngo Dinh Diem in Saigon. Diem's death profoundly destabilized South Vietnam; in the view of Kennedy's successor, Lyndon Johnson, it also obligated the United States to support any subsequent regime. "Though [Kennedy] privately thought the United States 'overcommitted' in Southeast Asia," Arthur Schlesinger, Jr., a historian who served on Kennedy's staff, has written, "he permitted the commitment to grow. It was the fatal error of his presidency." [22]

Yet Kennedy did not lack for notable accomplishments as president. During the Cuban missile crisis, in particular, he led brilliantly under the most difficult of circumstances. For seven days in October 1962, after the United States discovered Soviet nuclear missiles in Cuba, the world seemed poised on the brink of a nuclear war. Kennedy and Soviet premier Nikita Khrushchev engaged in what Secretary of State Rusk later called an "eyeball to eyeball" confrontation. The impasse was resolved only when, in response to a U.S. naval quarantine of Cuba, the Soviets agreed to dismantle their missiles. Throughout the crisis, Kennedy joined firmness to restraint, a course that allowed Khrushchev to yield to the president's demands without being humiliated. As Brauer has written of Kennedy's conduct, "He looked at things from the Soviet side, compromised on secondary issues, did not play politics, and when he succeeded in getting the missiles removed, did not gloat or boast." [23]

Kennedy's triumph in the missile crisis demonstrated that he had matured considerably since the Bay of Pigs fiasco. His growth in office also was apparent when he took measures to make another such crisis less likely. Speaking at American University on June 10, 1963, Kennedy called for an end to the cold war and, in particular, for a nuclear test ban treaty that would reduce tensions with the Soviet Union. He said that both the United States and the Soviet Union had a mutual interest in halting the arms race:

> For in the final analysis, our most basic common link is that we all inhabit this small planet. We all breathe the same air. We all cherish our children's future. And we are all mortal. . . . Let us reexamine our attitude toward the cold war, remembering that we are not engaged in a debate, seeking to pile up debating points.[24]

On August 5, 1963, the United States and the Soviet Union signed the nuclear test ban treaty, their first bilateral arms control agreement. The treaty was a small step forward (it did not ban underground tests, for example), but it raised hopes for more substantial progress in the future.

To supporters of the president, the test ban treaty and the missile crisis triumph were signs of developing greatness. But Kennedy's destiny, as the journalist Theodore White observed, was to be "cut off at the promise, not after the performance. . . ." [25] One of the most frequent criticisms of Kennedy, both when he was president and after his death, was that he offered much more in the way of domestic reform than he delivered. In particular, JFK was faulted for his failures as a legislative leader. Kennedy's New Frontier program embodied the high expectations he had articulated in his inaugural address. For example, in advocating medical insurance for the elderly (Medicare) and federal aid to education, he sought to consolidate and extend the accomplishments of Roosevelt and Truman, his most recent Democratic predecessors. In other ways, however, Kennedy sought to reshape his party's liberal tradition by offering initiatives, such as the Peace Corps and civil rights legislation, that reflected the themes of social justice and national service he had injected into the 1960 presidential campaign. Some of Kennedy's legislative initiatives, including the Peace Corps, became law. But most of his important bills—those representing the heart and soul of the New Frontier—were spurned by Congress.[26]

Indeed, Kennedy's relations with Congress were extraordinarily difficult throughout his abbreviated presidency. The Democrats had a 65-35 majority in the Senate and a 263-174 advantage in the House. But 21 of the Democratic senators and 99 of the Democratic representatives were southern conservatives, and most of them joined with the Republicans to oppose Kennedy's liberal agenda.

Kennedy's precarious position in Congress was revealed within days of his becoming president. The administration, with Speaker Sam Rayburn's support, moved to take control of the House Rules Committee, the conservative coalition's principal legislative stronghold. In the previous Congress, the Rules Committee, which had the power to prevent legislation from reaching the floor for debate, had eight

Democratic and four Republican members. But two of the Democrats were southern conservatives, who joined with Republicans to block reform legislation. At the outset of the Kennedy administration, Rayburn proposed to add three new members, two of them administration loyalists, to the committee, which would provide an 8-7 majority for most of Kennedy's bills. Yet even with the new president's open and active support and with Rayburn drawing on all his considerable accumulated store of good will, the administration won the House vote on expanding the committee by only five votes, 217-212. As Kennedy told one of his aides, the outcome was not so much a show of strength as a measure of "what we are up against." [27]

Kennedy's troubles in persuading Congress to enact his domestic program were not just a matter of stubborn legislative resistance to change. Although he was superb at planning and running a presidential campaign, Kennedy was bored by and impatient with congressional politics. "The very qualities of appearance, style and cast of mind that won [Kennedy] the admiration of the intellectual and diplomatic worlds somehow marked him as an outsider in his dealings with the Congress," noted Reston.[28] By 1963, the president's program was in deep trouble: several measures that Kennedy sought, particularly Medicare, federal aid to education, and civil rights, remained in legislative limbo at the time of his death.

Before he went to Dallas, JFK was looking forward to the 1964 election, which he hoped would bring enough new liberal Democrats into Congress to move the New Frontier forward. He also talked privately about a complete postelection military withdrawal from Vietnam. It is impossible to know whether Kennedy would have accomplished his domestic goals and avoided the travail of Vietnam had he lived. But the inability to deliver on promises was to become a recurring trait of the modern presidency.

Partly because of Kennedy, the evolution of the presidency had given rise to a more powerful, prominent, and yet politically isolated president. The modern executive was the object of expanding public expectations about government; it also had been transformed into an elaborate and far-reaching institution with considerable autonomous power. At the same time, however, the president was increasingly cut off from Congress and the party, which made it difficult to satisfy public demands by enacting lasting reforms. Kennedy did not create most of these conditions. But his legacy to his successors was a significant personalization of the presidency that greatly accentuated its separation from the other centers of American political power.

During Kennedy's one thousand days as president, the great promise of the personal presidency was widely celebrated. But developments within a few years of his death—the escalation of the Vietnam

War and the divisions it opened in American society, the growing tendency of both liberals and conservatives to discredit government, and the popular disillusionment with presidential power—were to reveal the less desirable consequences of the Kennedy administration's innovations.

Lyndon B. Johnson and Presidential Government

The tragedy in Dallas on November 22, 1963, left the presidency in the hands of Lyndon Johnson, a Texan whom Kennedy had selected as his vice-presidential running mate in 1960 to balance the ticket geographically. LBJ's effective campaigning in the South, especially in Texas and Louisiana, was crucial to the Democrats' narrow victory against Nixon. Before becoming vice president, Johnson was known as a consummate political operator in the Senate, where as majority leader he exercised enormous influence during the Eisenhower years. It remained to be seen, however, whether the quintessential legislative insider could adapt successfully to the requirements of the presidency.

Johnson's challenges as a successor president were compounded by the bitterness that many liberals felt about a southern power broker taking the place of their fallen leader. Blacks, especially, whose hopes for equality and justice had been raised by Kennedy, were disconcerted, as Johnson put it, to awake "one morning to discover that their future was in the hands of a President born in the South." [29] After all, it was southern Democrats in Congress, even more than conservative Republicans, who had blocked Kennedy's civil rights legislation.

Despite these obstacles, Johnson quickly grasped the reins of power. Indeed, he did more than reassure the nation and build confidence in his leadership. "In the wake of Kennedy's assassination," the presidential scholar Jeffrey Tulis has written, "Lyndon Johnson was able to turn the country's grief into a commitment to a moral crusade." [30] Nor did Johnson's crusade extend only to completing the New Frontier or even the New Deal. As the historian William Leuchtenburg has observed: "He aimed instead to be 'the greatest of them all, the whole bunch of them.' And to be the greatest president in history, he needed not to match Roosevelt's performance but to surpass it." [31]

In many ways Johnson was inadequate to the demands of the modern presidency, especially as a public educator. Unlike other twentieth-century presidents who wanted to remake the nation, LBJ neglected, even scorned, the "bully pulpit." Yet Johnson profoundly influenced the modern presidency in other ways. He more than continued the power and independence of the executive office. Regrettably, his failings also brought into serious question—for the first time since the 1930s—the widespread assumption that the public interest is served

On November 22, 1963, Lyndon Johnson took the presidential oath of office aboard *Air Force One* from federal district judge Sarah T. Hughes. On Johnson's left is Jacqueline Kennedy.

whenever the president dominates the affairs of state. The disillusionment with executive power that commenced late in Johnson's tenure actually began to unravel some of the conditions that had given rise to the modern presidency.

The Great Society

Johnson defined as his first task the enactment of Kennedy's New Frontier, including civil rights, a tax cut, and Medicare. He succeeded: Congress passed all of these controversial measures in short order. Especially notable was the Civil Rights Act of 1964. When Kennedy died, the bill was bogged down in the Senate. But, invoking the memory of the fallen leader and bringing to bear his own extraordinary skill and experience in legislative politics, Johnson prevailed. The new president's greatest strength as majority leader of the Senate had been personal persuasion, a talent he now used to convince the Senate Republican leader, Everett Dirksen, to support the bill and to enlist moderate Republicans in the cause. Dirksen's support sounded the death knell for the conservative coalition against civil rights. Congress passed the bill quickly, and Johnson signed it on July 2, 1964.[32]

The enactment of the Civil Rights Act of 1964 signaled a dramatic reinvigoration of the president's preeminence as legislative leader. Equally important in the long run was that the act enlisted the president and several executive agencies in the ongoing effort to ban racial discrimination. It empowered the federal bureaucracy—especially the Department of Justice, the Department of Health, Education and Welfare, and the newly formed Equal Employment Opportunity Commission—to assist the courts by creating parallel enforcement mechanisms for civil rights. These proved to be effective. For example, within four years the executive branch under Johnson accomplished more desegregation in the southern schools than the courts had in fourteen.[33]

Johnson's successful battle for civil rights dazzled the liberals in his party. The presidential scholar and self-professed Kennedy loyalist James MacGregor Burns wrote, "What will baffle the historian ... I think, will be how the complete Senate man moved so surely into the presidency and began to employ from the start the levers of presidential influence." [34] But civil rights was only the beginning. "Many people felt we should rest after the victory of the 1964 Civil Rights Act, take it easy on Congress, and leave some breathing space for the bureaucracy and nation," wrote Johnson. "But, there was no time to rest." [35]

Johnson's desire to move beyond Kennedy's agenda toward what he called the "Great Society" made him impatient to push on. The 1964 election, in which he and the Democrats won a resounding victory over the Republicans and their candidate, the arch-conservative senator Barry Goldwater of Arizona, provided the opportunity to do so. The election gave LBJ, who won more than 60 percent of the vote, the most convincing popular mandate in history—more decisive, even, than FDR's triumph in 1936. The Democrats gained thirty-seven seats in the House and one in the Senate, which left them with two-to-one margins in both houses of Congress.

Johnson had first unveiled his hopes for a Great Society on May 22, 1964, in a commencement speech at the University of Michigan. His bold vision took the reform aspirations of the past only as a point of departure:

> The Great Society rests on abundance and liberty for all. It demands an end of poverty and racial justice, to which we are totally committed in our time. But this is just the beginning. . . .
>   The Great Society is a place where every child can find knowledge to enrich his mind and to enlarge his talents. It is a place where

leisure is a welcome chance to build and reflect, not a feared cause of boredom and restlessness. It is a place where the city of man serves not only the needs of the body and the demands of commerce but the desire for beauty and the hunger of community.[36]

Johnson's vision gave rise to a legislative program of extraordinary breadth, which he placed before the Eighty-ninth Congress when it convened in January 1965. Congress responded enthusiastically. "No [Congress] since Reconstruction," Theodore White observed, "or perhaps since Roosevelt's seventy-third Congress of 1933-34, did more to reorder the nation...."[37] In 1965 alone, Congress passed eighty of Johnson's legislative proposals, denying him only three. The new laws included important policy departures such as Medicaid, the Voting Rights Act of 1965, the Older Americans Act, the Elementary and Secondary Education Act, the War on Poverty, the Air Pollution Control Act, and legislation to establish the Department of Transportation and the Department of Housing and Urban Development.

Johnson and the Institution of the Presidency

Johnson's domination of the political process had enduring effects on the presidency, some of which extended developments that had begun with Kennedy. Kennedy's ambition to "get this country moving again" had led him to design a freewheeling process of policy innovation that departed from the existing practice of letting domestic proposals evolve methodically through the departments and agencies, then undergo screening and clarification in the Bureau of the Budget. Johnson went much further. More and more, policies began to be invented by the White House staff, which was committed to moving quickly on the president's agenda. Concomitantly, career officials in the departments and agencies and professional policy analysts in the Budget Bureau became less influential.

The personalization of presidential policy making was not only extended during the Johnson years, it was institutionalized. Joseph Califano, the chief White House aide for domestic affairs, supervised the creation of several task forces, composed of government officials and prominent academics, which were charged to formulate innovative proposals for the president's domestic agenda. These task forces produced reports and recommendations in virtually every area of domestic policy, including poverty, environmental quality, urban planning, and aid to education. The Johnson administration took great care to protect the task forces from political pressures, even keeping their proceedings secret. Moreover, participants in the process were told not to worry about whether their recommendations would be acceptable to Congress or to party leaders.[38]

Several task force proposals became public policy; indeed, they formed the heart of the Great Society program. Almost as important, however, was the revolutionary character of the process itself. By placing policy development under White House supervision, free from traditional institutional restraints, the task force approach evaded what Johnson and his advisers regarded as the timidity and conservatism of the old system. Califano's group was the precursor of the Domestic Council, which was established by Johnson's successor, Richard Nixon, and of the domestic policy staffs that have been a part of subsequent administrations.[39] As James Gaither, an assistant to Califano, observed:

> I would have to say that I regard the change [in legislative program development] as one of the most significant institutional changes of the presidency. . . . I think it reflected the president's experience in the Congress as well as the Executive branch and his belief that the traditional processes were not producing the kind of innovative and imaginative new approaches that were necessary to deal with the very significant problems that were facing the country.[40]

The early years of the Johnson administration marked the historical height of "presidential government." To be sure, the White House and the Executive Office of the President had been increasingly active in formulating and carrying out programs since the administration of Franklin Roosevelt. Under Johnson, however, political and policy responsibility was concentrated in the presidency to an unprecedented extent. Major domestic policy departures were conceived in the White House, hastened through Congress by the extraordinary legislative skill of the president and his sophisticated congressional liaison team, and administered by new or refurbished executive agencies that had been designed to respond to the president's directives. Finally, Johnson established a personal governing coalition. As the columnist David Broder wrote in 1966, more than was true of any of his predecessors, including Kennedy, LBJ's leadership and program depended "for its success largely on the skill, negotiating ability, and maneuvering of the president."[41]

Soon, however, Johnson overextended himself. Ironically, the personalization of his presidency contributed to its undoing. Although LBJ was a gifted government insider, he could not rouse the public in the way that was required by the office he had helped to create. As his aide Harry MacPherson noted, Johnson was incapable of "rising above the dirt of 'political governing,' so that he could inspire the nation."[42] His best words and teachings were laws and policies, but he was unable to cultivate the stable base of popular support that his domestic program ultimately required in order to be implemented effectively. Even Johnson realized that his most serious weakness as president was "a general inability to stimulate, inspire, and unite all the public in the country. . . ."[43]

Since the days of its inception under Theodore Roosevelt and Woodrow Wilson, the modern presidency has been grounded in a concept of executive power that enjoins the president to be both the educator and the instrument of the popular will. Johnson, however, was inclined to ignore the normal tasks of public leadership in the pursuit of policies and programs that he hoped would serve the nation's long-term interests. Yet LBJ's "gargantuan aspirations" actually magnified the political burdens of the modern executive. His obvious domination of the political process ensured that he, not Congress, would be blamed if the Great Society programs failed. And fail many of them did, the victims of hasty packaging and unrealistic goals.[44]

The Fall of Lyndon Johnson

The war in Vietnam clearly demonstrated both Johnson's shortcomings and the more troubling aspects of presidential government. In 1965, the president concluded that a communist takeover in South Vietnam could be prevented only by committing a large contingent of U.S. forces to combat. Johnson's extraordinary ability to build a governing coalition in 1965 helped to sustain the Americanization of the war. With little resistance from either Congress, or, at the beginning, the public, the troop commitment rose from 23,000 at the end of 1964 to 181,000 a year later, to 389,000 a year after that, and to 500,000 by the end of 1967.

The war in Southeast Asia became, in an unprecedented way, the president's war. Harry Truman at least had been able to claim that the United States was "carrying out an obligation for the United Nations" when he deployed troops to Korea. But in Vietnam, the political scientist Richard Pious has written, "no treaty obligations or other commitments required the United States to intervene." [45] Nor did Congress ever declare war. It passed only the Gulf of Tonkin Resolution, which was rushed through both houses on August 7, 1964, after an alleged communist attack on two U.S. destroyers off the coast of North Vietnam. The resolution stated that Congress "approves and supports the determination of the President, as Commander-in-Chief, to take all necessary measures to repel any armed attack against the forces of the United States and to prevent further aggression." Johnson, who believed that Truman had erred politically in not asking Congress to support the Korean War, was anxious to have a legislative endorsement.

But the Gulf of Tonkin Resolution was hardly "the functional equivalent of a declaration of war," as Under Secretary of State Nicholas Katzenbach claimed at a Senate hearing in 1967.[46] Indeed, Johnson believed that although the resolution was a useful device to protect his political flank, he already had all the authority he needed to deploy troops in Vietnam. In March 1966, for example, the State Department's legal adviser wrote, "There can be no question in present circumstances of the President's authority to commit U.S. forces to the defense of South Vietnam. The grant of authority to the President in Article 2 of the Constitution extends to the actions of the United States currently undertaken in Vietnam." Johnson embraced this position at a news conference on August 18, 1967. Speaking of the Gulf of Tonkin Resolution, he said,

> We stated then and we repeat now, we did not think the resolution was necessary to do what we did and what we're doing. But we thought it was desirable and we thought if we were going to ask them [Congress] to stay the whole route and if we expected them to be there on the landing we ought to ask them to be there on the take off.[47]

By early 1968, however, the military situation in Vietnam had deteriorated and Johnson's political consensus at home had crumbled. On March 31, he announced that he would not be a candidate for reelection. But Johnson never lost his faith in the extraordinary powers of the presidency, nor, even under the stress of war, did he ever give up his dream of the Great Society. Indeed, his insistence on trying to have "guns and butter"—the Vietnam War *and* the Great Society—subjected the economy to strains of inflation that were aggravated by his reluctance to ask Congress to enact a tax increase.

The Twenty-fifth Amendment

One enduring legacy of the Johnson years was the Twenty-fifth Amendment, which was proposed by Congress in 1965 and ratified by the states in 1967. The main purpose of the amendment was to provide for two separate but related situations: vacancies in the vice presidency and presidential disabilities.[48]

The need for a reform like the Twenty-fifth Amendment was long-standing. The original Constitution had stated in Article II, section 1, paragraph 6, that, as with presidential deaths, resignations, and impeachments, "in Case of the . . . Inability [of the president] to discharge the Powers and Duties of the said Office, the Same shall devolve on the Vice President. . . ." The Constitution gave no guidance about what a disability was, how the vice president was to step in should the need arise, or even whether the vice president was actually to become president or was merely to assume the powers and duties of the office until the president recovered. (Did "the Same" refer to "the Powers and Duties" or to "the said Office"?) During the long disabilities of Presidents James A. Garfield and Woodrow Wilson, the problems raised by the Constitution's vagueness became dramatically apparent.[49]

Vice-presidential vacancies also were a frequent historical occurrence. The vice presidency becomes vacant when the president dies, resigns, or is impeached and removed, or when the vice president dies, resigns, or is impeached and removed. Such circumstances left the nation without a vice president sixteen times between 1789 and 1963: seven times because the vice president died, eight times because the president died, and once because the vice president resigned.[50] By merest chance, a double vacancy in the presidency and vice presidency never occurred.

Public and congressional concern about the problems of presidential disability and vice-presidential vacancy was minor and episodic through most of U.S. history, usually rising for brief periods while a president was disabled, then waning when the crisis passed. From 1945 to 1963, however, a combination of events took place that placed these problems high on the nation's constitutional agenda.

The invention and spread of nuclear weapons and intercontinental ballistic missiles after 1945 heightened concern that an able president be available at all times to wield the powers of the office. Then, in rapid succession, President Eisenhower suffered a series of temporarily disabling illnesses—a heart attack in 1955, an ileitis attack and operation in 1956, and a stroke in 1957. The assassination of President Kennedy in 1963 left the nation with a president, Lyndon Johnson, who had a history of heart trouble and whose legally designated successors, under the Presidential Succession Act of 1947, were an old and ailing Speaker of the House, John W. McCormack, and, as Senate president pro tempore, an even older and more ill Carl Hayden.

In December 1963, less than a month after the Kennedy assassination, Birch Bayh, a Democratic senator from Indiana and the chair of the Senate Judiciary Committee's Subcommittee on Constitutional Amendments, announced that he would hold hearings in early 1964 to consider constitutional remedies to the disability and vacancy problems. Coordinating his efforts with those of a special committee of the American Bar Association, Bayh drafted an amendment that formed the basis for the subcommittee's hearings and that, with minor modifications, later entered the Constitution as the Twenty-fifth Amendment.

The Senate approved the amendment on September 29, 1964, by a vote of 65-0. The House did not act in 1964, possibly because to propose an amendment to fill vice-presidential vacancies would be perceived as a slap at Speaker McCormack, who was first in line to succeed President Johnson. In 1965, however, after the election of Vice President Hubert H. Humphrey in November 1964, the House joined the Senate (which had reaffirmed its support of the amendment by a vote of 72-0 on February 19) and on April 13 voted its approval by a margin of 368-29.

Presidential Disabilities

From the beginning, most of Congress's concerns about the Twenty-fifth Amendment were directed at its disability provisions. As drafted by Bayh (and eventually enacted by Congress), three very different situations were covered by sections 3 and 4 of the amendment. In the first, the president is "unable to discharge the powers and duties of his office" and recognizes the condition, say, before or after surgery. A simple letter from the president to the Speaker of the House and the president pro tempore of the Senate is sufficient to make the vice president the acting president; a subsequent presidential letter declaring that the disability is ended restores the president's powers.

In the second situation, the president is disabled but, perhaps having lost consciousness, is unable to say so. Should this happen, either the vice president or the head of an executive department may call a meeting of the vice president and cabinet to discuss the situation. If both the vice president and a majority of the heads of the departments declare the president disabled, the vice president becomes acting president—again, until the president writes to congressional leaders to announce an end to the disability.

The third situation covered by the disability portions of the amendment is the most troubling. It involves instances (such as questionable mental health or sudden and severe physical disability) in which the president's ability to fulfill the office is in doubt—the president claims to be able, but the vice president and the cabinet judge differently. The amendment provides that should this happen, the vice president would become acting president pending a congressional resolution of the matter. Congress would have a maximum of three weeks to decide whether the president was disabled, with two-thirds votes of both the House and the Senate needed to overturn the president's judgment. But because the Twenty-fifth Amendment only transfers power to the vice president for as long as the president is disabled, a subsequent claim of restored health by the president would set the whole process in motion again.

Some critics of the Bayh proposal argued that it vested too much power in the executive branch to make disability determinations. Suggestions were offered to create a disability commission that included members of all three branches, perhaps joined by a number of physicians. Bayh defended his proposal by saying that any move to strip power from the president by officials outside the administration risked violating the constitutional principle of separation of powers. In the end, both to satisfy the critics and to preclude the possibility that a president might fire the cabinet in order to forestall a disability declaration, the amendment empowered Congress, at its discretion, to substitute another body for the cabinet.

Interestingly, the Twenty-fifth Amendment, although creating an elaborate set of procedures for disability determinations, includes no definition of *disability*. It is clear from the congressional debate that disability is not to be equated with incompetence, laziness, unpopularity, or impeachable conduct. As to what disability is, Congress thought that any definition it might write into the Constitution in 1965 would likely be rendered obsolete by changes in medical science and technology.

Vice-Presidential Vacancies

Widespread agreement existed in Congress about the need to replace the vice president when the office became vacant, both to increase the likelihood of a smooth succession to the presidency, if needed, by a member of the president's party and to ensure that the presidential disability provisions of the amendment would always have a vice president on hand to execute them. Bayh's proposal—that the president nominate a new vice president when the office becomes vacant and that a majority of both houses of Congress, voting separately, confirm the nomination—prevailed and became section 2 of the amendment, but not before consideration was given to a variety of other suggestions to have Congress or the electoral college from the previous election choose the vice president. Proposals to impose a time limit on Congress either to vote on a president's nominee for vice president or to forfeit its right to reject the nomination also were considered and rejected.

No serious opposition to the Twenty-fifth Amendment arose during the ratification process. The needed approval of thirty-eight states was attained on February 10, 1967, barely a year and a half after Congress proposed the amendment. Little did any of those who were involved in its passage realize that an extraordinary series of events would cause the vice presidency to become vacant twice in the next seven years.

The Presidency of Richard Nixon

The legacy of the Johnson years was more than legal and constitutional. Soon after LBJ left the White House, one of his assistants, George Reedy, wrote, "We may well be witnessing the first lengthening shadows that will become the twilight of the presidency." [51] The failure in Vietnam had fostered public cynicism about the merits of presidential policies, opposition to the unilateral use of presidential power, and a greater inclination in the press to challenge the wisdom and even the veracity of presidential statements and proposals.[52] Yet much still was demanded of presidents—they remained at the center of citizens' ever-expanding expectations of government.

The 1968 Election: Party Reform and Divided Government

The 1968 election dramatized the political disarray in which Johnson had left the country. The Democratic nominee for president, Vice President Hubert Humphrey, led a bitterly divided party. Its convention in Chicago was ravaged by controversy, both within the hall and out on the streets, where antiwar demonstrators clashed violently with the Chicago police. Without contesting a single primary, Humphrey was nominated by the regular party leaders, who still controlled a majority of the delegates and who preferred him to the antiwar candidate, Sen. Eugene McCarthy. (Humphrey's more powerful opponent, Sen. Robert Kennedy, had been assassinated on June 4, the night of the California primary.)

Politically, Humphrey was damaged goods. As Johnson's vice president, he found it difficult to distance himself from "Johnson's war." Unwilling to embrace the war, unable to make a clean break, he looked merely weak. Humphrey was rejected not only by the antiwar wing of his party but also by conservative Democrats, many of whom looked with favor upon the third-party candidacy of the segregationist Alabama governor, George Wallace.

Humphrey's controversial nomination and the failure of his general election campaign against the Republican candidate, former vice president Richard Nixon, gave rise to important institutional reforms. The rules of the Democratic party were revised to make its presidential nominating conventions more representative of the party's rank and file. The new rules eventually caused a majority of states to change from selecting delegates in closed councils of party regulars to electing them in direct primaries. Although the Democrats initiated these changes, many were codified in state laws that affected the Republican party almost as much.

The declining influence of the traditional party organizations was apparent not only in the new nominating rules but also in the perceptions and habits of voters. The 1968 election marked the beginning of an increased tendency for voters to "split their tickets"—that is, to divide their votes among the parties. The trend toward ticket splitting has continued into the present: since 1968, the electorate has tended to place the presidency in Republican hands and Congress under the control of Democrats, a historically unprecedented pattern of national politics.

Divided government profoundly affected the course of the Nixon administration, exacerbating the problems of modern presidential government that had become so obvious during the Johnson years. Despite the Democratic disarray in 1968, Nixon did not win a decisive mandate to govern. The Democrats retained clear control of both houses of Congress, making Nixon the first new president since Zachary Taylor in 1848 to be elected without a majority for his party in either the House or the Senate.

Congress was not the only rival for power within the government that the new president faced. Because the country had elected only one other Republican since 1932, the departments and agencies of the executive branch included a large number of Democrats. Most of them were protected by civil service procedures, which had been extended "upward, outward and downward" since the New Deal to encompass almost all of the federal work force. Moreover, as the administrative historian Paul Van Riper has observed, because patronage since the 1930s had been "a sort of intellectual and ideological patronage rather than the more traditional partisan type," the bureaucracy had been infused with a strong liberal bias.[53] Eisenhower had faced pockets of bureaucratic resistance, but the magnitude of the opposition was much more threatening to a conservative Republican president whose party did not control either house of Congress.

In his memoirs Nixon explained in colorful terms that one of his administration's most important tasks was to place its stamp on the federal bureaucracy as rapidly as possible:

> I urged the new Cabinet members to move quickly to replace holdover bureaucrats with people who believed in what we were trying to do. I warned that if we did not act quickly, they would become captives of the bureaucracy they were trying to change.... If we don't get rid of those people, they will either sabotage us from within, or they'll just sit back on their well-paid asses and wait for the next election to bring back their old bosses.[54]

All the more galling to the Nixon White House, then, was the ease with which the president's own appointees in the departments and agencies were coopted by the civil servants, who managed to enlist them as allies against the administration's policies. John Ehrlichman, who eventually became Nixon's domestic policy adviser, remarked at a press briefing late in 1972 that after the administration officials were appointed and had their pictures taken with the president, "we only see them at the annual White House Christmas Party; they go off and marry the natives." [55]

The New Federalism

The first Republican president of the New Deal era, Dwight Eisenhower, often spoke of "restoring the balance" between the branches by returning authority from the president to Congress. To be sure, Eisenhower eventually accepted the responsibilities of the modern executive, especially as he came to realize that even a conservative president had to exert strong leadership if he wanted to delimit the boundaries of the federal government's responsibility. But Eisenhower was a reluctant modern president: his "hidden-hand" approach emphasized both flexible accommodation to the New Deal and respect for the other institutions of American government.

Nixon, in contrast, aggressively sought to expand presidential power. At the time he took office, the New Deal approach to the modern welfare state was being seriously questioned, even by liberals. The new intellectual climate seemed to present an opportunity to change domestic policy significantly. Moreover, if Eisenhower was cautious almost to a fault, Nixon, as he told the journalist Stewart Alsop in 1958, was "a chance taker." [56] His entire political career was punctuated by personal crises and bold responses. "It is therefore not surprising," the historian Joan Hoff-Wilson has written, "that as president he rationalized many of his foreign and domestic initiatives as crises (or at least intolerable impasses) that could be resolved only by dramatic and sometimes drastic measures." [57]

Nixon made a more determined effort than Eisenhower to use the presidency as a lever for conservative public policy. Indeed, he was the first Republican president since Theodore Roosevelt to embrace a broad understanding of executive authority. But in contrast to TR, who also was the first chief executive of either party to regard the presidency as the cockpit of national leadership for social reform, Nixon sought to recast the office as the center of growing skepticism about reform.

Even Nixon, however, was not rigidly opposed to the welfare state. The main purpose of his major domestic policy initiative, the New Federalism, was to sort out the responsibilities of government so that national problems would be handled by the national government and problems that were more suited to decentralized solutions would be handled by state and local authorities. Welfare, which Nixon believed required a single set of standards, was an example of the former; job training, which he thought would benefit from a more flexible approach, typified the latter. As Nixon said of welfare in a March 1972 address to Congress:

> While decentralized management is highly desirable in many fields and is indeed central to my philosophy of government, I believe that many of these problems in welfare administration can best be solved by using a national automated payments system, which would produce economies and considerably increase both equity of treatment and tightened administration. [58]

Nixon's New Federalism was conservative mainly in its challenge to the New Deal presumption that social problems invariably are addressed most effectively at the national level. This challenge was enough, however, to provoke powerful opposition in the Democratic Congress and, especially, in the specialized bureaucracies of the executive branch, which would have lost power to the states and localities if the New Federalism had been enacted.[59]

Interestingly, Nixon's commitment to decentralization in the federal system went hand-in-hand with his desire to centralize power in the White House. He was convinced that the federal government and its special interests had grown so powerful that only a very strong president could "reverse the flow of power and resources from the states and communities to Washington." [60] Leonard Garment, a member of the president's legal staff, observed that "the central paradox of the Nixon administration was that in order to reduce *federal* power, it was first necessary to increase *presidential* power." Or, as Nixon himself said, "Bringing power to the White House was necessary to dish it out." [61]

Nixon and Vietnam

Nixon's aggrandizement of presidential power extended into foreign policy. Certainly it was in his political self-interest to end the war in Vietnam as soon as possible. "I am not going to end up like LBJ," Nixon once said, "holed up in the White House afraid to show my face on the street. I'm going to stop that war. Fast." [62]

But Nixon was no more successful than Johnson in obtaining what he called "peace with honor"—that is, a way to withdraw U.S. troops without losing South Vietnam to the Communists. The "honor" component of this goal was of primary importance to Nixon. He and his national security adviser, Henry Kissinger, believed that unless they could extricate the United States from the war in a manner that demonstrated resoluteness of purpose and certainty of action they would lose respect abroad from friends and foes alike. "Ending the war honorably," Kissinger argued, "is essential for the peace of the world. Any other solution may unloose forces that would complicate the prospects of international order." [63]

Vietnam consumed Nixon's first term, from January 20, 1969, until the war finally was concluded, at least formally, on January 27, 1973. In the interim, Nixon actually escalated the U.S. involvement by secretly bombing North Vietnamese military enclaves in Cambodia, a neighboring neutral country. When bombing failed to do the job, Nixon told the nation on April 30, 1970, that he was sending troops to invade Cambodia, a militarily futile venture that provoked massive antiwar demonstrations in the United States and an unprecedentedly hostile reaction in Congress.

Nixon's policies in Vietnam not only reinforced but made more rigid and controversial his aggressive use of presidential power. Like Truman and Johnson, he believed that in time of war the president may assume extralegal powers. But, although Nixon was a wartime president for all but twenty months of his five and a half years in the White House, he was to find, as Truman and Johnson had before him, that public acceptance of a claim to sweeping executive power does not redound automatically to a president who prosecutes an unpopular, undeclared war.

Nixon's determination to expand the boundaries of presidential power in the face of growing political resistance encouraged him to pursue his domestic and foreign policies by executive fiat. In doing so, he effected significant changes in the organization and conduct of the presidency. But he also planted the seeds of his own disgrace and resignation in 1974.[64]

Nixon and the Administrative Presidency

Nixon's "administrative presidency" was born of his inability to persuade Congress to enact the New Federalism. Although Nixon took a legislative approach during his first two years as president, most of his proposals bogged down on Capitol Hill. In response, he shifted to a strategy that would achieve his objectives through administrative action. As the scholar-practitioner Richard Nathan has noted, "Nixon came to the conclusion sometime in 1971 that in many areas of government, particularly domestic affairs, *operations is policy.* Many day-to-day management tasks for domestic programs—for example regulation writing, grant approval, and budget appointment—are substantive and therefore involve policy." [65]

The first phase of Nixon's administrative strategy was to expand and reorganize the Executive Office of the President (EOP) so that it could preempt the traditional responsibilities of the departments and agencies. The staff of the White House Office was doubled from 292 under Johnson to 583 by the end of Nixon's first term. With size came power. Nixon loyalists in the White House and in the other agencies of the EOP not only formulated policy, as had been the case in the Johnson administration, but tried to carry out policy as well.

In foreign affairs, Kissinger created the first completely White House-dominated system of policy making. Since Kennedy, the president's national security adviser and his aides had taken on an increasing share of the responsibilities of the State Department. But Nixon and

Kissinger built a foreign policy staff of unprecedented size and power. So marginal was the State Department that Secretary William Rogers was not even informed in advance of the administration's most innovative diplomatic initiative—the opening to China, which Nixon visited in February 1972 after nearly a quarter-century of fierce hostility between the United States and the communist Chinese government that had taken power in 1949.[66]

The staff of the newly formed Domestic Council, which was headed by John Ehrlichman, took charge of domestic policy making. In addition, the Bureau of the Budget was reorganized and expanded to strengthen the president's influence in domestic affairs. On July 1, 1970, by executive order, BOB became OMB, the Office of Management and Budget, with a new supervisory layer of presidentially appointed assistant directors for policy inserted between the OMB director and the office's senior civil servants. Consequently, the budget office not only assumed additional responsibility for administrative management but also became more responsive to the president.

By itself, the swelling of the Executive Office of the President did not effect full presidential control of public policy; recalcitrant bureaucrats and their allies in Congress still were able to resist many of Nixon's efforts to seize the levers of administrative power. Two weeks before the 1968 election, former president Eisenhower had written to Nixon that he hoped for, and expected, a victory so sweeping that it would give the president "a strong, clear mandate" and a Republican Congress. Eisenhower noted that such a victory would help Nixon to "change the ingrained power structure of the federal government (the heritage of the years of Democratic rule), placing more responsibility at state and local levels." [67] But, befitting his four-year-long emphasis on an autonomous presidency, even Nixon's landslide reelection in 1972 did little to help his party. The Republicans failed to make inroads in the House, the Senate, or the state legislatures.

Still lacking the support he needed from Congress to become an effective legislative leader, Nixon resolved to carry the administrative presidency one step further. Early in his second term he undertook a reorganization to re-create the bureaucracy in his own image. Making massive changes in personnel, the president moved proven loyalists into the departments and agencies, then consolidated the leadership of the bureaucracy into a "supercabinet" of four secretaries whose job was to implement all of the administration's policies. One of these "supersecretaries" was Kissinger, who became secretary of state while retaining his position as the assistant to the president for national security affairs. As such, Kissinger became fully responsible, in a formal as well as an informal sense, for foreign policy, second only to Nixon himself.

An Imperial Presidency?

Nixon's attempt to extend the bounds of presidential authority, and, by so doing, to achieve his political and policy objectives unilaterally, has been widely regarded as an unprecedented usurpation of power and, ultimately, as a direct cause of the Watergate scandal, which forced him to resign from office. It was, to be sure, both the improprieties of the president's personal reelection organization, the Committee to Re-elect the President (CREEP)—particularly its attempt to bug telephones in the offices of the Democratic National Committee—and the subsequent efforts by the president and his aides to cover up the break-in, that brought down the Nixon administration.

But Nixon's version of the administrative presidency was not entirely new; in important respects it was a logical extension of the evolving modern presidency. CREEP's complete autonomy from the regular Republican organization was merely the culmination of the recent history of presidential preemption of the traditional responsibilities of the national party committees. As for the post-reelection phase of Nixon's administrative reform strategy, in which the president concentrated managerial authority in the hands of a few White House aides and cabinet supersecretaries, it simply extended the recent practice of reconstructing the executive branch to be a more formidable instrument of presidential government. The irony was that the strategy of pursuing policy goals through administration, which had been invented mainly by Roosevelt, Johnson, and other Democrats, was considered especially suitable by a Republican president who faced a Congress and a bureaucracy that were determined to preserve those Democratic presidents' programs.

After witnessing the indiscretions of the Johnson and Nixon years, the historian Arthur Schlesinger, Jr., until then an eloquent defender of strong presidential leadership, wrote in 1973, "In the last years presidential primacy, so indispensable to the political order, has turned into presidential supremacy. The constitutional presidency—as events so apparently disparate as the Indochina War and the Watergate affair showed—has become the imperial presidency and threatens to be the revolutionary presidency." [68]

In truth, as Nixon learned to his regret, the federal government could not be remade by executive fiat. The modern presidency was never truly imperial; its power depended on broad agreement among Congress, the bureaucracy, and the courts that responsibilities should be delegated to the executive. By the time Johnson left office, the political environment of the presidency had become less supportive. Nixon only strengthened the opposition to the unilateral use of presidential power by further attenuating the bonds that tied the president to Congress, the party system, and the American people.

More than anything else, perhaps, Nixon's bitter relations with Congress were the source of his downfall. His early inability to win support on Capitol Hill led him to construe the powers of his office much too broadly, which only aggravated the relationship. Nixon's use of his power as commander in chief to bomb and invade Cambodia provoked a major legislative protest. So did his sweeping application of the president's traditional right to impound—that is, not spend—funds that had been appropriated by Congress.

Nixon's impoundment of funds, unlike the use of this power by several of his predecessors, was not for the purpose of economy and efficiency; it was an attempt to contravene the policies of the Democratic Congress by undoing the legislative process. Nixon's assault on the Office of Economic Opportunity (OEO), the agency responsible for leading the War on Poverty and a symbol of the Great Society, manifested his determination to challenge Congress for the right to govern. Congress had appropriated funds to continue the OEO, but Nixon had the agency's acting director, Howard Phillips, issue orders to dismantle it. At the same time, Nixon refused to nominate Phillips as the permanent OEO director, because the nomination would have been rejected by the Senate.[69]

Thus, Watergate or no Watergate, there still would have been a war between Nixon and Congress. Both sides had geared themselves up for a constitutional struggle before anything was known about the Watergate affair. Indeed, Congress's willingness to take the extraordinary step of removing a president in 1974 would be in part a response to Nixon's repeated efforts to circumvent the legislative process.[70]

Watergate and Its Legacy

The unsavory events that forced Nixon to resign as president created a political atmosphere so soured with disgust and disillusionment as to threaten the civility and public trust on which any government must depend.[71] The break-in at the Democratic National Committee was carried out by five members of a secret White House investigation unit (the "plumbers"), which originally had been formed to plug leaks to reporters that had compromised the Nixon administration's policy in Vietnam. In 1972, however, the plumbers' activities were extended to "campaign intelligence." On June 17, the five men who were trying to bug the Democrats' telephones were caught and arrested in the party's headquarters at the Watergate hotel in Washington.

"At its simple, most tangible level," the political scientist James Reichley has observed, "Watergate was nothing more than dirty politics.

A gang of officeholders, unsure of their chances of winning the next election, set out through illegal means to shift the odds in their favor." [72] Such behavior, however deplorable, was hardly unprecedented.

What made the Watergate scandal more than a "third rate burglary"—the characterization used by Nixon's press secretary, Ronald L. Ziegler—was its association with and profound effect on the development of the modern presidency. The malicious activities sanctioned by Nixon and some of his associates accelerated the existing trend toward political isolation, in which presidents were encouraged to try to run the government from the White House and to vest their political fortunes in a small circle of loyalists.

The planning of the break-in and of other acts of political sabotage, in which Attorney General John Mitchell and several White House aides participated, and the various efforts by the president and others to interfere with the investigation and prosecution of the case after the Watergate burglars were arrested, involved a logical, although perverse, abuse of the expanded powers of the modern presidency. Many of these powers had originated in wartime, and, not surprisingly, one of the Nixon administration's first lines of defense was to avow its concern for the national security in a perilous world. Nixon even justified his decision to fire Archibald Cox, the special Watergate prosecutor who had issued a subpoena to force the president to release certain secret White House tape recordings, by arguing that to acquiesce to Cox's aggressive investigation would make the president appear weak in the eyes of Soviet Communist party chief Leonid Brezhnev and other foreign leaders.[73]

The president invoked an absolute executive privilege in carrying out the "Saturday night massacre," as the firing of Cox on October 20, 1973, came to be called. Nixon also claimed executive privilege in response to the demands of the Senate select investigating committee, the Watergate grand jury, and the House Committee on the Judiciary. Presidents had always invoked executive privilege, and, historically, the claim that the president's confidential discussions and papers are exempt from examination by the other branches of the government had been constitutionally less controversial than the bounds of the president's removal power. But Nixon was the first president to argue that executive privilege has no limits, clearly confounding legitimate national security interests and his own political interest in staying in power.

The firing of Cox aroused a firestorm of protest, and Nixon eventually was forced to appoint a new special prosecutor, Leon Jaworski, and to give him the same powers that Cox had had, including specific authorization to go to court to contest the president's effort to withhold any evidence that the prosecution needed. On April 16, 1974, Jaworski asked that Nixon be subpoenaed to produce tapes and documents relating to sixty-four White House conversations that the special prosecutor believed he needed in order to try the seven associates of the president who had been indicted by the Watergate grand jury for conspiracy to defraud the United States and to obstruct justice. Jaworski also expected that the White House tapes would establish whether Nixon was part of the original Watergate conspiracy, the coverup, or both.

The controversy that was created by Jaworski's motion and Nixon's refusal to comply ultimately was settled by the Supreme Court. In *United States v. Nixon*, the Court rejected Nixon's claim to an absolute executive privilege and, specifically, to the exclusive right to determine when the privilege was properly employed. The Supreme Court's unanimous decision, issued on July 24, 1974, and written by Chief Justice Warren Burger, a Nixon appointee, stated that, "to read the Art. II powers of the President as providing an absolute privilege as against a subpoena essential to enforcement of criminal statutes . . . would upset the constitutional balance of 'a workable government'. . . . and cut deeply into the guarantee of due process of law." [74]

The Court agreed with Nixon that some form of executive privilege was "fundamental to the operation of government and inextricably rooted in the separation of powers under the Constitution." (This was the first time the justices had formally upheld any version of the privilege.)[75] But the Court brushed aside Nixon's argument that executive privilege could be invoked even in criminal proceedings that involved no issues of national security. It endorsed, instead, Justice Robert H. Jackson's statement in *Youngstown Sheet and Tube Co. v. Sawyer* that presidential claims of privilege must be balanced against the powers and duties of Congress and the courts. The *Youngstown* precedent led Chief Justice Burger to conclude

> that when the ground for asserting privilege as to subpoenaed materials sought for use in a criminal trial is based only on the generalized interest in confidentiality, it cannot prevail over the fundamental demands of due process of law in the fair administration of criminal justice. The generalized assertion of privilege must yield to the demonstrated specific need for evidence in a pending criminal trial.[76]

The Nixon presidency came to an end shortly after the House Judiciary Committee, acting on the heels of the Court's decision in the tapes case, voted to impeach him on August 4, 1974. The president's chances of surviving a Senate trial were dealt a further blow when he admitted that among the tapes he had been ordered to produce was one that clearly implicated him in the Watergate coverup. Even Nixon's Republican supporters on the Judiciary Committee conceded that the president virtually had confessed to obstruction of justice.[77]

On August 8, in a speech to the nation, Nixon sadly announced his decision to resign the next day. "Throughout the long and difficult period of Watergate, I have felt it was my duty to persevere; to make every possible effort to complete my term of office to which you elected me," he said. "In the past few days, however, it has become evident to me that I no longer have a strong enough political base in the Congress to justify continuing that effort." [78] Thus, the historian Alonzo Hamby has written, was Nixon's tenure as president "ended in personal disaster. Worse, he left the presidency itself an object of suspicion and scorn, awaiting a new Roosevelt or Eisenhower to restore its standing and provide a demoralized public with a sense of movement and purpose that could come only from the occupant of the White House." [79]

The Watergate scandal provoked Congress to pass a multitude of new laws to curb the powers of the presidency. More significant, Watergate shattered the recent consensus in American politics—already undermined by the controversies of the Johnson administration—that strong executive leadership embodied the public interest. When asked in 1959 whether the president or Congress should have "the most say in government," a representative sample of Americans had favored the president by 61 percent to 17 percent. A similar survey in 1977 indicated a striking reversal: 58 percent now believed that Congress should have the most say; only 26 percent supported presidential primacy. [80]

One important law that Congress passed to restrict the unilateral exercise of presidential power was the Congressional Budget and Impoundment Control Act of 1974, which required the president to obtain congressional approval before impounding any funds and which established Budget committees in both the House and the Senate to coordinate and strengthen the legislature's involvement in fiscal matters. The law also created the Congressional Budget Office, a legislative staff agency that would make available to Congress the same sort of fiscal expertise that the OMB provided to the executive branch. In a separate act, Congress modified the OMB. After fifty-three years as a purely presidential agency, the OMB's director and deputy directors were made subject to congressional confirmation. [81]

Congress also reasserted its influence in foreign affairs. The Case Act, passed in 1972 to curb the growing presidential tendency to engage in personal diplomacy, required that all executive agreements with foreign governments be reported to Congress. The War Powers Resolution, which Congress enacted over Nixon's veto in 1973, was intended to prevent a recurrence of Vietnam—that is, a prolonged period of presidential war making without formal authorization from Congress. The resolution required the president to consult Congress "in every possible instance" before committing troops to combat, then to submit a report within forty-eight hours of doing so. After sixty days, the troops were to be removed unless Congress voted to declare war or to authorize their continued deployment.

In and of themselves, these laws did not restrict the modern presidency severely. But their enactment expressed Congress's broader determination to reestablish itself as an equal, if not the dominant, partner in the governance of the nation. Congressional procedures were reformed to produce a more aggressive legislature. Decentralized since its rebellion against Speaker Joseph Cannon in the early twentieth century, Congress became even more so; in effect, the power of the standing committees devolved to the subcommittees, whose numbers, staff, and autonomy grew rapidly. The rise of subcommittee government posed a severe challenge to the modern president's preeminence in legislative and administrative affairs. As the political scientist Shep Melnick has written:

> Using subcommittee resources, members initiated new programs and revised old ones, challenging the president for the title of "Chief Legislator." No longer would Congress respond to calls for action by passing vague legislation telling the executive to do something. Now Congress was writing detailed statutes which not infrequently deviated from the president's program. Subcommittees were also using oversight hearings to make sure that administrators paid heed not just to the letter of legislation, but to its spirit as well.[82]

Gerald R. Ford and the Post-Watergate Era

Vice President Gerald Ford succeeded to the presidency on August 9, 1974, under some of the most difficult circumstances that any president ever has faced. Ford had never run for national or even statewide office; his electoral experience was confined to Michigan's fifth congressional district. He was representing this district in the House, which he served as the Republican leader, when, on October 10, 1973, Spiro T. Agnew was forced to resign as vice president in response to the revelation that he had been taking bribes ever since he was the county executive of Baltimore County, Maryland. Under the recently enacted Twenty-fifth Amendment, Nixon nominated Ford to replace Agnew.[83] The new vice president took office on December 6, after being confirmed by both houses of Congress. Thus, when the Watergate scandal later forced Nixon to resign, Ford became the first, and thus far the only, president not to have been elected either as president or as vice president.

Ford was a unique president in one other respect—never before had a vice president succeeded to the presidency because his predecessor had resigned. That Nixon left office in disgrace made the start of Ford's tenure especially inauspicious. Not only did Ford lack even a faint electoral mandate, he took office when the country was still deeply scarred and divided by the Vietnam War, when respect for the institution of the presidency was greatly diminished, and when the nation's economy and foreign relations were in disarray. Reflecting on this period, Kissinger later recalled, "The Presidency was in shambles." [84]

Both with symbolic actions and with changes in public policy and political style, Ford made an earnest effort to restore integrity to the presidency and to purge the nation of the effects of Watergate.[85] Invoking the Twenty-fifth Amendment to choose his own successor as vice president, Ford nominated Nelson A. Rockefeller, the long-respected former governor of New York. Many of the trappings of the so-called imperial presidency were removed. For example, within weeks Ford had reduced the White House staff by 10 percent, from 540 to 485. In addition, for certain kinds of occasions the Marine band was instructed to replace "Hail to the Chief" with the University of Michigan's fight song. Finally, the living quarters in the White House now were referred to officially as "the residence" rather than as "the mansion."

Symbolic changes were accompanied by new policies and a new presidential style. After three days in office Ford accepted the recommendation of a Senate resolution that he convene a White House "summit" on the economy. The Conference on Inflation, which included business and labor leaders and a bipartisan group of economists, and other events, such as numerous meetings between the new president and groups of governors, mayors, and county officials, were all part of Ford's attempt to open the doors of the recently isolated and insulated White House.

Perhaps Ford's most dramatic gesture to heal the nation's wounds was his plan of amnesty for the fifty thousand draft evaders and deserters from the Vietnam War. The president offered not an unconditional pardon but a program in which those who wanted amnesty could earn it. Ford moved quickly on the program, announcing it on August 19, 1974, the eleventh day of his presidency, before the most challenging of audiences, the annual convention of the Veterans of Foreign Wars in Chicago. "This decision," a Ford aide has written, "was not preceded by full or elaborate deliberations. His decision appears to have been driven not only by compassion but also by its symbolic value in helping to put the recent past behind the nation." [86]

Ford's innovations in symbols, style, and policy initially earned considerable good will for the administration. His self-effacing manner seemed less to diminish the presidency than to endow it with an endearing folksiness, which the press celebrated in favorable accounts of how the new president toasted his own English muffins in the morning and took a healthy swim at the end of the day. In his first week in office

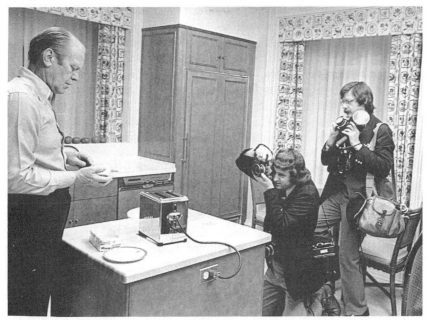

Gerald Ford tried to convey a simpler presidential image to the press to reverse the mutual distrust between the White House and the media that had built up during the Nixon administration. Here he is photographed as he makes his breakfast.

Ford received a 71 percent approval rating in the Gallup poll; only 3 percent disapproved of his performance, and 26 percent were undecided.[87]

Almost overnight, however, Ford's standing with the public and the press crumbled. On September 8, 1974, only four weeks after he became president, Ford granted Nixon "a full, free and absolute pardon." As with the Vietnam amnesty program, the Nixon pardon expressed Ford's desire to put behind the nation's recent unhappy past. Instead, it turned him into Watergate's final victim. As the political scientist Roger Porter, a member of the Ford administration, has noted, "For many Americans, this single act overwhelmed the aura of openness, accessibility, and candor that he had so successfully begun to establish." [88] By the end of September, Ford's approval rating had dropped to 50 percent.[89] The early press celebration of his unpretentious personal style was transformed into an attitude of scorn and ridicule: the president now was caricatured as a slow-witted bumbler.

Few challenged Ford's personal integrity, and, the outcry over the Nixon pardon notwithstanding, his plain, forthright manner did much, as his successor Jimmy Carter said in his inaugural address, "to heal our land." [90] But Ford was unable to restore the power of the modern presidency. The limits of his influence were revealed most clearly by his inability to work his will with an aggressive and sometimes hostile Democratic Congress. The 1974 congressional election, which swelled the Democratic majority by fifty-two seats in the House and four in the Senate, made the task of legislative leadership still more difficult.

Ford did not wilt in the face of partisan opposition; he even had some success with Congress in tax cutting and deregulation. But for the most part, Ford's influence was greatest when it was negative. He cast sixty-six vetoes, mostly against spending bills, during his twenty-nine months in office and was overridden only twelve times. As such, the Ford administration was more like the energetic late nineteenth-century executive than the modern presidency. "The strength of Congress consists in the right to pass statutes; the strength of the President in his right to veto them," the British scholar James Bryce had observed in 1890.[91]

Ford's difficulties with Congress did not stop at the water's edge. As in domestic policy, Congress was unwilling to let the Ford administration have its way in foreign affairs, the area in which presidents traditionally have operated from their strongest legal and political positions. The president was determined not to diminish the foreign policy powers of his office despite the Vietnam legacy and the War Powers Resolution. For example, he did not consult Congress in May 1975 when he sent troops to recover the merchant ship *Mayaguez* and its crew after they were seized by Cambodia. But Congress refused to respond to a number of Ford's most urgent proposals: his request for emergency assistance for the disintegrating government of South Vietnam, his plea to lift an embargo on aid to Turkey, and his plan to help the anti-Marxist guerrillas in Angola. More than anything, it was the lack of congressional support in foreign affairs that caused Ford to complain in March 1976 that "there had been a swing of the 'historic pendulum' toward Congress, raising the possibility of a disruptive erosion of the president's ability to govern." [92]

Ford's ability to govern also was weakened by the reformed presidential nominating process. He had barely become comfortable in the White House when his administration was forced to shift its attention from the politics of governing to the politics of election. Although Ford had hoped to win his party's nomination for president in 1976 by staying on the job in Washington, he had to campaign furiously to stave off defeat. The new primary-based, media-driven nominating process enabled Ronald Reagan, the conservative former governor of California, to mount a very strong challenge to the incumbent president within his own party. Reagan did not defeat Ford, but he came close, earning nearly half of the ballots that were cast at the Republican national convention and complicating the president's task of winning the fall campaign.

When Ford lost the general election to former Georgia governor Jimmy Carter, a man whom he viewed as "an outsider with little more going for him than a winning smile," he felt he had every reason to believe that the presidency was slipping into receivership.[93] Carter's four years as president did little to convince Ford that he was wrong.

A President Named Jimmy

James Earl Carter—he preferred "Jimmy"—embodied the extremes of promise and disappointment to which the contemporary executive office is prone. His elevation to the White House was a remarkable personal triumph, as was his initial popularity as president. Yet, so far did Carter fall politically that, as Greenstein has noted, "at the time he left office his reputation had nowhere to go but up." [94]

A one-term governor who was virtually unknown outside of Georgia before running for president, Carter won the 1976 Democratic nomination with little support from the leaders of his party. His campaign demonstrated how readily, under the new rules that governed the nominating process, a political outsider could win a party nomination by parlaying small state and regional primary victories into a national convention majority. After the election, in order to emphasize his personal relationship with the people, Carter went further than Ford to try to eliminate imperial trappings from the presidency. "Hail to the Chief" was banned temporarily from presidential appearances; Carter sometimes carried his own luggage; and at his inauguration he and his family stepped from their black limousines and walked the mile from the Capitol to the White House.

Carter's informality, which had appealed to many voters during the campaign, worked to his detriment once he became president. As with Ford, it did not take long for the iconoclastic White House press corps to begin treating the president's unpretentious manner as an expression of his modest talents. Carter's attempt to provide the televised equivalent of a fireside chat, for example, is remembered less for its content (the energy crisis) than for the unfavorable reviews that his appearance in a cardigan sweater received. In part, this reaction indicated, as the House Speaker Thomas P. (Tip) O'Neill observed, "that most people prefer a little pomp in their presidents." [95] More fundamentally, it reinforced the suspicion that Carter lacked what it takes to dominate the Washington community.

Unlike Eisenhower, Carter failed to recognize that presidential authority requires a certain measure of dignity. He eventually came to understand this, albeit too late. "In reducing the imperial presidency," Carter wrote in his memoirs, "I overreacted at first. We began to receive many complaints that I had gone too far in cutting back the pomp and ceremony, so after a few months I authorized the band to play 'Hail to the Chief' on special occasions. I found it to be impressive and enjoyed it." [96]

But Carter's problems went beyond style and symbolism. Before the end of his first year as president, it became obvious that he was having a terrible time with Congress. Nixon and Ford had experienced similar problems, but they had confronted a legislature that was controlled by the opposition party. Carter's presidency revealed that the tensions between the White House and Congress were not simply an artifact of divided partisan rule. Presidents and legislators had become, in effect, independent political entrepreneurs, each establishing their own constituencies. As a result, the two branches were even less likely than in the past to regard each other as partners in a shared endeavor— namely, to promote a party program. "I learned the hard way," Carter noted in his memoirs, "that there was no party loyalty or discipline when a complicated or controversial issue was at stake—none. Each legislator had to be wooed and won individually. It was every member for himself, and the devil take the hindmost!" [97]

Arguably, Carter contributed to the disarray he protested. He had run for president by building a personal electoral constituency; having won, he saw no need to court Congress. As the political scientist Larry Berman has written, "Carter believed that as an outsider the greatest advantage was that he could 'dance with the lady he came to the dance with.' He believed that the mere threat of going to the people would make Speaker Tip O'Neill or Senate Finance Committee Chairman Russell Long quiver." [98]

Carter's failures with Congress also may be attributed in part to the inexperience of his staff, which consisted mainly, Greenstein has observed, of "the provincial veterans of his campaign team." [99] But the Georgia loyalists' lack of schooling in the ways of Washington was less of a problem than their arrogance toward Congress as an institution. Assessing Carter's ineffective legislative liaison office, Speaker O'Neill complained:

> Frank Moore, a former public relations man from Georgia, was the [director of] congressional liaison, but he didn't know beans about Congress. On the other hand you don't have to be a legislative genius to figure out that Pennsylvania Avenue is a two-way street, and that members of Congress are entitled to certain basic courtesies. As Speaker, I didn't always have time to return my phone calls, either. But at least I made sure that somebody on my staff got back to the callers. [100]

Carter was able to learn from his mistakes and, after his first year in office, to establish better relations with Congress. The president's record with the Ninety-fifth Congress was, in fact, quite respectable. In 1978, Congress ratified the controversial Panama Canal treaties and enacted airline deregulation, civil service reform, and natural gas pricing legislation; it also eliminated some of the most egregious pork-barrel public works projects from the budget.

The improvements in Carter's performance as chief legislator can be explained in part by his creation of an effective White House Office of Public Liaison, a significant addition to the institutional presidency. The office, which was headed by Anne Wexler, made it possible for a president who lacked great rhetorical ability to rally public support. As the political scientist Erwin Hargrove has written: "The Wexler office compensated for Carter's limitations as a presidential persuader by institutionalizing the persuasion function, not with Congress, but by bringing groups of citizens to the White House for briefings by the president and others on current legislative issues." [101]

In addition to his occasional legislative achievements, Carter scored a personal diplomatic triumph with the September 17, 1978, signing of the Camp David Accords by Egyptian president Anwar Sadat and Israeli prime minister Menachim Begin. Frustrated with the difficulty of persuading Begin and Sadat to negotiate solutions to the conflicts of the Middle East, Carter boldly invited both of them to the presidential retreat at Camp David. Carter's unwavering determination to reach an agreement and his keen mind for detail, which he displayed throughout the thirteen days of diplomacy between the two Middle East leaders, were crucial to their success in bringing about the first rapprochement between Israel and an Arab nation.[102]

The accomplishments of his last three years in office notwithstanding, Carter never recovered fully from the confusion and ineptness of his early days as president. His poor start colored his relations with Congress and the public for the rest of his term.

Much of Carter's problem was that his outsider's approach to the presidency required effective popular leadership to appeal to the people over the heads of interest groups and legislators. Yet rousing the public was not Carter's style.[103] He was an effective campaigner in 1976, selling himself to the voters as a moral, trustworthy leader and a competent manager in a time of widespread disillusionment with dishonesty and inefficiency in Washington. But Carter lacked a unifying vision that would enable him to lead the nation in a particular direction. Having offered, during his first few months in office, a bewildering array of legislative proposals concerning energy, welfare, education, urban decay, and much more, Carter failed to provide any integrating themes that the public or his party could use to make sense of these measures. "I

Jimmy Carter brought together Egyptian president Anwar Sadat and Israeli prime minister Menachim Begin at Camp David in September 1978. Their signing of the Camp David Accords was a historic moment in the arduous process of bringing peace to the Middle East.

came to think," wrote his speechwriter James Fallows, "that Carter believes fifty things, but no one thing." [104]

The incoherence of Carter's early domestic program embodied the indecisive approach to politics and policy that permeated his entire presidency. Politically, Carter ostensibly wanted to move the Democratic party to the center so that it could compete more effectively in an era when New Deal and Great Society liberalism appeared to be losing support in the country. He said often and earnestly that he intended to cut government waste, run the bureaucracy efficiently, and balance the budget. In practice, however, Carter's relationship with his party was usually aloof, occasionally accommodating, but never purposeful.

In matters of public policy, the White House staff embodied the president's desire to be fiercely independent and a scourge to traditional Democratic approaches. But most of his cabinet appointees were liberal Washington insiders, such as Joseph Califano (Health, Education and Welfare) and Patricia Roberts Harris (Housing and Urban Development). Carter also appointed aggressive public-interest advocates to many regulatory agencies, such as Michael Pertschuk (Federal Trade Commission) and Joan Claybrook (National Highway Traffic Safety Administration). Not surprisingly, they proceeded to convert their strong commitments to social and economic regulation into government policy. The collective impression that Carter's appointees gave was of an irresolute leader who was eager to accommodate all factions of his party. Even when some of Carter's proposals were enacted, the public seldom believed that he deserved the credit. Yet, perversely, during the last two years of his presidency, when Carter was overcome by setbacks that really were beyond his control—notably the wildly inflationary OPEC oil price increases and the Iranian hostage crisis—he was roundly blamed. Any leader, no matter how gifted, would have had trouble dealing with these problems. But Carter's style of leadership brought the full brunt of adversity down upon him. His tendency to personalize the problems of state was especially damaging during the hostage crisis. "As the problem failed to go away," Hargrove has noted, "Carter became a prisoner in the White House, and the initial public favor that he had received by personalizing the issue turned sour." [105]

The consuming crises of Carter's presidency did not prevent him from fending off a serious challenge from Massachusetts senator Edward M. Kennedy for the 1980 Democratic nomination. But Carter entered the fall campaign burdened with a public image as a weak and indecisive leader. He was trounced by Ronald Reagan in the general election, the first time that a president had been denied reelection since Herbert Hoover lost to Franklin Roosevelt in 1932.

Notes

1. Richard G. Neustadt, *Presidential Power and the Modern Presidents: The Politics of Leadership from Roosevelt to Reagan*, 4th ed. (New York: Free Press, 1990), 8.
2. Ibid.
3. Ibid., 9.
4. Fred I. Greenstein, "Nine Presidents in Search of a Modern Presidency," in *Leadership in the Modern Presidency*, ed. Fred I. Greenstein (Cambridge, Mass.: Harvard University Press, 1988), 314.
5. John Eisenhower, the president's son and deputy chief of staff, reported that Eisenhower would have run again. Michael R. Beschloss, *Mayday: Eisenhower, Khrushchev, and the U-2 Affair* (New York: Harper and Row, 1986), 3.
6. John F. Kennedy, speech to the National Press Club, Washington, D.C., January 14, 1960, *"Let the Word Go Forth": The Speeches, Statements and Writings of John F. Kennedy*, ed. Theodore C. Sorensen (New York: Delacorte, 1988), 17-23.
7. William E. Leuchtenburg, *In the Shadow of FDR: From Harry Truman to Ronald Reagan*, rev. ed. (Ithaca, N.Y., and London: Cornell University Press, 1985), 119.
8. Cited in Larry Berman, *The New American Presidency* (Boston: Little, Brown, 1987), 237.
9. James Reston, "What Was Killed Was Not Only the President but the Promise," *New York Times Magazine*, November 15, 1964, 24, 127.

10. Carl M. Brauer, "John F. Kennedy: The Endurance of Inspirational Leadership," in Greenstein, *Leadership in the Modern Presidency*, 109.
11. John F. Kennedy, "Acceptance of Presidential Nomination," Democratic National Convention, Los Angeles, California, July 15, 1960, in Sorensen, *"Let the Word Go Forth,"* 101.
12. Kennedy, "The Inaugural Address," Washington, D.C., January 20, 1961, ibid., 14. See also James N. Giglio, *The Presidency of John F. Kennedy* (Lawrence: University Press of Kansas, 1991), 27-28.
13. Brauer, "John F. Kennedy," 119.
14. Giglio, *Presidency of John F. Kennedy*, 261.
15. Kennedy's preparation for press conferences involved his press secretary, Pierre Salinger, and cabinet members, who anticipated the questions that reporters would ask, gathered background information, and prepped the president in briefing sessions. Salinger occasionally prompted friendly reporters to ask certain questions, hinting that the president would have something important to say in response. On Kennedy's relationship with the press, see ibid., 255-275.
16. Brauer, "John F. Kennedy," 118.
17. Theodore J. Lowi, *The Personal President: Power Invested, Promise Unfulfilled* (Ithaca, N.Y., and London: Cornell University Press, 1985).
18. Ibid., 75-76; Harold F. Bass, "The President and the National Party Organization," in *Presidents and Their Parties: Leadership or Neglect?* ed. Robert Harmel (New York: Praeger, 1984), 62; and David Broder, *The Party's Over: The Failure of Politics in America* (New York: Harper and Row, 1972), 18-26.
19. Greenstein, "Nine Presidents," 325-326.
20. Quoted in Brauer, "John F. Kennedy," 131.
21. Desmond Ball, *Politics and Force Levels: The Strategic Missile Program of the Kennedy Administration* (Berkeley: University of California Press, 1980), esp. chap. 11.
22. Arthur Schlesinger, Jr., *The Cycles of American History* (Boston: Houghton Mifflin, 1986), 414.
23. Brauer, "John F. Kennedy," 132.
24. *Public Papers of the Presidents of the United States: John F. Kennedy, 1963* (Washington, D.C.: Government Printing Office, 1964), 462.
25. Theodore H. White, *In Search of History: A Personal Adventure* (New York: Harper and Row, 1978), 518.
26. On Kennedy's New Frontier program, see Giglio, *Presidency of John F. Kennedy*, 97-121.
27. Broder, *Party's Over*, 31; and James L. Sundquist, *The Decline and Resurgence of Congress* (Washington, D.C.: Brookings, 1981), 373-374.
28. Reston, "What Was Killed," 126.
29. Lyndon Baines Johnson, *The Vantage Point: Perspectives on the Presidency, 1963-1969* (New York: Holt, Rinehart, and Winston, 1971), 18.
30. Jeffrey Tulis, *The Rhetorical Presidency* (Princeton, N.J.: Princeton University Press, 1987), 162.
31. Leuchtenburg, *In the Shadow of FDR*, 142.
32. LBJ describes the legislative maneuvering that led to the enactment of the 1964 civil rights bill in his memoirs; see Johnson, *Vantage Point*, 159-160.
33. R. Shep Melnick, "The Courts, Congress, and Programmatic Rights," in *Remaking American Politics*, ed. Richard A. Harris and Sidney M. Milkis (Boulder, Colo.: Westview Press, 1989), 192-195. In 1954 in *Brown v. Board*

of Education, the Supreme Court had declared segregated public schools to be unconstitutional.

34. James MacGregor Burns, "Confessions of a Kennedy Man," in *To Heal and to Build: The Programs of President Lyndon B. Johnson,* ed. James MacGregor Burns (New York: McGraw Hill, 1968), 417.
35. Johnson, *Vantage Point,* 160.
36. *Public Papers of the Presidents of the United States: Lyndon Baines Johnson, 1963-1964* (Washington, D.C.: Government Printing Office, 1965), 1:704.
37. Theodore White, *America in Search of Itself: The Making of the President, 1956-1980* (New York: Harper and Row, 1982), 124.
38. William E. Leuchtenburg, "The Genesis of the Great Society," *Reporter,* April 21, 1966, 38.
39. Greenstein, "Nine Presidents," 329.
40. James Gaither, *Oral History,* interviewed by Dorothy Pierce (Tape 1: November 19, 1968, 24; Tape 4: January 17, 1969, 1-2), Lyndon Baines Johnson Library, Austin, Texas.
41. David Broder, "Consensus Politics: End of an Experiment," *Atlantic Monthly,* October 1966, 62.
42. Sidney M. Milkis, interview with Harry MacPherson, July 30, 1985.
43. *CBS Cronkite Interview with Lyndon Johnson,* no. 1, December 27, 1969, "Why I Chose Not to Run," 5. Lyndon Baines Johnson Library, Austin, Texas.
44. Tulis, *Rhetorical Presidency,* 172.
45. Richard M. Pious, *The American Presidency* (New York: Basic Books, 1979), 399.
46. Senate Foreign Relations Committee, "National Commitments," Senate Report 797, 90th Cong., 1st sess., 1967, 19-22.
47. Quoted in ibid., 21-22.
48. A third matter—the right of the vice president to succeed to the office, not just the powers, of the presidency—is also treated in the amendment. The original Constitution was vague as to whether the vice president was to become president or merely acting president when the president died, resigned, or was impeached and removed. John Tyler had asserted the vice president's right to full succession when he succeeded William Henry Harrison in 1841, which set the precedent for future successions. Section 1 of the Twenty-fifth Amendment simply wrote this precedent into the Constitution: "In case of the removal of the President from office or of his death or resignation, the Vice President shall become President."
49. Garfield lay dying for eighty days after he was shot in 1881. His cabinet met to discuss the situation but concluded that if Vice President Chester A. Arthur were to invoke paragraph 6, he would legally become president, thus barring Garfield from resuming the office should he recover. Woodrow Wilson's cabinet and many members of Congress were more disposed to transfer power temporarily to Vice President Thomas R. Marshall during Wilson's long disability in 1919 and 1920, but the Constitution's lack of guidance stayed their hands. When Secretary of State Robert Lansing raised the possibility with Joseph Tumulty, Wilson's secretary, Tumulty replied, "You may rest assured that while Woodrow Wilson is lying in the White House on the broad of his back I will not be a party to ousting him." Marshall confided to his secretary, "I am not going to seize the place and then have Wilson—recovered—come around and say, 'Get off, you

usurper.'" John D. Feerick, *The Twenty-Fifth Amendment* [New York: Fordham University Press, 1976], 9; Irving G. Williams, *The Rise of the Vice Presidency* [Washington, D.C.: Public Affairs Press, 1956], 112-114. Although Garfield's and Wilson's disabilities were unusual for their length, nearly one in three presidents has been disabled for at least a brief period of his term. In addition to Garfield and Wilson, there were James Madison, William Henry Harrison, Chester A. Arthur, Grover Cleveland, William L. McKinley, Warren G. Harding, Franklin D. Roosevelt, Dwight D. Eisenhower, John F. Kennedy, and Ronald Reagan. Feerick, *Twenty-Fifth Amendment*, chap. 1.

50. The seven vice presidents who died in office were: George Clinton, Elbridge Gerry, William R. King, Henry Wilson, Thomas A. Hendricks, Garret A. Hobart, and James S. Sherman. The eight presidents who died in office were: William Henry Harrison, Zachary Taylor, Abraham Lincoln, James A. Garfield, William L. McKinley, Warren G. Harding, Franklin D. Roosevelt, and John F. Kennedy. The vice president who resigned was John C. Calhoun.

51. George E. Reedy, *The Twilight of the Presidency* (New York: New American Library, 1970), xv.

52. Greenstein, "Nine Presidents," 330.

53. Paul P. Van Riper, *History of the United States Civil Service* (Evanston, Ill.: Row, Peterson, 1958), 327.

54. Richard Nixon, *RN: The Memoirs of Richard Nixon* (New York: Grosset and Dunlap, 1978), 352.

55. Quoted in Richard P. Nathan, *The Administrative Presidency* (New York: Wiley, 1983), 30.

56. Stewart Alsop, "Mystery of Richard Nixon," *Saturday Evening Post*, July 12, 1958, 28.

57. Joan Hoff-Wilson, "Richard M. Nixon: The Corporate Presidency," in Greenstein, *Leadership in the Modern Presidency*, 165.

58. "Special Message to Congress on Welfare Reform," March 27, 1972, *Public Papers of the Presidents of the United States, Richard Nixon, 1972* (Washington, D.C.: Government Printing Office, 1974), 504.

59. Nathan, *Administrative Presidency*, 27.

60. "Annual Message to Congress on the State of the Union," January 22, 1971, *Public Papers of the Presidents of the United States: Richard Nixon, 1971* (Washington, D.C.: Government Printing Office, 1972), 53; see also A. James Reichley, *Conservatives in An Age of Change: The Nixon and Ford Administrations* (Washington, D.C.: Brookings, 1985), 257-259.

61. Garment quoted in Reichley, *Conservatives in an Age of Change*, 259. Nixon quoted in Hoff-Wilson, "Richard M. Nixon," 177.

62. Quoted in George C. Herring, *America's Longest War: The United States and Vietnam* (New York: Wiley, 1979), 219.

63. Henry A. Kissinger, "The Viet Nam Negotiations," *Foreign Affairs* 47:2 (January 1969): 234.

64. Hoff-Wilson, "Richard M. Nixon," 165.

65. Nathan, *Administrative Presidency*, 45.

66. Greenstein, "Nine Presidents," 332. For a balanced account of Nixon's "administrative presidency," see Nathan, *Administrative Presidency*, 43-56; on Kissinger's NSC, see John D. Leecacos, "Kissinger's Apparat," *Foreign Policy*, no. 5 (Winter 1971-72): 3-27.

67. Cited in Stephen E. Ambrose, *Eisenhower: The President* (New York:

Simon and Schuster, 1984), 673.
68. Arthur M. Schlesinger, Jr., *The Imperial Presidency* (New York: Popular Library, 1973), 10.
69. Berman, *New American Presidency*, 263.
70. Greenstein, "Nine Presidents," 334; Stephen E. Ambrose, *Nixon: Ruin and Recovery, 1973-1990*, vol. 3 (New York: Simon and Schuster, 1991), 59-80.
71. This section draws on the insights of Reichley, *Conservatives in An Age of Change*, 250-261.
72. Ibid., 250.
73. Ibid., 259.
74. *United States v. Nixon*, 418 U.S. 683 (1974) 707, 712.
75. Ibid., 708.
76. Ibid., 713.
77. William M. Goldsmith, ed., *The Growth of Presidential Power: A Documented History* (New York and London: Chelsea, 1974), 3:2274; Pious, *American Presidency*, 75-78.
78. President Richard M. Nixon, "Resignation Address," August 8, 1974, printed in Goldsmith, *Growth of Presidential Power* 3:2275.
79. Alonzo L. Hamby, *Liberalism and Its Challengers: From FDR to Bush*, 2d ed. (New York: Oxford University Press, 1992), 338.
80. These surveys are discussed in James MacGregor Burns, J. W. Peltason, and Thomas Cronin, *Government by the People*, 11th ed. (Englewood Cliffs, N.J.: Prentice-Hall, 1981), 359.
81. Greenstein, "Nine Presidents," 335.
82. R. Shep Melnick, "The Politics of Partnership," *Public Administration Review* 45 (November 1985): 655.
83. In the absence of the Twenty-fifth Amendment, Agnew's resignation would have left Carl W. Albert, the Democratic Speaker of the House, next in the line of succession, immensely complicating the Nixon removal process.
84. Quoted in Roger Porter, "Gerald Ford: A Healing Presidency," in Greenstein, *Leadership in the Modern Presidency*, 199.
85. These changes are discussed in ibid., 206-213.
86. Ibid., 208.
87. Berman, *New American Presidency*, 293-294.
88. Porter, "Gerald Ford," 208-209.
89. Michael Nelson, ed., *Congressional Quarterly's Guide to the Presidency* (Washington, D.C.: Congressional Quarterly, 1989), 1470.
90. "Inaugural Address of President Jimmy Carter," January 20, 1977, *Public Papers of the Presidents of the United States: Jimmy Carter, 1977* (Washington, D.C.: Government Printing Office, 1977), 1:1.
91. James Bryce, *The American Commonwealth* (London: Macmillan, 1891), 1:221.
92. Quoted in Philip Shabecoff, "Presidency Is Found Weaker under Ford," *New York Times*, March 28, 1976, 1.
93. Gerald R. Ford, *A Time to Heal* (New York: Harper and Row, 1979), 378.
94. Greenstein, "Nine Presidents," 340.
95. Tip O'Neill, with William Novak, *Man of the House* (New York: St. Martin's Press, 1987), 376.
96. Jimmy Carter, *Keeping Faith: Memoirs of a President* (New York: Bantam Books, 1982), 27.
97. Ibid., 80.
98. Berman, *New American Presidency*, 315.

99. Greenstein, "Nine Presidents," 339.
100. O'Neill, *Man of the House*, 369.
101. Erwin C. Hargrove, "Jimmy Carter: The Politics of Public Goods," in Greenstein, *Leadership in the Modern Presidency*, 251.
102. William B. Quandt, *Camp David: Peacemaking and Politics* (Washington, D.C.: Brookings, 1986).
103. Hargrove, "Jimmy Carter," 233.
104. James Fallows, "The Passionless Presidency," *Atlantic Monthly*, May 1979, 42.
105. Hargrove, "Jimmy Carter," 254.

CHAPTER 13

A Restoration of Presidential Power?
Ronald Reagan and George Bush

In 1980, the political scientist Richard Neustadt wrote, "Watching President Carter in early 1979 sparked the question, is the Presidency possible?" [1] It seemed during the final days of the Carter administration that the presidency no longer worked, that presidents had become frustrated beyond hope of achievement by an attenuated party system, a hostile press, a congeries of powerful special-interest groups, an intransigent bureaucracy, an aggressive Congress, assertive courts, and a demoralized public. Of the five presidents who held office from 1961 to 1977, none completed two terms.

"Among the consequences of Reagan's election to the presidency," the political scientist Jeffrey Tulis wrote in 1987, "was the rewriting of textbooks on American government." No longer was it possible to claim that fragmented and demoralized political conditions "would frustrate the efforts of any president to accomplish substantial policy objectives, to maintain popularity, and to avoid blame for activities beyond his control." [2] In contrast to Gerald R. Ford and Jimmy Carter, Reagan successfully advanced an ambitious legislative program in 1981 and 1982, and was renominated without opposition and reelected handily in 1984. From the beginning of his first term until the damaging revelations of the Iran-contra affair in 1986, Reagan and his associates convinced most Americans that a strong, effective, popular leader had restored the presidency to preeminence in the political system. Even after the embarrassing disclosures of the scandal, Reagan was able to maintain control of the government's agenda, if not its policies. He retired from the White House as the most popular president since Franklin D. Roosevelt.

361

The Reagan Revolution

Reagan's political success prompted considerable speculation that the 1980 election, like the election of 1932, had begun a partisan realignment in American politics. Although the liberal consensus had been unraveling since 1968, Reagan was the first president to envision and work for an enduring national conservative Republican majority. Richard Nixon, Ford, and Carter were relatively conservative presidents, and each challenged certain policies of the New Deal and the Great Society. But they generally accommodated themselves to liberalism, seeking mainly to curb its excesses and to administer its programs more economically. Because Reagan, in contrast, had been outspokenly conservative for many years, some pundits quickly dubbed his landslide victory in 1980 the "Reagan Revolution."

In truth, the meaning of the 1980 election was somewhat ambiguous. In a three-candidate race among Reagan, Carter, and an independent, John Anderson, Reagan won by a landslide in the electoral college, sweeping forty-four states with 489 electoral votes. Yet he received only 51 percent of the popular vote, a three percentage point increase over Ford's tally in 1976. The results of the congressional elections, although not decisive, were quite impressive. For the first time since 1952, the Republicans won a majority in the Senate, and several prominent liberal Democrats were defeated. Nevertheless, although the ranks of House Republicans rose by thirty-five seats, the Democrats retained clear numerical control of the lower chamber.

Reagan's ability to transform his ambiguous electoral victory into concrete legislative achievements testified to his considerable rhetorical gifts. Critics dismissed his ability to communicate effectively as a former actor's trick of the trade—namely, to learn and deliver his lines. But Reagan's supporters maintained that there was logic and substance to his message, that he was not the "Great Communicator" but the "Great Rhetorician" who, like Woodrow Wilson, the two Roosevelts, and John F. Kennedy before him, articulated a vision that inspired the nation.[3]

Reagan's message as candidate and as president was but a variation on the theme that he had been enunciating ever since he gave a nationwide television address on behalf of the Republican party on October 27, 1964. "The Speech," as his writers referred to it, consisted of a single idea, universal in application: centrally administered government weakens a free people's character. A strong central state had so perverted the concept of rights in the United States, Reagan argued in 1964, that "natural unalienable rights" had come to be regarded as a "dispensation of government," stripping the people of their self-reliance and their capacity for self-government. "The real destroyer of the

Although critics accused former actor Ronald Reagan of making insubstantial speeches that glossed over the issues, others called him the "Great Rhetorician," pointing to his ability to inspire the nation with his ideas.

liberties of the people," Reagan warned, "is he who spreads among them bounties, donations, and benefits." [4] Seventeen years later, in his inaugural address—the first by a president in more than fifty years to appeal for limited government—Reagan sounded the same theme:

> In this present crisis, government is not the solution to our problem; government is the problem. From time to time we've been tempted to believe that society has become too complex to be managed by self-rule, that government by an elite group is superior to government for, by, and of the people. Well, if no one among us is capable of governing himself, then who among us has the capacity to govern someone else? All of us together—in and out of government—must bear the burden. The solutions we seek must be equitable with no one single group singled out to pay a higher price. [5]

Reagan's rhetoric challenged the fundamental principles of the New Deal. Yet the challenge was issued in terms that paid homage to Franklin Roosevelt. Indeed, Reagan made an extraordinary effort to associate himself with the New Deal president. In 1980, he referred to Roosevelt so frequently in his acceptance speech to the Republican national convention that the *New York Times* titled its next-day lead editorial "Franklin Delano Reagan." [6]

Quoting FDR did not mean that Reagan had "moved toward the center," as the *Times*'s editorial claimed. Rather, the historian William Leuchtenburg has observed, Reagan "exploited Roosevelt for conservative ends." He concluded his speech by calling on the delegates to fulfill the promise that FDR had made in his own acceptance speech to the Democratic convention in July 1932—"to eliminate unnecessary functions of government." Reagan's invocation of Roosevelt, then, was designed in part to dramatize the failures and false promises of the New Deal program and to highlight what Reagan had been saying for two decades: government had become too big and too remote from the people. [7]

But Reagan's identification with Roosevelt also expressed his desire to lead as FDR had led, exploiting fully the powers of the modern presidency to move the nation toward a new "rendezvous with destiny." Nixon had seen the possibility of using his office to take the country away from the New Deal, but not as fully as Reagan saw it. As for public policy, Reagan's agenda was less reminiscent of Nixon's than that of an earlier and less pragmatic defender of limited government—Calvin Coolidge. Coolidge had impressed Reagan the teenager; indeed, Coolidge's vision for America had a great influence on the rhetoric of the Reagan presidency. [8] Reagan's public addresses, like Coolidge's, conveyed the president's commitment to limited government in moral terms, as a righteous cause that served humankind at home and abroad.

Reagan's inclination to state his governing philosophy in exalted language shone forth most clearly in his March 8, 1983, speech to the National Association of Evangelicals. After expressing his disdain for the communist "evil empire" as another "sad, bizarre, chapter in human history," Reagan concluded:

> I believe ... the source of our strength in the quest for human freedom is not material, but spiritual. And because it knows no limitation, it must terrify and ultimately triumph over those who would enslave their fellow man. For in the words of Isaiah: "He giveth power to the faint; and to them that have no might He increased strength. ... But they that wait upon the Lord shall renew their strength; they shall mount up with wings as eagles; they shall run, and not be weary. ..."
>
> Yes, change your world. One of our Founding Fathers, Thomas Paine, said, "We have it within our power to begin the world over again." We can do it, doing together what no one church could do by itself." [9]

To his political opponents, Reagan's rhetoric was the cynical gloss on a harshly conservative public philosophy. But Reagan's words and the political vision they expressed stirred deeply rooted and widely shared American political values. As with Coolidge, the simplicity of Reagan's message, the dignity of his public demeanor, even the limitations of his faith in government, captivated the popular imagination.

Reagan and Congress

Reagan's rhetoric was matched by his skill as a legislative leader. Unlike the Carter administration, the Reagan administration, as one scholar has observed, "hit the ground running." Reagan's aides carefully studied Carter's errors and crafted a first-year strategy that would succeed in just those ways that Carter had failed. Thus, in contrast to Carter's bewildering array of early legislative proposals, Reagan concentrated on one theme: shrinking the welfare state.[10] His administration embodied this theme in two bold proposals: a large income tax cut and a major reduction in domestic spending.

Reagan's clear sense of direction was not his only point of contrast with Carter. Like Carter, Reagan had campaigned for president by running against the ills of Washington. But, once elected, Reagan recognized that it no longer made sense to continue to attack the Washington community. He lavished attention on members of Congress, frequently visiting Capitol Hill for meetings or telephoning members of the House and Senate on the eve of important votes. "We had to lasso him to keep him off the Hill," one close aide recalled about the first year.[11]

Reagan's personal relations with Congress were buttressed by a strong White House staff. In contrast to Carter, who had relied on the "parochial veterans" of his presidential campaign to organize and operate the executive office, the Reagan White House Office and the Office of Management and Budget (OMB) included not just personal loyalists but also skilled veterans from earlier Republican administrations. Reagan's able and experienced staff compensated for the president's own lack of interest in the details of public policy. Even his political opponents were impressed. "All in all, the Reagan team in 1981 was probably the best run political operation unit I've ever seen . . .," Speaker of the House Thomas P. (Tip) O'Neill noted in his memoirs. "I didn't like their mean-spirited philosophy, but they knew where they were going and they knew how to get there." [12]

The president's enormous popular appeal, his willingness to lobby Congress for his program, and the political skill of his staff enabled the Reagan administration to mount a legislative campaign in 1981 that rivaled the early breakthroughs of the New Freedom, the New Deal, and the Great Society. Reagan persuaded Congress to approve a dramatic departure in fiscal policy: more than $35 billion in domestic program reductions, a multiyear package of nearly $750 billion in tax cuts, and a three-year, 27 percent increase in defense spending. "In slightly more than six months," the journalist Hedrick Smith wrote in 1982, Reagan "had achieved more than political Washington had dreamed possible on the day of his inauguration." [13]

Reagan's first year as president seemed to restore the executive's preeminence as chief legislator. Both by courting members of Congress assiduously and by going over their heads to the people when necessary, Reagan worked his will on the legislative process, in spite of the Democratic majority in the House. In doing so, he actually turned the Congressional Budget and Impoundment Control Act, which Congress had enacted in 1974 to strengthen its hand in fiscal policy, on its head.

Reagan's OMB director, David Stockman, discovered a way that the administration could use one provision of the budget act—the "reconciliation" process, which Congress had created to coordinate its budget-making activities more effectively—to tie the legislature's hands. Reconciliation empowered the House and Senate Budget committees to bring together every proposed change in the budget in a single bill. The House Appropriations Committee belatedly described in a 1982 report how this approach played into the hands of the president:

> It is much easier for the Executive Branch to gain support for its program when it is packaged in one bill rather than pursuing each and every authorization and appropriation measure to insure compliance with the Executive's program. This device tends to aid the Executive Branch in gaining additional control over budget matters and to circumvent the will of Congress.[14]

After a dramatic televised speech to Congress on April 28, 1981, Reagan won a substantial legislative victory on a comprehensive budget resolution that incorporated every element of his budget policy: increases for defense, decreases for domestic programs, and a huge tax cut. The president's appearance, which came less than a month after he was wounded in a serious attempt on his life, produced what House Republican leader Robert Michel called "the kind of reception that makes a few of the waverers feel, 'Gosh, how can I buck that?' " [15] Yet Reagan's speech reached beyond the mostly Democratic Congress to the television audience at home:

> When I took the oath of office, I pledged loyalty to only one special interest group—"We the people." Those people—neighbors and friends, shopkeepers and laborers, farmers and craftsmen—do not have infinite patience. As a matter of fact, some eighty years ago Teddy Roosevelt wrote these instructive words in his first message to Congress: "The American people are slow to wrath, but when their wrath is once kindled, it burns like a consuming flame." [16]

The House majority leader, Jim Wright of Texas, was among those who lamented Reagan's budget victory as a dramatic setback in Congress's post-Watergate struggle to regain its independence. He complained bitterly that the administration was trying to "dictate every last scintilla, every last phrase" of legislation.[17] Even worse from Wright's standpoint, Reagan succeeded. As Tulis has written, "Like [Lyndon] Johnson's, this public policy was prepared hastily in the executive branch, and like the War on Poverty, the nation's legislature played no substantive role in planning the program. In short there was no public deliberation." [18]

Reagan's hastily conceived economic package suffered from some of the same defects as the Great Society. The justification for his substantial tax cuts, which exceeded by far the reductions in domestic spending and were accompanied by large increases in defense spending, was supply-side economic theory, which held that high levels of taxation stifle economic productivity. Economists such as Arthur Laffer and Paul Craig Roberts had argued that a large tax cut would so stimulate productivity that rising tax revenues would balance the budget by 1984. Inflation rates also would fall, along with interest rates. Savings, in turn, would increase because investors' fears of inflation would be allayed.[19] Yet, as Stockman privately admitted at the time, "None of us really understand what's going on with all these numbers." [20] As things turned out, the Reagan administration, contrary to the supply-side projections, saddled the country with the largest increase in the national debt in history.

Yet the unintended consequences of Reagan's fiscal program did not harm the president's standing with the public. Even when he faced political adversity, as during the severe recession of 1982, Reagan remained confident and on the march, vowing to "stay the course." Unlike Lyndon Johnson, he seldom agonized over his own or his office's legitimacy. As the political scientist Fred Greenstein has written, "Several of the modern presidents bore their responsibilities like crosses. Others, including Reagan for most of his presidency, were able to maintain control of the national political agenda, in part by concrete accomplishments, but also by exuding confidence and self-assurance." [21]

Reagan as Party Leader

Reagan's hope that his principles would animate a national political realignment never flagged, even after the Democrats rebounded in the 1982 congressional elections. His own reelection in 1984, in which he won 59 percent of the popular vote and all but thirteen electoral votes, convinced the president that events were moving in the right direction. In a speech to the Conservative Political Action Conference in March

1985, Reagan claimed that the triumphs of 1980 and 1984 had laid the foundation for a new conservative political orthodoxy that would endure well beyond his administration: "The tide of history is moving irresistibly in our direction. Why? Because the other side is virtually bankrupt of ideas. It has nothing more to say, nothing to add to the debate. It has spent its intellectual capital—such as it was—and it did its deeds." [22]

Reagan's efforts to inaugurate a new political era benefited from, and in turn helped to galvanize, the renewal of party politics. The development of the modern presidency had fostered a serious decline in the traditional, patronage-based parties. Yet institutional developments during the late 1970s and 1980s suggested that a new form of party politics had emerged. In effect, the erosion of old-style partisan politics had allowed a more national and issue-oriented party system to take shape, forging new links between presidents and their parties.

The Republican party, in particular, developed a strong institutional apparatus, which displayed unprecedented strength at the national level.[23] Because the reconstituted party system was associated less with patronage than with political issues and sophisticated fundraising techniques, it did not seem to pose as much of an obstacle to the personal and programmatic ambitions of presidents as did the traditional system. Indeed, by 1984 the Republican party had become a solidly right-of-center party, made over in Ronald Reagan's image.

Significantly, it was Reagan who broke with the tradition of the modern presidency and identified closely with his party. The president worked hard to strengthen the Republicans' organizational and popular base, surprising his own White House political director with his "total readiness" to make fund-raising and other appearances for the party and its candidates.[24] Even after the 1984 election, in which the Reagan campaign generally went its own way, Sen. Robert Dole said, "Nixon thought he could build a conservative majority that was above party, and Ford tried to strengthen the traditional Republican party. Reagan is trying to expand the Republican party to include a majority." [25]

The Reagan experience suggests how the relationship between the modern president and the modern political party can be mutually beneficial. Republican support solidified both the president's personal popularity and the political foundation for his program in Congress. In turn, the president served his fellow Republicans by strengthening their fund-raising efforts and by encouraging voters to extend their loyalties to include not just him but his party. Surveys taken after the 1984 election showed that the Republicans had attained virtual parity with the Democrats for the first time since the 1940s.

It may be, then, that the 1980s marked a watershed of renewed and strengthened ties between presidents and the party system. Unwilling to fall permanently behind the Republicans, the Democrats also became a more national and programmatic party, with an ideological center that was decidedly liberal. The playing out of the New Deal and the Great Society, and the conservative Republican response, had sharply reduced the presence of traditional southern Democrats in Congress, thus emancipating the party from the ball and chain that long had hobbled its forward liberal march. In the Seventy-fifth Congress (1937-1939) that balked at FDR's "Court-packing" plan, the thirteen southern states (the old Confederacy, plus Kentucky and Oklahoma), held 120 House seats, a full 117 of which were in Democratic hands. In the 100th Congress, near the end of the Reagan era, those same states had 124 seats. But only 85 of them were Democratic; nearly a third had migrated to the Republican side of the aisle. Moreover, the 1965 Voting Rights Act had substantially increased the number of African American voters in the South, thereby transforming the voting behavior of southern Democrats in Congress. "It was the sign of the times in 1983," *Congressional Quarterly*'s Alan Ehrenhalt wrote in 1987, "when Southern Democrats voted 78-12 in favor of the holiday honoring the Rev. Martin Luther King." [26] Taking account of the changes in the Democratic party wrought by the growing numbers of blacks and Republicans in the South, the political analyst James Sundquist speculated in 1988 that "the Democrats, if and when they elect a president, will demonstrate a cohesion that will astound those who recall the schismatic party of thirty or even twenty years ago." [27]

Reagan and the Administrative Presidency

Despite the recent changes in the party system, any celebration of the dawn of a new era of disciplined party government would be premature. Reagan's personal popularity never was converted into Republican control of the government. His landslide in 1984 did not prevent the Democrats from maintaining a strong majority in the House of Representatives, and, despite his plea to the voters to elect Republicans in the 1986 congressional elections, the Democrats recaptured control of the Senate.

To be sure, Reagan did enjoy considerably more support in the country and in Congress than his two Republican predecessors, Nixon and Ford. Although his 1981 tax and budget victories did not dismantle the welfare state, they did set the stage for a significant reordering of priorities in Washington. The enormous budget deficits that the tax cuts created limited Congress's ability to enact new spending programs. In 1986, the Reagan-sponsored Tax Reform Act further reduced congressional hopes of raising more revenues by lowering the basic income tax rates and by eliminating many of the exemptions, deductions, and preferences that traditionally had made it politically possible to increase the basic rates.

One effect of the budget deficit and the overhaul of the tax system was to "defund" the welfare state. During Reagan's first six years as president, Congress did not create a single major social program. This left the Democratic party, historically the party of domestic reform, in a serious bind. As former vice president Walter F. Mondale, the Democratic presidential nominee in 1984, lamented:

> Reagan has practiced the politics of subtraction. He knows the public wants to spend money on the old folks, protecting the environment and aiding education. And he's figured out the only way to stop it is to deny the revenues. No matter how powerful the argument the Democrats make for the use of government to serve some purpose, the answer must be no.[28]

The Reagan administration did spend money, of course; it oversaw the largest peacetime military buildup in history. The president also demonstrated that it was possible, despite the lingering trauma of Vietnam, to deploy troops abroad and increase his popularity. In 1983, acting with disregard for the War Powers Resolution, Reagan reasserted the president's powers as commander in chief by invading the Caribbean island of Grenada to depose its communist government; three years later, he ordered that Libya be bombed in retaliation for a terrorist attack in Germany. In both of these episodes, the duration of the military involvement was brief, casualties were few, victory was assured, and, consequently, public—and even congressional—support for the president was high.

Still, Reagan suffered a number of reversals on important matters. After 1982, Congress refused to cut domestic spending any further. It also required the administration to slow the pace of its rearmament program and restricted the president's ability to aid the anti-Marxist contra rebels in Nicaragua.

In the face of the mounting legislative opposition, the Reagan administration resorted to some of the same tactics of "institutional combat" that had been used during the Nixon years.[29] To support the Nicaraguan contras, it secretly built an alternative intelligence apparatus within the staff of the National Security Council, able to conduct covert operations that Congress either had refused to approve (such as continued military aid to the contras) or almost certainly would not have countenanced (such as the sale of weapons to Iran). These efforts exposed the administration to severe political risks and, eventually, to a damaging scandal, the Iran-contra affair. In November 1986, the nation learned that, with the president's approval, the United States had sold weapons to Iran and that, with or without the president's knowledge, some of the proceeds had been used by National Security Council staff members to assist the contras.

Public reaction to the Iran-contra affair was swift and dramatic—Reagan's approval rating fell from 67 percent to 46 percent in one month. Although the Iranian arms sales, which apparently were undertaken to secure the release of seven Americans who were being held hostage by terrorists in Beirut, Lebanon, were not illegal, they ran directly counter to the administration's hard-line antiterrorism policies. The diversion of funds to the contras, however, consistent as it may have been with the administration's anticommunist Central America policy, was, in view of the Boland Amendment (a 1985 ban on aid to the contras), widely regarded as illegal.

In response to political pressure, the president appointed former Texas Republican senator John Tower to chair a review board. The Tower Commission roundly criticized Reagan's management style, even suggesting that the president was blithely out of touch with the affairs of state, a mere figurehead who reigned at the mercy of his staff. But the Iran-contra affair was not simply a matter of the president being asleep on his watch. It also revealed the Reagan administration's determination to carry out its foreign policy without interference from Congress or any other source. Although the president may not have known about the diversion of funds to the contras, the news should not have come as a complete surprise: the so-called Reagan doctrine committed the United States to support insurrections against third world Marxist states, such as Nicaragua, Angola, and Afghanistan. As the minority (that is, Republican-written) report of the congressional committees that investigated the Iran-contra affair granted,

> President Reagan gave his subordinates strong, clear and consistent guidance about the basic thrust of the policies he wanted them to pursue toward Nicaragua. There is some question and dispute about *precisely* the level at which he chose to follow the operational details. There is no doubt, however, ... [that] the President set the U.S. policy toward Nicaragua, with few if any ambiguities, and then left subordinates more or less free to implement it.[30]

Many, if not most, of the Republican senators and representatives who signed the minority report supported Reagan's efforts to aid the contras. "Our *only* regret," read the report, "is that the administration was not open enough with Congress about what it was doing." Reagan's long-term efforts to build support for his policies would have been enhanced, they argued, if he had confronted Congress directly by vetoing the Boland Amendment and taking his case to the nation.[31]

The Reagan administration's strategy of circumventing rather than publicly confronting Congress testified to the continuing limits on presidential party leadership, as well as to the ineffectiveness of the statutory restraints that Congress had imposed on presidential preroga- tives in foreign affairs since the Watergate scandal. The prospects for a new spirit of cooperation and discipline within a revamped party system dissolved in the pursuit of policy through the deployment of the "administrative presidency." According to the political scientist Rich- ard Pious, "Iran-Contra was not due to a weak and uninvolved president mismanaging the national-security decision-making process," as the Tower Commission claimed. Rather, it was symptomatic of the restora- tion of presidential prerogative in foreign policy—the excesses of what Pious calls the "National Security Constitution." [32]

The Reagan administration's assertion of the "administrative presi- dency" in foreign policy was hardly an aberration. As a matter of course, when the president and his advisers confronted legislative resistance on an issue, they charted administrative avenues to advance their goals. Indeed, often they did not even try to modify the statutory basis of a liberal program, relying instead on administrative discretion as a first resort.

The Reagan presidency was the most administratively ambitious since the advent of the modern presidency. Not only was policy making concentrated in the White House Office and other units of the Execu- tive Office of the President, but care was taken to plant Reagan loyalists in the departments and agencies to ride herd on civil servants and carry forth the president's policies. As the political scientist Bert Rockman has noted, "It was the Nixon Presidency, particularly in its aborted second term, that became celebrated for its deployment [of the adminis- trative presidency]," but the Reagan Presidency intended to perfect the strategy and to do that from the beginning." [33]

Especially in the area of social regulation, "regulatory relief"—the Reagan administration's attempt to weaken environmental, consumer, and civil rights regulations—came not through legislative change but through administrative action, delay, and repeal. President Reagan's executive orders 12291 and 12498 mandated a comprehensive review of proposed agency regulations by the Office of Management and Budget. Reagan also appointed a Task Force on Regulatory Relief, headed by Vice President Bush, to apply cost-benefit analysis to existing rules. The task force's review included a reconsideration of the so-called midnight regulations of the Carter administration, upon which Reagan imposed a sixty-day freeze on January 29, 1981.[34]

In sum, Reagan advanced the development of the administrative presidency by resuming the long-standing trend toward concentrating power in the White House that had been suspended briefly in the aftermath of Vietnam and Watergate. He also confirmed dramatically conservatives' acceptance that centralization of power was essential to carry out their objectives. As Greenstein has written, "Nixon and Reagan had the courage to act on what once were the convictions of liberals, taking it for granted that the president should use whatever power he can muster, including power to administer programs, to shape policy." [35]

Despite the Iran-contra affair, the administrative presidency served Reagan's interests well. After the televised Iran-contra congressional hearings were concluded in the summer of 1987, Reagan recaptured a large measure of public approval. By the end of the year, with the signing of the Intermediate-range Nuclear Forces (INF) treaty in Washington, Reagan had fully resumed the political high ground. The treaty, which eliminated U.S. and Soviet intermediate-range nuclear missiles from Europe, enshrined him as a peacemaker on the great stage of East-West relations.[36] Throughout 1988, Reagan's approval rating improved steadily, eventually reaching 63 percent.

Underlying Reagan's political resilience was his ability to make his program the new foundation of national political discourse. As the political scientist Walter Dean Burnham has written, "Ronald Reagan was the most ideological President, and the leader of the most ideological administration, in modern American history." [37] To a remarkable extent, Reagan demonstrated that a firm ideological purpose could substitute for long hours, exhaustive attention to detail, and a dominant political party. Lacking an ideological agenda, Nixon's version of the administrative presidency was little more than a strategy to make the government respond to him personally. For Reagan, Rockman has noted, "the administrative presidency was a mechanism to ensure responsiveness to a political agenda that Reagan, and certainly his followers, hoped would outlast his own tenure in office." [38] Reagan's rhetoric defined the agenda during his presidency, and his reconstruction of the executive branch was the principal instrument by which his rhetoric gained force.

Yet for all of his popularity, and despite his policy successes at home and abroad, Reagan did not become, as he had hoped at the outset of his presidency, the "Roosevelt of the Right." "The one goal that consistently eluded him, and the one that Roosevelt achieved," the historian Alonzo Hamby has written, "was that of an enduring political realignment in the form of a broad coalition of interest groups loosely held together by an ideology." [39]

The importance of presidential politics and administration in the Reagan presidency may actually have reduced the prospects for a Republican realignment. The journalist Sidney Blumenthal has argued that Reagan "did not reinvent the Republican party so much as transcend it. His primary political instrument was the conservative movement, which inhabited the party out of convenience." [40] Blumenthal's observation is only partly correct: Reagan's commitment to strengthening his party was sincere and, in many respects, effective. Nevertheless, his administration's devotion to certain tenets of conservative ideology led it to rely on unilateral executive action and the mobilization of ad hoc citizens groups in ways that ultimately compromised the president's support for the Republican party. "Too many of those around [the president] seem to have a sense of party that begins and ends in the Oval Office," Secretary of Labor William Brock lamented in 1987. "Too many really don't understand what it means to link the White House to a party in a way that creates an alliance between the presidency, the House, and the Senate, or between the national party and officials at the state and local level." [41] Brock's criticism was echoed by many Republican officials as the Reagan years drew to a close.

To some extent, at least, Republican leaders were justified in blaming Reagan's personalistic style of leadership for his failure to convert his personal popularity into Republican control of government. From a broader historical perspective, however, Reagan's emphasis on presidential politics was a logical response to the New Deal and its consolidation of the modern presidency. Although Roosevelt's leadership had been the principal ingredient in a full-scale Democratic realignment, it had aimed to establish the president rather than the party as the steward of the public welfare. The New Deal, like its successor the Great Society in the 1960s, was less a partisan program than an exercise in expanding both the president's power and the nonpartisan administration of the affairs of state. It was not surprising, then, that the challenge to liberal policies that culminated in the elevation of Ronald Reagan to the White House in 1980 produced a conservative administrative presidency, which further retarded the revival of partisan politics.[42]

The Reagan Legacy and the Accession of George Bush

Reagan's politically successful tenure notwithstanding, the modern presidency of the 1980s did not, as it had during the early days of the Johnson administration, command the political system. Instead, the executive was challenged forcefully by a modern Congress that had developed its own tools of influence. Members of Congress, acting in partnership with the courts, bureaucratic agencies, interest groups, and the press, were able to circumscribe the Reagan administration's program of regulatory relief for corporations and other private institutions.

The embarrassing revelations of the Iran-contra affair also helped the Democratic Congress to weaken the Reagan administration during its final two years, although more in matters of personnel and policy than of politics. Among other things, the president was compelled to appoint a national security adviser, a director of the Central Intelligence Agency, and a White House chief of staff who were acceptable to Congress. In the realm of policy, the president was unable to advance his conservative agenda. Indeed, he found it possible to take only those initiatives—most notably arms control—that coincided with the agenda of the liberal opposition.[43]

A Reagan Court?

Reagan's effect on the federal judiciary is perhaps the best example of both the limitations and the force of the Reagan Revolution. During the 1960s and 1970s, the courts had joined liberal members of Congress and so-called public interest groups to broaden legal rules and procedures in ways that served the causes of African Americans, feminists, environmentalists, and other Democratic constituencies.[44] The Reagan administration worked hard to disrupt this alliance. By the end of Reagan's second term, it appeared that he had appointed enough conservative judges to move the federal courts considerably to the right.

In keeping with its effort to transform the terms of national political discourse, the Reagan administration, as the political scientists Benjamin Ginsberg and Martin Shefter have observed, "sought not simply to ensure that conservative judges would replace liberals on the federal bench, but sought also to stage an intellectual revolution by enhancing the impact of conservative ideas on American jurisprudence."[45] Prominent conservative legal scholars, such as Ralph K. Winter and Robert H. Bork of Yale University and Richard Posner of the University of Chicago, were appointed to the federal appeals courts. In 1986, when Chief Justice Warren Burger announced his retirement from the Supreme Court, Reagan promoted Justice William Rehnquist to chief justice and replaced him with Judge Antonin Scalia, who joined Reagan's earlier appointee, Sandra Day O'Connor, on the high bench. Rehnquist and Scalia were especially supportive of the administration's legal agenda; indeed, indirectly, they had helped to shape it. The administration had based many of its positions on separation of powers, federalism, and the competing claims of majority rule and minority rights on Rehnquist's and Scalia's legal writings and judicial opinions.[46]

The culmination of Reagan's effort to reconstitute the federal judiciary came in 1987, when he nominated Judge Bork to the Supreme Court. Bork was perhaps the leading conservative legal scholar in the country, a brilliant and outspoken critic of the liberals' recent procedural and programmatic judicial innovations. His appointment almost certainly would have tilted a closely divided Court decisively to the right on controversial issues such as abortion, affirmative action, and the death penalty.[47]

The controversy that greeted Bork's nomination was extraordinary. A public debate ensued that was without parallel in the history of judicial nominations for its partisanship and vitriol, stoked by extensive media and direct-mail campaigns by liberal and conservative interest groups. Equally incendiary were the Senate confirmation hearings, which were broadcast on national television. In five days of questioning before the mostly Democratic Judiciary Committee, Bork abandoned the practice of previous controversial nominees, such as Louis Brandeis in 1916, of letting their records speak for them. Instead, as the political scientist David O'Brien has noted, "Bork sought to explain, clarify, and amend his twenty-five year record as a Yale Law School professor, as a solicitor general, and as a judge. That broke with tradition and gave the appearance of a public relations campaign." [48]

In a resounding defeat for the Reagan administration, Bork became the twenty-eighth Supreme Court nominee in history—but only the fourth in the twentieth century—to fail to be confirmed by the Senate. No previous nominee had been battered quite so badly as Bork during his nearly thirty hours of testimony before the Judiciary Committee. The vote to reject him was 58-42, the widest margin of disapproval in the history of Supreme Court nominations.

In part, Bork's rejection testified to the widespread public resistance to the Reagan administration's social agenda. Although there was considerable popular support for cutting taxes and strengthening the nation's defenses, the administration's plan to restore "traditional" American values by retreating from liberal policies on civil rights, abortion, and prayer in the public schools was much more controversial. The breadth of the opposition to Reagan's social agenda was apparent in the nay votes of thirteen southern Democratic senators and six moderate Republicans.

Bork's rejection also testified to the heightened level of conflict over judicial nominations that marked the era of divided government. From 1900 to 1968, a period in which the same party usually controlled both the presidency and the Senate, the president's nominees almost always were confirmed; the approval rate was forty-two of forty-five, or 93 percent. From 1969 to 1992, however, institutional combat between the Republican executive and the Democratic legislature and the expanding policy activism of the judiciary combined to politicize the judicial appointment process in blatant ways. The battle over Bork was only the latest and most visible confrontation in the struggle between the Democrats and the Republicans to control the federal courts. [49]

Still, eight years of judicial appointments by Reagan left behind an important and perhaps an enduring legacy. A minor, although highly publicized, postscript to the Bork nomination was provided when Reagan's next nominee, Judge Douglas H. Ginsburg, a young protégé of

Bork, was forced to withdraw amid revelations that he had smoked marijuana not only as a student, but also as a law professor. Eventually, the administration nominated a moderate conservative jurist who was acceptable to the Senate, Judge Anthony M. Kennedy. Soon after, the Court, with Kennedy providing the decisive vote, moved to reconsider a 1976 pro-civil rights decision—rapid confirmation that Reagan had moved the Court in at least a slightly more conservative direction.[50]

Moreover, because Reagan was the first two-term president since Dwight D. Eisenhower, he was able to select 78 appeals court judges and 290 district court judges, nearly one-half of the federal judiciary. In the course of making these appointments, Reagan successfully challenged the tradition that lower court judgeships are mainly a matter of senatorial patronage. By strengthening the president's control over judicial selection, he ensured that the federal courts would issue more conservative rulings than in the past.

The 1988 Election and the Continuation of Divided Rule

Reagan never did transform Washington completely. Rather, he strengthened the Republican beachhead in the federal government, solidifying his party's recent dominance of the presidency and providing better opportunities for conservatives in the Washington community. Concomitantly, his two terms witnessed a revitalization of the struggle between the executive and the legislature; indeed, his programs laid the foundation for more fundamental conflicts between the branches.

The era of divided government that began in 1968 was marked not just by differences between the president and Congress over policy but also by each branch's harsh assaults on the other. Republican efforts to enhance the unilateral powers of the executive and to circumvent legislative restrictions on presidential conduct were matched by Democratic initiatives to burden the executive with smothering oversight by congressional committees and statutory limits on presidential power.

A major, if not the main, forum for partisan conflict during the Reagan years was a sequence of investigations in which the Democrats and the Republicans sought to discredit one another. For example, from the early 1970s to the mid-1980s a tenfold increase occurred in the number of indictments brought by federal prosecutors against national, state, and local officials, including more than a dozen members of Congress, several federal judges, and a substantial number of high-ranking executive officials. As the political scientist Morris Fiorina has written, "divided government encourages a full airing of any and all misdeeds, real and imagined."[51] Thus, in the 1980s disgrace and imprisonment joined electoral defeat as a risk of political combat in the United States, at least for some officeholders.

The pattern of institutional polarization and divided rule did not end with Reagan's retirement in 1989. On November 8, 1988, when the voters elected a Democratic Congress and a Republican president, George Bush, it was the fifth time in the last six presidential elections that they had divided the government between the parties. In contrast, when Eisenhower took the oath of office for the second time in 1957, he was the first president since Grover Cleveland in 1885 to begin his term with even one house of Congress controlled by the opposition party.

Vice President Bush's easy victory over his Democratic opponent, Massachusetts governor Michael Dukakis, was in one sense a triumph for Reagan. Bush won the support of almost 80 percent of the voters who approved of Reagan's performance as president.[52] Like Andrew Jackson, who in 1836 aided the last incumbent vice president to be elected president, Martin Van Buren, Reagan proved to be unusually helpful to his vice president, both in his popularity and in his active support during the campaign.[53]

Yet Bush's (and thus Reagan's) triumph was incomplete. Never before had a president been elected—by a landslide, no less—while the other party gained ground in the House, the Senate, the state governorships, and the state legislatures.[54] Never before had the voters given a newly elected president fewer fellow partisans in Congress than they gave Bush. Never, in short, had the American constitutional system of "separated institutions sharing powers" been characterized by such partisan segmentation. The incompleteness of the Reagan Revolution—and the major policy problems that President Reagan left behind for his successor—suggested that Bush might face a severe crisis of governance.

The Bush Presidency

The story of the Bush presidency is briefly, if oversimply, told: triumph in foreign affairs, failure in domestic policy. Unfortunately for Bush, in November 1992 the voters cared considerably more about the latter than they did about the former, and in his bid for reelection the president was soundly defeated by Bill Clinton, the Democratic governor of Arkansas.

Foreign Affairs

By experience and interest, George Bush was strongly oriented to foreign policy. Although international affairs had not been a prominent theme of his election campaign in 1988, it was in a sense the theme of his life: before becoming president, Bush had served as the U.S. ambassador to the United Nations, the director of the Central Intelligence Agency, the U.S. emissary to China, and the most active diplomatic traveler of any vice president in history. In these positions, he had cultivated a wide personal acquaintance among world leaders; as president, he spent hours at a time touching base with his fellow presidents and prime ministers by telephone. Bush also chose strong foreign policy advisers: former Reagan chief of staff and secretary of the Treasury (and, not incidentally, Bush friend and campaign manager) James A. Baker as secretary of state, former Ford chief of staff and Wyoming representative Richard Cheney as secretary of defense, former air force general and professor Brent Scowcroft as national security adviser (a position he had held in the Ford administration), and former Reagan national security adviser and army general Colin Powell as chairman of the Joint Chiefs of Staff.[55] Once selected, Bush forged his advisers into a cohesive team.

Bush's accomplishments in foreign policy nearly spanned the globe. He inherited two simmering problems in Latin America from the Reagan administration: one in Nicaragua, the other in Panama. In 1989, Bush was able to work out an agreement with the Democratic leaders of Congress concerning Nicaragua, the most acrimonious issue that had divided Reagan from Congress. Although Bush and Secretary of State Baker were contra supporters, they understood that, realistically, Congress could not be persuaded to approve new military assistance to the anticommunist Nicaraguan rebels. Determined to find a bipartisan solution that would end the long and enervating interbranch conflict over contra aid, Baker and the congressional leaders struck a deal to provide $4.5 million a month in nonlethal assistance to the contras for a limited period. The administration then roused sufficient pressure from Europe, the Soviet Union, Latin America, and Democratic members of Congress to persuade the Marxist Sandinista government of Nicaragua to conduct a fair election in February 1990, which it lost.

Bush acted militarily rather than diplomatically to accomplish his main objective in Panama, which was simply to remove the anti-American dictator, Gen. Manuel Noriega, from power. Noriega's offenses were several, in Bush's view: election fraud, money-laundering, clandestine arms trading, selling high-technology equipment to Cuba, and drug-trafficking. (He had been indicted on the latter charge by a federal grand jury in Miami in 1988.) Matters came to a head when Noriega annulled the results of a presidential election and, on December 15, 1989, the Panamanian legislature accorded him "maximum leader" status to handle a self-declared "state of war" with the United States. On December 20, Bush responded by sending in 12,000 troops (another 12,000 already were stationed in the Panama Canal Zone) to capture Noriega and return him to American soil to stand trial. Guillermo Endara, the winner of the annulled election, was sworn in as president.

"Operation Just Cause," as Bush dubbed the Panama invasion, not only was the largest U.S. military effort since Vietnam, it was considerably more successful.

In Europe, Bush oversaw the collapse of the Soviet empire and, soon after, of the Soviet Union itself. He was encouraging but not intrusive in 1989 and 1990 when first Poland, then East Germany and the other Soviet-dominated governments in Eastern Europe collapsed, followed in 1991 by the dissolution of the Soviet Union. Critics charged variously that the president was either too reticent in publicly celebrating communism's fall (Rep. Robert Torricelli, a New Jersey Democrat, complained, "We just won the Cold War, and rather than declaring victory, or even hinting this might be a success, we're lamenting what's going on") or too willing to interfere in other countries' affairs (conservative activist Patrick J. Buchanan ran against Bush in the 1992 Republican primaries as a "neo-isolationist" candidate in foreign policy). In truth, Bush adroitly avoided both extremes. A more assertive policy may well have provoked a defensive, even military, response from the Soviets; a less supportive one could have turned the newly free and democratic governments against the United States. Bush responded to the fall of communism with substantial but not draconian reductions in defense spending.

In the Middle East, Bush's major accomplishment was to assemble an unprecedentedly large and diverse multinational coalition to support and finance his Desert Storm campaign against Iraq and its leader, Saddam Hussein. The campaign, which culminated in the Gulf War, began within hours of Iraq's military occupation of Kuwait, a neighboring oil-rich state, on August 1, 1990. Working the telephone, Bush personally rallied the leaders of the Soviet Union, China, Europe, Japan, and several Arab nations in support of his strategy of diplomatic, economic, and military pressure on Iraq. During a period of six months, he dispatched nearly half a million U.S. soldiers to Saudi Arabia, then persuaded the other members of the alliance to pay $54 billion of the operation's $61 billion final cost. When Hussein remained adamant in his refusal to withdraw from Kuwait, Bush won strong approval from the United Nations on November 29, 1990, and narrow approval from Congress on January 12, 1991, to use military force to drive Iraq from Kuwait if it did not withdraw voluntarily by January 15. The deadline came and went. The next day, January 16, American and other allied bombers began a thirty-eight-day air campaign to cripple Iraq's military and communications infrastructure. On February 23, the ground invasion of Kuwait and Iraq was launched. In four days, the allies' military offensive drove the Iraqi forces out of Kuwait and severely weakened Iraq's capacity to threaten neighboring nations and dominate the world's petroleum markets.

George Bush saw the collapse of the Soviet Union during his time in office. Bush supported Boris Yeltsin, left, president of Russia, in his efforts to establish a new system of government.

Nonetheless, Hussein remained in power, much to Bush's surprise (he had expected that defeat would lead to Hussein's overthrow by the Iraqis themselves) and disappointment.

Substantively and politically, the victory over Iraq was the high-water mark of the Bush presidency—it was all downhill from there. The patriotic fervor aroused by the Gulf War served only to conceal fundamental differences about foreign policy between the president and Congress that foreshadowed a renewal of institutional conflict. The vote authorizing Bush to use troops against Iraq revealed a Congress that was deeply divided along partisan lines. Not since the War of 1812 had Congress so narrowly approved the use of military action: although Republicans lined up solidly for Bush (by 42-2 in the Senate and 165-3 in the House), Democrats voted against authorizing military action by large margins (45-10 in the Senate and 179-86 in the House). After the vote, the Democrats closed ranks behind Bush as the nation prepared for war, but a broader dispute about constitutional powers lingered in a reference in the Gulf War resolution to the War Powers Resolution, the statute passed in the wake of the Vietnam controversy that granted Congress specific roles in approving the use of force. Although Bush concluded that the deep divisions in the country required him to seek Congress's approval, he reasserted the claim of every president since the War Powers Resolution was passed that it was unconstitutional. The administration's pronouncements that it would welcome congressional support for the Gulf War were followed by a statement, released after Congress passed the war resolution, that explicitly denied that the president needed legislative support to implement the UN resolution authorizing force against Iraq. Viewing this conflict between Bush and Congress as another sorry episode of the "National Security Constitution," Pious criticized the administration's disavowal of the War Powers Resolution as the most recent example of "presidents ... playing a shell game, claiming to act according to law yet dispensing with statutory law at their convenience in national security matters." [56]

In truth, the "National Security Constitution" was but one element, albeit an extremely important one, of the institutional conflict spawned by the post-1968 era of divided government. This conflict would survive, even undermine, Bush's modest efforts to establish a new spirit of cooperation between the president and Congress. Consequently, far from creating the conditions for the restoration of consensus, the Gulf War set the stage for bitter conflicts in domestic affairs during the final two years of the Bush presidency that rivaled the ideological and institutional clashes of the Reagan years.

Despite these clashes and the damage they did to his presidency, Bush displayed a deft and steady hand in foreign policy throughout his one term in office. Even after losing the 1992 election, Bush continued to conduct a vigorous foreign policy; indeed, he was the most active lame duck president in history. In December 1992 and January 1993, Bush dispatched 25,000 American troops to restore social order and bring humanitarian relief to the starvation-plagued, warlord-dominated African nation of Somalia; signed the North American Free Trade Agreement (NAFTA) with Canada and Mexico; eased restrictions on U.S. trade with Vietnam; bombed Iraq to enforce compliance with the agreement that ended the Gulf War; and signed with Russian president Boris Yeltsin a second Strategic Arms Reduction Treaty (START II), which promised to reduce the number of nuclear warheads in the U.S. and former Soviet arsenals from nearly 24,000 to no more than 6,500. Finally, Bush outraged congressional Democrats by pardoning former secretary of defense Caspar W. Weinberger and five other high Reagan administration officials for any crimes they may have committed during the Iran-contra affair.

Domestic Affairs

In his 1988 presidential campaign, Bush had portrayed himself as the true heir to Reagan in domestic policy, albeit a "kinder and gentler" version, as he put it in his acceptance speech to the Republican national convention. His famous "Read my lips: no new taxes" campaign pledge was joined to a promise to be the "education president" and the "environmental president." Bush carried the theme of consolidation past the election. His inaugural address not only thanked Reagan "for the wonderful things that you have done for America" but also was laden with repeated invocations of words such as *continuity, continuance,* and *continuum*. In April 1989, Bush reaffirmed his status as Reagan's heir by telling reporters, "We didn't come in here throwing the rascals out." His chief of staff, former New Hampshire governor John Sununu, described the Bush administration as a "friendly takeover" of its predecessor.[57]

In contrast to Reagan, however, Bush gave almost all of his attention as president to his constitutional roles as chief diplomat and commander in chief. International triumphs aside, it is domestic rather than foreign policy that usually drives the electoral process.[58] National security and foreign policy had been Republican strong suits in recent elections and an important basis for attracting erstwhile Democrats— the so-called Reagan Democrats—into the party's presidential coalition. The collapse of the Soviet empire, however, removed the threat of communism and greatly reduced national security and foreign policy as important concerns in the 1992 election.[59] On election day only 8 percent of the voters said that foreign policy had been an important consideration in their choice of a presidential candidate. Eighty-seven percent of this group voted for Bush, but many more voters resented what they regarded as his concern for the world's problems at the expense of their own.[60] To be sure, Bush could have done things differently. Riding high politically after the triumph of Operation Desert Storm in March 1991 (his approval rating in a number of polls approached or exceeded 90 percent), Bush had enjoyed a rare opportunity to mobilize Congress in support of a domestic legislative agenda. But he had no such agenda. As Sununu had told a conservative audience in November 1990, "There's not a single piece of legislation that needs to be passed in the next two years for this president. In fact, if Congress wants to come together, adjourn, and leave, it's all right with us."[61]

To the extent that Bush did deal with domestic affairs, he was generally unsuccessful. His main challenge, coming after Reagan, was to smooth out the rough edges of his predecessor's dramatic economic policies, notably the budget deficits. But Bush failed miserably in this effort. In September 1990, he abandoned his "no new taxes" pledge in return for Congress's agreement to reduce federal spending over a five-year period. Announcing the budget deal at the White House, Bush proclaimed, "It is balanced, it is fair, and in my view, it is what the United States of America needs." A month later, inundated by criticism from conservative, antitax Republicans and from voters who were outraged that he had violated his main campaign promise, Bush told reporters that the agreement made him "gag," a sentiment that he maintained through the end of the 1992 election campaign.[62]

Meanwhile, the deficit actually continued to rise: the accumulated shortfalls of Bush's four years as president added another trillion dollars to the national debt, which already had risen from $1 trillion to $3 trillion under Reagan. The reason for the growing debt was that, although inflation remained low and the Federal Reserve Board had pushed down interest rates, the economy was suffering in other ways that had strong budgetary side effects. Real economic growth averaged around 1 percent a year during the Bush administration, the lowest rate in any four-year period since before World War II and about one-fourth the average annual rate of growth. In response, Americans' real per capita income fell, unemployment rose to 7.8 percent, and more businesses failed than in any administration since the Great Depression. Because of the weak economy, tax revenues decreased even as government expenditures increased to meet the rising demand for unemployment insurance, food stamps, and other forms of public assistance.

If Bush failed to smooth out the Reagan administration's rough spots, his record was at best mixed in his other domestic challenge: to soften its hard edges. Reagan's neglect of the environment and civil rights had been unpopular even when he was president.[63] Bush acted to remedy this neglect by signing the Clean Air Act of 1990 and the Civil Rights Act of 1991. But in each case, his commitment to reform was less than total. The Civil Rights Act became law only after a long and acrimonious squabble with Congress over the issue of racial quotas. The Clean Air Act soon was undermined by the antienvironmental Council on Competitiveness, a regulatory review board chaired by Vice President Dan Quayle, which became business's court of last resort in the Bush administration.

Bush's failures in domestic policy were failures of purpose and interest, not of political skill. The president wooed representatives and senators with an endless series of White House visits, games of golf and horseshoes, personal notes, and other favors and courtesies. To reach their constituents, he cultivated reporters in the same way. Such encounters, along with literally scores of formal and informal news conferences, helped Bush, who was a poor speechmaker, to get his message out to the American people. Partly as a result of these efforts, he was able to persuade Congress to sustain all but one of his vetoes—

Bush's 98 percent success rate (only one of forty-six vetoes was overridden) was historically unprecedented for a president with an opposition party-controlled Congress.[64] Bush also shepherded two Supreme Court nominees through the Democratic Senate, something Reagan had been unable to do. This was no easy task: New Hampshire judge David Souter (1990) was controversial because of his alleged lack of appropriate experience, and federal appeals court judge Clarence Thomas (1991), a black conservative, was charged with sexual harassment by a former employee, Anita Hill, in a series of televised public hearings. In addition, Bush named 37 federal appeals court judges and 148 federal district court judges during his presidency, all of them with Senate approval.

Although the White House boasted of securing a conservative majority on the Court, the fierce battle waged over the Thomas nomination left the nation in a state of profound unease. The Senate confirmed the nomination by a margin of 52-48, the closest Supreme Court vote in more than a century and one that reflected the same sort of bitter partisan division that had characterized the Bork hearings. Thomas was spared Bork's fate by the votes he received from eleven Democratic senators, most of them southerners, whose support was encouraged by the strong base that the judge, a Georgia native, had among southern blacks. Yet, as one journalist reported, the televised hearings that investigated Hill's charges "marked one of the wildest spectacles in modern congressional history, a subject for satire and scorn that rocked the Senate." [65]

It soon became clear that institutional conflict would not be confined to legislation and nominations. As the 1992 election approached in the midst of a serious recession, the Bush administration turned its attention to "liberating the economy" from new regulatory initiatives spawned by legislative measures—related to the environment, consumer protection, and discrimination against the disabled—that Bush had signed earlier.[66] The Council on Competitiveness assumed increasing importance in executive deliberations, putting regulatory agencies on notice that the administration expected them to justify the cost of existing and proposed regulations. Bush also imposed a ninety-day moratorium on new regulations as part of his 1992 State of the Union address, in which the administration sought to set the tone of its reelection campaign. One liberal public interest group complained that the president was "waging war" on his own agencies. "It is almost as if the President is choosing to run in this year's election as an outsider campaigning against the bureaucracy." [67]

Bush planned to run against Congress as well. Indeed, some Republican leaders hoped that the president would duplicate Harry Truman's feat in 1948, when the beleaguered heir to the Roosevelt

Revolution ran a spirited campaign against an opposition-controlled Congress and won a personal and party triumph. But Bush's attempt to mimic and repeat his Democratic predecessor's success by blaming Congress for all the nation's problems made a mockery of Truman's adage that "the buck stops here." Neither his leadership of his party nor his struggles with Congress gave the impression that Bush was resolutely committed to a program or a set of principles.

Bush castigated Congress for blocking some of his administration's more innovative proposals to give programmatic form to the positive aspirations of the Reagan revolution—individual opportunity, economic growth, and decentralization of power. As the political scientist Thomas Langston has observed, however, such proposals were not central to President Bush's ambitions, which in domestic policy were "directed more toward mere political survival than toward the redirection of government policy.[68]

To be sure, the Bush administration was rich in creative thinkers on domestic policy, such as Secretary of Housing and Urban Development Jack Kemp, Secretary of Education William J. Bennett, vice-presidential chief of staff William Kristol, and White House domestic policy adviser James Pinkerton. These so-called "New Paradigm" intellectuals believed that merely to advocate the destruction of existing government structures was an insufficient basis for a conservative return to power. Identifying a government role in creating or maintaining incentives for the expression of "middle-class values of ownership and responsibility," they offered "antibureaucratic" policies to foster these ideals, including the use of vouchers in secondary education and housing, extending tax credits for child care to low-income parents, selling public housing to tenants, reducing the capital gains tax, and lowering further the marginal rates of the personal income tax.[69]

But Bush's domestic gaze was backward rather than forward. He was encouraged in this tendency by other, more cautious aides, such as Sununu, Secretary of the Treasury Nicholas Brady, and OMB director Richard Darman. When Bush's advisers could not agree on a course of action (which, not surprisingly, was often the case), the president's inclination was to do nothing. "Do no harm" and "I don't want to do anything dumb" were the oft-repeated watchwords of the Bush domestic policy.[70]

In the elections of 1992, the Democrats not only captured the presidency but also managed to retain control of both congressional chambers, ending twelve years of divided rule in American politics. In his 1989 inaugural address, Bush had urged that the harsh ideological and partisan conflict that had characterized divided government during the past two decades give way to a new spirit of cooperation. Yet serious substantive disagreements between the president and Congress defied

Bush's efforts to make "the old bipartisanship new again." Some political analysts had regarded divided partisan control of the presidency and Congress as the healthy consequence of the voters' desire to mute the ideological polarization that characterizes modern party politics. Yet the Bush years dramatically revealed how thoroughly divided government obscures political responsibility and mires government in petty, virulent clashes that undermine respect for the nation's political institutions. Clinton's victory, then, seemed to represent more than a rejection of the incumbent president; in part, it expressed the voters' hope that the institutional combat they had witnessed during the era of divided government would now come to an end.

Notes

1. Richard G. Neustadt, *Presidential Power and the Modern Presidents: The Politics of Leadership from Roosevelt to Reagan,* 4th ed. (New York: Free Press, 1990), 230.
2. Jeffrey Tulis, *The Rhetorical Presidency* (Princeton, N.J.: Princeton University Press, 1987), 189.
3. On Reagan's use of rhetoric, see William Ker Muir, Jr., *The Bully Pulpit: The Presidential Leadership of Ronald Reagan* (San Francisco: Institute for Contemporary Studies, 1992).
4. Ronald Reagan, "A Time for Choosing," October 27, 1964, *Ronald Reagan Talks to America,* ed. Richard M. Scaife (Old Greenwich, Conn.: Devin Adair, 1983), 4-5; see also Muir, *Bully Pulpit,* 175-176.
5. "Inaugural Address of President Ronald Reagan," January 20, 1981, in Richard P. Nathan, *The Administrative Presidency* (New York: Wiley, 1983), 159.
6. *New York Times,* July 20, 1980, E20.
7. William E. Leuchtenburg, *In the Shadow of FDR: From Harry Truman to Ronald Reagan,* rev. ed. (Ithaca and London: Cornell University Press, 1985), 210. See also Alonzo L. Hamby, *Liberalism and Its Challengers: From F.D.R. to Bush,* 2d ed. (New York: Oxford University Press, 1992), chap. 8.
8. One of Reagan's speechwriters claimed that Calvin Coolidge—not FDR—was the president who most affected Reagan during both his early years and his presidency. In crafting Reagan's addresses, speechwriters often studied those of Coolidge. (Rep. Dana Rohrabacher [R-Calif.], former speechwriter to President Reagan, interview by Sidney M. Milkis, July 31, 1989.)
9. *Public Papers of the Presidents of the United States: Ronald Reagan, 1983* (Washington, D.C.: Government Printing Office, 1984), 1:364. See also Muir, *Bully Pulpit,* 74-78.
10. Marc Landy and Martin A. Levin, "The Hedgehog and the Fox," *Brandeis Review* 7:1 (Fall 1987): 17-19.
11. Charles O. Jones, "Ronald Reagan and the U.S. Congress," in *The Reagan Legacy,* ed. Charles O. Jones (Chatham, N.J.: Chatham House, 1988), 37.

12. Tip O'Neill, with William Novak, *Man of the House* (New York: St. Martin's Press, 1987), 410, 413.
13. Hedrick Smith, "The President As Coalition Builder: Reagan's First Year," in *Rethinking the Presidency*, ed. Thomas E. Cronin (Boston: Little, Brown, 1982), 274.
14. House of Representatives, Committee on Appropriations, *Views and Estimates on the Budget Proposed for Fiscal Year 1983*, 97th Cong., 2d sess., 1982, 12.
15. Quoted in Smith, "The President As Coalition Builder," 278.
16. *Public Papers of the Presidents of the United States: Ronald Reagan, 1981*, 1:393.
17. Quoted in Samuel Kernell, *Going Public: New Strategies of Presidential Leadership* (Washington, D.C.: CQ Press, 1986), 118.
18. Tulis, *Rhetorical Presidency*, 197.
19. James P. Pfiffner, *The President and Economic Policy* (Philadelphia: Institute for the Study of Human Issues, 1986), 122.
20. Quoted in William Greider, *The Education of David Stockman and Other Americans* (New York: Dutton, 1982), 33. See also David Stockman, *The Triumph of Politics: Why the Reagan Revolution Failed* (New York: Harper and Row, 1986), 79-99.
21. Fred I. Greenstein, "Nine Presidents in Search of a Modern Presidency," in Fred I. Greenstein, *Leadership in the Modern Presidency* (Cambridge, Mass.: Harvard University Press, 1988), 345.
22. "Remarks of the President to the 12th Annual Conservative Political Action Conference," March 1, 1985, Sheraton-Washington Hotel, Washington, D.C. (mimeographed copy provided to the authors by the White House).
23. On the transformation of party politics, see A. James Reichley, "The Rise of National Parties," in *The New Direction in American Politics*, ed. John E. Chubb and Paul E. Peterson (Washington, D.C.: Brookings, 1985). By the end of the 1980s, Reichley was much less hopeful that the emerging national parties were well suited to perform the historic partisan function of mobilizing public support for political values and governmental policies. See his richly detailed study, *The Life of the Parties: A History of American Political Parties* (New York: Free Press, 1992), esp. chaps. 18-21.
24. David S. Broder, "A Party Leader Who Works at It," *Boston Globe*, October 21, 1985, 14; Mitchell Daniels, assistant to the president for political and governmental affairs, interview by Sidney M. Milkis, June 5, 1986.
25. Robert Dole quoted in Reichley, "The Rise of National Parties," 176.
26. Alan Ehrenhalt, "Changing South Perils Conservative Coalition," *Congressional Quarterly Weekly Report*, August 1, 1987, 1704.
27. James L. Sundquist, "The New Era of Coalition Government in the United States," *Political Science Quarterly* 103:4 (Winter 1988-1989): 626 n. 39.
28. James M. Perry and David Shribman, "Reagan Era Restored Faith in Government until Recent Slippage," *Wall Street Journal*, November 30, 1987, 1, 13; see also William Schneider, "The Political Legacy of the Reagan Years," in *The Reagan Legacy*, ed. Sidney Blumenthal and Thomas Byrne Edsall (New York: Pantheon Books, 1988); and Walter Dean Burnham, "The Reagan Heritage," in *The Election of 1988: Report and Interpretations*, ed. Gerald M. Pomper (Chatham, N.J.: Chatham House, 1989).
29. Benjamin Ginsberg and Martin Shefter, *Politics by Other Means: The Declining Importance of Elections in America* (New York: Basic Books, 1990).

30. *Report of the Congressional Committees Investigating the Iran-Contra Affair*, with supplemental minority and additional views, H. Doc. 100-433, S. Doc. 100-216, 100th Cong., 1st sess., November 13, 1987, 501 (emphasis in original). See also Lou Cannon's biography of Reagan, which covers the Iran-contra episode in great detail. Cannon reports:

> Reagan, who knew little about how any federal program operated and was largely uninterested in matters of process, may not have known specifically that proceeds from the Iran arms sales were being placed into accounts for the contras. . . . But what Reagan certainly knew and consistently conveyed to his subordinates was that the contras needed far more help than Congress was willing to give them. Because of this knowledge and belief, Reagan encouraged Americans and friendly foreign leaders to help the contra cause. Oliver North may have gone beyond his instructions, but he was carrying out missions that Reagan wanted accomplished, both in his efforts to free the hostages and to help the Nicaraguan rebels. It is no wonder that Reagan considered North a national hero.

Cannon, *President Reagan: The Role of A Lifetime* (New York: Simon and Schuster, 1991), 718.

31. *Report of the Congressional Committees Investigating the Iran-Contra Affair*, 515 (emphasis in original). The division among those who served on the House and Senate select committees was highly partisan, but not completely so. Three Republican senators signed the majority document, which was far more condemning of the administration's actions: Sen. Warren Rudman, New Hampshire; Sen. William Cohen, Maine; and Sen. Paul Tribble, Virginia. The House committee divided strictly along party lines.

32. Richard M. Pious, "Prerogative Power and the Reagan Presidency: A Review Essay," *Political Science Quarterly* 106:3 (Fall 1991): 499-510.

33. Bert A. Rockman, "The Style and Organization of the Reagan Presidency," in Jones, *Reagan Legacy*, 10.

34. Richard A. Harris and Sidney M. Milkis, *The Politics of Regulatory Change: A Tale of Two Agencies* (New York: Oxford University Press, 1989). The "midnight rules" were issued by the Carter administration between December 29, 1980, and January 23, 1981. The strong disagreement in regulatory philosophy between Carter's appointees and the incoming conservative Republican administration intensified the traditional last-minute attempt by departing officials to push through favored policies. Carter's regulators essentially cleared their desks of all rules pending at the end of 1980, producing more than 200 new regulations in both proposed and final form. The rules, which represented a wide range of social causes for which Reagan and his regulatory task force had little sympathy, fell largely within the purviews of the Environmental Protection Agency and the Occupational Safety and Health Administration. See Edward Paul Fuchs, *Presidents, Management, and Regulation* (Englewood Cliffs, N.J.: Prentice Hall, 1988), 85-90.

35. Greenstein, "Nine Presidents," 345.

36. I. M. Destler, "Reagan and the World: An Awesome Stubbornness," in Jones, *Reagan Legacy*, 249-253.

37. Burnham, "The Reagan Heritage," 1.

38. Rockman, "The Style and Organization of the Reagan Presidency," 11.

39. Hamby, *Liberalism and Its Challengers*, 385.

40. Sidney Blumenthal, *The Rise of the Counterestablishment: From Conservative Ideology to Political Power* (New York: Times Books, 1986), 9.

41. William Brock, secretary, Department of Labor, interview by Sidney M. Milkis, August 12, 1987.
42. On the New Deal and its legacy for the presidency and party system, see Sidney M. Milkis, *The President and the Parties: The Transformation of the Americn Party System Since the New Deal* (New York: Oxford University Press, 1993).
43. Ginsberg and Shefter, *Politics by Other Means*, 148.
44. R. Shep Melnick, "The Courts, Congress, and Programmatic Rights," *Remaking American Politics*, ed. Richard A. Harris and Sidney M. Milkis (Boulder, Colo.: Westview, 1989); see also Mark Silverstein and Benjamin Ginsberg, "The Supreme Court and the New Politics of Judicial Power," *Political Science Quarterly* 102:3 (Fall 1987): 371-388.
45. Ginsberg and Shefter, *Politics by Other Means*, 154-156.
46. David M. O'Brien, "The Reagan Judges: His Most Enduring Legacy?" in Jones, *Reagan Legacy*, 86-87.
47. Ibid., 90.
48. Ibid., 91.
49. For a discussion of the politics of judicial appointments under the conditions of divided rule, see Michael Nelson, "Constitutional Aspects of the Elections," in *The Elections of 1988*, ed. Michael Nelson (Washington, D.C.: CQ Press, 1989), 201-205.
50. *Runyon v. McCrary*, 427 U.S. 160 (1976); see also Burnham, "The Reagan Heritage," 12-13.
51. Morris P. Fiorina, *Congress: Keystone of the Washington Establishment*, 2d ed. (New Haven and London: Yale University Press, 1989), 164 n. 27; Ginsberg and Shefter, *Politics by Other Means*, 4-6; and Nelson, "Constitutional Aspects of the Elections," 201. For an excellent account of the cultural and institutional bases of scandal in U.S. politics, see Suzanne Garment, *Scandal: The Culture of Mistrust in American Politics* (New York: Random House, 1991).
52. Nelson, "Constitutional Aspects of the Elections," 192.
53. Ibid., 191-192.
54. The Democrats gained two seats in the House, one in the Senate, one governorship, and more than a dozen seats in the state legislatures.
55. Cheney was not Bush's first choice as secretary of defense; former Texas Republican senator John Tower was. But in a partisan display characteristic of the divided government era, the Senate rejected Tower's nomination, the first time in history that a newly elected president's cabinet nominee had not been confirmed. Ironically, the Senate rejected Tower on the recommendation of the committee he formerly had headed—Armed Services.
56. Pious, "Prerogative Power and the Reagan Presidency," 510 n. 27.
57. Quoted in Michael Duffy and Dan Goodgame, *Marching in Place: The Status Quo Presidency of George Bush* (New York: Simon and Schuster, 1992), 19.
58. Stephen Hess and Michael Nelson, "Foreign Policy: Dominance and Decisiveness in Presidential Elections," in *The Elections of 1984*, ed. Michael Nelson (Washington, D.C.: CQ Press, 1985), 129-154.
59. James Ceaser and Andrew Busch, *Upside Down and Inside Out: The 1992 Elections and American Politics* (Lanham, Md.: Rowman and Littlefield, 1993), 15.
60. Laurence I. Barrett, "A New Coalition for the 1990s," *Time*, November 16, 1992, 47-48.

61. Duffy and Goodgame, *Marching in Place*, 70-71, 283.
62. Ibid., 83, 285.
63. Erwin C. Hargrove and Michael Nelson, "The Presidency: Reagan and the Cycle of Politics and Policy," in Nelson, *Elections of 1984*, 201-202.
64. Congress's one successful veto override came on a bill to reregulate cable television on October 5, 1992.
65. Joan Biskupic, "Thomas Victory Puts Icing on Reagan—Bush Court," *Congressional Quarterly Weekly Report,* Oct. 19, 1991, 3026.
66. Jonathan Rauch, "The Regulatory President," *National Journal,* November 30, 1991, 2902-2906.
67. OMB Watch, "President Bush's Regulatory Moratorium," *OMB Watch Alert,* January 24, 1992.
68. Thomas S. Langston, *Ideologues and Presidents: From the New Deal to the Reagan Revolution* (Baltimore, Md.: Johns Hopkins University Press, 1993), 193.
69. Ibid., 186-192.
70. Duffy and Goodgame, *Marching in Place*, 70-71, 283.

CHAPTER 14

Bill Clinton and the American Presidency

Viewed historically, the 1992 election seemed a rather ordinary affair. Certainly it did not inaugurate a critical transformation of the political landscape in the United States, as had the elections of 1800, 1828, 1860, 1896, and 1932. Nor was Arkansas governor Bill Clinton's victory as decisive as Ronald Reagan's in the 1980 election, which paved the way for important changes in the polity, if not for a partisan realignment. Still, taken on its own terms, the election of 1992 may prove to be profoundly important. "In the actual event," the political scientists Paul Quirk and Jon Dalager have noted, "the 1992 election was one of the most surprising and significant elections of the twentieth century." [1]

Perhaps the most remarkable development of the campaign was the precipitous decline in George Bush's fortunes. So formidable was his standing in the polls in 1991 that his reelection and a fourth consecutive Republican victory appeared all but inevitable. Bush's post-Gulf War popularity, however, masked a profound uneasiness in the country about his seeming indifference to domestic problems. Moreover, his successful foreign policy exploits only temporarily suppressed tensions within the Republican party, largely centered on cultural and social issues such as abortion and gay and lesbian rights, that had come to the fore with the end of the cold war.

The Bush presidency was a painful reminder of the modern executive's extraordinary isolation. Over the years, the presidency had been freed from the constraints of party, only to be constrained instead by a volatile political environment that often would rapidly undercut popular support. The twentieth-century evolution of the office had taught Americans that the president was to serve as their tribune, the embodiment of the popular will. Yet Bush was ill-suited to the tasks of public leadership. "When the weight of the [modern office] is put upon a figure as flimsy as George Bush," the conservative columnist George Will complained, "the presidency buckles. . . ." [2]

To be sure, Bush had revealed unexpected strengths as a leader. The Gulf War stirred his deepest commitments and allowed him to display considerable skills of crisis leadership. Yet he lacked the rhetorical flair and philosophical convictions needed to inspire and lead the public on a quest for domestic reform. Thus, the president who waged one of the nation's most successful wars became paralyzed in the presence of a stubborn recession and partisan estrangement from Congress. Hoping to be identified in history with the triumphant Harry Truman of 1948, Bush was forced to settle for the forlorn Winston Churchill of 1945. Quoting Churchill's mournful pronouncement after the British voters threw his party out of office at the end of World War II, Bush lamented that "he had been given the order of the boot." [3]

Bush's losing share of the popular vote in 1992, 37.7 percent, was by some measures the worst defeat of an incumbent president since Republican William Howard Taft finished third in 1912. Like Taft, whose reelection effort was plagued by the presence in the race of former Republican president Theodore Roosevelt, Bush was beset by a strong third candidate, Texas billionaire H. Ross Perot. In fact, Perot's 19 percent of the popular vote posed the most serious electoral challenge to the two-party system since TR's Progressive party campaign.

The comparison between TR and Perot is instructive. Roosevelt's campaign foretold not only of the emergence of an active and expansive national government, but also of presidential elections conducted less by parties than by candidates and their personal advisers. TR and his Democratic rival in the 1912 election, Woodrow Wilson, brought into being a new concept of presidential leadership that regarded the president, rather than the party or Congress, as the leading agent of representative government in the United States. Public acceptance of this concept set off a new dynamic, later enhanced by Franklin D. Roosevelt's political leadership and by the emergence of the broadcast media, that subordinated the collective responsibility of the political party to the president's leadership of public opinion. Ronald Reagan's presidency revealed that even conservative chief executives now considered it legitimate, indeed essential, to rouse the public in the service of their programs.

The Perot campaign suggested just how far presidential politics had been emancipated from the constraints of party. Perot had never held political office of any kind, and his campaign, dominated by thirty-minute commercials and hour-long appearances on talk shows, set a new standard for direct, plebiscitary appeals to the voters without even the pretense of a party campaign. Disdaining pleas to form a third party from those interested in party renewal, Perot required no nominating convention to launch his candidacy. Instead, he called his supporters to arms on the popular Cable News Network talk show "Larry King Live." [4]

A change in the structure of the media during the 1980s abetted Perot's circumvention of party politics. With the advent of cable television and the proliferation of talk shows that featured interviews and discussions with prominent individuals, unprecedented opportunities now existed to address the voters directly. These shows served as Perot's early primaries and caucuses; his ratings "victories" then sparked invitations to appear on the major network "infotainment" shows, such as "Good Morning America" and "Today," which in one instance allowed him two hours to answer viewers' questions. [5]

Thus, Perot represented not only a continuation of the long-term assault on political parties, but also an effort to usurp the mediating function of the major news organizations. "Perot is doing to the media, and with the aid of the media, what the media has done to political parties," the political philosopher Harvey Mansfield has written. [6]

Just as significant, Perot suggested a novel forum in which to link the presidency to public opinion. He proposed instituting "electronic town halls" as a means of governing. Somehow—in ways Perot never quite explained—public opinion would be used as a supplement to, or a substitute for, the deliberations of constitutional government. In the early summer, with polls showing that Perot was leading both Bush and Clinton, his novel concept of presidential leadership seemed destined to play an important and disconcerting part in American politics. [7] "Perot hints broadly at an even bolder new order," the historian Alan Brinkley wrote in July 1992, "in which Congress, the courts, the media, and the 'establishment' are essentially stripped of their legitimacy; in which the president, checked only by direct expressions of popular desire, will roll up his sleeves and solve the nation's problems. . . ." [8]

In the end, however, the American people invested their hopes for constructive change more cautiously, in the possibility that Bill Clinton represented a new form of Democratic politics that would cure the ills brought on by the ideological and institutional conflicts of the 1970s and 1980s. This hope was encouraged by the Democrats' surprising ability to take advantage of Bush's political misfortunes. Mindful that their own intractable factiousness had denied them control of the White House for twelve years, the Democrats ran a united, effective campaign. To be sure, Clinton's share of the popular vote was hardly a mandate. (His 43 percent was roughly the same percentage that losing Democratic candidates had received in the previous three elections.) But support for

Clinton was impressively broad. He won a strong electoral college majority by sweeping thirty-two states, many of which had not voted Democratic since 1964.

In the congressional elections, the Democrats preserved their majorities in both the House and the Senate. More than one hundred new members were elected to Congress, most of them willing to work cooperatively with the new president. Since 1968, the public's striking ambiguity about the parties usually had left the government in a cross-fire between a Republican president and a Democratic Congress. In 1992, however, an exit poll revealed that 62 percent of the voters now preferred to have the presidency and Congress controlled by the same party, in the hope that ideological polarization and institutional combat would be brought to an end.[9]

A plurality of the voters who sought a united party government voted for the Democrats. In addition, the level of straight-ticket voting was unusually high: 89 percent of Clinton's supporters voted for a Democratic House candidate.[10] Nevertheless, the 1992 election hardly represented, as the *Los Angeles Times* trumpeted in a postelection story, "a moment of redemption for the Democrats."[11] Rather, Clinton won because he presented himself as a "New Democrat," an "agent of change" who offered an alternative to both traditional Democratic liberalism and traditional Republican conservatism.[12] By large margins, voters in the election day 1992 exit polls rejected the traditional Democratic solution of "tax and spend." When asked whether they would rather have "government provide more services but cost more in taxes" or "government cost less in taxes but provide fewer services," voters chose less government and less taxes by a margin of 54 percent to 38 percent.[13]

The New Covenant

Clinton dedicated his campaign to principles and policies that "transcended," he claimed, the exhausted left-right debate that had immobilized the nation for two decades. During the mid-1980s, Clinton was a leader of the Democratic Leadership Council, a moderate group in the Democratic party that developed many of the ideas that became the central themes of his run for the presidency. As Clinton declared frequently during the campaign, his domestic agenda was neither trickle-down economics (the standard Republican approach) nor "tax and spend" government (the traditional Democratic solution) but rather "invest and grow." Using this approach, he said, his administration would channel federal money into new education, training, and infrastructure development programs designed to enhance U.S. competitiveness in an increasingly international economy.

Significantly, Clinton's program for economic renewal was joined with a vision to restore the frayed consensus of American political life. Clinton heralded a "new social contract" or "New Covenant" that in the name of responsibility and community would seek to constrain the demands for economic rights that had been unleashed by the New Deal. He promised that his administration would promote economic growth and a free market with tax incentives and a tough-minded trade policy; he also pledged that, in return, it was going to hold corporate leaders, and sometimes small employers, responsible for being "good corporate citizens." This responsibility would be exercised through government-imposed mandates on businesses to provide family and medical leave, job training, and health care for their workers.

The "sacred principles" of the New Covenant were first pronounced in a speech at Georgetown University on October 23, 1991. From then on, Clinton repeated them at every defining moment of his journey to the White House: the announcement of Sen. Albert Gore of Tennessee, who shared his ideas, as his running mate; the party platform; his acceptance speech at the Democratic convention in New York; and his victory remarks in Little Rock on election night. Invoking Roosevelt's Commonwealth Club address, in which FDR had outlined the "economic constitutional order" for the 1930s, Clinton said that the hopes of his generation rested on the possibility of "forming a New Covenant of change that will honor middle-class values, restore the public trust, create a new sense of community and make America work again." [14] The essence of Clinton's message was that the long-standing liberal commitment to guaranteeing economic welfare through entitlement programs such as Social Security, Medicare, Medicaid, and Aid to Families with Dependent Children had gone too far. The objective of the New Covenant was to correct the tendency of Americans to celebrate individual rights and government entitlements without any sense of the mutual obligations they have to each other and to their country. Clinton was a great admirer of John F. Kennedy, and his philosophy of government elaborated on Kennedy's call for a renewed dedication to national community and service, as exemplified by the Peace Corps.

Clinton's plan to enhance educational opportunity embodied most fully his commitment to restore the balance between rights and responsibilities. Its central feature, a national service corps, was emblematic of the core New Covenant principle—national community. According to Clinton, a federal trust fund would be created, out of which any and all Americans could borrow money for a college education, as long as they paid it back with two years of service as teachers, police officers, child care workers, or other activities that "our country desperately needs." [15]

To a great extent Bill Clinton's 1992 campaign focused on communicating directly with voters instead of working through the party apparatus. After the election, the administration continued to portray its accessibility by holding events such as public inaugural festivities on the Mall and a lottery for citizens to meet the Clintons at the White House.

The Early Months of the Clinton Presidency

The first hundred days of the Clinton presidency "diminished public expectations," the *Washington Post* reported, "that he—or anyone else—can do much to turn around a country that seven out of ten voters think is going in the wrong direction." [16] Hoping to be a dominating Democratic president in the FDR tradition, Clinton found himself the victim of the same sort of ridicule that had plagued his most recent Democratic predecessor, Jimmy Carter. Like Carter, Clinton was a former governor of a small southern state whom many believed to be in over his head. As the political scientist Walter Dean Burnham observed during the summer of 1993, "there has been no successful transition yet from the very small and parochial world of Little Rock to Big Time Washington." [17]

Clinton's weaknesses were amplified by the most hostile White House press corps faced by any president since Nixon. Because talk shows and local news programs allowed the new president to go directly to the American people, Washington correspondents were left largely out of the picture. (Indeed, Clinton held only one White House press conference during the first three months of his presidency.)[18] In response, the national press corps, frustrated by its diminishing influence, eagerly pounced on the administration's gaffes. News accounts of serious White House lapses in judgment, ranging from the eruption of gays and lesbians in the military as the administration's first major issue to the trashing of Clinton's first two nominees for attorney general—Zoë Baird and Kimba Wood—for employing illegal aliens as nannies, left the country both incredulous and angry. With the exception of Gerald Ford, who was not elected to office, Clinton's job approval rating for his first hundred days was the worst of any president in polling history.[19]

The transition from governor to president was made all the more difficult by Clinton's assembling of a White House staff—headed by close associates from Arkansas, such as Chief of Staff Thomas F. (Mack) McClarty and personnel director Bruce Lindsey, and by the talented but inexperienced communications director George Stephanopoulos (the only non-Arkansan on the senior staff)—that appeared to be unprepared for the complexity and toughness of Washington politics. Clinton did name some impressive figures to his cabinet, including Sen. Lloyd Bentsen as secretary of the Treasury, Rep. Les Aspin as secretary of defense, and former governor of Arizona Bruce Babbit as secretary of interior. But he centered political and policy decisions in the White House staff. The staff in turn manifested the virtues and flaws of the president, who, much more than his recent Republican predecessors, assumed the daily burden of decision making.[20]

In May 1993, Clinton brought David Gergen, a former employee of the Reagan administration, into the White House as an all-purpose adviser, with the hope that an experienced and pragmatic strategist would bring order from the cacophony of the administration's first three months. Gergen's presence did seem to calm somewhat the beleaguered White House staff. The staff problem was further ameliorated by a shuffling of aides that placed them in posts for which they seemed better suited. For example, Stephanopoulos, who was too easily ruffled for the communications role, moved to the less visible position of senior adviser to the president for policy and strategy. He was replaced as communications director by Mark Gearan, formerly a deputy chief of staff, whose outgoing, accessible manner was effective in cultivating good relations with the press. These changes appeared to yield a stronger White House organization—one that was better able to impose discipline in the use of Clinton's time and the messages he sought to deliver.[21]

But repairing the management of the White House staff could do only so much to right the Clinton presidency. At least part of Clinton's political difficulties originated with the president himself, especially his tendency to want to please all sides—an "innate indecisiveness," as one observer put it, that was magnified by a Democratic party fashioned from a demanding constellation of sometimes competing interest groups.[22] During the campaign, Clinton had professed to be a New Democrat who would challenge these groups and ignore their demands for more entitlement programs. But his commitment to control government spending and to recast the welfare state was obscured during the first hundred days by a number of traditional liberal actions. No sooner had he been inaugurated than Clinton announced his intention to issue executive orders to reverse Reagan and Bush's policy of forbidding abortion counseling at federally funded clinics—the so-called gag rule—and to lift the long-standing ban on homosexuals in the military. These policies could be carried out "with a stroke of the pen," Clinton believed, leaving him free, as he had promised during his quest for the presidency, to focus "like a laser" on the economy.

In truth, however, there was no prospect that such divisive social issues could be resolved through executive orders. The proposal to lift the ban on gays and lesbians in the military proved to be an especially explosive issue that plagued Clinton throughout the critical early months of his presidency. Intense opposition from the respected head of the Joint Chiefs of Staff, Gen. Colin Powell, and the influential chair of the Senate Armed Services Committee, Sam Nunn of Georgia, forced Clinton to defer his executive order for six months while he sought a compromise solution, thus arousing the ire of gay and lesbian activists who had given him strong financial and organizational support during the election.[23] Most damaging for Clinton was that the issue became a glaring benchmark of his inability to revitalize progressive politics in order to redress the economic insecurity and political alienation of the middle class.[24]

In his frustration, the president announced that he was "frankly appalled" at how much time was being spent on enervating social issues such as homosexuals in the military. In February, he appeared at a televised town meeting in Detroit to try to renew his rapport with the public and build support for his economic program.[25] But Clinton's plan to invest more money in the economy foundered on the rock of the budget deficit. Announcing that the fiscal 1993 deficit would be $50 billion higher than he had expected, Clinton withdrew his support for a middle-class tax cut. He then proposed a plan to cut $500 billion from the budget deficit in five years, a package that included additional taxes on energy that would, in fact, increase the tax burden on middle-class citizens. Some domestic programs were to be cut, but these reductions were less significant than the shift Clinton proposed in spending priorities from the Reagan and Bush years. The president's budget promised to transfer funds that had been part of the Republican military buildup to an array of traditional social programs intended to combat an "alarming rise in inequality." For example, Clinton's budget plan proposed a large expansion of federal tax credits for low-income working families with children, at a cost to the Treasury of $27 billion in five years. He also asked for an extra $13.8 billion for the Head Start program and $3.6 billion for the Special Supplemental Food Program for Women, Infants and Children.[26]

Such a plan, even though it promised to reduce the deficit, did not clearly distinguish Clinton from conventional "tax and spend" Democrats, a charge that congressional Republicans leveled at the president with alacrity. The Republicans marched in lock step opposition to Clinton's economic program, especially to his $16 billion stimulus package, which he offered as a partial antidote to the economic contraction that he feared deficit reduction would cause.

The idea behind the stimulus package was to win swift enactment of an emergency appropriation before Congress tackled the more complicated task of crafting a huge, multiyear deficit-reduction bill. As expected, a substantial part of the package's appropriations was devoted to construction projects, targeting an industry that had suffered continuing high unemployment. Yet about half the money in Clinton's proposal was assigned to programs other than jobs and construction—aid to the homeless, food assistance, housing loans, meat and poultry inspections, preventive medicine, and other social programs. Republicans argued that the economy would be better served by cutting, not increasing, federal spending; they also complained that social programs had no place in emergency legislation to spur employment and economic growth. The real purpose of the stimulus package, Republicans charged, was to appease Democratic legislators and interest groups, who championed the traditional liberal policies that candidate Clinton had promised to curtail.[27]

In April, Senate Republicans unanimously supported a filibuster that killed the stimulus package, setting off anew howls of "gridlock." As during the Carter era, Democratic control of the White House and Congress did not guarantee comprehensive action on the economy. But Carter's leadership had been undermined by fractious Democrats who resented his isolation from the party and its policy commitments. Clinton, in contrast, suffered from his identity with the Democratic leadership and its devotion to programmatic activism. With a Democrat in the White House—and one who seemed determined to fight "an exclusively Democratic holy war to reshape national economic policy"— Senate Minority Leader Robert Dole resorted to the filibuster as a tool of party opposition.[28] Such a course was virtually unprecedented;

historically, the filibuster had been employed by mavericks or regional minorities to obstruct party leaders.[29] That its use was orchestrated by the Republican party to ensnare President Clinton testified to the bitter partisanship that lingered from the Reagan-Bush era, as well as to Clinton's failure during the early days of his presidency to move the country beyond the institutional conflicts and budgetary evasions that were spawned by partisan estrangement. Had Clinton, upon assuming office, more clearly governed as a New Democrat, he might have been less vulnerable to the obstructionist tactics of the opposition party. Instead, the taxes and social policies that he supported enabled Republicans to tar him as a wolf in sheep's clothing—a conventional liberal whose commitment to reform had expired at the end of his presidential campaign.[30]

In truth, during his first hundred days Clinton said and did little about the New Covenant. He appointed Donna Shalala to head the Department of Health and Human Services, even though she had not expressed support for welfare reform. And in the February address to Congress in which he laid out his administration's goals, Clinton, instead of trumpeting the reciprocal obligations between citizens and their government, proposed a new set of entitlements in the form of expanded government support for health care, job training, and a college education. His proposal to make college loans available to all Americans did include the campaign-touted plan to form a national service corps, but the reciprocity he now expected of those who received college loans seemed almost apologetic—indeed, the option of paying the country back with a small percentage of one's income, thereby avoiding service as a teacher, police officer, or community service worker, greatly diluted the concept of national service.[31]

The acquiescence that Clinton displayed in the face of traditional liberal causes was, to a point, understandable; it was a logical response to the modern institutional separation between presidents and their parties. The centrist wing of the Democratic party that he represented—including the Democratic Leadership Council—was a minority wing. The majority of liberal interest group activists and Democratic members of Congress still preferred entitlements to obligations and regulations to responsibilities. Only the unpopularity of liberal groups and the emphasis on candidate-centered presidential campaigns had made Clinton's nomination and election possible. The media-driven caucuses and primaries that determine party nominations had given him the opportunity to seize the Democratic label as an outsider candidate but offered no means to effect a transformation of his party when he took office. To bring about the new agenda that he had advocated during the election, Clinton would have had to risk a brutal confrontation with the major powers in the Democratic party, a battle that might have left him as isolated as Carter had been.

Thus, the early Clinton presidency was a period of profound uncertainty. To be sure, there were some positive developments for the president. In June, for example, the Senate and House passed severely modified versions of his deficit-reduction plan, albeit by razor-thin margins and with important differences between the House and Senate bills. In August, Clinton successfully faced the challenge of forging a budget deal in a congressional conference committee without any support from the Republicans, who voted unanimously in both the House and the Senate against his package. (The House adopted the conference report by 218-216, and the Senate cleared the bill 51-50, with Vice President Gore casting the deciding vote.) Clinton won this narrow, bruising victory only after promising moderate Democrats that he would put together another package of spending cuts in the fall.[32]

The burden for achieving the new round of cuts fell on Gore, who headed a task force to "reinvent government" in order "to guarantee more effective, efficient, responsive government." The Gore report, released in early September, offered a set of proposals that it claimed would save $108 billion in five years by trimming 252,000 federal jobs, overhauling procurement laws, updating information systems, eliminating a few programs and subsidies, and cutting bureaucratic red tape.[33] But it remained to be seen whether such a complex plan, much of which required congressional approval, would be carried out. In addition, many Republicans and a few Democrats, with support from the Congressional Budget Office, said that the savings claims were exaggerated. Sounding an ominous note, Democratic representative Tim Penny complained that the reinventing government initiative was symptomatic of one of Clinton's most serious faults, the tendency to "oversell and underdeliver" his programs.[34]

Such exaggeration was born partly, perhaps, of the fragile support that Clinton was able to muster in Congress and the public for his budgetary program. Clinton's weak standing would be severely tested not only by the reinventing government initiative but also by the impending battles over health care reform and the North American Free Trade Agreement (NAFTA) with Canada and Mexico. In November, 1993, he faced the first of these tests, the NAFTA fight, knowing that a partisan approach would not work. Indeed, Democratic support for free trade was so weak that Clinton had to rely on winning more Republican than Democratic votes in Congress. Renewing his identity as an outsider, the president launched a successful campaign for the treaty by reaching beyond Congress to the American people. The turning point in the struggle came when the administration challenged Perot, the

In September 1992, Vice President Al Gore, left, issued the report of a
task force charged with initiating ideas to "reinvent government."
Here Clinton and Gore descend the Capitol steps with Speaker of the
House Thomas S. Foley.

leading opponent of NAFTA, to debate Gore on "Larry King Live."
Gore's forceful and optimistic defense of open markets was well received
by the large television audience, rousing enough popular support to
persuade a majority of legislators in both houses of Congress to approve
the trade agreement.[35]

With the successful fight for NAFTA, moderate Democrats began
to hope that Clinton had finally begun the task of dedicating his party
to the principles and policies that he had espoused during the campaign.
But the next major legislative battle would be for the administration's
health care program, which promised "to guarantee all Americans a
comprehensive package of benefits over the course of an entire lifetime." As such, it would create a new government entitlement program
and an administrative apparatus that would signal the revitalization
rather than the reform of traditional welfare state policy.[36] Although the
administration made conciliatory overtures to the plan's opponents,

hoping to forge bipartisan cooperation on Capitol Hill and a broad consensus among the general public, the possibilities for comprehensive reform hinged on settling fundamental disagreements about the appropriate role of government that long had divided the parties and the country. Thus, a year after being elected to the presidency, Clinton still faced the profound challenge of establishing the boundaries within which his party and national domestic policy could be reformed.

The risk always existed, of course, that a foreign policy crisis would deflect the president's attention from his political and economic problems at home. "No president in the last fifty years has tried to do what Bill Clinton has done in foreign policy," observed the presidential historian Michael Beschloss, "which is essentially to keep it away from the Oval Office as much as possible during his first six months." [37] But when he took office, Clinton found the international arena overflowing with actual and potential crises that demanded his attention. He faced a challenge from Saddam Hussein, whose alleged assassination plot against former president Bush provoked the president to order air strikes against an Iraqi intelligence installation in June. Clinton's action was supported by the public and by members of both parties in Congress, yet some observers warned that he eventually could become trapped by the same sort of Middle East conundrum that had long mystified previous administrations. As the *Boston Globe* reporter David Shribman wrote, "The President is gambling that he is not beginning a slow process of 'war by means' with Iraq, with U.S. action being followed by terrorist incidents that in turn are followed by more drastic American responses and more dramatic terrorist spectacles." [38]

The Clinton administration's long-term effectiveness in dealing with Iraq and other Middle East crises inevitably would be affected by its performance on the Israeli-Palestinian issue. The Arab-Israeli negotiations concerning the future of the West Bank and Gaza Strip that had been initiated with the encouragement of the Bush administration were at a standstill when Clinton took office. Then, to the surprise of the White House and the rest of the world, Israeli prime minister Yithzak Rabin and Palestinian Liberation Organization chief Yasir Arafat announced at the end of August that they had reached an agreement that would lay the foundation for mutual recognition and peace. Although the United States had been left out of the secret negotiations, which were mediated by Norwegian foreign minister Johan Jorgen Holst, Clinton hosted and orchestrated a White House ceremony on September 13 at which the two once-bitter enemies shook hands and signed a Declaration of Principles for Palestinian self-rule in lands that Israel had occupied since 1967. Clearly, as the political scientist Seyom Brown has written, "Clinton's role was more that of after-the-fact implementor and facilitator than superpower impresario—a not unwelcome gift to a president who would rather concentrate on domestic affairs." [39] But having enthu-siastically endorsed the agreement and committed the United States to raising a multinational fund to underwrite economic reconstruction in the new Palestinian-controlled areas, the Clinton administration is likely to see its role in Middle East affairs expand.[40] By becoming the guarantor of the agreement, Clinton risked that the antipeace extremists on both sides again would get the upper hand.

There was no prospect, then, that this domestically-honed presi-dent would be able to avoid close involvement in foreign policy. Indeed, savage conflict in the former Yugoslavia constantly threatened to intrude upon Clinton's determination to keep his gaze fixed on domestic affairs. Even more prepossessing was the turbulent transition that Russia and other former Soviet states were undergoing from commu-nism to democratic capitalism. Russia suddenly became a front-burner issue in September when its president, Boris Yeltsin, vented his frustration with legislative opposition to his economic reforms by summarily dismissing the Russian parliament and calling for a new parliament to be elected in December. When his opponents responded by naming their own leader as "acting president" of Russia, raising the prospect of civil war, Clinton and other high administration officials reiterated their long-standing support for Yeltsin. This support re-mained firm even after Yeltsin suppressed the revolt militarily on October 4. "But underneath the administration's publicly-expressed confidence that Yeltsin would prevail," Brown observed, "officials were taking a second look at the United States grand strategy toward the former Communist countries." [41]

The Clinton administration faced its most troubling foreign policy predicament in Somalia, where the troops deployed at the end of the Bush administration to feed starving people had become part of a more dangerous and controversial United Nations peace-keeping mission. Operating under the authority of Security Council resolutions that ordered the capture of warlord Mohammed Aidid, the UN forces became the target of violent attacks in which U.S. soldiers were wounded, captured, and killed. In October, Clinton faced strong pres-sure from Congress to withdraw from Somalia, but his first response was to reinforce the U.S. troops with additional personnel and weaponry. Finally, with Congress threatening to cut off funding for the mission by February 1, 1994, two months earlier than the president intended, the Clinton administration agreed to limit its goals to protecting American forces and securing supply lines for relief aid.[42]

Like Bush, Clinton had settled for a case-by-case, pragmatic approach to developments in the post-cold war world. Yet hard-pressed by Congress on Somalia and challenged by the dramatic events in Russia and the Middle East, the Clinton administration groped for an understanding of foreign policy that would define the place of the United States in the new world order. Just as Truman, seeking the moral authority and bipartisan support he needed to act effectively in the era of global politics that began after World War II, had presented Congress with the "containment" doctrine in 1946, so Clinton may also need to develop a doctrine to relate the country's interests and basic values to the changed world of the 1990s.[43]

The Presidency and Democratic Discourse

From the beginning, the challenge of the Clinton presidency has been to revive the impression, created during the 1992 campaign, that Clinton stood for a new philosophy of government and knew how to translate it into action. Such a rediscovery of his philosophical compass will not be easy, however. The modern presidency operates in a political arena that is seldom congenial to serious political debate and that all too often deflects attention from painful but necessary struggles about the appropriate meaning of classical liberalism and the relative merits of contemporary liberalism and conservatism. Since the beginning of the nineteenth century, political parties have been vehicles for democratic debate and choice in the United States. Indeed, the major parties—the Democrats and the Republicans since the Civil War—have organized political debate so that the ambitions of individual candidates have been joined to, and restrained by, collective organizations with a past and a future.[44] For all their faults, political parties, until recently, provided voters with the same sort of chaotic but heartfelt participation in presidential politics that sports fans experience in cheering for the Chicago Bulls or the Phoenix Suns.

But with the recent liberation of the presidency from many of the constraints of party leadership and the rise of the mass media, party politics has been displaced by a form of television democracy. The homage paid to the techniques of mass manipulation in modern campaigns is not the stuff of democratic debate and choice. Indeed, it leads to a plebiscitary form of democracy, in which citizens directly invest their support in an individual leader.

Much celebration occurred after the 1992 campaign about the voters purportedly taking back the political process—they forced the candidates to talk about the issues, it was said, and then turned out on election day in greater force (55 percent) than in any election since 1972. Indeed, not only were the party organizations largely irrelevant to the campaign, so were the major news organizations. In 1992, politics came directly to the voters: on radio talk shows, on television talk and entertainment shows, even in supermarket tabloids. Yet discussion of the issues sometimes was lost amid the personal appeals and feel-good babble of television politics. Perot, of course, surpassed Clinton and Bush in avoiding the restraints of political parties and the tough questions of reporters. But Clinton, too, was eager during the campaign to reach out to the voters through talk shows, and, as president, he has continued to seek direct communication with them.

The embarrassing defeat that Perot suffered at the hands of Gore in their debate over NAFTA was unlikely to put an end to the form of politics that the Texas billionaire represented. Indeed, the administration's resort to a televised dialogue with Perot on such an important issue testified to the extent to which "Perotism" set the tone of political life during the first year of the Clinton presidency. This was evident not only in the importance of talk shows in public policy debates but also in the use of electronic town halls by the administration and its critics in seeking to gain favor with the public. As a presidential candidate Perot had proposed that the electronic town meeting be used to govern the nation. The television spectacle in Detroit that launched Clinton's campaign for budget reform gave effect to Perot's proposal and raised to a new level the concern with public opinion polls that contemporary presidents have displayed.

Warning against this obsession, former vice president Walter F. Mondale admonished that

> every new president would do well, as his first official act, to sit down alone and have a talk with himself about what it means to be president, what he wants to accomplish, and what it will take to do it. A President should be thinking about his place in history, not his ranking in polls or whether or not everybody likes him.[45]

The presidents who do enjoy a prominent place in history have taken the people to school, educating them about new policy proposals and persuading them to make difficult choices. Public education of this sort, however, is rarely encountered on talk shows, or even in electronic town meetings. Instead, in such forums candidates and presidents are tempted to seek the devotion of the American people in order to manipulate them.

Talk show politics exposes the people to exactly the demagogy that the Framers of the Constitution feared, as well as to the sort of public figures who will exploit citizens' impatience with the difficult tasks involved in sustaining a healthy democracy. Such an approach brings to mind Alexander Hamilton's two-centuries-old warning about those who make the challenges of politics sound too easy. "[Of] those men who have overturned the liberties of republics," Hamilton cautioned in *Federalist* No. 1, "the greatest number have begun their career by paying an obsequious court to the people, commencing demagogues, and ending tyrants." [46]

Notes

1. Paul J. Quirk and Jon K. Dalager, "The Election: A 'New Democrat' and a New Kind of Presidential Campaign," in *The Elections of 1992*, ed. Michael Nelson (Washington, D.C.: CQ Press, 1993), 57.
2. George Will, "The Veep and the Blatherskite," *Newsweek*, June 29, 1992, 72.
3. Sidney Blumenthal, "The Order of the Boot," *New Yorker*, December 7, 1992, 55-63.
4. See, for example, Theodore J. Lowi, "The Party Crasher," *New York Times Magazine*, August 23, 1992, 28, 33.
5. James Ceaser and Andrew Busch, *Upside Down and Inside Out: The 1992 Elections and American Politics* (Lanham, Md.: Rowan and Littlefield, 1993), 105. See also Philip Meyer, "The Media Reformation: Giving the Agenda Back to the People," in Nelson, *Elections of 1992*, 89-108.
6. Harvey Mansfield, "Only Amend," *New Republic*, July 6, 1992, 14.
7. Paul Starobin, "President Perot?" *National Journal*, July 4, 1992, 1567-1572.
8. Alan Brinkley, "Roots," *New Republic*, July 27, 1992, 45.
9. William Schneider, "A Loud Vote for Change," *National Journal*, November 7, 1992, 2544.
10. Ibid.
11. "From Bush to Clinton: Continuity Versus Change," *Los Angeles Times*, January 20, 1993, B6.
12. E. J. Dionne, Jr., *Why Americans Hate Politics* (New York: Simon and Schuster, 1991).
13. Schneider, "A Loud Vote for Change," 2542.
14. Bill Clinton, "The New Covenant: Responsibility and Rebuilding the American Community," speech delivered at Georgetown University, Washington, D.C., October 23, 1991.
15. Similar ideas and attendant policy proposals in such areas as welfare and business regulation are spelled out in detail in Will Marshall and Martin Schramm, eds., *Mandate for Change* (New York: Berkley Books, 1993).
16. Dan Balz and David Broder, "President Clinton's First Hundred Days," *Washington Post*, April 29, 1993, A1. The first one hundred days of an administration are an early benchmark of presidential performance that Franklin Roosevelt inadvertently bequeathed to his successors.
17. Walter Dean Burnham, "On the Shoals, Nearing the Rocks," *American Prospect* 14 (Summer 1993): 10-11.
18. Sidney Blumenthal, "The Syndicated Presidency, *New Yorker*, April 5, 1993, 42-47.
19. Of the last nine presidents at this point in their terms, only Ford (47 percent) had a lower approval rating than Clinton (55 precent). But Ford's *disapproval* rating (33 percent) was four points lower than Clinton's (37 percent). *Gallup Poll Monthly*, April 1993, 4.
20. Burt Solomon, "A One-Man Band," *National Journal*, April 24, 1993, 970-974.
21. Burt Solomon, "Musical Chairs in the West Wing May Bring Order from Cacophany," *National Journal*, June 26, 1993, 1660-1661; and Fred Barnes, "The Turn," *New Republic*, October 18, 1993, 10-12.
22. James W. Cicconi, a former member of the Reagan and Bush White Houses, cited in Solomon, "Musical Chairs," 1661.

23. Thomas L. Friedman, "Ready or Not, Clinton Is Rattling the Country," *New York Times*, January 31, 1993, sec. 4, 1.

24. Richard L. Berke, "Clinton in Crossfire," *New York Times*, July 20, 1993, A16. President Clinton arrived at a compromise plan in July 1993. It will permit homosexuals to serve in the military if they do not engage in homosexual behavior on or off base and remain quiet about their sexual identity. It also will make it difficult for commanders to initiate investigations without clear evidence of homosexual behavior. Thomas L. Friedman, "President Admits Revised Policy Isn't Perfect," *New York Times*, July 20, 1993, A1, A16.

25. Thomas L. Friedman, "Clinton Lays Base for New Sacrifice in TV 'Town Hall,' *New York Times*, February 11, 1993, A1, A27.

26. Robert Pear, "Clinton's Bold Plan Sets Social Policy His Way," *New York Times*, February 21, 1993, sec. 4, 1, 3.

27. Jon Healey, "Spending Increases Come First in Rush to Pass Package," *Congressional Quarterly Weekly Report*, February 22, 1993, 365-369; Healey, "Democrats Look to Salvage Part of Stimulus Plan," *Congressional Quarterly Weekly Report*, April 24, 1993, 1001-1002.

28. George Hager and David S. Cloud, "Test for Divided Democrats: Forge a Budget Battle," *Congressional Quarterly Weekly Report*, June 26, 1993, 1631-1635.

29. Alan Brinkley, "The 43% President," *New York Times Magazine*, July 4, 1993, 22.

30. Sidney Blumenthal, "Bob Dole's First Strike," *New Yorker*, May 3, 1993, 40-46.

31. William Clinton, "Address before a Joint Session of Congress on Administration Goals," February 17, 1993, *Weekly Compilation of Presidential Documents*, February 17, 1993, 215-224.

32. Douglas Jehl, "Rejoicing Is Muted for the President in Budget Victory," *New York Times*, August 8, 1993, 1, 23; David Shribman, "Budget Win a Hollow One for President," *Boston Globe*, August 8, 1993, 1, 24.

33. Vice President Al Gore, *Creating a Government that Works Better and Costs Less* (Report of the National Performance Review), September 7, 1993 (Washington, D.C.: Government Printing Office, 1993).

34. Penny cited in Fred Barnes, "Gored," *New Republic*, September 20 and 27, 1993, 12.

35. David Shribman, "A New Brand of D.C. Politics," *The Boston Globe*, November 18, 1993, 15; Gwen Ifill, "56 Long Days of Coordinated Persuasion," *New York Times*, November 19, 1993, A27.

36. William Clinton, Address to Congress on Health Care Plan, printed in *Congressional Quarterly Weekly Report*, September 25, 1993, 2582-2586; Robin Toner, "Alliance to Buy Health Care: Bureaucrat or Public Servant?" *New York Times*, December 5, 1993, 1, 38.

37. CNN transcripts, July 5, 1993.

38. David Shribman, "The Middle East Tests Another President," *Boston Globe*, June 28, 1993, 1.

39. Seyom Brown, *The Faces of Power: Constancy and Change in United States Foreign Policy from Truman to Clinton* (New York: Columbia University Press, forthcoming), chap. 13.

40. Carroll J. Doherty, "Lawmakers Struggle for Footing in Whirlwind of Mideast Peace," *Congressional Quarterly Weekly Report*, September 18, 1993, 2469-2472.

41. Brown, *Faces of Power*, chap. 13.
42. Clifford Krauss, "White House Reaches a Deal with Byrd on Role in Somalia," *New York Times*, October 15, 1993, A12.
43. Brown, *Faces of Power*, chap. 13.
44. Wilson Carey McWilliams, "Parties as Civic Associations," in *Party Renewal in America*, ed. Gerald Pomper (New York: Praeger, 1980).
45. Walter F. Mondale, "Two Views from Pennsylvania Avenue," *American Prospect* 14 (Summer 1993): 16.
46. Alexander Hamilton, James Madison, and John Jay, *The Federalist Papers*, introduction by Clinton Rossiter (New York: New American Library, 1961), 35.

CHAPTER 15

The Vice Presidency

Like the presidency, the vice presidency has been shaped by a combination of constitutional design, changing historical circumstances, and individual initiatives. Like the presidency, too, the vice presidency has grown in prestige and influence and in the expectations that the public has of the office. The history of the vice presidency may be organized usefully into four main periods: the Constitutional Convention, the nineteenth century, the first half of the twentieth century, and the modern era.

The Constitutional Convention

The vice presidency was invented late in the Constitutional Convention, not because the delegates saw any need for such an office, but rather as a means to perfect the arrangements they had made for presidential election and succession and, to some degree, for leadership of the Senate.[1] The original Constitution provided that the vice presidency was to be awarded to the person who received the second highest number of electoral votes for president. If two or more candidates finished in a second-place tie in the presidential election, the Senate would choose among them.

The only ongoing responsibility that the Constitutional Convention assigned to the vice president was to preside over the Senate, casting tie-breaking votes. The vice president's more important duty was to stand by as successor to the presidency in the event of the president's death, impeachment, resignation, or "inability to discharge the Powers and Duties" of the office. But the Constitution was vague about whether the vice president was to become the new president in these circumstances or was only to assume the office's powers and duties; it also left unclear whether the succession was to last until the end of the departed president's four-year term or until a special election could be held to choose a new president. In addition, the Constitution neglected to define the term *inability* or to provide a procedure for the vice president to take power in the event that the president became disabled. Finally, by giving the vice president both legislative and executive responsibilities, the Constitution deprived the office of solid moorings in either Congress or the presidency.

Thus, although the vice presidency solved several constitutional design problems that inhered in the presidency and the Senate, it was plagued from birth by inherent problems of its own. The office's hybrid status was bound to make it an object of suspicion in legislative councils because it was partly executive and in executive councils because it was partly legislative. The vice president's responsibility to preside over the Senate was not very important. The poorly defined successor role was to be an inevitable source of confusion and, perhaps, of tension between presidents and vice presidents: the fabled "heartbeat away" that separates the vice president from the presidency is, after all, the president's. Finally, more than any other institution of the new government, the vice presidency required the realization of the convention's hope that political parties would not develop. The office would seem less a brilliant than a rash improvisation if it were occupied as a matter of course by the president's leading partisan foe.

The Nineteenth Century

John Adams, who was elected to serve with President George Washington in 1789 and 1792, was the first vice president. Midway through his tenure, Adams lamented to his wife, Abigail Adams, that "my country has in its wisdom contrived for me the most insignificant office that ever the invention of man contrived or his imagination conceived." [2] Little did Adams realize that the vice presidency was at a peak of influence during the period he served. Because the Senate had only twenty-six members and still was relatively unorganized, he was able to cast twenty-nine tie-breaking votes (still the record) and to guide the upper house's agenda and intervene in debate. Adams was respected and sometimes consulted on diplomatic and other matters by Washington, who invited him to meet with the cabinet in the president's absence. Moreover, having won the vice presidency by receiving, at least technically, the second largest number of electoral votes for president in each of the nation's first two elections, it is not surprising that Adams was elected president in 1796 after Washington left office.

Adams's election as president was different from Washington's, however. The hopes of the Constitutional Convention notwithstanding, two political parties, the Federalists and the Democratic-Republicans, emerged during the Washington administration. The result in 1796 was the election as vice president of the Democratic-Republicans' presidential nominee, Thomas Jefferson. Adams tried to lure Jefferson into the administration's fold by urging him to undertake a diplomatic mission to France, but Jefferson, eager to build up his own party and win the presidency away from Adams, would have no part of it. He justified his refusal by claiming that, constitutionally, the vice presidency was a legislative office. By Jefferson's own testimony, that was the end of his dealings with President Adams, except on formal occasions. He did make a mark as Senate president, writing a book—*Manual of Parliamentary Practice*—that, although never formally adopted by the Senate, became its working procedural guide. But most of Jefferson's congressional activities involved behind-the-scenes opposition to President Adams and the Federalists.

Unsatisfied with the divided partisan outcome of the 1796 election, each party nominated a complete ticket in 1800, instructing its electors to cast their two votes for its presidential and vice-presidential candidates. The intent was that both would be elected; the result was that neither was. Jefferson and his running mate, Aaron Burr, ended up with an equal number of votes for president. The House of Representatives eventually chose Jefferson, but not before Federalist mischief-makers kept the election uncertain through thirty-six ballots. Burr became vice president.

One result of the election of 1800 was the Burr vice presidency, which was marked by bad relations between Burr and Jefferson (they were personally incompatible and represented different factions of the party) and by various misdeeds, including a duel in which Burr shot and killed former Treasury secretary Alexander Hamilton. Another result was the widespread realization that something had to be done about the electoral college so that it could accommodate party competition. Vice-presidential selection was the problem; requiring electors to vote separately for president and vice president was one obvious solution.

In opposing the proposal for a separate ballot, some members of Congress argued that it would create a worse problem than it solved. Because "the vice president will not stand on such high ground in the method proposed as he does in the present mode of a double ballot [for president]," Massachusetts representative Samuel Taggart predicted, the nation could expect that "great care will not be taken in the selection of a character to fill that office." Sen. William Plumer of New Hampshire warned that such care as was taken would be "to procure votes for the president." [3] In truth, as the nomination of Burr indicated, the parties already had begun to degrade the vice presidency into a device for balancing the ticket in the election.

In 1804, motions were made in Congress to abolish the vice presidency rather than continue it in a form reduced from its original constitutional status as the position awarded to the second-most-qualified person to be president. These motions failed. In their place, the Twelfth Amendment was passed and entered the Constitution later that year. The amendment provided that electors "shall name in their ballots the person voted for as President, and in distinct ballots the person voted for as Vice President." It also stipulated that if no one received a majority of electoral votes for vice president, then "from the two highest numbers on the list, the Senate shall choose the Vice President." Finally, the Twelfth Amendment extended the Constitution's original age, citizenship, and residency qualifications for president to the vice president.

The development of political parties and the enactment of the Twelfth Amendment sent an already constitutionally weak vice presidency into a political tailspin that lasted until the end of the nineteenth century. Party leaders, not presidential candidates (who often were not even present at national nominating conventions and who, if present, were expected to be seen and not heard), chose the nominees for vice president, which certainly did not foster trust or respect between the president and the vice president in office. Aggravating the tension were the main criteria that party leaders applied to vice-presidential selection. One criterion was that the nominee placate the region or faction of the party that had been most dissatisfied with the presidential nomination, which led to numerous New York-Virginia, North-South, Stalwart-Progressive, hard money-soft money, and other such pairings. Another was that the nominee be able to carry in the general election a swing state where the presidential candidate was not popular.

In addition to fostering tension within the government, ticket balancing as the main basis for vice-presidential selection also placed such a stigma on the office that many political leaders were unwilling to accept a nomination. Daniel Webster, declining the vice-presidential place on the Whig party ticket in 1848, said, "I do not propose to be buried until I am dead." [4] Those who did accept a nomination and were elected found that fresh political problems four years later invariably led party leaders to balance the ticket differently: no first-term vice president in the nineteenth century ever was renominated for a second term by a party convention. Nor, after Vice President Martin Van Buren in 1836, was any nineteenth-century vice president elected or even nominated for president. Finally, the vice president's role as Senate president (which most vice presidents, following Jefferson's lead and for want of anything else to do, spent considerable time performing) became more ceremonial as the Senate took greater charge of its own affairs, developing an extensive committee system and a number of leadership positions. John C. Calhoun, who served from 1825 to 1833, was the last vice president whom the Senate allowed to appoint its committees.

Not surprisingly, the nineteenth-century vice presidents make up a virtual rogues' gallery of personal and political failures. Because the office was so unappealing, an unusual number of the politicians who could be enticed to run for vice president were old and in bad health. Six died in office, all of natural causes: George Clinton, Elbridge Gerry, William R. King (who took his oath of office in Cuba and died there a month later), Henry Wilson, Thomas A. Hendricks, and Garret A. Hobart. Some vice presidents became embroiled in financial scandals: Daniel D. Tompkins was charged with keeping inadequate financial records while serving as governor of New York during the War of 1812, and Schuyler Colfax and Henry Wilson were implicated in the notorious Crédit Mobilier stock scandal of the 1870s.

Other vice presidents fell prey to personal weaknesses or political jealousies. Tompkins and Andrew Johnson were heavy drinkers. (Johnson's first address to the Senate was a drunken harangue.) Richard M. Johnson kept a series of slave mistresses, educating the children of one but selling another when she lost interest in him. Clinton, Calhoun, and Chester A. Arthur each publicly expressed his dislike for the president with whom he served. Clinton refused to attend President James Madison's inauguration and openly attacked the administration's foreign and domestic policies. Calhoun alienated two presidents, John Quincy Adams and Andrew Jackson, by using his position as Senate president to subvert their policies and appointments, then resigned in 1831 to accept South Carolina's election as U.S. senator. Arthur attacked President James A. Garfield over a patronage quarrel. "Garfield has not been square, nor honorable, nor truthful . . .," he told the *New York Herald*. "It's a hard thing to say of a president of the United States, but it's only the truth." [5] Finally, some vice presidents did not even live in Washington—Richard Johnson left to run a tavern.[6]

The history of the nineteenth-century vice presidency is not entirely bleak. A certain measure of comity existed between a few presidents and vice presidents—notably Jackson and Van Buren, James K. Polk and George M. Dallas, Abraham Lincoln and Hannibal Hamlin, Rutherford B. Hayes and William A. Wheeler, and William McKinley and Hobart—but even in their administrations, the vice president was not invited to cabinet meetings or entrusted with important tasks. What strengthened most of these relationships was the president's respect for the vice president's advice, which was sought informally, and the vice president's willingness and effectiveness as an advocate of the administration's policies in the Senate.

In one area of vice-presidential responsibility—presidential succession—the nineteenth century witnessed a giant step forward. The succession question did not even arise until 1841, when William Henry Harrison became the first president to die in office. The language of the Constitution provided little guidance about whether the vice president, John Tyler, was to become president for the remainder of Harrison's term or merely acting president until a special election could be held. The records of the Constitutional Convention, which could have helped to clarify the delegates' intentions (they had wanted a special election), had long been kept secret by James Madison and still were not available. In this uncertain situation, Tyler's claim to both the presidency and the balance of Harrison's term was accepted with little debate, setting a precedent that the next successor president was able to follow without any controversy at all. Vice President Millard Fillmore succeeded to the presidency in 1850, after President Zachary Taylor died.

But even this bright spot in the early history of the vice presidency was tarnished. Tyler's tenure as president was marred by debilitating disagreements with the party, especially in Congress, and with the late president's cabinet. Fillmore and the two other nineteenth-century successor presidents, Andrew Johnson and Arthur, encountered similar problems. (Johnson was impeached by the House and came within one vote of being removed by a two-thirds majority of the Senate.) None of the four is regarded as having been a successful president. In the most recent round of historians' rankings, Johnson was rated a failure, Tyler and Fillmore as below average, and Arthur as average.[7] Nor were any of the nineteenth-century successor presidents even nominated for a full term as president in their own right.

Unresolved issues of succession and disability also vexed the vice presidency during the nineteenth century. Taken together, six vice-presidential deaths, one vice-presidential resignation, and four presidential deaths left the nation without a vice president during eleven of the century's twenty-five presidential terms. President Taylor's death in July 1850 and Vice President King's in April 1853 meant that, with the exception of the month that King spent in Cuba after taking the oath of office in March 1853, there was no vice president for seven consecutive years, until March 1857. Fortunately, no president died while the vice presidency was vacant.

The issue of vice-presidential responsibility in periods of presidential disability also remained unresolved. Five nineteenth-century presidents seem to have been disabled for measurable lengths of time.[8] In 1881, for example, during the seventy-nine days that President Garfield lay comatose before dying from an assassin's bullet, Vice President Arthur stood by helplessly, unwilling to act and thus risk being accused of coveting the presidency.

Theodore Roosevelt to Harry S. Truman

By the start of the twentieth century, the vice presidency had become an easy and frequent target of political humor. Mr. Dooley, the invented character of the writer Finley Peter Dunne, described the office as "not a crime exactly. Ye can't be sint to jail f'r it, but it's kind iv a disgrace. It's like writin' anonymous letters." Thomas R. Marshall, who occupied the vice presidency during Woodrow Wilson's two terms as president, said that the vice president is like "a man in a cataleptic fit; he cannot speak; he cannot move; he suffers no pain; he is perfectly conscious of all that goes on, but has no part in it." (Marshall also told the story of the two brothers: "One ran away to sea; the other was elected vice president. And nothing was heard of either of them again.") John Nance Garner was a fairly active vice president during the first two terms of Franklin D. Roosevelt's administration, but the G-rated version of his pithy assessment of the office is probably the most frequently quoted of all: "The vice presidency isn't worth a pitcher of warm spit." [9]

Gibes such as these now seem antiquated. Far from being "kind iv a disgrace," the vice presidency is one of the most prestigious offices in the United States. If Marshall's vice president was "cataleptic" and anonymous, his modern successors are active, often influential, and almost universally recognized. A party's nomination to run for vice president is highly coveted by most modern politicians, partly (perhaps mostly) as a steppingstone to the presidency.

The advance of the vice presidency from opprobrium to approbation has occurred most rapidly since World War II, but it began during the first years of the twentieth century with the rise of mass-circulation magazines and newspaper wire services, a new style of active presidential campaigning, and changes in the vice-presidential nominating process. In 1900, the Republican nominee, Theodore Roosevelt, became the first vice-presidential candidate (and, other than William Jennings Bryan, the Democratic nominee for president in 1896, the first member of a national party ticket) to campaign vigorously nationwide. While President William McKinley waged a sedate "front-porch" reelection campaign, Roosevelt gave 673 speeches to three million listeners in twenty-four states.

The national reputation that Roosevelt gained through travel and the media stood him in good stead with both his party and the country when he succeeded to the presidency after McKinley was assassinated in 1901. Roosevelt was able to reverse the earlier pattern of successor presidents and begin a new one: unlike Tyler, Fillmore, Andrew Johnson, and Arthur, Roosevelt was nominated by his party to run for a full term as president in 1904, thus setting the precedent for Calvin

Coolidge in 1924, Harry S. Truman in 1948, Lyndon B. Johnson in 1964, and Gerald R. Ford in 1976. Roosevelt's success also may help to explain another new pattern that contrasts sharply with nineteenth-century practice. Starting with James S. Sherman in 1912, every first-term vice president in the twentieth century who has sought a second term has been nominated for reelection.

In addition to the political precedents he established, Roosevelt helped to lay the intellectual groundwork for an enhanced role for the vice president in office. In an 1896 article, he argued that the president and vice president should share the same "views and principles" and that the vice president "should always be . . . consulted by the president on every great party question. It would be very well if he were given a seat in the Cabinet . . . a vote [in the Senate], on ordinary occasions, and perchance on occasion a voice in the debates." [10]

Roosevelt was unable as vice president (and unwilling as president) to practice what he preached about the vice presidency. Just as party leaders imposed the vice-presidential nomination of Charles W. Fairbanks on him to balance the ticket in 1904 (Roosevelt was from the progressive wing of the party, Fairbanks from the Old Guard), so had Roosevelt's nomination as vice president been forced on McKinley in 1900, and for roughly the same reason. Neither McKinley nor Roosevelt liked or trusted his vice president, much less assigned him responsibilities. Roosevelt often repeated the humorist Dunne's response when the president said that he was thinking of going down in a submarine: "Well, you really shouldn't do it—unless you take Fairbanks with you." [11]

Still, the enhanced political status of the vice presidency soon began to make it a more attractive office to at least some able and experienced political leaders, including Charles Dawes, who had served in three administrations and won a Nobel Prize; Charles Curtis, the Senate majority leader; and Garner, the Speaker of the House. With somewhat more talent to offer, some vice presidents were given new responsibilities by the presidents they served. John Adams had been the last vice president to meet with the cabinet, for example, but when President Wilson went to Europe in 1918 to negotiate the treaty that ended World War I, he asked Vice President Marshall to preside in his absence. Wilson's successor, Warren G. Harding, invited Vice President Coolidge to meet with the cabinet as a matter of course, as has every president since Franklin Roosevelt. [12]

FDR, like his cousin Theodore, had both run for vice president before becoming president (he lost in 1920) and written an article to urge that the responsibilities of the vice presidency be expanded. In the article, Roosevelt had identified four roles that the vice president could perform helpfully: cabinet member, presidential adviser, liaison to

Congress, and policy maker in areas "that do not belong in the province" of any particular department or agency.[13]

As president, Roosevelt initially had so much respect for Garner that, even though the conservative Texan's nomination had been imposed on him at the 1932 Democratic convention, the president relied on the vice president during the first term as "a combination presiding officer, cabinet officer, personal counselor, legislative tactician, Cassandra, and sounding board."[14] Most significant, the vice president served as an important liaison from Roosevelt to Congress—it was Garner's suggestion that led to the practice, which subsequent presidents have preserved, of meeting weekly with congressional leaders. Garner also undertook a goodwill mission abroad at Roosevelt's behest, another innovation that virtually all later administrations have continued.

During the second term, Roosevelt and Garner had a falling out over the president's Court-packing plan, support for organized labor, and other liberal policies—Garner even challenged Roosevelt for the party's 1940 presidential nomination. The rupture between the president and the vice president set the stage for an important modification of the vice-presidential selection process that was designed to foster greater harmony between presidents and vice presidents. In 1936, at Roosevelt's insistence, the Democrats already had abolished their two-thirds rule for presidential nominations, which meant that candidates for president no longer had to engage in as much trading of delegate votes for vice-presidential nominations and other administration posts in order to win at the convention. (The party also abolished the two-thirds rule for vice-presidential nominations, reducing the degree of consensus needed for that choice as well.) In 1940, Roosevelt completed his coup by seizing the party leaders' traditional power to determine nominations for vice president and making it his own. His tactic was simple: he threatened that unless the convention nominated Secretary of Agriculture Henry A. Wallace for vice president (which it was loath to do), he would not accept the Democratic nomination for president.

Unlike Garner and many of his other predecessors, Wallace had never been a member of Congress and, while in office, spent little time on Capitol Hill. But he did become the only vice president to be appointed as head of a government agency. In July 1941, Roosevelt named Wallace to chair the new Economic Defense Board, a three-thousand-member wartime preparation agency that, after World War II was declared in December, was renamed the Board of Economic Warfare and assigned major procurement responsibilities. Unfortunately, the powers and duties of Wallace's agency overlapped with those of several cabinet departments, notably State and Commerce. These overlaps generated interagency conflicts over jurisdiction and policy that weakened both the war effort and Wallace's authority. But because the vice president is a constitutionally independent official whom the president cannot command or remove, at least not in the usual sense, Roosevelt felt compelled to abolish the warfare board rather than fire Wallace, which left the vice president embarrassed and devoid of function. What initially had seemed to be a new birth of vice-presidential power turned out to be false labor. No subsequent president has ever asked the vice president to head an executive agency.

Nevertheless, the steadily growing involvement of the vice president in other executive branch activities continued under Wallace. He sat with the cabinet, advised the president, and traveled abroad as an administration emissary. Even Wallace's distant relationship with Congress exemplified a developing characteristic of the twentieth-century vice presidency: the atrophy of the office's role as the president of the Senate. To some degree, the first development explained the second; to the extent that vice presidents became more involved with the presidency, they had less time to spend on the floor of the Senate and less ability to win senators' trust. But changes in the Senate also helped to account for the decline of the vice president's constitutional responsibilities in that institution. For one thing, with the admission of new states, the Senate had grown larger, making tie votes statistically less probable. The Senate also had become more institutionalized, developing its own body of rules and procedural precedents, which the president of the Senate was expected merely to announce, on the advice of the parliamentarian.

Advances in the visibility, stature, and extraconstitutional responsibilities of the vice presidency may help to explain the office's improved performance of its main constitutional duty: to provide an able successor to a departed president. Historians rate two of the five twentieth-century successor presidents (Theodore Roosevelt and Truman) as near-great, one as above average (Johnson), and only Coolidge as below average.[15]

For all its gains, however, the vice presidency on the eve of midcentury remained a fundamentally weak office. Its constitutional status was substantially unaltered, although in 1933 the Twentieth Amendment did establish the full successorship of the vice president-elect in the event of the president-elect's death. Ticket balancing to increase the party's appeal on election day continued to dominate vice-presidential selection. All the ambiguities of the vice president's rights and duties in times of presidential disability still were unresolved, as dramatized by the passive role that Marshall felt compelled to play (lest he be branded a usurper) during the prolonged illness of Woodrow Wilson. Tension continued to mark some presidential-vice presidential pairings, although less frequently after Franklin Roosevelt won for presidential candidates the right to choose their running mates.

Even the glimmerings of enhanced vice-presidential influence sometimes seemed to be no more than that. Roosevelt replaced the unpopular Wallace with Senator Truman when he ran for a fourth term in 1944. On inauguration day 1945, the president was ill, and World War II was racing to a close. Yet Truman later was to say that in his eighty-two days as vice president, "I don't think I saw Roosevelt but twice . . . except at cabinet meetings." [16] Truman was at most dimly aware of the existence of the atomic bomb, the Allies' plans for the postwar world, and the serious deterioration of the president's health. In this woeful state of ignorance and unpreparedness, Truman, upon Roosevelt's death on April 12, 1945, immediately succeeded to the office of the president and to its full range of powers and duties. He told a friend later that day, "I feel like I have been struck by a bolt of lightning." [17]

The Modern Vice Presidency

Truman's lack of preparation in 1945, along with the subsequent development of an ongoing cold war between the United States and the Soviet Union and the proliferation of intercontinental ballistic missiles armed with nuclear warheads, heightened public concern that the vice president should be someone who is not just willing but also ready and able to step into the presidency at a moment's notice. This concern has had important consequences for vice-presidential selection, activities, and succession and disability, as well as for the political status of the vice presidency.

Selection

To meet the new public expectations about vice-presidential quality, most modern presidential candidates have paid considerable attention to experience, ability, and political compatibility in selecting their running mates. Winning votes on election day is still as much the goal as in the days of old-style ticket balancing, but presidential nominees realize that voters now care more about competence and loyalty—a vice-presidential candidate's ability to succeed to the presidency ably and to carry on the departed president's policies faithfully—than they do about having all regions of the country or factions of the party represented on the ticket. This realization has helped to create a climate for a more influential vice presidency. As Joel Goldstein has shown, the president is most willing to assign responsibilities to vice president when the two are personally and politically compatible and when the president believes that the vice president has talents the administration needs.[18] These conditions are now likely to be met (and have been, in every administration since 1974) as a consequence of the new selection criteria.

Little is left to chance in modern vice-presidential selection, at least when the presidential nominating contest is settled, as has been typical since 1952, well in advance of the convention. Jimmy Carter set a precedent in 1976 when he conducted a careful, organized preconvention search for a running mate. A list of four hundred Democratic officeholders was compiled and scrutinized by aides, then winnowed down to seven finalists who were investigated and, ultimately, interviewed by Carter. (He tapped Sen. Walter F. Mondale at the convention.) Mondale, Gov. Michael S. Dukakis, and Bill Clinton followed similar procedures as the Democratic presidential nominees in 1984, 1988, and 1992, respectively. Ronald Reagan did nothing so elaborate in 1980 because he hoped to lure former president Ford onto the ticket, but he and his aides did give considerable thought to the kind of running mate they wanted. George Bush searched widely before choosing Indiana senator Dan Quayle in 1988.[19]

The fruit of both the new emphasis on loyalty and competence and the new care that is invested in the selection process can be seen in the roster of postwar vice-presidential nominees. The modern era has been marked by an almost complete absence of ideologically opposed running mates, and those vice-presidential candidates who have differed on certain issues with the heads of their tickets have hastened to gloss over past disagreements and to deny that any would exist in office. The record is even more compelling with regard to competence. From 1948 to 1992, the vice-presidential candidate as often as not was the more experienced member of the ticket in high government office, including John Sparkman in 1952, Estes Kefauver in 1956, Johnson and Henry Cabot Lodge in 1960, Mondale in 1976, Bush in 1980, Lloyd Bentsen in 1988, and Albert Gore in 1992.[20]

No guarantee exists, of course, that reasoned, responsible vice-presidential nominations will be made on every occasion. Politicians do not always see their interests clearly. Nixon, the Republican presidential nominee in 1968, was too clever by half when, acting on the theory that a relatively unknown running mate would have few enemies and cost the ticket few votes, he chose Spiro T. Agnew as his candidate for vice president. In 1984, many observers thought Mondale seemed too eager to placate feminist groups within the party when he selected Geraldine A. Ferraro, a three-term member of the House of Representatives with no notable foreign affairs experience, as his running mate, just as George McGovern may have been overly concerned about satisfying organized labor when he picked Sen. Thomas Eagleton in 1972. It was revealed soon after Eagleton's nomination for vice president that he had undergone electroshock treatment for a nervous breakdown, a fact that he withheld from McGovern and that led to his being dropped from the ticket.

On April 12, 1945, Vice President Truman took the presidential oath of office as his wife and daughter looked on. Later that day he told a friend, "I feel like I have been struck by a bolt of lightning."

What seems certain, however, is that the presidential candidate who pays insufficient attention to competence and loyalty in choosing the vice-presidential nominee will pay a price in the election. The news media will present critical stories, the other party will run harsh commercials, and the now-traditional vice-presidential debate, which is nationally televised, may reveal the nominee as an unworthy presidential successor. Bush's selection of the inexperienced Quayle may have reduced his margin of victory in the popular vote by as much as four to eight percentage points in the 1988 election.[21] In contrast, the nomination of Albert Gore defied all the conventions of ticket-balancing—like Clinton, he was a southerner, a Baptist, a moderate, and a baby-boomer—but Gore's obvious intelligence and ability appealed to many voters.[22]

A concern for competence and loyalty in the vice presidency also characterized the solution Congress invented to a recurring problem of the executive that the challenges of the postwar era had made urgent: vice-presidential vacancies. The Twenty-fifth Amendment, which was ratified in 1967, established a procedure to select vice presidents in unusual circumstances.[23] The amendment stated that "whenever there is a vacancy in the office of the Vice President, the President shall nominate a Vice President who shall take office upon confirmation by a majority vote of both Houses of Congress," voting separately. This procedure came in handy, albeit in circumstances its authors scarcely had imagined, in 1973, when Vice President Agnew resigned as part of a plea bargain to reduce bribery charges and was replaced by Ford, and in 1974, when Ford became president after President Nixon resigned to avert impeachment proceedings and appointed former New York governor Nelson A. Rockefeller to fill the vacated vice presidency.

Activity

One thing modern presidents do to reassure the nation that the vice president is prepared to succeed to the presidency is to keep them informed about matters of state. As President Dwight D. Eisenhower's remark at a news conference indicates, to do otherwise would invite public criticism: "Even if Mr. Nixon and I were not good friends, I would still have him in every important conference of government, so that if the grim reaper would find it time to remove me from the scene, he is ready to step in without any interruption." [24] In 1949, at President Truman's request, the vice president was made a statutory member of the National Security Council. (The only other task that is assigned to the vice president by law is to serve on the Board of Regents of the Smithsonian Institution.) Vice presidents also receive full national security briefings as a matter of course.

As a further means of public reassurance, most presidents now encourage the vice president to stay active and in the public eye. Since Garner began the practice, vice presidents have traveled abroad in the president's behalf with growing frequency in pursuit of a variety of diplomatic missions, ranging from simple expressions of American good will to actual negotiations. Vice presidents since Garner also have met regularly with the cabinet and have served, to some degree, as a legislative liaison from the president to Congress—counting votes on Capitol Hill, lobbying discreetly, and listening to complaints and suggestions.

Alben W. Barkley, who served as vice president in the Truman administration, elevated the ceremonial duties of the vice presidency to center stage. Some of these, such as crowning beauty queens (a Barkley favorite), have been inconsequential, but others, such as college commencement addresses and appearances at events that symbolize administration goals, have not been. Nixon, serving a president who did not enjoy partisan politics, carved out new vice-presidential roles that were as insignificant as chair of a study commission and as important as public advocate of the administration's policies, leadership, and party. The advocacy role exposes the vice president to a wide range of politically important audiences, including interest groups, party activists, journalists, and the general public.

During the 1960s and 1970s, vice presidents began to accumulate greater institutional resources to help them fulfill their more extensive duties. Johnson, the vice president to Kennedy, gained for the vice presidency an impressive suite of offices in the Executive Office Building, adjacent to the White House. Agnew won a line item in the executive budget. Between them, the two vice presidents freed their successors from the traditional dependence on Congress for office space and operating funds.

Even more significant institutional gains were registered by Ford and Rockefeller, the two vice presidents who were appointed under the Twenty-fifth Amendment and whose agreements to serve were urgently required by their presidents, for political reasons. Ford, who feared becoming too dependent on a president who might be removed from office, persuaded Nixon to increase dramatically his budget for hiring staff. The new personnel included support staff for press relations, speech writing, scheduling, and administration (which meant the vice president no longer had to depend on the often-preoccupied White House staff for those functions), policy staff (enabling vice presidents to develop useful ideas and advice on matters of presidential concern), and political staff (to help vice presidents protect their interests and further their ambitions). Rockefeller secured a weekly place on the president's calendar for a private meeting. He also enhanced the perquisites of the vice presidency—everything from a better airplane to serve as *Air Force Two* to an official residence (the Admiral's House at the Naval Observatory) and a redesigned seal for the office. The old seal had shown an eagle at rest; the new one displayed a wingspread eagle with a claw full of arrows and a starburst at its head.[25]

The vice presidency came into full flower during Mondale's tenure in the Carter administration. As a candidate in 1976, Mondale participated in the first nationally televised debate between the vice-presidential candidates. His most tangible contributions to the institution during his term as vice president, building on earlier gains, were the authorization he won to attend all presidential meetings, full access to the flow of papers to and from the president, and an office in the West Wing of the White House. Most important, perhaps, Mondale demonstrated that the vice president could serve the president (who, as noted earlier, had selected him with unprecedented care and attention) as a valued adviser on virtually all matters of politics and public policy. Some vice presidents in each of the earlier eras of the office's history, and most vice presidents in the modern era, had been consulted by their presidents on at least a few important matters—Johnson on space issues, Humphrey on civil rights, Rockefeller on domestic policy. But no vice president ever had attained Mondale's status as a wide-ranging senior adviser to the president.

President Jimmy Carter regarded his vice president, Walter Mondale, left, as a valued adviser on virtually all matters of politics and public policy, a status no earlier vice president had attained. Mondale also was authorized to attend all presidential meetings and was allowed full access to the flow of papers to and from the president.

Bush, as vice president to President Reagan, was heir to all the institutional gains in roles and resources that his recent predecessors had won. Although he did not enter office enjoying the same sort of personal relationship with Reagan that Mondale had with Carter, Bush worked hard and, for the most part, successfully to win the president's confidence. As president, Bush fostered an even stronger relationship with Quayle.[26] From the beginning, Clinton's relationship with Gore rivaled Carter's with Mondale for trust and responsibility.

Every vice president realizes that the extent to which the new activities of the office translate into real influence within the White House still depends in large part on the president's perception of the vice president's ability, energy, and, perhaps most important, loyalty. But, because of the new vice-presidential selection criteria, this perception is more likely to be favorable than at any previous time in history. And, because of the institutionalization of numerous roles and resources in the vice presidency, the vice president has a greater opportunity than ever to be of real service to a president.

Succession and Disability

In addition to creating a procedure to fill vice-presidential vacancies, the Twenty-fifth Amendment accomplished two other purposes. One was to state explicitly the right of the vice president to assume the presidency if the president dies, resigns, or is removed and to serve for the remainder of the departed president's term, an uncontroversial measure that conferred constitutional sanction on a long-settled tradition. The other was to establish a set of procedures to handle situations of presidential disability. The amendment provided constitutional methods both for the president, by means of a letter to the leaders of Congress, to name the vice president as acting president during a time of disability and for the vice president and a majority of the heads of the departments to make that decision if the president were unable to do so. The amendment even created a procedure to be followed if the vice president and the cabinet believed the president to be disabled and the president disagreed: the vice president would become acting president, but the president would be restored to power within twenty-one days unless two-thirds of both the House and the Senate voted to the contrary.

Only two clear situations of presidential disability have arisen since the Twenty-fifth Amendment was passed, both during the Reagan administration.[27] The first occurred when Reagan was shot on March 30, 1981. Some thought was given, then and in the days afterward, to naming Vice President Bush as acting president. But White House aides discouraged any such action for fear that to do so would make Reagan appear weak or would confuse the nation.[28]

Criticism of the administration's failure to act shaped its preparation for the second instance of presidential disability, Reagan's scheduled cancer surgery on July 13, 1985. This time Reagan did relinquish his powers and duties to Bush before undergoing anesthesia. Curiously, he did not explicitly invoke the Twenty-fifth Amendment in doing so, saying instead that he was not convinced that the amendment was meant to apply to "such brief and temporary periods of incapacity" as his surgery. Still, a precedent was established, raising expectations that the Twenty-fifth Amendment would work as intended in future administrations. This precedent was followed in May 1991 when President Bush announced a plan to turn power over to Vice President Quayle in the event that his irregular heartbeat required electric shock therapy. (It did not.)

Political Status

The vice president enjoys a curious political status. Until Bush's victory in 1988, no incumbent vice president had become president by the ballot since 1836, when Van Buren was elected. Yet, in a marked departure from previous political history, the vice presidency has become an effective steppingstone to a major party presidential nomination in the postwar era. Of the modern vice presidents, Nixon, Hubert Humphrey, Mondale, and Bush were nominated directly for president, and Truman, Johnson, and Ford were nominated for a full term after succeeding to the presidency. Three others—Barkley, Agnew, and Rockefeller—did not actively seek a presidential nomination.[29]

What accounts for the recent ascendancy of the vice presidency in the politics of presidential nominations? First, the two-term limit that was imposed on presidents by the Twenty-second Amendment (1951) made it possible for the vice president to step forward as a presidential candidate during the president's second term, as Nixon did in 1960 and Bush did in 1988, without alienating the president. (This effect of the amendment was wholly unanticipated.) Second, the roles that Vice President Nixon developed, with Eisenhower's encouragement, as party builder (campaigning during election years, raising funds between elections) and as public advocate of the administration and its policies uniquely situate the vice president to win friends among the party activists who influence presidential nominations. Finally, the recent growth in diplomatic travel and other vice-presidential activities has made it a more prestigious office and thus a more plausible stepping-stone to the presidency. Even the trappings of the modern vice presidency—the airplane, mansion, seal, Secret Service contingent, and West Wing office—are physical symbols of prestige.[30]

Perhaps more important, in their efforts to ensure the nation that they are fulfilling their responsibility to prepare for a possible emergency succession, presidents may make inflated claims about the participation of the vice president in the administration. Thus, the typical modern vice president can argue plausibly, as Mondale frequently did, that the vice presidency "may be the best training of all" for the presidency:

> I'm privy to all the same secret information as the president. I have unlimited access to the president. I'm usually with him when all the central decisions are being made. I've been through several of those crises that a president inevitably confronts, and I see how they work. I've been through the budget process. I've been through the diplomatic ventures. I've been through a host of congressional fights as seen from the presidential perspective.[31]

Yet vice presidents who are nominated by their party for president carry certain disadvantages into the fall campaign that are as surely grounded in the office as are the advantages they bring to the nominating contest. Indeed, some of the very activities of the modern vice presidency that are most appealing to the party activists who influence nominations may repel members of the broader electorate that decides the general election. Days and nights spent fertilizing the party's grass roots with fervent, sometimes slashing rhetoric can alienate voters who look to the presidency for unifying, not partisan, leadership.

In addition, although only the president can plausibly take credit for an administration's successes, the vice president is fair game for attacks by the other party's presidential candidate for its shortcomings. (Because of the Vietnam War, that was the fate of Vice President Humphrey in 1968.) Such attacks allow no good response. A vice president who tried to stand apart from the administration would alienate the president and cause voters to wonder why the criticisms were not voiced earlier, when they might have made a difference. The vice president may say instead that loyalty to the president forecloses public disagreement (an argument that Bush made frequently in 1988), but that course is no less perilous. Strength, independence, vision, and integrity are the qualities voters most seek in a president, not loyalty to the boss.

To be sure, future vice presidents are not destined to lose presidential elections any more than they are destined to win presidential nominations. Before Bush was elected in 1988, Nixon (in 1960) and Humphrey (in 1968) each came within a percentage point of victory. But the electoral tensions that vice presidents face, which inhere in the office, were well stated by President Eisenhower: "To promise and pledge *new* effort, *new* programs, and *new* ideas without appearing to criticize the current party and administration—that is indeed an exercise in tightrope walking."[32]

Conclusion

In selection, activity, succession and disability, and political status, the vice presidency has come a long way during the twentieth century, especially since 1945. But the curious electoral history of the vice-presidents-turned-presidential-candidates is a reminder that, for all its progress as an institution, some weaknesses of the office endure. Although new selection criteria make the nomination of vice-presidential candidates who are qualified to be president more likely, the recent examples of William E. Miller in 1964, Agnew in 1968, Eagleton in 1972, Ferraro in 1984, and Quayle in 1988 indicate that older patterns of choice are not yet extinct.

New selection criteria may foster greater harmony in office between the president and the vice president, but they do not guarantee it. Perhaps it is not surprising that the two modern presidents who inflicted the greatest pain on their vice presidents, Johnson and Nixon, once were vice presidents themselves.[33] Finally, although vice presidents enjoy more resources, responsibilities, and influence than ever before, they do so mainly at the sufferance of the president. The price of power for a vice president can be high—unflagging loyalty, sublimation of one's own views and ambitions, and willing receptiveness to the president's beck and call. But, in view of the inherent constitutional weakness of the office, no other path to influence exists.

Notes

1. See Chapter 2.
2. Quoted in Paul C. Light, *Vice-Presidential Power: Advice and Influence in the White House* (Baltimore: Johns Hopkins University Press, 1984), 13.
3. Quoted in Joel K. Goldstein, *The Modern American Vice Presidency* (Princeton, N.J.: Princeton University Press, 1982).
4. Quoted in Thomas E. Cronin, "Rethinking the Vice Presidency," in *Rethinking the Vice Presidency*, ed. Thomas E. Cronin (Boston: Little, Brown, 1982), 326. Rather than being buried, of course, Webster would have succeeded to the presidency when Zachary Taylor died in 1850.
5. Quoted in Irving G. Williams, *The Rise of the Vice Presidency* (Washington, D.C.: Public Affairs Press, 1956), 66.
6. Johnson was the protagonist in two other unique events in the history of the vice presidency. In the election of 1836, Virginia's Democratic electors refused to vote for Johnson because they objected to his interracial sexual extravagances. This left Johnson one vote short of the required electoral vote majority, so the Senate elected him by 33-16. Four years later, Johnson refused to withdraw as a candidate for the Democratic nomination for vice president, dividing the party convention to such an extent that it selected no vice-presidential candidate at all. The Democrats lost the election.
7. Robert K. Murray and Tim H. Blessing, "The Presidential Performance Study: A Progress Report," *Journal of American History* 70 (December 1983): 535-555.
8. The five nineteenth-century presidents who were disabled for a measurable period of time were Madison, William Henry Harrison, Arthur, Garfield, and Grover Cleveland (John D. Feerick, *The Twenty-fifth Amendment* [New York: Fordham University Press, 1976], chap. 1).
9. These familiar quotations about the vice presidency may be found in Michael Dorman, *The Second Man: The Changing Role of the Vice Presidency* (New York: Delacorte Press, 1968), 6-7. Garner actually referred to a bodily fluid other than spit.
10. Theodore Roosevelt, "The Three Vice-Presidential Candidates and What They Represent," *Review of Reviews*, September 1896, 289.
11. Quoted in Williams, *Rise of the Vice Presidency*, 89.
12. Marshall's decision to accept Wilson's invitation to meet with the cabinet was made with some misgivings. Although he once had described the president as "my commander-in-chief" whose "orders would be obeyed," Marshall believed that, constitutionally, the vice president, as president of the Senate, was a "member of the legislative branch," ill-suited to executive responsibilities. Thus, he told the cabinet, he wanted it clearly understood

that he was present only "informally and personally" and would "preside in an unofficial and informal way." Before his inauguration in 1925, Vice President Dawes said publicly that he would not accept an invitation from President Coolidge to meet with the cabinet, if, as seemed likely, one were forthcoming. "The cabinet and those who sit with it should always do so at the discretion and inclination of the president . . .," Dawes told reporters, neglecting the possibility that Coolidge might wish to exercise his discretion to have the vice president present. "No precedent should be established which creates a different and arbitrary method of selection" (Williams, *Rise of the Vice Presidency*, 108-110, 134).

13. Franklin D. Roosevelt, "Can the Vice President Be Useful?" *Saturday Evening Post*, October 6, 1920, 8.
14. Williams, *Rise of the Vice Presidency*, 158-159.
15. Murray and Blessing, "The Presidential Performance Study," 535-555.
16. Quoted in Williams, *Rise of the Vice Presidency*, 219.
17. Quoted in Robert J. Donovan, *Conflict and Crisis: The Presidency of Harry S Truman, 1945-1948* (New York: Norton, 1977), 15.
18. Goldstein, *Modern American Vice Presidency*, 147-148.
19. Michael Nelson, "Choosing the Vice President," *PS: Political Science and Politics* 21 (Fall 1988): 858-868.
20. Goldstein, *Modern American Vice Presidency*, 85.
21. Michael Nelson, "Constitutional Aspects of the Elections," in *The Elections of 1988*, ed. Michael Nelson (Washington, D.C.: CQ Press, 1989), 190.
22. Michael Nelson, "The Presidency: Clinton and the Cycle of Politics and Policy," in *The Elections of 1992*, ed. Michael Nelson (Washington, D.C.: CQ Press, 1993), 125-132.
23. Vice-presidential vacancies occurred seven times because the vice president died, once because he resigned, and eight times because the president died.
24. *Public Papers of the Presidents* (Washington, D.C.: Government Printing Office, 1957), 132.
25. Rockefeller also headed the White House Domestic Council, an assignment that, like Henry Wallace's, ended in failure (Michael Nelson, "Nelson A. Rockefeller and the American Vice Presidency," in *Gerald R. Ford and the Politics of Post-Watergate America*, vol. 1, ed. Bernard J. Firestone and Alexej Ugrinsky [Westport, Conn.: Greenwood Press, 1993], 139-160).
26. Fred Barnes, "Danny Gets His Gun," *New Republic*, June 26, 1989, 10-11.
27. Reportedly, some White House aides regarded Reagan as mentally incapable in 1987. See Jane Mayer and Doyle McManus, *Landslide: The Unmaking of a President, 1984-1988* (Boston: Houghton Mifflin, 1988), vii-xi.
28. Lawrence I. Barrett, *Gambling with History: Ronald Reagan in the White House* (Garden City, N.Y.: Doubleday, 1983), chap. 7.
29. Quayle and Gore are widely thought to have presidential ambitions.
30. As Vice President Ford remarked in 1974, "I am now surrounded by a clutch of Secret Service agents, reporters and cameramen, and assorted well-wishers. When I travel I am greeted by bands playing 'Hail Columbia' and introduced to audiences with great solemnity instead of just as 'my good friend, Jerry Ford' " (quoted in Light, *Vice-Presidential Power*, 10).
31. Quoted in Cronin, "Rethinking the Vice Presidency," 338.
32. Dwight D. Eisenhower, *Waging Peace* (Garden City, N.Y.: Doubleday, 1965), 596.
33. Paul Light calls this the "abused child syndrome" (*Vice-Presidential Power*, 108).

APPENDIX

Constitution of the United States

We the People of the United States, in Order to form a more perfect Union, establish Justice, insure domestic Tranquility, provide for the common defence, promote the general Welfare, and secure the Blessings of Liberty to ourselves and our Posterity, do ordain and establish this Constitution for the United States of America.

Article I

Section 1. All legislative Powers herein granted shall be vested in a Congress of the United States, which shall consist of a Senate and House of Representatives.

Section 2. The House of Representatives shall be composed of Members chosen every second Year by the People of the several States, and the Electors in each State shall have the Qualifications requisite for Electors of the most numerous Branch of the State Legislature.

No Person shall be a Representative who shall not have attained to the age of twenty five Years, and been seven Years a Citizen of the United States, and who shall not, when elected, be an Inhabitant of that State in which he shall be chosen.

[Representatives and direct Taxes shall be apportioned among the several States which may be included within this Union, according to their respective Numbers, which shall be determined by adding to the whole Number of free Persons, including those bound to Service for a Term of Years, and excluding Indians not taxed, three fifths of all other Persons.][1] The actual Enumeration shall be made within three Years after the first Meeting of the Congress of the United States, and within every subsequent Term of ten Years, in such Manner as they shall by Law direct. The Number of Representatives shall not exceed one for every thirty Thousand, but each State shall have at Least one Representative; and until such enumeration shall be made, the State of New Hampshire shall be entitled to chuse three, Massachusetts eight, Rhode-Island and Providence Plantations one, Connecticut five, New-York six, New Jersey four, Pennsylvania eight, Delaware one, Maryland six, Virginia ten, North Carolina five, South Carolina five, and Georgia three.

When vacancies happen in the Representation from any State, the Executive Authority thereof shall issue Writs of Election to fill such Vacancies.

The House of Representatives shall chuse their Speaker and other Officers; and shall have the sole Power of Impeachment.

Section 3. The Senate of the United States shall be composed of two Senators from each State, [chosen by the Legislature thereof,][2] for six Years; and each Senator shall have one Vote.

Immediately after they shall be assembled in Consequence of the first Election, they shall be divided as equally as may be into three Classes. The Seats of the Senators of the first Class shall be vacated at the Expiration of the second Year, of the second Class at the Expiration of the fourth Year, and of the third Class at the Expiration of the sixth Year, so that one third may be chosen every second Year; [and if Vacancies happen by Resignation, or otherwise, during the Recess of the Legislature of any State, the Executive thereof may make temporary Appointments until the next Meeting of the Legislature, which shall then fill such Vacancies.][3]

No Person shall be a Senator who shall not have attained to the Age of thirty Years, and been nine Years a Citizen of the United States, and who shall not, when elected, be an Inhabitant of that State for which he shall be chosen.

The Vice President of the United States shall be President of the Senate, but shall have no Vote, unless they be equally divided.

The Senate shall chuse their other Officers, and also a President pro tempore, in the Absence of the Vice President, or when he shall exercise the Office of President of the United States.

The Senate shall have the sole Power to try all Impeachments. When sitting for that Purpose, they shall be on Oath or Affirmation. When the President of the United States is tried, the Chief Justice shall preside: And no Person shall be convicted without the Concurrence of two thirds of the Members present.

Judgment in Cases of Impeachment shall not extend further than to removal from Office, and disqualification to hold and enjoy any Office of honor, Trust or Profit under the United States: but the Party convicted shall nevertheless be liable and subject to Indictment, Trial, Judgment and Punishment, according to Law.

Section 4. The Times, Places and Manner of holding Elections for Senators and Representatives, shall be prescribed in each State by the Legislature thereof; but the Congress may at any time by Law make or alter such Regulations, except as to the Places of chusing Senators.

The Congress shall assemble at least once in every Year, and such Meeting shall [be on the first Monday in December],[4] unless they shall by Law appoint a different Day.

Section 5. Each House shall be the Judge of the Elections, Returns and Qualifications of its own Members, and a Majority of each shall constitute a Quorum to do Business; but a smaller Number may adjourn from day to day, and may be authorized to compel the Attendance of absent Members, in such Manner, and under such Penalties as each House may provide.

Each House may determine the Rules of its Proceedings, punish its Members for disorderly Behaviour, and, with the Concurrence of two thirds, expel a Member.

Each House shall keep a Journal of its Proceedings, and from time to time publish the same, excepting such Parts as may in their Judgment require Secrecy; and the Yeas and Nays of the Members of either House on any question shall, at the Desire of one fifth of those Present, be entered on the Journal.

Neither House, during the Session of Congress, shall, without the Consent of the other, adjourn for more than three days, nor to any other Place than that in which the two Houses shall be sitting.

Section 6. The Senators and Representatives shall receive a Compensation for their Services, to be ascertained by Law, and paid out of the Treasury of the United States. They shall in all Cases, except Treason, Felony and Breach of the Peace, be privileged from Arrest during their Attendance at the Session of their respective Houses, and in going to and returning from the same; and for any Speech or Debate in either House, they shall not be questioned in any other Place.

No Senator or Representative shall, during the Time for which he was elected, be appointed to any civil Office under the Authority of the United States, which shall have been created, or the Emoluments whereof shall have been encreased during such time; and no Person holding any Office under the United States, shall be a Member of either House during his Continuance in Office.

Section 7. All Bills for raising Revenue shall originate in the House of Representatives; but the Senate may propose or concur with Amendments as on other Bills.

Every Bill which shall have passed the House of Representatives and the Senate, shall, before it become a Law, be presented to the

President of the United States; If he approve he shall sign it, but if not he shall return it, with his Objections to that House in which it shall have originated, who shall enter the Objections at large on their Journal, and proceed to reconsider it. If after such Reconsideration two thirds of that House shall agree to pass the Bill, it shall be sent, together with the Objections, to the other House, by which it shall likewise be reconsidered, and if approved by two thirds of that House, it shall become a Law. But in all such Cases the Votes of both Houses shall be determined by yeas and Nays, and the Names of the Persons voting for and against the Bill shall be entered on the Journal of each House respectively. If any Bill shall not be returned by the President within ten Days (Sundays excepted) after it shall have been presented to him, the Same shall be a Law, in like Manner as if he had signed it, unless the Congress by their Adjournment prevent its Return, in which Case it shall not be a Law.

Every Order, Resolution, or Vote to which the Concurrence of the Senate and House of Representatives may be necessary (except on a question of Adjournment) shall be presented to the President of the United States; and before the Same shall take Effect, shall be approved by him, or being disapproved by him, shall be repassed by two thirds of the Senate and House of Representatives, according to the Rules and Limitations prescribed in the Case of a Bill.

Section 8.   The Congress shall have Power To lay and collect Taxes, Duties, Imposts and Excises, to pay the Debts and provide for the common Defence and general Welfare of the United States; but all Duties, Imposts and Excises shall be uniform throughout the United States;

To borrow Money on the credit of the United States;

To regulate Commerce with foreign Nations, and among the several States, and with the Indian Tribes;

To establish an uniform Rule of Naturalization, and uniform Laws on the subject of Bankruptcies throughout the United States;

To coin Money, regulate the Value thereof, and of foreign Coin, and fix the Standard of Weights and Measures;

To provide for the Punishment of counterfeiting the Securities and current Coin of the United States;

To establish Post Offices and post Roads;

To promote the Progress of Science and useful Arts, by securing for limited Times to Authors and Inventors the exclusive Right to their respective Writings and Discoveries;

To constitute Tribunals inferior to the supreme Court;

To define and punish Piracies and Felonies committed on the high Seas, and Offences against the Law of Nations;

To declare War, grant Letters of Marque and Reprisal, and make

Rules concerning Captures on Land and Water;

To raise and support Armies, but no Appropriation of Money to that Use shall be for a longer Term than two Years;

To provide and maintain a Navy;

To make Rules for the Government and Regulation of the land and naval Forces;

To provide for calling forth the Militia to execute the Laws of the Union, suppress Insurrections and repel Invasions;

To provide for organizing, arming, and disciplining, the Militia, and for governing such Part of them as may be employed in the Service of the United States, reserving to the States respectively, the Appointment of the Officers, and the Authority of training the Militia according to the discipline prescribed by Congress;

To exercise exclusive Legislation in all Cases whatsoever, over such District (not exceeding ten Miles square) as may, by Cession of particular States, and the Acceptance of Congress, become the Seat of the Government of the United States, and to exercise like Authority over all Places purchased by the Consent of the Legislature of the State in which the Same shall be, for the Erection of Forts, Magazines, Arsenals, dock-Yards, and other needful Buildings; —And

To make all Laws which shall be necessary and proper for carrying into Execution the foregoing Powers, and all other Powers vested by this Constitution in the Government of the United States, or in any Department or Officer thereof.

Section 9. The Migration or Importation of such Persons as any of the States now existing shall think proper to admit, shall not be prohibited by the Congress prior to the Year one thousand eight hundred and eight, but a Tax or duty may be imposed on such Importation, not exceeding ten dollars for each Person.

The Privilege of the Writ of Habeas Corpus shall not be suspended, unless when in Cases of Rebellion or Invasion the public Safety may require it.

No Bill of Attainder or ex post facto Law shall be passed.

No Capitation, or other direct, Tax shall be laid, unless in Proportion to the Census or Enumeration herein before directed to be taken.[5]

No Tax or Duty shall be laid on Articles exported from any State.

No Preference shall be given by any Regulation of Commerce or Revenue to the Ports of one State over those of another; nor shall Vessels bound to, or from, one State, be obliged to enter, clear, or pay Duties in another.

No Money shall be drawn from the Treasury, but in Consequence of Appropriations made by Law; and a regular Statement and Account of the Receipts and Expenditures of all public Money shall be published from time to time.

No Title of Nobility shall be granted by the United States: And no Person holding any Office of Profit or Trust under them, shall, without the Consent of the Congress, accept of any present, Emolument, Office, or Title, of any kind whatever, from any King, Prince, or foreign State.

Section 10. No State shall enter into any Treaty, Alliance, or Confederation; grant Letters of Marque and Reprisal; coin Money; emit Bills of Credit; make any Thing but gold and silver Coin a Tender in Payment of Debts; pass any Bill of Attainder, ex post facto Law, or Law impairing the Obligation of Contracts, or grant any Title of Nobility.

No State shall, without the Consent of the Congress, lay any Imposts or Duties on Imports or Exports, except what may be absolutely necessary for executing it's inspection Laws: and the net Produce of all Duties and Imposts, laid by any State on Imports or Exports, shall be for the Use of the Treasury of the United States; and all such Laws shall be subject to the Revision and Controul of the Congress.

No State shall, without the Consent of Congress, lay any Duty of Tonnage, keep Troops, or Ships of War in time of Peace, enter into any Agreement or Compact with another State, or with a foreign Power, or engage in War, unless actually invaded, or in such imminent Danger as will not admit of delay.

Article II

Section 1. The executive Power shall be vested in a President of the United States of America. He shall hold his Office during the Term of four Years, and, together with the Vice President, chosen for the same Term, be elected, as follows:

Each State shall appoint, in such Manner as the Legislature thereof may direct, a Number of Electors, equal to the whole Number of Senators and Representatives to which the State may be entitled in the Congress: but no Senator or Representative, or Person holding an Office of Trust or Profit under the United States, shall be appointed an Elector.

[The Electors shall meet in their respective States, and vote by Ballot for two Persons, of whom one at least shall not be an Inhabitant of the same State with themselves. And they shall make a List of all the Persons voted for, and of the Number of Votes for each; which List they shall sign and certify, and transmit sealed to the Seat of the Government of the United States, directed to the President of the Senate. The President of the Senate shall, in the Presence of the Senate and House of Representatives, open all the Certificates, and the Votes shall then be counted. The Person having the greatest Number of Votes shall be the President, if such Number be a Majority of the whole Number of Electors appointed; and if there be more than one who have such

Majority, and have an equal Number of Votes, then the House of Representatives shall immediately chuse by Ballot one of them for President; and if no Person have a Majority, then from the five highest on the list the said House shall in like Manner chuse the President. But in chusing the President, the Votes shall be taken by States, the Representation from each State having one Vote; A quorum for this Purpose shall consist of a Member or Members from two thirds of the States, and a Majority of all the States shall be necessary to a Choice. In every Case, after the Choice of the President, the Person having the greatest Number of Votes of the Electors shall be the Vice President. But if there should remain two or more who have equal Votes, the Senate shall chuse from them by Ballot the Vice President.][6]

The Congress may determine the Time of chusing the Electors, and the Day on which they shall give their Votes; which Day shall be the same throughout the United States.

No Person except a natural born Citizen, or a Citizen of the United States, at the time of the Adoption of this Constitution, shall be eligible to the Office of President; neither shall any Person be eligible to that Office who shall not have attained to the Age of thirty five Years, and been fourteen Years a Resident within the United States.

In Case of the Removal of the President from Office, or of his Death, Resignation, or Inability to discharge the Powers and Duties of the said Office,[7] the Same shall devolve on the Vice President, and the Congress may by Law provide for the Case of Removal, Death, Resignation or Inability, both of the President and Vice President, declaring what Officer shall then act as President, and such Officer shall act accordingly, until the Disability be removed, or a President shall be elected.

The President shall, at stated Times, receive for his Services, a Compensation, which shall neither be increased nor diminished during the Period for which he shall have been elected, and he shall not receive within that Period any other Emolument from the United States, or any of them.

Before he enter on the Execution of his Office, he shall take the following Oath or Affirmation:—"I do solemnly swear (or affirm) that I will faithfully execute the Office of President of the United States, and will to the best of my Ability, preserve, protect and defend the Constitution of the United States."

Section 2. The President shall be Commander in Chief of the Army and Navy of the United States, and of the Militia of the several States, when called into the actual Service of the United States; he may require the Opinion, in writing, of the principal Officer in each of the executive Departments, upon any Subject relating to the Duties of their respective Offices, and he shall have Power to grant Reprieves and

Pardons for Offences against the United States, except in Cases of Impeachment.

He shall have Power, by and with the Advice and Consent of the Senate, to make Treaties, provided two thirds of the Senators present concur; and he shall nominate, and by and with the Advice and Consent of the Senate, shall appoint Ambassadors, other public Ministers and Consuls, Judges of the supreme Court, and all other Officers of the United States, whose Appointments are not herein otherwise provided for, and which shall be established by Law: but the Congress may by Law vest the Appointment of such inferior Officers, as they think proper, in the President alone, in the Courts of Law, or in the Heads of Departments.

The President shall have Power to fill up all Vacancies that may happen during the Recess of the Senate, by granting Commissions which shall expire at the End of their next Session.

Section 3. He shall from time to time give to the Congress Information of the State of the Union, and recommend to their Consideration such Measures as he shall judge necessary and expedient; he may, on extraordinary Occasions, convene both Houses, or either of them, and in Case of Disagreement between them, with Respect to the Time of Adjournment, he may adjourn them to such Time as he shall think proper; he shall receive Ambassadors and other public Ministers; he shall take Care that the Laws be faithfully executed, and shall Commission all the Officers of the United States.

Section 4. The President, Vice President and all civil Officers of the United States, shall be removed from Office on Impeachment for, and Conviction of, Treason, Bribery, or other high Crimes and Misdemeanors.

Article III

Section 1. The judicial Power of the United States, shall be vested in one supreme Court, and in such inferior Courts as the Congress may from time to time ordain and establish. The Judges, both of the supreme and inferior Courts, shall hold their Offices during good Behaviour, and shall, at stated Times, receive for their Services, a Compensation, which shall not be diminished during their Continuance in Office.

Section 2. The judicial Power shall extend to all Cases, in Law and Equity, arising under this Constitution, the Laws of the United States, and Treaties made, or which shall be made, under their Authority; — to all Cases affecting Ambassadors, other public Ministers and Consuls; — to all Cases of admiralty and maritime Jurisdiction; — to Controversies to which the United States shall be a Party; — to

Controversies between two or more States; — between a State and Citizens of another State;[8] — between Citizens of different States; — between Citizens of the same State claiming Lands under Grants of different States, and between a State, or the Citizens thereof, and foreign States, Citizens or Subjects.[8]

In all Cases affecting Ambassadors, other public Ministers and Consuls, and those in which a State shall be Party, the supreme Court shall have original Jurisdiction. In all the other Cases before mentioned, the supreme Court shall have appellate Jurisdiction, both as to Law and Fact, with such Exceptions, and under such Regulations as the Congress shall make.

The Trial of all Crimes, except in Cases of Impeachment, shall be by Jury; and such Trial shall be held in the State where the said Crimes shall have been committed; but when not committed within any State, the Trial shall be at such Place or Places as the Congress may by Law have directed.

Section 3. Treason against the United States, shall consist only in levying War against them, or in adhering to their Enemies, giving them Aid and Comfort. No Person shall be convicted of Treason unless on the Testimony of two Witnesses to the same overt Act, or on Confession in open Court.

The Congress shall have Power to declare the Punishment of Treason, but no Attainder of Treason shall work Corruption of Blood, or Forfeiture except during the Life of the Person attainted.

Article IV

Section 1. Full Faith and Credit shall be given in each State to the public Acts, Records, and judicial Proceedings of every other State. And the Congress may by general Laws prescribe the Manner in which such Acts, Records and Proceedings shall be proved, and the Effect thereof.

Section 2. The Citizens of each State shall be entitled to all Privileges and Immunities of Citizens in the several States.

A Person charged in any State with Treason, Felony, or other Crime, who shall flee from Justice, and be found in another State, shall on Demand of the executive Authority of the State from which he fled, be delivered up, to be removed to the State having Jurisdiction of the Crime.

[No Person held to Service or Labour in one State, under the Laws thereof, escaping into another, shall, in Consequence of any Law or Regulation therein, be discharged from such Service or Labour, but shall be delivered up on Claim of the Party to whom such Service or Labour may be due.][9]

Section 3. New States may be admitted by the Congress into this

Union; but no new State shall be formed or erected within the Jurisdiction of any other State; nor any State be formed by the Junction of two or more States, or Parts of States, without the Consent of the Legislatures of the States concerned as well as of the Congress.

The Congress shall have Power to dispose of and make all needful Rules and Regulations respecting the Territory or other Property belonging to the United States; and nothing in this Constitution shall be so construed as to Prejudice any Claims of the United States, or of any particular State.

Section 4. The United States shall guarantee to every State in this Union a Republican Form of Government, and shall protect each of them against Invasion; and on Application of the Legislature, or of the Executive (when the Legislature cannot be convened) against domestic Violence.

Article V

The Congress, whenever two thirds of both Houses shall deem it necessary, shall propose Amendments to this Constitution, or, on the Application of the Legislatures of two thirds of the several States, shall call a Convention for proposing Amendments, which, in either Case, shall be valid to all Intents and Purposes, as Part of this Constitution, when ratified by the Legislatures of three fourths of the several States, or by Conventions in three fourths thereof, as the one or the other Mode of Ratification may be proposed by the Congress; Provided [that no Amendment which may be made prior to the Year One thousand eight hundred and eight shall in any Manner affect the first and fourth Clauses in the Ninth Section of the first Article; and][10] that no State, without its Consent, shall be deprived of its equal Suffrage in the Senate.

Article VI

All Debts contracted and Engagements entered into, before the Adoption of this Constitution, shall be as valid against the United States under this Constitution, as under the Confederation.

This Constitution, and the Laws of the United States which shall be made in Pursuance thereof; and all Treaties made, or which shall be made, under the Authority of the United States, shall be the supreme Law of the Land; and the Judges in every State shall be bound thereby, any Thing in the Constitution or Laws of any State to the Contrary notwithstanding.

The Senators and Representatives before mentioned, and the Members of the several State Legislatures, and all executive and judicial

Officers, both of the United States and of the several States, shall be bound by Oath or Affirmation, to support this Constitution; but no religious Test shall ever be required as a Qualification to any Office or public Trust under the United States.

Article VII

The Ratification of the Conventions of nine States, shall be sufficient for the Establishment of this Constitution between the States so ratifying the Same.

Done in Convention by the Unanimous Consent of the States present the Seventeenth Day of September in the Year of our Lord one thousand seven hundred and Eighty seven and of the Independence of the United States of America the Twelfth. IN WITNESS whereof We have hereunto subscribed our Names,

George Washington,
President and
deputy from Virginia.

New Hampshire: John Langdon,
Nicholas Gilman.

Massachusetts: Nathaniel Gorham,
Rufus King.

Connecticut: William Samuel Johnson,
Roger Sherman.

New York: Alexander Hamilton.

New Jersey: William Livingston,
David Brearley,
William Paterson,
Jonathan Dayton.

Pennsylvania: Benjamin Franklin,
Thomas Mifflin,
Robert Morris,
George Clymer,
Thomas FitzSimons,
Jared Ingersoll,
James Wilson,
Gouverneur Morris.

Delaware: George Read,
Gunning Bedford Jr.,
John Dickinson,
Richard Bassett,
Jacob Broom.

Maryland:	James McHenry, Daniel of St. Thomas Jenifer, Daniel Carroll.
Virginia:	John Blair, James Madison Jr.
North Carolina:	William Blount, Richard Dobbs Spaight, Hugh Williamson.
South Carolina:	John Rutledge, Charles Cotesworth Pinckney, Charles Pinckney, Pierce Butler.
Georgia:	William Few, Abraham Baldwin.

[The language of the original Constitution, not including the Amendments, was adopted by a convention of the states on September 17, 1787, and was subsequently ratified by the states on the following dates: Delaware, December 7, 1787; Pennsylvania, December 12, 1787; New Jersey, December 18, 1787; Georgia, January 2, 1788; Connecticut, January 9, 1788; Massachusetts, February 6, 1788; Maryland, April 28, 1788; South Carolina, May 23, 1788; New Hampshire, June 21, 1788.

Ratification was completed on June 21, 1788.

The Constitution subsequently was ratified by Virginia, June 25, 1788; New York, July 26, 1788; North Carolina, November 21, 1789; Rhode Island, May 29, 1790; and Vermont, January 10, 1791.]

Amendments

Amendment I

(First ten amendments ratified December 15, 1791.)

Congress shall make no law respecting an establishment of religion, or prohibiting the free exercise thereof; or abridging the freedom of speech, or of the press; or the right of the people peaceably to assemble, and to petition the Government for a redress of grievances.

Amendment II

A well regulated Militia, being necessary to the security of a free State, the right of the people to keep and bear Arms, shall not be infringed.

Amendment III

No Soldier shall, in time of peace be quartered in any house, without the consent of the Owner, nor in time of war, but in a manner to be prescribed by law.

Amendment IV

The right of the people to be secure in their persons, houses, papers, and effects, against unreasonable searches and seizures, shall not be violated, and no Warrants shall issue, but upon probable cause, supported by Oath or affirmation, and particularly describing the place to be searched, and the persons or things to be seized.

Amendment V

No person shall be held to answer for a capital, or otherwise infamous crime, unless on a presentment or indictment of a Grand Jury, except in cases arising in the land or naval forces, or in the Militia, when in actual service in time of War or public danger; nor shall any person be subject for the same offence to be twice put in jeopardy of life or limb; nor shall be compelled in any criminal case to be a witness against himself, nor be deprived of life, liberty, or property, without due process of law; nor shall private property be taken for public use, without just compensation.

Amendment VI

In all criminal prosecutions, the accused shall enjoy the right to a speedy and public trial, by an impartial jury of the State and district wherein the crime shall have been committed, which district shall have been previously ascertained by law, and to be informed of the nature and cause of the accusation; to be confronted with the witnesses against him; to have compulsory process for obtaining witnesses in his favor, and to have the Assistance of Counsel for his defence.

Amendment VII

In Suits at common law, where the value in controversy shall exceed twenty dollars, the right of trial by jury shall be preserved, and no fact tried by a jury, shall be otherwise re-examined in any Court of the United States, than according to the rules of the common law.

Amendment VIII

Excessive bail shall not be required, nor excessive fines imposed, nor cruel and unusual punishments inflicted.

Amendment IX

The enumeration in the Constitution, of certain rights, shall not be construed to deny or disparage others retained by the people.

Amendment X

The powers not delegated to the United States by the Constitution, nor prohibited by it to the States, are reserved to the States respectively, or to the people.

Amendment XI *(Ratified February 7, 1795)*

The Judicial power of the United States shall not be construed to extend to any suit in law or equity, commenced or prosecuted against one of the United States by Citizens of another State, or by Citizens or Subjects of any Foreign State.

Amendment XII *(Ratified June 15, 1804)*

The Electors shall meet in their respective states and vote by ballot for President and Vice-President, one of whom, at least, shall not be an inhabitant of the same state with themselves; they shall name in their ballots the person voted for as President, and in distinct ballots the person voted for as Vice-President, and they shall make distinct lists of all persons voted for as President, and of all persons voted for as Vice-President, and of the number of votes for each, which lists they shall sign and certify, and transmit sealed to the seat of the government of the United States, directed to the President of the Senate; — The President of the Senate shall, in the presence of the Senate and House of Representatives, open all the certificates and the votes shall then be counted; — The person having the greatest number of votes for President, shall be the President, if such number be a majority of the whole number of Electors appointed; and if no person have such majority, then from the persons having the highest numbers not exceeding three on the list of those voted for as President, the House of Representatives shall choose immediately, by ballot, the President. But in choosing the President, the votes shall be taken by states, the representation from each state having one vote; a quorum for this purpose shall consist of a member or members from two-thirds of the states, and a majority of all the states shall be necessary to a choice. [And if the House of Representatives shall not choose a President whenever the right of choice shall devolve upon them, before the fourth day of March next following, then the Vice-President shall act as President, as in the case of the death or other constitutional disability of the President. —][11] The person having the greatest number of votes as Vice-President, shall be the Vice-President, if such number be a majority of the whole number of Electors appointed, and if no person have a majority, then from the two highest numbers on the list, the Senate shall choose the Vice-President; a quorum for the purpose shall consist of two-thirds of the whole number of Senators, and a majority of the whole number shall be necessary to a choice. But no person constitutionally ineligible to the office of President shall be eligible to that of Vice-President of the United States.

Amendment XIII *(Ratified December 6, 1865)*

Section 1. Neither slavery nor involuntary servitude, except as a punishment for crime whereof the party shall have been duly convicted, shall exist within the United States, or any place subject to their jurisdiction.

Section 2. Congress shall have power to enforce this article by appropriate legislation.

Amendment XIV *(Ratified July 9, 1868)*

Section 1. All persons born or naturalized in the United States, and subject to the jurisdiction thereof, are citizens of the United States and of the State wherein they reside. No State shall make or enforce any law which shall abridge the privileges or immunities of citizens of the United States; nor shall any State deprive any person of life, liberty, or property, without due process of law; nor deny to any person within its jurisdiction the equal protection of the laws.

Section 2. Representatives shall be apportioned among the several States according to their respective numbers, counting the whole number of persons in each State, excluding Indians not taxed. But when the right to vote at any election for the choice of electors for President and Vice President of the United States, Representatives in Congress, the Executive and Judicial officers of a State, or the members of the Legislature thereof, is denied to any of the male inhabitants of such State, being twenty-one years of age,[12] and citizens of the United States, or in any way abridged, except for participation in rebellion, or other crime, the basis of representation therein shall be reduced in the proportion which the number of such male citizens shall bear to the whole number of male citizens twenty-one years of age in such State.

Section 3. No person shall be a Senator or Representative in Congress, or elector of President and Vice President, or hold any office, civil or military, under the United States, or under any State, who, having previously taken an oath, as a member of Congress, or as an officer of the United States, or as a member of any State legislature, or as an executive or judicial officer of any State, to support the Constitution of the United States, shall have engaged in insurrection or rebellion against the same, or given aid or comfort to the enemies thereof. But Congress may by a vote of two-thirds of each House, remove such disability.

Section 4. The validity of the public debt of the United States, authorized by law, including debts incurred for payment of pensions and bounties for services in suppressing insurrection or rebellion, shall not be questioned. But neither the United States nor any State shall assume or pay any debt or obligation incurred in aid of insurrection or rebellion against the United States, or any claim for the loss or emancipation of any slave; but all such debts, obligations and claims shall be held illegal and void.

Section 5. The Congress shall have power to enforce, by appropriate legislation, the provisions of this article.

Amendment XV *(Ratified February 3, 1870)*

Section 1. The right of citizens of the United States to vote shall not be denied or abridged by the United States or by any State on account of race, color, or previous condition of servitude.

Section 2. The Congress shall have power to enforce this article by appropriate legislation.

Amendment XVI *(Ratified February 3, 1913)*

The Congress shall have power to lay and collect taxes on incomes, from whatever source derived, without apportionment among the several States, and without regard to any census or enumeration.

Amendment XVII *(Ratified April 8, 1913)*

The Senate of the United States shall be composed of two Senators from each State, elected by the people thereof, for six years; and each Senator shall have one vote. The electors in each State shall have the qualifications requisite for electors of the most numerous branch of the State legislatures.

When vacancies happen in the representation of any State in the Senate, the executive authority of such State shall issue writs of election to fill such vacancies: *Provided,* That the legislature of any State may empower the executive thereof to make temporary appointments until the people fill the vacancies by election as the legislature may direct.

This amendment shall not be so construed as to affect the election or term of any Senator chosen before it becomes valid as part of the Constitution.

Amendment XVIII *(Ratified January 16, 1919)*

Section 1. After one year from the ratification of this article the manufacture, sale, or transportation of intoxicating liquors within, the importation thereof into, or the exportation thereof from the United States and all territory subject to the jurisdiction thereof for beverage purposes is hereby prohibited.

Section 2. The Congress and the several States shall have concurrent power to enforce this article by appropriate legislation.

Section 3. This article shall be inoperative unless it shall have been ratified as an amendment to the Constitution by the legislatures of the several States, as provided in the Constitution, within seven years from the date of the submission hereof to the States by the Congress.][13]

Amendment XIX *(Ratified August 18, 1920)*

The right of citizens of the United States to vote shall not be denied or abridged by the United States or by any State on account of sex.

Congress shall have power to enforce this article by appropriate legislation.

Amendment XX *(Ratified January 23, 1933)*

Section 1. The terms of the President and Vice President shall end at noon on the 20th day of January, and the terms of Senators and Representatives at noon on the 3d day of January, of the years in which such terms would have ended if this article had not been ratified; and the terms of their successors shall then begin.

Section 2. The Congress shall assemble at least once in every year, and such meeting shall begin at noon on the 3d day of January, unless they shall by law appoint a different day.

Section 3.[14] If, at the time fixed for the beginning of the term of the President, the President elect shall have died, the Vice President elect shall become President. If a President shall not have been chosen before the time fixed for the beginning of his term, or if the President elect shall have failed to qualify, then the Vice President elect shall act as President until a President shall have qualified; and the Congress may by law provide for the case wherein neither a President elect nor a Vice President elect shall have qualified, declaring who shall then act as President, or the manner in which one who is to act shall be selected, and such person shall act accordingly until a President or Vice President shall have qualified.

Section 4. The Congress may by law provide for the case of the death of any of the persons from whom the House of Representatives may choose a President whenever the right of choice shall have devolved upon them, and for the case of the death of any of the persons from whom the Senate may choose a Vice President whenever the right of choice shall have devolved upon them.

Section 5. Sections 1 and 2 shall take effect on the 15th day of October following the ratification of this article.

Section 6. This article shall be inoperative unless it shall have been ratified as an amendment to the Constitution by the legislatures of three-fourths of the several States within seven years from the date of its submission.

Amendment XXI *(Ratified December 5, 1933)*

Section 1. The eighteenth article of amendment to the Constitution of the United States is hereby repealed.

Section 2. The transportation or importation into any State, Territory, or possession of the United States for delivery or use therein of intoxicating liquors, in violation of the laws thereof, is hereby prohibited.

Section 3. This article shall be inoperative unless it shall have been ratified as an amendment to the Constitution by conventions in the several States, as provided in the Constitution, within seven years from the date of the submission hereof to the States by the Congress.

Amendment XXII *(Ratified February 27, 1951)*

Section 1. No person shall be elected to the office of the President more than twice, and no person who has held the office of President, or acted as President, for more than two years of a term to which some other person was elected President shall be elected to the office of the President more than once. But this Article shall not apply to any person holding the office of President when this Article was proposed by the

Congress, and shall not prevent any person who may be holding the office of President, or acting as President, during the term within which this Article become operative from holding the office of President or acting as President during the remainder of such term.

Section 2. This article shall be inoperative unless it shall have been ratified as an amendment to the Constitution by the legislatures of three-fourths of the several States within seven years from the date of its submission to the States by the Congress.

Amendment XXIII *(Ratified March 29, 1961)*

Section 1. The District constituting the seat of Government of the United States shall appoint in such manner as the Congress may direct:

A number of electors of President and Vice President equal to the whole number of Senators and Representatives in Congress to which the District would be entitled if it were a State, but in no event more than the least populous State; they shall be in addition to those appointed by the States, but they shall be considered, for the purposes of the election of President and Vice President, to be electors appointed by a State; and they shall meet in the District and perform such duties as provided by the twelfth article of amendment.

Section 2. The Congress shall have power to enforce this article by appropriate legislation.

Amendment XXIV *(Ratified January 23, 1964)*

Section 1. The right of citizens of the United States to vote in any primary or other election for President or Vice President, for electors for President or Vice President, or for Senator or Representative in Congress, shall not be denied or abridged by the United States or any State by reason of failure to pay any poll tax or other tax.

Section 2. The Congress shall have power to enforce this article by appropriate legislation.

Amendment XXV *(Ratified February 10, 1967)*

Section 1. In case of the removal of the President from office or of his death or resignation, the Vice President shall become President.

Section 2. Whenever there is a vacancy in the office of the Vice President, the President shall nominate a Vice President who shall take office upon confirmation by a majority vote of both Houses of Congress.

Section 3. Whenever the President transmits to the President pro tempore of the Senate and the Speaker of the House of Representatives his written declaration that he is unable to discharge the powers and duties of his office, and until he transmits to them a written declaration to the contrary, such powers and duties shall be discharged by the Vice President as Acting President.

Section 4. Whenever the Vice President and a majority of either the principal officers of the executive departments or of such other body as Congress may by law provide, transmit to the President pro tempore of the Senate and the Speaker of the House of Representatives their written declaration that the President is unable to discharge the powers and duties of his office, the Vice President shall immediately assume the powers and duties of the office as Acting President.

Thereafter, when the President transmits to the President pro tempore of the Senate and the Speaker of the House of Representatives his written declaration that no inability exists, he shall resume the powers and duties of his office unless the Vice President and a majority of either the principal officers of the executive department or of such other body as Congress may by law provide, transmit within four days to the President pro tempore of the Senate and the Speaker of the House of Representatives their written declaration that the President is unable to discharge the powers and duties of his office. Thereupon Congress shall decide the issue, assembling within forty-eight hours for that purpose if not in session. If the Congress, within twenty-one days after receipt of the latter written declaration, or, if Congress is not in session, within twenty-one days after Congress is required to assemble, determines by two-thirds vote of both Houses that the President is unable to discharge the powers and duties of his office, the Vice President shall continue to discharge the same as Acting President; otherwise, the President shall resume the powers and duties of his office.

Amendment XXVI *(Ratified July 1, 1971)*

Section 1. The right of citizens of the United States, who are eighteen years of age or older, to vote shall not be denied or abridged by the United States or by any State on account of age.

Section 2. The Congress shall have power to enforce this article by appropriate legislation.

Amendment XXVII *(Ratified May 7, 1992)*

No law varying the compensation for the services of the Senators and Representatives shall take effect, until an election of Representatives shall have intervened.

Notes

1. The part in brackets was changed by section 2 of the Fourteenth Amendment.
2. The part in brackets was changed by the first paragraph of the Seventeenth Amendment.
3. The part in brackets was changed by the second paragraph of the Seventeenth Amendment.
4. The part in brackets was changed by section 2 of the Twentieth Amendment.
5. The Sixteenth Amendment gave Congress the power to tax incomes.
6. The material in brackets has been superseded by the Twelfth Amendment.
7. This provision has been affected by the Twenty-fifth Amendment.
8. These clauses were affected by the Eleventh Amendment.
9. This paragraph has been superseded by the Thirteenth Amendment.
10. Obsolete.
11. The part in brackets has been superseded by section 3 of the Twentieth Amendment.
12. See the Nineteenth and Twenty-sixth Amendments.
13. This Amendment was repealed by section 1 of the Twenty-first Amendment.
14. See the Twenty-fifth Amendment.

Source: U.S. Congress, House, Committee on the Judiciary, *The Constitution of the United States of America, as Amended,* 100th Cong., 1st sess., 1987, H Doc 100-94.

U.S. Presidents and Vice Presidents

President and political party	Born	Died	President's term of service	Vice president	Vice president's term of service
George Washington (F)	1732	1799	April 30, 1789-March 4, 1793	John Adams	April 30, 1789-March 4, 1793
George Washington (F)			March 4, 1793-March 4, 1797	John Adams	March 4, 1793-March 4, 1797
John Adams (F)	1735	1826	March 4, 1797-March 4, 1801	Thomas Jefferson	March 4, 1797-March 4, 1801
Thomas Jefferson (DR)	1743	1826	March 4, 1801-March 4, 1805	Aaron Burr	March 4, 1801-March 4, 1805
Thomas Jefferson (DR)			March 4, 1805-March 4, 1809	George Clinton	March 4, 1805-March 4, 1809
James Madison (DR)	1751	1836	March 4, 1809-March 4, 1813	George Clinton[a]	March 4, 1809-April 12, 1812
James Madison (DR)			March 4, 1813-March 4, 1817	Elbridge Gerry[a]	March 4, 1813-Nov. 23, 1814
James Monroe (DR)	1758	1831	March 4, 1817-March 4, 1821	Daniel D. Tompkins	March 4, 1817-March 4, 1821
James Monroe (DR)			March 4, 1821-March 4, 1825	Daniel D. Tompkins	March 4, 1821-March 4, 1825
John Q. Adams (DR)	1767	1848	March 4, 1825-March 4, 1829	John C. Calhoun	March 4, 1825-March 4, 1829
Andrew Jackson (DR)	1767	1845	March 4, 1829-March 4, 1833	John C. Calhoun[b]	March 4, 1829-Dec. 28, 1832
Andrew Jackson (D)			March 4, 1833-March 4, 1837	Martin Van Buren	March 4, 1833-March 4, 1837
Martin Van Buren (D)	1782	1862	March 4, 1837-March 4, 1841	Richard M. Johnson	March 4, 1837-March 4, 1841
W. H. Harrison[a] (W)	1773	1841	March 4, 1841-April 4, 1841	John Tyler[c]	March 4, 1841-April 6, 1841
John Tyler (W)	1790	1862	April 6, 1841-March 4, 1845		
James K. Polk (D)	1795	1849	March 4, 1845-March 4, 1849	George M. Dallas	March 4, 1845-March 4, 1849
Zachary Taylor[a] (W)	1784	1850	March 4, 1849-July 9, 1850	Millard Fillmore[c]	March 4, 1849-July 10, 1850
Millard Fillmore (W)	1800	1874	July 10, 1850-March 4, 1853		
Franklin Pierce (D)	1804	1869	March 4, 1853-March 4, 1857	William R. King[a]	March 24, 1853-April 18, 1853
James Buchanan (D)	1791	1868	March 4, 1857-March 4, 1861	John C. Breckinridge	March 4, 1857-March 4, 1861
Abraham Lincoln (R)	1809	1865	March 4, 1861-March 4, 1865	Hannibal Hamlin	March 4, 1861-March 4, 1865
Abraham Lincoln[a] (R)			March 4, 1865-April 15, 1865	Andrew Johnson[c]	March 4, 1865-April 15, 1865
Andrew Johnson (R)	1808	1875	April 15, 1865-March 4, 1869		
Ulysses S. Grant (R)	1822	1885	March 4, 1869-March 4, 1873	Schuyler Colfax	March 4, 1869-March 4, 1873
Ulysses S. Grant (R)			March 4, 1873-March 4, 1877	Henry Wilson[a]	March 4, 1873-Nov. 22, 1875

President (party)	Born	Term of office	Vice President	Term of office
Rutherford B. Hayes (R)	1822	March 4, 1877-March 4, 1881	William A. Wheeler	March 4, 1877-March 4, 1881
James A. Garfield[a] (R)	1831	March 4, 1881-Sept. 19, 1881	Chester A. Arthur[c]	March 4, 1881-Sept. 20, 1881
Chester A. Arthur (R)	1830	Sept. 20, 1881-March 4, 1885		
Grover Cleveland (D)	1837	March 4, 1885-March 4, 1889	Thomas A. Hendricks[a]	March 4, 1885-Nov. 25, 1885
Benjamin Harrison (R)	1833	March 4, 1889-March 4, 1893	Levi P. Morton	March 4, 1889-March 4, 1893
Grover Cleveland (D)	1837	March 4, 1893-March 4, 1897	Adlai E. Stevenson	March 4, 1893-March 4, 1897
William McKinley (R)	1843	March 4, 1897-March 4, 1901	Garret A. Hobart[a]	March 4, 1897-Nov. 21, 1899
William McKinley[a] (R)		March 4, 1901-Sept. 14, 1901	Theodore Roosevelt[c]	March 4, 1901-Sept. 14, 1901
Theodore Roosevelt (R)	1858	Sept. 14, 1901-March 4, 1905		
Theodore Roosevelt (R)		March 4, 1905-March 4, 1909	Charles W. Fairbanks	March 4, 1905-March 4, 1909
William H. Taft (R)	1857	March 4, 1909-March 4, 1913	James S. Sherman[a]	March 4, 1909-Oct. 30, 1912
Woodrow Wilson (D)	1856	March 4, 1913-March 4, 1917	Thomas R. Marshall	March 4, 1913-March 4, 1917
Woodrow Wilson (D)		March 4, 1917-March 4, 1921	Thomas R. Marshall	March 4, 1917-March 4, 1921
Warren G. Harding[a] (R)	1865	March 4, 1921-Aug. 2, 1923	Calvin Coolidge[c]	March 4, 1921-Aug. 3, 1923
Calvin Coolidge (R)	1872	Aug. 3, 1923-March 4, 1925		
Calvin Coolidge (R)		March 4, 1925-March 4, 1929	Charles G. Dawes	March 4, 1925-March 4, 1929
Herbert Hoover (R)	1874	March 4, 1929-March 4, 1933	Charles Curtis	March 4, 1929-March 4, 1933
Franklin D. Roosevelt (D)	1882	March 4, 1933-Jan. 20, 1937	John N. Garner	March 4, 1933-Jan. 20, 1937
Franklin D. Roosevelt (D)		Jan. 20, 1937-Jan. 20, 1941	John N. Garner	Jan. 20, 1937-Jan. 20, 1941
Franklin D. Roosevelt (D)		Jan. 20, 1941-Jan. 20, 1945	Henry A. Wallace	Jan. 20, 1941-Jan. 20, 1945
Franklin D. Roosevelt[a] (D)		Jan. 20, 1945-April 12, 1945	Harry S Truman[c]	Jan. 20, 1945-April 12, 1945
Harry S Truman (D)	1884	April 12, 1945-Jan. 20, 1949		
Harry S Truman (D)		Jan. 20, 1949-Jan. 20, 1953	Alben W. Barkley	Jan. 20, 1949-Jan. 20, 1953
Dwight D. Eisenhower (R)	1890	Jan. 20, 1953-Jan. 20, 1957	Richard Nixon	Jan. 20, 1953-Jan. 20, 1957
Dwight D. Eisenhower (R)		Jan. 20, 1957-Jan. 20, 1961	Richard Nixon	Jan. 20, 1957-Jan. 20, 1961
John F. Kennedy[a] (D)	1917	Jan. 20, 1961-Nov. 22, 1963	Lyndon B. Johnson[c]	Jan. 20, 1961-Nov. 22, 1963
Lyndon B. Johnson (D)	1908	Nov. 22, 1963-Jan. 20, 1965		
Lyndon B. Johnson (D)		Jan. 20, 1965-Jan. 20, 1969	Hubert H. Humphrey	Jan. 20, 1965-Jan. 20, 1969
Richard Nixon (R)	1913	Jan. 20, 1969-Jan. 20, 1973	Spiro T. Agnew	Jan. 20, 1969-Jan. 20, 1973
Richard Nixon[b] (R)		Jan. 20, 1973-Aug. 9, 1974	Spiro T. Agnew[b]	Jan. 20, 1973-Oct. 10, 1973
			Gerald R. Ford[c]	Dec. 6, 1973-Aug. 9, 1974

President and political party	Born	Died	President's term of service	Vice president	Vice president's term of service
Gerald R. Ford (R)	1913		Aug. 9, 1974-Jan. 20, 1977	Nelson A. Rockefeller	Dec. 19, 1974-Jan. 20, 1977
Jimmy Carter (D)	1924		Jan. 20, 1977-Jan. 20, 1981	Walter F. Mondale	Jan. 20, 1977-Jan. 20, 1981
Ronald Reagan (R)	1911		Jan. 20, 1981-Jan. 20, 1985	George Bush	Jan. 20, 1981-Jan. 20, 1985
Ronald Reagan (R)			Jan. 20, 1985-Jan. 20, 1989	George Bush	Jan. 20, 1985-Jan. 20, 1989
George Bush (R)	1924		Jan. 20, 1989-Jan. 20, 1993	Dan Quayle	Jan. 20, 1989-Jan. 20, 1993
William J. Clinton (D)	1946		Jan. 20, 1993-	Albert Gore	Jan. 20, 1993-

Sources: Presidential Elections Since 1789, 4th ed. (Washington, D.C.: Congressional Quarterly, 1987), 4.; Daniel C. Diller, "Biographies of the Vice Presidents," in *Guide to the Presidency*, ed. Michael Nelson (Washington, D.C.: Congressional Quarterly, 1989), 1319-1346.

Note: D—Democrat; DR—Democratic-Republican; F—Federalist; R—Republican; W—Whig.

a. Died in office.
b. Resigned.
c. Succeeded to the presidency.

Summary of Presidential Elections, 1789-1992

Year	No. of states	Candidates	Electoral vote	Popular vote
1789[a]	10	*Fed.* George Washington	*Fed.* 69	—[b]
1792[a]	15	*Fed.* George Washington	*Fed.* 132	—[b]
1796[a]	16	*Fed.* John Adams *Dem.-Rep.* Thomas Jefferson	*Fed.* 71 *Dem.-Rep.* 68	—[b]
1800[a]	16	*Fed.* John Adams Charles Cotesworth Pinckney *Dem.-Rep.* Thomas Jefferson Aaron Burr	*Fed.* 65 *Dem.-Rep.* 73	—[b]
1804	17	*Fed.* Charles Cotesworth Pinckney Rufus King *Dem.-Rep.* Thomas Jefferson George Clinton	*Fed.* 14 *Dem.-Rep.* 162	—[b]
1808	17	*Fed.* Charles Cotesworth Pinckney Rufus King *Dem.-Rep.* James Madison George Clinton	*Fed.* 47 *Dem.-Rep.* 122	—[b]
1812	18	*Fed.* George Clinton Jared Ingersoll *Dem.-Rep.* James Madison Ellbridge Gerry	*Fed.* 89 *Dem.-Rep.* 128	—[b]

Year	No. of states	Candidates	Electoral vote	Popular vote
1816	19	*Dem.-Rep.* James Monroe / Daniel D. Tompkins	*Dem.-Rep.* 183	—[b]
		Fed. Rufus King / John Howard	*Fed.* 34	—[b]
1820	24	*Dem.-Rep.* James Monroe / Daniel D. Tompkins	*Dem.-Rep.* 231	—[b]
		—[c]	—[c]	
1824[d]	24	*Dem.-Rep.* Andrew Jackson / John C. Calhoun	*Dem.-Rep.* 99	*Dem.-Rep.* 151,271 41.3%
		Dem.-Rep. John Q. Adams / Nathan Sanford	*Dem.-Rep.* 84	*Dem.-Rep.* 113,122 30.9%
1828	24	*Dem.-Rep.* Andrew Jackson / John C. Calhoun	*Dem.-Rep.* 178	*Dem.-Rep.* 642,553 56.0%
		Nat.-Rep. John Q. Adams / Richard Rush	*Nat.-Rep.* 83	*Nat.-Rep.* 500,897 43.6%
1832[e]	24	*Dem.* Andrew Jackson / Martin Van Buren	*Dem.* 219	*Dem.* 701,780 54.2%
		Nat.-Rep. Henry Clay / John Sergeant	*Nat.-Rep.* 49	*Nat.-Rep.* 484,205 37.4%
1836[f]	26	*Dem.* Martin Van Buren / Richard M. Johnson	*Dem.* 170	*Dem.* 764,176 50.8%
		Whig William H. Harrison / Francis Granger	*Whig* 73	*Whig* 550,816 36.6%
1840	26	*Dem.* Martin Van Buren / Richard M. Johnson	*Dem.* 60	*Dem.* 1,275,390 52.9%
		Whig William H. Harrison / John Tyler	*Whig* 234	*Whig* 1,128,854 46.8%
1844	26	*Dem.* James Polk / George M. Dallas	*Dem.* 170	*Dem.* 1,339,494 49.5%
		Whig Henry Clay / Theodore Frelinghuysen	*Whig* 105	*Whig* 1,300,004 48.1%

Year	No. of states	Dem.	Rep.	Electoral vote Dem.	Electoral vote Rep.	Popular vote Dem.	Popular vote Rep.
1848	30	*Dem.* Lewis Cass, William O. Butler	*Whig* Zachary Taylor, Millard Fillmore	*Dem.* 127	*Whig* 163	*Dem.* 1,361,393 47.3%	*Whig* 1,223,460 42.5%
1852	31	*Dem.* Franklin Pierce, William R. King	*Whig* Winfield Scott, William A. Graham	*Dem.* 254	*Whig* 42	*Dem.* 1,607,510 50.8%	*Whig* 1,386,942 43.9%
1856[g]	31	James Buchanan, John C. Breckinridge	John C. Fremont, William L. Dayton	174	114	1,836,072 45.3%	1,342,345 33.1%
1860[h]	33	Stephen A. Douglas, Herschel V. Johnson	Abraham Lincoln, Hannibal Hamlin	12	180	1,380,202 29.5%	1,865,908 39.8%
1864[i]	36	George B. McClellan, George H. Pendleton	Abraham Lincoln, Andrew Johnson	21	212	1,812,807 45.0%	2,218,388 55.0%
1868[j]	37	Horatio Seymour, Francis P. Blair, Jr.	Ulysses S. Grant, Schuyler Colfax	80	214	2,708,744 47.3%	3,013,650 52.7%
1872[k]	37	Horace Greeley, Benjamin Gratz Brown	Ulysses S. Grant, Henry Wilson		286	2,834,761 43.8%	3,598,235 55.6%
1876	38	Samuel J. Tilden, Thomas A. Hendricks	Rutherford B. Hayes, William A. Wheeler	184	185	4,288,546 51.0%	4,034,311 47.9%
1880	38	Winfield S. Hancock, William H. English	James A. Garfield, Chester A. Arthur	155	214	4,444,260 48.2%	4,446,158 48.3%
1884	38	Grover Cleveland, Thomas A. Hendricks	James G. Blaine, John A. Logan	219	182	4,874,621 48.5%	4,848,936 48.2%

Year	No. of states	Candidates Dem.	Candidates Rep.	Electoral vote Dem.	Electoral vote Rep.	Popular vote Dem.	Popular vote Rep.
1888	38	Grover Cleveland Allen G. Thurman	Benjamin Harrison Levi P. Morton	168	233	5,534,488 48.6%	5,443,892 47.8%
1892[l]	44	Grover Cleveland Adlai E. Stevenson	Benjamin Harrison Whitelaw Reid	277	145	5,551,883 46.1%	5,179,244 43.0%
1896	45	William J. Bryan Arthur Sewall	William McKinley Garret A. Hobart	176	271	6,511,495 46.7%	7,108,480 51.0%
1900	45	William J. Bryan Adlai E. Stevenson	William McKinley Theodore Roosevelt	155	292	6,358,345 45.5%	7,218,039 51.7%
1904	45	Alton B. Parker Henry G. Davis	Theodore Roosevelt Charles W. Fairbanks	140	336	5,028,898 37.6%	7,626,593 56.4%
1908	46	William J. Bryan John W. Kern	William H. Taft James S. Sherman	162	321	6,406,801 43.0%	7,676,258 51.6%
1912[m]	48	Woodrow Wilson Thomas R. Marshall	William H. Taft James S. Sherman	435	8	6,293,152 41.8%	3,486,333 23.2%
1916	48	Woodrow Wilson Thomas R. Marshall	Charles E. Hughes Charles W. Fairbanks	277	254	9,126,300 49.2%	8,546,789 46.1%
1920	48	James M. Cox Franklin D. Roosevelt	Warren G. Harding Calvin Coolidge	127	404	9,140,884 34.2%	16,133,314 60.3%
1924[n]	48	John W. Davis Charles W. Bryant	Calvin Coolidge Charles G. Dawes	136	382	8,386,169 28.8%	15,717,553 54.1%
1928	48	Alfred E. Smith Joseph T. Robinson	Herbert C. Hoover Charles Curtis	87	444	15,000,185 40.8%	21,411,991 58.2%

Year	States	Democratic candidates	Electoral vote	Popular vote	Republican candidates	Electoral vote	Popular vote
1932	48	Franklin D. Roosevelt John N. Garner	472	22,825,016 57.4%	Herbert C. Hoover Charles Curtis	59	15,758,397 39.6%
1936	48	Franklin D. Roosevelt John N. Garner	523	27,747,636 60.8%	Alfred M. Landon Frank Knox	8	16,679,543 36.5%
1940	48	Franklin D. Roosevelt Henry A. Wallace	449	27,263,448 54.7%	Wendell L. Willkie Charles L. McNary	82	22,336,260 44.8%
1944	48	Franklin D. Roosevelt Harry S. Truman	432	25,611,936 53.4%	Thomas E. Dewey John W. Bricker	99	22,013,372 45.9%
1948[o]	48	Harry S. Truman Alben W. Barkley	303	24,105,587 49.5%	Thomas E. Dewey Earl Warren	189	21,970,017 45.1%
1952	48	Adlai E. Stevenson II John J. Sparkman	89	27,314,649 44.4%	Dwight D. Eisenhower Richard M. Nixon	442	33,936,137 55.1%
1956[p]	48	Adlai E. Stevenson II Estes Kefauver	73	26,030,172 42.0%	Dwight D. Eisenhower Richard M. Nixon	457	35,585,245 57.4%
1960[q]	50	John F. Kennedy Lyndon B. Johnson	303	34,221,344 49.7%	Richard M. Nixon Henry Cabot Lodge	219	34,106,671 49.5%
1964	50*	Lyndon B. Johnson Hubert H. Humphrey	486	43,126,584 61.1%	Barry Goldwater William E. Miller	52	27,177,838 38.5%
1968[r]	50*	Hubert H. Humphrey Edmund S. Muskie	191	31,274,503 42.7%	Richard M. Nixon Spiro T. Agnew	301	31,785,148 43.4%
1972[s]	50*	George McGovern Sargent Shriver	17	29,171,791 37.5%	Richard M. Nixon Spiro T. Agnew	520	47,170,179 60.7%
1976[t]	50*	Jimmy Carter Walter F. Mondale	297	40,830,763 50.1%	Gerald R. Ford Robert Dole	240	39,147,793 48.0%

		Candidates		Electoral vote		Popular vote	
Year	No. of states	Dem.	Rep.	Dem.	Rep.	Dem.	Rep.
1980	50*	Jimmy Carter Walter F. Mondale	Ronald Reagan George Bush	49	489	35,483,883 41.0%	43,904,153 50.7%
1984	50*	Walter F. Mondale Geraldine Ferraro	Ronald Reagan George Bush	13	525	37,577,185 40.6%	54,455,075 58.8%
1988[u]	50*	Michael S. Dukakis Lloyd Bentsen	George Bush Dan Quayle	111	426	41,809,083 45.6%	48,886,097 53.4%
1992	50*	William J. Clinton Albert Gore	George Bush Dan Quayle	370	168	43,728,275 43.2%	38,167,416 37.7%

Sources: Harold W. Stanley and Richard G. Niemi, *Vital Statistics on American Politics*, 2d ed. (Washington, D.C.: CQ Press, 1990), 102-106; *Guide to U.S. Elections*, 2d ed. (Washington, D.C.: Congressional Quarterly, 1985), 329-366; Federal Election Commission.

Note: Dem.-Rep.—Democratic-Republican; Fed.—Federalist; Nat.-Rep.—National-Republican; Dem.—Democratic; Rep.—Republican.

a. Elections of 1789-1800 were held under rules that did not allow separate voting for president and vice president.
b. Popular vote returns are not shown before 1824 because consistent, reliable data are not available.
c. One electoral vote was cast for John Adams and Richard Stockton, who were not candidates.
d. 1824: All four candidates represented Democratic-Republican factions. William H. Crawford received 41 electoral votes and Henry Clay received 37 votes. Because no candidate received a majority, the election was decided (in Adams's favor) by the House of Representatives.
e. 1832: Two electoral votes were not cast.
f. 1836: Other Whig candidates receiving electoral votes were Hugh L. White, who received 26 votes, and Daniel Webster, who received 14 votes.
g. 1856: Millard Fillmore, Whig-American, received 8 electoral votes.
h. 1860: John C. Breckinridge, Southern Democrat, received 72 electoral votes. John Bell, Constitutional Union, received 39 electoral votes.
i. 1864: Eighty-one electoral votes were not cast.
j. 1868: Twenty-three electoral votes were not cast.
k. 1872: Horace Greeley, Democrat, died after the election. In the electoral college, Democratic electoral votes went to Thomas Hendricks, 42 votes; Benjamin Gratz Brown, 18 votes; Charles J. Jenkins, 2 votes; and David Davis, 1 vote. Seventeen electoral votes were not cast.
l. 1892: James B. Weaver, People's party, received 22 electoral votes.
m. 1912: Theodore Roosevelt, Progressive party, received 88 electoral votes.

n. 1924: Robert M. La Follette, Progressive party, received 13 electoral votes.
o. 1948: J. Strom Thurmond, States' Rights party, received 39 electoral votes.
p. 1956: Walter B. Jones, Democrat, received 1 electoral vote.
q. 1960: Harry Flood Byrd, Democrat, received 15 electoral votes.
r. 1968: George C. Wallace, American Independent party, received 46 electoral votes.
s. 1972: John Hospers, Libertarian party, received 1 electoral vote.
t. 1976: Ronald Reagan, Republican, received 1 electoral vote.
u. 1988: Lloyd Bentsen, the Democratic vice-presidential nominee, received 1 electoral vote for president.
*   Fifty states plus District of Columbia.

Fair Deal, 295-297
Fairbanks, Charles W., 418
Fall, Albert B., 260-261, 275-276n18
Fallows, James, 354
Faubus, Orval, 309
Fausold, Martin, 270, 271
FDR. *See* Roosevelt, Franklin D.
Federal Farm Board, 271
Federal government
  Federalist party view of, 100
  framers' ideas, 13-14
  Hoover's political philosophy, 270,
    273
  impetus for forming, 5
  in industrial era, 205-206
  in Jacksonian philosophy, 123-125,
    128
  Jefferson view of, 103-105, 109
  in New Paradigm philosophy, 386
  in Nixon's political philosophy, 338-
    339
  origin of separation of powers, 38-39
  in post-Revolutionary period, 6, 7
  in Reagan political philosophy, 362-
    363
  in Franklin D. Roosevelt's political
    philosophy, 278-279, 284-285
  in Theodore Roosevelt's political
    philosophy, 215-216
Federal Reserve Board, 243, 282, 384
Federal Trade Commission, 243
Federalist No. 1, 407
Federalist No. 47, 38, 45
Federalist No. 64, 54
Federalist No. 68, 64-65, 107
Federalist No. 69, 62
Federalist No. 70, 62
Federalist No. 71, 63
Federalist No. 72, 36, 63
Federalist No. 73, 63, 78
Federalist No. 74, 47
Federalist Papers, The, 61, 82
Federalist party
  in John Adams administration, 95-
    96, 98
  in election of 1796, 90, 93-94, 413
  in election of 1800, 99, 413
  Jefferson's objections to, 100-101
  on role of executive, 100, 103
  on role of judiciary, 101
  in War of 1812, 111

Whiskey Rebellion of 1794 and, 84,
  85-86
Feerick, John D., 64, 68n71
Ferraro, Geraldine, 423, 429
Fifteenth Amendment, 182-183
Filibusters, 400-401
Fillmore, Millard, 144-145, 416
Fiorina, Morris, 377
Forbes, Charles, 260
Ford, Gerald, 347-351, *349,* 408n19,
  418, 422, 424, 425, 428, 431n30
Foreign affairs/policy
  Bush, 378-382
  Clinton, 404-406
  development of executive authority,
    82-83, 115, 311, 371-372
  Eisenhower, 307, 311
  Ford, 350
  Harding, 259
  House of Representatives in, 119n10
  League of Nations, 250-252
  Legislative role in, 82-83, 91, 92,
    346-347
  McKinley, 198-199
  Monroe, 115
  Nixon, 339-341
  in post-Revolutionary period, 7-8
  Reagan, 370-372
  receiving of ambassadors, 51
  recognition of countries, 246
  Roosevelt, Franklin D., 291-294
  Roosevelt, Theodore, 218-224,
    233n64n65, 245
  Supreme Court on authority for,
    292-293
  Truman Doctrine, 297
  Washington, 79, 80, 81-83
  Wilson, 245-253
Foulke, William Dudley, 217
Fourteen Points, 250
Fourteenth Amendment, 173, 182
Fourth Amendment, 107
France, 81-82, 90, 94-95, 96-97, 106,
  115
Frankfurter, Felix, 286
Franklin, Benjamin, 11, 23-24, 28-29,
  30, 37, 39, 42, 46, 55
Frederick (Duke of York), 54
Free Soil party, 143-144
Freedman's Bureau, 173
Freedom of speech, 97